The Men Who Made

LEYTON ORIENT
FOOTBALL CLUB
1904 – 2002

Neilson N. Kaufman
Assisted by Alan E. Ravenhill

TEMPUS

First published 2002

PUBLISHED IN THE UNITED KINGDOM BY:

Tempus Publishing Ltd
The Mill, Brimscombe Port
Stroud, Gloucestershire, GL5 2QG

PUBLISHED IN THE UNITED STATES OF AMERICA BY:

Tempus Publishing Inc.
2 Cumberland Street
Charleston, SC 29401
USA

British Library Cataloguing in Publication Data.
A catalogue record for this book is available from the British Library.

ISBN 0 7524 2412 2

Typesetting and origination by Tempus Publishing.
PRINTED AND BOUND IN GREAT BRITAIN.

FOREWORD

I have no voice this morning. This is unfortunate because I am supposed to be playing and talking on a TV programme in Manchester this lunch-time. I am not sure that Manchester is the best city in which to croak the explanation that I shouted myself dumb at Leyton Orient last night. Supporters of both United and City would think that dumb full stop, but they don't understand. You see, last night was the return leg of the Division Three play-off semi-finals. We started the game 1-0 down to Hull City, yet ran out 2-1 winners on aggregate, which gave us another chance to get out of this awful division.

Of course, United would never have allowed themselves to get there in the first place. They would have bought a few million-pound players to get out of trouble. But that is the point. Where is the joy in supporting a team that buys its way to success? Sure, their supporters will get to see 'glamour' clubs and 'glamour' players, but they will never know the magic of a night like last night, which is all about what can be achieved by astute management and the sheer hard work of players who – between them – cost less than a few weeks' wages of just one of United's fat-cat superstars.

Six years ago, Leyton Orient couldn't afford the milk for their half-time cuppas, but now they have a foot in the door that leads to the Premier League. Fantasy football? Maybe. But after the excitement of last night's game, I awoke from a dream about one of my first visits to the O's with my brother during the early 1960s. Our young left-winger, Terry McDonald, scored a brilliant last-minute goal and we won 1-0. Who were we playing that day? Yes, it was Manchester United.

Julian Lloyd Webber,
17 May 2001.

ACKNOWLEDGEMENTS

First and foremost, I would like to thank All Mighty God for giving me the opportunity to complete this book. Although both authors have spent many years working on this project, their task was made so much easier by the assistance of many that have contributed generously of their time, expertise and photographs. There have been a number of football historians whose help has been invaluable: Jim Creasy (a great help to many club historians), Terry Frost (sorry Bradford were relegated), Andy Porter (can Spurs rise under Hoddle?), Gordon Macey (can QPR get back to the top?), Mike Peterson and Trevor Bugg (guys, will Hull make it this season?), Trefor Jones (will Watford get to the top under Elton?) and Alex White (will Fulham survive in the Premiership?).

The following have given generously of their time: Peter Allen, Stu M. Allen, David Bloomfield, Eddie Brown, Andrew Buonocore, Tim Carder, Stan Charlton, Scott Cheshire, David Dodd, Jason Forrester, Richard Godwin, Graham Goodall, David Gould, Malcolm Graham, Don Hales, Alan J Harvey, Barry Hearn, Anne Holman, Keith Howard, Terry Howard, David Hyams, Steve Jenkins, Neil Johnston, Tommy Johnston, Colin Jose, Alan Kaufman, Eddie Lewis, John Maddocks, Nick Madden, Terry 'Henry' Mancini, Wade Martin, Terry McDonald, Tony McDonald, Len Mitty, Ken Mortimer, Donald Nannstead, Lynne Newman, Kirstine Nicholson, Fred Ollier, Ian Ochiltree, Richard J. Owen, Ian Page, James Pope, Matthew Porter, Mark Priddy, Luke Riches, Matthew Roper, Andy Shalders, Colin Shaw, Ian Sheen, Martin Strong, Nicola Struthers at Manchester United FC, Roger J. Triggs, Chris Unwins, Julian Lloyd Webber, Roger Wedge, Paul West, Steve Whitney, Mark Wilson, Brian B. Winston, Frank Woolf, Jonathan Wren, Chris Zoricich and Delia Zussman.

The following clubs were helpful in supplying player information: Aldershot Town, Arsenal, Aston Villa, Barnet, Barry Town, Barnsley, Blackpool, AFC Bournemouth, Brentford, Brighton & Hove Albion, Bristol City, Bristol Rovers, Bromley, Burnley, Cardiff City, Carlisle United, Celtic, Chelmsford City, Chelsea, Chesterfield, Colchester United, Coventry City, Crewe Alexandra, Dundee, Dunfermline, East Fife, Enfield, Everton, Exeter City, Folkestone Invicta, Fulham, Gillingham, Glasgow Rangers, Gravesend & Northfleet, Halifax Town, Harlow Town, Hartlepool United, Harrow Borough, Heart of Midlothian, Hendon, Huddersfield Town, Hull City, Ipswich Town, Kings Lynn, Leeds United, Leyton, Lincoln City, Liverpool, London Maccabi Lions, Luton Town, Maidstone United, Manchester City, Manchester United, Margate, MCC, Middlesbrough, Motherwell, Newcastle United, Northampton Town, Notts County, Paris St Germain, Partick Thistle, Peterborough United, Port Vale, Portsmouth, Queens Park Rangers, Reading, Rhyl Athletic, Rochdale, Rotherham United, Scunthorpe United, Sheffield United, Sheffield Wednesday, Southampton, Southend United, Southport, Stoke City, Sunderland, Surrey CCC, Swansea City, Swindon Town, Tottenham Hotspur, Walsall, Watford, West Bromwich Albion, West Ham United, Wimbledon, Wingate & Finchley, Wolverhampton Wanderers, Wycombe Wanderers, Yeading and York City.

As with previous books, a special thank-you must go to my loving wife, Debbie, and our twin daughters, Amy and Samantha, and all family members for their constant prayers, support and understanding.

The design and layout of the book are largely the results of the efforts of Tempus Publishing, and a big thank-you goes to James Howarth, Becky Gadd and Rosie Knowles for their assistance, co-operation and support.

To all those people who have played a part in this book, the authors are more grateful than this simple acknowledgement implies. And last but not least, to all those players, managers, officials, owners and supporters over 120 years of this grand club – this book is dedicated to you all. Research is never-ending and already I'm keeping tabs of all the changes in personnel at the club over the coming years in preparation for the next *Men Who Made* volume on the new players of this great club.

PICTURE CREDITS

Special thanks and gratitude to the following in allowing me to reproduce their photographs: O's former photographer Tim Reder, George Bodnar, Mike Childs, George Flower, Tony Furby, Arthur Griffiths, Trefor Jones, Linda Mabbott (aka species 8472), John Munday, David Read, Martin P. Smith, Mark S. Waters, Alex White and Dave Winter, the *Hackney Gazette*, the *Ilford Recorder* and the *Walthamstow Guardian*. Thanks also go to Leyton Orient Football Club, who hold the copyright for the Orient crest and a number of photographs, but have kindly given permission for these images to be used in this book.

ABOUT THE AUTHORS

Alan E. Ravenhill
Alan was born in Walthamstow in 1937. He first supported O's as a nine-year-old, and has since seen them play at fifty-one grounds around the country, and says, 'I couldn't have enjoyed following any club more than Orient'. He has written numerous articles on the O's and is also a writer of poetry.

Neilson N. Kaufman
Neil was born in the old Barts Hospital, central London on 3 October 1950, and first watched the O's back in 1958 when players like Eddie Brown, Tommy Johnston, Eddie Lewis, Phil White and Phil Woosnam were doing their thing. He moved to South Africa in July 1981, when the O's were still in the 'old' Second Division, but remains in daily e-mail contact with the club.

Alan and Neil have often written to each other over the years about doing a book on the players who have served the club throughout its history. This is a particularly appropriate time to produce this volume because in 2001 the club celebrated its 120th anniversary.

INTRODUCTION

It is now more than twenty-seven years since Alan Ravenhill and myself completed the original history of Leyton Orient Football Club – *A Pictorial History* – and over eleven years since the *Complete Record* was published. I'm happy that my friend and co-author of the these two books has joined me to assist with this new book on all the players, managers and coaches who have performed for O's since entering the FA Cup in 1904 and becoming members of the Football League the following year.

The club's story began in 1881 when members from Homerton College, a theological college for Nonconformists and Puritans, formed themselves into the Glyn Cricket Club. In March 1888, they started a football section and changed their name to Orient, after the ship *SS Orient*, when one Jack Dearing, a club committee man and worker for the Orient Steamship Navigation Company (later the P&O Group), suggested that name be adopted.

Though the years, players such as Herbert Kinagby, Fred Parker, Richard McFadden, Owen Williams, Arthur Wood, John Townrow, Ted Crawford, Frank Neary, Stan Aldous, Tommy Johnston, Dave Dunmore, Terry Mancini, Peter Allen, Barrie Fairbrother, Peter Kitchen, Alan Comfort, Mark Cooper, Terry Howard, and more recently, Carl Griffiths, Matty Lockwood, Dean Smith, Steve Watts, and new young star Jabo Ibehre have played for London's so-called 'unfashionables'.

The club has taken some hard knocks over the years, yet there have been many wonderful moments to savour, and now under new manager Paul Brush and his assistant Martin Ling, can they do what Tommy Taylor failed to achieve, having missed out on promotion via the play-offs twice in recent years? Will the new managerial team manage to avoid the dreaded drop into the Nationwide Conference and be able to go for promotion in 2002/03?

Front cover
Top left: Tommy Johnston, O's all-time goalscoring record holder.
Bottom left: Peter Allen, O's all-time appearance record holder.
Main picture: Mark Warren celebrates a goal by Darren Purse in August 1994, one of 4603 League goals from 3607 games between 1905 and 2001.

Back cover
William Henderson, O's captain during the 1907/08 season.

A

Kenneth ACHAMPONG, 1990-93

Kenny Achampong was born of Ghanaian parents in Kilburn, London on 26 June 1966 and later attended Tulse Hill School. This talented 5ft 9in midfielder joined Orient for £25,000 in July 1990 from Charlton Athletic after a brief loan spell. He started his career with Fulham in 1983, making his League debut aged eighteen. He spent five seasons at Craven Cottage and made 77(15) senior appearances, scoring 15 goals. He walked out of Craven Cottage criticizing their training methods, and was suspended by the FA for not honouring his contract. He went to West Ham United for a trial in January 1989, but then moved across London to Charlton Athletic in September 1989, where he played just 10 times. Achampong made his O's debut at Tranmere Rovers on 17 September 1990. Manager Frank Clark stated that Achampong 'had a tremendous amount of ability, just waiting to be fulfilled'. Unfortunately, he never quite fulfilled that promise with O's. He was in and out of the team, and even had to be substituted a number of times for bizarre reasons, including the breaking of a contact lens. During an FA Cup tie against Oldham Athletic, he couldn't see physio Bill Songhurst hold up a board for him to come off because he had lost a lens. It was only minutes later that he left the field, when Steve Castle told him he had to get off. He missed the start of the 1991/92 season when contracting malaria during a visit to his parents in Ghana. He was called up for the Ghanaian World Cup squad in January 1993, but unfortunately he had to drop out

Kenny Achampong

after undergoing knee surgery; he was not chosen again. Achampong was released in May 1993 because he could not get on with the team manager, Peter Eustace. Achampong's skill appeared to be lost amidst the confusing tactical formations of Eustace and a welter of crunching tackles. He later had an unsuccessful trial in France with Marseilles, and then played in Ghana and Belgium.

SEASON	LEAGUE		FA CUP		L. CUP	
	Apps	Gls	Apps	Gls	Apps	Gls
1990/91	25(9)	4	2	0	2(1)	0
1991/92	20(4)	2	3(1)	0	2	0
1992/93	19(6)	1	2	0	1(1)	0
TOTAL	64(19)	7	7(1)	0	5(2)	0

TOTAL APPS	76(22)
TOTAL GOALS	7

* Kenny Achampong also appeared in 6(1) Auto Windscreens Shield matches, scoring a single goal.

Anthony Alan ACKERMAN, 1966-68

Tony Ackerman, a 6ft tall centre half, joined O's from West Ham United's youth side during May 1966. Born in Islington, London on 20 February 1948, he made his League debut against Watford on 29 October 1966. However, Ackerman never quite made the grade, and after a loan spell with Corby Town, he decided to give up the game in 1968 for a job in the printing trade.

SEASON	LEAGUE		FA CUP		L. CUP	
	Apps	Gls	Apps	Gls	Apps	Gls
1966/67	3	0	0	0	0	0
1967/68	1	0	0	0	0	0
TOTAL	4	0	0	0	0	0

TOTAL APPS	4
TOTAL GOALS	0

George ADAMS, 1949-50

Born in Falkirk, Scotland on 16 October 1926, wing-half Adams joined O's from Chelmsford City in May 1949. His League debut came on 25 March 1950 against Newport County. He was unable to gain a regular place in the first team and joined Southern League side Bath City in 1950. In March 1954, he had a spell in Crystal Palace reserves.

SEASON	LEAGUE		FA CUP		TOTAL	
	Apps	Gls	Apps	Gls	Apps	Gls
1949/50	4	0	0	0	4	0
TOTAL	4	0	0	0	4	0

David Roy AFFLECK, 1935-37

Dave Affleck was a strong fair-haired centre half with good heading ability, and he had two good seasons with O's. Born in Coylton, Ayrshire, Scotland on 26 July 1912, he graduated from Scottish junior football with Crosshouse Castle Rovers.

After a short spell with Notts County, he made his League debut with Bristol City, making 3 appearances in 1934/35. Affleck joined O's in July 1935, taking over the central defender's berth from William Fellowes, who was transferred to Luton Town. He proved a very capable replacement and a most effective defender. Due to financial problems, he was sold to Southampton in May 1937 for a substantial fee, and went on to make 51 appearances at the Dell up until the Second World War. He was given a free transfer in June 1946, and went on to join Yeovil Town. After retiring from the game, he became a policeman. Affleck died in Stoke-sub-Haddon, Somerset on 11 August 1984.

SEASON	LEAGUE		FA CUP		TOTAL	
	Apps	Gls	Apps	Gls	Apps	Gls
1935/36	25	0	3	0	28	0
1936/37	41	0	2	0	43	0
TOTAL	66	0	5	0	71	0

* Dave Affleck also appeared in 2 Third Division Cup matches 1935/36 and made a solitary appearance in 1936/37.

Stanley Elvey Reginald ALDOUS, 1950-58

Stan Aldous was born in Northfleet on 10 February 1923, and was one of five footballing brothers. Aldous was a tough centre half who captained O's in some of their greatest triumphs, including the Third Division Championship in 1956. He started his career with Erith & Belvedere, but it was whilst with Bromley that he gained a wonderful reputation. Aldous joined O's almost by default. He was with Gravesend & Northfleet FC, who for some reason forgot to register him for the 1950/51 season, so he became a free agent. Fulham were interested in his signature,

Stan Aldous

but it was O's manager Les Gore (who had previously played alongside Aldous in the Gravesend side) who persuaded him to join Orient, so at the age of twenty-five he became an 'Oriental'. Aldous, being such a strong and powerful central defender, dominated in the air and proved to be very difficult to beat on the deck. He was one of a handful of players to have made over 300 League appearances during his eight-year stay. He moved on to Headington United (now Oxford United) and was later a coach with QPR and a manager with his old club, Gravesend. During the late 1970s, he owned the Royal Bingo and Social Club in Littleport, Cambridgeshire. Aldous made a great contribution to the history of the club. He discussed his career with the author just before his death, and said that the most disappointing moment was the 1-0 defeat by Port Vale in the sixth round of the FA Cup, in front of 31,000 fans in March 1954. Aldous stated: 'We domi-

nated the whole match but could not find the net.' He went on to say 'I suppose the greatest and most exciting moment was when we won promotion into the Second Division back in 1956. There was always a great friendship about the club from the top – chairman Harry Zussman – to the lads who cleaned the boots. I was proud to be associated with the O's during the 1950s when I feel, at last, we shook off the tag of being a music hall joke and took our rightful place in the Second Division.' Stan Aldous died in Ely on 17 October 1995.

SEASON	LEAGUE		FA CUP		TOTAL	
	Apps	Gls	Apps	Gls	Apps	Gls
1950/51	30	0	0	0	30	0
1951/52	46	0	9	0	55	0
1952/53	45	2	2	0	47	2
1953/54	43	1	7	0	50	1
1954/55	45	0	2	0	47	0
1955/56	42	0	4	0	46	0
1956/57	40	0	1	0	41	0
1957/58	11	0	0	0	11	0
TOTAL	302	3	25	0	327	3

Douglas Stewart ALLDER, 1975-77
Doug Allder, the former England youth international, became an 'Oriental' in July 1975 as part of the deal that took Terry Brisley to Millwall. Unfortunately, he never quite settled in East London and his form was a great disappointment. Born in Hammersmith, London on 30 December 1951, the left-winger and midfielder made his debut for the Lions as an amateur in October 1969. He made a total of 191(11) League appearances, scoring 11 goals. After leaving O's, he went on trial with both Torquay United and Watford. He found his form again with Brentford, and was a regular in their Fourth Division promotion-winning side. Allder made a career total of 332 League

Doug Allder

joined O's in December 1933, and made his solitary senior appearance on the wing (aged eighteen and a half) in a 5-1 victory over Northampton Town on 24 February 1934. He could not break into the first team and joined Leytonstone a few months later. In May 1934, he turned professional with Fulham, making 11 League appearances during his three-year stay at Craven Cottage. In June 1937, he signed for Doncaster Rovers for £350, playing 31 times. He joined Brentford from Dartford in June 1938, in a season which was stopped due to the onset of the Second World War. After hostilities ceased, he played for Northampton Town (making 5 appearances), before joining Southern League Colchester United in May 1947 and appeared in the 1947/48 FA Cup side that defeated several League teams, including Huddersfield Town of the First Division. He also played for the Essex club in their inaugural season in the League during 1950/51, making a total of

appearances, before moving into non-League with Tooting & Mitcham, and then Walton & Hersham. In 1992 he became coach at the Millwall School of Excellence, and more recently, he has worked as a shopfitter with a Surrey firm.

SEASON	LEAGUE		FA CUP		L. CUP	
	Apps	Gls	Apps	Gls	Apps	Gls
1975/76	19(4)	0	1	0	0(1)	0
1976/77	15(3)	0	2(1)	0	1(1)	0
TOTAL	34(7)	0	3(1)	0	1(2)	0

TOTAL APPS	38(10)
TOTAL GOALS	0

* Doug Allder also appeared in 5(1) matches in the Anglo-Scottish Cup.

Albert Robert ALLEN, 1933-34

Bob Allen was born in Bromley-by-Bow, London on 11 October 1916. The former England schoolboy and Tottenham junior

Bob Allen

29 League appearances and scoring a single goal. Allen died in Epping Forest in February 1992.

SEASON	LEAGUE		FA CUP		TOTAL	
	Apps	Gls	Apps	Gls	Apps	Gls
1933/34	1	0	0	0	1	0
TOTAL	1	0	0	0	1	0

James ALLEN, 1937-38

James Allen was born in Amble, Northumberland, on 18 August 1913. He is often confused with another player from the same era: Joseph Allen, who played for Mansfield Town, Spurs, QPR and Racing Club De Rouxbai in France. Joseph Allen was born in Nottingham on 30 December 1909. Right half-back James Allen (sometimes his surname was recorded as Allan) stood 5ft 10in and started his career with Northumberland club Stakeford Albion. He joined Huddersfield Town in March 1934, making his League debut against Preston North End in January 1935. After a year he moved south, joining QPR in April 1935 for a small fee, and making 45 senior appearances before joining O's on a free transfer in May 1937. He made his O's League debut against Notts County on 13 November 1937, but did not make a great impression and moved into non-League a year later. He died in Hammersmith, London in 1979, aged sixty-six.

SEASON	LEAGUE		FA CUP		TOTAL	
	Apps	Gls	Apps	Gls	Apps	Gls
1937/38	5	0	3	0	8	0
TOTAL	5	0	3	0	8	0

* James Allen also appeared in a single Third Division Cup match in 1937/38.

Peter Charles ALLEN, 1965-78

Peter Allen, the 5ft 9in midfielder holds the O's League appearance record, finally breaking Arthur Wood's total on 13 March 1976 against Sunderland, and he became the first O's player to break the 400 League appearance barrier on 26 April 1977 against Southampton. Allen left the club in March 1978, having made 428(8) League appearances – a record unlikely ever to be broken with the advent of the Bosman transfer ruling. Born in Hove, Sussex on 1 November 1946, he excelled academically, gaining seven 'O' levels and three 'A' levels at grammar school in Brighton. Allen joined Tottenham Hotspur as an associated schoolboy, but he was still at school when the O's manager, Dave Sexton, spotted him playing and, after a brief spell on amateur forms with the club, he decided to turn professional in July 1965, in preference to entering Birmingham University or the London School of Economics. He made his debut as a nineteen-year-old in the League Cup tie against Coventry City on 22 September 1965, and his Second Division debut came three days later at Portsmouth. Unfortunately, his first season was not a happy one – Dave Sexton had resigned by Christmas, and O's were relegated to the Third Division. The following season, the club nearly went out of business. This was not an ideal time for the young player, but Allen stayed loyal and battled on and off the field to improve O's fortunes. He regularly impressed as a constructive midfield player with a good firm tackle, and played a vital role in O's avoiding relegation over the next few seasons. The 1969/70 season saw a great improvement at Brisbane Road, and it was no coincidence that Allen had a won-

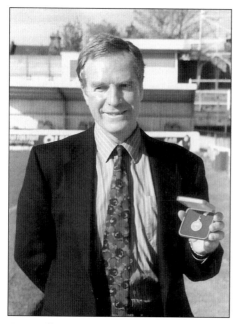

Peter Allen

derful season, playing in all 46 matches en route to winning the Third Division Championship. Second Division football seem to bring out the very best in Allen's all-round play, and it was no surprise when First Division Everton came in with a big offer for his services, but he decided to stay in London, and over the next few seasons was a model of consistency. During this period, he had an unbroken run of 116 League appearances that ended in August 1971. He led the team superbly during 1973/74, with O's pushing for promotion to the First Division, but they missed out by a single point and he was very disappointed. As he became unsettled at the club, rumours became rife that he would leave, but manager George Petchey persuaded him to stay, and his old enthusiasm returned. Allen's last three seasons at the club were often troubled by injury problems. He was awarded a testimonial year in 1975/76,

culminating in a match against West Ham United. It came as a real surprise that he was allowed to leave by O's boss Jimmy Bloomfield, in order to join former O's boss George Petchey at Millwall (the last club you would expect Allen to play for) during March 1978. This was also at a time when O's were awaiting an FA Cup quarter-final match at Middlesbrough with a number of players out with injury problems. In football there are usually two types of midfield players: there is the hard-tackling aggressive player with a high work-rate, and there is the calm ball-playing type, who distributes the ball to colleagues accurately. What made Peter Allen so special was that he had a bit of both in him. He never shirked an opportunity to make a telling tackle when it was required, and when in possession of the ball he always attempted to use it methodically. He never appeared in the top division, but it would have been very interesting to see how he would have fared. One thing is for certain: there have been many less talented players who have played in the top flight. Allen was hard, but always a fair and sporting player. He did get sent off once in a League match at Walsall, but the decision was so ridiculous that, quite rightly, no action was taken against him. He captained the team for over three seasons and always led by example, both on and off the field. When he joined O's, he was thought of more as an attacking player, and he did go onto score a number of goals, none more pleasing than the very early goal at Millwall in May 1971 to secure the points. But his defensive qualities came to the fore under George Petchey. One also recalls him having a wonderful match at Tottenham Hotspur when he filled in as a central defender. He also filled in admirably at full-back on a number of occasions. Therefore versatility, leadership and sportsmanship can all be ascribed to Peter Allen. After a short period at the Den – where he made 16(2) appearances – he suffered two serious injuries, which forced him to retire from the game at the age of thirty-two. He declined an offer of a coaching post with the Lions in order to undertake a three-year course to complete his articles. He qualified as a solicitor in 1984, worked for a large firm of attorneys to gain experience, then set up his own partnership in 1988 with John Diebel (named Diebel & Allen and based in Portslade, East Sussex). Recently he completed a course on the legal aspects of sports management and still plays the odd game of five-a-side soccer.

SEASON	LEAGUE		FA CUP		L. CUP	
	Apps	Gls	Apps	Gls	Apps	Gls
1965/66	21(2)	3	0	0	1	0
1966/67	34	2	2	0	0	0
1967/68	34(2)	4	5	0	1	0
1968/69	43	3	2	0	3	0
1969/70	46	3	2	0	2	0
1970/71	42	2	3	0	1	0
1971/72	40	5	4	1	2	0
1972/73	42	3	1	0	2	0
1973/74	37	1	0	0	4	0
1974/75	31(1)	0	2	0	1	0
1975/76	7	0	0	0	0	0
1976/77	29	1	3	0	4	0
1977/78	18(3)	0	1	0	3	1
TOTAL	424(8)	27	25	1	24	1

TOTAL APPS   473(8)

TOTAL GOALS   29

* Peter Allen also appeared in 9 matches in the Anglo-Scottish Cup.

William Martin Laws ALLISON, 1931-32

Billy Allison was born in Shildon on 13 January 1908, but he never really settled down south and seemed to play his best football back home in the north-east. The 5ft 9in left-back joined Arsenal from Shildon FC on 9 May 1929 for £50. He stayed at Highbury for two seasons and made 39 reserve appearances before his move to O's on 2 May 1931. He made his League debut against Crystal Palace on 31 August 1931. Laws left in 1932 for Darlington, where he made 52 senior appearances. After a short spell with Eden Colliery FC, he joined Hartlepool United in May 1935 where he had a long association, playing 119 senior games before ending his career with Spenymoor United. Allison died in Shildon during 1981.

SEASON	LEAGUE		FA CUP		TOTAL	
	Apps	Gls	Apps	Gls	Apps	Gls
1931/32	14	0	0	0	14	0
TOTAL	14	0	0	0	14	0

Leslie Ethelbert George AMES, 1926-31

Leslie Ames was better known for his wonderful exploits on the cricket field with both Kent and England than as a footballer! He was a high-class wicket-keeper/batsman, playing 47 tests for England between 1929 and 1939, and scoring 2,434 runs at an average of 40.56. During this time he scored 8 centuries, took 74 catches and made 24 stumpings. Ames scored a career total of 32,248 runs (102 centuries) with 703 catches and 418 stumpings. He also took 24 bowling wickets. Born in Eltham, Kent on 3 December 1905, the 5ft 9in outside right started his football career with Folkestone, before joining O's in 1926. He was registered for five seasons, but his cricketing commitments restricted his football career. He made his League debut against Preston North End on 15 January 1927 and he stayed with O's until joining Gillingham in September 1931, playing 5 matches and scoring once for the Gills. Ames was manager-secretary for Kent CCC between 1960 and 1974, and in 1950 he became the first professional cricketer to be appointed as an England selector, serving eight seasons. Ames died in Canterbury on 27 February 1990.

SEASON	LEAGUE		FA CUP		TOTAL	
	Apps	Gls	Apps	Gls	Apps	Gls
1926/27	5	0	0	0	5	0
1927/28	6	0	0	0	6	0
1928/29	0	0	0	0	0	0
1929/30	1	0	0	0	1	0
1930/31	2	0	0	0	2	0
TOTAL	14	0	0	0	14	0

Kwame Ampadu

Patrick Kwame AMPADU, 1998-2000

Kwame Ampadu was born in Bradford on 20 December 1970 of Irish parentage. This creative midfielder started his career with Arsenal, gaining international caps for Eire at youth, under-17 and under-21 levels. He signed professional forms at Highbury in November 1988, but never broke into the first-team squad, making just 2 League substitute appearances. After a loan spell with Plymouth Argyle in October 1990, he went on loan to West Bromwich Albion and was then signed for £50,000 on 24 June 1991. Ampadu made 27(22) League appearances with 4 goals at the Hawthorns before his move to Swansea City on 16 February 1994 for £15,000, where he made 128(9) League appearances and scored 12 goals. He played for the Swans in a Division Three play-off final at Wembley Stadium on 24 May 1998, losing to a last-minute goal

against Northampton Town. He struggled to hold down a regular first-team place with Swansea City in his last season at the Vetch due to a number of injuries including a broken toe. He joined O's on a free transfer on 22 May 1998 and started quite well, making his League debut at Chester City on 8 August 1998. He played in the first 15 senior matches, but then suffered from a loss of form and sat on the bench. He came back early in the second half of the season to find better form, but injury curtailed his season and led to him missing O's promotion play-off matches in May 1999. During the following season he missed just 3 League matches, but this was due mainly to injury to other players rather than his own form. He was given a free transfer in May 2000, and on 1 July joined former fellow 'Oriental' Alex Ingelthorpe at Exeter City, where he was a regular throughout the 2000/01 season with over 30 senior appearances without finding the net. He was placed on the transfer list in May 2001, but was still in their side during the following season.

SEASON	LEAGUE		FA CUP		L. CUP	
	Apps	Gls	Apps	Gls	Apps	Gls
1998/99	26(3)	1	2(1)	0	4	0
1999/2000	43	1	2	1	4	0
TOTAL	69(3)	2	4(1)	1	8	0

TOTAL APPS	82(4)
TOTAL GOALS	3

* Kwame Ampadu also appeared in a single Auto Windscreens Shield match in 1999/2000.

Thomas Cowan ANDERSON, 1967-68

Tommy Anderson wandered far and wide throughout his footballing career, eventually settling in Australia as a soccer reporter and radio personality. Born in Haddington, East Lothian, Scotland on 24 September 1934, the speedy striker made a few senior appearances for O's in 1967 after joining from the Melbourne George Cross Club in Australia. He left O's in December 1967, and the following month was appointed player- manager with Irish club Limerick. He moved to Australia in 1970 to join South Coast United as player-coach, but after only a single match – a loss to Hakoah – he left to join the St Georges club. He played there for a few seasons before retiring from playing and moving in coaching with Pan Hellenic FC, APIA and Marconi. In 1978 he joined Sydney Olympic as coach. Anderson made 205 League appearances during a career that spanned some eleven seasons with numerous clubs including Watford (twice), Bournemouth, QPR, Torquay United, Stockport County, Doncaster Rovers, Wrexham and Barrow.

SEASON	LEAGUE		FA CUP		L. CUP	
	Apps	Gls	Apps	Gls	Apps	Gls
1967/68	8(1)	0	0	0	1	0
TOTAL	8(1)	0	0	0	1	0

TOTAL APPS	9(1)
TOTAL GOALS	0

James Patrick ANDREWS, 1956-59

Born in Invergordon, Scotland on 1 February 1927, Jimmy Andrews was a very small, yet tricky inside or outside left. He started his career with Dundee FC and moved south of the Border in November 1951 to join West Ham United for a fee of £4,750, quite a substantial fee in those days. He gave the Hammers good service, playing in 120 senior matches and netting 21 goals. He moved to O's for the Second Division campaign in June 1956, but found he could not hold down a regular first-team place. However, when called upon he performed well with his clever ball-playing ability. Andrews joined QPR in June 1959, teaming up with former O's boss Alec Stock. He made 87 senior appearances and scored 17 goals, before taking up a coaching job with Rangers. Andrews went on to gain quite a reputation as coach with Luton Town and Tottenham Hotspur. He managed Cardiff City in their 1975/76 promotion and Welsh Cup double triumph, but was sacked in November 1978. Soon afterwards, he went on to be a scout for Southampton.

SEASON	LEAGUE		FA CUP		TOTAL	
	Apps	Gls	Apps	Gls	Apps	Gls
1956/57	14	4	0	0	14	4
1957/58	16	1	0	0	16	1
1958/59	6	3	0	0	6	3
TOTAL	36	8	0	0	36	8

Andrew ANSAH, 1996-97

Andy Ansah, a much-travelled striker, was born in Lewisham, London on 19 March 1969. He began his League career with Brentford in March 1989, making 3(5) League appearances before moving to Southend United in March 1990. There he spent five seasons, scoring 33 League goals from 141(16) starts, however, after a contractual dispute he was twice loaned to Brentford, and then experienced non-contract spells with both Peterborough United and Gillingham. He joined O's (also on a non-contract basis) in December 1996 after a spell in Hong Kong, and made just 2 appearances as a substitute against Mansfield Town and Scarborough in January 1997. Ansah decided to leave the club for a better deal with Hayes, then he played with Heybridge Swifts for a time, before moving back into the League (again on a non-contract basis) with Brighton & Hove Albion in November 1997, making 10(15) League appearances and netting 3 goals. In July 1999 he was on the books of Farnborough Town. Ansah's League career, which spanned some 10 years, totalled 162(41) appearances with 41 goals. He later embarked on an acting career, appearing in Sky's *Dream Team* programme.

SEASON	LEAGUE		FA CUP		L. CUP	
	Apps	Gls	Apps	Gls	Apps	Gls
1996/97	0(2)	0	0	0	0	0
TOTAL	0(2)	0	0	0	0	0

TOTAL APPS	0(2)
TOTAL GOALS	0

Robert Leonard ARBER, 1968-74

Full-back Bobby Arber was born in Poplar, London on 13 January 1951, and came to O's from Arsenal's youth set-up on 1 March 1968. This steady defender got his first-team chance when Dennis Rofe was transferred to Leicester City in August 1972, but he could not keep a regular place in the side and went on loan to Southend United, before leaving to play in South Africa. After his playing days were over, he returned to England and worked as a coach with Essex-based clubs Barking and Woodford Town. Later he became youth coach at Tottenham Hotspur and in 1999 was appointed by Arsenal as a full-time scout.

SEASON	LEAGUE		FA CUP		L. CUP	
	Apps	Gls	Apps	Gls	Apps	Gls
1971/72	3	0	0	0	0	0
1972/73	28	0	1	1	1	0
1973/74	0	0	1	0	0	0
TOTAL	31	0	2	1	1	0

TOTAL APPS	34
TOTAL GOALS	1

Bobby Arber

A

Graham Leonard ARCHELL, 1965-69

Born in Islington, London on 8 February 1950, inside forward Archell came through O's youth ranks during the mid 1960s, turning professional in 1967. He was a clever forager who made his League debut on the left wing against Barrow on 11 November 1967. Despite his early progress, he did not fulfil his potential and moved to Folkestone Town in May 1970.

SEASON	LEAGUE		FA CUP		L. CUP	
	Apps	Gls	Apps	Gls	Apps	Gls
1967/68	3	0	0	0	0	0
1968/69	2(2)	0	0	0	2	0
1969/70	0	0	0	0	0	0
TOTAL	5(2)	0	0	0	2	0

TOTAL APPS	7(2)
TOTAL GOALS	0

Jack ARCHER, 1895-1905

Born in Hackney, London, right full-back Jack Archer joined O's in July 1895 and played in the club's London League campaigns until entering the Second Division of the London League in 1904. He appeared for O's in their first Southern League match, a goal-less home draw against Brighton & Hove Albion on 8 October 1904, in front of more than 3,000 spectators. He also featured in all 6 FA Cup ties during the 1904/05 season, but upon O's election into the League in May 1905 he was not retained, and continued a career in non-League football.

SEASON	LEAGUE		FA CUP		TOTAL	
	Apps	Gls	Apps	Gls	Apps	Gls
1904/05*	-	-	6	0	6	0
TOTAL	-	-	6	0	6	0

* Clapton Orient first entered the League in the 1905/06 season.

James Mitchell ARCHIBALD, 1923-26

Born in Dunfermline, Scotland on 18 September 1892, Jimmy Archibald – a lively wing-half – started his career with Motherwell, but came south to join Spurs on trial after the First World War in July 1919. The deal was made permanent on 10 September for a £100 fee, and he went on to make 25 senior appearances, scoring a single goal. In 1923 he was transferred to League outfit Aberdare Athletic, scoring twice in 30 appearances. He then became an 'Oriental' in June 1923, proving to be more than a useful performer with his constructive and forceful play. He eventually lost his place to Tommy Dixon and moved to Southend United. In later years he played for both Margate FC and for Tunbridge Wells Rangers FC. James Archibald died in Waltham Forest on 25 January 1975.

SEASON	LEAGUE		FA CUP		TOTAL	
	Apps	Gls	Apps	Gls	Apps	Gls
1923/24	36	0	3	0	39	0
1924/25	6	0	0	0	6	0
1925/26	7	1	0	0	7	1
TOTAL	49	1	3	0	52	1

Kenneth ARMITAGE (see FENTON)

James Harris ARMSTRONG, 1926-28

This tall commanding centre half joined O's in November 1926 from Easington Colliery FC, but it was whilst with both Queens Park Rangers and Watford that he made his mark. Born in Lemington-upon-Tyne on 8 March 1904, Jimmy Armstrong was mostly a reserve with O's, finally making his senior debut on 2 April 1927 in the 4-5 home defeat against Portsmouth. Armstrong joined QPR in May 1928, where he enjoyed a long spell that yielded 112 League appearances. In May 1933 he signed for Watford, making a further 201 senior appearances with 2 goals. He continued to turn out for the Hornets during the Second World War, playing 52 wartime matches. In 1941 he retired to take up a job with Universal Asbestos Ltd, where he remained for the next twenty-eight years. He died in Watford on 13 April 1971.

SEASON	LEAGUE		FA CUP		TOTAL	
	Apps	Gls	Apps	Gls	Apps	Gls
1926/27	2	0	0	0	2	0
1927/28	0	0	0	0	0	0
TOTAL	2	0	0	0	2	0

Andrew John ARNOTT, 1995-97

Andy Arnott, a very determined and industrious 6ft 1in central defender, joined O's from Gillingham after a two-month wait for a tribunal to fix his transfer fee. Previously he had an unsuccessful loan spell with Manchester United in March 1993. Born in Chatham, Kent on 18 October 1973, he made 60(22) senior appearances with the Gills, scoring 12 goals before becoming an 'Oriental' on 25 January 1996. The tribunal fixed his fee at £10,000, with a further £5,000 to be paid after 50 first-team appearances, as well as a 25 per cent sell-on clause. Arnott, who made his debut at Darlington on 3 February 1996, once deputised in goal for Luke Weaver for more than thirty minutes in a League match at Exeter City on 9 November 1996 without conceding a goal, but O's lost 3-2. After two seasons with O's, he was transferred to Fulham on 17 June 1997 for £23,000, but had an unproductive spell at Craven Cottage, making just a single solitary substitute

Andy Arnott

appearance against Bournemouth on 18 October 1997. He went on loan to Rushden & Diamonds, before a £20,000 move took him to Brighton & Hove Albion on 23 October 1998. He was sent off in a match against the O's in February 1999 for punching the ball into the Leyton net with his hand. He made 27(1) appearances and scored 2 goals for the Seagulls, before joining Colchester United in September 1999 on loan. That deal was later made permanent during October 1999, as he signed on a free transfer. He made his debut against Millwall, but his progress at Layer Road was hampered by injury. Arnott announced his retirement from the League in February 2001 at the age of twenty-seven, due to a recurring groin injury, after 5(10) League appearances for Gillingham. He then joined Nationwide Conference side Stevenage Borough in August 2001.

SEASON	LEAGUE		FA CUP		L. CUP	
	Apps	Gls	Apps	Gls	Apps	Gls
1995/96	19	3	0	0	0	0
1996/97	28(3)	3	2	0	2	0
TOTAL	47(3)	6	2	0	2	0

TOTAL APPS	51(3)
TOTAL GOALS	6

* Andy Arnott also appeared in a single Auto Windscreens Shield match.

Sir Hubert ASHTON, 1926-27

Hubert Ashton, one of three brilliant sporting brothers, found his greatest success away from the football field. He won a Military Cross for 'Bravery on the Western Front' in the First World War. Between 1930 and 1964, he was Conservative MP for Chelmsford, working for four years as Personal Private Secretary to the Chancellor of the Exchequer and the Home Secretary. In 1943 he served as the Sheriff of Essex, and was the brother-in-law of political rival Sir Hugh Gaitskell. In 1956 Ashton was made a Knight of the British Empire. Born on 13 February 1898 in Calcutta, India he moved to Manchester whilst still a young boy. In 1920 he was regarded as one of the most promising amateur cricketers around, and he won Cambridge blues for cricket, football and hockey. Ashton remained an amateur throughout his football career, which started with the Corinthians Club. He played for West Bromwich Albion during the 1919/20 season, but the 5ft 10in full-back did not make his League debut with Bristol Rovers until 2 May 1925 against Reading – it was his only senior appearance. He became an 'Oriental' on 21 August 1926, making his O's debut in a 6-0 defeat at Blackpool

on 11 December 1926. His final match for O's was at Middlesbrough on 26 February 1927, another 6-0 defeat. In May 1927 he joined Gillingham, but soon retired from the game to concentrate on his cricketing career with Essex CCC. He had 35 innings with them, scoring 819 runs at an average of 24.08 between 1921 and 1939. In 1941 he was elected chairman of Essex CCC and also served as president of the MCC. Hubert Ashton died in South Weald, Essex on 17 June 1979, aged eighty-one.

SEASON	LEAGUE		FA CUP		TOTAL	
	Apps	Gls	Apps	Gls	Apps	Gls
1926/27	5	0	0	0	5	0
TOTAL	5	0	0	0	5	0

Paul Anthony ATKIN, 1997 (loan)

This 6ft central defender came to O's on loan from York City on 21 March 1997. Born in Nottingham on 3 September 1969, Atkin started as an apprentice with Notts County. He moved to Bury in March 1989, playing 14(7) games and scoring once. He signed for York City on a free transfer in July 1991, and made 131(22) appearances, scoring 3 goals. He was part of the York team to gain promotion via the play-offs in 1993. Atkins joined O's on 21 March 1997, and made his debut against Lincoln City. Atkin joined Scarborough in August 1997, making a further 26(8) appearances and scoring once. He moved to Gainsborough Trinity on 27 July 1998. In 1999 he worked at the FA School of Excellence based at Lilleshall.

SEASON	LEAGUE		FA CUP		L. CUP	
	Apps	Gls	Apps	Gls	Apps	Gls
1996/97	5	0	0	0	0	0
TOTAL	5	0	0	0	0	0

Kevin Austin

Kevin Levi AUSTIN, 1993-96

Austin was born in Hackney, London on 12 February 1973. This consistent 6ft 2in central defender was good in the air and surprisingly fast on the ground for his size. He joined O's from non-League Saffron Walden Town on 19 August 1993 for £1,000. On 31 July 1996 he joined Lincoln City for £30,000, where he continued to be a model of consistency, playing 127(1) League matches and scoring 2 goals for the Imps. Lincoln City wanted Austin so badly that their fans set up a 'Buy Kevin Austin' appeal, raising thousand of pounds towards his transfer fee. Later Lincoln valued Austin at around £300,000, but he left them under the Bosman ruling in July 1999 after rejecting a £40,000 move to Bristol City. He then joined Barnsley on a free transfer, but after just a handful of matches disaster struck against his old club, Lincoln, in

a Worthington Cup tie. Austin suffered a serious Achilles tendon injury, which ruled him out for the reminder of the 1999/2000 season. He joined Brentford on loan on 27 October 2000, making just 3 League appearances. He was expected to join Oxford United in January 2001, but failed a medical. He played just 5(1) senior matches at Oakwell and left Barnsley in 2001. Austin, who had made 3 appearances for Trinidad & Tobago, continued his rehabilitation with Cambridge United, making his reserve debut in November 2001.

SEASON	LEAGUE		FA CUP		L. CUP	
	Apps	Gls	Apps	Gls	Apps	Gls
1993/94	30	0	3	0	0	0
1994/95	39	2	2	0	2	0
1995/96	32(8)	1	1	0	2	1
TOTAL	101(8)	3	6	0	4	1

TOTAL APPS	111(8)
TOTAL GOALS	4

* Kevin Austin also appeared in 7 Auto Windscreens Shield matches.

Samuel Tayo AYORINDE, 1995-97

Sammy Ayorinde was born in Lagos, Nigeria on 20 October 1974 and came to O's from Austrian club Sturm Graz in September 1995. Ayorinde had to wait a number of months before obtaining a work permit from the Department of Employment, and he was only given the all-clear on 24 April 1996, once he married his long-time girlfriend Beatrice. However, he was allowed to play reserve football during his wait, scoring 19 goals from 21 starts for the O's. He made his long-awaited League debut on 4 May 1996 at Cambridge United. Ayorinde never quite lived up to all the expectations, although he did score one great goal at Exéter City on 9 November 1996 – with his back to goal, he flicked the ball onto his chest before executing a perfect overhead kick from the edge of the area and into the net. In May 1996 he was called up for the Nigerian under-23 squad for the Olympic Games in Atlanta, USA. He went on loan to numerous clubs in Finland and England (including Altrincham and Rushden & Diamonds), before a permanent move took him to Dover Athletic on 2 December 1997 for an undisclosed fee. He went on to score 5 goals from 18(1) Conference appearances. He later played for Bangor City in 1998, where he gained some Nigerian under-21 caps and his first Nigerian international cap, and was the First League of Wales player to gain international honours against Burkina Faso. He briefly appeared for Hampton in the Ryman Isthmian League, and in the year 2000 he played for Tunisian First Divison side Stade Tunisien, followed by Swedish side Djurgaarden. In 2001 Ayorinde played for Swedish side Assyriska Fotboliforening from the Superettan League and scored 8 goals before he moved back to England to join Nationwide Conference side Stalybridge Celtic FC, for whom he signed on 29 November. Also in their side was former 'Oriental' Paul Beesley.

SEASON	LEAGUE		FA CUP		L. CUP	
	Apps	Gls	Apps	Gls	Apps	Gls
1995/96	1	0	0	0	0	0
1996/97	6(6)	2	1	0	1(1)	0
TOTAL	7(6)	2	1	0	1(1)	0

TOTAL APPS	9(7)
TOTAL GOALS	2

B

Cyril William BACON, 1946-50

Fair-haired Cyril Bacon, an all-action wing-half, was born in Hammersmith, London on 9 November 1919. He joined O's in June 1946, having been spotted playing for the Royal Air Force. Cyril Bacon had previously guested for Hayes and Chelsea. He made his O's debut against Southend United on 4 September 1946. A most energetic and enthusiastic performer, it was these qualities which helped to save O's from the embarrassment of having to apply for re-election to the League at the League's AGM in 1947, scoring twice in the penultimate match at Mansfield Town. Bacon was released by O's in May 1950 and joined Brentford on trial.

Cyril Bacon

SEASON	LEAGUE		FA CUP		TOTAL	
	Apps	Gls	Apps	Gls	Apps	Gls
1946/47	40	3	1	0	41	3
1947/48	27	0	0	0	27	0
1948/49	41	0	2	0	43	0
1949/50	10	0	0	0	10	0
TOTAL	118	3	3	0	121	3

Daniel BAILEY, 1922-23

Born East Ham, London on 26 May 1893, Dan Bailey started his career with Custom House before joining West Ham United in 1912. There he made 49 Southern League appearances, and the inside forward proved he had an eye for goal netting 13 times. After returning from service in Egypt during the First World War, he played in the Hammers' first season in the League (1920/21), making 38 senior appearances and scoring 4 goals. He joined Charlton in 1922, scoring 8 goals from 33 appearances. He moved to O's along with Joseph Hughes in July 1922 from Charlton Athletic, playing just one

Dan Bailey

season before retiring aged thirty. The following year he returned to action, joining Margate FC. Bailey died in Norwich on 3 April 1967.

SEASON	LEAGUE		FA CUP		TOTAL	
	Apps	Gls	Apps	Gls	Apps	Gls
1922/23	18	4	1	0	19	4
TOTAL	18	4	1	0	19	4

Edward Francis BAILY, 1958-60

Eddie Baily's spell with O's was brief, but those supporters who saw the thirty-three-year-old play will never forget his cajoling and coaxing of his colleagues. He was affectionately nicknamed 'the cheeky chappie', on account of his Cockney wit and one-touch creative skills. Born in Clapton, London on 6 August 1925, he started as a junior with Tottenham Hotspur after playing with Finchley FC and representing Hackney Schools. During the Second World War he was registered with Chelsea, but they cancelled his registration after an Army error which reported him missing in action. Thus he became a free agent and signed for Spurs. He made 325 senior appearances whilst at White Hart Lane, scoring 69 goals, and was an important cog in their famous push-and-run style of play during the 1950s. Baily was involved in one of the most controversial goals in League history on 2 April 1952 against Huddersfield Town, when his re-taken corner kick rebounded to him off the back of the unsighted referee, allowing him to cross the ball for the goal – a player touching the ball twice while taking a corner kick infringes rule seventeen. He was transferred to Port Vale in January 1956 for £6,000, but after just 26 League matches with 8 goals, he moved onto Nottingham Forest for £7,000 and was part of their

1957 side which gained promotion to the First Division. After 68 League appearances and 14 goals, he became an 'Oriental' in December 1958, his play inspiring the team to avoid what looked certain relegation. He linked up well with two other veterans, Tommy Johnston and Eddie Brown. Baily decided to retire in 1960, in order to take up a coaching position with the club, and his influence was there for all to see when O's were promoted (for the only time in the club's history) to the First Division in the 1961/62 season. He left the club in October 1963, and was appointed assistant manager at Spurs, a position he held until September 1974. After a short spell as scout with West Ham United, he became coach with Chesham United. He returned to the Hammers as chief scout in August 1976, but resigned during October 1977 to become assistant manager at Birmingham City and assistant manager to the England national team. Baily retired from the game in 1996, aged seventy-one. Nowadays he is living in Enfield. He won numerous representative honours, including 9 full England caps, scoring 5 times for his country.

Joe Baker

SEASON	LEAGUE		FA CUP		TOTAL	
	Apps	Gls	Apps	Gls	Apps	Gls
1958/59	18	3	1	0	19	3
1959/60	11	0	0	0	11	0
TOTAL	29	3	1	0	30	3

Joseph Philip BAKER, 1995-99

Joe Baker, a 5ft 8in right-winger ,had great pace and ball control and yet struggled to break into the O's first-team squad during the four years he was at Brisbane Road. Born in Kentish Town, London on 19 April 1977, the former Chelsea junior came to O's on 15 May 1995 from Charlton Athletic on a three-and-a-half year contract. However, he made just a handful of starts for O's, but does hold one record – he made 52 League appearances as a substitute, beating the previous record of 49 substitute appearances held by Lee Harvey. He had a couple of loan spells with Derby County and Portsmouth, and when he was left out of the O's tour to Uganda during the summer of 1998, many thought he was on the way out, yet he was still at the club for the start of the 1998/99 season. Baker's first League goal came in O's 8-0 drubbing of Doncaster Rovers on 28 December 1997, and he also scored in O's 4-4 League Cup draw at Bolton Wanderers on 30 September 1997. In 1998/99 he did not find favour with manager Tommy Taylor, playing only a handful of games. Later that season a foot injury restricted his appearances, and he also had an operation to remove a piece of skin from his windpipe to help him breathe more easily. Baker did not go on O's tour of Antigua in July 1999, and Barry Hearn stated that he would be released from his contract if he found another club. Baker went on trial with Billericay and played as a second-half substitute against O's in a friendly in July 1999. A month later he was on trial with Welling United, managed by former 'Oriental' Kevin Hales, but he returned to O's in September 1999. He could not even make it on to the bench with the club having twelve first-team players on the injured list. He was released at the end of October 1999 and joined Sutton United. More recently he has played for Billericay Town, making over 100 appearances and scoring 40 goals, and was voted their best player of the 2000/01 campaign.

Steve Baker

SEASON	LEAGUE		FA CUP		L. CUP	
	Apps	Gls	Apps	Gls	Apps	Gls
1995/96	4(16)	0	0(1)	0	0(2)	0
1996/97	15(5)	0	0(1)	0	0	0
1997/98	4(27)	3	0(2)	0	1(1)	2
1998/99	0(4)	0	0(1)	0	0	0
1999/2000	0	0	0	0	0	0
TOTAL	23(52)	3	0(5)	0	1(3)	2

TOTAL APPS	24(60)
TOTAL GOALS	5

* Joe Baker also appeared in 2(3) Auto Windscreens Shield matches.

Stephen BAKER, 1988-91

Steve Baker joined O's from Southampton in March 1988 for £50,000, after having made 85(13) senior appearances at the Dell. He scored on his O's debut against Swansea City on 26 March 1988. Born in Newcastle on 16 June 1962, he started with Wallsend Boys Club, joining Southampton as an apprentice in July 1978 and signing pro forms the following December. During his stay at the Dell, he went on loan to Burnley in February 1983. Baker played mostly at right full-back for O's. This attacking player, who stood just 5ft 5in tall, was ever-present in the promotion season of 1988/89 and featured in all 4 play-off matches. In the 1990/91 season, he was playing on a week-by-week contract basis, and the following season he did not report back for training. He joined AFC Bournemouth on a permanent basis in September 1991, making 5(1) League appearances. After a spell with Aldershot Town, he joined Farnborough Town in the Vauxhall Conference, making 16 appearances. He was still playing for Farnborough in 1998/1999, but after having made over 150 appearances for the Hampshire club, Baker re-joined Aldershot in May 1999. In July 2000 the veteran defender joined Basingstoke and remained with them for the 2001/02 season. However, the thirty-nine-year-old has been out for most of 2002 with an Achilles injury.

SEASON	LEAGUE		FA CUP		L. CUP	
	Apps	Gls	Apps	Gls	Apps	Gls
1987/88	9	3	0	0	0	0
1988/89*	50	3	1	0	5	0
1989/90	27(5)	0	0(1)	0	3(1)	0
1990/91	23(2)	0	3(1)	0	5	0
TOTAL	109(7)	6	4(2)	0	13(1)	0

TOTAL APPS   126(10)

TOTAL GOALS   6

* The 1988/89 season includes 4 promotion play-off matches.

** Steve Baker also appeared in 7 Auto Windscreens Shield matches.

Edgar Albert BALLARD, 1946-47, 1952-53

Wing-half Ted Ballard is one of a handful of players to have two spells as an 'Oriental'. Born in Brentford, London on 16 June 1920, and having started his football career with Hayes FC, he joined Brentford as an amateur in September 1943, playing in 5 regional matches during the Second World War for the Bees. He joined O's in May 1946, staying just one season before an exchange deal involving Billy Stroud, which took him to Southampton in June 1947. Ballard was at the Dell for five seasons, making 47 League appearances as understudy to Alf Ramsey. He returned to O's in July 1952 on a free transfer, but failed to make a first-team appearance. In 1953 he joined Snowdon Colliery FC, and then in June 1956 he joined Hastings United and was appointed their player-manager in June 1957. A year later he retired from playing, and in June 1961 he became their secretary-manager. On leaving full-time football, he served for a few years as landlord of the Clarence Public House in Hastings, and during the early 1970s, he was employed as a franchise officer for the Green Shield Stamp Company, before retiring in April 1991 to live in St Leonards-on-Sea, Sussex, where he still resides.

SEASON	LEAGUE		FA CUP		TOTAL	
	Apps	Gls	Apps	Gls	Apps	Gls
1946/47	26	1	1	0	27	1
1952/53	0	0	0	0	0	0
TOTAL	26	1	1	0	27	1

Neil Anthony BANFIELD, 1983-85

Neil Banfield was born in Poplar, London on 20 January 1962. Having gained District and England schoolboy and youth honours, he became an apprentice with Crystal Palace in August 1979. The defender was released by the Eagles after endless reserve outings and just 2(1) first-team appearances during 1980/81. In June 1981, he decided to try his fortune in Australia with Adelaide City FC, where he stayed for two seasons. He joined O's in December 1983, making his League debut against Preston North End on 6 March 1984. Banfield played more regularly the following season, but was released in May 1985 and joined Dagenham & Redbridge FC. He was later Charlton Athletic's youth-team coach and then Arsenal's under-17 coach.

SEASON	LEAGUE		FA CUP		L. CUP	
	Apps	Gls	Apps	Gls	Apps	Gls
1983/84	6	0	0	0	0	0
1984/85	24(1)	0	3	0	2	0
TOTAL	30(1)	0	3	0	2	0

TOTAL APPS   35(1)

TOTAL GOALS   0

* Neil Banfield also appeared in 4 Auto Windscreens Shield matches.

Tunji Babajide BANJO, 1977-82, 1987-88
This busy and nimble midfield player was born in Kensington, London on 19 February 1960. He represented Brent, Middlesex and London Schools, and was spotted by O's player Bobby Fisher whilst he was representing London against Liverpool Schools during a match at Brisbane Road. He was invited to attend a training session with O's and Banjo signed apprentice forms in 1977. After numerous youth and reserve matches and 2 substitute appearances in the first team, he made a brilliant 'full' first-team debut against Burnley in a 3-0 win on 18 April 1978 – his display was possibly one of the finest by a youth player making his debut. Remarkably, before his dream League debut he came on as a substitute in the sixty-eighth minute in O's FA Cup semi-final match against Arsenal at Stamford Bridge a few weeks earlier. Banjo later stated: 'Although I came on wearing the number 12 shirt for only about twenty minutes in the semi-final, it was the highlight of my career and the moment led to my recognition by the Nigerian FA.' Banjo was a player full of flair who did not fit into the rigid system of football that was rife at the time. He was good in two aspects of the game – intelligent off-the-ball running with great acceleration, and excellent accurate passing. He made his Nigerian international debut – with fellow 'Oriental' John Chiedozie – in Lagos during 1981, making both of their goals against Tunisia. Banjo went on to win a total of 7 Nigerian caps (the most international caps by any O's player, along with Chiedozie and Tony Grealish of Eire). Banjo was released in May 1982 to join AEL Limasol in Greece. He returned to O's in 1987 on a non-contract basis, but never played in the first team. After his playing days he worked as a bus driver in North London, as well as being appointed in July 2001 as reserve-team coach (under another former 'Oriental', Bobby Fisher) at Jewish club London Maccabi Lions of the Herts Senior County League.

SEASON	LEAGUE		FA CUP		L. CUP	
	Apps	Gls	Apps	Gls	Apps	Gls
1977/78	3(3)	0	0(1)	0	0	0
1978/79	13(4)	1	0(1)	0	1	0
1979/80	1	0	0	0	1	0
1980/81	0	0	0	0	0	0
1981/82	3	0	0	0	0	0
1987/88	0	0	0	0	0	0
TOTAL	20(7)	1	0(2)	0	2	0

TOTAL APPS   22(9)
TOTAL GOALS   1

* Tunji Banjo also appeared in 3(1) Anglo-Scottish Cup matches, scoring once.

Tunji Banjo

Arthur BANNER, 1947-53

Arthur Banner was voted by supporters as one of the all-time great O's players in a special Millenium poll conducted by the club in December 1999. Banner was an excellent captain during the late 1940s, and will be remembered by older fans for the way he would roll up his sleeves and encourage his teammates. Born in Sheffield on 28 June 1918, he started his career with local junior side Lopham FC, before joining Doncaster Rovers in March 1937. He could never break into their senior side, so he came south and joined West Ham in May 1938. After 27 League appearances for the Hammers, he became an 'Oriental' during February 1948, signing on a free transfer, and he formed a wonderful partnership with Ledger Ritson. Banner only scored 2 senior goals, yet he also netted 2 from the penalty spot in friendlies in 1951 against Racing Club of Haarlem from Holland in a Festival of Britain match (a 3-1 win) and against Scottish side Airdrieonians (a 2-5 home defeat). Banner proved a loyal servant and was awarded with a benefit match in 1953. He joined Sittingbourne as player-manager in May 1953 and later coached Ilford FC. Banner retired to Thorpe Bay, where he died at his home on 30 April 1980.

Arthur Banner

William BARKE (see NAYLOR)

Donny BARNARD, 2001-present

Donny (not Donald) Barnard was born in Forest Gate, London on 1 July 1984. The 6ft tall left-back graduated through O's youth ranks, appearing in the highly successful under-19 side. He also made 19 appearances for the under-17 side. He made his League debut when coming on as a substitute in the sixty-ninth minute during a 2-1 win at Southend United on 1 September 2001. He was brought on to replace Scott Oakes in a reshuffle after Dave McGhee was sent off, and looked like being a fine, assured passer of the ball, with plenty of pace. Barnard made his full debut in a 2-1 win over Rushden & Diamonds two weeks later. After breaking a leg, he started his recovery by making his return on 1 December 2001 for half-an-hour in a training match.

SEASON	LEAGUE		FA CUP		TOTAL	
	Apps	Gls	Apps	Gls	Apps	Gls
1947/48	12	0	0	0	12	0
1948/49	30	0	2	0	23	0
1949/50	36	1	1	0	37	1
1950/51	22	0	0	0	22	0
1951/52	40	0	9	1	49	1
1952/53	24	0	2	0	26	0
TOTAL	164	1	14	1	178	2

SEASON	LEAGUE		FA CUP		L. CUP	
	Apps	Gls	Apps	Gls	Apps	Gls
2001/02	6(4)	0	0(1)	0	0	0
TOTAL	6(4)	0	0(1)	0	0	0

TOTAL APPS	6(5)
TOTAL GOALS	0

Gary Lloyd BARNETT, 1993-95

This diminutive but busy forward – he stood just 5ft 6in tall and weighed 9st 4lb – was to join O's in August 1989, but failed a medical test which showed a hole in the heart and returned to his club, Fulham. It wasn't until 1993 that he did eventually join O's in a £30,000 deal from Huddersfield Town. Born in Stratford-upon-Avon on 11 March 1963, he started his career as a trainee with Coventry City, but in 1984 moved on to Oxford United, playing 45 League matches and scoring 9 goals. He moved to Fulham in September 1985 for £20,000, making 193(16) appearances and scoring 35 goals. In July 1990 he joined Huddersfield Town for £30,000, making a further 100 League appearances. The thirty-two-year-old started off well in his first season at Brisbane Road by scoring 7 goals, but in 1994/95 he was in and out of the side, and was released by manager Holland in May 1995, joining Scunthorpe United two months later. A disappointed Barnett said at the time: 'I've got to accept it and gradually the pain will go away. I've got to be positive and find myself another club.' After a short spell with Worcester City, he became a successful player-coach at Welsh club Barry Town in September 1995, and was appointed manager in the summer of 1996. Under his leadership they have won the Welsh League twice and qualified for European competition.

Gary Barnett

In August 1999 he was appointed assistant manager with Kidderminster for their new adventure in the League.

SEASON	LEAGUE		FA CUP		L. CUP	
	Apps	Gls	Apps	Gls	Apps	Gls
1993/94	32(4)	7	2	0	1	0
1994/95	15(12)	0	2	0	2	0
TOTAL	47(16)	7	4	0	3	0

TOTAL APPS	54(16)
TOTAL GOALS	7

* Gary Barnett also appeared in 5(2) Auto Windscreens Shield matches, scoring once.

John Victor BARR, 1922-23

Born in Medway, Kent in 1902, John Barr became an 'Oriental' after joining from Folkestone in August 1922. He made his debut in the 2-0 win over Leicester City on 9 September 1922. However, the right-winger could never establish himself as a first-teamer and eventually left the club in July 1923, joining Chatham Town.

SEASON	LEAGUE		FA CUP		TOTAL	
	Apps	Gls	Apps	Gls	Apps	Gls
1922/23	8	0	0	0	8	0
TOTAL	8	0	0	0	8	0

Scott BARRETT, 1998-present

Goalkeeper Scott Barrett was born in Ilkeston on 2 April 1963. Who would have thought back then that Barrett's heroic saves would ultimately take O's to their third Wembley appearance? His brilliant save in the dying minutes of the second leg of the Division Three play-off at Rotherham took the match into extra time and then into a penalty shoot-out. He saved Rotherham's second and third penalties to take O's to a Wembley play-off final against Scunthorpe United in May 1999, which was, unfortunately, lost 1-0. This was Barrett's second appearance at Wembley, having previously helped Colchester United beat Witton Albion to lift the FA Trophy in 1992. He began his eighteen-year career with Ilkeston Town. His League career started in 1984 with Wolverhampton Wanderers, where he ended up playing 32 senior matches. In a League career which featured spells at Wolves, Stoke City, Colchester United, Stockport County Gillingham and Cambridge, this excellent shot-stopper made 275 senior appearances before joining O's on a free transfer from Cambridge United on 25 January 1999. He is also on record as having scored a goal for Colchester United in a GM Vauxhall Conference clash against Wycombe Wanderers in 1991 – the opposing goalkeeper that day was former 'Oriental' Chris Mackenzie. Barrett made

his O's debut against Darlington on 30 January 1999. (In fact, he was expected to join O's in the summer of 1997, but manager Taylor refused to pay a fee for the experienced 'keeper.) Barrett has performed consistently well since replacing the out-of-form Mackenzie in goal during the club's push for promotion in 1999. He shared the jersey in 1999/2000 with Ashley Bayes and signed a new one-year contract, but during the 2000/01 season he has sat on the bench as understudy to Bayes. He came back into the side in March 2001, after Bayes looked a little weary and was rested, but Barrett was back on the bench during O's run to the play-off final in May 2001. Thirty-eight-year-old Barrett signed another one-year contract in June 2001 and also agreed to act as the club's goalkeeping coach. He had an unexpected run in the first team in 2001/02 when first-choice goalkeeper Ashley Bayes went out with a long-term shoulder injury.

Scott Barrett

SEASON	LEAGUE		FA CUP		L. CUP	
	Apps	Gls	Apps	Gls	Apps	Gls
1998/99*	23	0	0	0	0	0
1999/2000	29	0	2	0	1	0
2000/01	7	0	0	0	0	0
2001/02	32	0	4	0	0	0
TOTAL	91	0	5	0	2	0

TOTAL APPS	98
TOTAL GOALS	0

* Barrett's League total includes 3 promotion play-off matches in 1998/99.

George BARRY, 1994-95

This 5ft 8in full-back joined O's from Fisher 93 FC of the Beazer Homes League on 16 March 1995, at the age of twenty-seven, on a non-contract basis until the end of that season. Born in Islington, London on 19 September 1967, Barry started his career in 1984 as an apprentice with Crystal Palace, playing at centre forward during his two years at Selhurst Park. He had previously spent three seasons playing in Cyprus and for the past two years he had been turning out for Fisher. He impressed the O's management during three reserve trial matches and was thrown into action in an away fixture against Cambridge United, which resulted in a 0-0 draw on 21 March 1995. Barry later returned to the Fisher club on 31 May 1995. In January 1998, Barry joined Cheshunt.

SEASON	LEAGUE		FA CUP		L. CUP	
	Apps	Gls	Apps	Gls	Apps	Gls
1994/95	5(1)	0	0	0	0	0
TOTAL	5(1)	0	0	0	0	0

TOTAL APPS	5(1)
TOTAL GOALS	0

Christopher BART-WILLIAMS, 1989-91

Chris Bart-Williams made his full League debut for O's at the age of 16 years and 232 days against Tranmere Rovers on 2 February 1991, although he had previously come on as a substitute at Grimsby Town on 23 October 1990. He made an instant impression playing in midfield and showing tremendous maturity and ability with a wonderful temperament. He signed YTS forms with O's and earned £27.50 per week. It was O's scout Jimmy Hallybone who first spotted Bart-Williams playing for Sunday side Grasshoppers in New Southgate, and he himself acknowledged the assistance he received from the youth coach at the time, John Gorman. Born in Freetown, Sierra Leone on 16 June 1974, manager Eustace said of him: 'If he maintains the improvement he's shown so far, he is going to be an exceptional player.' A week before his seventeenth birthday he gained England under-19 honours whilst with O's, starring in a 2-1 win over Iceland (and was the youngest player on the field), and on his return he signed a two-year contract with the club. After just making 34(2) League appearances for O's, he moved to Sheffield Wednesday on 21 November 1991 for £350,000 (this fee included the transfer of 'keeper Chris Turner). O's also stood to pick up another £225,000 divided into three equal payments, the last of which would be paid after he had played 60 games for the club. That took the final deal to £575,000, but added on was another £100,000 for an England cap as well as a percentage of the profit, should Wednesday sell him. Bart-Williams, a 5ft 11in midfielder, had shone in the 2 League cup ties against Wednesday a few months earlier. O's boss Eustace said: 'We did not want to push

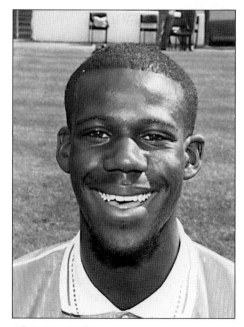

Chris Bart-Williams

Chris out anywhere for a quick cash return, but he loved his two-week training spell at Hillsborough and wanted to sign for them. We are delighted with the deal and so are they, and most importantly, Chris himself.' Bart-Williams made his meteoric rise from playing for Arvensdale FC on Hackney Marshes during February 1990 to Hillsborough in just 18 months. He made 95(29) appearances, scoring 16 goals for the Owls before joining Nottingham Forest, now under their new manager Frank Clark, on 1 July 1995 for £2.5 million (with O's picking up a percentage of that fee). He has appeared 16 times for the England under-21 side, although he has never won a full cap. Bart-Williams, after seven years of service with Forest, handed in a transfer request during May 2001, wanting to move back into the Premiership. The Forest skipper was top scorer with 15 goals during the 2000/01 season, and made a total of 200(7) League appearances with 30 goals. He was briefly linked with a £1 million move to Birmingham City, but after that fell through, the Forest directors informed their manager, Paul Hart, during November 2001 that he should not pick Bart-Williams again for first-team duty, so that he could be on his way as soon as possible. Shortly after the directors took this step, Bart-Williams moved to Premiership side Charlton Athletic on 3 December for a month's loan. He later made the move permanent, signing in January 2002 on a free transfer.

SEASON	LEAGUE		FA CUP		L. CUP	
	Apps	Gls	Apps	Gls	Apps	Gls
1990/91	19(2)	2	0	0	0	0
1991/92	15	0	0	0	4	0
TOTAL	34(2)	2	0	0	4	0

TOTAL APPS	38(2)
TOTAL GOALS	2

* Chris Bart-Williams also appeared in 2 Auto Windscreens Shield matches.

Frederick Leslie BARTLETT, 1937-48

Fred Bartlett was born in Reading on 5 March 1913. This tall, elegant centre half joined O's in May 1937 from Queens Park Rangers (after playing 50 senior matches for them between October 1932 and May 1937), as a replacement for Dave Affleck. His O's debut was in the first match played at Brisbane Road (Osborne Road, as it was then known) against Cardiff City on 28 August 1937. During the Second World War, he played in a club record 207 regional fixtures between 1939 and 1946 and was one of a small number of players to be retained for the 1946/47 season. During the first season after the Second World War, he played 36 times in the League and also made an FA Cup appearance. However, the following season he played only once – at Port Vale in January 1948. He enjoyed a benefit match against QPR with William P. Wright on 2 May 1949, and soon after joined Southern League outfit Gloucester City. Bartlett died in Henley-on-Thames in 1968.

SEASON	LEAGUE		FA CUP		TOTAL	
	Apps	Gls	Apps	Gls	Apps	Gls
1937/38	20	0	1	0	21	0
1938/39	39	0	2	0	41	0
1945/46*	-	-	2	0	2	0
1946/47	36	0	1	0	37	0
1947/48	1	0	0	0	1	0
TOTAL	96	0	6	0	102	0

* There was no League competition in 1945/46.

** Fred Bartlett also appeared in 2 Third Division Cup matches between 1937 and 1939.

Herbert George BATTEN, 1927-29

Bert Batten was born in Bedminster, Bristol on 14 May 1898. The forward joined Bristol City from Paulton Rovers in July 1920, making 7 League appearances. In May 1921 he moved on to Plymouth Argyle where he had a most successful stay, playing 89 League matches and scoring 27 goals between 1921 and 1926. Whilst with Argyle, he went to Australia with an FA touring team during 1925. After 51 League matches, including spells with Everton, Bradford City and Reading, he joined O's in January 1927 but didn't really settle at the club and moved on to Northfleet United on 8 October 1929. Batten died in Chelsea, London on 15 May 1956.

SEASON	LEAGUE		FA CUP		TOTAL	
	Apps	Gls	Apps	Gls	Apps	Gls
1927/28	10	1	0	0	10	1
1928/29	21	5	0	0	21	5
TOTAL	31	6	0	0	31	6

Ashley John BAYES, 1999-present

Ashley Bayes was born in Lincoln on 19 April 1972, and he started his career as a trainee with Brentford, turning professional on 5 July 1990. The 6ft 1in tall goalkeeper made just 4 senior appearances for the Bees (including a match against O's) before a free transfer took him to Torquay United on 13 August 1993. He made 119 senior appearances for the Gulls during his three-year stay. He moved to Exeter City on 31 July 1996 and proved to be consistent and enthusiastic, showing what a good shot-stopper he is, with excellent reflexes. He missed very few games for the Grecians, playing 144 senior matches. It was Bayes who pulled off some good saves against O's to

Ashley Bayes

deny Tommy Taylor his first points as manager during his first match in charge during November 1996. He remained a crowd favourite throughout his stay at St James Park and was voted their Player of the Year for the 1997/98 season. He signed for O's on 6 June 1999 under the Bosman ruling as cover for Scott Barrett, however, he made his debut at the start of the 1999/2000 season at Carlisle United on 7 August. He began the 2000/01 season as first-choice 'keeper, and gave a first-class showing in the FA Cup tie against Tottenham Hotspur in January 2001. He seemed to lose form and looked a little weary after a long season and was replaced by Scott Barrett in March 2001, but returned to the fray to see O's reach their second play-off final in three years. He missed much of the start of the 2001/02 season with a long-term shoulder injury. He made his return as first-team goalkeeper when coming on as a substitute for the injured Scott Barrett against Macclesfield Town on 9 March 2002. This is the first time a goalkeeper has come on for O's in a League game as a playing substitute.

SEASON	LEAGUE		FA CUP		L. CUP	
	Apps	Gls	Apps	Gls	Apps	Gls
1999/2000	17	0	1	0	2	0
2000/01*	42	0	4	0	4	0
2001/02	12(1)	0	0	0	1	0
TOTAL	71(1)	0	5	0	7	0

TOTAL APPS   83(1)

TOTAL GOALS   0

*Bayes' League record includes 3 play-off matches in 2000/01.

** Ashley Bayes also made a single appearance in both the Auto Windscreens Shield in 1999/2000 and the LDV Vans Trophy in 2000/01.

Johnny Baynham

John BAYNHAM, 1946-48

Welshman Johnny Baynham was born in Rhondda, South Wales on 21 April 1918. He started his career with Acton United before moving onto Brentford and then joining O's in March 1946. There he played in the latter part of the 1945/46 season, scoring against Northampton Town in a wartime regional fixture in April 1946. This fast-raiding left-winger had a straightforward style with not too many frills, but on his day proved to be a tricky wingman to stop. He scored direct from a corner kick on his League debut at Southend United on 4 September 1946. In August 1948 he joined Swindon Town, in a deal that brought Jackie Dryden to Brisbane Road. Baynham made 4 appearances for the Wiltshire club scoring once. He then played for Guildford City in 1949 and managed Chesham United between 1958 and 1966. Baynham died in Hillingdon during February 1995.

SEASON	LEAGUE		FA CUP		TOTAL	
	Apps	Gls	Apps	Gls	Apps	Gls
1946/47	36	4	1	0	37	4
1947/48	24	3	1	0	25	3
TOTAL	60	7	2	0	62	7

Peter Edward BEALE, 1908-09

Londoner Peter Beale started his playing career with Peterborough Loco FC before moving to Southern League outfit Leyton FC. The left-winger joined O's in 1908, making his League debut against Hull City on 2 January 1909, replacing the injured Felix Ward. He scored later that month at Blackpool. Beale was largely a reserve player with O's, and left in 1909 to join Southern League team New Brompton, after Gillingham and Northampton Town.

SEASON	LEAGUE		FA CUP		TOTAL	
	Apps	Gls	Apps	Gls	Apps	Gls
1908/09	5	1	1	0	6	1
TOTAL	5	1	1	0	6	1

Matthew John BEALL, 1998-2002

The long-running saga of Beall's transfer from Cambridge United was eventually resolved on 26 October 1998 when he was finally allowed to put pen to paper, after Cambridge refused to release his registration for six months. A tribunal ordered O's to pay £25,000, with another £12,500 to be paid after a further 20 appearances and another £12,500 after 40 appearances, with a 20 per cent sell-on fee in the contract. Born in Enfield on 4 December 1977, this diminutive tough-tackling defensive midfielder started out with Norwich City as a schoolboy. He joined Cambridge United as a YTS player in August 1995 and made his first-team debut as a substitute in the AWS in September 1995. His full League debut came in January 1996 whilst still a trainee, and he signed professional forms on 28 March 1996. He was an immediate hit with the United fans and made 73(8) League appearances, scoring 7 goals at the Abbey Stadium. He also played in 6 FA Cup matches, scoring twice. He refused to sign a new contract at Cambridge, and even threatened to quit football rather than play for the U's again. He made his O's debut against Scunthorpe United on 31 October 1998, and he scored the winning goal a week later at Hull City. He played in the 3 play-off matches in May 1999. Beall missed the start of the 2000/01 season due a stress fracture in his shin, incurred during the summer, returning to a position on the bench only in October. With an influx of new players at Brisbane Road, Beall went on loan to Conference side Dover Athletic on 16 February 2001 He should have felt at home teaming up with three former 'Orientals' in their squad – namely Paul Hyde, Danny Chapman and Lee Shearer – as well as Danny Hockton, who was with O's on loan. He made his debut in a 1-1 draw at Doncaster Rovers on 17 February, making 2 further appearances before returning to O's and playing in the 1-1 draw at Shrewsbury Town on 17 March 2001, looking a lot sharper after his spell away. He was an unused substitute in the play-off final against Blackpool at the Millennium Stadium in May 2001. Beall signed a new one-year contract in June 2001, but was released in January 2002 and joined Dr Marten's Premier League side Cambridge City in February.

SEASON	LEAGUE		FA CUP		L. CUP	
	Apps	Gls	Apps	Gls	Apps	Gls
1998/99*	24(2)	2	5	0	0	0
1999/2000	22(11)	1	1	0	2	0

SEASON	LEAGUE		FA CUP		L. CUP	
2000/01	12(5)	0	0(2)	0	0	0
2001/02	7(4)	0	0	0	0	0
TOTAL	65(22)	3	6(2)	0	2	0

TOTAL APPS	73(24)
TOTAL GOALS	3

* Beall's League total includes 3 promotion play-off matches in 1998/99.

** Beall also appeared in 2 LDV Vans Trophy matches between 2000 and 2002.

Malcolm Lloyd BEASON, 1975-76

Born in Dulwich, London on 1 December 1955, this constructive midfield player started as an apprentice with Crystal Palace in August 1973, joining O's from Palace in September 1975. He showed considerable promise during his stint in the reserves, but made just one League appearance as a playing substitute in the 2-0 victory over Oldham Athletic on 1 November 1975, replacing Peter Bennett. After suffering a serious injury in a reserve match, he was out for five months and became disillusioned with the game and decided to retire from football.

SEASON	LEAGUE		FA CUP		L. CUP	
	Apps	Gls	Apps	Gls	Apps	Gls
1975/76	0(1)	0	0	0	0	0
TOTAL	0(1)	0	0	0	0	0

TOTAL APPS	0(1)
TOTAL GOALS	0

Paul BEESLEY, 1988-90

Paul Beesley still holds the club record for the highest transfer fee paid for an incoming player. O's boss Frank Clark paid out £175,000 for the central defender from Wigan Athletic on 20 October 1988. He went on to have a long and industrious career, making over 450 senior appearances, before joining Conference side Chester City on 4 July 2000. He stayed with O's for just one season and was sold for a handsome profit to Sheffield United on 10 July 1990 for £300,000. Born in Liverpool on 21 July 1965, the 6ft 1in player started his career with Marine FC, before joining Wigan on a free transfer on 22 September 1984, making 172(2) appearances before his move to East London. However, life in the capital did not suit his family, and when Dave Bassett at newly-promoted Sheffield United came in with a big-money offer, everyone was happy with the deal. After 168 games for the Blades, he returned to the Premiership with Leeds United in a £250,000 deal during August 1995, making 29(4) senior appearances and 2(2) appearances in UEFA Cup matches. After George Graham took over at Elland Road, Beesley lost his way and it was Frank Clark at Manchester City who paid £600,000 for the thirty-two-year-old player during

Paul Beesley, O's £175,000 record signing

February 1997. After Clark left Maine Road, Beesley could not find a regular place, making just 10(3) appearances for the Blues. After a couple of loan spells in 1998 (with Port Vale and West Bromwich Albion), he signed for Port Vale in August 1998 on a free transfer. Beesley spent just one season with Vale, making 34 senior appearances and scoring 3 goals. He joined Blackpool in May 1999, and after 15(3) League matches came his move to Football Conference side Chester City on 4 July 2000, replacing former 'Oriental' Stuart Hick who left Chester after they lost their League status. He was appointed assistant manager and made 35 senior appearances before being sacked in May 2001 for failing to turn up for post-season training. However, he was reinstated the following month at the troubled club. The thirty-six-year-old Beesley eventually left Chester City and moved across the water to Ireland with Ballymena United on a month's contract, before signing for Nationwide Conference side Stalybridge Celtic on 18 October 2001 and making his debut in a 1-0 win over Yeovil two days later. It was quite a career for O's record signing.

SEASON	LEAGUE		FA CUP		L. CUP	
	Apps	Gls	Apps	Gls	Apps	Gls
1988/89	32	1	1	0	0	0
TOTAL	32	1	1	0	0	0

TOTAL APPS	33
TOTAL GOALS	1

* Paul Beesley also appeared in 2 Auto Windscreens Shield matches, scoring once.

Joseph BELL, 1924-26
Born in Shettleston, Scotland Joe Bell became an 'Oriental' in July 1924, joining from Dumbarton, having played one season with the Scottish side and making 16 Scottish League appearances during 1923/24. A player who could play at wing-half or on the wing, he made just a single League appearance in each of his seasons at Millfields Road. Bell was transferred to Welsh club Aberdare Athletic in July 1926, making 23 Third Division (South) appearances, including playing in their final ever League match on 7 May 1927 against Brighton.

SEASON	LEAGUE		FA CUP		TOTAL	
	Apps	Gls	Apps	Gls	Apps	Gls
1924/25	1	0	0	0	1	0
1925/26	1	0	0	0	1	0
TOTAL	2	0	0	0	2	0

Mark Dickson BELL, 1907-10
One of the more talented and famous Scottish-born players to have played for O's in the Edwardian era, Mark Bell was born in Edinburgh on 8 February 1881.

Mark Bell

Gary Bellamy

Bell started his career as a nippy winger with Roseberry FC and then Edinburgh Hibernians. His professional career commenced as a seventeen-year-old with the Edinburgh side St Barnards FC in 1898, where he made 24 Scottish League appearances. In October 1900 he joined Heart of Midlothian, making 29 senior appearances and scoring 9 goals. He also gained a Scottish Cup winners' medal and a Scottish international cap in March 1901 against Wales. During May 1902 he moved south of the Border to play for Southern League Southampton, and bagged 2 goals in their 11-0 victory over Watford in December 1902. After just 9 Southern League appearances with a return of 6 goals, he returned to Hearts in April 1903 to make 17 senior appearances, scoring 3 goals. In May 1904 Bell joined Fulham of the Southern League and stayed for 3 years, making 58 appearances and scoring 6 goals. He joined O's in August 1907 and operated at right-half, and took over the captaincy from Jumbo Reason in 1909. He remained at O's for three seasons before returning to the Southern League with Leyton FC. Mark Bell was a constructive player whose best years were probably just behind him when at Millfields Road. During the First World War he guested for Fulham in 1915. He then emigrated to Australia in 1919, but returned to Edinburgh after the war, where he died on 26 October 1961, aged eighty-one.

SEASON	LEAGUE		FA CUP		TOTAL	
	Apps	Gls	Apps	Gls	Apps	Gls
1907/08	36	3	5	2	41	5
1908/09	28	1	1	0	29	1
1909/10	24	0	1	0	25	0
TOTAL	88	4	7	2	95	6

Gary BELLAMY, 1992-96

Gary Bellamy was a player who had been watched by O's for some time before he was signed by manager Eustace on a month's loan. He then stayed for four seasons. This 6ft 2in defender was born in Worksop on 4 July 1962. He started as an apprentice with Chesterfield in 1980, making 184 League appearances and contributing 7 goals. He moved on to join Wolverhampton Wanderers, accumulating 136 appearances and scoring 9 goals. He played in their 2-0 victory at Wembley over Burnley in the Sherpa Van Trophy in front of 82,000 fans. Bellamy signed for O's on 17 November 1992 for £30,000, and proved to be a very good professional who brought quality and sureness to the team. He became the first player to be released by new manager Pat Holland, after having made 140 senior appearances, when Holland surprisingly revealed: 'He's on a free transfer, I will not be using him any more.' His professional career spanned some sixteen years and included 452(9) League appearances and 22 goals. After a spell with Braintree Town, Bellamy then became player-manager of Chelmsford City in August 1997 and held that position until May 2001. However, after taking them from the Eastern Counties League into the Dr Martens League Premier Division, he was next appointed as the new boss of Dover Athletic on 5 June 2001. Bellamy was fired from that role on 9 November 2001 after having been in charge of the club for just 19 matches, of which 13 were lost. Bellamy himself was unhappy at the financial situation at the club.

SEASON	LEAGUE		FA CUP		L. CUP	
	Apps	Gls	Apps	Gls	Apps	Gls
1992/93	38(1)	4	2	0	0	0
1993/94	27(2)	1	2	0	1	0
1994/95	32	0	2	0	0	0
1995/96	32	1	1	0	1	0
TOTAL	129(3)	6	7	0	2	0

TOTAL APPS 138(3)

TOTAL GOALS 6

* Gary Bellamy also appeared in 14 Auto Windscreens Shield matches.

Michael Richard BENNETT, 1997-98

Born in Camberwell, London on 27 July 1969, Mickey Bennett joined O's from non-League Cambridge City after playing for a number of League clubs including Charlton Athletic, Wimbledon, Brentford, Millwall and Cardiff City, in a League career that spanned ten years and 139 matches. 'Beno' a midfielder, started his career as an apprentice with Charlton in April 1987, making 24(11) League appearances and representing the England under-19 side on

a tour of Brazil, before a £60,000 move took him to Brentford in July 1992. He made 40(6) League appearances for the Bees. His O's debut came at Exeter City, where he played for twenty-two minutes before being substituted. He made just a single further appearance as a playing substitute, but was released in June 1998 and joined Brighton & Hove Albion on a one-year contract, where he made 37(1) appearances and was voted their Player of the Year in 1999. In August 1999 he joined Canvey Island FC.

SEASON	LEAGUE		FA CUP		L. CUP	
	Apps	Gls	Apps	Gls	Apps	Gls
1997/98	1(1)	0	0	0	0	0
TOTAL	1(1)	0	0	0	0	0

TOTAL APPS 1(1)

TOTAL GOALS 0

* Mickey Bennett also appeared in a single Auto Windscreens Shield match.

Peter Leslie BENNETT, 1970-79

Born in Hillingdon on 24 June 1946, this former England schoolboy came to O's as part of the £78,000 deal that took Tommy Taylor to West Ham United in October 1970. 'Les' Bennett joined the Hammers as an apprentice in July 1963, making 39 League appearances and scoring 3 goals. He made his debut a few days after his arrival at Brisbane Road against Sheffield Wednesday, and soon after was appointed club captain. He played a major part in O's run to the semi-final of the FA Cup in 1978. Bennett proved a very versatile player, playing at centre-half, midfield and centre forward. Alas, he was hit by a number of serious injuries, including a pelvic injury which eventually forced him to retire from the game in 1980. He later

Peter Bennett

held a coaching position with the club and was awarded a well-deserved testimonial in 1982. Bennett now lives in West London and works as a carpenter.

SEASON	LEAGUE		FA CUP		L. CUP	
	Apps	Gls	Apps	Gls	Apps	Gls
1970/71	30	0	3	0	0	0
1971/72	35	0	4	0	0	0
1972/73	25	1	0	0	2	0
1973/74	2	0	0	0	0	0
1974/75	15(1)	0	2	0	1	0
1975/76	33(1)	5	0	0	1	0
1976/77	25(2)	5	4	0	2	0
1977/78	24	2	5	0	1	1
1978/79	6	0	0	0	1	0
TOTAL	195(4)	13	18	0	8	1

TOTAL APPS	221(4)
TOTAL GOALS	14

* Peter Bennett also played in 1(1) Texaco Cup match in 1974/75 and 6(1) Anglo-Scottish Cup matches.

Charles George BENSON, 1912-13

Sunderland-born Charles Benson came to O's in July 1912 from Sunderland College. The right-winger played once in the League on 28 December 1912 in a 2-1 defeat by Preston North End, replacing the injured Joe Dix. He was released in May 1913 and returned to the north-east.

SEASON	LEAGUE		FA CUP		TOTAL	
	Apps	Gls	Apps	Gls	Apps	Gls
1912/13	1	0	0	0	1	0
TOTAL	1	0	0	0	1	0

Daniel BENSTOCK, (1992-94)

Before joining O's, Danny Benstock was cleaning windows for a living and playing part-time football with Barking in the Diadora League. He was the second player in recent years to arrive from Mayersbrook Park, Alan Hull being the other. Born in Hackney, London on 10 July 1970, he started playing football with Hoxton Lion Boys Club, after playing representative football for East London and London Schools. Benstock had a short spell as a junior with Gillingham, before moving into non-League football with Enfield. After a couple of seasons he joined Barking, where he played at left-back. He signed an eighteen-month contract on a five-figure deal and made his O's debut in the AWS match against Wrexham, the twenty-two-year-old winning the Man of the Match award with a swash-buckling midfield performance. He was not a regular first-teamer during his stay, and was released in May 1994. He later played for Purfleet and also the reformed Collier Row & Romford Club in 1996/97 (for whom he made a total of 197 appearances), helping them to win the ICIS League Second Division title. He signed for Bishop Stortford in February

Danny Benstock

1999, where he could be found playing alongside former O's youth player Scott Honeyball. He joined Ford United in January 2000.

SEASON	LEAGUE		FA CUP		L. CUP	
	Apps	Gls	Apps	Gls	Apps	Gls
1992/93	8(1)	0	0	0	0	0
1993/94	9(3)	0	0	0	0(2)	0
TOTAL	17(4)	0	0	0	0(2)	0

TOTAL APPS	17(6)
TOTAL GOALS	0

* Danny Benstock also appeared in a single Auto Windscreens Shield match.

Claude BERRY, 1900-05

Londoner Claude Berry joined O's when still a non-League side in 1900 from local amateur football. The right half was in the side that won the Middlesex Charity Cup and the West Ham Charity Cup in 1901/02. Berry also played in O's first match in the Second Division of the Southern League as well as playing in all 6 FA cup ties in 1904/05. He was not retained for the 1905/06 season, and a local newspaper reported that he had returned to play non-League football in the Clapton area.

SEASON	LEAGUE		FA CUP		TOTAL	
	Apps	Gls	Apps	Gls	Apps	Gls
1904/05*	-	-	6	0	6	0
TOTAL	-	-	6	0	6	0

* Clapton Orient first played in the League in 1905/06.

Gregory BERRY, 1989-92, 1995-96 (loan)

Greg Berry was plucked from non-League obscurity as an eighteen-year-old, having played with East Thurrock United in the Essex Senior League. He joined O's for a £2,000 fee (plus 10 per cent of any future transfer) on 3 July 1989, leaving behind a 'safe' career with NatWest Bank. Berry made an indelible mark by scoring on his home League debut and making another in a 4-1 win over Reading on 21 October 1989. During that summer he went on loan to Swedish side Grebbstaad. Born in Linford, Essex on 5 March 1971, he first played at centre forward and was then moved onto to the wing. He was placed on the transfer list in October 1991, but responded two months later with a brace of goals that knocked West Bromwich Albion out of the FA Cup. His first came just after thirty-five seconds, as he smashed the ball into the roof of the net, and he snatched a second late on to cap a most memorable performance. Berry scored a fine hat-trick against Bury on 24 March 1992. He soon caught the eye of Premiership scouts, and on 14 August

Greg Berry

1992 he signed for Premier League Wimbledon for £250,000 (with Vaughan Ryan coming to O's). His stay with the Dons was not a happy one, and he made just 6(1) League appearances for them before joining Millwall in March 1994 for £200,000, scoring 4 goals from 21 Division One outings. He went on loan to Brighton & Hove Albion in August 1995, but he left the Albion scene on a stretcher, rather sadly sustaining an ankle ligament injury. Berry returned to O's for a loan spell in March 1996 and left the Lions for good in 1997. He moved into non-League with Essex side Purfleet. After a spell in America, he re-joined Purfleet in July 2001.

SEASON	LEAGUE		FA CUP		L. CUP	
	Apps	Gls	Apps	Gls	Apps	Gls
1989/90	6(3)	1	1	0	0	0
1990/91	32(3)	5	4(1)	0	5	2
1991/92	30(6)	8	3(1)	2	1	1
1995/96	4(3)	0	0	0	0	0
TOTAL	72(15)	14	8(2)	2	6	3

TOTAL APPS	86(17)
TOTAL GOALS	19

* Greg Berry also appeared in 5(3) Auto Windscreens Shield matches, scoring once.

Jeremiah BEST, 1931-33

Born in Mickley, Northumberland on 23 January 1901, Jerry Best signed for Newcastle United from Mickley FC in December 1919. The speedy inside forward played only twice before joining Leeds United in July 1920 for £100, and appeared in their first ever League match. After just 11 matches he returned to the non-League game, after failing to get regular first-team football. In December 1920 he emigrated to the USA, where he played for the New Bedford Whalers and then Falls River FC.

He returned to England in 1931 and signed for O's, proving to be a versatile and skilful player, and an asset during two difficult seasons for the club. Best left the club in 1933, joining Darlington where he top-scored for three seasons, netting over 70 goals from 109 League appearances. Thirty-six-year-old Best moved to Hull City in October 1936, and was released by the Tigers after netting 11 goals from 31 League appearances before retiring. Best died in Darlington during 1975.

SEASON	LEAGUE		FA CUP		TOTAL	
	Apps	Gls	Apps	Gls	Apps	Gls
1931/32	31	10	3	0	34	10
1932/33	20	7	1	0	21	7
TOTAL	51	17	4	0	55	17

Frederick Walter BEVAN, 1909-13

Burly centre forward Fred Bevan was born in Poplar, London on 27 February 1879. Bevan had a long and distinguished career, starting with amateurs Millwall St Johns FC before joining 'big brother' Millwall Athletic on 12 August 1899 and making 17 Southern League appearances (scoring 7 goals). He moved to Manchester City in May 1901, but after just 8 League games he moved back into the Southern League with Reading, scoring 20 goals from just 36 appearances. In June 1904 he went to Queens Park Rangers and netted a further 30 goals from 58 appearances. In July 1906 he was off to Bury, who paid £340 for his services, ending as their leading goalscorer in 1906/07 with 18 goals from 34 senior appearances. He was with Fulham when they played their first League fixture in September 1907, but after only 5 games he moved to Derby County during October 1907. He stayed for two seasons with the Rams, making 50 League appearances and netting 17 goals. Bevan, although a heavy man, was not a battering-ram type of player, but showed neat skills and deft touches. He became an 'Oriental' in November 1909, and although he was near the veteran stage of his career, he led O's line well, with the likes of McFadden and Dalrymple alongside him. He, in fact, was picked to represent the Football League against the Southern League in 1910, and he skippered the club between 1910 and 1913, before Fred Parker took over. Although not as prolific as in his younger days he still weighed in with 36 goals during his four seasons at Millfields Road. Bevan left O's in 1914 to join Chatham FC, but returned to the club as reserve-team coach and stayed from 1920 until 1923. Fred Bevan died in Poplar on 10 December 1935, aged fifty-six.

SEASON	LEAGUE		FA CUP		TOTAL	
	Apps	Gls	Apps	Gls	Apps	Gls
1909/10	20	7	1	0	21	7
1910/11	37	12	1	0	38	12
1911/12	34	11	1	1	35	12
1912/13	27	5	1	0	28	5
TOTAL	118	35	4	1	122	36

Anthony BIGGS, 1958-61

Tony Biggs, a tall fair-haired centre forward, came to O's on 27 December 1958, as part of the deal that took Len Julians to Arsenal. The former England amateur international came with an extremely good reputation, having scored 44 reserve goals for the Gunners from 64 appearances, but he made just 4 senior appearances and registered a single goal. Born in Greenford, Middlesex on 17 April 1936, he started as a junior with Brentford, then moved on Bexleyheath FC and Hounslow Town, before moving to Highbury on 25 July 1955. Whilst at O's he had the

Fred Bevan

daunting task of trying to displace the splendid Tommy Johnston. Although a good header of the ball, Biggs was a bit ungainly on the deck, but proved to be a very good reserve. He moved to Guildford in 1961, and later played for Hereford United. He then went to Folkestone where he played for several years, scoring many goals. He also was a fair cricketer, having played for the Middlesex Second XI.

SEASON	LEAGUE		FA CUP		TOTAL	
	Apps	Gls	Apps	Gls	Apps	Gls
1958/59	2	0	0	0	2	0
1959/60	2	1	0	0	2	1
1960/61	0	0	0	0	0	0
TOTAL	4	1	0	0	4	1

Sid Bishop

Sidney Harold Richard BISHOP, 1953-65
The wonderful 6ft tall centre half, along with John Townrow, would probably be ranked as one of the best ever to play for O's. He was a major factor in the club attaining promotion to the First Division. Indeed, not one centre forward scored against him for half a season in 1961/62, and he formed part of the formidable half-back line of Lucas-Bishop-Lea. Born in Tooting on 8 April 1934, his parents were supporters of Tooting & Mitcham FC, and young Sid was often their team mascot. He joined O's groundstaff in June 1952 from the club's nursery side (Chase of Chertsey FC) and turned professional six months later. During the promotion season of 1955/56 he made a number of appearances, including one in the 2-1 victory over Millwall that clinched the Second Division Championship. During the promotion campaign of 1961/62, he was ever-present. Bishop was no failure in the First Division, playing in 39 matches. Although not noted for his scoring attributes, he probably netted one of the longest goals ever seen at Brisbane Road, when striking a forty-yard drive past the startled Bristol Rovers 'keeper (Howard Radford) in a 3-2 win on 4 February 1961. He also scored another memorable goal from a long shot against Liverpool in a 2-1 victory on 2 May 1963. He spent his last season with the club (1964/65) as a part-time player. After thirteen years with O's, he was released by new boss Dave Sexton in May 1965, joining Southern League Hastings United as player-manager. Later he held a similar position with Guildford City. Sid Bishop was a beautifully balanced player and majestic in the air, and was unlucky not to be capped for England. He is seen regularly at various O's player reunions. Sid is still involved in football as the coach of an amateur Harlow-based side called Links FC, for whom his son, Warren, plays on the right wing.

SEASON	LEAGUE		FA CUP		L. CUP	
	Apps	Gls	Apps	Gls	Apps	Gls
1953/54*	8	0	0	0	-	-
1954/55	0	0	0	0	-	-
1955/56	15	0	1	0	-	-
1956/57	4	0	0	0	-	-
1957/58	31	0	2	0	-	-
1958/59	29	0	0	0	-	-
1959/60	42	0	1	0	-	-
1960/61	40	3	3	0	2	0
1961/62	42	0	4	0	3	0
1962/63	39	1	4	0	3	0
1963/64	42	0	3	0	1	0
1964/65	4	0	0	0	0	0
TOTAL	296	4	18	0	9	0

TOTAL APPS	323
TOTAL GOALS	4

* The League Cup competition only began in the 1960/61 season.

Robert Watson BLACK, 1938-46

Rugged wing-half Bobby Black joined O's from near-neighbours West Ham United in 1938, where he had managed to make just 2 League appearances. Born in Washington, Co. Durham on 17 July 1915, he came into the O's team midway through the 1938/39 season and looked to be a very useful player. He played at left half in the 3 League matches in August 1939, before the League was suspended due to the Second World War and all playing records expunged. Black played in a total of 81 regional matches during the war, scoring twice. He also appeared in the two FA cup matches of November 1945 against Newport Isle of Wight. Thirty-one-year-old Black was not retained for League football after the Second World War in 1946/47. He died in the Bridgnorth area during 1979.

SEASON	LEAGUE		FA CUP		TOTAL	
	Apps	Gls	Apps	Gls	Apps	Gls
1938/39	23	0	0	0	23	0
1939/40*	3	0	0	0	3	0
1945/46**	-	-	2	0	2	0
TOTAL	23	0	2	0	25	0

* The 1939/40 season was suspended after 3 matches due to the Second World War and all records were expunged.

** No League matches were played in 1945/46 due to the war.

Mark Christopher BLACKHALL, 1977-83

Mark Blackhall came through the club's youth ranks and made his full League debut in the final match of the 1981/82 season – a 3-0 victory over Leicester City on 18 May 1982. The 6ft striker was born in Upney, Essex on 17 November 1960. He played in the first team for a short while, but in truth was never quite up to League standard. His only goal, a spectacular diving header, came in a 5-2 defeat

Mark Blackhall (on right of picture)

at Brentford on 22 January 1983. He did, however, draw praise from O's boss at the time, Ken Knighton, for his attitude in training, when apparently some other players around him had lax attitudes. Blackhall moved into non-League football with Chelmsford City in 1983. More recently, it was reported he owns a night club in Southend.

SEASON	LEAGUE		FA CUP		L. CUP	
	Apps	Gls	Apps	Gls	Apps	Gls
1981/82	1(3)	0	0(1)	0	0	0
1982/83	11(3)	1	1	0	1(1)	0
TOTAL	12(6)	1	1(1)	0	1(1)	0

TOTAL APPS		14(8)
TOTAL GOALS		1

* Mark Blackhall also appeared in 1(2) Football League Group Cup matches.

Clifford Harold BLACKWELL, 1930-32

Harry Blackwell, a goalkeeper, joined O's in July 1930 from Aberdeen (although the club programme at the time stated he came from Blackpool FC, but that club had no record of him on their books!). He played a few matches after Arthur Wood had broken his collarbone in an FA Cup tie against Luton Town in December 1930. Born in Wortley near Sheffield in 1902, he started with Scunthorpe & Lindsay United (playing 2 matches for them in the Midlands League during 1920) and found himself alongside another former 'Oriental', Robert Duffus. Blackwell moved to Aberdeen in August 1921 and made 252 senior appearances for the Dons. On 10 February 1923 in a Scottish FA Cup Tie at Pittodrie against Peterhead in driving rain and a gale force wind, Blackwell set a new fashion between the sticks when wearing a rain-

coat and raising a spectator's umbrella, whilst he stood and watched his team-mates score 13 goals against their opponents. He left the Dons in 1929. After his spell with O's he joined Preston North End in June 1932.

SEASON	LEAGUE		FA CUP		TOTAL	
	Apps	Gls	Apps	Gls	Apps	Gls
1930/31	12	0	1	0	13	0
1931/32	3	0	0	0	3	0
TOTAL	15	0	1	0	16	0

James Alfred BLAIR, 1949-53

Jimmy Blair, whose grandfather, father and brother were all professional footballers, was born in Whiteinch, Glasgow on 6 January 1918. As a boy he lived in South Wales, and represented Wales at schoolboy level. He signed for Blackpool as an amateur from Cardiff City in June 1935, having played some games for Birmingham City in the Central League. He made his League debut against Stoke City in September 1937, a few months before his nineteenth birthday. The *Blackpool News Chronicle* reported: 'Young Jimmy Blair filled the stage and captured the limelight, a tall, well-built athlete who is surely destined for international honours'. Well, all those expectations never really materialised and he had an 'up and down' career with 'Pool between 1935 and 1947, making 51 League appearances and scoring 8 goals. However, he did obtain one Scottish international cap against Wales in October 1946. He was transferred to Bournemouth for £4,150 in October 1947, and after 80 League matches that yielded 8 goals, he became an 'Oriental' over Christmas 1949. He excelled at Brisbane Road, showing some wonderful skill to delight the O's fans over four sea-

Jimmy Blair

sons, topping the goalscoring charts with 16 goals in 1950/51. He was one of the scorers when O's beat Dutch side Racing Club of Haarlem 3-1 in a 1951 Festival of Britain match. When O's transfer-listed him in October 1951, a national newspaper wrote: 'It doesn't make sense, he could have been one of the greatest of his time but his football refuses to conform to the orthodox'. He ended up staying with O's for a further two years, only moving to Kent League side Ramsgate Athletic as player-manager in May 1953. Jimmy Blair died in Llanelli on 12 July 1983.

SEASON	LEAGUE		FA CUP		TOTAL	
	Apps	Gls	Apps	Gls	Apps	Gls
1949/50	23	3	0	0	23	3
1950/51	45	16	1	0	46	16
1951/52	21	5	1	0	22	5
1952/53	15	2	2	0	17	2
TOTAL	104	26	4	0	108	26

Patrick John BLATCHFORD, 1951-54

Paddy Blatchford was born in Plymouth on 28 December 1925. The outside left joined Plymouth Argyle from Cornish club Saltash United in November 1948, and made 19 League appearances, scoring 2 goals. He joined O's as a part-timer in May 1951, being otherwise employed as a civil servant. A small and nippy fast-raiding outside left, he immediately won a place in O's first XI, making his debut against his former club. He figured prominently in O's great FA Cup run in 1951/52, then lost his a way a little, but had a great day at home to Ipswich Town on Boxing Day 1952, scoring a couple of brilliant opportunist goals. He failed to get into the side during the 1953/54 season, due to the form of George Poulton, so he left in May 1954 and played for Bideford Town and later for Bridgewater. Paddy Blatchford died in 1981 at the age of fifty-six.

Paddy Blatchford

SEASON	LEAGUE		FA CUP		TOTAL	
	Apps	Gls	Apps	Gls	Apps	Gls
1951/52	42	5	9	1	51	6
1952/53	18	3	0	0	18	3
1953/54	0	0	0	0	0	0
TOTAL	60	8	9	1	69	9

Herbert BLISS, 1922-25

Bertie Bliss was born in Willenhall, Staffordshire on 29 March 1890. He was first spotted by Tottenham Hotspur whilst playing for the Birmingham & District League representative side against Scotland juniors in March 1912, signing for them a month later from Willenhall Swifts FC. This small player – he stood just 5ft 6 in tall – was famed for his powerful shoot-on-sight attitude, his drives often proving unstoppable. He had a long and distinguished career with Spurs, winning a Second Division Championship medal in 1921 and scoring 31 goals. He also won an England cap against Scotland in April 1921 (playing alongside his Spurs colleague, and later O's player-manager, Arthur Grimsdell). He scored a hat-trick against O's in 1919/20 and netted 168 goals for Spurs from 315 senior matches. By the end of 1921/22, his form began to wane, and he joined O's in December 1922 for a reported £2,000. His appearance at Millfields helped to increase attendances, scoring 20 goals in his three seasons with the club. He was given a free transfer in July 1925, ending his career with a single season at Bournemouth & Boscome Athletic. Bliss died in Wood Green, London on 14 June 1968.

SEASON	LEAGUE		FA CUP		TOTAL	
	Apps	Gls	Apps	Gls	Apps	Gls
1922/23	18	6	1	0	19	6
1923/24	35	9	0	0	35	9
1924/25	17	5	0	0	17	5
TOTAL	70	20	1	0	71	20

Les Blizzard

Leslie William BLIZZARD, 1950-56

Six-footer Les Blizzard became an 'Oriental' during May 1950, when he joined from Yeovil Town, and he proved to be a wonderful servant to the club. He also kept his colleagues entertained on away trips, being a fine pianist and vocalist. Born in Acton on 13 March 1923, he started his professional career in 1946/47 with Queens Park Rangers, for whom he appeared 4 times. In May 1947 he joined Bournemouth, playing just once before breaking his leg, and then he moved into the Southern League with Yeovil, featuring in their great FA Cup run in 1949 (alongside Alec Stock) when they defeated both Bury and Sunderland. Blizzard, an excellent right half who got up well for the ball and had his own way of 'selling a dummy', appeared in both of O's great FA Cup runs of 1951/52 and 1953/54. He appeared in the game against Nottingham Forest in August 1956, on O's return to the Second Division. That was his only appearance that season, but he moved to Headington United (later Oxford United) in December 1956, before retiring at the end of that season, aged thirty-four. Blizzard died in Northampton during 1996.

SEASON	LEAGUE		FA CUP		TOTAL	
	Apps	Gls	Apps	Gls	Apps	Gls
1950/51	26	1	1	0	27	1
1951/52	40	2	9	0	49	2
1952/53	32	3	2	0	34	3
1953/54	37	2	7	0	44	2
1954/55	46	4	2	0	48	4
1955/56	41	0	4	0	45	0
1956/57	1	0	0	0	1	0
TOTAL	223	12	25	0	248	12

Note: In the 1990 book *The Complete Record of Leyton Orient FC*, it shows Blizzard as having made 31 League appearances in 1952/53, with a total of 33 senior appearances that season. It also shows a grand total of 222 League appearances and a final total of 247 senior appearances. These figures are incorrect. The totals should have read as above. His appearance against QPR on 25 September 1952 was incorrectly given to Deverall.

James Henry BLOOMFIELD, 1968-69

Jimmy Bloomfield came to O's as player-manager from Plymouth Argyle on 8 March 1968, changing the course of the club's history. After having just escaped relegation in 1968/69, they became champions of the Third Division in 1969/70, his first season as full-time boss. The 5ft 9in player was a midfield general and a beautiful passer of the ball, with a wonderful body-swerve that kept defenders guessing all the time. He was unlucky not to gain the international recognition his play deserved. Bloomfield, who was born in Kensington, London on 15 February

Jimmy Bloomfield

1934, started his career with Athenian League side Hayes, before moving to Brentford in October 1952, where he made 42 League appearances and scored 5 goals. His big chance came with an £8,000 move to Arsenal in July 1954. He stayed at Highbury for six years, making 210 League appearances and scoring 54 goals before a £30,000 move took him to Birmingham City in November 1960. After 123 matches and 28 goals, he returned to Brentford for £15,000 in June 1964. He later had a short spell with West Ham United, before his move to Plymouth during September 1966, where he made 25 League appearances and scored once between 1966 and 1968. Bloomfield's playing career spanned some seventeen years and totalled 494 League appearances and 93 goals. He returned to Brisbane Road on 23 May 1977 after the sacking of George Petchey, following a spell as manager of Leicester

City. He resigned in May 1981 and was then appointed part-time scout with Luton Town. After a long battle against cancer, Jimmy Bloomfield died at his north London home on 3 April 1983, aged just forty-nine.

SEASON	LEAGUE		FA CUP		L. CUP	
	Apps	Gls	Apps	Gls	Apps	Gls
1967/68	14(1)	0	0	0	0	0
1968/69	29(1)	3	2	1	2	0
TOTAL	43(2)	3	2	1	2	0

TOTAL APPS	47(2)
TOTAL GOALS	4

John Arthur BODEN, 1905-06

John Boden, a well-built centre half, appeared in O's first ever League match at Leicester Fosse on 2 September 1905. Boden stayed just seven months there before a transfer took him to Aston Villa as a result of the club's desperate financial plight. Born in Northwich in 1881, he started his League career in 1902 with Glossop North End, making 91 League appearances and scoring 4 goals before becoming an 'Oriental', having been signed by manager Sam Ormerod in May 1905 on a weekly wage of £4. He was credited with converting O's first penalty in the League at Port Vale on 30 September 1905. His transfer to Villa took place during March 1906, but he couldn't settle at the club, playing just 18 matches before moving into the Southern League in 1907 and making 65 appearances for Reading. He joined Croydon Common, making 20 Southern League appearances and scoring 2 goals, before joining Plymouth Argyle in June 1911. He made 67 appearances and scored 39 goals for the Devon club (as a centre forward), before moving to New

Brighton in October 1912, where he made a further 17 appearances and scored 5 times. Boden died in 1942.

SEASON	LEAGUE		FA CUP		TOTAL	
	Apps	Gls	Apps	Gls	Apps	Gls
1905/06	27	5	6	3	33	8
TOTAL	27	5	6	3	33	8

Ian BOGIE, 1993-95

This small, skilful midfield player joined O's from Millwall on 14 October 1993, and had two good seasons at Brisbane Road. Born in Newcastle on 6 December 1967, he became an apprentice with his home-town club on 18 December 1985, where he played alongside Paul Gascoigne, winning an England schools cap. Bogie followed 'Gazza' into the Magpies first team in 1986/87, making 7(7) League appearances before moving to Preston North End in February 1989. After making 67(12) appearances and weighing in with 12 goals, he came south to join

Ian Bogie

Millwall during August 1991 for £145,000. After 44(7) appearances and a single goal, he became an 'Oriental' on 14 October 1993. With O's hard-pressed for cash, he was allowed to move to Port Vale for £50,000 on 23 March 1995, and had a long and successful career at Vale Park. He played for there for five seasons, making 150(22) senior appearances. The thirty-three-year-old then joined Kidderminster Harriers on a free transfer in June 2000 for their new adventure in the League. After 18(7) senior appearances, he left them at the end of March 2001, asking to be released because he was missing his family (who were still living in the north-east) and it was having an effect on his game. So ended a senior career of 262 appearances.

SEASON	LEAGUE		FA CUP		L. CUP	
	Apps	Gls	Apps	Gls	Apps	Gls
1993/94	34	3	0	0	0	0
1994/95	28(3)	2	2	0	2	0
TOTAL	62(3)	5	2	0	2	0

TOTAL APPS	66(3)
TOTAL GOALS	5

* Ian Bogie also appeared in 8(1) Auto Windscreens Shield matches.

Gordon Edward BOLLAND, 1962-64

Gordon Bolland, a long-striding 6ft tall inside forward, came to O's from Chelsea as a nineteen-year-old in March 1962 for a fee of £8,000 after 2 League appearances. This was an exciting time in the club's history as they were on the verge of promotion to the First Division, and he made his League debut against Sunderland. Born in Boston, Lincolnshire on 12 August 1943, he started out with home club Boston United, joining Chelsea in February 1959. He appeared in O's First Division campaign and was the leading goalscorer during the following season on 17 goals, but he was transferred to Norwich City for a reported £31,500 during March 1964. One of his feats whilst at Carrow Road was scoring one of the goals that knocked Manchester United out of the FA Cup at Old Trafford in 1967. He made 104(1) League appearances for the Norfolk club, netting 29 goals. After a brief spell with Charlton Athletic, he joined Millwall for £10,000 and there re-captured some of his best form, playing some 267(6) senior matches for the Lions and notching 66 League goals. In June 1975 he moved back to his local club Boston United as player-manager and made 24(2) appearances, scoring 5 goals. Bolland was a top-class striker, making a total of 417(8) career League appearances and scoring 112 goals. He now lives in his native Boston, working as a sales rep for a tyre company.

Gordon Bolland

Bolland in action for O's

SEASON	LEAGUE		FA CUP		L. CUP	
	Apps	Gls	Apps	Gls	Apps	Gls
1961/62	8	0	0	0	0	0
1962/63	24	3	4	0	2	2
1963/64	31	16	3	0	1	1
TOTAL	63	19	7	0	3	3

TOTAL APPS	73
TOTAL GOALS	22

James McFarlane BOLTON, 1930-32

Jimmy Bolton was born in Clydebank on 22 March 1906. The 5ft 7in tall left half became an 'Oriental' in July 1930, after joining from St Johnstone, having made 60 senior appearances for the Scottish side between 1926 and 1930. He did well for O's in the 1930/31 season – his only goal came in the 4-0 win over Torquay United in November 1930 – but he lost his place the following season to Joe Peacock. He joined York City in July 1932, playing the opening 7 matches, but after

a serious injury he was eventually forced to retire from the game.

SEASON	LEAGUE		FA CUP		TOTAL	
	Apps	Gls	Apps	Gls	Apps	Gls
1930/31	29	1	2	0	31	1
1931/32	8	0	3	0	11	0
TOTAL	37	1	5	0	42	1

Richard Arthur BOURNE, 1905-07

Dick Bourne was a player of pedigree who was on the verge of an England cap when he became O's most expensive player. He joined from Preston North End after a League tribunal fixed his fee at £100 in June 1905 (Orient had offered £50 and Preston wanted £150). Bourne was born in Roundle during January 1881, and started his career with local side Roundle FC, before moving to Sheffield United in 1900 and making 12 League appearances (scoring one goal). He moved to Barnsley in 1902, and after 18 League appearances he moved on to Preston in 1902 and played 62 times, scoring 7 goals. Bourne was an outstanding outside left, who coupled both skill and speed, and on his day, he was a very dangerous forward. It was his ability to waltz around defenders and make goals for others that made him very popular with the Millfields Road fans. In February 1907 with the club again desperate to raise cash, he was sold to West Bromwich Albion for £135. He made just 9 appearances and scored a solitary goal whilst with Albion. He ended his career with Walsall as coach in 1908. Bourne made around 150 League appearances throughout his career, but besides being an excellent footballer he also excelled at cricket and as an oarsman. He retired from football in 1920 and died in 1944, aged sixty-two.

SEASON	LEAGUE		FA CUP		TOTAL	
	Apps	Gls	Apps	Gls	Apps	Gls
1905/06	37	1	6	1	43	2
1906/07*	19	1	-	-	19	1
TOTAL	56	2	6	1	62	3

* Clapton Orient did not enter into the FA Cup in 1906/07.

James BOW, 1934-35

Jimmy Bow was born in Lochore, Fife on 14 December 1910. The outside left (and sometime centre forward) started his career with Lochore Welfare FC, moved to Hamilton Academicals in 1929, and then progressed on to Edinburgh side St Barnards in 1932. He became an 'Oriental' in 1934, but could never break into the first team. His only senior appearance (in an FA Cup tie against Chester on 8 December 1934) came about only because of injuries to forwards Crawford, Farrell, Miles, Rigby, Smith and Taylor. O's lost 1-3. Bow, who was also a very good golfer, moved on to Gateshead in November 1936, playing just a single League match against Halifax Town on 19 December 1936, a few days after his twenty-sixth birthday.

SEASON	LEAGUE		FA CUP		TOTAL	
	Apps	Gls	Apps	Gls	Apps	Gls
1934/35	0	0	1	0	1	0
TOTAL	0	0	1	0	1	0

William BOWER, 1905-15

Billy Bower, a 6ft 1in and 14st 7lb goalkeeper, had the distinction of being the only O's player to appear in at least one League match during the first ten seasons of the club's League campaigns. Born in Dalston, London in 1888, Bower was a member of the Hackney District side and also gained 2 England schoolboy caps. He supported the O's in their non-League days, and a local newspaper reported in an article that as a boy he always dreamt of playing for the O's. He signed for them in May 1905 from Peel Institute FC, making his League debut on 10 March 1906, after regular 'keeper Joe Redding had conceded 17 goals in 4 League matches. Bower did not fare much better, with 7 goals going past him in 2 matches. His final League appearance came on 17 October 1914, a 1-0 home defeat by Derby. However, he turned out to be a very capable custodian and a grand servant to the club. He left in 1915 to join non-League outfit New Brompton. Bower died in February 1954, aged sixty-six.

SEASON	LEAGUE		FA CUP		TOTAL	
	Apps	Gls	Apps	Gls	Apps	Gls
1905/06	11	0	0	0	11	0
1906/07*	35	0	-	-	35	0
1907/08	6	0	1	0	7	0
1908/09	9	0	0	0	9	0
1909/10	8	0	0	0	8	0
1910/11	37	0	1	0	38	0
1911/12	20	0	1	0	21	0
1912/13	28	0	0	0	28	0
1913/14	16	0	2	0	18	0
1914/15	1	0	0	0	1	0
TOTAL	171	0	5	0	176	0

* Clapton Orient did not enter into the FA Cup in 1906/07.

Stanley BOWLES, 1980-81

Stan Bowles arrived at the club in July 1980 as Jimmy Bloomfield's biggest name signing for £90,000, although he was never quite the same outstanding player that he had been in his earlier days. However, the 5ft 10in midfielder still showed plenty of quality touches in

Stan Bowles

his play. Born on 24 December 1948 in Manchester, he started his career as an apprentice with Manchester City in January 1967. He spent nearly four years at Maine Road, playing just 15(2) League games and scoring twice, but netting 34 goals from 117 appearances for their reserve side. After playing 5 times on loan with Bury during early 1970, he signed on a free transfer to Crewe Alexandra on 24 September 1970. He went on to net 18 goals from 51 League appearances. After a spell with Carlisle United (joining for £12,000, playing 33 League appearances and scoring 12 goals), it was with Queens Park Rangers that he really made his name. After joining on 16 September 1972 for £112,000, he scored 96 goals from 315 senior appearances and whilst with the club gained 5 full England caps. Brian Clough brought to him to Nottingham Forest in December 1979 for over

£200,000, but after only 19 League outings and 2 goals for Forest, he was snapped up by Bloomfield to become an 'Oriental'. He netted one particularly memorable goal against Preston North End in October 1980, when he nonchalantly ghosted past three defenders and hit a great left-foot shot on the turn into the roof of the net. However, Stan Bowles had gained himself a reputation of being a somewhat wayward character with a weakness for gambling, and it was really no surprise when Ken Knighton took over as manager with his strong disciplinary code, that Bowles would be one of the first players to be on their way. He joined Brentford in September 1981 and did wonderfully well with the Bees, being voted their Player of the Year. He netted 16 goals from 80(1) League outings before calling it a day at the end of the 1986/87 season. Although there was always doubt about his temperament, Bowles was indeed a wonderful player and left many magical moments for all supporters to savour over the years. He made a total of 507 career League appearances, netting 127 goals. Presently he acts as 'mine host' on matchdays in QPR's hospitality suites, and he is as popular as ever at that club.

SEASON	LEAGUE		FA CUP		L. CUP	
	Apps	Gls	Apps	Gls	Apps	Gls
1980/81/	39	6	1	0	2	0
1981/82	7	1	0	0	1	0
TOTAL	46	7	1	0	3	0

TOTAL APPS	50
TOTAL GOALS	7

* Stan Bowles also appeared in 3 Anglo-Scottish Cup matches and 3 Football League Group Cup matches.

Stephen John BOWTELL, 1968-73

Steve Bowtell, a tall, slim goalkeeper, was an England schoolboy and youth international when with O's. Born in Bethnal Green, London on 2 December 1950, after his apprenticeship he turned professional on 1 January 1968. A great career was predicted for him, and he made his League debut at just seventeen years of age in the 0-4 defeat by Gillingham on 7 May 1968. However, he found it difficult to displace Ray Goddard, and eventually joined Margate FC in July 1973. He spent six seasons at Margate, making 285 senior appearances. In February 1979 he joined Dulwich Hamlet, and after spells with Woking and Fisher Athletic, he retired in 1987. Bowtell later moved into coaching.

SEASON	LEAGUE		FA CUP		L. CUP	
	Apps	Gls	Apps	Gls	Apps	Gls
1967/68	1	0	0	0	0	0
1968/69	2	0	0	0	0	0
1969/70	2	0	0	0	0	0
1970/71	0	0	0	0	0	0
1971/72	3	0	0	0	0	0
1972/73	0	0	0	0	0	0
TOTAL	8	0	0	0	0	0

TOTAL APPS	8
TOTAL GOALS	0

Steve Bowtell

Ian BOWYER, 1971-1973

Ian Bowyer burst onto the scene as a teenager with Manchester City in the 1969/70 season, scoring 12 goals. The following campaign was not very successful, and he was allowed to leave Maine Road after making 42(8) first-team appearances and 88 appearances for their reserves (scoring 23 goals). He joined O's for £25,000 in June 1971 as Jimmy Bloomfield's final signing before he departed as manager to Leicester City. Born in Little Sutton, Ellesmere Port on 6 June 1951, he played impressively for two seasons, appearing both as a striker and on the left-side of midfield. At the start of the 1973/74 season he was in dispute with the club and moved to Nottingham Forest during October 1973 for £40,000. He stayed there for seven seasons and was a key figure in some of their more successful years. He made 222(17) League appearances, scoring 49 goals, before joining Sunderland for £50,000 in January 1981. He never settled in the north-east, and after just 15 League appearances he returned to the City Ground in January 1982 and was appointed captain. During his two spells with Forest, he won 2 First Division Championship medals, 2 European Cup medals and a League Cup medal. He made a total of 425(20) appearances, netting 68 goals. He moved to Hereford

Ian Bowyer

He resigned from the St Andrews management team in August 2001 after his demotion to reserve-team manager, and then moved on to take over as coach at his former club Nottingham Forest.

SEASON	LEAGUE		FA CUP		L. CUP	
	Apps	Gls	Apps	Gls	Apps	Gls
1971/72	42	15	4	2	2	0
1972/73	33(3)	4	1	0	2	1
1973/74	0	0	0	0	1	1
TOTAL	75(3)	19	5	2	5	2

TOTAL APPS	85(3)
TOTAL GOALS	23

Thomas William BOWYER, 1919-20

Tommy Bowyer, born in Stoke-on-Trent, joined O's from Stoke City reserves in April 1919, scoring on his club debut for the reserves against Arsenal in a London Combination match. The inside forward also scored O's first goal on their return to League football after the end of the First World War at Huddersfield Town on 30 August 1919. Bowyer stayed just one season with O's before moving to Gillingham in May 1920, but it was with Walsall that he made his mark, scoring 13 goals from 32 Birmingham League appearances. He appeared in the Saddlers' inaugural Third Division (North) fixture in August 1921, making 34 League appearances and scoring 5 goals for them before joining Birmingham League outfit Shrewsbury Town in May 1922 for £150.

SEASON	LEAGUE		FA CUP		TOTAL	
	Apps	Gls	Apps	Gls	Apps	Gls
1919/20	21	6	0	0	21	6
TOTAL	21	6	0	0	21	6

United as player-manager in July 1987 and stayed for three years, taking them to a Welsh Cup final on 13 May 1990 – it turned out to be his last match in charge. Ian Bowyer cost no more than £175,000 throughout his playing career, which spanned some twenty-two seasons. He made over 600 senior appearances, scoring more than 100 goals. He also left some wonderful memories for O's to savour, such as his hat-trick on his home debut against Cardiff City during August 1971, and his glorious goal at Leicester City in O's 2-0 FA Cup victory at Filbert Street in February 1972. He was assistant-manager at both Plymouth Argyle and Rotherham United. More recently he was joint assistant-manager with Mick Mills under Trevor Francis at Birmingham City, who narrowly lost to Liverpool in a close encounter in the League Cup Final in February 2001 in a penalty shoot-out.

Hugh BOYD, 1936-37

Glasgow-born wing-half Hugh Boyd, who had started his career with East Stirling, came south of the Border to join O's from the Irish club Portadown, after failing a trial with Luton Town in October 1936. He played just 2 League matches during December 1936 – both defeats – and was not chosen again. After his unsuccessful stay at Lea Bridge Road, he re-joined East Stirling in November 1937.

SEASON	LEAGUE		FA CUP		TOTAL	
	Apps	Gls	Apps	Gls	Apps	Gls
1936/37	2	0	0	0	2	0
1937/38	0	0	0	0	0	0
TOTAL	2	0	0	0	2	0

John Boyle

John BOYLE, 1973-75

John Boyle was born in Motherwell, Scotland on 25 December 1946, He became an 'Oriental' towards the end of a very successful career with Chelsea, and it was apparent that he was not at his best, suffering during his stay with injuries. The sturdy hard-working midfielder joined Chelsea as a junior during August 1964, making his senior debut on 20 January 1965 in a League Cup semi-final against Aston Villa, scoring a goal in their 3-2 victory. He stayed at Stamford Bridge for nine seasons, making 253(13) senior appearances and scoring 12 goals. During September 1973 he joined Brighton & Hove Albion, playing 10 matches during his four-month loan stay before signing for O's in December 1973, where he made his debut two days before his twenty-seventh birthday. After struggling to get back into the side after a cartilage operation, he went to play in America with Tampa Bay Rowdies during 1975. He later worked as a security officer in central London.

SEASON	LEAGUE		FA CUP		L. CUP	
	Apps	Gls	Apps	Gls	Apps	Gls
1973/74	13	0	4	0	0	0
1974/75	5	0	0	0	0	0
TOTAL	18	0	4	0	0	0

TOTAL APPS	22
TOTAL GOALS	0

* John Boyle also appeared in 1(1) Texaco Cup matches in 1974/75.

Peter BOYLE, 1905-06

Irishman Peter Boyle was one of the more famous players to appear in O's inaugural League side of 1905/06, having won 5 Irish international caps between 1901 and 1904. Born in Carlingford, Co. Louth in 1877, Boyle was brought up in Scotland and started his career with Coatbridge Juniors. In 1895 he was a player with Albion Rovers in the Scottish Alliance League. During December 1896 he joined Sunderland for £50 and stayed at Roker Park for two years, making 32 senior appearances. In December 1898 Sheffield United offered £200 for his services, and he had an illustrious career in Sheffield, winning two FA Cup medals and making 184 senior appearances for the Yorkshire club. In May 1904 he returned to Scotland to play for Motherwell, where he made 14 appearances. He became an 'Oriental' in May 1905, but the twenty-eight-year-old player only stayed for four months before he joined Wigan Town. He later appeared for Chorley FC and Eccles Borough. In May 1912 he became player-manager of Midlands League side York City. Boyle died on 24 June 1939, aged sixty-two.

SEASON	LEAGUE		FA CUP		TOTAL	
	Apps	Gls	Apps	Gls	Apps	Gls
1905/06	11	0	2	0	13	0
TOTAL	11	0	2	0	13	0

Peter BRABROOK, 1968-71

The speedy and experienced 5ft 11in right-winger came to O's in July 1968, making a major contribution to O's Third Division Championship campaign of 1969/70. Born in Greenwich, London on 28 November 1937, he joined Chelsea as a junior and signed as a professional in March 1955, making 271 senior appearances and scoring 57 goals. He appeared for England in the 1958 World Cup finals, winning 3 caps. He was transferred to West Ham United for £35,000 in October 1962, and scored in the first minute of his Hammers debut. He won an FA Cup winner's medal in 1964 and also played in the two-legged League Cup final against West Bromwich Albion in 1966. Altogether he made 214 senior appearances (netting

43 goals) before joining O's. During his debut against Rotherham United in August 1968, he showed all his old skill and trickery before a serious Achilles tendon injury put paid to his season after just 10 senior matches. He came back the following season, and with Mark Lazarus on the left wing they supplied plenty of good football for the O's fans to enjoy, both playing a prominent part in O's successful season. However, Brabrook played just a single season in the Second Division, and at the age of thirty-four he moved to Southern League side Romford. He later had two spells as manager with Diadora League side Billericay. Brabrook has since owned a butchery in Hornchurch, Essex, and after that he worked for former O's chairman Neville Ovenden's paper company, as well as looking after the under-17 squad at West Ham United.

SEASON	LEAGUE		FA CUP		L. CUP	
	Apps	Gls	Apps	Gls	Apps	Gls
1968/69	7	2	0	0	3	0
1969/70	37	3	2	0	2	0
1970/71	26(2)	1	0(1)	0	1	0
TOTAL	70(2)	6	2(1)	0	6	0

TOTAL APPS	78(3)
TOTAL GOALS	6

George BRADBURY, 1920-22

Defender George Bradbury was born in Matlock on 26 April 1897. He joined O's from Hartshay Colliery in May 1920 and stayed with them for two seasons before a £300 transfer took him to Chesterfield in 1922. He made 4 senior appearances there before joining Scunthorpe & Lindsey United in June 1923, where he stayed for two seasons. Bradbury died in Bakewell during 1974.

SEASON	LEAGUE		FA CUP		TOTAL	
	Apps	Gls	Apps	Gls	Apps	Gls
1920/21	10	2	0	0	10	2
1921/22	22	0	1	0	23	0
TOTAL	32	2	1	0	33	2

Terence Eugene BRADBURY, 1966-67

Terry Bradbury was born in Paddington, London on 15 November 1939. The former England schoolboy left half started with Chelsea in July 1957, making 29 appearances in 1960/61. He moved to Southend United in September 1962, staying for four years and making 175(1) senior appearances (scoring 19 goals). He arrived at O's in June 1966 as part of a swap deal with Colin Flatt. Bradbury had a turbulent stay at Brisbane Road (he did not get on with O's boss Dick Graham) and was suspended by the club for an incident that occurred at Colchester United during October 1966. However, he remained until the close of the season before joining Wrexham in June 1967. He was appointed player-coach at Chester City in 1971, and later had spells with both Weymouth and Northwich Victoria. Bradbury's career spanned some eleven years and included 381(4) appearances and 26 goals.

SEASON	LEAGUE		FA CUP		L. CUP	
	Apps	Gls	Apps	Gls	Apps	Gls
1966/67	25(2)	0	3	0	1	0
TOTAL	25(2)	0	3	0	1	0

TOTAL APPS	29(2)
TOTAL GOALS	0

James Leslie BRADLEY, 1920-21

Jimmy Bradley was born in Lesmahagow, Lanarkshire in 1892. He started playing in Scottish junior football, and after earning quite a reputation, the sixteen-year-old came south of the Border in 1908 to play for Southern League side Luton Town, where he made 11 appearances and scored 6 goals. He returned to Scotland to join Dundee Hibernians in 1909. In July 1920 he returned south to Luton Town, and made his League debut for the Hatters in their 9-1 defeat at Swindon Town during August. He played just 5 matches before becoming an 'Oriental' in February 1921, and his O's debut came in the 3-0 defeat at South Shields. He went on to score the winner against Leeds later that month. He was subsequently dropped, due to the return of James Forrest, and returned home to Scotland, a very unhappy man.

SEASON	LEAGUE		FA CUP		TOTAL	
	Apps	Gls	Apps	Gls	Apps	Gls
1920/21	5	1	0	0	5	1
TOTAL	5	1	0	0	5	1

Marcel Eric Louis BRAHAN, 1955-56

Born in Stepney, London on 3 December 1926, Lou Brahan, a very tall and powerful centre half, joined O's on 1 July 1955 as an amateur from Walthamstow Avenue. Having started his career with Briggs Sports FC, he was noted as one of the best amateur pivots of his era. He made his O's debut against Southend United on 3 September 1955, when both Aldous and Bishop were injured. However, he could not retain his place and eventually moved back to Avenue during that season. He later played with both Tooting & Mitcham and Carshalton FC. Brahan died in Epping Forest during December 1995.

SEASON	LEAGUE		FA CUP		TOTAL	
	Apps	Gls	Apps	Gls	Apps	Gls
1955/56	1	0	0	0	1	0
TOTAL	1	0	0	0	1	0

John Lewis BRATBY, 1920-23

Born in Belper on 15 May 1895, Bratby proved to be an energetic forward during his stay at Millfields Road. He joined from Matlock Town during June 1920, after a short trial with Luton. His only League goal came against Bury in the opening fixture of the 1921/22 season, O's winning 3-1. He was forced to retire due to a serious injury sustained during a match for the reserves during 1924. Bratby died in Peacehaven, Sussex on 12 December 1982.

SEASON	LEAGUE		FA CUP		TOTAL	
	Apps	Gls	Apps	Gls	Apps	Gls
1920/21	3	0	0	0	3	0
1921/22	19	1	0	0	19	1
1922/23	5	0	0	0	5	0
TOTAL	27	1	0	0	27	1

Matthew Ronald BRAZIER, 2002-present

Matt Brazier was born in Whipps Cross on 2 July 1976. He began his career playing for Redbridge United and Hyde Rovers as a boy, before joining QPR as an apprentice in 1993 and turning professional two years later. A left-sided midfielder, Brazier made 36(13) League appearances and scored 2 goals, before a £65,000 took him to Fulham in March 1998. His stay at Craven Cottage lasted just four months, however, and he made 6(6) senior appearances and scored once before going on loan to Cardiff City in August 1998. He eventually signed a permanent deal with the Welsh club for £100,000 in July 1999. Brazier initially made a big impression, playing an important part in Cardiff's promotion campaign of the 2000/01 season, in which they finished as Division Three runners-up. However, the following season he fell out of favour after having made a total of 54(13) League appearances and having scored 3 goals. In December 2001, both he and Kevin Nugent were close to sealing a joint £70,000 move to Division Two side Colchster United, but talks broke down and O's boss Paul Brush snapped up both players on free transfers on 31 January 2002.

SEASON	LEAGUE		FA CUP		L. CUP	
	Apps	Gls	Apps	Gls	Apps	Gls
2001/02	8	0	0	0	0	0
TOTAL	8	0	0	0	0	0

TOTAL APPS	8	
TOTAL GOALS	0	

John Victor BRINTON, 1948-49

John Brinton (also known as Jack) was a well-built but speedy winger, who was born in Avonmouth on 11 July 1916. He started his career with Avonmouth Town before joining Bristol City during August 1935, where he made 12 League appearances and scored once. He moved to Newport County in July 1937, but after just 6 appearances he signed for Derby County for £1,000 in January 1938, scoring twice in 8 appearances. The thirty-two-year-old joined O's in August 1948 from Stockport County, after making 58 League appearances at Edgerley Park and scoring 9 goals. After a single unsuccessful season at Brisbane Road, he left in July 1949 for Streets FC. Brinton died in Leigh, Bristol on 22 February 1997.

SEASON	LEAGUE		FA CUP		TOTAL	
	Apps	Gls	Apps	Gls	Apps	Gls
1948/49	4	1	0	0	4	1
TOTAL	4	1	0	0	4	1

Terence William BRISLEY, 1966-75

Terry Brisley joined the club as a thirteen-year-old schoolboy, along with another future O's star – Denis Rofe – in 1966.

Terry Brisley

£20,000, where he played 44(4) League matches and notched 5 goals. He was subsequently signed by Portsmouth for £25,000, and went on to play a major part in Pompey gaining promotion from the Fourth Division in 1980. He made a total of 55 League appearances and scored 13 goals before joining Maidstone United in the Alliance League in 1981. Brisley now lives in Brentwood, Essex and works in London as a foreign exchange broker.

SEASON	LEAGUE		FA CUP		L. CUP	
	Apps	Gls	Apps	Gls	Apps	Gls
1970/71	18(4)	1	3	0	0	0
1971/72	25(3)	2	0(1)	0	2	0
1972/73	38(1)	5	1	0	2	0
1973/74	38(1)	0	3	0	3	0
1974/75	14	1	0	0	2	0
TOTAL	133(9)	9	7(1)	0	9	0

TOTAL APPS	149(10)
TOTAL GOALS	9

* Terry Brisley also appeared in a single Texaco Cup match in 1974/75.

Jason Curtis BRISSETT, 2000

Jason Brissett was born in Redbridge, Essex on 7 September 1974 and began his career as a trainee with Arsenal in August 1992. The speedy 5ft 10in tall right-winger sustained a serious injury in the 1996/97 season and made few League appearances for the club after that. He became an 'Oriental' on 2 July 2000, after making a total of 160(51) League appearances with Peterborough United, AFC Bournemouth, Walsall and Cheltenham (on loan), since his League debut in June 1993. It was reported soon after he joined the club that he had been arrested in August 2000 for various firearm offences and for the supply of drugs. Leyton

Born in Stepney, London on 4 July 1950, he was on the small side at just 5ft 6in tall, yet he was new O's boss Jimmy Bloomfield's first signing during March 1968. Brisley made steady progress through the youth and reserve ranks before making his League debut, when he came on as a substitute against Carlisle United in September 1970. He was an industrious midfield player who was very effective in the build-up of attacks, proving most effective between 1972 and 1974. Brisley was in the side that won the national five-a-side competition in the mid-1970s by defeating QPR 6-1 in the final. He had a loan spell with Southend United in March 1975, making 8 League appearances before a permanent move took him to Millwall in July 1975, as part of a deal that brought Doug Allder to Leyton. He made 106(1) League appearances and scored 14 goals before joining Charlton Athletic in January 1978 for

Orient FC issued a statement that Brissett was not out on bail, but that he had been released without any further charges, and press reports stating otherwise were, in fact, incorrect. However, he struggled to find his form early on, but did show what he was capable of with a good performance in the Worthington Cup win at Reading on 5 September 2000. He never really settled, falling out of favour with O's boss Tommy Taylor, and was released from his contract on 24 December 2001. He moved down the football ladder to join Football Conference side Stevenage Borough in January 2001. His stay did not last too long when, after just 2(1) appearances, he was shown the door by their management team of Paul Fairclough and former 'Oriental' Kevin Hales. He had a trial with QPR – playing alongside another former 'Oriental' Ahmet Brkovic – at the end of July 2001, in a friendly against Luton Town, in which former O's star Carl Griffiths netted the only goal of the match for his new club. Neither player was signed.

SEASON	LEAGUE		FA CUP		L. CUP	
	Apps	Gls	Apps	Gls	Apps	Gls
2000/01	2(2)	0	0	0	1(1)	0
TOTAL	2(2)	0	0	0	1(1)	0

TOTAL APPS	3(3)
TOTAL GOALS	0

Ahmet BRKOVIC, 1999-2001

The skilful midfielder was born in Dubrovnik, Croatia on 23 September 1974. He came to O's on trial on 16 October 1999 as a free agent, before signing a six-month contract on 5 November 1999, after impressing manager Taylor. This was after he had attended trials for both Millwall and Luton Town. The former Dubrovnik, Prevlaka, Junak-Split and Varteks-Varazdin player came to England after meeting a Romford girl who was on holiday in Croatia – they got married and settled in Essex. 'Brko', as he is affectionately known, sparked an O's revival in 1999, a time at which O's were at the bottom of the table. His spectacular overhead kick at Darlington and a scissors kick goal against Plymouth Argyle were both delights to watch. He was one of the bright spots in what proved to be a dismal 1999/2000 season. After protracted discussions, he eventually signed a new one-year contract in July 2000 saying: 'With all my heart, I want to stay with the Orient'. He played regularly in 2000/01 and did his part in taking O's to a play-off final at the Millennium Stadium in May, where O's lost 4-2 to Blackpool. His contract expired on 30 May 2001 and he was not offered a new contract. He went on trial with Stoke City and played for forty-five minutes in their 3-0 win over

Ahmet Brkovic

non-League side Newcastle Town on 15 July 2001. It was reported that he would sign a one-year contract, but in the end the deal died a mysterious death. He then played in a trial match for QPR on 31 July (a 1-0 defeat by Luton Town) but, once again, no deal was struck. He then went to Luton Town and starred for their reserves against O's reserves at Brisbane Road, scoring twice in a 3-2 win. After two further reserve outings, he signed a three-month contract for the Hatters on 4 October 2001. The Hatters boss said of his new charge: 'He is an intelligent foot-baller, who works well up and down the right flank and looks confident on the ball.' He has been an instant hit at Kenilworth Road and has been a regular in the promotion-chasing first team in 2002.

SEASON	LEAGUE		FA CUP		L. CUP	
	Apps	Gls	Apps	Gls	Apps	Gls
1999/2000	25(4)	5	2	0	0	0
2000/01*	34(8)	2	2	2	3	0
TOTAL	59(12)	7	4	2	3	0

TOTAL APPS	66(12)
TOTAL GOALS	9

* Brkovic's record includes 0(2) appearances in the play-offs during 2000/01.

** Brkovic also played in a single Auto Windscreens Shield match in 1999/2000 and also made an appearance in an LDV Vans Trophy match in 2000/01.

William Henry BROADBENT, 1925-32

Billy Broadbent was born in Chaddleston, Oldham on 20 November 1901 and started his career with Wellington Athletic. He went on to make 12 League appearances for Oldham Athletic between January 1920 and April 1923, before joining Brentford in June 1924 and making 17 League appear-ances. The right half joined O's during June 1925, and although not a regular in his first season, he did feature in O's great 2-0 FA Cup victory over Newcastle United in February 1926, when he came in as a last-minute replacement for the injured Bert Rosier. A good reliable professional who performed well during his seven-year stay at Millfields, he left to join Preston North End in March 1932, but played just 3 matches. Broadbent died in Lancaster on 14 February 1979.

SEASON	LEAGUE		FA CUP		TOTAL	
	Apps	Gls	Apps	Gls	Apps	Gls
1925/26	9	2	2	0	11	2
1926/27	29	3	2	0	31	3
1927/28	40	1	1	0	41	1
1928/29	24	0	0	0	24	0
1929/30	27	2	3	0	30	2
1930/31	32	0	0	0	32	0
1931/32	37	0	3	0	40	0
TOTAL	198	8	11	0	209	8

Charles Edward BROOKS, 1937-38

Kent-born Charlie Brooks, a 5ft 11in full-back, started his career with Folkestone Town in March 1931. Briefly, he joined Arsenal as an amateur in March 1931, but returned to Folkestone soon after. He became an 'Oriental' in May 1937, but could not command a regular place in the side. He then joined Crystal Palace in June 1938, but could only find a place in their reserve side. He made 30 wartime appearances for O's in 1941/42.

SEASON	LEAGUE		FA CUP		TOTAL	
	Apps	Gls	Apps	Gls	Apps	Gls
1937/38	4	0	1	0	5	0
TOTAL	4	0	1	0	5	0

* Charles Brooks also appeared in a Third Division Cup match in 1937/38.

Shaun BROOKS, 1983-87 and 1994-96
Cultured midfielder Shaun Brooks had two spells with O's, joining an elite band of players to play more than 200 senior games for the club. Born in south London on 9 October 1962, this midfielder often showed a skilful touch. He first joined the O's in November 1983 from Crystal Palace, where he made 54 League appearances scoring 4 goals. He enjoyed some good seasons at Brisbane Road, before declining a new contract in 1987 and transferring to AFC Bournemouth for £20,000. He amassed 114(14) League appearances for the Cherries, scoring 4 goals. During his time there, he also went on loan to Stockport County in December 1992 after a bust-up with their boss Terry Purlis, which left Brooks with facial cuts. Pullis was reprimanded over the incident. Brooks went on trial with Everton, but was not offered a contract. He then went to Crewe Alexandra, but decided not accept their offer. In the end, he joined Dorchester Town. During

Shaun Brooks

October 1994 he went back to AFC Bournemouth on trial, but after just a solitary League appearance, he re-joined O's in November 1994 to bring some experience to a struggling team at the foot of the table. In May 1996 he was given a free transfer by O's and joined Poole Town. During a professional career that spanned some seventeen seasons, he played 394(40) matches and scored 52 goals. During the 1999/2000 season, thirty-seven-year-old Brooks was playing for Wimborne Town in the Wessex League.

SEASON	LEAGUE		FA CUP		L. CUP	
	Apps	Gls	Apps	Gls	Apps	Gls
1983/84	33(3)	9	1	0	0	0
1984/85	27(2)	5	1	0	4	0
1985/86	35(3)	7	6	3	4	1
1986/87	45	5	4	1	2	0
1994/95	8(1)	0	0(1)	0	0	0
1995/96	34(7)	2	1	0	2	0
TOTAL	182(16)	28	13(1)	4	12	1

TOTAL APPS	207(17)
TOTAL GOALS	33

* Shaun Brooks also appeared in 11(3) Auto Windscreens Shield matches, scoring 2 goals.

Charles George BROWN, 1936-37
Charles Brown (not to be confused with Charles George Brown of Hayes, Crystal Palace and Watford fame between 1930 and 1935) was born in Earslford, London on 7 December 1909. He started with Dartford in August 1935 and stayed for a year before going on loan to Aldershot – the 6ft tall wing-half became an 'Oriental' in May 1936. His only appearance came in the 2-1 defeat at Queens Park Rangers on 19 September 1936. He later served on the committee of the Chase of Chertsey club from January 1947.

SEASON	LEAGUE		FA CUP		TOTAL	
	Apps	Gls	Apps	Gls	Apps	Gls
1936/37	1	0	0	0	1	0
TOTAL	1	0	0	0	1	0

SEASON	LEAGUE		FA CUP		L. CUP	
	Apps	Gls	Apps	Gls	Apps	Gls
2001/02	0	0	0	0	0	0
TOTAL	0	0	0	0	0	0

TOTAL APPS	0
TOTAL GOALS	0

Craig BROWN, 2001-present

Eighteen-year-old Craig Brown became O's boss Tommy Taylor's sixth summer signing on 31 July 2001, after producing some impressive displays during his trial period when he scored 4 goals in as many games. He netted twice against Saffron Waldon in a 9-0 victory, and also scored against Crawley Town and Kings Lynn. Born in Kingston-on-Thames, London on 13 January 1983, Craig Brown started his career as a right full-back as a ten-year-old with West Ham United's School of Excellence. Two years later he joined the Millwall Centre of Excellence, spending five years at the New Den. In 2000 he moved to Reading's Academy as a scholar, where he was converted into an attacking mid-fielder and forward. He was released in May 2001, and although offered a chance with Ryman Premier League side Sutton United, he jumped at a chance with O's instead. O's boss Taylor stated: 'I think that Brown has what it takes to make the grade. He's got plenty of pace and he has shown during his trial that he knows where the goal is. I'm sure he'll become a useful member of the first-team squad.' Up to the end November 2001, Brown had not featured as a first-team squad member, but had played 6(1) matches for O's under-19 youth side and made a lone reserve appearance as a substitute. He joined Sutton United on a month's loan in December 2001, but after a short time he returned to the club on the injured list.

Edwin BROWN, 1959-1961

Eddie Brown was one of the most colourful characters ever to wear an O's shirt, and he would brighten up the dullest of matches with his eccentric, clowning antics. He would chat with the fans on the terraces, do a celebration jig around a corner flag every time he scored a goal, and I even heard him quoting Shakespeare to his opposition marker in many a match, that is if they could catch him, which many couldn't because of his remarkable speed! Off the field, Brown even had time to work as a male model. He was one of the great clowns of the modern game, yet what a grand player Eddie Brown was. He hit an incredible 200 League goals from a total of 399 career outings. He was born in Preston, on 28 February 1926, and his early life makes remarkable reading. He spent eight years as a religious brother at the De La Salle College in Guernsey and he was known as 'Brother John'. It was reported that his football career started in September 1948, when he walked into the offices of Preston North End and asked for a trial. He impressed them so much that he signed professional forms with the Deepdale club, making 36 appearances with 6 goals. He became known as the 'Brown bomber', because of his great speed, and he went onto to play for Southampton between 1950 and 1952, making 57 appearances and scoring 32 goals. He then played for Coventry City (1951-1955), where he made 85 League appearances and netted

60 goals, and then for Birmingham City (1955-1959), where he made 158 appearances and hit 74 goals. He moved to O's in January 1959 for £6,000, after an impressive reserve match for City against O's at Brisbane Road. He made his debut in a friendly at Leyton against QPR, a remarkable 9-1 victory. He built up a wonderful relationship with veteran players Eddie Baily and Tommy Johnston – between the three of them, their ages totalled ninety-eight years, and yet they still managed to steer O's clear of relegation. Brown recorded the 200th senior goal of his career for O's against Middlesborough on 30 April 1960. He had previously put four goals past Sunderland in March 1959, and scored a hat-trick against Boro in October 1959. After three seasons with O's, Brown joined Scarborough for a four-year spell as player-manager, followed by a similar position at Stourbridge in the Lancashire League. When approaching forty years of age, he went to Wigan Athletic, also in the Lancashire League. He retired three years later to become a part-time French tutor at All Hallows School. He was still managing Broughton Amateurs in 2001, as well as working in the family carpet business. He also acts as a successful compère on the after-dinner circuit. Thanks for wonderful memories, Eddie Brown.

SEASON	LEAGUE		FA CUP		L. CUP	
	Apps	Gls	Apps	Gls	Apps	Gls
1958/59	16	10	0	0	-	-
1959/60	35	12	1	0	-	-
1960/61*	12	6	0	0	2	1
TOTAL	63	28	1	0	2	1

TOTAL APPS	66
TOTAL GOALS	29

* The League Cup commenced in 1960/61.

Thomas Law BROWN, 1950-53

Tommy Brown was born in Glenbuck, Ayrshire, on 17 April 1921, and started his career with Cambuslang Rangers. The 5ft 10in player joined Heart of Midlothian in 1938, making 27 Scottish League appearances and scoring 4 goals. He played for a Scottish representative side at the age of seventeen on 2 December 1939 in a wartime international against England at Newcastle United. He won 3 caps in total. Hailed as a 'brilliant prospect', like so many of his contemporaries, his professional career was curtailed by the onset of the Second World War. After the war he joined Millwall in January 1945, making 68 League appearances and scoring 7 goals for them. He then moved to Charlton Athletic in October 1948 for a large fee for those days of £8,500, making 36 senior appearances and scoring just once. He joined O's on 4 August 1950 for just £300, and proved to be a bargain

Tom Brown

buy, delighting O's fans for three seasons. One of his best displays was at Birmingham City in the fourth round of the FA Cup during February 1952, when his brilliant scheming wrought havoc in the City defence. Brown was a master-tactician and excellent ball distributor, and captained the team in the 1951/52 season. Sadly, he sustained a serious leg injury against Bristol Rovers on 7 March 1953, which eventually forced him to retire. He became coach with Dartford in July 1953. A benefit match was staged for him in April 1954, when many top players of the day – including Sir Stanley Matthews – appeared for him. Tommy Brown died in Edinburgh on 10 May 1966, aged forty-five.

SEASON	LEAGUE		FA CUP		TOTAL	
	Apps	Gls	Apps	Gls	Apps	Gls
1950/51	30	0	1	0	31	0
1951/52	39	3	9	2	48	5
1952/53	30	2	0	0	30	2
TOTAL	99	5	10	2	109	7

William Charles BROWN, 1946-47

Born in Canning Town, London on 24 April 1920, Bill Brown, a tall centre forward, joined O's from Romford FC in August 1946, after showing distinct promise in a trial match. He scored on his League debut against Ipswich Town on 31 August 1946. He did not progress as well as expected, playing only in the reserves, and was released in May 1947 before moving back in to non-League football. Brown died in 1982, aged sixty-two.

SEASON	LEAGUE		FA CUP		TOTAL	
	Apps	Gls	Apps	Gls	Apps	Gls
1946/47	2	1	0	0	2	1
TOTAL	2	1	0	0	2	1

William Ian BROWN, 1947-48

Billy 'Buster' Brown, was a big strong defender, who joined O's as a veteran in March 1947. Aged thirty-seven, he showed all the cunning with which years of experience in First Division football had equipped him. Brown was born in Silverton, London on 6 September 1910. He started with Fairburn House FC, then moved on to Luton Town in 1930, where he made 49 League appearances before moving to Huddersfield Town in 1934. After three seasons and 41 appearances for the Yorkshire club, he signed for Brentford in March 1937 for £3,000, chalking up 92 League appearances and playing over 270 Second World War regional matches for the Bees. The balding Brown made his O's debut in June 1947 against Cardiff City – O's first ever League match to be played in the month of June, in a season severely affected by bad weather. He left O's in May 1948, joining former O's manager William Peter Wright and former O's coach William Bulloch Wright at Southern League club Chingford Town. 'Buster' Brown died in Ealing, London on 15 January 1993, aged eighty-three.

SEASON	LEAGUE		FA CUP		TOTAL	
	Apps	Gls	Apps	Gls	Apps	Gls
1946/47	1	0	0	0	1	0
1947/48	25	0	1	0	26	0
TOTAL	26	0	1	0	27	0

John Jack BRUCE, 1932-33

Jack Bruce, a goalkeeper, was born in Trimdon, Co. Durham in December 1908, joining O's from non-League Tunbridge Wells Rangers in July 1932. He showed considerable promise for a time, winning his first-team colours after some stirring displays in the reserves, and he vied for the first-team jersey with Bert Emery. Bruce was released in October 1933 and joined Whitecrofts FC on the Isle of Wight. He later worked for Leavesden mental hospital from September 1934. Bruce died in Nottingham in December 1998, aged ninety.

SEASON	LEAGUE		FA CUP		TOTAL	
	Apps	Gls	Apps	Gls	Apps	Gls
1932/33	19	0	1	0	20	0
TOTAL	19	0	1	0	20	0

Robert BRUCE, 1951-52

Bobby Bruce, a tricky outside left, started with Larne Town FC before joining Leicester City in March 1950, but he never made an impression at Filbert Street. Born in Belfast, Ireland on 14 October 1928, he joined O's on an extended trial in November 1951. After a few reserve games, he made his League debut at Bristol Rovers on 27 February 1952, where he gave experienced Rovers full-back Harry Bamford some anxious moments. Bruce was not retained after his trial and returned home to Ireland.

SEASON	LEAGUE		FA CUP		TOTAL	
	Apps	Gls	Apps	Gls	Apps	Gls
1951/52	1	0	0	0	1	0
TOTAL	1	0	0	0	1	0

Eric BRYANT, 1951-52

Born in Birmingham on 18 November 1921, Bryant, a lively centre forward, started his career as an amateur with Gillingham in 1939. He joined Mansfield Town, and between May 1946 and 1948 he made 35 League appearances, scoring 17 goals, before joining Yeovil & Petters United. He signed for Plymouth Argyle in October 1949 for £3,000, but after just

Eric Bryant

11 appearances which yielded 4 goals, he became an 'Oriental' in July 1951. Oddly enough, his debut came a month later against his former club, Plymouth, but he soon lost his first-team place. He moved to Chelmsford City in 1952, and later played for Poole Town, Dorchester Town and Bideford. Bryant died in Wareham on 2 December 1995.

SEASON	LEAGUE		FA CUP		TOTAL	
	Apps	Gls	Apps	Gls	Apps	Gls
1951/52	12	1	0	0	12	1
TOTAL	12	1	0	0	12	1

David BUCHANAN, 1906-08

Born in Bellshire, Scotland in 1873, Dave (or 'Buck', as he was known) is reported as having been the only known outfield player to have worn a black skullcap whilst on the field of play. He was one of the real characters in O's early League days, and he stood just 5ft 7in tall.

Dave Buchanan

SEASON	LEAGUE		FA CUP		TOTAL	
	Apps	Gls	Apps	Gls	Apps	Gls
1906/07*	31	2	-	-	31	2
1907/08	34	0	5	3	39	3
TOTAL	65	2	5	3	70	5

* Clapton Orient did not enter the FA Cup in 1906/07.

Buchanan started his career with Third Lanark, moving to Southern League club Brentford in 1903, and then on to Middlesbrough in 1904, for whom he only played reserve football. He joined Plymouth Argyle in 1905, making 17 Southern League and 12 Western League appearances and scoring twice. The thirty-three-year-old proved to be a clever, grafting and consistent right half or inside forward, and joined O's from Argyle in July 1906. Buchanan was completely bald, and it was written that he wore the skullcap everywhere he went, being a very sensitive chap. After 2 successful seasons with O's, he moved to Southern League outfit Leyton FC as player-manager in June 1908. It was Buchanan who first signed a young Charles Buchan, later to become a very famous player with Sunderland, Arsenal and with England. He left Leyton in 1912.

Michael Edwin BULLOCK, 1968-76

Mickey Bullock was born in Stoke on 2 October 1946. The 5ft 11in striker joined O's as a twenty-two-year-old from Oxford United for £8,000 during October 1968. The former England schoolboy became an apprentice at Birmingham City in June 1962, turning professional in October 1963, and made his League debut as a sixteen-year-old, scoring the winner against Manchester United in January 1964. After 27 appearances and 10 goals for the Blues, he was transferred to Oxford in June 1967 for £10,000. He became their top scorer with 13 goals from 45 appearances that season, helping them to win the Third Division Championship. Bullock had some wonderful seasons with O's, scoring 19 goals in the Third Division Championship-winning side of 1969/70. He also hit 16 goals when O's missed out on promotion to the First Division in 1973/74 by a single point. He scored in the vital match against Aston Villa, but his last-minute effort that could have given O's a First Division place, was tipped over the bar. Mickey Bullock was never the dashing type of centre forward, more the subtle player who seemed to 'hang' in the air when jumping for a header, and he was able to lay off the ball very well. He was a grand club servant, an impeccably fair sportsman, and rated after Tommy Johnston as one of the finest headers of a ball to play for O's. It was with sadness that he left the club to join Halifax Town in February 1976, where he stayed for nine years. Initially, he joined as a player – making 119(9) senior appearances and scoring 21 goals – and then in 1979 progressed on to the role of coach, finally becoming manager on 13 July 1981. Bullock was sacked as manager on 22 October 1984. He later managed Goole Town and Ossett Town, and was a scout for Hereford United, Portsmouth and Crystal Palace. Mickey Bullock scored 109 League goals in a career which totalled 450(19) appearances. He now works as an insurance consultant.

SEASON	LEAGUE		FA CUP		L. CUP	
	Apps	Gls	Apps	Gls	Apps	Gls
1968/69	33	6	2	0	0	0
1969/70	42	19	2	0	2	0
1970/71	41(1)	5	3	0	1	0
1971/72	42	11	4	1	2	1
1972/73	25(6)	4	0	0	2	0
1973/74	40(1)	16	4	0	4	2
1974/75	28	3	0	0	2	0
1975/76	16(2)	1	1	0	1	0
TOTAL	267(10)	65	16	1	14	3

TOTAL APPS	297(10)
TOTAL GOALS	69

* Mickey Bullock also appeared in a Texaco Cup match in 1974/75.

Mickey Bullock

Michael Rupert BURGESS, 1953-56

The Canadian-born 6ft 1in tall left half, Mike Burgess, joined O's from the groundstaff of Bradford Park Avenue in July 1953, and at twenty-one years old became the youngest member of O's first-team squad, having turned professional with the Yorkshire club on 1 August 1952. Born in Montreal on 17 April 1932, he was a slightly awkward-looking player, who nevertheless was big and strong with a powerful left-foot shot, and was later converted by O's boss Alec Stock to an inside forward. He scored an important goal in a FA Cup fifth round tie against Doncaster Rovers in 1954, and netted 24 goals for O's reserves in 1954/55. Burgess was involved in the deal that brought in Tommy Johnston from Newport County in February 1956, and he went on to make 24 appearances and score 7 goals for County. In June 1957 he moved to Bournemouth, where he made 109 League appearances and scored 34 goals, including finishing as top scorer in 1958/59 with 24 goals. He then moved on to Halifax Town during July 1961 (34 appearances and 3 goals), followed by Gillingham during March 1963 for £250. There he made 109(1) appearances and scored twice, and he appeared at centre half in every League match (46) of their

Fourth Division Championship-winning team in 1963/64. His last League club was Aldershot, whom he joined in November 1965, making just 6 appearances. He made a career total of 314 League appearances and scored 58 goals. He moved on to play for Canterbury City in November 1967.

SEASON	LEAGUE		FA CUP		TOTAL	
	Apps	Gls	Apps	Gls	Apps	Gls
1953/54	13	5	1	1	14	6
1954/55	7	1	0	0	7	1
1955/56	11	6	4	1	15	7
TOTAL	31	12	5	2	36	14

Wayne BURNETT, 1989-92

Burnett, a former YTS player, made his full League debut in the final match of the 1989/90 season at Fulham, but then spent a frustrating year dogged by injury. He had been capped at youth level by England, playing at Wembley against Poland in a 3-0 win. Born in Lambeth, London on 4 September 1971, this skilful midfielder came back and scored his only League goal for the club on the opening day of the 1991/92 season at Brentford, when heading home a Ricky Otto cross. (Some reports credited the goal to Kevin Nugent.) He followed up with a goal against Northampton Town in a 5-0 victory in the League Cup. After a successful campaign, he became Kenny Dalglish's thirteenth signing for Blackburn Rovers on 19 August 1992 for £80,000. He never made it at Ewood Park and remained stuck in the reserves. During August 1993 he joined Plymouth Argyle for £100,000, making 61(9) appearances and scoring 3 goals, after which he moved to Bolton Wanderers in December 1995, but stayed only a short while, making only 3 appearances as substitute. During September 1996 he joined Huddersfield Town for £150,000, playing 43(6) times, but was on the move again to Grimsby Town in February 1998 for £100,000. He had a successful time with them, playing in the Auto Windscreen Final on 19 April 1998 and scoring a sudden-death goal in the 112th minute to secure a 2-1 win over AFC Bournemouth. The match took place in front of 62,432 fans and meant that Burnett obtained legendary status in the history of Blundell Park. One month later, he was back at the famous stadium in a Division Two play-off final when Grimsby completed a great Wembley 'double', beating Northampton Town 1-0. Burnett had made 59(11) League appearances for Grimsby up to the end of the 2000/01 season, and scored 3 goals. Rumours abounded that twenty-nine-year-old Burnett might return to O's, but in the end he signed a new one-year contract with Grimsby and scored their winner on the opening day of the new season.

Wayne Burnett

SEASON	LEAGUE		FA CUP		L. CUP	
	Apps	Gls	Apps	Gls	Apps	Gls
1989/90	1(2)	0	0	0	0	0
1990/91	0(1)	0	0	0	0	0
1991/92	33(3)	1	3(1)	0	3(1)	0
TOTAL	34(6)	1	3(1)	0	3(1)	0

TOTAL APPS	40(8)
TOTAL GOALS	2

* Wayne Burnett also appeared in 4 Auto Windscreens Shield matches.

Peter John BURRIDGE, 1958-61

Born in Harlow, Essex on 30 December 1933, Burridge was a player who only came to the fore once leaving Brisbane Road. Burridge joined O's from non-League Barnet in April 1958. Usually a centre forward, despite being very good with his left foot, he could never displace Tommy Johnston, yet he did score in the first minute of his O's debut on 27 December 1958 at Stoke City. He also scored twice in O's 4-3 win, a friendly at Scottish side Montrose in 1959/60. He could only manage a handful of appearances before moving to Millwall (two divisions lower than O's) in August 1960 for £2,000. He played very well for the Lions and scored 58 goals in 87 League appearances – including 38 goals in one season – and won a Fourth Division Championship medal. He moved to Crystal Palace in June 1962 for £10,000, and also performed very well there, scoring 42 goals in 114 appearances. During November 1965 he moved to Charlton Athletic, where he found it more difficult to score, with just 4 goals from 42(2) appearances. He joined Southern League side Bedford Town in May 1966. Burridge was yet another player who, because of the wonderful achievements of Tommy Johnston, had to go elsewhere to show his true capabilities. He totalled 106 career League goals from 249(2) appearances. After his retirement, he ran a public house in Harlow, Essex and also worked in a printing business during the 1990s.

SEASON	LEAGUE		FA CUP		TOTAL	
	Apps	Gls	Apps	Gls	Apps	Gls
1958/59	2	1	1	0	3	1
1959/60	4	1	0	0	4	1
TOTAL	6	2	1	0	7	2

Joseph BUTLER, 1905-06

Born in Lawleybank, Telford, Shropshire in 1879, before entering the football arena Butler worked as a miner. Goalkeeper Joe Butler started his League career with Stockport County, and between 1900 and 1905 played over 100 senior matches. O's needed a top-class 'keeper for their first campaign in the League in 1905/06, and Butler was the man signed. He appeared in O's first League fixture at Leicester Fosse on 2 September 1905, a 2-1 defeat. He did quite well, but with the club in dire straits financially, a number of players had to sold and Butler was one, returning to Stockport at the end of January 1906 for a substantial fee. He made a further 74 appearances for County before he was off to Glossop North End in March 1908 for £150, where he went for four seasons without missing a match, notching up 161 League appearances. He was signed by Sunderland for a large fee in October 1912, and performed very well for the club. In his two seasons he made 78 senior appearances, appeared in their 6-0 FA Cup victory over O's in January 1913, and in the played in the 1913 FA Cup final at Crystal Palace (which Aston Villa won 1-0). In May 1914 he joined Lincoln

City, where he made a further 37 League appearances. Butler, although he was only 5ft 9in, proved to be a very capable custodian, and his old Sunderland team-mate, Charlie Buchan, once described Butler as being a very reliable rather than spectacular goalkeeper. He made a total of 457 League appearances throughout his fifteen-year career. Joseph Butler died in August 1941.

SEASON	LEAGUE		FA CUP		TOTAL	
	Apps	Gls	Apps	Gls	Apps	Gls
1905/06	20	0	4	0	24	0
TOTAL	20	0	4	0	24	0

Richard Cadette

Richard Raymond CADETTE, 1984-85
Born in Hammersmith, London on 21 March 1965, Richard Cadette joined O's from Wembley FC on 1 August 1984, after a trial with Luton Town. The 5ft 8in striker proved fast and agile. Only nineteen at the time, he did well when chosen by boss Frank Clark, and although small in stature, he was fast and agile. However, his stay was short-lived and he joined Bobby Moore at Southend United on a free transfer on 15 August 1985, promptly scoring 4 goals against O's in their 5-1 victory. He was Southend's top scorer at the end of the 1985/86 season with 25 goals, and went on to total 49 goals from 90 games before a £130,000 move to Sheffield United in July 1987. He moved to Brentford in July 1988 for £77,500, where he netted a further 20 goals from 67(20) League appearances. After that he had loan spells with Bournemouth (4(4) appearances and a single goal) and Falkirk, with whom he

was voted Scottish First Division Player of the Year in 1993, having scored 18 goals. He signed for Millwall for £135,000 during October 1994, but made just 20(5) senior appearances and scored 5 goals before joining Irish club Shelbourne. Cadette ended his professional career at Clyde-bank in Scotland, but after a solitary goal in just 4 appearances and, he left that club in September 1997. After his retirement he worked as a coach at the Millwall Youth Academy.

SEASON	LEAGUE		FA CUP		L. CUP	
	Apps	Gls	Apps	Gls	Apps	Gls
1984/85	19(2)	4	1	1	4	0
TOTAL	19(2)	4	1	1	4	0

TOTAL APPS	24(2)
TOTAL GOALS	5

* Richard Cadette also appeared in 2 Auto Windscreens Shield matches.

Frederick CADIOU, 2000 (trial)

Frenchman Freddie Cadiou, a forward, was born in Paris on 20 April 1969. The thirty-one-year-old joined O's on a month's trial on 6 October 2000, with a view to a longer contract. He had previously played for French Second Division side BS Wasquehal, where he netted 12 goals in 19 games during 1999/2000. Before this, he had a two-week trial with Scottish club Dundee United, but didn't make any first-team appearances. Not only a footballer, he also completed a master's degree in education science. Cadiou made his League debut as substitute against Cardiff City on 14 October 2000, replacing Carl Griffith in the ninetieth minute. He made a total of 3 substitute appearances – all O's victories – and yet was not retained, leaving the club at the end of October. With new £25,000 signing Chris Tate occupying his place on the bench, Cadiou returned to his French club, BS Wasquehal. In July 2001 he joined French Fourth Division side Valenciennes on a one-year contract.

SEASON	LEAGUE		FA CUP		L. CUP	
	Apps	Gls	Apps	Gls	Apps	Gls
2000/01	0(3)	0	0	0	0	0
TOTAL	0(3)	0	0	0	0	0

TOTAL APPS	0(3)
TOTAL GOALS	0

Charles CAIRNEY, 1950-51

Born in Blantyre, Lanarkshire on 21 September 1926, 'Chic' (as he was known) started with Cambuslang in 1947 before joining Celtic in March 1949. He moved to O's on 27 July 1950, having played just one Scottish League match against Raith Rovers on 1 October 1949. Right-half Cairney was confined mainly to the O's reserve team, making his League debut in a 2-1 defeat at Bristol Rovers in November 1950. In 1951 he joined Southern League side Barry Town, but during July 1953 he returned to the League with Bristol Rovers, playing 14 matches and scoring once. He later had spells with Headington United, Worcester City, and in October 1957, he moved to East Stirling. Chic always gave 100 per cent wherever he played, showing neatness and constructive ability. He died in Scotland on 25 March 1995.

SEASON	LEAGUE		FA CUP		TOTAL	
	Apps	Gls	Apps	Gls	Apps	Gls
1950/51	4	0	0	0	4	0
TOTAL	4	0	0	0	4	0

David CALDERHEAD Jnr, 1919-20

Born in Dumfries, Scotland in 1889, he started playing football with junior sides Dumfries Primrose FC and Maxwell Town Volunteers FC. Calderhead Jnr was educated at St Peter's school in Lincoln after his father was appointed manager with Lincoln City. Calderhead Jnr joined his father when he became the manager at Chelsea, and made his League debut for the Blues at centre half against Leicester Fosse in January 1911. He made 43 senior appearances during his stay at Stamford Bridge, before joining Motherwell in April 1914. During the First World War, he guested for Chelsea, Leicester Fosse and Notts County. He joined O's in June 1919 without having much success, and his only appearance came against Wolverhampton Wanderers on 13 September 1919. He joined Lincoln City in April 1921 and was appointed their secretary-manager. On leaving full-time football in May 1924, he became licensee of the Newmarket Hotel in Lincoln.

SEASON	LEAGUE		FA CUP		TOTAL	
	Apps	Gls	Apps	Gls	Apps	Gls
1919/20	1	0	0	0	1	0
TOTAL	1	0	0	0	1	0

James CALDWELL, 1907-08

London-born winger Jimmy Caldwell was brother of another 'Oriental', Tommy Caldwell, who joined O's a year later after his brother's departure. He started with Willsden FC before joining O's in June 1907, and made his League debut at West Bromwich Albion on 21 September 1907, the same day the O's first team were defeating Custom House FC in an FA Cup first round qualifying tie. He left O's in 1908, having been replaced by his more famous brother, joining Southern League side Hastings & St Leonards FC. He later played for Queens Park Rangers in 1908, and in 1911 played for Reading.

SEASON	LEAGUE		FA CUP		TOTAL	
	Apps	Gls	Apps	Gls	Apps	Gls
1907/08	12	0	0	0	12	0
TOTAL	12	0	0	0	12	0

Peter James CALDWELL, 1995-97

Born in Dorchester, near Oxford on 5 June 1972, the goalkeeper started as an associated schoolboy with Queens Park Rangers in 1988, and turned professional in March 1990, but played only reserve football. He became an 'Oriental' on 3 July 1995 spending two seasons with the club, however, with the arrival of veteran 'keepers Les Sealey, and later Peter Shilton, he decided to pack his bags to continue his career in America in March 1997.

Peter Caldwell (diving at feet of striker)

SEASON	LEAGUE		FA CUP		L. CUP	
	Apps	Gls	Apps	Gls	Apps	Gls
1995/96	28	0	0	0	2	0
1996/97	3	0	0	0	0	0
TOTAL	31	0	0	0	2	0

TOTAL APPS	33
TOTAL GOALS	0

* Peter Caldwell also appeared in an Auto Windscreens Shield match.

Thomas CALDWELL, 1907-08

Tommy Caldwell was born in the East End of London in 1886. He started his career with Ilford Alliance FC, and later played for West Ham St Pauls FC. He joined O's in 1908, replacing his younger brother James. The winger made his League debut at Fulham on 18 March 1908, but left O's to join Southend United in May 1908/09. There he scored 5 goals in 21 Southern

League and FA Cup appearances. In August 1909 he joined West Ham United, bagging a-hat-trick against Bristol Rovers in October 1909, and scoring the match-winner in an FA Cup victory over Manchester United in February 1911. He played 96 Southern League and FA Cup matches for the Hammers, scoring 14 goals. In 1912 he joined Southern League New Brompton, and later played for Reading.

SEASON	LEAGUE		FA CUP		TOTAL	
	Apps	Gls	Apps	Gls	Apps	Gls
1907/08	7	0	0	0	7	0
TOTAL	7	0	0	0	7	0

Alexander CAMPBELL, 1926-28

Glasgow-born Alex Campbell started his career with Parkhead FC, and in 1921 he joined Albion Rovers. The full-back came south of the Border to become an 'Oriental' in July 1926, showing some good ability at the end of the 1926/27 season. He played in a run of 5 unbeaten matches to help save O's from the embarrassment of having to apply for re-election to the League. He continued his fine form at the start of the following season when O's went 5 matches unbeaten, but a bad injury sustained at Blackpool during September 1927 saw him return to League action a full three months later. He left O's in 1928 to join Connah's Quay and Shotton FC, a club he later went on to coach.

SEASON	LEAGUE		FA CUP		TOTAL	
	Apps	Gls	Apps	Gls	Apps	Gls
1926/27	5	0	0	0	5	0
1927/28	18	0	0	0	18	0
TOTAL	23	0	0	0	23	0

Gary CAMPBELL, 1990

Born in Belfast, Northern Ireland on 4 April 1966, Gary Campbell commenced his career on 1 January 1984 as an apprentice with Arsenal. After spells with the likes of Finchley FC and Boreham Wood FC, as well as a short trial with West Bromwich Albion, the winger joined O's on trial from near neighbours Leyton-Wingate FC in February 1990. After a match at Swansea in April 1990, he was not feeling well and was diagnosed as suffering from shingles. Campbell was not on the retained list for May, and he later played for Bromley.

SEASON	LEAGUE		FA CUP		L. CUP	
	Apps	Gls	Apps	Gls	Apps	Gls
1989/90	4(4)	0	0	0	0	0
TOTAL	4(4)	0	0	0	0	0

TOTAL APPS	4(4)
TOTAL GOALS	0

Gary Campbell

C

Hugh CAMPBELL, 1935-36

Glasgow-born Hugh Campbell came down south to O's in August 1935, after a brief spell with Glasgow Rangers, and the left-winger made his debut against Reading on 5 September 1935. He could not hold down a regular first-team place and moved to Cardiff City in July 1936, playing just once for them in the final fixture of the 1936/37 season at Bristol City on 1 May. He joined Ballymena in June 1937, moving later that season to Distillery FC. During 1938/39 he was at Halifax Town, making 25 League appearances and scoring once.

SEASON	LEAGUE		FA CUP		TOTAL	
	Apps	Gls	Apps	Gls	Apps	Gls
1935/36	8	1	0	0	8	1
TOTAL	8	1	0	0	8	1

* Hugh Campbell also appeared in a Third Division Cup match in 1935/36, scoring once.

John CAMPBELL, 1929-30

Born in South Shields, Co. Durham on 12 May 1901, Johnny Campbell began as a schoolboy goalkeeper, but was successfully converted to a centre forward during his time with a local works team. He continued his career north of the border with Berwick Rangers in the Scottish Border League. He later returned to his native north-east with Jarrow FC. In June 1923 he joined West Ham United, making 28 League appearances and scoring 11 goals. He once scored 5 goals for Hammers reserves against Fulham in December 1928 in a 13-2 win. The livewire striker looked impressive for O's, netting a hat-trick for the club in a 5-0 win at Torquay United on 18 January 1930, after signing in September 1929. He left O's in May 1930, retiring due to an injury. Campbell died in Newcastle-upon-Tyne in January 1983.

SEASON	LEAGUE		FA CUP		TOTAL	
	Apps	Gls	Apps	Gls	Apps	Gls
1920/30	25	9	6	2	31	11
TOTAL	25	9	6	2	31	11

Joseph CAMPBELL, 1949-50

Joe Campbell was born Glasgow on 28 March 1925, and the inside forward came down south to join O's in July 1949 from Glasgow Celtic, after playing for St Marks FC and St Anthony's FC. He was a neat player who only managed to get into the first team on the odd occasion, but when O's signed another Scotsman – Jimmy Blair – Campbell was transferred to Gillingham in September 1950 for £2,000, making 12 League appearances for the Gills and scoring twice. In August 1951 he joined Bedford Town.

SEASON	LEAGUE		FA CUP		TOTAL	
	Apps	Gls	Apps	Gls	Apps	Gls
1949/50	5	1	0	0	5	1
TOTAL	5	1	0	0	5	1

Kevin Joseph CAMPBELL, 1989 (loan)

Campbell proved to be an inspiration when joining O's on loan from Arsenal for three months in January 1989, scoring on debut at Crewe Alexandra which helped O's in their push to the promotion play-off, one could see that he was destined for greater things. He returned to Highbury before O's won promotion over Wrexham in the play-off final during June 1989, he went to Leicester City the following season netting 5 goals from 11 appearances. Born in Lambeth,

Kevin Campbell

London on 4 February 1970, the striker progressed through Arsenal's youth ranks. He was a big strong striker who made 124(42) appearances for the Gunners, scoring 46 goals. He signed for Nottingham Forest for £280,000, making 79 appearances and scoring 32 goals. He went to play in Turkey in July 1998 with Trabzoyspor for a £250,000 fee, but came back to England joining Everton on loan in March 1999, and netting 9 goals from 8 League appearances. He eventually joined them for £300,000 on 14 July 1999, hitting a further 21 goals from 52(2) appearances up to the end of the 2000/01 season. He netted a goal against O's in Everton's 4-1 FA Cup victory at Goodison Park on 26 January 2002. Kevin Campbell will not be forgotten for the part he played in O's attaining promotion. He has always been a dangerous striker and a good goalscorer, as his record proves.

SEASON	LEAGUE		FA CUP		L. CUP	
	Apps	Gls	Apps	Gls	Apps	Gls
1988/89	16	9	0	0	0	0
TOTAL	16	9	0	0	0	0

TOTAL APPS	16
TOTAL GOALS	9

George Walter CANDY, 1908-09

Londoner George Candy was born in 1886. The outside left joined O's in 1908 from Salisbury Town as cover for Felix Ward. He made his League debut against Glossop North End on 3 October 1908, but did not get much of a look-in and played the season out in the reserves, leaving in 1909.

SEASON	LEAGUE		FA CUP		TOTAL	
	Apps	Gls	Apps	Gls	Apps	Gls
1908/09	3	0	0	0	3	0
TOTAL	3	0	0	0	3	0

Scott CANHAM, 1998-2000, 2001-present

Scott Canham was born in Newham, London on 5 November 1974. He started his career as a trainee on 2 July 1993 with West Ham United. After loan spells with Torquay United in November 1995 and Brentford in January 1996, he joined the Bees on 29 August 1996 for £25,000 and spent three seasons with them, making 24(11) League appearances and scoring once. He played as a subsitute for Brentford in a Division Two play-off final at Wembley Stadium in May 1998, which they lost 1-0. O's boss Tommy Taylor signed Scott Canham as a utility defender in August 1998 on a one-year contract. Canham made his O's debut as a substitute at Torquay United on 1 September 1998, replacing Danny Morrison in the eighty-seventh minute. His full debut came in January 1999 at right wing-back

C

against Darlington, and he had an excellent match. He could never get a decent run and was released in May 2000, joining Chesham United after a previous loan spell. The twenty-six-year-old surprisingly re-joined O's on a one-year contract in June 2001. O's boss Tommy Taylor saw enough in the midfielder to give him another chance of making a name for himself in Division Three. Canham was rewarded with a new one-year contract in February 2002 after some wonderful displays, none more so than the brace he scored against Halifax Town on 2 March 2002 in O's 3-1 victory – the first of the new year.

SEASON	LEAGUE		FA CUP		L. CUP	
	Apps	Gls	Apps	Gls	Apps	Gls
1998/99	2(6)	0	0	0	0	0
1999/2000	1	0	0	0	1	0
2001/02	23(1)	4	1	1	0	0
TOTAL	26(7)	4	1	1	0(1)	0

TOTAL APPS 27(8)

TOTAL GOALS 5

* Scott Canham also appeared in an Auto Windscreens Shield match.

Cyril Edward CANVIN, 1946-1947

Born in Hemel Hempstead on 23 January 1924, Cyril Canvin, a hard-as-nails inside forward, came to O's in March 1947 from Aspley FC. He scored a few goals for the reserves and got his chance for the final 3 matches of the 1946/47 season. He got into trouble quite often with referees (before the days when bookings became a regular occurrence), and he was not retained for the following season and returned to non-League football. Canvin died in Hemel Hempstead on 3 November 1950, aged just twenty-six.

SEASON	LEAGUE		FA CUP		TOTAL	
	Apps	Gls	Apps	Gls	Apps	Gls
1946/47	3	0	0	0	3	0
TOTAL	3	0	0	0	3	0

Melvyn CAPLETON, 1997-98, 1998-99

The 5ft 11in and 12st goalkeeper Mel Capleton was at the club in 1997, as cover for Paul Heald, but he left after a few months. He returned on 1 August 1998, when both O's 'keepers – Hyde and Mackenzie – had injuries. He played in a Worthington Cup tie at Nottingham Forest in September 1998, and had a blinder, making many splendid saves in a 0-0 draw. Born in Hackney, London on 24 October 1973, he started his career in July 1992 as a youth trainee with Southend United. However, he was released and moved to Blackpool in August 1993, making 9(2) League appearances in two seasons and conceding a total of 29 goals. He joined Cork City in Ireland, and then in October 1995, he spent two seasons with Grays Athletic. During October 1998 he re-joined Southend, before going on loan to Ryman League club Canvey Island. Capleton had an impressive match for the Shrimpers at Brisbane Road in April 1999, saving a Dean Smith penalty to help the visitors to a surprise 3-0 League victory. In a career that has spanned some eight years, Capleton had made just 63(5) League appearances up to 1999/2000 season, but with the arrival of Mark Prudhoe in November 1999 he was dropped and sat on the bench. He played just once as a substitute goalkeeper in the 2000/01 season – at Halifax Town in September 2000 – and he was on the bench a further 11 times. Capleton broke his leg in a reserve match that season, and after a lengthy period of rehabilitation, he eventually went on loan to Grays Athletic on

4 September 2001. At the end of November he cancelled his contract with Southend United and joined Grays on a permanent basis.

SEASON	LEAGUE		FA CUP		L. CUP	
	Apps	Gls	Apps	Gls	Apps	Gls
1997/98	0	0	0	0	0	0
1998/99	0	0	0	0	1	0
TOTAL	0	0	0	0	1	0

TOTAL APPS	1
TOTAL GOALS	0

Peter Richard CAREY, 1956-1960

Peter Carey, an Essex FA representative, came to O's on trial and went on tour with the team to Malta in May 1956. He first signed as an amateur from Barking FC in October 1956, after a trial with Portsmouth. Born in Barking, Essex on 14 April 1933, the tall, fair-haired, and some-what slow-moving defender proved to be a very thoughtful and constructive type of modern midfield player, who also led the front-line on the odd occasion. He made his League debut at Grimsby Town on 8 September 1956. After four seasons with the club, he joined Queens Park Rangers on 20 May 1960, making 17 League appearances and scoring once. During November 1960 he moved to Colchester United, making a further 10 League appearances. August 1961 saw him on the books of Aldershot, where he played a further 48 League matches. After his playing days was over, he managed a number of non-League sides, including Walthamstow Avenue in the early 1970s.

SEASON	LEAGUE		FA CUP		TOTAL	
	Apps	Gls	Apps	Gls	Apps	Gls
1956/57	2	0	0	0	2	0
1957/58	24	2	2	0	26	2
1958/59	5	0	0	0	5	0
1959/60	3	0	0	0	3	0
TOTAL	34	2	2	0	36	2

William Anderson CAREY, 1926-27

Right half Billy Carey was born in Govan, Scotland on 14 August 1898. He was employed by Harland & Wolff, and fig-ured regularly in their works side. He then moved to Killintilloch Rob Roy FC, the Scottish junior club that had pro-duced many fine players that have gone on to make it in a higher level. After two seasons he moved to Glasgow junior side Benburn FC. His next move was to Peebles Rovers, who were a Scottish Third Division side. He was spotted by O's boss Peter Proudfoot, and came south to join O's in July 1926, as a stand-in for Tommy Dixon. He made his League debut at Notts County on 25 September 1926, but after a poor display in a 6-1 defeat at Manchester City on 30 October, was promptly dropped. He proved to be a hard-working and stylish player, but was unable to gain a regular first-team place after that. He returned home to his native Scotland in 1927.

SEASON	LEAGUE		FA CUP		TOTAL	
	Apps	Gls	Apps	Gls	Apps	Gls
1926/27	3	0	0	0	3	0
TOTAL	3	0	0	0	3	0

George Albert CARRINGTON, 1919-20

Born in Poplar, London on 20 June 1888, George Carrington joined O's from local Essex side Ford Sports in 1919. A third-choice goalkeeper – behind Jimmy Hugall and Tommy Gray – he played just once in the League, a 0-1 home defeat by Fulham on 4 September 1919. He left O's in 1920, joining Millwall on trial, but he never featured for the Lions.

SEASON	LEAGUE		FA CUP		TOTAL	
	Apps	Gls	Apps	Gls	Apps	Gls
1919/20	1	0	0	0	1	0
TOTAL	1	0	0	0	1	0

Daniel Stephen CARTER, 1988-95

Danny Carter was born in Hackney, London on 29 June 1969. The wingman started his career with Brighton & Hove Albion as a sixteen-year-old. A couple of years later he left England to play in Sweden with the IS Nornan club, who finished as runners-up in the Swedish Third Division. On his return to the UK, he joined Diadora League side Billericay before he became an 'Oriental' in July 1988. He made his League debut as a substitute against Scunthorpe United, and also played as a substitute in O's first promotion play-off match at Scarborough in May 1989. Carter played regularly and consistently for six seasons, although he suffered a nasty injury at Hull City in March 1992, which kept him on the sidelines for nearly six months. His most successful season was in 1993/94, but like the rest of his team-mates he suffered a loss of form in the relegation battle of 1994/95, although he did play well in the Cup run to the Southern Area semi-final of the Auto Windscreens Shield. Carter was in the process of signing for Peterborough United in June 1995 for £35,000 when new O's boss Pat Holland was appointed. He wanted him to stay, but Carter had already put pen to paper. He made 45 League appearances for Posh which yielded a single goal. He was given a free transfer and joined former 'Oriental' Gary Barnett – manager with Barry Town in Wales – on 1 September 1997, playing 31(3) matches and scoring 5 goals. He was voted their Player of the Year for 1997/98. He joined Merthyr Tydfil on 8 January 1998, and the thirty-year-old made 83(2) senior appearances, scoring

Danny Carter

10 goals up to the end of 2000/01 season. After being released from his contract in August 2001, he stayed at the club to assist with first-team coaching duties.

SEASON	LEAGUE		FA CUP		L. CUP	
	Apps	Gls	Apps	Gls	Apps	Gls
1988/89*	0(2)	0	0	0	0	0
1989/90	29(2)	5	1	0	4	2
1990/91	38(4)	5	5	1	4(1)	0
1991/92	15(5)	2	0	0	3(1)	0
1992/93	26(3)	3	0	0	0	0
1993/94	35(1)	7	2	1	2	0
1994/95	25(4)	0	2	1	0(1)	0
TOTAL	168(21)	22	10	3	13(3)	2

TOTAL APPS	191(24)
TOTAL GOALS	27

* Included in 1988/89 season is a single play-off appearance as a substitute.

** Danny Carter also appeared in 17(1) Auto Windscreens Shield matches, scoring once.

Robert Hector CARTER, 1999-2001

Born in Stepney, London on 23 April 1982, Rob Carter (who attended Langdon School) was a former YTS player who signed as a professional in July 1999. The strong and competitive central midfielder made his League debut as a substitute in the fiftieth minute against Torquay United on 18 September 1999. Carter made his full debut in the second leg Worthington Cup tie (a 1-0 victory) against Grimsby Town four days later. Carter was released in May 2001, but came back on trial having had some impressive displays in pre-season friendlies. However, despite scoring once in a 3-1 win at Crawley Town, he was not retained by boss Taylor.

SEASON	LEAGUE		FA CUP		L. CUP	
	Apps	Gls	Apps	Gls	Apps	Gls
1999/2000	0(2)	0	0	0	1	0
2000/01	0	0	0	0	0	0
TOTAL	0(2)	0	0	0	1	0

TOTAL APPS	1(2)
TOTAL GOALS	0

William John CARTER, 1964-67

Born in Woking on 14 September 1945, Billy Carter was a member of O's youth side before signing professional forms on 1 October 1964. He operated as a wing-half or inside forward, and played for the club at a time when they were in deep financial trouble. Never a regular first-teamer, he did, however, play over 30 senior matches for the side during his two seasons. He left in May 1967, joining Southern League Hillingdon Borough, and playing for them in the 1971 non-League Cup final (later the FA Trophy).

SEASON	LEAGUE		FA CUP		L. CUP	
	Apps	Gls	Apps	Gls	Apps	Gls
1965/66	11(1)	0	1	0	0	0
1966/67	15(2)	3	2(1)	0	1	0
TOTAL	26(3)	3	3(1)	0	1	0

TOTAL APPS	30(4)
TOTAL GOALS	3

David William Royce CASS, 1987-88

David Cass was born in Forest Gate, London on 27 March 1962, A tall, well-built goalkeeper, he came to O's as a part-timer. He was signed as understudy to Peter Wells in March 1987, and had played for Billericay Town before his move to Brisbane Road. He was a carpenter by trade. During April 1988 he did not really expect to get into the side, but when Wells suffered a broken leg, it meant that Cass played the final seven League matches of the 1987/88 season. He looked a bit shaky under pressure, but didn't let the side down with O's

David Cass

winning 4 and losing 3 of those matches. His final match was in front of a 15,781 crowd at Burnley, who had to win to avoid the drop into the Conference. O's lost 2-1, and the second half of the match was broadcast live around the world on BBC World Service. In August 1988 he went for a trial with Colchester United, but soon moved back to Billericay.

SEASON	LEAGUE		FA CUP		L. CUP	
	Apps	Gls	Apps	Gls	Apps	Gls
1986/87	7	0	0	0	0	0
TOTAL	7	0	0	0	0	0

TOTAL APPS	7
TOTAL GOALS	0

Steve Castle

Stephen CASTLE, 1984-92, 1996-97, 2000-02
Steve Castle, a tenacious and tireless midfielder, always gave 100 per cent and was not afraid to go in where the boots were flying. He is one of just a handful to have had three spells with the club, after returning 'home' on 2 July 2000 from Peterborough United. Castle had a tremendous goalscoring record for a midfielder, and it was hoped he would be able to improve on his overall ranking of seventh on O's all-time goalscoring list. He was also ranked eighteenth on the all-time appearances list, but ongoing injuries curtailed his progress through his stay. Born in Barkingside, Essex on 17 May 1966, he joined O's as a schoolboy, being apprenticed on 18 May 1984. His League debut came at full-back against Bradford City in September 1984. He had a memorable match at Rochdale in May 1985, scoring 4 goals, and he played a vital role in O's promotion season of 1988/89. In 1990 it appeared he would be on his way with a move to

Wimbledon, but the deal fell through and he signed a new two-year contract. He was O's top goalscorer in 1990/91. After becoming a free agent in 1992, he refused a new deal and he joined Peter Shilton at Plymouth Argyle on 2 June 1992. O's evaluation was £250,000, but Shilton's offer fell well short. In the end, a tribunal fixed his fee at £195,000. He finished joint top scorer at Home Park with another former 'Oriental', Kevin Nugent, both on 11 goals He netted 35 goals from 98(3) League appearances, before joining Birmingham City on 21 July 1995 for £225,000. After just 16(7) League appearances and a single goal, he went on loan to Gillingham and then to O's on 3 February 1997. After five years away from the club, he scored in his third match back against Rochdale (O's first win from 7 starts) with a rare headed goal. His loan spell was cut short after he needed cartilage surgery. O's boss Taylor wanted to sign Castle, but in the end he joined his former Birmingham boss, Barry Fry, at Peterborough United as player-coach on 14 May 1997 on a free transfer. He continued his scoring ways with Posh, reaching a wonderful career milestone of 100 League goals in 1999. He ended his career with Posh in a promotion play-off final victory at Wembley in May 2000. He declined a new contract after playing 102 matches and netting 17 goals and re-signed for O's, returning back to where he started his career. Unfortunately, he underwent knee surgery during the summer, but the problem was slow to clear and he had further minor surgery in October 2000. It was hoped he would return to the fray in 2001 after the Barkingsider came through a reserve match on 14 February 2001 unscathed. He played in the first half against AFC Bournemouth and came on as a substitute for the final 5 minutes in the 3-2 win at Lincoln City ten days later, but he struggled with fitness and made just a handful of appearances in the season. Castle was hoping to have made it third time lucky in the play-offs – having previously been promoted with O's and Peterborough United – but it was not meant to be, with O's losing 4-2 to Blackpool in the play-off final at the Millennium Stadium in Wales. Castle was awarded a testimonial match against Tottenham Hotspur on 17 July 2001, which attracted a sizeable Brisbane Road crowd of 6,636. The match ended in a 2-0 victory for the visitors, and Castle left the field to a standing ovation. He stated: 'I'm obviously very pleased with the turnout tonight. I'd like to thank the fans for their support.' Thirty-five-year-old Castle could not find a regular spot in the team, and on 25 September he went on

loan to Nationwide Conference side Stevenage Borough. He stayed for just over two months, playing 5(1) matches before returning to Brisbane Road during mid-November. After a long fight to regain his fitness, Castle decided to retire from playing in February 2002 and helped out with youth-team coaching duties at West Ham. He made a career total of 458(37) League appearances and scored a remarkable 110 goals from his midfield position during his eighteen-year career. He will be remembered fondly by all O's supporters.

SEASON	LEAGUE		FA CUP		L. CUP	
	Apps	Gls	Apps	Gls	Apps	Gls
1984/85	20(1)	1	3	0	0	0
1985/86	19(4)	4	1(1)	1	1	0
1986/87	22(2)	5	4	1	0(1)	0
1987/88	42	10	4	0	2	0
1988/89*	26(2)	6	0	0	0	0
1989/90	27	7	1	0	4	2
1990/91	45	12	5	3	6	3
1991/92	35(2)	10	5	1	2	0
1996/97	4	1	0	0	0	0
2000/01**	4(8)	0	0(1)	0	0	0
2001/02	0(1)	0	0	0	0(1)	0
TOTAL	244(20)	56	23(2)	6	15(2)	5

TOTAL APPS	282(24)
TOTAL GOALS	67

* Includes 4 promotion play-off matches in 1988/89.

** Includes 2(1) promotion play-off matches in 2000/01.

*** Steve Castle also appeared in 14(2) Auto Windscreens Shield matches.

Ronald CATER, 1951-52
Born in Fulham, London on 2 February 1922, Cater joined West Ham United's groundstaff as a fifteen-year-old in 1937.

Although born in West London, he turned out for the East Ham Boys side. He turned professional in 1944, after a short spell with Leytonstone. During the Second World War, he enlisted with the Royal Artillery, and in April 1939 he joined the Essex Regiment. He made 70 senior appearances for the Hammers, and then took the same short journey to the O's that so many players have taken over the years, on a free transfer. A player with a conspicuous crew-cut hairstyle, he was mostly a reserve with O's. However, he was a most useful player to have in that he could play in many positions and never let the team down. He was always a great trier and strong tackler.

SEASON	LEAGUE		FA CUP		TOTAL	
	Apps	Gls	Apps	Gls	Apps	Gls
1951/52	13	0	1	0	14	0
TOTAL	13	0	1	0	14	0

Sidney William CAVENDISH, 1904-05

Sid Cavendish was born in Overseal, Staffordshire in October 1876. He joined O's in July 1904, and ended as top scorer in O's only season in the Southern League Second Division campaign in 1904/05, scoring 26 Southern and London League goals. He never figured in O's first League campaign in 1905/06, appearing in one FA Cup tie against Felstead in 7 October 1905. He left O's in June 1906 for Salisbury City, and stayed with that club as trainer up until the late 1920s. Cavendish started his career with Overseal FC, but made his name whilst with Southern Leaguers Southampton, becoming their reserve-team top scorer in 1898/99 with 22 goals. He also hit 2 goals from 8 Southern League appearances. In 1902 he joined Freemantle FC in the Hampshire League. Cavendish died in Salisbury July 1954, aged seventy-seven.

SEASON	LEAGUE		FA CUP		TOTAL	
	Apps	Gls	Apps	Gls	Apps	Gls
1904/05*	-	-	3	0	3	0
1905/06	0	0	1	0	1	0
TOTAL	0	0	4	0	4	0

* Clapton Orient only entered the League in 1905/06.

Justin Andrew CHANNING, 1996-98

Born in Reading on 19 November 1968, Justin Channing joined O's from Bristol Rovers on a free transfer on 8 July 1996. Channing, a 5ft 11in defender, started his career as an apprentice with Queens Park Rangers on 27 August 1986, winning England youth caps during his time there. He made 42(13) League appearances that yielded 5 goals, and then a £250,000 transfer took him to Bristol Rovers on 7 January 1993, where he made 121(9) League appearances and scored 10 goals before his move to Brisbane Road. He stayed with O's for two seasons, before being released by boss Tommy Taylor in May 1998, and went on to join Ryman Premier League side Purfleet before later playing for Slough Town. In November 1999 he signed for Ryman League First Division side Harlow Town with former 'Oriental' Tony Kelly.

SEASON	LEAGUE		FA CUP		L. CUP	
	Apps	Gls	Apps	Gls	Apps	Gls
1996/97	40	5	2	1	1	0
1997/98	29(5)	0	2	0	2(1)	0
TOTAL	69(5)	5	4	1	3(1)	0

TOTAL APPS	76(6)
TOTAL GOALS	6

* Justin Channing also appeared in 3 Auto Windscreens Shield matches.

Daniel Graham CHAPMAN, 1995-97

This strong defender/midfielder was born in Greenwich, London on 21 November 1974. Danny Chapman started his career with Millwall as a trainee, making 4(8) League appearances for the Lions between March 1993 and July 1995. He was snapped up on a free transfer by the O's on 1 July 1996, and spent 2 successful seasons at Brisbane Road, but was released by new boss Taylor in July 1977 because he refused to sign a new contract. Chapman launched a stinging attack on the club stating. ' I thought I had done well for the club, but according to the new boss (Taylor) I have to go, so I'll live with it.' Taylor, in response, said: 'I had no choice but to let him go, it is all I could do.' Chapman then joined Peterborough United for a short period, before he decided to move on and join former 'Oriental' Kevin Hales at Football Conference side Welling United, playing 31(1) times in 1997/98. The following season he played for Hastings United, but twenty-four-year-old Chapman was back at Welling in May 1999, and then the following season moved to Dover Athletic. In August 2001 he was at Dr Martens Premier League side Folkestone Invicta.

SEASON	LEAGUE		FA CUP		L. CUP	
	Apps	Gls	Apps	Gls	Apps	Gls
1995/96	38	2	1	0	2	0
1996/97	31(9)	2	1(1)	0	0(1)	0
TOTAL	69(9)	4	2(1)	0	2(1)	0

TOTAL APPS	73(11)
TOTAL GOALS	4

* Danny Chapman also appeared in 3 Auto Windscreens Shield matches.

John CHAPMAN, 1919-20

Born in Islington, London in 1895, John Chapman came to O's from Southall FC in October 1919 on amateur forms, having previously been on Brentford's and Arsenal's books. He also guested for O's during the First World War. He impressed O's manager Billy Holmes – playing at centre forward – and scored on his League debut against Port Vale on 15 November 1919, a 2-1 victory. After a short run in the side, he was confined to the reserves and left the club in August 1921, joining the Middlesex-based club Excelsior.

SEASON	LEAGUE		FA CUP		TOTAL	
	Apps	Gls	Apps	Gls	Apps	Gls
1919/20	9	2	0	0	9	2
TOTAL	9	2	0	0	9	2

Vernon William CHAPMAN, 1947-49

Born in Leicester on 9 May 1921, he played for a number of non-League clubs (including Aylestone United, Leicester Nomads, Ibstone Penistone Rovers and Bath City) before joining Leicester City in March 1941. He was a very quick right-winger, who played 11 wartime games and scored 6 goals. He set one City record by scoring 10 goals for their reserves in a 17-0 victory against Holwell Works in September 1941. However, he made just a single League appearance for City before a £550 move to O's in July 1947, where he linked up well with big centre forward Frank Neary. Chapman scored some grand goals, and none were better than the twenty-five-yarder at Torquay United that won the match. He left O's in 1949 to join Brush Sports FC, and in 1951 he was at Burton Albion until his appointment as manager of Midland club Tamworth.

SEASON	LEAGUE		FA CUP		TOTAL	
	Apps	Gls	Apps	Gls	Apps	Gls
1947/48	28	6	0	0	28	6
1948/49	3	1	0	0	3	1
TOTAL	31	7	0	0	31	7

Stanley CHARLTON, 1952-56, 1958-65

Stan Charlton was one of the most popular players to wear an O's shirt since the Second World War. He was a fine left-back with a unique sliding tackle, as well as the only O's captain to lead his men into the First Division. Born in Exeter, Devon on 28 June 1929, he started out with Spartan Boys before establishing himself with Athenian League side Bromley (with whom he won 3 England amateur caps) and he was a member of the Great Britain squad for the Helsinki Olympic Games in 1952. Charlton, who stood 5ft 10in and weighed 12st – joined O's as an amateur in July 1952, and he was ever-present throughout his first season.

Stan Charlton, one of O's greatest captains

Stan Charlton

During October 1955 he and Vic Groves moved to Arsenal for a joint fee of £30,000. He stayed three seasons at Highbury, playing 99 First Division games before returning to Brisbane Road during December 1958. The highlight of his career was being chaired off the pitch after the match against Bury that clinched O's promotion to the First Division in April 1962. He left in 1965 to take over as manager of Weymouth. A benefit match was staged for his service to the club in April 1970. Charlton was recently honoured by the club with a celebration in May 2000 for his seventieth birthday. Also in attendance was Malcolm Graham, the man whose goals took O's to promotion to the First Division One all those years ago. After retiring from the game, he was a district manager for a major pools company, and nowadays lives in Weymouth, Dorset.

SEASON	LEAGUE		FA CUP		L. CUP	
	Apps	Gls	Apps	Gls	Apps	Gls
1952/53	46	0	2	0	-	-
1953/54	43	0	7	0	-	-
1954/55	46	1	2	0	-	-
1955/56	16	0	0	0	-	-
1958/59	17	0	1	0	-	-
1959/60	29	0	1	0	-	-
1960/61*	31	0	3	0	3	0
1961/62	41	0	4	0	3	0
1962/63	42	0	4	0	5	0
1963/64	42	1	3	0	1	0
1964/65	14	0	1	0	1	0
TOTAL	367	2	28	0	13	0

TOTAL APPS	408
TOTAL GOALS	2

* First year of the League Cup competition.

John Okay CHIEDOZIE, 1976-81

Born in Owerri, Nigeria on 18 April 1960, his family relocated to England to avoid the Nigerian civil war when he was just thirteen years old. He was one of many youngsters developed by O's boss George Petchey, who was never afraid to plunge the 'boys' into first-team action. 'Chidders', as he was affectionately known, was thrown into a Second Division match against Millwall on 8 March 1977, just before his a seventeenth birthday, after another youngster (Laurie Cunningham) was sold to West Bromwich Albion. 'Chidders' had made a rapid rise through schoolboy football and was offered a trial with West Ham United, but he left and signed for the O's on apprentice forms in July 1976. He showed plenty of pace and soon established himself as a first-team regular in the 1977/78 season. At the start of O's great FA Cup run, he laid on the pass for Peter Kitchen to score at Norwich City, but the next day he broke his leg when coming on as a substitute at Ipswich Town in a Southern Floodlit youth cup match. That put paid to his season and allowed another young winger, Kevin Godfrey, to get his chance of stardom. Upon his return after that injury, he continued to excel on the wing, and it was no surprise that newly-elected First Division outfit Notts County came in with a £600,000 record bid that was too good to refuse, although it was reported that O's boss Jimmy Bloomfield was against the deal. John Chiedozie won 7 Nigerian caps – alongside another 'Oriental' Tunji Banjo – during his stay at Brisbane Road, the first being in 1981 against Tunisia. 'Chidders' performed extrememly well in the top grade, making 110(1) appearances and weighing in with 16 goals. During August 1984 he joined Tottenham Hotspur for £350,000, but suffered with injuries at White Hart Lane, making only 45(8) League appear-

John Chiedozie

C

ances and bagging 12 goals. However, he did win 2 further Nigerian caps – against Liberia in October 1984 and against Tunisia during July 1995. He was given a free transfer and played out his career with Derby County, Notts County and Chesterfield, before having to retire through another injury in 1990. During a career that spanned some thirteen years, he made a total of 293(18) League appearances and scored 48 goals. Nowadays, 'Chidders' is living near the New Forest area and running a company that hires out bouncy castles for parties.

SEASON	LEAGUE		FA CUP		L. CUP	
	Apps	Gls	Apps	Gls	Apps	Gls
1976/77	6(9)	0	0	0	0	0
1977/78	21	2	2	0	3	0
1978/79	33(3)	6	3	1	1	0
1979/80	35(2)	3	1	1	2	1
1980/81	36	9	1	0	2	0
TOTAL	131(14)	20	7	2	8	1

TOTAL APPS	146(14)
TOTAL GOALS	23

* John Chiedozie also appeared in 7 Anglo-Scottish Cup matches (scoring once) and 2 Football League Groups Cup matches (scoring once).

Frank CHISEM, 1932-33

Born in Darlington on 4 October 1907, right-back Frank Chisem joined O's in August 1932 from Tunbridge Wells Rangers, along with goalie Jack Bruce. His only League outing came in the 3-3 draw at Swindon Town on 9 September 1932. He stayed a number of seasons at Lea Bridge Road playing in the reserves, until leaving in December 1935 and joining Shildon Railway Athletic. He died in Newcastle-upon-Tyne during February 1978.

SEASON	LEAGUE		FA CUP		TOTAL	
	Apps	Gls	Apps	Gls	Apps	Gls
1932/33	1	0	0	0	1	0
TOTAL	1	0	0	0	1	0

Iyesden CHRISTIE, 1999-present

Iyesden Christie was born in Coventry on 14 November 1976. He joined O's in June 1999 from Mansfield Town, with a tribunal fixing his fee at a bargain £40,000. (O's offered £20,000 but the Stags wanted over £100,000.) Christie was a product of Coventry City's youth scheme, joining in 1973 and turning professional on 22 May 1995. He was reported to be quite an outstanding youth player, who was never given a chance in the first team. He made just 2 substitute appearances – in a League match on 23 September 1995 at Blackburn Rovers , when he came on for Dion Dublin, and on 4 October 1995, when he came on at Hull City in the League Cup. He went on loan to AFC Bournemouth in November 1996, and to Mansfield Town during February 1997. 'Izzy', as he was nicknamed by the Stags' fans, joined Mansfield from Coventry for £15,000 (plus half of any future transfer fee) in May 1997. Pace was his biggest asset – he can be devastating and has the talent to turn a game. He became a real crowd favourite, scoring 12 goals before Christmas 1997, including a brilliant hat-trick against Stockport County in the League Cup. His finest goal for the Stags' came in September 1998 against Hull City, when he picked the ball up just past the halfway line and tore into the City defence to unleash an unstoppable shot into the corner of the net. His record with them was 57(40) appearances and 23 goals. Unfortunately, he got injured at the start of the 1999/2000 season, which restricted his progress, yet he still finished as the top League scorer. The following season after a bright start, he sustained a very bad knee injury after a challenge on Newcastle United goalie Shay Given during a Worthington Cup tie during September 2000, and was out of action for the remainder of the season. After fourteen months on the sidelines, he made his welcome return when playing the final twenty minutes in an Avon Insurance Combination fixture at Brisbane Road on 30 October 2001 against Brentford. He scored O's fourth goal at Portsmouth in the dying seconds of O's wonderful FA Cup win in January 2002.

Jamie Clapham

SEASON	LEAGUE		FA CUP		L. CUP	
	Apps	Gls	Apps	Gls	Apps	Gls
1999/2000	22(14)	7	2	0	1(1)	0
2000/01	1(6)	2	0	0	2(1)	1
2001/02	9(6)	3	0(1)	1	0	0
TOTAL	32(26)	12	1(2)	1	4(1)	1

TOTAL APPS	37(29)
TOTAL GOALS	14

* Iyesden Christie also appeared in an Auto Windscreens Shield match in 1999/2000.

James Richard CLAPHAM, 1997 (loan)
Jamie Clapham came on loan from Tottenham Hotspur on 29 January 1997. This attacking left-sided midfield player was born in Lincoln on 7 December 1975. He joined Spurs as a trainee in 1992, turning professional in July 1994. He joined O's on 28 January 1997, making his debut on 1 February 1997 against Exeter City, but was recalled by Spurs in March 1997 after 6 appearances for the O's. He made just one substitute appearance for Spurs against Coventry in May 1997. After another loan spell at Bristol Rovers in March 1997, he went for a trial at Ipswich Town during January 1998. Their manager George Burley was so impressed that he splashed out £300,000 for him on 13 March 1998. He appeared in their return to the Premiership in August 2000 (a 3-1 defeat at Tottenham Hotspur) and has made a total of 140(17) League appearances at Portman Road and scored 6 goals up until mid-February 2002.

SEASON	LEAGUE		FA CUP		L. CUP	
	Apps	Gls	Apps	Gls	Apps	Gls
1996/97	6	0	0	0	0	0
TOTAL	6	0	0	0	0	0

TOTAL APPS	6
TOTAL GOALS	0

David George CLARK, 1961-65
Dave Clark, was born in Ilford, Essex on 19 January 1938. He joined O's from their near neighbours, Leyton Amateurs, in

David Clark

December 1961. He looked to be a good player, making his League debut at left-back when he came on in place of Eddie Lewis at Brighton in a 1-0 win on 7 April 1962. He also appeared in 3 matches in the First Division. A twice-broken leg ended his playing career and he was appointed trainer in 1965, but lost his job during a financial crisis a year later.

SEASON	LEAGUE		FA CUP		L. CUP	
	Apps	Gls	Apps	Gls	Apps	Gls
1961/62	1	0	0	0	0	0
1962/63	3	0	0	0	2	0
TOTAL	4	0	0	0	2	0

TOTAL APPS	6
TOTAL GOALS	0

Joseph Thomas Henry CLARK, 1946-47

Born in Bermondsey, London on 2 March 1920, Joe Clark, a rugged full-back, joined O's from Gravesend & Northfleet in February 1946 and made a dozen Second World War regional appearances. He played almost half the 1946/47 season, the first season back after the war, but he was released in May 1947.

SEASON	LEAGUE		FA CUP		TOTAL	
	Apps	Gls	Apps	Gls	Apps	Gls
1946/47	18	0	1	0	19	0
TOTAL	18	0	1	0	19	0

Simon CLARK, 1997-2000

Born on 12 March 1967 in Boston, Lincolnshire, Simon Clark started his career at Kings Lynn, went on to play for Yeading FC and later moved to Stevenage Borough. He moved to Hendon, making 120 appearances between February 1991 and 1994, before joining Peterborough United on a free transfer on 25 March 1994. The big strong central defender came from Posh on May 31 1997 for £20,000, after having made 119(3) appearances and scored 3 goals. He proved to be an excellent capture and became renowned for being a strong tackler and good in the air – attributes which spell danger to opposing defenders at set pieces. Clark scored a hat-trick of headers at Doncaster Rovers on 2 September 1997 (some reports credited one of the goals to Hicks, but it was later confirmed that Clark scored all 3). His tough-tackling approach sometimes proved his undoing, and he obtained a large number of bookings whilst with O's. He headed O's sixth goal on fifty-two minutes in a 6-1 win over Shrewsbury in April 1999. He formed part of the 'three Amigos' defence partnership with both Hicks and Smith, and was voted Player of the Year for the 1998/99 season. Clark missed most of the latter part of the

1999/2000 season through injury, and the thirty-three-year-old defender was given a free transfer. He joined Division Two side Colchester United in June 2000, and made his debut for the U's at Swindon Town during August 2000. He made 37(2) senior appearances during the season, proving himself an important part in the U's back four. Clarke left Colchester by mutual consent in January 2002 – after 52(3) League appearances – because his wife wanted to return home to Singapore. He joined Woodlands Wellington FC of Singapore's S-League.

SEASON	LEAGUE		FA CUP		L. CUP	
	Apps	Gls	Apps	Gls	Apps	Gls
1997/98	39	5	2	0	3	0
1998/99*	43	4	5	0	2	0
1999/2000	19	1	1	0	2	0
TOTAL	101	10	8	0	7	0

TOTAL APPS	116
TOTAL GOALS	10

Simon Clark

* Simon Clark's League total includes 3 promotion play-off matches in 1998/99.
** Clark also appeared in 2 Auto Windscreens Shield matches.

William CLARK, 1924-25

Born in Beith, Ayrshire on 16 September 1900, the left-winger joined O's in July 1924 from Beith FC. He made his debut in the 1-1 draw at Barnsley on 4 April 1925. After just a handful of matches, he returned to his former club in May 1925.

SEASON	LEAGUE		FA CUP		TOTAL	
	Apps	Gls	Apps	Gls	Apps	Gls
1924/25	4	0	0	0	4	0
TOTAL	4	0	0	0	4	0

Derek CLARKE, 1976-79

Derek Clarke was a member of a remarkable footballing family with five brothers – Frank, Wayne, Kelvin, and the most famous of the brothers, Allan, of Leeds and England fame – all professional footballers with 589 League goals from 1555(85) matches between them, from the 1960s right up to the early 1990s. Born in Willenhall, Staffordshire on 19 February 1950, Derek Clarke started with Walsall, where he played 6 games (scoring twice), before a £20,000 transfer took him to Wolverhampton Wanderers. After two years and only 2(2) League appearances, he joined Oxford United for £11,000, and from 172(7) League appearances, he netted 35 goals. Clarke joined O's in 1976 for £10,000, making his debut when he came on as a substitute at Bolton in August 1976. He was a member of the side that reached the semi-final of the Anglo-Scottish Cup, but a serious leg ligament injury against Fulham in December 1976 kept him out for the remainder of the season, therefore miss-

C

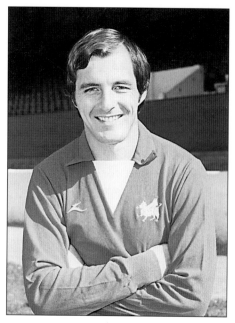

Derek Clarke

SEASON	LEAGUE		FA CUP		L. CUP	
	Apps	Gls	Apps	Gls	Apps	Gls
1976/77	14(1)	2	0	0	0	0
1977/78	12(3)	4	1	0	0	0
1978/79	4(2)	0	0	0	0	0
TOTAL	30(6)	6	1	0	0	0

TOTAL APPS	31(6)
TOTAL GOALS	6

* Derek Clarke also appeared in 4 Anglo-Scottish Cup matches, scoring once.

John CLEGG, 1913-14

Born in Sheffield on 1 January 1890, goalkeeper John Clegg first joined Bristol City as a seventeen-year-old in July 1908, making his League debut against Sheffield United on 5 April 1909. After making 126 League appearances, he moved on to Barnsley in December 1910, making a further 33 appearances. After a brief spell with the Wednesday (who later on became Sheffield Wednesday), he became an 'Oriental' during December 1913, making his O's debut in the 1-0 win over Woolwich Arsenal on 13 December. Clegg proved a capable last line of defence, but found it difficult to displace O's two fine custodians, Bower and Hugall. He left the club in 1914 to join Bradford Park Avenue.

SEASON	LEAGUE		FA CUP		TOTAL	
	Apps	Gls	Apps	Gls	Apps	Gls
1913/14	8	0	1	0	9	0
TOTAL	8	0	1	0	9	0

Ralph COATES, 1978-81

Born in Hetton-le-Hole on 26 April 1946, he started his career as an apprentice with Burnley in October 1961, after working as a colliery fitter

ing the two-legged final against Nottingham Forest. Only his immense personal determination saw him overcome an injury that threatened to end his career prematurely. He returned the following September (1977), scoring in the exciting 5-3 win over Oldham Athletic, when Peter Angell was in charge as acting manager after George Petchey had been fired as week or so before. Clarke obtained a surprise recall, ahead of Kevin Godfrey, in the FA Cup semi-final against Arsenal in April 1978, but Clarke could never recapture his early form after his long-term injury. He went on loan to Carlisle United in October 1978, making just a single substitute appearance. He was eventually released in May 1979 and joined Crewe Alexandra. After his retirement, Clarke ran his own builders merchants company in London for five years, before returning to the Midlands to work as a machine operator.

94

and playing for Eppleton Colliery Welfare. He was one of a number of young talented players to come through the Turf Moor youth ranks. The stocky little winger had seven wonderful years with the Clarets, making 214 League appearances and scoring 26 goals. He also won 2 full England caps. Coates moved to Tottenham Hotspur for £190,000 in May 1971, and he netted the goal that won the League Cup final in 1972, as well as winning 2 further England caps. He also appeared in the 1972 and 1974 EUFA Cup finals, gaining a winners' medal in the former. After making 173(15) senior appearances and scoring 14 goals at White Hart Lane, he was signed on a free transfer by O's boss Jimmy Bloomfield during October 1978, along with Ian Moores, after Coates came back from a loan spell with the St George's club in Australia. He had two splendid seasons at Brisbane Road, and although aged thirty-two, he was a key

figure over that period, always giving 100 per cent in his new midfield role, even when playing in the reserves as player-coach. Coates excelled when running with the ball and scored some grand goals, including a couple against his former club Burnley in August 1979. He retired from professional football in 1982 and moved into the non-League circuit with Hertford Heath, Ware FC and finally Nazeing FC. Upon retirement he managed two leisure centres – the Marconi Sports Club in Potters Bar and the Elliott Sports & Social Club in Borehamwood. He also trained as a sports psychology counsellor. Ralph Coates was a credit to the game, not only for his total commitment, but also for his impeccable fair play.

SEASON	LEAGUE		FA CUP		L. CUP	
	Apps	Gls	Apps	Gls	Apps	Gls
1978/79	30	3	2	0	0	0
1979/80	42	9	3	0	2	0
1980/81	4	0	0	0	1	0
TOTAL	76	12	5	0	3	0

TOTAL APPS	84
TOTAL GOALS	12

* Ralph Coates also appeared in 3 Anglo-Scottish Cup matches.

Paul Mark COBB, 1990-92

A natural nippy striker, who was born in Tilbury, Essex on 13 December 1972, Cobb started his career as a sixteen-year-old with Purfleet. It was O's youth-team coach John Gorman who brought him to Brisbane Road during November 1990. He was given his first-team chance as a substitute at home against Southend United in April 1991, but played just a handful of first-team

Ralph Coates

games. The striker, diminutive at just 5ft 6in, then moved into non-League football enjoying spells with Enfield and with his first club Purfleet, until in July 1997, a £14,000 fee took him to Dagenham & Redbridge. During recent times, Cobb has proved to be a prolific non-League scorer, netting 35 goals in 1996/97 for Purfleet in the ICIS League, and a club record 84 senior goals during his three-year stay with Dagenham & Redbridge (a record equalled by Danny Shipp in September 2001). Cobb moved to Canvey Island on 9 August 2001 for £4,000.

SEASON	LEAGUE		FA CUP		L. CUP	
	Apps	Gls	Apps	Gls	Apps	Gls
1990/91	2(2)	0	0	0	0	0
1991/92	1	0	0	0	0	0
TOTAL	3(2)	0	0	0	0	0

TOTAL APPS	3(2)
TOTAL GOALS	0

Paul Cobb

Albert George COCHRAN, 1960-63

Albert Cochran was a very agile goalkeeper, and it would be true to say that only lack of height prevented him from going further in the game. Born in Ebbw Vale, Wales on 26 November 1939, he started as a junior with Plymouth Argyle and joined O's in July 1960. He made just a single League appearance in the 2-0 defeat at Lincoln City in the final match of the 1960/61 season and departed to Folkestone in May 1963, where he enjoyed a long and successful stay.

SEASON	LEAGUE		FA CUP		L. CUP	
	Apps	Gls	Apps	Gls	Apps	Gls
1960/61	1	0	0	0	0	0
1961/62	0	0	0	0	0	0
1962/63	0	0	0	0	0	0
TOTAL	1	0	0	0	0	0

TOTAL APPS	1
TOTAL GOALS	0

Donald James COCK, 1925-27

Donald Cock had a distinguished career before joining O's from Arsenal in October 1925 for a fee of £1,500. Born in Hayle, Cornwell on 8 July 1896, Donald was the brother of Jack Cock – of Huddersfield, Chelsea and England fame. He commenced his football career during the First World War by guesting for Brentford. He then joined Fulham in June 1919, and was their leading scorer for the 1919/20 season, scoring 25 goals in the Second Division. In total, he netted 43 goals from 86 League appearances for the Craven Cottage club. During October 1922, he was transferred to Notts County for £1,750 and helped them win a Second Division title. He was their leading

Donald Cock

SEASON	LEAGUE		FA CUP		TOTAL	
	Apps	Gls	Apps	Gls	Apps	Gls
1925/26	31	13	4	3	35	16
1926/27	33	15	2	0	35	15
TOTAL	64	28	6	3	70	31

scorer both in 1922/23 (with 13 goals) and 1923/24 (with 11 goals). He joined Arsenal on 5 March 1925 for a then club record fee of £4,000, but he managed only 3 League appearances before becoming an 'Oriental'. Cock was one of O's best forwards during the 1920s, and he starred in the great FA Cup victory over Newcastle United in February 1926, scoring O's second goal on forty-five minutes. A strong attacker, he scored a splendid hat-trick against Stoke City in March 1926, and O's boss Peter Proudfoot told reporters that he (Cock) was one of the best signings he had ever made for the club. Cock joined Wolverhampton Wanderers in July 1927 for over £2,000. but after just 3 appearances and a single goal, he moved on to Newport County just three months later. Donald Cock died in Bradmore, near Wolverhampton on 31 August 1974.

Glenn COCKERILL, 1993-96

Glenn Cockerill joined O's in December 1993 from Southampton, after a very long and distinguished career, and stayed for three years. This popular and very talented midfielder was born in Grimsby on 25 August 1959. He started his career with non-League Louth United. He joined O's from Southampton in 1993 – the Saints had paid £225,000 to acquire him from Sheffield United. He stayed at Brisbane Road for three seasons. He even became joint caretaker-manager (after the Sitton/Turner duo were sacked) for the fixture at Bristol Rovers on 22 April 1995, along with youth coach Tom Loizou. Cockerill ruled himself out of the gaffer's job on a full-time basis when he said 'I enjoyed the manager's role at Bristol, but I enjoy playing more. Even though I'm thirty-six years old, I can carry on playing for a few more years'. Cockerill would have certainly been a popular choice of manager with the fans. He enjoyed one more season at the club, but in May 1996 he was amongst a group of eight players to be released by new O's boss Pat Holland. The departure of Cockerill came as big disappointment to the fans. Holland stated: 'The decision to release Cockerill was taken by the board, even after he had offered to take a drop in salary to stay with the club. He has carried our midfield for the past two seasons. He's got so much experience and he could have given us another year'. A shocked Cockerill said: 'I would have loved to stay at Orient another year because things could have come right at the club'. He joined Fulham on 5 July 1996 and, despite his age, he did extremely well at Craven Cottage, when Fulham clinched the runners-up spot in Division Three in 1996/97. He was awarded a testimonial for his achievements in football, having made a total of 771(49) senior appearances and scored 95 goals in a twenty-year career, and then followed Mickey Adams to Brentford as assistant player-manager on 6 November 1997. Cockerill became assistant manager with Bashley FC in July 1998. In 2000 he was on the coaching staff at Crystal Palace (alongside Ray Houghton) under Palace boss Alan Smith, but was sacked as their assistant manager on 18 March 2001. Cockerill was appointed as temporary coach to Woking on 24 January 2002 and became their head coach two months later.

Glenn Cockerill

SEASON	LEAGUE		FA CUP		L. CUP	
	Apps	Gls	Apps	Gls	Apps	Gls
1993/94	19	2	0	0	0	0
1994/95	32(1)	4	2	0	2	1
1995/96	38	1	1	0	2	0
TOTAL	89(1)	7	3	0	4	1

TOTAL APPS	96(1)
TOTAL GOALS	8

* Glenn Cockerill also appeared in 10 Auto Windscreens Shield matches.

Ernest Samuel COCKLE, 1920-21

Born on 12 September 1896 in West Ham, London, Ernie Cockle, a centre forward, came to O's from the East London works side Green & Siley Weir in August 1920. He did well for a time, but was not quite the answer to O's centre forward problems (6 different players being chosen in that position during the 1920/21 season). He scored the winner on his debut in a 2-1 win over Nottingham Forest on 2 October 1920. Cockle moved to non-League Margate FC in June 1921, and later played for Northampton Town. He died in Thornton Heath, Surrey on 11 June 1966.

SEASON	LEAGUE		FA CUP		TOTAL	
	Apps	Gls	Apps	Gls	Apps	Gls
1920/21	20	4	2	0	22	4
TOTAL	20	4	2	0	22	4

Allan CODLING, 1936-38

Born in Guisborough on 24 February 1911, Allan Codling showed good form on the left wing for Folkestone, the O's liked the look of him and brought him to Lea Bridge Road in May 1936. He played in half of the 1936/37 season, and was in the team for O's first League fixture at Brisbane Road against Cardiff City on

28 August 1937. Codling gradually fell out of favour to the more experienced Les Dodds, and in August 1938 he was transferred to Darlington, where he made just 7 League appearances. He was a good winger who had a fair spell as an 'Oriental'. He died on 24 February 1991 – his eightieth birthday – in Saltburn.

SEASON	LEAGUE		FA CUP		TOTAL	
	Apps	Gls	Apps	Gls	Apps	Gls
1936/37	21	2	0	0	21	2
1937/38*	11	1	0	0	11	1
TOTAL	32	3	0	0	32	3

* Allan Codling also appeared in a Third Division Cup match in 1937/38.

Roland John CODLING, 1905-06

Ralph Codling, as he was known, was an attacking left half. He was a stern tackler who had a good shot, one of the more experienced players who signed up for O's first League campaign in 1905/06 from Stockport County, for whom he had made 28 League appearances. Born in Durham in October 1879, he started out with Stockton before commencing his career with Southern League side Swindon Town in 1901/02, making 12 appearances before joining Stockport in 1903. He appeared in O's first League match at Leicester Fosse during September 1905. He was an ever-present in the side until being sold to Aston Villa for a substantial fee in March 1906, in order to ease the club's financial crisis. He made 82 senior appearances for Villa. and was a first-team player for two seasons until joining Northampton Town in 1909, where he made 3 appearances. After a spell with Southern League side Croydon Common (making 29 appearances) he joined Manchester City in August 1910, where he played a further

5 League matches. Codling died in 1940, aged sixty-two.

SEASON	LEAGUE		FA CUP		TOTAL	
	Apps	Gls	Apps	Gls	Apps	Gls
1905/06	28	1	6	0	34	1
TOTAL	28	1	6	0	34	1

Lee COLKIN, 1997 (loan)

Born in Nuneaton on 15 July 1974, Colkin started his career as a trainee with Northampton Town in July 1990. This quick left-sided defender joined O's on loan from the Cobblers on 29 August 1997, where he had been voted their Young Player of the Year in 1996. He stayed with O's for a couple of months and made some solid displays. He made his full debut against Cambridge United on 5 September 1997, after a couple of appearances as a playing substitute. He returned to Northampton on 2 November 1997 and made 74(25) League appearances (as well as scoring 3 goals), and also appeared for the Cobblers in a Division Three play-off final against Swansea City. He signed for non-Leaguers Hednesford Town in March 1998, and made 53(2) appearances and scored once before joining Nationwide Conference side Morecambe on 17 May 2001 on a free transfer.

SEASON	LEAGUE		FA CUP		L. CUP	
	Apps	Gls	Apps	Gls	Apps	Gls
1997/98	5(6)	0	0	0	0(1)	0
TOTAL	5(6)	0	0	0	0(1)	0

TOTAL APPS	5(7)
TOTAL GOALS	0

William Charles Elvet COLLINS, 1927-29

Elvet Collins was born in Rymney, Wales on 16 October 1902, and played for his local team, Rymney FC, in the Welsh League in 1922/23. He moved to Cardiff City in 1924, and during his four-year stay he made just 13 League appearances. He played for Wales in what was described as a junior international – he was twenty-four at the time. Despite not being a very tall player (standing just 5ft 8in tall), he was, however, a very tricky outside right. He joined O's in May 1929, making his debut on the opening day of 1927/28 and was a regular in that campaign. He played in both FA Cup ties against Aston Villa during January 1929 – the first tie at Villa Park attracted 53,086 fans (the biggest ever crowd to witness an O's match), but the match ended goalless. The replay was a different matter, O's losing by a record 0-8, in front of a 27,532 midweek crowd at Millfields Road. Collins left the club in August 1929 joining Lovells Athletic. In 1930 he played for Llanelli FC and won a Welsh cap against Scotland. In 1932 he moved to Newport County and in 1936 he retired from football and went to work for a local coliery. He died in Blackwood, Monmouthshire, Wales on 23 January 1977.

Alan Comfort

SEASON	LEAGUE		FA CUP		TOTAL	
	Apps	Gls	Apps	Gls	Apps	Gls
1927/28	35	1	1	0	36	1
1928/29	4	0	2	0	6	0
TOTAL	39	1	3	0	42	1

Alan COMFORT, 1986-89

Alan Comfort joined O's in March 1986 for a small fee from Cambridge United, after making 61(3) appearances and netting 5 goals – it was good to see a decent old-fashioned winger back at the club. Comfort was born in Aldershot on 8 December 1964. He started his career as an apprentice with QPR in October 1982, but finding his opportunities limited, he joined Cambridge in October 1984, scoring on his League debut against the O's. Comfort missed very few matches and can be compared with another former great O's wingman Owen Williams – both players with their exciting wing play would create a buzz around the ground with exhilarating left-wing dribbles. After O's great victory over Wrexham in the promotion play-off final at Brisbane Road in June 1989, he was rushed off to Ireland to be married! He scored 18 goals that season, a wonderful return for a winger. Like Owen Williams, back in March 1924, Comfort joined Middlesbrough in July 1989 for £175,000. He had been close to signing for AFC Bournemouth, but O's boss Frank Clark set up the Middlesbrough deal. However, on 4 November 1989 tragedy occurred in a League match at Newcastle United. In trying to retrieve a ball, he fell badly and twisted his knee, but after three knee operations his professional career was over after just 18 senior appearances and 2 goals for Boro. He received a cash pay-off instead of the testimonial he requested. Comfort decided to enter the clergy, and in December 1990 it was announced that he had become a vicar, after studying theology in Durham. He said at the time: 'I would love one day to return to East London. I feel there is a job to be done there. It is where I played most of my football with Orient. When I was badly injured, it was Frank Clark who was always good to me. I don't really think there is a nicer person or club in football – when I got injured, a lot of people disappeared, but Frank always kept in touch.' Comfort became curate at St Chad's, Chadwell Heath, and more recently was vicar of St Stephen's church in Albert Road, Buckhurst Hill, Essex. Appropriately enough, Reverend Alan Comfort is today the chaplain of Leyton Orient Football Club. On the football front, he was voted into second place (behind the legendary Tommy Johnston) as one of O's all-time greatest players in a Millennium poll, receiving 11 per cent of all votes cast.

SEASON	LEAGUE		FA CUP		L. CUP	
	Apps	Gls	Apps	Gls	Apps	Gls
1985/86	15	5	0	0	0	0
1986/87	40(5)	11	2(1)	0	2	0
1987/88	46	12	4	1	2	0
1988/89	48	18	3	0	5	1
TOTAL	149(5)	46	9(1)	1	9	1

TOTAL APPS	167(6)
TOTAL GOALS	48

* Alan Comfort also appeared in 7 Auto Windscreens Shield matches, scoring twice.

Edward John CONNELLY, 1948-49

Eddie Connelly was born in Dumbarton, Scotland on 9 December 1916. He started with Fife club Rosslyn Park Juniors, and a great future was predicted for him. Newcastle United paid £90 for his services in March 1935, but despite showing great skill he never quite fulfilled his early potential, making just 25 League appearances with 8 goals during his three-year stay. He moved to Luton Town in March 1938 for £2,100, and netted 16 goals from 50 League appearances for the Hatters. He joined West Bromwich Albion in August 1939 for £4,150. Connelly was suspended indefinitely by the League in November 1940, after having been sent off twice whilst playing for WBA – the ban was finally lifted in October 1941. During the Second World War he guested for both Luton and Dumfermline. He returned to WBA for the 1945/46 season, but he soon after re-joined Luton to make a further 38 League appearances before becoming an 'Oriental' in June 1948 for £2,000. The inside forward was a splendid little ball-player, who did well for O's in his first season. The thirty-two-year-old moved to Brighton & Hove Albion in October 1949 on a free transfer, making just 7 senior appearances and scoring once before retiring at the end of the season. Connelly died on 16 February 1990 in Luton.

SEASON	LEAGUE		FA CUP		TOTAL	
	Apps	Gls	Apps	Gls	Apps	Gls
1948/49	31	5	2	1	33	6
1949/50	1	0	0	0	1	0
TOTAL	32	5	2	1	34	6

Michael George CONROY, 1987-88

Mike Conroy was born in Johnstone, Scotland on 31 July 1957. The midfielder

Mike Conroy

SEASON	LEAGUE		FA CUP		L. CUP	
	Apps	Gls	Apps	Gls	Apps	Gls
1987/88	2(1)	0	0	0	0	0
TOTAL	2(1)	0	0	0	0	0

TOTAL APPS	2(1)
TOTAL GOALS	0

* Mike Conroy also appeared in 0(1) Auto Windscreens Shield match.

started his career with Port Glasgow FC, before moving to Glasgow Celtic in April 1978, where he played 89 senior matches and scored 14 goals between 1978 and 1982. He left with two Scottish League Championship medals (1979 and 1981) and also a 1980 Scottish Cup winners' medal. He moved to Hibernian in June 1981, where he played 31 matches and scored 9 goals. In September 1984 the hard-grafting midfielder moved south of the Border to join Blackpool, where he made 66 appearances and scored 2 goals. In July 1986 he moved to Wrexham, where a further 25 appearances were made. The thirty-year-old was then released, and he joined O's in June 1987 on a three-month contract. He missed the start of the 1987/88 season after being troubled with an injury to the sole of his foot. He was not retained, and was appointed player-assistant manager with Cork City in 1988. He was dismissed during May 1993.

Leon CONSTANTINE, 2001 (loan)

Twenty-three-year-old Leon Constantine joined O's on an month's loan from Millwall on 27 August 2001. The loan deal came completely out of the blue. O's boss Taylor spoke to his Lions' counterpart, Mark McGhee, during a coach trip home from a League match at York City and the deal was agreed. Taylor spoke to Constantine and he was at the ground at 9.30 a.m. the following Monday, and was signed in time to play in the League match against Hartlepool United that Bank Holiday afternoon. Born in Hackney, London on 24 February 1978, the striker started off his career with Ryman League side Edgware Town in August 1999. He moved to the New Den on 31 August 2000 for £20,000, having previously spent seven weeks on trial with Charlton Athletic (as well as having also turned down a chance to train with the O's). Constantine impressed the Lions management in friendlies against Luton Town and O's, and they offered him a one-year contract with an option for a further year. He made his League debut for Millwall as a playing substitute in a 4-1 victory at Peterborough United on 30 September 2000. He also appeared in a 0-0 draw in an LDV Vans Trophy match against Swindon Town in January 2001. When he came to O's on loan, Taylor said of his new charge's debut performance: 'He didn't know any of the players, only meeting them a few hours before kick-off. He was just brilliant.' The following week he scored the opener in a 2-1 win at Southend United. He scored again the following week with a wonderful effort, jinking around a number of players on the edge of the area to score from fifteen yards in a 3-1 win over Bristol Rovers. As a result, his loan period was extended for a further month. The striker returned to Millwall on 23 October 2001 after his loan spell was cut short by new O's boss Paul Brush, who explained: 'Although Leon had done ever so well for us in his first 4 games, like a number of the players he has lost confidence. He looked like he had the weight of the world on his shoulders, and his performance dropped. The fact that he played in the League will stand him in good stead with the Lions.' He joined Scottish First Division side Partick Thistle on 10 January 2002 on a three-month loan contract.

SEASON	LEAGUE		FA CUP		L. CUP	
	Apps	Gls	Apps	Gls	Apps	Gls
2001/02	8(1)	3	0	0	0	0
TOTAL	8(1)	3	0	0	0	0

TOTAL APPS	8(1)
TOTAL GOALS	3

* Constantine also played in 0(1) LDV Vans Trophy cup match.

Reuben COOK, 1956-58

Ben Cook was born in Dunston-on-Tyne, Co. Durham on 9 March 1933. The 5ft 11in tall wing-half started his playing career with Bleach Green Juniors, and then played for Tow Law Town in the Northern League. He came south to join Arsenal on 26 November 1951, but two years of national service and various injuries restricted his appearances at Highbury. He played in 28 Combination matches and 64 Eastern Counties League games for the Gunners before he became an 'Oriental' on 19 January 1956. He made his senior debut eleven days later in the Southern Floodlight Cup match at Aldershot, a 1-0 defeat. A tall, stylish player, he found it difficult to displace the regulars in O's squad, not making his League debut until the 2-1 home win over Lincoln City on 6 April 1957. He moved into non-League football with Tonbridge in 1958, and a year later went to Yiewsley.

SEASON	LEAGUE		FA CUP		TOTAL	
	Apps	Gls	Apps	Gls	Apps	Gls
1955/56	0	0	0	0	0	0
1956/57	2	0	0	0	2	0
1957/58	0	0	0	0	0	0
TOTAL	2	0	0	0	2	0

Kenneth Herbert COOPER, 1932-33

Ken Cooper was an amateur who joined O's in July 1932 whilst still on the books of the Corinthians Club. Born in Romford, Essex on 20 February 1911, he played at either inside forward or centre forward. He only had a handful of matches with O's before returning to Corinthians in 1933. He was a more than capable player, who could have done well, had he decided to turn professional. Cooper died in Westminster, London on 14 July 1971.

SEASON	LEAGUE		FA CUP		TOTAL	
	Apps	Gls	Apps	Gls	Apps	Gls
1932/33	4	0	0	0	4	0
TOTAL	4	0	0	0	4	0

C

Mark David COOPER, 1989-94

Mark Cooper will go down in the annals of O's history as the player who scored the goal against Wrexham to take O's to promotion in a play-off final at Leyton in June 1989, when shooting home from twelve yards with just eight minutes remaining. The striker proved to be a brilliant signing by O's boss Frank Clark, and Cooper went on to score over 50 senior goals for the club. Born in Watford, Hertfordshire on 5 April 1967, he joined the O's in February 1989 as a twenty-one-year-old who had already crammed an enormous amount of action into a career which included spells with Cambridge United, Tottenham Hotspur, Shrewsbury Town and Gillingham. This big bustling striker – he stood 6ft 2in tall and weighed over 13st 4lb – made his League debut for Cambridge at just seventeen years of age and went on to score 17 goals from 62(9) appearances. He was snapped up by Spurs in April 1987 for £50,000, but it

Mark Cooper

was an unhappy period in his career and there were times when he couldn't even make the reserve team. He moved to Shrewsbury Town on loan, and when playing against Gillingham, Cooper impressed them so much that they paid Spurs their club record fee of £102,500. He made 38(11) senior appearances for the Gills, scoring 11 goals. He joined O's in February 1989 for £21,500, and went onto achieve fourteenth place in O's all-time club senior scoring chart, with 54 goals over six seasons at Brisbane Road. None of his goals was more valuable than the two he scored against Scarborough in the play-offs and the winner (already mentioned) against Wrexham in the play-off final. His goalscoring achievements were quite remarkable, considering he had a number of long-term injuries. Fittingly, he scored the club's 4,000th League goal (against Wigan Athletic on 14 April 1990), when he turned and slammed the ball from fully twenty yards into the net – a pity it was not photographed! He left O's to join Barnet on 13 July 1994 on a free transfer, and hit two against the O's in their 4-0 win in the Coca-Cola League Cup on 16 August 1994. Also in the Barnet side that night were two other former 'Orientals' – Carl Hoddle and Mickey Tomlinson. Cooper scored 23 goals for the Bees from 64(12) senior appearances. However, this was not the end of 'Coops': he moved to Northampton Town in August 1996 on a free transfer, and spent a successful season with the Cobblers that saw them reach the play-off final. He played 37(4) League matches and scored 10 goals. He played in a single play-off match at Cardiff City on 9 May 1997, but he sustained a serious injury, missing their victory in the final at

Mark Cooper is mobbed after scoring the goal against Wrexham that won promotion for O's in June 1989

SEASON	LEAGUE		FA CUP		L. CUP	
	Apps	Gls	Apps	Gls	Apps	Gls
1988/89*	14(4)	7	0	0	0	0
1989/90	38(1)	11	1	0	4	1
1990/91	18(4)	9	0	0	0	0
1991/92	11(7)	6	2(2)	1	0	0
1992/93	20(8)	7	2	2	2	1
1993/94	20(9)	8	3	1	0	0
TOTAL	121(33)	48	8(2)	4	6	2

TOTAL APPS	135(35)
TOTAL GOALS	54

* Mark Cooper's record includes 4 appearances and 3 goals in promotion play-off games in 1988/89.

** Cooper also appeared in 6(2) Auto Windscreens Shield matches, scoring once.

Wembley Stadium. His League career ended on a total of 107 League goals from 348 appearances, but his goalscoring achievements did not stop there. Cooper continued to knock in the goals when he moved to Welling United, scoring 19 goals from 40(1) appearances in 1997/98 and 4 goals from 22(4) appearances in 1998/99. In January 1999 he went on a month's loan to Bishop Stortford. The thirty-two-year-old then joined Gravesend & Northfleet on a free, scoring on his debut against Bishop Stortford on 30 March 1999. He ranks – along with Colin West and Carl Griffiths – as being one of the three most prolific strikers for O's over this past decade. Mark Cooper has been a prolific goalscorer at all levels of the game, and was a master of his art. Cooper retired from the game in May 2000 after a series of injuries.

Mark Nicholas COOPER, 1997-98

Mark Cooper is the son of former Leeds United and England full-back Terry Cooper, but is not related to Mark Cooper, O's prolific goalscorer mentioned above. This attacking midfielder started his career as a young trainee with Bristol City in September 1987, and he went onto have a long career with a number of clubs before joining O's on a non-contract basis on 1 December 1997. Born in Wakefield on 18 December 1968, he played 217(31) League career matches and scored 52 goals during spells with Exeter City (twice), Southend United, Birmingham City, Fulham, Huddersfield Town, Wycombe Wanderers, Hartlepool United, Maidstone United and, finally, O's. He played just once for the O's as a substitute at Cardiff City on 10 January 1988, before joining Rushden & Diamonds in February 1988, where he went on to make 14(3) appearances and score 3 goals. He joined Hednesford on 8 June 2000, and in March 2001 the thirty-three-year-old veteran joined Forest Green

Rovers on a fourteen-month contract and scored on his debut against Kettering Town FC.

SEASON	LEAGUE		FA CUP		L. CUP	
	Apps	Gls	Apps	Gls	Apps	Gls
1997/98	0(1)	0	0	0	0	0
TOTAL	0(1)	0	0	0	0	0

TOTAL APPS	0(1)
TOTAL GOALS	0

* Mark Cooper also appeared in an Auto Windscreens Shield match.

Patrick Avalon CORBETT, 1983-86

Born on 12 February 1963 in Hackney, London, Pat Corbett signed for Spurs as an apprentice in July 1979, before turning professional during October 1980. He was a good athlete and became a district schools champion at both the 400 metres and the long jump. Corbett progressed through their youth ranks

Pat Corbett

and scored a goal on his League debut as a substitute at Southampton. During the summer of 1981 he went on loan to GAIS in Sweden. After a further 4 first-team appearances, Spurs did not renew his contract and he considered leaving the game and going back to college. However, he decided to join O's in May 1983 instead. He looked to be a good versatile player with good ball distribution skills, performing well both as a full-back and as a central defender. He was a regular for two seasons, but lost his place in the 1985/86 season, and in April 1986 he was released and went to play in Finland. One unusual incident concerning Pat Corbett occurred during a match on 27 October 1984, when the referee sent him to the touchline to change his shirt after thirty-six minutes of a League game at Wigan Athletic. The official happened to notice that both he and Colin Foster were wearing number 6 shirts!

SEASON	LEAGUE		FA CUP		L. CUP	
	Apps	Gls	Apps	Gls	Apps	Gls
1983/84	43	1	1	0	2	0
1984/85	24	1	1	0	4	0
1985/86	10	0	0	0	3	0
TOTAL	77	2	2	0	9	0

TOTAL APPS	88
TOTAL GOALS	2

* Pat Corbett also appeared in 6(1) Auto Windscreens Shield matches, scoring once.

William Joseph CORKINDALE, 1926-29

'Corky', as he was affectionately known, was born on 9 May 1901 in Langley Green, Birmingham. He started out with Wellington Town, joining Swansea City in November 1923 for £250 and making 19 appearances, but he could never establish himself with the Welsh club and joined O's in June 1926. He was a regular during his three seasons at Millfields Road. A bandy-legged 5ft 10in outside left who liked to cut in for a shot on goal, he became extremely popular with the fans. He appeared in O's relegation season of 1928/29, and he was present in the team at Reading on 4 May 1929, which was to be its last match in the Second Division for a further twenty-seven years. Corkindale joined Millwall in May 1929 and made 40 senior appearances for the club, scoring 5 goals. In later years he was involved in the restaurant business. Corkindale died on 3 August 1972 in Ampthill, Bedfordshire, aged seventy-one.

David Corner

SEASON	LEAGUE		FA CUP		TOTAL	
	Apps	Gls	Apps	Gls	Apps	Gls
1926/27	35	7	2	0	37	7
1927/28	22	3	0	0	22	3
1928/29	39	7	4	1	43	8
TOTAL	96	17	6	1	102	18

David Edward CORNER, 1988-89

This central defender, who looked good in the air but a little unsteady on the ground, joined O's from Sunderland in July 1988, having made 42(3) senior appearances and scored 3 goals. Born in Sunderland on 15 May 1966, he started as an associate schoolboy with Oldham Athletic in 1982, but turned professional with Sunderland during April 1984. He was thrown in to the deep end when selected to play as an eighteen-year-old in the 1985 League Cup final against Norwich City, replacing the suspended Sunderland skipper, Shaun Elliott. However, it was Corner's mistake that led to City's goal, and ultimately to them winning the cup, and his Sunderland career appeared to be over. Shortly after representing England in the Youth World Cup in Russia in August 1995, he was loaned to Cardiff City where he made six appearances. He went on loan to Peterborough United in March 1988 (playing 9 matches) before joining O's. He could not find a regular spot and joined Darlington, where he earned a Fourth Division Championship winners' medal. He was reported to be working in the North-East as an insurance salesman during the late 1990s.

SEASON	LEAGUE		FA CUP		L. CUP	
	Apps	Gls	Apps	Gls	Apps	Gls
1988/89	4	0	0	0	2	0
TOTAL	4	0	0	0	2	0

TOTAL APPS	6
TOTAL GOALS	0

C

John Anthony CORNWELL, 1981-87

Blond-haired John Cornwell appears in the record books as the scorer of O's fastest-ever League goal – this took place against Torquay United on 18 March 1986, and was witnessed by just 1,828 spectators. The goal was recorded as having been scored after just fourteen seconds. Born in Bethnal Green, London on 13 October 1964, Cornwell was yet another youngster from West Ham's youth ranks. He was signed by Jimmy Bloomfield in July 1981, after representing both Essex and London schoolboys. A player who had a good, biting tackle and was good at running off the ball, Cornwell is one of only forty or so players to have made more than 200 senior appearances for the club. He signed a professional contract on his eighteenth birthday and made his League debut at Norwich City in May 1982. The midfielder, although often troubled by injuries, was a regular for the following

Cornwell scored 39 goals for O's

John Cornwell

five seasons, before being signed by Newcastle United on 9 July 1987 for £50,000. The Magpies saw him as a utility player. He never settled at St James' Park, making just 28(5) League appearances and scoring once, before a £50,000 transfer to Second Division Swindon Town occurred during December 1988. However, he never managed to settle at the County Ground either, making just 7(18) League appearances. In August, he joined Southend United for £45,000, and during his four-year spell on the coast, he played in 92(9) matches and scored 5 goals. Later he had loan spells with Cardiff City in August 1993 (5 appearances, 2 goals); Brentford in September 1993 (4 appearances); and, finally, with Northampton Town in February 1994 (13 appearances, 1 goal). More recently, he has been running a public house in Black Notley, and coaching the local Sunday football side in the village.

SEASON	LEAGUE		FA CUP		L. CUP	
	Apps	Gls	Apps	Gls	Apps	Gls
1981/82	3	0	0	0	0	0
1982/83	30(2)	3	1	0	0	0
1983/84	42	7	1	0	2	1
1984/85	33(3)	10	2	1	2(1)	1
1985/86	41(3)	8	6	1	3	0
1986/87	45(1)	7	4	0	2	0
TOTAL	194(9)	35	14	2	9(1)	2

TOTAL APPS	217(10)
TOTAL GOALS	39

* John Cornwell also appeared in 7 Auto Windscreens Shield matches, scoring twice.

Roy William COTTON, 1974-76

Born on 14 November 1955 in Fulham, London, Roy Cotton, a former youth international whilst with Brentford, joined O's from the West London club in July 1974, after playing 2 League games in 1973/74 for the Bees. He played mostly on the left wing and scored reg-

Roy Cotton

ularly for the reserves. His only full appearance came in a League Cup match against Birmingham City in September 1975, but he made 3 appearances in the League as a substitute. He was transferred to Aldershot in July 1976, with whom he made 5 League appearances in 1977/78.

SEASON	LEAGUE		FA CUP		L. CUP	
	Apps	Gls	Apps	Gls	Apps	Gls
1974/75	0	0	0	0	0	0
1975/76	0(3)	0	0	0	1	0
TOTAL	0(3)	0	0	0	1	0

TOTAL APPS	1(3)
TOTAL GOALS	0

Charles COULL, 1934-35, 1936-37

Charlie 'Chic' Coull, a centre half, was born on 27 November 1912 in East End, Dundee. He played first for Stobswell Juniors and then Arden Lea FC, before joining Glasgow Celtic in 1933. He joined O's on 14 June 1934, but played mostly in the reserve side, making his League debut against Bournemouth on 19 January 1935. He left London for Southport on 12 June 1935 (2 League appearances), but sustained a knee injury during November 1935, which kept him out of the side for the remainder of the season. He re-joined O's in July 1936 as a reserve for Dave Affleck in 1936, however, in March 1937 he left to become player-manager of Portadown. In later years he worked as a tram and bus driver for the Dundee Corporation. Coull died in Charleston, Dundee on 7 May 1991.

SEASON	LEAGUE		FA CUP		TOTAL	
	Apps	Gls	Apps	Gls	Apps	Gls
1934/35	4	0	0	0	4	0
TOTAL	4	0	0	0	4	0

Edmund Charles CRAWFORD, 1933-35

Big, tough centre forward Ted Crawford joined O's from Liverpool in July 1933 after making just 7 appearances and scoring 4 goals at Anfield. He previously hit the headlines with Halifax Town, where he netted 22 goals from 35 senior matches in his one season at that club, 1932/33. Born in Filey, Yorkshire on 31 October 1906, he began his playing career with Scarborough Town in the Northern League. He then moved to the unusually-named Scarborough Penguins from the Yorkshire League, and then on to Filey Town in the East Riding League, where it was reported that he scored over 150 goals. Twenty-eight-year-old Crawford broke O's scoring record with 25 senior goals in 1935/36 with some fierce left-foot shooting. He notched 3 hat-tricks during his time at the club, and there was always a chance of a goal when Crawford got into the penalty area – indeed, he ranks as one of O's best ever strikers. He is in third spot on O's all-time goalscoring list, and is one of only nine players to have recorded more than 20 League goals in a season. He also scored the only goal of the game in a friendly against Motherwell in 1935/36. Besides his League effort, he also played in 51 wartime regional matches, netting 9 goals. He retired from football in May 1945 to take up an appointment as coach with Swedish side Dagerfors. In 1949 he left to become coach of Italian club Bologna, leaving in 1952. Crawford died in Hendon during 1977.

SEASON	LEAGUE		FA CUP		TOTAL	
	Apps	Gls	Apps	Gls	Apps	Gls
1933/34	32	10	1	0	33	10
1934/35	29	9	0	0	29	9
1935/36	41	23	5	2	46	25
1936/37	33	11	2	2	35	13
1937/38	36	6	2	0	38	6
1938/39	29	8	2	2	31	10
TOTAL	200	67	12	6	212	73

* Ted Crawford also appeared in 6 Third Division Cup matches between 1933 and 1939, without scoring.

Wynn CROMPTON, 1933-35

This sturdy defensive-minded left full-back was born in Cefn-y-Bedd, near Wrexham on 11 February 1907. He started his career with Oak Alyn FC in the Welsh League. He then moved to Wrexham in 1927 and stayed for five seasons, making 64 League appearances and winning 3 full Welsh caps. He moved south on loan with Tunbridge Wells Rangers in 1932, but soon afterwards signed for O's, on 14 July 1933, where he teamed up with the veteran England international and ex-Liverpool full-back, Tommy Lucas. He proved to be an excellent defender and was one of the players to lift O's out of the doldrums during the mid-1930s. He was transferred to Crystal Palace in 1935, before moving to Exeter City and making 7 appearances in 1935/36 before retiring. He was the grandfather of Steve Crompton, who played for Wolves and Hereford United in the 1970s. Wynn Crompton died in Wrexham on 28 May 1988.

SEASON	LEAGUE		FA CUP		TOTAL	
	Apps	Gls	Apps	Gls	Apps	Gls
1933/34	42	0	4	0	46	0
1934/35	37	0	2	0	39	0
TOTAL	79	0	6	0	85	0

* Wynn Crompton also appeared in 3 Third Division Cup matches between 1933 and 1935.

Arthur CROPPER, 1930-32

Born in Brimington, near Chesterfield on 2 January 1906, the inside forward started with Luton Town, but soon moved on to Matlock & Stavely FC. During December 1927 he signed for Norwich City, and made 23 League appearances from which he scored 3 goals. He became an 'Oriental' in October 1930 and had a good run in the team. He scored twice in a 3-0 win over Brentford on 27 November 1930, a League match played at the famous Wembley Stadium. In July 1932 he moved onto Gillingham, making 16 League appearances and scoring twice. He played for Yarmouth Town between September 1933 and April 1936, and later ran a pub in Yarmouth. Cropper died in Hellesdon, Norfolk on 25 October 1949.

SEASON	LEAGUE		FA CUP		TOTAL	
	Apps	Gls	Apps	Gls	Apps	Gls
1930/31	25	10	2	1	27	11
1931/32	2	0	0	0	2	0
TOTAL	27	10	2	1	29	11

Roger George CROSS, 1968 (loan)

Born in East Ham, London on 20 October 1948, Roger Cross, a big bustling striker, joined O's as an eighteen-year-old on loan from West Ham United during October 1968. He had joined the Hammers staff in 1964 after playing schools football with East Ham and Essex, and had become their top youth and reserve scorer for two consecutive seasons. His stay at Brisbane Road was brief, and he returned to Upton Park before joining Brentford for £12,000 in March 1970, where he scored 18 goals from 62 appearances. He went to Fulham for £30,000 in September 1971, but was not a great success at Craven Cottage. Cross returned to Griffin Park in December 1972, and netted 79 goals from

223(5) senior matches. After a spell in America with Seattle Sounders, he later had coaching jobs with Millwall, QPR and Spurs. In February 1998 he became the first-team coach with West Ham.

SEASON	LEAGUE		FA CUP		L. CUP	
	Apps	Gls	Apps	Gls	Apps	Gls
1968/69	4(2)	2	0	0	0	0
TOTAL	4(2)	2	0	0	0	0

TOTAL APPS	4(2)
TOTAL GOALS	2

Errol Gilmour CROSSAN, 1960-61

Born on 6 October 1930 in Montreal, Canada, Crossan came to England as a youngster and joined Manchester City on trial in January 1954, after playing with Westminster Royals FC in Canada. The right-winger joined Gillingham in July 1955, and made 75 appearances from which he scored 16 goals. He joined Southend United during August 1957, and after 40 League games and 11 goals, he was transferred to Norwich City in September 1958. During a four-year stay, he notched 28 League goals from 112 appearances, and played in their great FA Cup run in 1958/59 that took them to the semi-final. Crossan became an 'Oriental' in January 1961, in a deal that took George Waites to Carrow Road. However, he did not stay long before he retired from the game and returned to Canada in July 1961.

SEASON	LEAGUE		FA CUP		L. CUP	
	Apps	Gls	Apps	Gls	Apps	Gls
1960/61	8	2	2	0	0	0
TOTAL	8	2	2	0	0	0

TOTAL APPS	10
TOTAL GOALS	2

Laurie Cunningham

Laurence Paul CUNNINGHAM, 1974-77
Laurie Cunningham (the 'black pearl', as he was known) was one of the most exciting talents ever to grace Brisbane Road. He was voted into joint third place (with Peter Allen) by O's fans in a Millennium poll of greatest O's players. He was born in Archway, near Holloway, London on 8 March 1956. He was on Arsenal's books as a junior along with another former 'Oriental' Glenn Roeder – both failed to make it at Highbury and were snapped up by O's scout Len Cheeswright within eighteen months, and both went on to become first-team regulars. Cunningham first came to the attention of the footballing public on 3 August 1974 in a Texaco Cup match at West Ham in front of 16,338 spectators. His brilliant touch, natural ball control and pace were all there for all to see. His League debut came in a 3-1 win at Oldham Athletic the following October. The O's management nursed him along slowly, but when the time was right, Barrie Fairbrother was sold to Millwall and Cunningham was brought into the side. During the final match of the 1974/75 season against Southampton, he walked into the dressing-room late for the match and was told by Petchey that unless he scored a goal, his first in the League, he would be heavily fined and suspended. It seemed to do the trick, as he scored the winning goal! He went on to play many magical games for O's, but on the eve of the March 1977 transfer deadline, he moved to West Bromwich Albion for £110,000, with both Joe Mayo and Allan Glover joining O's as part of the deal. He became the first black player to represent an England side when selected by Ron Greenwood for the under-21s, and he proved his worth by scoring with a downward header against Scotland at Bramall Lane in April 1977. He became the second black player to win a full England cap, soon after Viv Anderson.

Cunningham goes on another dazzling run

Tommy Cunningham

Cunningham made 81(5) appearances for Albion that yielded 15 goals, before joining Real Madrid for £995,000 in 1979. There he scored on his debut in front of 100,000 Bernabeau fans, and went on to score 15 goals to help them win the Spanish League and Cup double. After gaining 6 full England caps between 1979 and 1982, he seemed to lose interest in football and spent more time as a male model, fashion designer and boutique owner in Europe. He drifted from club to club, playing for Manchester United during 1983 (3(2) League appearances, 1 goal); Marseilles; Leicester City during 1985 (13(2) League matches); Sporting Gijon; and Charleroi in Belgium. At the age of thirty-two he returned to London in February 1988 to play for Wimbledon, and came on as a substitute in the Dons' famous FA Cup final victory over Liverpool in May 1988. He returned to Spain to play for Second Division side Rayo Vallecano of Madrid. Sadly, during the early hours of 15 July 1989, he was killed in a car crash in Madrid. Laurie Cunningham may not have fulfilled his early promise, but O's fans who were privileged enough to witness his talent will never forget this graceful player.

SEASON	LEAGUE		FA CUP		L. CUP	
	Apps	Gls	Apps	Gls	Apps	Gls
1974/75	15(2)	1	0(1)	0	0	0
1975/76	33(1)	8	1	0	1	0
1976/77	24	6	4	0	4	1
TOTAL	72(3)	15	5(1)	0	5	1

TOTAL APPS	82(4)
TOTAL GOALS	16

* Laurie Cunningham also appeared in 1(1) matches in the Texaco Cup during 1974/75 and 8 matches in the Anglo-Scottish Cup, scoring twice.

Thomas Edward CUNNINGHAM, 1981-87
Tommy Cunningham spent six seasons with the club between 1981 and 1987, having been signed by Paul Went. He later returned as coach in 1995, and when Pat Holland was fired, he became acting manager for 2 home League matches (against Scarborough and Torquay United) in October 1996. The latter – a 1-0 win – was the first victory in 7 matches, and the goal was scored by loanee Carl Griffiths in his first match for O's. Born in Bethnal Green, London on 7 December 1955, the big, strong defender started with Chelsea as an apprentice during October 1973, but joined QPR on a free transfer during May 1975. He made 27(3) League appearances for Rangers, before becoming a £50,000 record signing for Wimbledon in March 1979, where he went on to make 99 League appearances and score 12 goals. He joined O's for £46,000 in September 1981, and remained captain

C

for more than three seasons. He was a player who always gave 100 per cent, and probably his most memorable day came at Exeter City in February 1984, where he scored a hat-trick from the centre half position in a 4-3 win. Cunningham joined Fisher Athletic in June 1987, but left the club after the appointment of Tommy Taylor as boss in November 1996. In 1998/99 he was the youth coach at Barnet, and later was appointed assistant-manager to John Still in September 1999. Barnet were relegated to the Football Conference in May 2001. He was appointed as manager of Jewish Third Division Ryman League club Wingate & Finchley FC in July 2001, and brought in young O's star Niam Uka on loan.

SEASON	LEAGUE		FA CUP		L. CUP	
	Apps	Gls	Apps	Gls	Apps	Gls
1981/82	18	1	0	0	1	0
1982/83	28	3	2	0	0(1)	1
1983/84	36	6	1	0	2	0
1984/85	36	1	4	0	1	1
1985/86	13	2	3	0	1	0
1986/87	31	4	2	0	2	0
TOTAL	162	17	12	0	7(1)	2

TOTAL APPS 181(1)
TOTAL GOALS 19

* Tommy Cunningham also appeared in 0(1) Football League Groups Cup match and 5 Auto Windscreens Shield matches, scoring once.

Daniel Lee CURRAN, 1998-2000

Danny Curran was born in Brentwood, Essex on 13 June 1981. This quick two-footed small-built striker scored 22 youth League and cup goals and 5 goals for the reserves in 1998/99, and he was also was voted Youth Player of the Year in 1997/98. He first played junior football with

Corringham Cosmos and Balstonia, and gained representative honours for Basildon District. He made his first-team debut when coming on as a fifty-fifth-minute substitute in the Auto Windscreen Trophy match at Peterborough United on 8 December 1988. His League debut came in the home match against Darlington on 28 December 1998, when he came on to replace Amara Simba in the sixty-second minute. He also came on as a substitute in the seventy-eighth minute in the FA Cup tie at Bristol Rovers on 23 January 1999. The eighteen-year-old scored in a pre-season friendly against Antigua in July 2000 with a header, but never quite lived up to his early promise. He went on loan to Purfleet on 8 January 2000, signing with them on a permanent basis in May 2000. After a spell with Aveley, he joined East Thurrock United in August 2001. He trained with O's to keep fit and played in a friendly against Enfield in February 2002. He has since been released by East Thurrock.

SEASON	LEAGUE		FA CUP		L. CUP	
	Apps	Gls	Apps	Gls	Apps	Gls
1998/99	0(1)	0	0(1)	0	0	0
1999/2000	0	0	0	0	0(1)	0
TOTAL	0(1)	0	0(1)	0	0(1)	0

TOTAL APPS 0(3)
TOTAL GOALS 0

* Danny Curran also appeared in 0(1) Auto Windscreens Shield match.

Darren CURRIE, 1995-96 (loan)

Darren Currie, the nephew of former star Tony Currie, was born in Hampstead, London on 29 November 1974. He joined O's on a three-month loan period from West Ham United on 16 November 1995. This attacking midfield player, who started as a trainee with the Hammers on 2 July 1993 (making 18 reserve appearances and scoring 4 goals), made a 'hot' start to his loan spell with O's against Cambridge United on 18 November 1995. With his first touch, Currie performed a fancy twist-and-turn past two defenders and put over a perfect lob to set up Colin West to curl home the opener after just three minutes. After only 10 League appearances, he was recalled to Upton Park because Shrewsbury Town were impressed with his displays with O's – he had also had a couple of loan spells with them the previous season. He joined the Gay Meadow club in a £70,000 deal in February 1996, making 46(20) League appearances that yielded 8 goals. On 26 March 1998 he joined Plymouth Argyle on a non-contract basis, and made 5(2) appearances without scoring. In July 1998 he joined Barnet on a free transfer, and was a regular during the 1998/99 season, making 128(7) senior appearances for the Bees up to May 2001, scoring 20 goals. Currie was chosen for the PFA Division Three team in the 2000/01 season; this was particularly remarkable as Barnet were relegated to the Football Conference the same year. He was the target of O's boss Tommy Taylor who put in a £125,000 bid to get his man from the Bees in June 2001, but when it was reported that they wanted in excess of £200,000, he was snapped up by Wycombe Wanderers in July 2001.

SEASON	LEAGUE		FA CUP		L. CUP	
	Apps	Gls	Apps	Gls	Apps	Gls
1995/96	9(1)	0	0	0	0	0
TOTAL	9(1)	0	0	0	0	0

TOTAL APPS	9(1)
TOTAL GOALS	0

Guy Paul DALE, 1920

Born in Barnsley in 1894, Guy Dale, the tall, promising goalkeeper came south to join O's from Barnsley's reserve side in July 1920. He played just once in the League for O's, in a 1-0 win at Bury on 9 October 1920. On 14 December 1920 came the tragic news that Dale had been killed in a motorcar accident in Framingham, Kent. It was difficult to say what he might have achieved, but he certainly looked a good prospect in the few reserve matches he played in.

SEASON	LEAGUE		FA CUP		TOTAL	
	Apps	Gls	Apps	Gls	Apps	Gls
1920/21	1	0	0	0	1	0
TOTAL	1	0	0	0	1	0

Robert Rodie DALRYMPLE, 1911-1920

Bob Dalrymple, or 'Dally' as he was known, was a very classy inside forward who was born in Glasgow, Scotland on 2 January 1880. He started his career with Westmarch & Abercom FC in May 1890, and at twenty-two years old he turned professional with Hearts, and went on to win a Scottish Cup runners-up medal in 1903, when they lost to Rangers. He made 13 appearances and scored 3 goals before he came south of the Border to join Southern League outfit Plymouth Argyle in 1904, where he made 92 senior appearances and netted 29 goals. After a brief spell with Glasgow Rangers (15 appearances, 8 goals), he joined Portsmouth in 1906 (40 appearances, 8 goals). It was whilst he was with Fulham, whom he joined in 1907, that he

Bob Dalrymple

SEASON	LEAGUE		FA CUP		TOTAL	
	Apps	Gls	Apps	Gls	Apps	Gls
1910/11	17	6	0	0	17	6
1911/12	31	13	1	0	32	13
1912/13	18	3	0	0	18	3
1913/14	36	9	2	0	38	9
1914/15	30	7	1	0	31	7
1919/20	7	0	0	0	7	0
TOTAL	139	38	4	0	143	38

David Blyth Logie DAVIDSON, 1946-50
Born in Lanark, Scotland on 25 March 1920, David Davidson started with Douglas Water Thistle FC, before joining Bradford Park Avenue in May 1938. A versatile defender, he could play in several positions, but enjoyed most being at centre half or at left half. He joined O's in January 1947, after making 13 League appearances for the Yorkshire club, and he had several good seasons at Brisbane Road. In 1949/50, however, he played in a couple of heavy home defeats – 4-1 by Notts County, and the following week,

came to prominence, netting 44 goals from 108 senior appearances before his record transfer to O's for £300 on 28 January 1911, a large fee for a thirty-one-year-old player. He joined the likes of McFadden, Dix, Bevan Parker and Jonas in the forward line, and the O's were in line for promotion to the First Division for two seasons running, finishing both times in fourth position. He returned to O's in 1919 after the First World War, and his last League match was at Bury on 22 November 1919, when he was approaching his thirty-ninth birthday. Dalyrmple was probably one of the most stylish players to appear for O's up to the First World War, and gave grand service to all the clubs he played for. After six seasons at Millfields Road, he retired due to an injury, and joined Welsh side Ton Pentre as coach in January 1920. He died, aged ninety, in Worthing, Sussex during July 1990.

David Davidson

7-2 by Aldershot – and over 30,000 spectators witnessed the 2 home matches. Davidson left the club under a cloud, dismissed for a breach of club discipline in 1950. He died in Hackney, London during 1954, aged just thirty-four.

SEASON	LEAGUE		FA CUP		TOTAL	
	Apps	Gls	Apps	Gls	Apps	Gls
1946/47	19	1	0	0	19	1
1947/48	19	0	1	0	20	0
1948/49	37	0	2	0	39	0
1949/50	9	0	1	0	10	0
TOTAL	84	1	4	0	88	1

David Ivor DAVIES, 1952-54

Born in Bridgend, Wales on 21 July 1932, centre forward David (or 'Dai') Davies came to O's from South Wales amateur side Pyle in 1952. He was mostly confined to the reserves, and was loaned out to Harwich & Parkeston for whom he played in the 1953 Amateur Cup final at Wembley against Pegasus, although he got injured early on and limped through most of the match. He turned professional in July 1953, but only achieved a handful of League outings. However, he had one memorable day when he hit the winner in a FA Cup tie against Fulham in a 2-1 win in January 1954. A player who suffered badly with injuries, breaking his leg a couple of times during his career. He moved to Ramsgate Athletic (managed by former 'Oriental' Jimmy Blair) in 1954, and later played for Tunbridge Wells. In 1964/65 he joined former 'Orientals' Brian Webb and Tommy Long at Woodford Town.

SEASON	LEAGUE		FA CUP		TOTAL	
	Apps	Gls	Apps	Gls	Apps	Gls
1952/53	0	0	0	0	0	0
1953/54	4	0	1	1	5	1
TOTAL	4	0	1	1	5	1

Dudley Davies

Dudley DAVIES, 1950-52

Born in Shoreham, Sussex on 27 December 1924, he started off as a junior with Brighton & Hove Albion, before joining Lancing Town as an amateur. He then moved to Charlton Athletic, but never featured in their first team. The winger joined O's from Charlton in May 1950. A player who always tried hard and was full of energy down the wing, he was a regular in 1950/51 until youngster Brian Jackson displaced him, and he left the club in May 1952.

SEASON	LEAGUE		FA CUP		TOTAL	
	Apps	Gls	Apps	Gls	Apps	Gls
1950/51	14	1	1	0	15	1
1951/52	3	1	0	0	3	1
TOTAL	17	2	1	0	18	2

Reginald Walter DAVIES, 1963-64, 1965-66

Born in Tipton, Staffordshire on 9 October 1933, goalkeeper Reg Davies started his career as an apprentice with West Brom in

January 1951 (4 League appearances), before joining Walsall in July 1955 for £400 (53 League appearances). Davies was an agile goalie who had two spells with O's. He joined from Millwall in July 1963, where he had been very successful, making 199 League appearances between 1958 and 1962, and he became known as 'the Cat' at the Den. He could not find a regular place with O's, being second choice behind Mike Pinner. He left in July 1964 to join Port Vale after just 11 League matches, but he re-joined O's for his second spell in March 1965. However, he could not oust Welsh international 'keeper Vic Rouse, and he eventually retired in 1966 at the age of thirty-three.

SEASON	LEAGUE		FA CUP		L. CUP	
	Apps	Gls	Apps	Gls	Apps	Gls
1963/64	11	0	0	0	1	0
1964/65	11	0	0	0	0	0
1965/66	5	0	0	0	0	0
TOTAL	27	0	0	0	1	0
TOTAL APPS			28			
TOTAL GOALS			0			

Martin DAVIN, 1933-34

Scotsman Martin Davin, an inside right, was born in Dumbarton on 9 September 1905. He started off with the Vale of Clyde club, before joining Dumbarton in June 1926. He moved south of the Border in August 1927 to play for Bury, and made 38 League appearances, scoring 9 goals. In July 1930 he moved to Bolton Wanderers, but played just 3 League matches and was soon off again to join Hull City that November as a utility player during an injury crisis, making a further 8 League and scoring once over the next two seasons. He moved to Yeovil & Petters United in 1931/32, playing under manager David

Pratt, and in 1932/33 he played for Scottish side Airdrieonians. He became an 'Oriental' in August 1933, again signed by Pratt, and made his debut in a 3-0 defeat at Norwich City on the opening day of the season. He went on to score in a 4-0 win over Bristol City and a 2-1 victory over Brighton & Hove Albion, but after manager Pratt left the club and was replaced by Peter Proudfoot, he only played twice more. In August 1933, he joined Ashford Town. Davin died in Romford, Essex on 9 November 1957, aged fifty-two.

SEASON	LEAGUE		FA CUP		TOTAL	
	Apps	Gls	Apps	Gls	Apps	Gls
1933/34	15	2	0	0	15	2
TOTAL	15	2	0	0	15	2

Edwin DAVIS, 1912-13

The 6ft tall goalkeeper Ted Davis was born in Bedminster, Bristol in January 1892. He began his career with Bristol City in 1911, and then went to Brentford on trial, before becoming an 'Oriental' in December 1912. His chances were limited, with both Billy Bower and James Hugall in front of him, and he had just a handful of League outings when both were injured in 1913. He also appeared in the 6-0 defeat at Sunderland in the FA Cup in January 1913. He joined Portsmouth in May 1913, appearing just once in the Southern Alliance. He moved to Huddersfield Town on 7 February 1914 (where he made 57 appearances) and then moved to Blackburn Rovers in July 1922 (making a further 25 appearances). In May 1925 he joined Bristol City where he made 3 League appearances. In 1930 he was appointed player-manager of Bath City. Davis died in his native Bristol on 6 March 1954, aged sixty-two.

SEASON	LEAGUE		FA CUP		TOTAL	
	Apps	Gls	Apps	Gls	Apps	Gls
1912/13	4	0	1	0	5	0
TOTAL	4	0	1	0	5	0

Frederick DAVIS, 1936

Fred Davis was born in Hackney, London during 1913. He was a splendid amateur player for Walthamstow Avenue, and went on to sign amateur forms with O's in February 1936. Nicknamed 'twinkle toes' for his nippy and exciting wing runs, he played against both Crystal Palace and Millwall in 1936, making the goals for Ted Crawford in the two 1-0 victories. O's were keen to sign him up as a professional, but he preferred to remain an amateur, and returned to Walthamstow Avenue at the end of the season.

Tommy Dawson

SEASON	LEAGUE		FA CUP		TOTAL	
	Apps	Gls	Apps	Gls	Apps	Gls
1935/36	2	0	0	0	2	0
TOTAL	2	0	0	0	2	0

Thomas DAWSON, 1932-33

Born in Springwell, Co. Durham on 15 December 1901, Tommy Dawson worked as a pit miner before turning to football. The left full-back started with Copwell Institute and then Washington Colliery in the Northern League, but after a short spell with Darlington he joined Stoke City in June 1924, making 24 senior appearances between 1924 and 1932. He also captained the Stoke reserve side for two seasons, playing over 100 matches. He became an 'Oriental' in May 1932 on a free transfer. During August 1933 he joined Gateshead and later became their trainer. Dawson died in Washington, Co. Durham on 30 November 1977.

SEASON	LEAGUE		FA CUP		TOTAL	
	Apps	Gls	Apps	Gls	Apps	Gls
1932/33	19	0	1	0	20	0
TOTAL	19	0	1	0	20	0

Keith David DAY, 1987-93

The precarious career of a professional footballer is perfectly encapsulated in Keith Day. The long-serving 6ft 1in central defender was sweeping all before him in the 1991/92 season, winning O's Player of the Year award, only to be released on a free transfer twelve months later. Born in Grays, Essex on 29 November 1962, he started his career with Aveley FC in the Diadora League. He then went on to join Colchester United in August 1984, making 113 League appearances and scoring 12 goals. He joined O's in July 1987 and played a key role in the promotion side of 1988/89. He didn't score many goals for O's, but his most memorable was a stunning volley for a home victory over

Keith Day

Huddersfield Town in 1991/92. After being left out of the side in 1992/93, the thirty-year-old defender handed in a transfer request and was released in May 1993. He joined Beazer League side Sittingbourne in June 1993. During March 1999 it was reported that he had been appointed joint caretaker-manager (with Dean Coney) at Farnborough Town.

SEASON	LEAGUE		FA CUP		L. CUP	
	Apps	Gls	Apps	Gls	Apps	Gls
1987/88	41	2	4	0	2	0
1988/89*	49	2	3	0	4	0
1989/90	39	1	1	0	4	1
1990/91	21(3)	1	0	0	2	0
1991/92	31(2)	2	5	1	3	0
1992/93	7(3)	1	1(1)	0	2	0
TOTAL	188(8)	9	14(1)	1	17	1

TOTAL APPS	219(9)
TOTAL GOALS	11

* Day played in 4 promotion play-off matches in 1988/89.

** Keith Day also appeared in 13(2) Auto Windscreens Shield matches, scoring twice.

Mervyn Richard DAY, 1979-83

Mervyn Day became O's most expensive goalkeeper when he joined from West Ham United in July 1979 for £100,000. His arrival saw the departure of John Jackson, after his remarkable run of 222 consecutive League appearances over five seasons. Born in Chelmsford, Essex on 26 June 1955, Day excelled as an all-round sportsman at King Edward VI Grammar School in Chelmsford. The 'keeper signed as an apprentice with the Hammers in July 1971, turning professional during March 1973. He totalled 233 senior appearances at Upton Park, before losing his place to Phil Parkes. He won 5 England under-23 caps, an FA Cup winner's medal in 1975 and a European Cup runners-up' medal in 1976. He started off well at Brisbane Road, but lost form as the club drifted down to the Third Division. He was skipper in 1982, and was chosen as a substitute 'keeper to Nigel Spinks for England 'B' against New Zealand, a match played at Brisbane Road in October 1979. Day was transferred to Aston Villa for £25,000 in May 1983, where he made 33 appearances. After loan spells at Coventry City, Leicester City, Luton Town and Sheffield United, he signed for Leeds United in February 1985 for £30,000 and had a successful 'second' career. He won a Second Division Championship medal in 1989/90, and made 260 senior appearances at Elland Road. He joined Carlisle United on a free transfer in July 1993, and after 16 League appearances, he was appointed manager in January 1996. Unfortunately, he could not prevent them from relegation to Division Three, but proved his managerial acumen by leading them straight back up again. Day was dismissed in controversial circumstances in 1997 by Carlisle chairman Michael Knighton, who wanted a more hands-on role for himself. He was appointed goalkeeping coach at Everton, but moved on to join Alan Curbishley as first-team coach at Charlton Athletic in May 1998, and he has remained with them throughout their ups and downs en route to the Premiership. Mervyn Day made a total of 642 League appearances in a career than spanned some twenty-three years.

SEASON	LEAGUE		FA CUP		L. CUP	
	Apps	Gls	Apps	Gls	Apps	Gls
1979/80	42	0	2	0	2	0
1980/81	40	0	1	0	2	0
1981/82	42	0	5	0	2	0
1982/83	46	0	2	0	2	0
TOTAL	170	0	10	0	8	0

Mervyn Day

TOTAL APPS	188
TOTAL GOALS	0

* Mervyn Day also appeared in 3 Anglo-Scottish Cup matches and 6 Football League Groups Cup matches.

Norman Victor DEELEY, 1961-64

Little Norman Deeley – he stood less than 5ft 5in tall, yet he was a thrusting goalscoring winger, who joined O's in February 1962 for £12,000, as a replacement for the injured Phil White. He assisted O's efforts in achieving promotion to the First Division in April 1962. Born in Wednesbury, West Midlands on 30 November 1933, he was the smallest player ever to be capped for England schoolboys in 1947/48. His size did not daunt Wolverhampton Wanderers, who signed him in May 1948. He made his League debut against Arsenal in August 1951 at right half, but he switched to the wing after his demob in 1957 and netted 75 goals from 237 senior appearances between 1951 and 1961. Deeley won 2 England caps in 1959 (against Brazil and Peru) and he scored twice as Wolves took the FA Cup in 1960. His dash and verve was a great asset as the club strived to stay in the First Division, and he netted one of the goals in a 9-2 League Cup victory over Chester. As the following season progressed, he lost some of his sparkle and pace, but did score twice in a 5-0 win over Maltese side Sliema Wanderers, a friendly match played in 1963/64. Deeley was transferred to Worcester City in July 1964. He later played for Bromsgrove Rovers (from August 1967) and Darlaston (from September 1971). Living in his native Wednesbury, he became manager of the Caldmore Community Agency in Walsall,

D

Norman Deeley

scoring 3 goals. He stayed just a single season at Brisbane Road, before being transferred to Shrewsbury Town for £25,000 on 4 July 1995, where he made 62(18) League appearances and scored three goals. He became a victim of Shrewsbury's bad run in 1997/98, and moved to Football Conference side Dover Athletic on loan in January 1998. In May 1998 he joined Welsh side Barry Town, and more recently he moved to Irish side Bohemians in May 1999, later playing alongside two other former 'Orientals' Dave Morrison and Simon Webb. He starred in their 2 European games against Aberdeen in August 2000, but cracked the fibula in his right leg during the second match and was ruled out for the remainder of the Gypsies' 2000/01 season.

SEASON	LEAGUE		FA CUP		L. CUP	
	Apps	Gls	Apps	Gls	Apps	Gls
1994/95	43	1	1(1)	0	2	0
TOTAL	43	1	1(1)	0	2	0

TOTAL APPS	46(1)
TOTAL GOALS	1

* Mark Dempsey also appeared in 5 Auto Windscreens Shield matches, scoring once.

and later held a post as steward for the Walsall FC VIP lounge on match-days.

SEASON	LEAGUE		FA CUP		L. CUP	
	Apps	Gls	Apps	Gls	Apps	Gls
1961/62	14	2	0	0	0	0
1962/63	36	5	4	1	5	2
1963/64	23	2	3	1	1	0
TOTAL	73	9	7	2	6	2

TOTAL APPS	86
TOTAL GOALS	13

Mark Anthony DEMPSEY, 1994-95

A determined and committed left-sided midfielder who joined O's from Gillingham in July 1994, Dempsey missed just 3 matches in the relegation season of 1994/95. Born in Dublin on 9 December 1972, he started as a trainee with Gillingham in August 1990. The Eire youth and under-21 international made 32(22) senior appearances for the Gills,

Robert DENNISON, 1926-29

Bob Dennison was born in Arnold, Nottinghamshire on 16 October 1900, and started his long career with local side Arnold St Mary's FC. The inside forward first showed his promise with Norwich City in 1920/21, where he made 25 appearances and scored 10 goals. He joined Brighton & Hove Albion in May 1924, where he scored 34 goals from 114 appearances. His next club was Manchester City, with whom he stayed for a short period, playing just 7 matches and scoring 4 goals. He scored 9 goals from 20 reserve appearances at Maine Road. Dennison became an 'Oriental' on 26 August 1926, and proved to be a lively and dangerous forward, netting a hat-trick against Bristol City in October 1927. With the arrival of Reg Tricker in 1929, he was not a regular and joined Chesterfield in June 1929, appearing in 28 League matches and netting 7 goals. During August 1933 he played for Yarmouth Town. Dennison died in Norwich on 24 June 1973.

SEASON	LEAGUE		FA CUP		TOTAL	
	Apps	Gls	Apps	Gls	Apps	Gls
1926/27	30	13	2	2	32	15
1927/28	26	10	0	0	26	10
1928/29	14	5	4	1	18	6
TOTAL	70	28	6	3	76	31

Frederick George DENTON, 1920-21

Born in Barnet, Hertforshire on 7 May 1899, Fred Denton, a 5ft 8in inside forward, was signed from local amateur football during August 1920, after catching the eye with his goalscoring feats. He was mainly a reserve, making his League debut at Blackpool in a 2-2 draw on 13 September 1920, before moving to Chatham Town in May 1921. Denton died in Lee-on-Solent on 26 September 1969.

SEASON	LEAGUE		FA CUP		TOTAL	
	Apps	Gls	Apps	Gls	Apps	Gls
1920/21	3	0	0	0	3	0
1921/22	0	0	0	0	0	0
TOTAL	3	0	0	0	3	0

Harold Reginald DEVERALL, 1948-53

Jackie Deverall was born in Petersfield, near Reading on 5 May 1916, and was one of just a few players to be allowed to remain as a part-timer throughout his playing career, being a chartered accoun-tant by profession. As a schoolboy he won 2 England caps and later played for Maidenhead United in an FA Amateur Cup semi-final match, before signing part-time professional forms with Reading during November 1939. He went on to make 74 senior appearances and score 9 goals. The wing-half joined O's in May 1948 and figured prominently in O's 1951/52 FA Cup run. He had a splendid never-say-die attitude, and was a great example to the younger players. He had a benefit match staged for him after retiring from playing in 1953, and he went on to join Sittingbourne as coach. After retiring altogether from football, he ran a newsagent's business in Tilehurst. He died in Reading on 11 June 1999.

SEASON	LEAGUE		FA CUP		TOTAL	
	Apps	Gls	Apps	Gls	Apps	Gls
1948/49	29	1	2	1	31	2
1949/50	7	0	0	0	7	0
1950/51	30	1	1	0	31	1

Jackie Deverall

1951/52	22	0	8	0	30	0
1952/53	26	0	2	0	28	0
TOTAL	114	2	13	1	127	3

Note: In the 1990 book *The Complete Record of Leyton Orient*, it stated that Deverall made 27 League appearances in 1952/53, with a total that season of 29 senior appearances, a grand total of 115 League appearances, and a final total of 128 senior appearances. These figures are incorrect. His total appearance figures should read as printed above, as the 1990 book wrongly included an appearance by Deverall on 25 September 1952, an appearance, in fact, made by Blizzard.

Kevin James DICKENSON, 1985-92

Although Kevin Dickenson signed for O's during the summer of 1985, his association with the O's goes back a lot further than that. Having been born in Hackney (on 24 November 1962), as a youngster his father took him down to Brisbane Road to watch the O's, even though Kevin supported Spurs at the time and was on their books as a junior between 1977 and 1979. Dickinson was small in stature – standing just 5ft 6in tall – but he proved to be a reliable and splendid servant to the club, and was voted Player of the Year by the fans in 1985/86. He spent seven seasons at the club. Dickenson turned professional with Charlton Athletic on 21 May 1980, and made 72(3) League appearances as well as scoring once. He was snapped up by O's boss Frank Clark on 1 July 1985 on a free transfer, and went on to star in O's promotion season of 1988/89, playing in all 4 of the play-off matches. His last couple of seasons with O's proved to be a real nightmare, and he suffering some serious injuries, which eventually forced the tenacious left-back to retire.

Kevin Dickenson

SEASON	LEAGUE		FA CUP		L. CUP	
	Apps	Gls	Apps	Gls	Apps	Gls
1985/86	46	1	6	0	4	0
1986/87	39	0	4	0	2	0
1987/88	22	1	4	0	0	0
1988/89*	42(1)	1	2	0	5	0
1989/90	31	0	1	0	4	0
1990/91	6(1)	0	1	0	0	0
1991/92	8	0	0	0	2	0
TOTAL	194(2)	3	18	0	17	0

TOTAL APPS	229(2)
TOTAL GOALS	3

* Kevin Dickenson's record includes 4 promotion play-off matches in 1988/89.
** Dickenson also appeared in 11 Auto Windscreens Shield matches.

James Henry DIMMOCK, 1932-34

Jimmy Dimmock was born in Edmonton, London on 5 December 1900. He found fame with Tottenham Hotspur and spent twelve seasons with them. The left-winger was the first Spurs player to reach the milestone of 400 League appearances, and also the first to score 100 League goals. Dimmock, who won 3 full England caps and scored the FA Cup-winning goal in 1921, started his career with Edmonton Ramblers, joining Spurs in December 1918. He moved to Thames Association on 13 August 1931, making 37 League appearances and scoring 12 goals. During the First World War he guested for O's, and the thirty-two-year-old was signed up on 23 September 1932 by O's boss (and former colleague) Jimmy Seed. He was not the same player as in his younger days at White Hart Lane, but still he looked very useful at times. In March 1934 he joined Ashford Town, and was later a player with Tunbridge Wells Rangers. Dimmock had one leg amputated in December 1958 and the other leg removed during the late 1960s. He died in Edmonton on 23 December 1972. In recognition of his wonderful achievements at Spurs, local schools in Cheshunt and Enfield competed for 'The Jimmy Dimmock Cup'.

SEASON	LEAGUE		FA CUP		TOTAL	
	Apps	Gls	Apps	Gls	Apps	Gls
1932/33	18	3	1	0	19	3
1933/34	0	0	0	0	0	0
TOTAL	18	3	1	0	19	3

Joseph Charles DIX, 1910-15

Born in Geddington, Kettering in 1886, Joe Dix started his professional career with Kettering Town before he joined Portsmouth on 13 April 1906, where he played in 82 Southern League matches and 8 FA Cup ties, scoring 24 goals. He joined O's in June 1910 on a controver-

sial note. Dix had not told the Hampshire club of his move and they complained to the League. O's were ordered to pay a fine, as well as a transfer fee of £100. The outside left played a major part in one of the club's best periods of their history, and he performed well over five seasons. He will go down as one of O's best left-wingers, making many of the goals scored by the prolific goalscorer Richard McFadden. However, one of the negative parts of his game was that he did not score enough goals himself. After the First World War, he retired from the game altogether.

SEASON	LEAGUE		FA CUP		TOTAL	
	Apps	Gls	Apps	Gls	Apps	Gls
1910/11	22	3	1	0	23	3
1911/12	38	5	1	0	39	5
1912/13	35	0	1	0	36	0
1913/14	32	1	3	0	35	1
1914/15	21	2	1	0	22	2
TOTAL	148	11	7	0	155	11

Thomas Henry DIXON, 1919-27

Tommy Dixon was born in Seaham on 17 September 1899. The former coal miner joined O's in June 1919 from Murton Colliery Welfare FC, after failing a trial with Sunderland, and had 8 wonderful seasons at Millfields Road. Dixon was a very hard-working player, and the wing-half figured prominently in O's great FA Cup run of 1925/26. He had a brilliant game when O's shocked the football world by knocking Newcastle United (2-0) out of the cup in a fifth round tie during February 1926. He was a player who would have fared very well in the modern game with his dynamic midfield play. Dixon moved on to Southend in June 1927, and made 249 League and 16 FA Cup matches, scoring 7 goals. After retiring, he went to live in Australia for a while. In 1955 it was reported that he was running the Bay Horse public house in Chelmsford.

SEASON	LEAGUE		FA CUP		TOTAL	
	Apps	Gls	Apps	Gls	Apps	Gls
1919/20	9	2	0	0	9	2
1920/21	17	3	0	0	17	3
1921/22	34	0	1	0	35	0
1922/23	32	1	1	0	33	1
1923/24	38	1	3	0	41	1
1924/25	42	2	1	0	43	2
1925/26	40	4	4	0	44	4
1926/27	22	2	0	0	22	2
TOTAL	234	15	10	0	244	15

Leslie Smith DODDS, 1937-39

Les Dodds was born in Patishead, Newcastle-upon-Tyne on 20 September 1912. The outside left started his career with Newcastle Swifts – the Newcastle United youth team – and, at the age of seventeen, he moved to Grimsby Town, and stayed there until March 1934, making 14 League appearances and scoring once for the club. He joined Hull City for £75 in March 1934 (scoring 4 goals from 20 Second Division appearances), prior to joining Torquay United in June 1935 (for whom he made 35 League appearances and scored 3 goals) and then Wellington Town. He became an 'Oriental' in July 1937 – he had a straightforward-looking style, running down the wing to get his centres across. He had 2 good seasons with O's before moving to Hartlepool United in July 1939, where he netted 4 goals from 53 wartime outings. During 1941/42, he was a wartime guest player for his former club Grimsby Town. Leslie Dodds died in Humberstone, Lincolnshire on 29 November 1967.

SEASON	LEAGUE		FA CUP		TOTAL	
	Apps	Gls	Apps	Gls	Apps	Gls
1937/38	24	1	2	0	26	1
1938/39	29	3	2	0	31	3
TOTAL	53	4	4	0	57	4

* Les Dodds also appeared in a Third Division Cup match in 1938/39.

William DODGIN Snr, 1937-39

Bill Dodgin Snr, was born in Gateshead on 17 April 1909, and his football career spanned more than fifty years as a player and manager. A workmanlike wing-half, who started his career with Lincoln City in 1933 (45 League outings), he was part of the revival at Charlton Athletic, who rose from the Third Division to the First in consecutive seasons from 1934/35, making 29 League appearances. He joined O's in July 1937, and had two good seasons with them, before joining Southampton in May 1939. During the war years he was a guest player for O's, making 29 appearances in the 1942/43 season, but was recalled to the Dell in 1943. Dodgin was appointed as Southampton manager on 1 January 1946, and he went on to become manager of Fulham on 1 August 1949. After his four-year spell at Craven Cottage, Dodgin Snr was appointed manager at Brentford in October 1953, before holding similar positions with Yiewsley and Sampdoria in Italy. He was appointed as boss of Bristol Rovers in August 1969, and in November 1970 his Rovers side faced Fulham in an FA Cup tie, who were by then managed by his son, William Jnr! William Dodgin Snr died in Godalming on 16 October 1999, at the age of ninety. His son died in June 2000, aged sixty-eight.

SEASON	LEAGUE		FA CUP		TOTAL	
	Apps	Gls	Apps	Gls	Apps	Gls
1937/38	23	1	0	0	23	1
1938/39	39	0	2	0	41	0
TOTAL	62	1	2	0	64	1

* Bill Dodgin also appeared in 2 Third Division Cup matches between 1937 and 1939.

Arthur Albert DOMINY, 1929-30

Born in South Stoneham, Wollston, Hampshire on 11 February 1893, Arthur 'Art' Dominy first came to prominence at county level during 1911/12. In spells at Weston Grove FC, Peartree Athletic and Bitterne Guild FC, he scored a total of over 50 goals, and after a short spell with Wollston FC he was snapped up by Southampton in March 1913. During the First World War, he was a guest player with Glasgow Rangers, Arsenal and the Harland & Wolff works team. He captained the Saints in their promotion to the Second Division in 1922,

Arthur Dominy

and made 222 League appearances (scoring 68 goals) in his six seasons with them. He joined Everton in 1926 on a free transfer, and made a further 29 appearances from which he scored 12 goals. During 1927 he moved to Gillingham and made 52 League appearances, netting 17 goals. Dominy became an 'Oriental' at the age of thirty-six in July 1929, but after a handful of matches he dropped down into non-League football with Newport. At his best, he was a very good inside forward. After retiring he had a spell between 1943 and 1946 as scout and manager with Southampton. He died in Mitcham, Surrey on 23 September 1974.

SEASON	LEAGUE		FA CUP		TOTAL	
	Apps	Gls	Apps	Gls	Apps	Gls
1929/30	5	1	2	0	7	1
TOTAL	5	1	2	0	7	1

Nigel DONN, 1982-83

The 5ft 10in midfielder came to O's in August 1982, after completing a spell with Finnish side Karpalo FC. Born in Maidstone, Kent on 2 March 1962, he started off his career as an apprentice with Gillingham (making 2(1) League appearances), and representing Kent at youth level. Donn was a hard-working player, who got into a rather weak-looking O's side in 1982. He joined Maidstone United in May 1983, and was a member of their Alliance Premier League Championship-winning side. During the summer of 1988 he joined Dover Athletic, and later acted as their caretaker manager. He has subsequently held managerial positions with Ashford Town, Margate and Tonbridge Angels.

Nigel Donn

SEASON	LEAGUE		FA CUP		L. CUP	
	Apps	Gls	Apps	Gls	Apps	Gls
1982/83	22(1)	2	1	0	2	0
TOTAL	22(1)	2	1	0	2	0

TOTAL APPS	25(1)
TOTAL GOALS	2

* Nigel Donn also appeared in a Football League Groups Cup match.

Leopold DONNELLAN, 1984-85 (loan)

Leo Donnellan was a Chelsea reserve player who came on loan to O's in December 1984. After returning to Stamford Bridge, he signed for Fulham in August 1985. Born of Irish parentage in Willesdon, London on 19 January 1965, he represented the Ireland under-21 side against England in March 1985. He left Craven Cottage after three seasons (having made 61(30) senior appearances) to join Wealdstone, and later had spells with Hendon and Farnborough.

SEASON	LEAGUE		FA CUP		L. CUP	
	Apps	Gls	Apps	Gls	Apps	Gls
1984/85	6	0	2	0	0	0
TOTAL	6	0	2	0	0	0

TOTAL APPS	8
TOTAL GOALS	0

* Leo Donnellan also appeared in 2 Auto Windscreens Shield matches.

Christopher DORRIAN, 1998-2002

Chris Dorrian, a right full-back, signed for O's on YTS forms on 1 July 1998, and he was a non-playing substitute against Barnet in the final match of the 1999/2000 season. Born in Harlow, Essex on 3 April 1982, he made his League debut on the first day of the following season with a five-star performance at Plymouth Argyle on 12 August 2000. He was one of the most consistent players in the O's youth side, playing 25 games in 1998/99 and 30 games in 1999/2000, as well as making 5 starts for the reserves. Dorrian, who is understudy to Matthew Joseph, has shown great potential – he is solid in the tackle, and much is expected of him in future years. He made his League debut against Plymouth Argyle in August 2000. He was a member of the youth side that won the FA Alliance Cup final at the Millennium Stadium in Cardiff, a 1-0 victory against Bradford City on 22 April 2001. He was rather surprisingly loaned out to Nationwide Conference side Dover Athletic for three months in August 2001, making his debut in a 1-0 home defeat by Telford United. He was re-called from his loan stay at Dover after making 14 Nationwide Conference appearances. After a late withdrawal by Billy Beall through illness, he made a surprise appearance in the excellent 1-0 win against Bristol City in the FA Cup on 17 November 2001. He was released from his contract in March 2002.

SEASON	LEAGUE		FA CUP		L. CUP	
	Apps	Gls	Apps	Gls	Apps	Gls
1999/2000	0	0	0	0	0	0
2000/01	2	0	0	0	1	0
2001/02	2(1)	0	2	0	0	0
TOTAL	4(1)	0	2	0	1	0

TOTAL APPS	7(1)
TOTAL GOALS	0

David Wishart DOUGAL, 1905-07

Dave Dougal was born in Dundee on 22 March 1882. The outside right began his career with Dundee Hibernians (a junior side) in August 1902, and then moved to Dundee FC in May 1903. He decided to come south of the Border, but made little impression with either Preston North End or Grimsby Town. He became an 'Oriental' in October 1905 for the club's first season in the League, and played regularly for two seasons. He left O's and joined Southern League outfit Reading in June 1907, in exchange for goalkeeper Walter Whittaker. He played in 20 Southern League matches before moving to Brighton & Hove Albion in February 1908, where he made a further 14 senior appearances and scored once. During June 1908 he joined his former Seagulls boss Frank Scott-Walford at Leeds City, making his debut against Clapton Orient in September 1908. He remained there for two seasons, making 25 League appearances and scoring twice. In November 1910 he returned to Scotland to play for Montrose. On leaving the game, he worked for many years in the confectionery trade. Dougal died in Dundee on 5 March 1937.

SEASON	LEAGUE		FA CUP		TOTAL	
	Apps	Gls	Apps	Gls	Apps	Gls
1905/06	17	1	5	3	22	4
1906/07*	33	2	-	-	33	2
TOTAL	50	3	5	3	55	6

* Clapton Orient did not enter the FA Cup in 1906/07.

Simon DOWNER, 1998-present

Downer, a product of O's YTS scheme, was born in Rush Green, Romford, Essex on 19 October 1981. He started as a junior with Barking Colts, and represented Barking Districts. As a young boy, Downer supported Arsenal. This quick, strong central defender was a regular in O's South East Counties side during 1998/99, making 34 League and cup appearances and scoring 6 goals. He played in 8 games in 1999/2000, also playing in 5 reserve matches. He has shown himself to be a good defender with an impressive passing technique, and he should have an excellent future ahead of him. He made his first-team debut in an Auto Windscreen Trophy first round cup tie at Peterborough United on 8 December 1998. Downer came on as a substitute for Steve Watts in the eighty-ninth minute of the final League match of the season against Barnet on 8 May 1999. He was voted the Youth Player of the Year for 1998/99, and made his full League debut at the start of the 1999/2000 season at Carlisle United on 7 August 1999. He appeared regularly that season, having signed a professional contract on 1 October 1999, which was extended in October 2000 by a further two years as a reward for his obvious potential. Being so highly regarded, it is thought that Downer may become O's first million-pound player. He went to Newcastle United on

26 February 2001 for them to see how he performs within a Premiership coaching environment. Downer signed a new three-year extension to his contract for O's in March 2001. Downer appeared in the play-off final in May 2001 (a 4-2 defeat by Blackpool) at the Millennium Stadium in Cardiff, and looked set for a regular place in 2001/02, but in October 2001, news came that he would unfortunately miss the remainder of the season due to tendonitis in his left knee.

SEASON	LEAGUE		FA CUP		L. CUP	
	Apps	Gls	Apps	Gls	Apps	Gls
1998/99	0(1)	0	0	0	0	0
1999/2000	24	0	1	0	1(1)	0
2000/01*	23(11)	0	2(1)	0	1(1)	0
2001/02	11(1)	0	0	0	1	0
TOTAL	58(13)	0	3(1)	0	3(2)	0

TOTAL APPS	64(16)	
TOTAL GOALS	0	

* Downer's League record includes 3 play-off appearances in 2000/01.

** Simon Downer also appeared in 2 Auto Windscreens Shield matches.

Derrick Graham DOWNING, 1972-75

Derrick Downing was a joy to watch. He was a hard, crisp tackler with excellent shooting power, who never stopped chasing and running throughout the ninety minutes. He started as a winger, but was converted to an attacking left wing-back by O's boss George Petchey. Born in Doncaster on 3 November 1945, he started his career with Doncaster Rovers reserve side, but moved to Frickley Colliery after just nine weeks. Middlesbrough offered £1,000 for his services in February 1965, when he was only nineteen years old, and he spent 7 years

Derrick Downing

at Ayresome Park, making 171(11) League appearances for them and scoring 39 goals. He became an 'Oriental' in May 1972 for £25,000. He played many splendid matches, and it was a sad day when he left the club to join York City in July 1975 on a free transfer. He stayed at Bootham Crescent for a single season, making 44(3) League appearances and scoring twice. In July 1977 he signed for Hartlepool United, making a further 40 League appearances and scoring 4 goals. In 1977 he dropped out of the League to play for Scarborough and then Mexborough. Later he was player-manager of Hatfield Main, and in 1990 he became manager of Sutton Coldfield Town in the Doncaster Premier League.

SEASON	LEAGUE		FA CUP		L. CUP	
	Apps	Gls	Apps	Gls	Apps	Gls
1972/73	38	6	1	0	2	2
1973/74	35(2)	3	1(2)	0	4	0

1974/75	27(2)	3	2	0	2	0
TOTAL	100(4)	12	4(2)	0	8	2

TOTAL APPS	112(6)
TOTAL GOALS	14

John George DRYDEN, 1948-50

Jackie Dryden, as he was known, was born in Sunderland on 16 September 1919, and played his early football for the Washington Chemical works side. The outside right joined Charlton Athletic in March 1946 from Bexleyheath FC. He couldn't get into their first team and joined Hylton Colliery. During May 1947 he moved to Swindon Town, playing 21 League matches and scoring 3 goals – one of which was against O's in their 3-0 win at Brisbane Road in December 1947. In June 1948 he joined O's in an exchange deal that took O's winger John Baynham to Swindon Town. The thrusting winger had a good first season at the club, but failed to gain a regular place in his second term and moved into non-League football with Tonbridge in 1950.

SEASON	LEAGUE		FA CUP		TOTAL	
	Apps	Gls	Apps	Gls	Apps	Gls
1948/49	30	8	2	0	32	8
1949/50	10	2	1	0	11	2
TOTAL	40	10	3	0	43	10

William DRYDEN, 1912-13

Born in Amble, Northumberland, Billy Dryden started playing his career by playing for a number of non-League sides, before joining O's in November 1912. In August 1906 he played for Broomhill FC, he joined Blyth Spartans the following year, and then moved on to Ashington of the Northern Alliance League in May 1908. He joined O's from Choppington FC in November 1912, and the centre forward performed well for O's, scoring on League debut at Fulham and twice at Barnsley during December 1912. However, he couldn't keep his place in the side, so he moved to Southern League outfit Watford for £25, making 20 appearances and scoring 8 goals. During January 1914, he was transferred to Portsmouth for £100, where he scored a total of 6 goals from 13 matches.

SEASON	LEAGUE		FA CUP		TOTAL	
	Apps	Gls	Apps	Gls	Apps	Gls
1912/13	13	6	1	0	14	6
TOTAL	13	6	1	0	14	6

Samuel DUDLEY, 1930-32

Sam Dudley was appropriately born in Dudley Port, Tipton, Staffordshire on 26 November 1907. A useful-looking left half, he joined O's from Coleraine in Ireland during July 1930, having previously been on the books of Preston North End (as an amateur) and Bournemouth (for whom he made just 2 League appearances). He scored on his O's debut in a 1-0 win at Luton Town in March 1931 – his only senior goal – and played just a handful of matches, before joining Chelsea in June 1932, where he appeared just once in the League. In 1934 he moved to Exeter City, playing in 8 League games and scoring once. His brother, Jim, played for West Bromwich Albion. Sam Dudley died in Dudley on 14 January 1985.

SEASON	LEAGUE		FA CUP		TOTAL	
	Apps	Gls	Apps	Gls	Apps	Gls
1930/31	8	1	0	0	8	1
1931/32	4	0	0	0	4	0
TOTAL	12	1	0	0	12	1

John 'Jack' Murison DUFFUS, 1922-23

John Duffus (younger brother of another 'Oriental', Robert) was born in Aberdeen on 9 May 1901. The 5ft 10in centre forward, was also very capable at playing in the centre of defence, possessing good ball control and a fiery nature. He did the rounds in Scottish football, starting with Aberdeen Richmond FC, and moving on via Dumbarton and Dundee. He moved south of the Border in 1920 to Scunthorpe & Lindsey United, where he played 5 Midlands League matches alongside his brother and 15 matches in total, scoring 9 goals in 1920/21. In 1921 he moved to Wales and played for Llanelli and then Caerau FC, before becoming an 'Oriental' in October 1922. He was generally a reserve, but he played once alongside his brother against Bury at Millfields Road on 9 December 1922, a 0-2 defeat. Also in the side that day were brothers Jack and Samuel Tonner. Duffus was troubled by injury throughout the season, and joined Tottenham Hotspur on 9 May 1923, but never featured in their first team. A £75 move to Norwich City took place on 27 May 1924, and this move was more agreeable to him. In three seasons with the Canaries, he made 79 senior appearances at centre half, scoring 4 goals. He signed for Stockport County in July 1927, playing in just 6 League matches and scoring 4 goals. During August 1928 he joined Hyde United, and a year later moved to Hurst FC. On leaving football he moved to Stockport, Cheshire in 1928, where he worked as a churchwarden in Bramhall. He also ran a market garden nursery business until his retirement in 1966. He died in Stockport on 18 September 1975.

SEASON	LEAGUE		FA CUP		TOTAL	
	Apps	Gls	Apps	Gls	Apps	Gls
1922/23	6	0	0	0	6	0
TOTAL	6	0	0	0	6	0

Robert Morrice Duncan DUFFUS, 1922-23

The elder brother of John, Bob Duffus was born in Aberdeen on 28 February 1891. The defender played for Aberdeen, Dundee and Dumbarton, and then with his brother at Scunthorpe in 1920/21. Next he joined Millwall in May 1921 for £200, making 6 senior appearances for the Lions. He joined O's on 9 September 1922, but could never replace regular centre half John Townrow. After a handful of League appearances, he joined Northern League side Accrington Stanley in July 1923, making 31 senior appearances. The following year he was appointed player-manager of Welsh side Bangor City. Bob Duffus died whilst watching an Aberdeen match on 19 March 1948, aged fifty-eight.

SEASON	LEAGUE		FA CUP		TOTAL	
	Apps	Gls	Apps	Gls	Apps	Gls
1922/23	5	0	0	0	5	0
TOTAL	5	0	0	0	5	0

Bernard DUFFY, 1927-29

Born in Uddingston, near Glasgow on 7 July 1900, Bernard Duffy started with Glasgow side Bellshire Athletic, before moving to Chelsea in June 1923. He made just a single League appearance during each of his three seasons at Stamford Bridge. The wing-half joined O's in March 1927, proving to be a really tough character who never shirked a tackle. In fact, his biting tackle was probably his main asset. His forceful play was a big factor in O's escaping relegation in 1926/27 and

1927/28, but when O's were finally relegated to the Third Division (South) in 1928/29, he moved on to Shelbourne FC in Dublin during June 1929. Duffy was a bustling player with a hard tackle, and who would have performed very well in recent years when individual ball skills seemed to become of secondary importance.

SEASON	LEAGUE		FA CUP		TOTAL	
	Apps	Gls	Apps	Gls	Apps	Gls
1926/27	12	0	0	0	12	0
1927/28	28	1	0	0	28	1
1928/29	30	0	4	0	34	0
TOTAL	70	1	4	0	74	1

David Gerald Ivor DUNMORE, 1961-65

Big centre forward Dave Dunmore was born in Whitehaven, Cumberland on 8 February 1934. He played for York Boys and Cliftonville Minors. During May 1952 he joined York City, scoring 25 goals from 48 senior starts, before signing for First

Dave Dunmore

Division Tottenham Hotspur in February 1954 for £10,500. During six seasons at White Hart Lane, he made 97 senior appearances and scored 34 goals. He moved to West Ham during March 1960, in a deal that took Johnny Smith to Spurs. During his two-year stay at Upton Park, he acquitted himself very well and scored 18 goals from 39 games. He became an 'Oriental' in March 1960, in an exchange deal that took young Alan Sealey to the Hammers, and it was Dunmore who eventually replaced the legendary Tommy Johnston the following season. The 5ft 11in striker made a dramatic impact at Brisbane Road, and it was his 22 League goals that helped O's to promotion to the First Division in 1961/62 with some glorious goals, none better that his forty-yard screamer against Liverpool at Anfield in a 3-3 draw. Dunmore was playing so well, that he was even mentioned as a possible England candidate. In June 1965, the thirty-one-year-old Dunmore was given a free transfer by new O's manager Dave Sexton, and returned to York City to score 13 goals from 61(2) League appearances. He moved into non-League football with Worcester City in May 1967, and ended his playing career with a team called Bridlington Trinity. At his best, Dave Dunmore was a top-class forward, who ranks alongside such former O's greats as Richard McFadden, Tommy Johnston and Peter Kitchen, and he is one of only nine players to bag 20 or more League goals in a season for O's. During a career that spanned some thirteen years, he made 369 League appearances and scored 132 goals. During the late 1990s Dunmore was still living in his native York and working as a sheet metal worker.

SEASON	LEAGUE		FA CUP		L. CUP	
	Apps	Gls	Apps	Gls	Apps	Gls
1960/61	11	3	0	0	0	0
1961/62	39	22	4	0	2	0
1962/63	37	11	4	1	5	2
1963/64	28	9	3	0	0	0
1964/65	32	9	1	1	2	0
TOTAL	147	54	12	2	9	2

TOTAL APPS	168
TOTAL GOALS	58

* Dave Dunmore also scored a number of goals in friendly matches including 3 goals against Wormatia Worms FC of Germany in 1960/61 (O's won 5-1); 2 goals against ADO of Hague, Holland in 1962/63 (a 2-1 win); and a goal against Scottish side Morton in 1962/63 (a 4-0 win).

Herbert Bertram DUNN, 1924-26

Bertie Dunn was born in Carshalton, Surrey on 15 August 1895, although some sources state incorrectly that Dunn was born in Montrose, Scotland. He started playing for his local side – Carshalton Athletic – in 1911. Having enlisted with the Kings' Royal Rifles in August 1914, he spent a number of years as a gym instructor whilst also playing for Carshalton. The right-winger joined Southern League outfit Charlton Athletic in 1919, and was in the side for their first ever professional fixture (against Norwich City on 28 August 1920) and was again present for their first ever League match (against Exeter City during August 1921). Dunn made 23 Southern League and 13 League and cup appearances, before joining Scottish side Alloa Athletic in May 1922. He returned south to become an 'Oriental' during May 1924, but was never able to gain a regular first-team place.

SEASON	LEAGUE		FA CUP		TOTAL	
	Apps	Gls	Apps	Gls	Apps	Gls
1924/25	3	0	0	0	3	0
1925/26	1	0	0	0	1	0
TOTAL	4	0	0	0	4	0

Thomas Joseph DUNNE, 1964-65

Tommy Dunne was a clever inside forward. Born in Glasgow on 22 June 1946, he joined O's from Scottish junior side St Anthony's in June 1964, having previously been a youth player on Celtic's books. His only League appearance came against Cardiff City on 14 November 1964. He showed plenty of constructive, scheming ability in the reserve side, but was released in May 1965 and moved back to Scotland to join Albion Rovers.

SEASON	LEAGUE		FA CUP		L. CUP	
	Apps	Gls	Apps	Gls	Apps	Gls
1964/65	1	0	0	0	0	0
TOTAL	1	0	0	0	0	0

TOTAL APPS	1
TOTAL GOALS	0

John Barry DYSON, 1968-73

Barry Dyson, was a quick, thrusting forward, who forced his way to the top with some sensational scoring feats with Tranmere Rovers between 1962 and 1966. Few clubs can have discovered a more valuable nugget of gold in the free transfer dross. The goals flowed with abundance whilst with the Rovers, and he twice hit 30 senior goals in a season. The blond bombshell (as he was known) was born on 6 September 1942 in Oldham, Lancashire. He started his career as a junior with Bury, but it was with Tranmere that he notched 106 goals from 183 senior appearances. He was sold to Crystal Palace for £15,000 in September 1966

SEASON	LEAGUE		FA CUP		L. CUP	
	Apps	Gls	Apps	Gls	Apps	Gls
1968/69	25	10	0	0	0	0
1969/70	46	6	2	0	2	0
1970/71	41	3	3	2	1	0
1971/72	34(3)	9	4	1	2	0
1972/73	8(3)	0	0	0	1	0
TOTAL	154(6)	28	9	3	6	0

TOTAL APPS   169(6)

TOTAL GOALS   31

E

Barry Dyson

(scoring a hat-trick in only his second game) and made 33(1) League appearances with 9 goals. He moved to Watford for £9,000 in January 1968 (scoring twice on debut), and went on to net 19 goals from 38 League appearances. He joined O's for £8,000 in December 1968, and was converted to midfield by O's boss Jimmy Bloomfield, where he enjoyed a wonderful run of 112 consecutive League matches. He also captained the side when Terry Mancini was sidelined through injury during the promotion campaign of 1969/70. He was released in July 1973, joining Colchester United where he made 41(1) League appearances and scored 6 goals. In 1975 he joined Chelmsford City, and in 1984 he became manager of Borehamwood FC. Upon retirement from football, he ran a haulage business in Colchester until he died on 26 February 1995, aged fifty-three, a month after suffering a heart attack.

Douglas EADIE, 1967 (loan)

Doug Eadie came to O's on loan from West Ham United in September 1967 after an injury crisis at the club, but returned to Upton Park before his loan period expired. He made his O's debut in a 4-2 defeat at Reading in September 1967. The flying winger was born in Edinburgh on 22 September 1946. His first-team opportunities with the Hammers were limited to just 2 League appearances between 1966 and 1968. After a short spell with Bournemouth, he returned to his native Scotland to play with Greenock Morton.

SEASON	LEAGUE		FA CUP		L. CUP	
	Apps	Gls	Apps	Gls	Apps	Gls
1967/68	2	0	0	0	0	0
TOTAL	2	0	0	0	0	0

TOTAL APPS   2

TOTAL GOALS   0

Alan James EAGLES, 1957-61

Big, burly player Alan Eagles was born in Edgware, London on 6 September 1933.

He joined O's from Athenian League club Carshalton Athletic in May 1957 on amateur forms, before turning professional in September of that year. He was hailed as a second Stan Charlton, and his displays at right-back suggested he might live up to that reputation. He had a grand League debut against Barnsley in October 1957, and became a regular choice until being displaced by George Wright in November 1958. During the latter part of his stay, he put on a considerable amount of weight and the fans nicknamed him the tank, as he was known for his crunching tackles and fearless play. But he was never a dirty player, just powerful and unflinching. He may not have fulfilled his early promise, but he was still a useful squad player. His best display was certainly in a 1-0 win against Liverpool in February 1958, when he didn't put a foot wrong. Eagles moved to Colchester United in January 1961 for £3,000, making 16 League appearances and scoring once. In August 1961 he joined Queens Park Rangers, but before he could make his senior debut, he moved to Aldershot in November 1961 and made 14 League appearances, scoring once. After leaving the Shots, he played for several non-League clubs, including Yiewsley, Hillingdon, Deal Town, Gravesend & Northfleet and Pembroke Borough in Wales. Upon giving up football, he was appointed harbour superintendent at Tenby, Wales – a job he performed for twenty-five years until his retirement in 1993. He had success with his local pub side, New Hedges in Tenby and also officiated in the administration of the Pembrokeshire Football Association, as well as running a hotel in Saundersfoot for a number of years. Eagles died in South Pembroke, Wales on 6 November 1995.

SEASON	LEAGUE		FA CUP		L. CUP	
	Apps	Gls	Apps	Gls	Apps	Gls
1957/58	29	0	2	0	-	-
1958/59	14	0	0	0	-	-
1959/60	17	0	1	0	-	-
1960/61*	15	0	0	0	2	0
TOTAL	75	0	3	0	2	0

TOTAL APPS	80
TOTAL GOALS	0

* The League Cup competition began in the 1960/61 season.

Stanley James William EARL, 1953-57

Born in Alton, Hampshire on 9 July 1929, Stan Earl started his career with local side Alton Town. In November 1949 he joined Portsmouth, making 8 appearances between 1950 and 1952. He joined O's in July 1953 from Pompey, and was a solidly-built left-back, who seldom used his weight in his play. Although excellent with his left foot, he didn't really get a reg-

Stan Earl

ular place until Stan Charlton moved to Arsenal in October 1955. Thought to be a little slow for Second Division football in 1956/57, after Stan Willemse was signed during the summer, he never got a look-in. He was transferred (along with Jimmy Lee) to Third Division (South) side Swindon Town in November 1956, where he made 23 League appearances. He joined Yeovil Town in January 1958. In 2001, he resided in Brympton, Yeovil.

SEASON	LEAGUE		FA CUP		TOTAL	
	Apps	Gls	Apps	Gls	Apps	Gls
1953/54	7	0	0	0	7	0
1954/55	3	0	0	0	3	0
1955/56	23	0	4	0	27	0
1956/57	0	0	0	0	0	0
TOTAL	33	0	4	0	37	0

Stan Earle

Stanley George James EARLE, 1932-33

Inside forward Stan Earle joined O's in May 1932 from West Ham United, at the age of thirty-five. This was after he had spent eight wonderful years at Upton Park, making 273 senior appearances and scoring 58 goals. Born in Stratford, London on 6 September 1897, This superbly creative 6ft 2in inside right started out with Clapton FC. There he won a FA Amateur Cup winner's medal in 1922 and he also gained 12 England amateur international caps. He joined Arsenal as an amateur in March 1922, scoring 3 goals from just 4 League appearances. He joined the Hammers in August 1924, turning professional a year later. He was not a regular in O's side, but performed with considerable skill when called upon. He moved to Walthamstow Avenue as coach in 1932, and later managed Leyton FC. Earle died in Brightlingsea on 26 September 1971, after a long illness.

SEASON	LEAGUE		FA CUP		TOTAL	
	Apps	Gls	Apps	Gls	Apps	Gls
1932/33	15	1	1	0	16	1
TOTAL	15	1	1	0	16	1

George Frederick EASTMAN, 1928-30

Born in Leyton, London on 7 April 1903, Eastman started his career with West Ham United. Remarkably, the centre half's only 2 League outings for the Hammers occurred in 2 consecutive seasons, and both took place against an Everton side starring the legendary Dixie Dean. After failing a trial with Norwich City, he joined O's from Chatham Town in 1928. He was not a regular in the side, but did play in both FA Cup ties against Aston Villa that season. In August 1931 he moved to France to play for FC Sachoux. Eastman was also a good cricketer, playing 48 matches as wicketkeeper for Essex CCC between 1926 and 1929. Eastman died in Eastbourne, Sussex in March 1991.

SEASON	LEAGUE		FA CUP		TOTAL	
	Apps	Gls	Apps	Gls	Apps	Gls
1928/29	9	0	4	0	13	0
1929/30	4	0	1	1	5	1
TOTAL	13	0	5	1	18	1

William EDLEY, 1907-08

Lancashire-born Billy Edley, a reserve wing-half with Stockport County, came to London to join O's in August 1907. He was mainly a reserve-team player and featured just once for the first team. This was in an FA Cup match against Southern League side Southend on 2 November 1907, when both Liddell and Thacker were injured. Edley left the club shortly after his one day of fame to return home.

SEASON	LEAGUE		FA CUP		TOTAL	
	Apps	Gls	Apps	Gls	Apps	Gls
1907/08	0	0	1	0	1	0
TOTAL	0	0	1	0	1	0

Alfred John EDMONDS, 1929-32

Born in Brighton, Sussex on 16 October 1902, Alf Edmonds came to O's in August 1929 from Brighton & Hove Albion. Educated at St Luke's Terrace School in Brighton, he gained fame as one of the best young players in Sussex whilst playing for his local side Vernon Athletic, and for Allen West FC in the Sussex County League. He turned out for Brighton reserves in 1922, but only turned professional in 1925, making 14 League appearances during his four-year stay with the club. Whilst with O's he was very versatile, and played in a number of different positions, including at centre forward, at inside right, and at right, left and centre half. He was a great trier, and was O's top scorer in 1929/30. After three excellent seasons,

he left to join Bury in June 1932, and two years later moved to Mansfield Town. He finished his playing career with Manchester North End in the Manchester League. Edmonds retired in 1935 to become a publican in Bury. He died in that town during March 1942, aged just thirty-nine.

SEASON	LEAGUE		FA CUP		TOTAL	
	Apps	Gls	Apps	Gls	Apps	Gls
1929/30	28	14	4	0	32	14
1930/31	28	2	0	0	28	2
1931/32	33	2	0	0	33	2
TOTAL	89	18	4	0	93	18

Edmund Clifford EDWARDS, 1935-36

Born in Thurcroft, Yorkshire in 1912, Edmund Edwards – a 6ft tall inside forward – was a player who spent much of his career on trial with a number of clubs. He started with Thurcroft Main FC, and then, between 1931 and 1934, had trials with Rotherham United, Sheffied United and Bury. He joined O's during August 1935, after his short stay with Bury. He played for O's in the opening fixture on 31 August 1935, a 3-0 win over Luton Town – his only League appearance. He went to Hull City on trial in May 1936, but moved on to Mossley, and later to Carlisle United in August 1938, where he played in 2 League games. Edwards died in Sheffield during August 1991.

SEASON	LEAGUE		FA CUP		TOTAL	
	Apps	Gls	Apps	Gls	Apps	Gls
1935/36	1	0	0	0	1	0
TOTAL	1	0	0	0	1	0

* Edmund Edwards also appeared in a Third Division Cup match in 1935/36 against Bournemouth on 26 September 1935.

Evan Jenkins EDWARDS, 1929-32

Born in Bedlinog, near Merthyr Tydfil, Wales on 14 December 1896, left-winger Evan Edwards – a Welsh amateur international player – joined O's at the end of a long and successful career in July 1929. He began with Merthyr Town, where he made 57 League appearances and scored 8 times between 1920 and 1923. He then moved on to join Wolverhampton Wanderers, where he made 63 League outings, scored a dozen goals, and won a Third Division Championship medal in just two seasons. In 1925 he joined Swansea Town, playing in just 10 senior matches and scoring twice. The following term he went to Northampton Town, where he played in 11 matches and scored twice. The next year he moved to Halifax Town, but without any first-team outings to his name, he left to play for Ebbw Vale. In 1928 he returned to the League with Darlington, scoring 3 goals from 25 appearances. The thirty-three-year-old Edwards stayed with O's for almost three years, and yet made only a handful of appearances. During his stay he assisted the club in first-team coaching duties.

SEASON	LEAGUE		FA CUP		TOTAL	
	Apps	Gls	Apps	Gls	Apps	Gls
1929/30	4	0	0	0	4	0
1930/31	0	0	0	0	0	0
1931/32	0	0	0	0	0	0
TOTAL	4	0	0	0	4	0

Stanley Llewellyn EDWARDS, 1953-56

Born in Dawdon on 17 October 1926, Stan Edwards was on the books of Hawdon Colliery FC and Chelsea between 1949 and 1952. The centre forward made no impression at Stamford Bridge, and joined Colchester United in June 1952, making 16 League appearances and scoring 5 goals. O's boss Alec Stock brought him to Brisbane Road in exchange for Tommy Harris in September 1953. He was mainly a reserve player, and played really well for the second-string, scoring a number of goals with some powerful right-foot shooting. His 2 League outings were a result of an injury to Billy Rees – he did quite well and scored on his debut in a 3-3 draw at Shrewsbury Town in October 1953. He was unlucky not to have had a better run in the side, and his luck really turned sour during his time at Brisbane Road when he broke his leg on two occasions whilst playing for the reserves, forcing him to retire from the game. His overall record does not do justice to his ability. Edwards later became a sales representative for a rubber company. He died in Bromley, Kent on 14 January 1989.

SEASON	LEAGUE		FA CUP		TOTAL	
	Apps	Gls	Apps	Gls	Apps	Gls
1953/54	2	1	0	0	2	1
1954/55	0	0	0	0	0	0
1955/56	0	0	0	0	0	0
TOTAL	2	1	0	0	2	1

Robert ELLIOTT, 1905-06

Bobby Elliott was born in Clapton, London. He was an amateur player, who appeared just once for O's – on 7 October 1905 in an FA Cup qualifying round tie at Felstead. His appearance only came about because the first team were on duty the same day in a Second Division home fixture against Barnsley, so a set of reserves (as well as a couple of amateur players) were used for the FA Cup match. He returned to non-League football after being released in May 1906.

SEASON	LEAGUE		FA CUP		TOTAL	
	Apps	Gls	Apps	Gls	Apps	Gls
1905/06	0	0	1	0	1	0
TOTAL	0	0	1	0	1	0

SEASON	LEAGUE		FA CUP		TOTAL	
	Apps	Gls	Apps	Gls	Apps	Gls
1932/33	27	0	0	0	27	0
1933/34	0	0	0	0	0	0
TOTAL	27	0	0	0	27	0

Frederick Charles ELLIS, 1932-33

Born in Kent on 7 November 1900, Fred Ellis started off as a left-winger with his local side Sheppey United. During 1924/25 he had a trial with Aston Villa, but in June 1925 he joined Gillingham and spent six years at the Priestfield Stadium, making 104 League appearances and scoring once. In June 1931 he joined Watford, making 37 senior appearances at wing-half and scoring once. He became an 'Oriental' in July 1932, and played regularly for the first team at full-back throughout that season. He left O's in October 1933 to join Ashford Town, after O's had signed Eddie Ware from Brentford. Ellis died during 1970 on the Isle of Sheppey, the place of his birth.

Fred Ellis

Joseph Patrick ELWOOD, 1958-66

Forward Joe Elwood was overlooked far too often during his seven-year stay at the club. Born in Belfast on 26 October 1939, he was first spotted by O's boss Alec Stock when captaining Ireland against England, in a youth international at Brisbane Road in May 1957. He scored twice that day, but he was overshadowed by a lad named Jimmy Greaves, who notched 4 goals in England's 6-2 victory. Elwood joined O's on 24 April 1958 from Irish League side Glenavon. He bagged all 4 goals against high-flying Bristol City during November 1958, and soon after was chosen to represent an Irish FA XI against the Army at Windsor Park, Belfast. He continued his good form, and after netting a hat-trick against Charlton Athletic in April 1959, he earned himself a Northern Ireland under-23 cap. He netted a few goals against foreign opposition in friendly matches with 2 goals against Maltese side Sliema Wanderers (a 5-0 victory in 1963/64) a goal in the 4-3 win at Montrose in 1959/60, and the opener in a 4-0 win over Greenock Morton in 1962/63. Elwood was O's first ever League playing substitute – Jimmy Scott was the first player ever to sit on the bench during the previous month against Huddersfield Town, but never came onto the field of play – coming on against Preston North End on 4 September 1965. In May 1966 he moved back to Ireland to join Ards. Between 1979 and 1984, Elwood was the PE master at Upton House School in

Joe Elwood

Homerton, and then moved to the Homerton House Secondary School, where he stayed for over five years and is still seen at O's matches and player reunions.

SEASON	LEAGUE		FA CUP		L. CUP	
	Apps	Gls	Apps	Gls	Apps	Gls
1958/59*	28	10	1	0	-	-
1959/60	18	4	0	0	-	-
1960/61	11	2	3	2	0	0
1961/62	10	2	2	1	0	0
1962/63	11	1	2	1	0	0
1963/64	7	1	0	0	0	0
1964/65	11	5	0	0	0	0
1965/66	5(2)	0	0	0	0	0
TOTAL	101(2)	25	8	4	0	0

TOTAL APPS	109(2)
TOTAL GOALS	29

* The League Cup competition began in the 1960/61 season.

Herbert John EMERY, 1928-29, 1931-33

Goalkeeper Bert Emery was born in Bristol on 18 February 1910. He first joined O's as an amateur from amateur side Cardiff Corries in August 1928, but after several reserve appearances he was not retained, and joined Rotherham United in May 1929, where he made 36 League appearances. He rejoined O's in May 1931, as the replacement for the long-serving Arthur Wood, who had decided to move into non-League football after holding down the last line of defence for over ten years. Emery performed well at times, and in one match at Bournemouth & Boscome on Boxing Day 1931, he was clapped off the field after an excellent display had earned O's a 1-0 victory. He shared the jersey with Jack Bruce in 1932/33, and left the club in June 1933 to join Newport County. Emery died in Cheltenham on 13 August 1995, aged eighty-five.

SEASON	LEAGUE		FA CUP		TOTAL	
	Apps	Gls	Apps	Gls	Apps	Gls
1928/29	0	0	0	0	0	0
1931/32	39	0	3	0	42	0
1932/33	23	0	0	0	23	0
TOTAL	62	0	3	0	65	0

John Alwyn EVANS, 1950-54

Stocky John 'Taffy' Evans was one of the smallest full-backs – at 5ft 7in – in the League during his era, yet what he lacked in inches, he made up for in speed and great anticipation. Born in Aberystwyth, Wales on 22 October 1922, after a spell with his local side, he joined Millwall in September 1943 and did well for the Lions, playing 73 times and scoring twice. He joined O's in June 1950, and appeared on the right wing on 3 occasions when O's had injury problems. He featured in

John Evans

O's great FA Cup run of 1951/52, and enjoyed 4 wonderful seasons until illness struck him down in the summer of 1954, forcing him to retire from the game. O's boss Alec Stock signed Jimmy Lee from Chelsea as his replacement. Evans was always a sporting player, who rarely gave away a foul. He died on 24 February 1956 after his long illness, aged just thirty-four.

SEASON	LEAGUE		FA CUP		TOTAL	
	Apps	Gls	Apps	Gls	Apps	Gls
1950/51	44	0	1	0	45	0
1951/52	42	0	9	0	51	0
1952/53	27	0	2	0	29	0
1953/54	36	0	7	0	43	0
TOTAL	149	0	19	0	168	0

Nolan EVANS, 1912-15

Born Ashton-in-Makerfield, near Wigan, left-back Nolan was known as 'Peggy' by his team-mates. He started his career with Bryn Central and then St Helen's Recreation FC, before joining Exeter City in 1910, for whom he made 63 Southern League and 7 FA Cup appearances, scoring twice. He joined O's on 6 May 1912, and proved to be a very capable defender and partner to John Johnston. He starred in the 2-2 draw at Arsenal in the final match of the 1913/14 season, which dented the Gunners' promotion aspirations. He was a regular for three seasons leading up to the First World War. His only goal came in the controversial 3-1 win over Leeds City on 2 March 1914, when the second half was played in poor light with O's fans lighting up newspapers to witness proceedings. Not many fans, and not even the visiting goalkeeper, saw Evans' shot thunder into the net. Leeds boss Herbert Chapman complained to the League, and although the result stood, O's were fined for having such a late mid-week kick-off. Evans was one of ten O's players and officials who received serious wounds during the First World War hostilities, which ended his playing career.

SEASON	LEAGUE		FA CUP		TOTAL	
	Apps	Gls	Apps	Gls	Apps	Gls
1912/13	37	0	1	0	38	0
1913/14	37	1	3	0	40	1
1914/15	37	0	1	0	38	0
TOTAL	111	1	5	0	116	1

Thomas John EVANS, 1924-28, 1930-31

Born in Maerdy, Wales on 7 April 1903, Tom Evans, a 6ft 1in tall, athletic and skilful left-back, joined O's from Maerdy FC in May 1924. He was injured during his first appearance at Southampton in September 1924, and after recovering from a knee injury, he went on loan to Aberdare Athletic where he made 5 League appearances, before returning to O's in December 1925. He played splendidly in O's great FA Cup run of 1925/26, and he went on to become O's third full international player and the first to play for Wales, appearing against Scotland at Ibrox on 30 October 1926. After 2 further Welsh caps (against England and Scotland), he was transferred to Newcastle United in December 1927 for £3,650. A player who suffered with knee injuries throughout his career, he was restricted to just 13 First Division appearances and a single goal for the Magpies, but he did become their first player ever to be capped for Wales. The classy player returned to O's in May 1930 on a free transfer. He stayed for 2 further seasons before joining South Wales side Merthyr Town in July 1932, retiring soon after.

SEASON	LEAGUE		FA CUP		TOTAL	
	Apps	Gls	Apps	Gls	Apps	Gls
1924/25	1	0	0	0	1	0
1925/26	20	1	4	0	24	1
1926/27	21	0	2	0	23	0
1927/28	11	0	0	0	11	0
1930/31	23	0	2	0	25	0
1931/32	3	0	0	0	3	0
TOTAL	79	1	8	0	87	1

Isaac EVENSON, 1905-07

Ike Evenson was born in Manchester during November 1882, and started his career as a centre forward with schools side Gorton & Audenshaw. He joined O's from Leicester Fosse in July 1905. Evenson played with Tonge FC, before joining Glossop North End in 1898. In 1900 he was at Stockport County when they entered the League, and netted 9 goals from 36 League appearances. During 1903 he moved to Leicester Fosse, making 52 senior appearances and

scoring 20 goals. With O's he moved into a more attacking centre-half role, and became the first O's player to bag a hat-trick in the League, against Chesterfield in a 3-3 draw at Millfields Road on 23 September 1905. He had a three-month spell as acting manager, when O's player-manager Billy Holmes was suspended by the League. This was whilst they investigated the Billy Meredith affair of bribery and match-fixing by a large number of Manchester City players. The O's directors recognised his effort by presenting him with a framed resolution inscribed on vellum. He enjoyed a regular place in the side until his transfer to West Brom on 29 April 1907 for £225. He made just 8 League appearances and scored once for Albion, before joining Plymouth Argyle in July 1908, for whom he made 47 appearances and scored twice. He moved to Nottingham Forest in 1909. Evenson was an unselfish player, who gave the club good service. He died in Manchester in 1954.

SEASON	LEAGUE		FA CUP		TOTAL	
	Apps	Gls	Apps	Gls	Apps	Gls
1905/06	30	5	4	2	34	7
1906/07*	33	3	-	-	33	3
TOTAL	63	8	4	2	67	10

* Clapton Orient did not enter the FA Cup in 1906/07.

Michael Richard EVERITT, 1976

Mike Everitt was born in Mile End, London on 21 March 1958. The inside forward was an apprentice with Crystal Palace from March 1975. He joined O's in February 1976, and showed enough promise to make a substitute appearance the same month, replacing Tony Grealish in the 2-0 win over Fulham.

Unfortunately, he was injured in a reserve match and did not make the expected progress. He left in May 1977 and joined Hornchurch FC. A year later he returned to O's on a non-contract basis, but only stayed for a very brief period.

SEASON	LEAGUE		FA CUP		L. CUP	
	Apps	Gls	Apps	Gls	Apps	Gls
1975/76	0(1)	0	0	0	0	0
TOTAL	0(1)	0	0	0	0	0

TOTAL APPS	0(1)
TOTAL GOALS	0

Ken Facey

Kenneth William FACEY, 1952-61

Ken Facey is the only O's player to appear in the top ten of both the O's leading goalscoring and all-time appearances charts. It is quite remarkable that he is second on the goalscoring charts, considering he played the latter part of his career at wing-half. Another record held by Facey is that he is O's penalty king, with 23 converted spot-kicks and only 4 misses. Born in Millfields Road, Clapton – a stone's throw from O's second ground – on 12 October 1927, as a sixteen-year-old, he played for Leyton Amateurs and also had spells with Walthamstow Avenue, St Albans and Tottenham Hotspur. He spent some time on O's books, but returned to Leyton FC to feature in their 1952 FA Amateur Cup final appearance against Walthamstow Avenue. Facey re-joined O's on 12 May 1952, feeling that there would be a far greater opportunity for him at a smaller club than with one of the bigger clubs.

Facey scored on his League debut in December 1952 in a 1-1 draw against Reading. His most productive season was 1954/55, when he netted 22 League goals – one of only nine O's players to score more than 20 in a season. He featured in O's Third Division (South) Championship-winning side of 1955/56, and skippered the team for almost three seasons. Ken Facey retired from football in 1963, and went on to work for the Post Office until his retirement in 1992.

SEASON	LEAGUE		FA CUP		L. CUP	
	Apps	Gls	Apps	Gls	Apps	Gls
1952/53	22	8	1	0	-	-
1953/54	43	12	7	2	-	-
1954/55	44	22	2	1	-	-
1955/56	26	12	3	2	-	-
1956/57	40	2	1	0	-	-
1957/58	30	2	1	0	-	-
1958/59	37	4	1	0	-	-
1959/60	38	9	1	0	-	-

1960/61*	21	3	2	0	3	0
TOTAL	301	74	19	5	3	0

TOTAL APPS	323
TOTAL GOALS	79

* The League Cup competition started in the 1960/61 season.

Barrie Edward FAIRBROTHER, 1968-75
Barrie Fairbrother proved to be one of the most popular players of the modern era. A real bundle of energy, he was a very speedy and a dangerous player, particularly in and around the penalty area. Born in Hackney, London on 30 December 1950, he joined O's in 1967, after a short spell as a youth player with Tottenham Hotspur. He scored over 150 youth and reserve-team goals during his time with O's. He scored on his League debut with a lovely half-volley against Mansfield Town during August 1969, and he went on to play a major part in O's champi-

Fairbrother celebrates promotion in April 1970

onship side of 1969/70. No older O's fan will ever forget his last-gasp winner over Chelsea in the FA Cup fifth round match in February 1972. He was voted the first ever O's Player of the Year in 1974, but that meant little to him after O's had failed by a single point to gain a place in the First Division, and only his tears in the dressing room after the dramatic match against Aston Villa will be remembered. He lost heart after that disappointment, and with the introduction of young Laurie Cunningham, he joined Millwall in June 1975. His stay at the Den was hampered by a groin injury that required two operations, and he made just 12(3) League appearances for the club. He did, however, score a goal against the O's in a dramatic League Cup replay at Highbury in October 1975, which the Lions won 3-0. During his time in the League, he was only booked once, when Johnson of West Brom was weaving in

Barrie Fairbrother

and out of tackles and seemed to trip over his own feet. Fairbrother moved to Australia in 1976 and played a few matches for Queensland. He still wears his Third Division Championship medal as a reminder of the wonderful first season he had as a League player.

SEASON	LEAGUE		FA CUP		L. CUP	
	Apps	Gls	Apps	Gls	Apps	Gls
1969/70	35(4)	13	2	0	0	0
1970/71	31(4)	2	3	1	0(1)	0
1971/72	17(3)	0	4	2	0	0
1972/73	24(3)	11	0	0	1	0
1973/74	41	14	4	3	4	2
1974/75	23(3)	1	2	1	2	0
TOTAL	171(17)	41	15	7	7(1)	2

TOTAL APPS	193(18)
TOTAL GOALS	50

* Barrie Fairbrother also appeared in 3 Texaco Cup matches in 1974/75, scoring once.

Alexander FARLEY, 1945-48

Alex Farley was born in Finchley, London on 11 May 1925, and the left-back started his career with Finchley FC. He joined O's from Cromwell Athletic in November 1945, and proved to be a very useful defender, and if not for the form of Ledger Ritson, he would surely have made more first-team appearances. Farley appeared in both FA Cup ties in 1945/46 against Newport Isle of Wight, who knocked O's out of the competition. After two seasons at Brisbane Road, he joined Bournemouth in June 1948, but failed to break into their first team. He was ever-present in their reserve side until the thirteenth match, which proved to be 'unlucky' for him. He received a nasty injury in a reserve match at Highbury on 2 October 1948, and

although he tried to resume playing after half-time, he collapsed on the pitch and was never to play football again.

SEASON	LEAGUE		FA CUP		TOTAL	
	Apps	Gls	Apps	Gls	Apps	Gls
1945/46*	-	-	2	0	2	0
1946/47	11	0	1	0	12	0
1947/48	4	0	0	0	4	0
TOTAL	15	0	3	0	18	0

* There was no League competition in 1945/46.

Francis FARRELL, 1937-39

Born in Wishaw, Lanarkshire, Scotland in 1916, Frank Farrell, as he was known (not to be confused with Vince Farrell, who left O's in 1937), was a Scottish amateur international who moved down south to play for O's, after playing for Hibernian reserves during August 1937. The inside forward stayed at Brisbane Road for two seasons, playing in the reserves before returning home to his native Scotland.

SEASON	LEAGUE		FA CUP		TOTAL	
	Apps	Gls	Apps	Gls	Apps	Gls
1937/38	0	0	0	0	0	0
1938/39	2	0	0	0	2	0
TOTAL	2	0	0	0	2	0

Vincent FARRELL, 1934-37

Born in Preston on 11 September 1908, Vince Farrell, the Lancashire schoolboy player, started with local side Dick Kerrs, before joining Preston North End in 1930 and scoring 5 goals from 16 League appearances. The 5ft 10in player moved to O's in June 1934 to replace Tommy Mills, and performed credibly at inside forward for two seasons. In his final season, he was converted to a scheming wing-half. He netted a hat-trick against Brighton & Hove Albion at Lea Bridge

Road in April 1936. He moved to Exeter City in May 1937, scoring twice on his debut, and netted 4 goals from 6 League appearances. He later played for the Leyland Motors works side. Farrell died in Preston on 25 April 1987, aged seventy-eight.

SEASON	LEAGUE		FA CUP		TOTAL	
	Apps	Gls	Apps	Gls	Apps	Gls
1934/35	28	8	0	0	28	8
1935/36	29	9	3	0	32	9
1936/37	22	4	0	0	22	4
TOTAL	79	21	3	0	82	21

* Vince Farrell also appeared in a Third Division Cup match in 1936/37.

Justinus Soni FASHANU, 1990 (trial)

Justin Fashanu was a player of pedigree with 11 England under-21 caps and an England 'B' cap. He came to O's in March 1990, after short spells with Manchester City and West Ham United in the latter part of 1989, and coaching both in the USA and Canada. Sadly, he committed suicide in 1998. Born in Hackney, London on 19 February 1961, the former Barnado's boy was brought up with his younger brother, John, by their adopted white parents in rustic Attleborough, Norfolk. He began his career as an apprentice in December 1978 with Norwich City, and he finished as their top scorer with 11 goals in 1979/80. The following season he topped the scoring again, with 19 goals, and there was a stunning long-range effort against Liverpool, which was replayed on television many times as a goal of the season. After 84(6) League appearances for the Canaries, which yielded 35 goals, he moved to Nottingham Forest in August 1981 for £1 million, but he could only manage

Justin Fashanu

3 goals from 31(1) starts, before moving to Southampton on loan and netting 3 goals from 9 starts. Fashanu moved on to Notts County in December 1982 for £150,000, and he scored 20 goals from 63(1) matches, before injury put paid to his career at Meadow Lane. He made a comeback with Brighton & Hove Albion in 1985/86, but after 16 matches and 2 goals he crossed the Atlantic. After his short stay at Brisbane Road, he went back to Canada for a while, but was appointed player-manager with Torquay United in December 1991 and made a total of 41 appearances (scoring 15 goals), before leaving in 1993 for first Leatherhead, and then Scottish side Airdrie during February 1993, where he played 16 matches and scored 5 goals. In 1994 he went to Hearts, where he made 11 appearances and scored once, after which he left and returned to the USA to take up a coaching position with Maryland Mania FC. He

F

made a total of 229(12) League career appearances and scored 90 goals. Fashanu's suicide in a grubby garage in Shoreditch, London on 2 May 1998 was a tragic end to a man who had succeeded in life against tremendous odds. The thirty-seven-year-old thought he would be facing gay sex allegations in the USA but, in fact, no warrant of arrest has ever been issued against him.

SEASON	LEAGUE		FA CUP		L. CUP	
	Apps	Gls	Apps	Gls	Apps	Gls
1989/90	3(2)	0	0	0	0	0
TOTAL	3(2)	0	0	0	0	0

TOTAL APPS	3(2)
TOTAL GOALS	0

Ron Fearon

Ronald FEARON, 1991-92, 1995-96

Fearless goalkeeper Ron Fearon was much-travelled, having played for fifteen different clubs over a nineteen-year career, before joining O's in August 1995. Having previously been at O's in January 1992 (on loan from Ipswich Town, as cover for Chris Turner and Paul Newell), he returned to Portman Road without making a first-team appearance. Born in Romford, Essex on 19 November 1960, Fearon started his walkabout football career in 1977 as an apprentice at Queens Park Rangers. In 1979, he moved to Reading, where he spent four years making 61 League appearances – his longest spell with any single club. The goalkeeper spent the next decade flying around the world – he took his trade to America playing for San Diego Sockers, and he was also player-coach of semi-professional outfit Newport Beach FC. Upon his return to England, he spent a couple of seasons with Sutton United, kept goal for Ipswich Town in the First Division between 1987 and 1989 (making a total of 28 League appearances), and in between he made 7 appearances loan appearances for Brighton in September 1988. It was then back to the States to the Wichita Wings in Kansas, before spells at Walsall, FC Berlin (Germany), Hearts (Scotland), Oldham Athletic, then Walsall again, and finally back to Wichita Wings. In 1985, Fearon had plans to play in the Continental Indoor League in the States, but he missed the registration cut-off date, so he came to East London, having known O's coach Tommy Cunningham. He made his O's debut in the Auto Windscreen Shield match against Shrewsbury Town on 7 November 1995, and he was the star of the show in O's 3-1 League win over Cambridge United eleven days later. At the conclusion of the season, he moved to Ashford Town, and then on to Barkingside and Dover Athletic (where he played 15 matches). At the age of thirty-eight, he played a further dozen matches in 1997/98 for Dover, in amongst which came yet another loan spell, this time with Gravesend & Northfleet! In December 1998, he was on the books of Barnet and in August 1999, he joined Hendon. Nowadays, he is a teacher at Davenaut School.

SEASON	LEAGUE		FA CUP		L. CUP	
	Apps	Gls	Apps	Gls	Apps	Gls
1991/92	0	0	0	0	0	0
1995/96	18	0	1	0	0	0
TOTAL	18	0	1	0	0	0

TOTAL APPS 19

TOTAL GOALS 0

* Ron Fearon also appeared in an Auto Windscreens Shield match.

Gregory Paul FEE, 1990-91 (loan)

Greg Fee was born in Halifax on 24 June 1964. The defender joined O's on a month's loan from Sheffield Wednesday in March 1991. Fee started his career with Bradford City as a youth trainee in May 1983, making 6(1) appearances. He moved to Sheffield Wednesday in August 1987 (making 16(10) League appearances), but then gave up football to attend university, and played part-time with Boston United. Thereafter, he had loan spells with Preston North End, Northampton Town, Mansfield Town and O's During his loan spell in East London, Fee was unfortunate to score an own goal at Shrewsbury Town on 19 March 1991. He played in 5 matches – all defeats. He later joined Mansfield Town for £20,000 in March 1991, where he played 50(4) matches and scored 7 goals. In December 1992, he went on loan to Chesterfield and made 10 appearances.

He joined Telford United in the Football Conference in July 1998, having signed from Boston United where he had made 244 appearances and scored 38 goals. He moved to Telford United and later had spells with Emley and Harrogate Town. Later Fee became player-manager of Gainsborough Trinity in July 2000, but retired three months later. On his retirement from the game, he worked for BP and also for the FA.

SEASON	LEAGUE		FA CUP		L. CUP	
	Apps	Gls	Apps	Gls	Apps	Gls
1990/91	4(1)	0	0	0	0	0
TOTAL	4(1)	0	0	0	0	0

TOTAL APPS 4(1)

TOTAL GOALS 0

William James FELLOWES, 1933-35

Billy Fellowes (sometimes incorrectly shown as Fellows) was born in Bradford on 15 March 1910. He started his career in the Plymouth & District League with Tavistock Town, before moving onto Plymouth Argyle in July 1927, where he made five 5 appearances. The sturdily-built centre half and wing-half joined O's in July 1933, and had an excellent first season, proving to be a strong and commanding player in the side that hammered Aldershot 9-2 in February 1934. He moved to Luton Town (along with O's colleague John Finlayson) in May 1935, and made 41 League appearances in the Hatters' 1936/37 Third Division (South) Championship-winning team. He made 110 League appearances in total for the club, scoring 3 goals. He joined Exeter City in July 1938, making 58 League appearances and scoring once. (He also played 3 matches in 1939/40, which were later expunged from the record books due to the outbreak of the Second World War). Fellowes was appointed Exeter's first assistant manager, but he resigned in September 1949. He went on to run a sports business in Plymouth until his death in November 1987.

SEASON	LEAGUE		FA CUP		TOTAL	
	Apps	Gls	Apps	Gls	Apps	Gls
1933/34	41	1	4	0	45	1
1934/35	37	0	2	0	39	0
TOTAL	78	1	6	0	84	1

* Billy Fellowes also appeared in 3 Third Division Cup matches between 1933 and 1935.

Neale Michael FENN, 1997-98 (loan)

This Eire under-21 international central striker came to O's on 1 February 1998, on loan from Tottenham Hotspur, but never really showed his full potential. He had made a total of 10 senior appearances as a substitute for Spurs (scoring

Neale Fenn (left)

once) between August 1995 and May 2001. Born in Edmonton, London on 18 January 1977, he made his O's League debut at Exeter City on 31 January 1998 – the same match in which the tragic injury to O's goalie Paul Hyde occurred, which eventually ended his League career. Due to a niggling injury, Fenn had a very disappointing loan spell with O's. Boss Taylor said. 'It is a shame because the boy has so much talent, but he has not performed or scored for us, and that is what I brought him here to do.' He went on loan to Norwich City on 26 March 1998, making 6(1) appearances, and he scored in their 5-0 win over Swindon Town. In November 1998 he joined Swindon on loan, making 4 appearances without scoring. In December 1998 he moved to Lincoln City on loan. Throughout a League career that began in 1995, he has made only 13(3) appearances and scored just once. He enjoyed a loan period at Peterborough United – where he scored 5 goals in 4 reserve games – and he signed for them on a free transfer in May 2001.

SEASON	LEAGUE		FA CUP		L. CUP	
	Apps	Gls	Apps	Gls	Apps	Gls
1997/98	3	0	0	0	0	0
TOTAL	3	0	0	0	0	0

TOTAL APPS	3
TOTAL GOALS	0

Kenneth James FENTON, 1946-47

Centre half Ken Fenton was born in Bramley, Sheffield on 23 October 1920. He joined O's from Gainsborough Trinity in April 1946, having previously been an amateur with Barnsley. Fenton played only a few first-team games at

Brisbane Road. During March 1947, Fenton changed his surname to Armitage, and all his first-team appearances for O's occurred under his previous name. He was transferred to Oldham Athletic in July 1947 and made 5 League appearances for the club, but he was not retained in May 1948. He died in Sheffield in 1952, at the young age of thirty-two.

SEASON	LEAGUE		FA CUP		TOTAL	
	Apps	Gls	Apps	Gls	Apps	Gls
1946/47	7	0	0	0	7	0
TOTAL	7	0	0	0	7	0

Gordon FERRY, 1965-67

Gordon Ferry was born in Sunderland on 22 December 1943. He joined O's from Arsenal in June 1965, having made 11 League appearances for the Gunners since signing in January 1961. The steady centre half established himself as a first-team choice, and was ever-present in 1965/66, a season in which O's were relegated. He had the misfortune to score two own goals in the home fixture against Wolverhampton Wanderers in October 1965. The following season, with Paul Went in the side, he left the club during November 1966, and moved to the USA to play for Atlanta Chiefs, for whom he made 38 appearances. He returned to England in 1968 to play for non-League outfit Barnet.

SEASON	LEAGUE		FA CUP		L. CUP	
	Apps	Gls	Apps	Gls	Apps	Gls
1965/66	42	0	1	0	1	0
1966/67	0	0	0	0	0	0
TOTAL	42	0	1	0	1	0

TOTAL APPS	44
TOTAL GOALS	0

William FINDLAY, 1926-27

Born in Motherwell, Scotland in 1901, Bill Findlay joined O's from Peebles Rovers in September 1926. The wing-half made his League debut in the 0-4 home defeat by Darlington on 6 November 1926, but he remained a reserve at Milfields Road until returning home in May 1927.

SEASON	LEAGUE		FA CUP		TOTAL	
	Apps	Gls	Apps	Gls	Apps	Gls
1926/27	2	0	0	0	2	0
TOTAL	2	0	0	0	2	0

John FINLAYSON, 1933-35

Born in Cowdenbeath, Scotland on 14 June 1912, defender John Finlayson joined O's from Cowdenbeath in July 1933. He was a versatile player who could play at full-back, half-back and inside forward. However, he could never quite manage to hold down a regular first-team place and was snapped up by Luton Town in June 1935. He had a very successful career at right half with the Bedfordshire club, whom he joined along with fellow 'Oriental' William Fellowes. Finlayson made 154 League appearances for Luton and scored 9 goals for the Hatters between 1935 and 1939, and both men were members of the 1936/37 Luton side that became the champions of the Third Division (South).

SEASON	LEAGUE		FA CUP		TOTAL	
	Apps	Gls	Apps	Gls	Apps	Gls
1933/34	1	0	0	0	1	0
1934/35	10	0	0	0	10	0
TOTAL	11	0	0	0	11	0

* John Finlayson also appeared in a Third Division Cup match in 1934/35.

William FINLAYSON, 1924-25

Born in Thornliebank, Renfrewshire, Scotland on 29 March 1899, Bill Finlayson started with local side Ashfield FC in Glasgow, and then played for Thornliebank FC. The light-weight centre forward – he was only 5ft 7in tall and weighed just 9st 7lb – came south of the Border to join Chelsea in June 1920, making his League debut against Bolton Wanderers in January 1922. He had just 5 League outings and scored once for the West London club, before becoming an 'Oriental' in May 1924. After just one season at Millfields Road, he moved across London to join Brentford in May 1925, playing 18 matches and scoring 5 goals. The following year, he moved back to Scotland.

Steve Finney

SEASON	LEAGUE		FA CUP		TOTAL	
	Apps	Gls	Apps	Gls	Apps	Gls
1924/25	21	2	1	0	22	2
TOTAL	21	2	1	0	22	2

Stephen Kenneth FINNEY, 1998-99

Steve Finney – a 5ft 10in striker – joined O's on 25 March 1999 on a free transfer from Carlisle United, to replace Carl Griffith, who had been sold for £100,000 to Port Vale the previous day. O's boss Tommy Taylor agreed to take over Finney's contract until the end of the 1998/99 season, but he proved not to be the man for the job. Born in Hexham on 31 October 1973, he was brought up in Penrith, near Carlisle. He started his career as a trainee with Preston North End on 2 May 1992, making 1(5) League appearances and scoring once. On 12 February 1993 he joined Manchester City, but never played first-team football. Finney's best spell was with Swindon Town, where he became a crowd favourite following his goalscoring exploits in their 1996 Division Two Championship success, when he scored 16 goals, playing alongside midfielder Martin Ling. He lost his form the following season and went on loan to Cambridge United on 9 October 1997, scoring twice from 4(3) starts. He returned to Swindon in November 1997, netting 3 times. During the summer he asked for a transfer, and joined Carlisle United in June 1998 – a club he had supported as a boy – having turned down both Northampton Town and Walsall. He made 38 senior appearances for Carlisle during 1998/99, scoring 6 goals, including one against O's in February 1999. He scored in his last appearance for the Cumbrians at Darlington on 23 March 1999. Finney made his O's League debut against Southend United on 4 April 1999. It was reported that Finney was not happy being on the subs' bench for the match against Cardiff City in April 1999, and he was subsequently dropped by O's boss Taylor. Finney was released by O's in May 1999, and joined Exeter City on trial in June 1999, which did not work out, and he then joined Northern Unibond First Division side Gretna. He was later on the books of Barrow and then Chester City, whom he joined in October 1999, making 4(9) League appearances and scoring once. He joined Altrincham in December 2000, but didn't stay long.

SEASON	LEAGUE		FA CUP		L. CUP	
	Apps	Gls	Apps	Gls	Apps	Gls
1998/99	2(3)	0	0	0	0	0
TOTAL	2(3)	0	0	0	0	0

TOTAL APPS	2(3)
TOTAL GOALS	0

Paul FISHENDEN, 1986 (loan)

Born in Hillingdon on 2 August 1963, Paul Fishenden, a striker, came to O's on loan from Wimbledon in October 1986, after having previously had loan spells with both Fulham and Millwall. Unfortunately, he didn't cut much ice at Brisbane Road – in fact, he looked somewhat cumbersome – yet he did well with the Dons, with whom he turned professional in January 1981, and for whom he made 57(19) appearances and scored 22 goals. After he returned to them, he was then transferred to Crewe Alexandra in 1988 and was their top scorer with 16 goals. That form did not last, and he moved into non-League football with Wokingham, Crawley Town and Sutton United.

SEASON	LEAGUE		FA CUP		L. CUP	
	Apps	Gls	Apps	Gls	Apps	Gls
1986/87	4	0	1	0	0	0
TOTAL	4	0	1	0	0	0

TOTAL APPS	5
TOTAL GOALS	0

Frederick William FISHER, 1936-37

Born in Hucknall, Nottinghamshire during 1910, Fred Fisher started his career with Staveley Town in 1928. He then had spells as a reserve with Notts County, Torquay United, Mansfield Town and Swindon Town, before joining Gillingham in July 1935, where he made 17 League appearances and scored 6 goals. The 5ft 10in inside forward joined O's from the Gills in 1936. He looked a lively player, but was mostly confined to O's reserve side, making little headway at Lea Bridge Road. However, he did score twice in a first round Third Division Cup match at Southend United on 28 October 1936 to secure a 2-0 victory. He joined Newport Isle of Wight in June 1937.

SEASON	LEAGUE		FA CUP		TOTAL	
	Apps	Gls	Apps	Gls	Apps	Gls
1936/37	2	0	0	0	2	0
TOTAL	2	0	0	0	2	0

* Fred Fisher also appeared in a Third Division Cup match in 1936/37, scoring twice.

Frederick FISHER, 1954-56

Freddy Fisher was born in Hetton-le-Hole on 28 November 1924. The fast, tricky outside right started his career with Slough Town, and then guested for Reading in wartime matches during August 1944, eventually signing for them in May 1946 as a professional. He did very well at Elm Park, making 152 senior appearances and scoring 24 goals. He once broke a leg at Brisbane Road whilst playing for Reading reserves in 1950. He moved to Shrewsbury Town in July 1952, making 64 League appearances and scoring 9 goals. He had an outstanding game in Jackie Deverall's testimonial match for an all-star XI in April 1953. He joined O's in May 1954, and was brilliant in O's reserve side, partnering Phil White on the right wing. He was an O's player during some of their most successful seasons, otherwise this clever little footballer would surely have played more League games and made a bigger impact. Fisher scored on his first-team debut at Southend United in April 1955, but was not retained and moved into non-League football.

SEASON	LEAGUE		FA CUP		TOTAL	
	Apps	Gls	Apps	Gls	Apps	Gls
1954/55	2	1	0	0	2	1
TOTAL	2	1	0	0	2	1

Robert Paul FISHER, 1971-83

Bobby Fisher, the Brent schools captain, was brought to the club by his uncle, Mark Lazarus, in August 1971. He signed as a associate schoolboy, after he had spells in the youth sides of both Queens Park Rangers and Watford. Born in Wembley on 3 August 1956, Fisher was groomed by manager George Petchey for a midfield berth, but after David Payne broke his leg in April 1974, he was switched to the vacant full-back position, and at the age of sixteen, he had already sat on the substitute's bench. He came on for his League debut as a substitute against Sunderland in August 1973, and his first full appearance came against Bolton Wanderers the following month. He showed composure beyond his years, establishing himself in the side for eight seasons. He appeared in all 8 FA Cup ties in the 1977/78 run to the semi-final. Fisher left the club in November 1982, joining Cambridge

United, where he made 42 League appearances. He moved on to Brentford in February 1984, making his Bees debut against O's in an Associate Members Cup tie. After a further 45 appearances, he moved into non-League football with Maidstone United in December 1985. Fisher's style of play was not always to O's fans' liking. He was the type of defender who held off from making rash tackles, but there is no denying that he was a neat, polished player, who proved to be a grand servant with the club. He is one of only a small band of players to have made in excess of 300 League appearances for O's. After retiring from football, he became an author, journalist and actor. In July 2001, Fisher was appointed director of football of Jewish club London Maccabi Lions, of the Herts Senior County League. His reserve coach was Tunji Banjo, and it was Fisher who had first introduced Banjo to Orient some twenty-four years previously. He also works with another former 'Oriental' – Barry Silkman – as a players' agent.

SEASON	LEAGUE		FA CUP		L. CUP	
	Apps	Gls	Apps	Gls	Apps	Gls
1973/74	4(4)	0	0	0	2	0
1974/75	42	0	2	0	2	0
1975/76	36(1)	0	1	0	1	0
1976/77	31(1)	0	4	0	3(1)	0
1977/78	42	1	8	0	3	0
1978/79	37	0	3	0	1	1
1979/80	42	3	3	0	2	0
1980/81	41	0	0	0	2	0
1981/82	31	0	5	0	2	0
1982/83	2	0	0	0	1	0
TOTAL	308(6)	4	26	0	19(1)	1

TOTAL APPS	353(7)
TOTAL GOALS	5

Bobby Fisher

before he was transferred to his former club, Wisbech Town, in June 1967. He later played for Romford.

SEASON	LEAGUE		FA CUP		L. CUP	
	Apps	Gls	Apps	Gls	Apps	Gls
1965/66	32(1)	8	1	0	0	0
TOTAL	32(1)	8	1	0	0	0

TOTAL APPS	33(1)
TOTAL GOALS	8

* Bobby Fisher also appeared in 3 Texaco Cup matches in 1974/75, 14(1) Anglo-Scottish Cup matches and 6 Football League Group Cup matches.

Colin Harold FLATT, 1965-66

Born in Blyth on 30 January 1940, Colin Flatt was a strong, powerful centre forward, who was signed by O's boss Dave Sexton from Wisbech Town in May 1965, having previously played for Woodford Town and Ilford FC. He made a good start to his O's career, but as the team slid down the table, so his form also faltered. His best match was when he netted twice in the 2-1 win over Birmingham City in September 1965 on a very muddy pitch. He finished the season as joint top scorer with Dave Metchick on 8 goals, but left O's in a swap deal for Southend United's Terry Bradbury in June 1966. He played a single season at Roots Hall, making 20(2) League appearances and scoring 8 goals,

Charles FLETCHER, 1927-28, 1930-33

Born on 28 October 1905 in Homerton, London, Charlie Fletcher was famed for his powerful shooting, particularly from dead-ball situations, and there was always a buzz when he strode up to take a free-kick. He actually started his career with O's in 1927/28, but didn't get a first-team chance and so moved on to Crystal Palace in June 1928. He made his League debut for Palace that September, and went on to make a total of 7 League appearances. During June 1929, he moved to Third Division (South) outfit Merthyr Town, and scored once in 24 League games. Fletcher became an 'Oriental' for the second time in June 1930. He really blossomed in 1931/32, appearing mostly on the left wing. He bagged 22 senior goals, and is one of just nine players to have recorded 20 League goals or more in a season for O's. At the start of the following season, manager Jimmy Seed bought veteran Charlie Dimmock and Fletcher, not to his liking, was deployed in a more defensive role than before. He was sold to Brentford in June 1933, and became a member of their Second Division Championship-winning side of 1934/35, making a total of 104 appearances for the Bees and scoring 24 goals. He later played for Burnley (65 appearances and 22 goals), Plymouth Argyle (23 League appearances and 6 goals), and in July 1939, he joined Ipswich Town (36 senior appearances and 11 goals). He guested for O's during wartime football, making 68 appearances and scoring 13 goals. Throughout his League career, he made a total of 369 appearances and scored 93 goals. He played in a further 24 FA Cup ties, netting 5 goals. Charlie Fletcher died in Lewisham, London on 22 August 1980.

SEASON	LEAGUE		FA CUP		TOTAL	
	Apps	Gls	Apps	Gls	Apps	Gls
1927/28	0	0	0	0	0	0
1930/31	38	3	2	0	40	3
1931/32	41	20	3	2	44	22
1932/33	41	9	1	0	42	9
TOTAL	120	32	6	2	126	34

Gary FLETCHER, 2001-present

Little did young striker Gary Fletcher know when he scored a brace against O's for Northwich Victoria in December 2000, that a few months later he was to be signed by O's boss Tommy Taylor. He signed for a reported fee of £50,000, a few days after his twentieth birthday, and Taylor acted quickly to clinch the deal, following interest from Everton. Born in Widnes, Liverpool on 4 June 1981, he started off as a youth player with Northwich Victoria and signed as a professional on 1 August 1999 with the Football Conference side, having represented English Universities. Fletcher went on to score 15 goals from 37(11) senior appearances, and in December 2000, the highly-rated player was linked with Lou Macari at Huddersfield Town. On 16 March 2001, he joined Hull City on loan, with Northwich Victoria receiving a compensation payment for the loss of

their star player. The striker, who can also play down the wing, was to sign for £150,000 at the end of the season, making way for former 'Oriental' Jason Harris to move on loan to Shrewsbury Town. Fletcher made 1(4) League appearances, but failed to break into their side. Hull boss Brian Little felt the asking fee was too much, and concluded: 'For that sort of money, I'd be hoping to get someone that I could pick week in and week out without hesitation, and I don't believe Gary (Fletcher) falls into that category yet.' O's boss Taylor snapped him up in 2001, but, unfortunately, he suffered a serious kidney injury and missed most of the first half of the 2001/02 season. In December 2001, the 6ft striker moved to Grays Athletic on loan to get match-fit, netting 3 times.

SEASON	LEAGUE		FA CUP		L. CUP	
	Apps	Gls	Apps	Gls	Apps	Gls
2001/02	3(6)	0	0	0	0	0
TOTAL	3(6)	0	0	0	0	0

TOTAL APPS	3(6)
TOTAL GOALS	0

John Jack FLETCHER, 1936-38

Stocky, fair-haired Jack Fletcher was born in Tyne Dock, South Shields during 1910. After playing junior football in the North-East, he started his professional career with Guildford City. He moved to Bournemouth & Boscombe Athletic in November 1933, making 26 League appearances and scoring 3 goals. His next move was to Queens Park Rangers in September 1935, where he played 20 games. The inside forward became an 'Oriental' in May 1936, and was a regular in his first season. He was in the side for O's first ever League match at Brisbane

Road on 28 August 1937, against Cardiff City. A few weeks later, he scored a hat-trick against Bournemouth, but he lost form the following season, and was sold to Southampton in June 1938, where he played only reserve football. During September 1938, he joined Barrow and made 18 Third Division (North) appearances, scoring 5 times. He ended his career with Winchester City. Fletcher was a difficult player to judge – on his day, he looked a fine player, but he lapsed into spells of very ordinary play all too often.

SEASON	LEAGUE		FA CUP		TOTAL	
	Apps	Gls	Apps	Gls	Apps	Gls
1936/37	38	6	0	0	38	6
1937/38	17	5	1	0	18	5
TOTAL	55	11	1	0	56	11

* Jack Fletcher also appeared in 3 Third Division Cup matches between 1936 and 1938.

Kenneth FLINT, 1958-59

Born in Selston, Kirkby on 12 November 1923, Ken Flint, a really nippy outside left, joined Tottenham Hotspur in June 1947 from Bedford Town. He worked as a part-time miner during his early days at White Hart Lane, for whom he made just 5 League appearances during 1947/48, being mostly a reserve player. He moved to Aldershot in July 1950, in a part-exchange deal involving goalie Ron Reynolds and £3,000, and between 1950 and 1957, he made 324 League appearances for the Shots, scoring 70 goals. He was awarded a testimonial by Aldershot in October 1955. He came to O's in June 1958 at the age of thirty-five, and although he had put on a little weight, he still looked useful when called upon. However, O's boss Alec Stock released him in October 1958, and he joined

Southern League side Bath City, and he later played for Sittingbourne. After retiring from football, he worked for many years for an Enfield bookie.

SEASON	LEAGUE		FA CUP		TOTAL	
	Apps	Gls	Apps	Gls	Apps	Gls
1958/59	4	0	0	0	4	0
TOTAL	4	0	0	0	4	0

William Henry FOGG, 1933-36

Born in Birkenhead on 9 March 1903, Bill Fogg started playing football with Wirrall Railways works. The forceful right half played for Tranmere Rovers early in his career, and scored on his League debut in January 1925, against Ashington in a Third Division (North) match. He made a total of 22 League appearances, scoring 6 goals. He moved to Welsh side Bangor City in May 1926, and then joined Huddersfield Town in May 1928 for £20, starring in their FA Cup run in 1929/30 and playing in all 6 matches leading up to

Bill Fogg

the FA Cup final. Unfortunately, he got injured in the semi-final and missed the Wembley final against Arsenal, but with special permission from the FA, he received a winner's medal. He made 69 senior appearances for the Terriers, scoring on 3 occasions. He joined O's on 16 August 1933, and stayed for three seasons – he was a member of the side that thrashed Aldershot 9-2 in February 1934. During his final season, his form seemed to wane, and his final 3 appearances were on the right wing – all defeats. He was transferred to New Brighton on 20 August 1936, where he played a further 77 senior matches and scored once. William Fogg died in Barnston, near Oxton, Cheshire on 29 July 1966, aged sixty-three.

SEASON	LEAGUE		FA CUP		TOTAL	
	Apps	Gls	Apps	Gls	Apps	Gls
1933/34	27	1	3	0	30	1
1934/35	39	0	2	0	41	0
1935/36	15	1	0	0	15	1
TOTAL	81	2	5	0	86	2

* William Fogg also appeared in 5 Third Division Cup matches between 1933 and 1936.

Alexander Rooney FORBES, 1956-57

Born in Dundee on 21 January 1925, Alex Forbes started his career with Ashdale boys' club, and then moved to Dundee North End. The half-back joined Sheffield United in June 1946, making 61 League appearances and scoring 6 goals. Forbes joined Arsenal on 19 February 1948 for £12,500, and went onto make 240 senior appearances, scoring 20 goals. Forbes, who gained 14 Scottish caps, played in the Gunners' 2-0 FA Cup final victory over Liverpool at Wembley in 1950, and also

in their 1952 FA Cup final defeat by Newcastle United (1-0). He joined O's on a free transfer on 1 August 1956 for the club's return to the Second Division. He didn't really settle at Brisbane Road, and soon lost his place to Phil McKnight. Injury hampered his progress, and he was mostly confirmed to the reserves. Forbes showed plenty of ability, but moved on to Fulham in September 1957, where he made just 4 League appearances. After that, he moved into non-League football with Gravesend & Northfleet. During 1962 he returned to Highbury as coach to their junior side, before emigrating to South Africa, where he both played and coached. More recently, he has been running a business in Johannesburg with former Stoke City and England star, George Eastham. Forbes has retired and now lives in Cape Town.

SEASON	LEAGUE		FA CUP		TOTAL	
	Apps	Gls	Apps	Gls	Apps	Gls
1956/57	8	0	0	0	8	0
TOTAL	8	0	0	0	8	0

Nicolas FORGE, 2001

Nicolas Forge was born in Roanne, France on 13 May 1971. He joined O's on a non-contract basis on 5 March 2001, after a couple of reserve outings on trial. The left-back made his League debut at Cardiff City the following evening, and by all accounts, he showed good ball control and skill, although O's boss Taylor disagreed, and Forge was soon on his way. Last season, the midfielder could be found playing for ASOA Valenciennes FC (making 21 appearances and scoring 3 goals), but they were relegated from the French Second Division. Two of Forge's former colleagues at Valenciennes – David Friio and Romain Larrieu – joined Plymouth Argyle, where they have both become first-team regulars. Forge came to Brisbane Road after having a trial with Darlington a few weeks previously, but he reported didn't sign because he wanted to return to France.

SEASON	LEAGUE		FA CUP		L. CUP	
	Apps	Gls	Apps	Gls	Apps	Gls
2000/01	1	0	0	0	0	0
TOTAL	1	0	0	0	0	0

TOTAL APPS	1
TOTAL GOALS	0

James Jack Henry FORREST, 1913-22

Born in Shildon, near Sunderland in 1891, Jack Forrest joined O's from Shildon FC in 1913. He was yet another in a line of North-Easterners to join during the era. He proved to be a very hard-working wing-half with a firm tackle, who could attack and defend with equal skill. He made his League debut in September 1913 against Fulham, and was a regular member of the first team for the following four seasons. After fierce competition for places (with Dixon and Nicholson) in 1921, he spent over a year in the reserves, before leaving to join Northampton Town on trial in November 1922. He made his League debut for the Cobblers in their 5-2 win over Southend United on 11 November. He played just once more, but was not offered a contract and moved on to join Spennymoor United in May 1923. Forrest played consistently well for the O's before the First World War, but like many footballers of his generation, he lost his best years due to the hostilities in Europe.

SEASON	LEAGUE		FA CUP		TOTAL	
	Apps	Gls	Apps	Gls	Apps	Gls
1913/14	35	3	3	0	38	3
1914/15	31	2	1	0	32	2
1919/20	36	3	1	0	37	3
1920/21	24	2	2	0	26	2
1921/22	0	0	0	0	0	0
1922/23	0	0	0	0	0	0
TOTAL	126	10	7	0	133	10

David FORYSTH, 1964-67

Born in Falkirk, Scotland on 5 May 1945, Dave Forsyth joined O's in May 1964 from Scottish junior side Kirkintilloch Rob Roy – a club which has produced many fine players who have gone on to senior football, both in Scotland and England, over the years. The 6ft tall player, a centre half in his youth days, was converted to full-back by O's. He had a long run in the reserves, but broke into the first team in 1965/66, a season that saw O's relegated to the Third Division. In March 1967 he moved to South Africa to play for Durban FC, and still resides in KwaZulu Natal. Forysth did quite well during a difficult time for the club.

SEASON	LEAGUE		FA CUP		L. CUP	
	Apps	Gls	Apps	Gls	Apps	Gls
1964/65	0	0	0	0	0	0
1965/66	17	0	1	0	0	0
1966/67	15	0	3	0	1	0
TOTAL	32	0	4	0	1	0

TOTAL APPS	37
TOTAL GOALS	0

Leopold FORTUNE-WEST, 1997 (loan)

Leo Fortune-West – a big, tall striker – came to O's on loan from Gillingham on 27 March 1997, having had just a couple of games for the Gills that season, after breaking his leg in mid-September 1996.

Born in Stratford, London on 9 April 1971, Fortune-West started his career with Stevenage Borough, before joining Gillingham on 12 July 1995 for £5,000, and netting 18 goals from 48(19) League starts. He made his O's League debut as a substitute at Scunthorpe United, and made his single full League appearance at Chester City on 3 May 1997. However, Fortune-West did score O's winning goal in the Vauxhall President's Cup Final over Peterborough United. He returned to the Gills, but during October 1997, he went on loan to Rotherham United, scoring 4 times in 5 appearances. In June 1998 he moved to Lincoln City on a free transfer, scoring once in 11 appearances. In November 1998, a surprise £60,000 move took him to Brentford, where he made only 2(10) senior appearances. In February 1999 he moved to Rotherham United for £35,000, and he netted 26 League goals from 61 outings. He appeared against O's in both Division Three play-off semi-final matches in May 1999. He was sent off against O's in a Division Three match in November 1999 for elbowing Dean Smith. A player who has made a habit of scoring against the O's in recent years, Fortune-West joined Cardiff City on 8 September 2000 for £300,000.

Colin Foster (left) signs for O's

SEASON	LEAGUE		FA CUP		L. CUP	
	Apps	Gls	Apps	Gls	Apps	Gls
1996/97	1(4)	0	0	0	0	0
TOTAL	1(4)	0	0	0	0	0

TOTAL APPS	1(4)
TOTAL GOALS	0

Colin John FOSTER, 1981-87

'Fozzie', as he was affectionately known, was born in Chislehurst, Kent on 16 July 1964, and the central defender jumped quickly into O's first team at the tender age of seventeen. As a schoolboy, due to his physique and outstanding ability, he tended to be picked for teams in advance of his years. He made his debut in an FA Cup tie against Charlton Athletic in January 1982, and his League debut came against Grimsby Town a week later. He played regularly for six seasons, and it was no surprise that he moved into the First Division, with Nottingham Forest's Brian Clough paying £50,000 in March 1987, in a deal which sent Mark Smalley to Brisbane Road. Foster remained at the City Ground for three seasons, making 81(4) senior appearances and scoring 6 goals. He returned to East London to join Second Division West Ham United for £750,000 in September 1989, and made 88(5) League appearances, scoring 5 goals. A planned £400,000 return move to Forest in 1992 fell through, and he went on loan to Notts County in January 1994, making 9 League appearances. He eventually left Upton Park for Division One side Watford in March 1994, for a give-away £100,000, and enjoyed 3 good seasons at Vicarage Road, making 66 League appearances and netting 8 goals. After a loan spell with Cambridge United in 1997, he joined them on a non-contract basis in August 1997, but after 34 League appearances and a single goal, he was forced to retire from the game through injury in July 1998.

SEASON	LEAGUE		FA CUP		L. CUP	
	Apps	Gls	Apps	Gls	Apps	Gls
1981/82	23	2	5	1	0	0
1982/83	43	2	2	1	2	0
1983/84	10(1)	1	0	0	2	0
1984/85	42	1	4	1	4	0
1985/86	36	2	4	1	2	0
1986/87	19	2	4	1	2	0
TOTAL	173(1)	10	19	5	12	0

TOTAL APPS	204(1)
TOTAL GOALS	15

* Colin Foster also appeared in 3 Football League Groups Cup matches and 5 Auto Windscreens Shield matches, scoring once.

Ronald Edmund FOSTER, 1956-63

Tall, slim and slightly-built – he stood 5ft 9in tall and weighed 10st 3lbs – Ronnie Foster was born in Islington, London on 22 November 1938. He came to O's as an amateur from Clapton FC in March 1957, and appeared in the reserves along with another player named Ron Foster (an industrious little wing-half, who never appeared in the first team and drifted into non-League football). Foster was making progress in the reserves whilst doing his national service, and his first-team chance came when Eddie Baily stood down, and he took over the schemer role from October 1959. His quick, clever ball-playing skills contributed greatly to the team's improving form. He scored O's first ever goal in the League Cup at Chester on 12 October 1960. He played a major part in the promotion season of 1961/62, but, sadly, had to pull out in the last minute of the vital last match of the season against Bury in April 1962 due to injury, as he did not want to let the side down. His place was taken by Malcolm Graham, who stole the limelight with 2 goals to take O's to promotion. He only had a handful of outings in O's First Division campaign of 1962/63, and during December 1962 he moved to Grimsby Town for £11,500, where he made 129 League appearances and scored 24 goals. He moved to Reading in July 1966 for £6,000, and bagged 5 goals from 45 appearances. Foster went out to America in 1968 to join Dallas Tornados

Ronnie Foster

for £3,000, but returned in March 1969 to join Brentford, playing just 3(1) matches. Upon retirement from the game, he worked as a black-cab driver in London.

SEASON	LEAGUE		FA CUP		L. CUP	
	Apps	Gls	Apps	Gls	Apps	Gls
1956/57	0	0	0	0	-	-
1957/58	0	0	0	0	-	-
1958/59	0	0	0	0	-	-
1959/60	24	6	1	1	-	-
1960/61*	11	1	1	0	3	1
1961/62	33	10	4	3	3	0
1962/63	4	0	0	0	1	2
TOTAL	72	17	6	4	7	3

TOTAL APPS	85
TOTAL GOALS	24

* The League Cup competition began in the 1960/61 season.

Thomas Curtis FOSTER, 1934-36

Born on 30 June 1908 in Easington, Sunderland, Tommy Foster joined O's from Reading in June 1934, for whom he had made a single League appearance in 1933/34. Mainly a reserve with O's, the strong centre forward seemed to score dramatic goals whenever chosen for the first team. He was the reserve side's top scorer in 1934/35, with 34 goals. He scored on his League debut against Crystal Palace in October 1934, and the following April, he netted a hat-trick against Brighton & Hove Albion in a 6-0 victory. Another memorable feat was fine brace which knocked high-flying Charlton Athletic out of the FA Cup in January 1936 in a brilliant 3-0 victory in front of a record attendance of 18,658 at the Lea Bridge Road ground. He was transferred to Swansea Town in May 1936, where he netted 4 goals from 13 League

starts. The following year he moved to Crewe Alexandra, where his two-year stay brought him 26 goals from 62 senior appearances. Foster died in Congleton during 1982.

SEASON	LEAGUE		FA CUP		TOTAL	
	Apps	Gls	Apps	Gls	Apps	Gls
1934/35	11	10	2	0	13	10
1935/36	8	1	3	2	11	3
TOTAL	19	11	5	2	24	13

John Jack FOWLER, 1930-32

Born in Cardiff on 3 December 1899, Jack Fowler was a versatile player who could play equally well at centre forward or at centre half. He started his career with Maerdy FC in 1919 before moving on to Plymouth Argyle in 1921, where he hit 25 goals in 39 senior appearances. He moved to Swansea Town in February 1924 for a record fee of £1,280. He stayed at the Vetch for over five seasons, scoring 101 League goals in 160 appearances. During his stay, he won 6 full Welsh caps. He featured in their Third Division (South) Championship-winning side of 1925. He also featured in the Swans' run to the FA Cup semi-final in 1926, and was their top scorer in both 1924/25 and 1925/26, scoring 28 goal in each of those seasons. He hit 5 goals against Charlton in September 1924, and recorded a remarkable 9 hat-tricks for the Swans. Fowler joined O's in June 1930, at the age of thirty-two, and was appointed club captain immediately. In his first 3 League matches, he netted 5 goals, including a hat-trick against Coventry City in September 1930. He also hit the first ever goal at the new Lea Bridge Road Ground on 4 September 1930, against Newport County, in a 3-1 win in front of 5,550 fans. In the 1931/32 season, he moved to centre half, and proved very effective. Unfortunately, age and injuries took their toll, forcing him to retire in 1932. Fowler returned to Swansea to manage the Rhyddings Hotel for thirty-five years. He died in Swansea on 26 February 1975, aged seventy-five.

SEASON	LEAGUE		FA CUP		TOTAL	
	Apps	Gls	Apps	Gls	Apps	Gls
1930/31	40	12	2	0	42	12
1931/32	35	3	3	0	38	3
TOTAL	75	15	5	0	80	15

George James FRANCIS, 1919-20

Born in Poplar, London on 18 June 1896, centre half George Francis joined O's from non-League football in September 1919. He played just one home League match – a 1-0 defeat by Huddersfield Town on 6 September 1919. He moved to Folkestone FC in August 1920. Francis died in Maidstone, Kent on 29 September 1923, aged just twenty-seven.

SEASON	LEAGUE		FA CUP		TOTAL	
	Apps	Gls	Apps	Gls	Apps	Gls
1919/20	1	0	0	0	1	0
TOTAL	1	0	0	0	1	0

Keith Roy FRANCIS, 1950-52

Born in Yeovil on 22 July 1929, Francis joined O's from his local side – Yeovil Town – in June 1950, as a very promising midfield player. However, his opportunities were limited. He made his League debut in the 2-1 victory over Brighton & Hove Albion on 21 April 1951, but despite playing very well for the reserves, he moved back into non-League football during May 1952. It was Francis who visited former O's boss Alex Stock in the nursing home in Wimborne on a regular basis before Stock died on 16 April 2001.

SEASON	LEAGUE		FA CUP		TOTAL	
	Apps	Gls	Apps	Gls	Apps	Gls
1950/51	3	0	0	0	3	0
1951/52	0	0	0	0	0	0
TOTAL	3	0	0	0	3	0

James John Buchanan FRENCH, 1933-34

Jimmy French was born in Tannochside, Scotland on 31 December 1907. The centre forward started out with Scottish side Airdrionians. He moved on to Gillingham in June 1930, making 19 senior appearances and scoring once. During July 1931 he joined Kent non-League side Tunbridge Wells Rangers. French became an 'Oriental' in August 1933, but only got the occasional first-team outing, although he bagged 32 goals for the reserves in the 1933/34 season. He scored on his League debut on 23 September 1933 in a 2-1 win over Brighton & Hove Albion. He appeared in a Third Division Cup second round match at Norwich City on 8 February 1934 – a 3-0 reverse in front of 2,561 Carrow Road midweek fans. He left the club in May 1934 and returned to play in Kent.

SEASON	LEAGUE		FA CUP		TOTAL	
	Apps	Gls	Apps	Gls	Apps	Gls
1933/34	4	1	0	0	4	1
TOTAL	4	1	0	0	4	1

* Jimmy French also appeared in a Third Division Cup match in 1933/34.

Raymond FROOM, 1945-46

Londoner Ray Froom, an amateur wing-half, joined O's from Southall FC in 1945 and performed well when called upon during the season, playing in 8 regional wartime matches and scoring once. He appeared in both FA Cup ties against Newport Isle of Wight during November

1945, which O's lost 2-3 on aggregate. He was not retained for the commencement of the League in 1946, and went back into non-League football.

SEASON	LEAGUE		FA CUP		TOTAL	
	Apps	Gls	Apps	Gls	Apps	Gls
1945/46*	-	-	2	0	2	0
TOTAL	-	-	2	0	2	0

* There were no League matches in 1945/46 due to the Second World War.

Barry Francis FRY, 1966-67 and 1967-68
Barry Fry, a stocky inside forward, was born in Bedford on 7 April 1945. He started as an apprentice with Manchester United in April 1960, gaining England schoolboy recognition, but he could never break into their first team and moved on to Bolton Wanderers in May 1964, making 3 League appearances and scoring once. July 1965 saw a move to his local side Luton Town (6 League appearances), before he joined Gravesend & Northfleet during May 1966, and then became an 'Oriental' in December 1966. Fry was mostly a reserve at the club, and helped out O's boss Dick Graham with the coaching and training duties. He joined Bedford Town for a short while, but returned to O's in June 1967, playing in the 2-0 defeat at Brisbane Road by Torquay United on 26 August 1967. However, with O's still going through a financial crisis, Fry was not retained, and he joined Romford in May 1968. He then moved on to Stevenage Borough and later Dunstable, and it was with the latter that he gained his first managerial experience, steering them to promotion in his debut campaign as player-manager. Other managerial spells – with Hillingdon Borough, Barnet and Maidstone United –

Barry Fry

followed before he went back to Barnet in August 1986 for a second stint. Three times the North Londoners were runners-up in the GM Vauxhall Conference, before finally gaining a place in the League as a semi-professional outfit. He steered them into the play-offs in their first League season and gained promotion a year later. Fry was appointed manager of Southend United in April 1993 when seven points adrift at the bottom of the table. Remarkably, he steered them clear with 6 wins and 2 draws. He then joined Birmingham City, and in his two-and-a-half years at St Andrews, he achieved an Auto Windscreen Shield final win – defeating O's in the two-legged semi-final – and promotion in 1995. In May 1996 he was dismissed, and three weeks later he was installed as manager with Peterborough United, leading them to promotion to Division Two (via a Wembley play-off) in 1999/2000. Barry Fry, one of football's most flamboyant and animated characters, has woven his magic and enjoyed success with most of the clubs he has managed. His managerial career has spanned more than fifteen years in both non-League and League football.

SEASON	LEAGUE		FA CUP		L. CUP	
	Apps	Gls	Apps	Gls	Apps	Gls
1966/67	2(1)	0	0	0	0	0
1967/68	5(5)	0	0	0	1	0
TOTAL	7(6)	0	0	0	1	0

TOTAL APPS	8(6)
TOTAL GOALS	0

John Frederick FULLBROOK, 1946-48

John Fullbrook was born in Grays, Essex on 15 July 1918, and was yet another player whose early career was interrupted by the Second World War. He joined Plymouth Argyle in 1945 from the Royal Navy, and made 8 Southern League appearances before returning to the Navy the following year. The right-back joined O's as an amateur from Plymouth Argyle in March 1946, and appeared for O's at the close of the last wartime season of 1945/46, playing in 5 matches. He featured at right half in O's first League match after the war (against Ipswich Town in August 1946), and he even appeared at centre forward at Brighton in November 1946, and was a regular throughout that campaign. During the following season, the arrival of thirty-seven-year-old William 'Buster' Brown from Brentford meant that he lost his place and remained in the reserves all season. He joined Dartford in June 1948, appearing for them against O's in an FA Cup first round home tie in November 1948, O's winning 4-1. Fullbrook died in March 1992.

SEASON	LEAGUE		FA CUP		TOTAL	
	Apps	Gls	Apps	Gls	Apps	Gls
1946/47	34	1	1	0	35	1
1947/48	2	0	0	0	2	0
TOTAL	36	1	1	0	37	1

Raymond Hamilton FULTON, 1972-73

Ray Fulton was born in Hendon on 24 September 1953. The red-haired left-back joined O's from near neighbours West Ham United, where he was an apprentice in August 1972. Despite being small in stature, he looked a neat defender. He was unable to break into the first team, making a single League appearance against Swindon Town on 18 November 1972. Fulton remained in the reserves throughout the season, then joining Folkestone Town in June 1973.

SEASON	LEAGUE		FA CUP		L. CUP	
	Apps	Gls	Apps	Gls	Apps	Gls
1972/73	1	0	0	0	0	0
TOTAL	1	0	0	0	0	0

TOTAL APPS	1
TOTAL GOALS	0

G

John McDonald GALBRAITH, 1921-31

John Galbraith was born in Renton, Scotland. The defender started his career with the Vale of Leven junior club, before he moved to Shawfield FC from whom he joined O's in July 1921. He soon impressed as a skilful, hard-working player, and remained with O's for ten seasons. He will remembered by older fans for scoring a beauty against Newcastle United in the 2-0 FA Cup fifth round vic-

G

John Galbraith

tory in February 1926. He also scored in O's final League match at the Millfields Road ground on 3 May 1930, a 4-1 win over Brighton & Hove Albion. With the club seeking urgent funds during a cash crisis, Galbraith was sold to Cardiff City in February 1931 for £2,000. He played in 143 senior games, scoring twice at Ninian Park before becoming manager of Milford United in July 1935. He returned to O's as coach in 1938.

SEASON	LEAGUE		FA CUP		TOTAL	
	Apps	Gls	Apps	Gls	Apps	Gls
1921/22	37	3	1	0	38	3
1922/23	24	1	1	0	25	1
1923/24	4	0	0	0	4	0
1924/25	25	0	1	0	26	0
1925/26	32	1	4	1	36	2
1926/27	41	1	2	0	43	1
1927/28	33	0	1	0	34	0
1928/29	22	0	2	0	24	0
1929/30	38	1	5	0	43	1

1930/31	21	2	2	0	23	2
TOTAL	277	9	19	1	296	10

David Wilson GALLOWAY, 1938-39

Dave Galloway was born in Kirkaldy, Fife, Scotland on 6 May 1910. The small, slightly-built inside forward, who stood just 5ft 5in tall, signed for Raith Rovers on 29 October 1927 from nearby Wellesley Juniors. He appeared in 98 Scottish League and 10 Scottish Cup matches, scoring 21 goals. He joined Aberdeen in April 1931, however, he had hardly kicked a ball for the Dons when a number of players were dropped, after what was stated in the local press as 'some internal club trouble'. Galloway joined Preston North End, and also had a spell with Port Vale in 1934/35. He moved to Carlisle United, where he made 109 League appearances and scored 11 goals. In August 1938, the thirty-three-year-old became an 'Oriental', and was included for the start of the campaign but was soon replaced by Ted Crawford. During February 1939 he joined Tunbridge Wells Rangers. He died in 1979.

SEASON	LEAGUE		FA CUP		TOTAL	
	Apps	Gls	Apps	Gls	Apps	Gls
1938/39	2	0	0	0	2	0
TOTAL	2	0	0	0	2	0

Bradley David GAMBLE, 1991-94

Bradley Gamble was born on 4 February 1975 in Southwark, London. He was spotted by O's scout Roy Cook whilst playing for Fisher Athletics' junior side, having first started out with Sunday morning side Kennington Rovers along with another former O's youth player Mickey Tomlinson. He represented South London Schools at every level from the under-12s up to the under-16s.

A left-winger with good dribbling and crossing skills, he signed with O's as a YTS player in 1991, and then signed professional forms in July 1993. Bradley Gamble made his League debut in a 2-1 home win over Cambridge United on 27 December 1993. He had previously come on as a substitute in the Autoglass Trophy match at AFC Bournemouth six days earlier to replace Mark Cooper. He was never seen in the O's first team again, and was eventually released in May 1994.

SEASON	LEAGUE		FA CUP		L. CUP	
	Apps	Gls	Apps	Gls	Apps	Gls
1993/94	1	0	0	0	0	0
TOTAL	1	0	0	0	0	0

TOTAL APPS	1
TOTAL GOALS	0

* Bradley Gamble also appeared in 0(1) Auto Windscreens Shield match.

Bradley Gamble

Henry Penty GARBUTT, 1930-31

Inside forward Henry Garbutt was born in Pontefract on 12 November 1907. He started his career with Castleford Town FC, and then moved to Tottenham Hotspur in March 1927. He went on tour with Spurs to Malta, scoring 4 goals in 3 matches, but made no League appearances, remaining a reserve player through out his stay at White Hart Lane. He became an 'Oriental' on 12 June 1930, when the club had just moved their headquarters to Lea Bridge Road. However, he was given a limited number of League outings and had to be satisfied with reserve football. Garbutt moved to Accrington Stanley in September 1931, making 12 League appearances and netting 7 goals. He died in Nottingley during February 1986.

SEASON	LEAGUE		FA CUP		TOTAL	
	Apps	Gls	Apps	Gls	Apps	Gls
1930/31	9	1	0	0	9	1
1931/32	0	0	0	0	0	0
TOTAL	9	1	0	0	9	1

Richard GARCIA, 2000 (loan)

Richie Garcia was born in Perth, Australia on 4 September 1981. The whiz-kid from 'Down Under' had been a prolific goalscorer for the West Ham youth side, and established an FA Youth Cup record when he scored in every round, as the Hammers stormed to victory in the competition in 1998. He joined O's on a month-by-month loan period at the start of August 2000. An impressive product of the Australian Soccer Academy, he played for Western Australian State League club Kingsway Olympic, before leaving for the UK at the age of fifteen in July 1997. He signed apprentice forms with the Hammers on

Richard Garcia

4 September 1997 – on his sixteenth birthday – and then turned professional two years later. He scored 13 reserve and 11 youth League goals over the two years. Garcia played very well for Australia in the Youth World Cup in 1999, which the Aussies eventually lost to Brazil on penalties. He made his O's debut in the 1-0 win at Plymouth Argyle on 12 August 2000, and over the following weeks looked to be fast and skilful with the ability to beat men; not only a provider, but also capable of finding the net. Two weeks later he netted twice at Blackpool, the second a spectacular overhead kick, to secure O's a point. All O's fans were thankful to receive the news that Garcia had decided to sign a one-year loan agreement in November 2000, but, sadly, days later in a League match at Cheltenham, he turned away after a tackle, and his feet seemed to go one way and his body the other way on

a wet pitch. A scan revealed the worst, showing snapped cruciate knee ligaments, which virtually ended his stay at Brisbane Road. He returned to Perth, Australia to undergo specialised keyhole surgery on his injury and was expected to return to Upton Park to start pre-season training – a sad season for a player who looked a little bit special. Garcia signed a new one-year contract with the Hammers in May 2001. He made his League debut as a playing substitute at Leeds United on 1 January 2002.

SEASON	LEAGUE		FA CUP		L. CUP	
	Apps	Gls	Apps	Gls	Apps	Gls
2000/01	18	4	0	0	3	0
TOTAL	18	4	0	0	3	0

TOTAL APPS 21
TOTAL GOALS 4

James Robert GARDNER, 1926-29

Jimmy Gardner, a small outside right, was born in Felixstowe on 29 July 1901. He started his career with Walton United, before playing for Ipswich Town in 1921 in the Southern Amateur League, making 20 appearances during 1921/22 and winning a championship winners' medal. After a trial with Norwich City, he joined Southern League outfit Yeovil & Petters United in August 1922. He joined Bristol Rovers for a £50 fee on 5 August 1925, making 32 League appearances and scoring 4 goals. Gardner became an 'Oriental' in June 1926, gaining hero status in his first season when he netted 7 times in just 9 games. He also converted a penalty in the final game of the 1926/27 season, for a 1-0 win to save O's from relegation – much to the delight of the O's travelling fans amongst the 8,908 Elm Park crowd. Gardner was involved in a car accident in August 1927, and after returning he found it difficult to replace Turnbull in the first team. He did score 21 goals for the reserves during that season, but whenever he did play in the first team, he often grabbed vital goals. He left the club in August 1929 to join Western League side Lovells Athletic, netting 60 goals in all competitions in 1930/31. He came back into the League whilst on loan with Newport County, notching 12 goals from just 13 League appearances, but returned to Lovells in June 1933. Thereafter, he did the rounds with a number of non-League clubs, including Felixstowe Town, Parklands Welfare FC and Billingham FC. In 1936 he became coach of Basle FC in Switzerland. Gardner was a straightforward, no-nonsense player, whose important contribution in 1926/27 will go down in the annals of the club's history.

SEASON	LEAGUE		FA CUP		TOTAL	
	Apps	Gls	Apps	Gls	Apps	Gls
1926/27	16	9	0	0	16	9
1927/28	9	7	1	0	10	7
1928/29	6	1	0	0	6	1
TOTAL	31	17	1	0	32	17

Peter John GARLAND, 1996-97

Midfielder Peter Garland's only real claim to fame with O's was as a trial player, with his last-minute goal in a friendly against the Welsh national side in May 1996 that secured a surprise 2-1 victory. Born in Croydon on 20 January 1971, Garland started his career with Tottenham Hotspur as a trainee, with whom he gained England youth caps. After a lone senior appearance, he was surprisingly signed by Newcastle United for a reported £35,000 on 24 March 1992. He played just twice for the Magpies as a substitute, before a move back to London took him to Charlton Athletic on 18 December 1992 for an undisclosed fee. There he made 40(13) League appearances and scored twice. After a loan spell with Wycombe Wanderers in March 1995 – where he made 5 appearances – he joined O's on 4 July 1996. His weight was a concern – he was more than 14st – and O's chairman Barry Hearn's own personal trainer worked with the player, so he could lose over 2st. O's boss Pat Holland joked: 'Either way the club can't lose with Peter's signing: if he doesn't slim down, we'll open a pie and mash shop with him!'. The rotund Garland just couldn't make it, and was released on 31 May 1997. O's new boss Tommy Taylor said of Garland: 'He was probably one of the most gifted players at the club, but also the least professional. He was told to lose weight in order to obtain a new contract, but it just never happened.' In recent years, Garland has played for Crawley Town and Dulwich Hamlet. He joined Croydon FC in December 2000, some fourteen years after his debut for Croydon's youth team, which earned him a Southern League Youth Cup winner's medal.

SEASON	LEAGUE		FA CUP		L. CUP	
	Apps	Gls	Apps	Gls	Apps	Gls
1996/97	13(8)	0	2	0	1	0
TOTAL	13(8)	0	2	0	1	0

TOTAL APPS	16(8)
TOTAL GOALS	0

Herbert GARLAND-WELLS, 1929-30

Born on 14 November 1907 in Brockley, London, Monty Garland-Wells was a real all-round sportsman, who also played cricket and rugby, as well as football. The goalkeeper joined O's in November 1920, having represented Pembroke College at

Oxford University, and having gained an England amateur international cap. He made his O's debut in the 3-1 win over Coventry City in February 1929. He left in September 1930 to join Fulham, but had no League outings and moved on to Corinthians. In cricket, Garland-Wells was an attacking middle-order batsman with Surrey CCC, and in 190 first-class matches, he scored 6,086 runs. Apart from his batting, he was also a medium-pace bowler with a mean leg-cutter, taking 185 wickets. He probably bowled his most satisfying delivery in May 1930, when he bowled the legendary Don Bradman for 32 runs. Between 1934 and 1938, Garland-Wells was Surrey's vice-captain, taking over the leadership in 1939. Like so many others, he had his career cut short by the Second World War. He joined his father's law firm, but in 1963 he was struck off for seven years for accounts irregularities. He became a well-known figure at Wentworth Golf Club until he gave up golf to retire to Brighton, where he took up bowls and represented his county. It was Garland-Wells who played a part in the development of greyhound racing at the Millfields Road ground, which eventually forced the club to leave that ground after many years. He died in Hove, Sussex on 6 June 1992, aged eighty-five.

SEASON	LEAGUE		FA CUP		TOTAL	
	Apps	Gls	Apps	Gls	Apps	Gls
1929/30	11	0	0	0	11	0
TOTAL	11	0	0	0	11	0

George John GATES, 1906-09

Hammersmith-born Gates started his professional career with Brentford in the Southern League, playing 15 matches and scoring twice between 1904 and 1906. He

moved across London to become an 'Oriental' in June 1906. He looked to be a dangerous forward, having three seasons with O's before being transferred to Grimsby Town in September 1909, where he made 18 senior appearances and scored once. In 1911 he joined Merthyr Town, winning a Southern League Second Division Championship winner's medal in 1912, and making a total of 63 appearances and scoring 6 goals for the Welsh side between 1911 and 1914. After the First World War, he retired from football to become a publican, after turning down the chance to return to football with Swindon Town.

SEASON	LEAGUE		FA CUP		TOTAL	
	Apps	Gls	Apps	Gls	Apps	Gls
1906/07*	26	0	-	-	26	0
1907/08	8	0	3	0	11	0
1908/09	19	7	0	0	19	7
TOTAL	53	7	3	0	56	7

* Clapton Orient did not enter into the FA Cup competition in 1906/07.

Peter GAVIGAN, 1925-26

Born on 11 December 1897 in Gorbals, Glasgow, Gavigan was quite a skilful right-winger, who really loved to take on his opposing full-back and beat him with skill and pace, and then make goals for his fellow forwards. He had five seasons with Fulham, having joined them from Vale of Clyde FC in December 1920, and made 78 senior appearances (scoring once), but he broke his knee-cap at Plymouth Argyle in an FA Cup tie in January 1922 and could not regain his place in the side. He became an 'Oriental' in August 1925, and his fast-raiding, zippy entertaining style of play made him a firm favourite with the O's fans. He had an excellent

Peter Gavigan

match against Newcastle United in the FA Cup fifth round victory in February 1926. He left the club in July 1927, and after a brief spell with Bilston United, he joined St Johnstone. He later played for Dundee in July 1930, before moving on to Dundee United. He died in Dundee on 2 March 1977, aged seventy-nine.

SEASON	LEAGUE		FA CUP		TOTAL	
	Apps	Gls	Apps	Gls	Apps	Gls
1925/26	34	1	4	0	38	1
1926/27	28	3	2	0	30	3
TOTAL	62	4	6	0	68	4

James McLean GAY, 1928-31

Jimmy Gay was born in Stanley, Perthshire, Scotland on 17 March 1897. He started playing with Perth Celtic FC, before he joined Clydebank in the Scottish League in September 1920. He then played for a number of clubs, including St Barnards, Lochgelly United,

Dunfermline Athletic, Rhyl Athletic and Aberdeen. In June 1926 he came south of the Border to join Coventry City, making 31 League appearances. He became an 'Oriental' in May 1928, and quickly set up a good full-back partnership with Ernie Morley. Gay played in both memorable FA Cup ties against Aston Villa during January 1929. The following season he lost his place to Bert Lyons, making his final League appearance in February 1930 against Queens Park Rangers. The steady defender joined Watford on a free transfer in May 1930, and he began his time there with a 6-0 win over Torquay and a 5-1 FA Cup win over Walthamstow Avenue. During August 1931 he returned to Scotland to play 3 Scottish League matches with Raith Rovers, before eventually retiring from the game. He died in Blairgowrie, Perthshire, Scotland on 31 August 1967 aged seventy.

SEASON	LEAGUE		FA CUP		TOTAL	
	Apps	Gls	Apps	Gls	Apps	Gls
1928/29	33	0	4	0	37	0
1929/30	7	0	0	0	7	0
TOTAL	40	0	4	0	44	0

Frank Richard GEORGE, 1957-63

Born on 20 November 1933 in Stepney, London, goalkeeper Frank George – who stood 5ft 11in and weighed nearly 14st – joined O's on amateur forms from Athenian League side Carshalton Athletic, turning professional on 9 April 1957. George hit the headlines with a wonderful display on his League debut against Fulham in April 1957. Very daring and quick off his line, he had to compete for the jersey with two long-standing O's 'keepers: Pat Welton and Dave Groombridge. He finally gained a regular place during November 1957, but could never quite recapture his early form and was replaced by Bill Robertson in March 1961. He played in O's promotion season of 1961/62, and made 7 First Division appearances. He left the club in 1963 to become understudy to Watford's ever-present Pat Jennings. There he made 10 League appearances, the last being a 6-2 defeat at Reading. During July 1965, he joined Southern League side Worcester City.

SEASON	LEAGUE		FA CUP		L. CUP	
	Apps	Gls	Apps	Gls	Apps	Gls
1956/57*	1	0	0	0	-	-
1957/58	23	0	2	0	-	-
1958/59	34	0	1	0	-	-
1959/60	2	0	0	0	-	-
1960/61	26	0	3	0	3	0
1961/62	26	0	4	0	3	0
1962/63	7	0	2	0	2	0
TOTAL	119	0	12	0	8	0

TOTAL APPS	139
TOTAL GOALS	0

* The League Cup competition commenced in the 1960/61 season.

Stanislaw Eugeniusz GERULA, 1948-50
Stan Gerula was born in Poland on 21 February 1924. The Polish amateur international goalkeeper, who also represented the Polish Army, joined O's in May 1948, having played for non-League side Carpathians. The club needed a 'keeper as cover for first-team man Stan Tolliday, who was out for long periods through illness and injury. He competed well for the first-team spot with Reg Newton, but with the emergence of Pat Welton, he went on loan to Southern League side Guildford City, and eventually left the club in 1950 to join top amateur side (and near neighbours) Walthamstow Avenue. He was the first ever Polish-born player to appear in a Wembley Cup final for Avenue against Leyton in 1952, and will be remembered for his superb display for Avenue in an FA Cup fourth round tie against Manchester United in 1953. He left Avenue in 1956, and played Sunday football for a time, before being appointed as Avenue's groundsman in later years. Gerula died in Shepherds Bush, London on 29 August 1979, aged fifty-five.

SEASON	LEAGUE		FA CUP		TOTAL	
	Apps	Gls	Apps	Gls	Apps	Gls
1948/49	15	0	0	0	15	0
1959/50	15	0	1	0	16	0
TOTAL	30	0	1	0	31	0

Derek William GIBBS, 1960-63
Derek Gibbs a tall, strong inside forward, holds one record that can never be broken – he scored O's first ever goal in the

Derek Gibbs

First Division on 18 August 1962, against Arsenal at Brisbane Road. Born in Fulham, London on 22 December 1934, Gibbs signed for Chelsea as a junior in April 1955. He played mostly reserve football during his stay at Stamford Bridge, making just 25 senior appearances with 6 goals during a five-year stay. He joined O's as a utility player on a free transfer during November 1960, and although his opportunities were restricted, he did score some vital goals. He notched a couple of crucial goals at Luton Town in O's 1961/62 promotion season, and played in the penultimate match of the campaign against Bury that secured promotion. Another highlight of his O's career, was a brilliant strike for the winning goal at the Dell, which knocked Southampton out of the FA Cup in January 1961. Gibbs moved to Queens Park Rangers with Malcolm Graham for a combined fee of £10,000 in August 1963, making 29 senior appearances before moving into the Southern League with Romford.

SEASON	LEAGUE		FA CUP		L. CUP	
	Apps	Gls	Apps	Gls	Apps	Gls
1960/61	13	1	2	1	0	0
1961/62	3	2	0	0	1	1
1962/63	17	1	3	1	3	0
TOTAL	33	4	5	2	4	1

TOTAL APPS	42
TOTAL GOALS	7

Harold Thomas GIBSON, 1913-15
Harry Gibson was born in Hoxton, London. He joined O's from Hoxton Hall FC in 1913, and although not a regular player, he proved to be an industrious and energetic wing-half during the two seasons leading up to the First World War. Like most players, he joined the Footballers Battalion, but, sadly, he was seriously injured in the hostilities, and forced to retire from the game. However, he was often spotted at the ground in later years, supporting the boys in white and red.

SEASON	LEAGUE		FA CUP		TOTAL	
	Apps	Gls	Apps	Gls	Apps	Gls
1913/14	15	0	0	0	15	0
1914/15	15	0	0	0	15	0
TOTAL	30	0	0	0	30	0

Kenneth GIBSON, 1905-06
Quick-raiding outside right Ken Gibson came to O's for the inaugural season in the League in 1905 from non-League side Saracens, as cover for Herbert Kingaby. He scored on his League debut in a 3-0 victory over Lincoln City on 20 January 1906. Gibson returned to the Saracens club in May 1906.

SEASON	LEAGUE		FA CUP		TOTAL	
	Apps	Gls	Apps	Gls	Apps	Gls
1905/06	5	1	0	0	5	1
TOTAL	5	1	0	0	5	1

Thomas Richard GIBSON, 1960-61
Don Gibson, as he was always known, was born Manchester on 12 May 1929. The fair-haired player was later to become the son-in-law of the late Sir Matt Busby. He signed for Manchester United in November 1946, and turned professional the following August, making his League debut at full-back in August 1950. He was a member of United's 1951/52 League Championship side, playing in 17 matches, which was enough to qualify him for a League Championship medal. After 108 League appearances at Old Trafford with no goals, he joined Sheffield Wednesday in June 1955 for £8,000. He

was dogged by injuries, but played in 83 senior games, scored 3 times and won a Second Division Championship medal. Gibson joined O's in June 1960 on a free transfer, but was confined to the reserves (due to the form of Ken Facey) and acted as reserve team captain. A wing-half who was strong in the tackle, he made his League debut for O's in a 3-1 win at Leeds United during September 1960. He moved to Buxton FC as player-manager in May 1961, but resigned the following January, and went into business as a shop-keeper.

SEASON	LEAGUE		FA CUP		L. CUP	
	Apps	Gls	Apps	Gls	Apps	Gls
1960/61	8	0	0	0	0	0
TOTAL	8	0	0	0	0	0

TOTAL APPS	8
TOTAL GOALS	0

David Charles GILES, 1981 (loan)

Welshman David Giles came to O's on loan in November 1981, and the midfielder scored a brace in his final match at Oldham on 19 December 1981. He holds a unique record, having played for all three Welsh League Clubs – plus former members Newport County – and was capped for Wales at all international levels. Born in Cardiff on 21 September 1956, he started his long career as an apprentice with Cardiff City in September 1974, and made 51(8) League appearances which yielded 3 goals. He moved to Wrexham in December 1978 for £30,000, making 38 appearances and scoring twice. He moved to Swansea City in November 1979 for £70,000, and featured prominently in their 1980/81 promotion success, but after 130 appearances he joined Crystal Palace in March

1982, and later played for Birmingham City, Newport County and Cardiff City. He ended his playing career with Barry Town, and later became their coach. Giles won 12 Welsh international caps, and made a total of 302(22) League appearances (scoring 28 goals) throughout a career that spanned some twelve years. After his retirement from football, he became a double glazing salesman in Wales.

SEASON	LEAGUE		FA CUP		L. CUP	
	Apps	Gls	Apps	Gls	Apps	Gls
1981/82	3	2	0	0	0	0
TOTAL	3	2	0	0	0	0

TOTAL APPS	3
TOTAL GOALS	2

James Joshua Allison GILL, 1933-34

Born in Bear Park, near Crook, Co. Durham on 21 July 1903, he started his career as a centre half with Crook Town, and then moved to Bear Park Welfare FC. He was then converted to goalkeeper, and joined Bolton Wanderers in August 1926, for whom he made 42 senior appearances. Afterwards, he moved on to Bradford City in June 1930 for £500, where he played 89 matches. Thirty-year-old Gill joined Orient on 18 July 1933, starting off as a first-team choice, but soon losing his place to Alf Robertson in December 1933. He moved to Accrington Stanley on 26 June 1934, and his move to Peel Park meant he had appeared in every division of the League. He made 62 appearances for Accrington, before going on to join Great Harwood Town in September 1936, retiring two years later. Gill died in Blackburn on 6 September 1985, aged eighty-two.

SEASON	LEAGUE		FA CUP		TOTAL	
	Apps	Gls	Apps	Gls	Apps	Gls
1933/34	19	0	3	0	22	0
TOTAL	19	0	3	0	22	0

Kenneth Ernest GILLATT, 1920-23

Born in Wensleydale, Derbyshire in 1897, Ernie Gillatt served in France during the First World War, and was awarded a DCM for heroism in Ypres. The forward joined O's in June 1920 from Matlock Town, having previously played for Hartsay Colliery. He can hardly be recalled as one of O's great players of the 1920s, yet he was speedy and a useful squad member. He had a reasonable first season at Millfields Road, and starred in the 3-0 victory over Notts County in April 1920 (a match attended by the Prince of Wales), weighing in with a goal. He also hit a couple of wonderful goals in a 4-2 win over Fulham in December 1921. He moved to Burnley on trial in September 1923, playing just once on the right wing against Liverpool. He was not offered a contract, and joined Mansfield Town of the Midlands League in November 1923. He had 2 successful seasons with them, gaining 2 championship medals in 1924 and 1925, and making 35 appearances as well as scoring 10 goals. Gillatt joined Barnsley in February 1925 for £175, scoring once in 13 League appearances.

SEASON	LEAGUE		FA CUP		TOTAL	
	Apps	Gls	Apps	Gls	Apps	Gls
1920/21	30	2	0	0	30	0
1921/22	16	4	1	0	17	4
1922/23	15	0	1	0	16	0
TOTAL	61	6	2	0	63	6

Thomas Aubrey GILSON, 1905-06

Born in Lichfield, Staffordshire on 1 June 1879, Alf, as he was often affectionately known, started his career with Burton United. In 1900 he joined Aston Villa, but after just 2 First Division appearances, he moved to Southern League Brentford in 1902. Gilson returned to the League with Bristol City in June 1903, scoring once in 52 senior appearances. The right-back became an 'Oriental' in May 1905, as cover for George Lamberton, and made his League debut for O's in a 6-1 defeat at Leeds City in March 1906. His only other senior appearance was two weeks later, another 6-1 defeat, this time at Chelsea. He never appeared for the club again, and he re-joined Brentford in 1906. Gilson died in Waddleston on 2 March 1912, aged thirty-two.

SEASON	LEAGUE		FA CUP		TOTAL	
	Apps	Gls	Apps	Gls	Apps	Gls
1905/06	2	0	0	0	2	0
TOTAL	2	0	0	0	2	0

Gilbert Swinburne GLIDDEN, 1950-51

Gil Glidden was born in Sunderland on 15 December 1915. He joined O's in November 1950 from Reading as a trainer, where he had enjoyed a successful career. However, he was called upon to play at left-back for the League match at Newport County on 28 April 1951, due to an injury crisis at the club, at the age of thirty-five. He started off as a junior with Sunderland in 1932, and made his League debut with Port Vale in 1935. He went on to make 5 League appearances and score once for Vale. In May 1936 he joined Reading, and was one of four players to appear for them either side of the Second World War. He played for them in both legs of the 1938 Southern Section Cup Final, as Reading became the last winners of that competition. He scored a total of 24 goals in 122 League appearances for Reading, and was often referred to as one of the fittest players in the League. After leaving O's in 1951, he become a physical training instructor at a school. Glidden died on Staffordshire Moors during October 1988.

SEASON	LEAGUE		FA CUP		TOTAL	
	Apps	Gls	Apps	Gls	Apps	Gls
1950/51	1	0	0	0	1	0
TOTAL	1	0	0	0	1	0

Allan Richard GLOVER, 1976-78

Born on 21 October 1950 in Laleham, near Staines, Glover started off as an apprentice with Queens Park Rangers in 1966, but his chances were limited. The midfielder decided to move on to West Bromwich Albion as part of a £70,000 deal (involving winger Clive Clark), and went on to make 84 League appearances and score 8 goals. He had a loan spell with Southend United in January 1976, which lasted all of 30 seconds before he was stretchered off with an injury. He was part of the Laurie Cunningham deal (with Joe Mayo) that brought them to Brisbane Road in March 1977, and both scored on their O's debut at Blackburn Rovers in a 2-2 draw. Glover also scored a vital goal against Hull City in May 1977, that spared them from going down to the Third Division. Unfortunately, he was dogged by injury during his stay, and moved to Brentford in November 1988, where he made a further 21(2) League appearances. During 1980 he joined Staines FC, but was forced to retire through injury in 1981 after making 165 career League appearances and scoring 16 goals.

Allan Glover

SEASON	LEAGUE		FA CUP		L. CUP	
	Apps	Gls	Apps	Gls	Apps	Gls
1976/77	16	2	0	0	0	0
1977/78	21	3	0	0	1	0
TOTAL	37	5	0	0	1	0

TOTAL APPS	38
TOTAL GOALS	5

* Allan Glover also appeared in 3 Anglo-Scottish Cup matches.

Terence Robert GLYNN, 1976-77

Terry Glynn was born in Hackney, London on 17 December 1958. He came though O's junior ranks, signing as an apprentice in March 1975. Although starting off as a defender, he later converted to a striking role. He made his full League debut in the 1-1 draw with Millwall on 8 March 1977. Glynn was not retained, and he left in May 1977. After a trial with Brentford, he moved into non-League football, where he played for Ilford and then Wycombe Wanderers. In later years, he played for the Old Parmitarians.

SEASON	LEAGUE		FA CUP		L. CUP	
	Apps	Gls	Apps	Gls	Apps	Gls
1976/77	1(1)	0	0	0	0	0
TOTAL	1(1)	0	0	0	0	0

TOTAL APPS	1(1)
TOTAL GOALS	0

Raymond GODDARD, 1967-74

Goalkeeper Ray Goddard was born in Fulham, London on 13 February 1949. He joined O's from Fulham in March 1967, where he began as an apprentice but never featured in their League side. He was given his O's League debut against Workington on 27 May 1976, replacing Ron Willis. The eighteen-year-old was soon to make the position his own, and he become one of O's best ever 'keepers. He was a regular in O's Third Division Championship-winning side of 1969/70, but was upset when O's boss George Petchey signed John Jackson from Crystal Palace in October 1973. However, he did appear in the vital promotion-clinching match against Aston Villa in April 1974. Unfortunately, the match was drawn, and it was Carlisle United who were promoted to the First Division. After a short loan spell with Scottish League side Greenock Morton, he joined Millwall in November 1974, and made 80 League appearances for the Lions. He was transferred to Wimbledon for £45,000 in February 1978, where he made a further 119 League appearances and won a championship medal. He scored a vital penalty goal against Bury in May 1981 to help secure the Dons the championship. Older O's fans will also remember Goddard for fir-

ing the winning penalty past O's goalie Mervyn Day in a League Cup shootout, just moments after saving Joe Mayo's kick. He ended his career with Wealdstone, whom he joined in July 1981. After his retirement, he owned a bar in sunny Spain.

SEASON	LEAGUE		FA CUP		L. CUP	
	Apps	Gls	Apps	Gls	Apps	Gls
1966/67	1	0	0	0	0	0
1967/68	41	0	5	0	0	0
1968/69	44	0	2	0	4	0
1969/70	44	0	2	0	2	0
1970/71	42	0	3	0	1	0
1971/72	39	0	4	0	2	0
1972/73	42	0	1	0	2	0
1973/74	25	0	3	0	2	0
TOTAL	278	0	20	0	13	0

TOTAL APPS	311
TOTAL GOALS	0

* Ray Goddard also appeared in 0(1) Texaco Cup match in 1974/75.

Ray Goddard

G

Kevin GODFREY, 1976-88

Born on 24 February 1960 in Kennington, London, Kevin Godfrey represented South London schools, becoming an apprentice with O's in June 1976. He was just sixteen-and-a-half when he made his O's first-team debut in a Anglo-Scottish Cup tie against Chelsea at Brisbane Road in August 1976. He turned professional in March 1977, and remarkably went onto to achieve fourth place in O's all-time goalscoring charts with 72 senior goals. Two of his most memorable matches were against Bolton Wanderers in April 1985 (where he scored a hat-trick in a 4-3 win) and against Tottenham Hotspur in the first leg of the League Milk Cup in September 1985 (where he scored both goals in a 2-0 victory). His biggest disappointment was being left out of the FA Cup semi-final against Arsenal in April 1978, when the more experienced Derek Clarke was chosen ahead of him. Wingman Godfrey was quick, with good ball control, but in his

Kevin Godfrey

early days, he often let himself down with weak crosses. However, he was a loyal clubman. He went on loan to Plymouth Argyle in February 1986, where he made 7 League appearances and scored once. After a short spell with Maidenhead United, he joined Brentford on a free transfer in October 1988, making 101(39) League appearances and scoring 17 goals. In May 1993 he joined non-League Yeading FC, and nowadays, he is a taxi-driver in London.

SEASON	LEAGUE		FA CUP		L. CUP	
	Apps	Gls	Apps	Gls	Apps	Gls
1977/78	11	0	5	0	0	0
1978/79	3(3)	0	0	0	0(1)	0
1979/80	2(3)	1	2	0	0	0
1980/81	5(4)	2	0	0	0	0
1981/82	42	8	5	0	2	0
1982/83	42(3)	11	2	2	2	0
1983/84	39(2)	10	1	0	2	1
1984/85	36(4)	10	4	1	3	0
1985/86	13(3)	4	4	1	3	3
1986/87	34(2)	10	2	0	1(1)	0
1987/88	28(6)	7	3(1)	1	2	0
TOTAL	255(30)	63	28(1)	5	15(2)	4

TOTAL APPS	298(33)
TOTAL GOALS	72

* Kevin Godfrey also appeared in 1 Anglo-Scottish Cup match, 3 Football League Groups Cup matches and 6(2) Auto Windscreens Shield matches.

Richard Robert GOFFIN, 1907-1911

Born in Clapton, London during 1886, inside forward Dick Goffin began his career with Eton Mission FC in the Clapton & District League in 1902, and later played for Peel Institute. He joined O's in 1907, and although not a regular first-team choice, he performed well for the reserves. Goffin's first League goal was in the 5-1 win over Chesterfield during November 1907. He stayed at Millfields Road for four seasons, before his move to Southern League side New Brompton (later Gillingham) during July 1911, where he made 78 appearances and scored 11 goals. During the First World War, he guested for Chelsea. After the war, he was one of a few players to be reinstated by the League, as an amateur playing for Uxbridge. After retiring from playing, he acted for many years as a trainer to the RAF.

SEASON	LEAGUE		FA CUP		TOTAL	
	Apps	Gls	Apps	Gls	Apps	Gls
1907/08	26	8	0	0	26	8
1908/09	7	0	0	0	7	0
1909/10	8	2	0	0	8	2
1910/11	24	2	1	1	25	3
TOTAL	65	12	1	1	66	13

Anthony GOODGAME, 1966-67

Tony Goodgame, a defender, was born in Hammersmith, London on 19 February 1946. He started off as an apprentice with Fulham in February 1964 and became an 'Oriental' in August 1966, but only managed a handful of appearances. He was a great trier with a very hard tackle, but perhaps with limited ability. He made his League debut against Peterborough United in September 1966. Goodgame moved to Southern League outfit Hillingdon Borough on a free transfer in May 1967.

SEASON	LEAGUE		FA CUP		L. CUP	
	Apps	Gls	Apps	Gls	Apps	Gls
1966/67	7(1)	0	0	0	0	0
TOTAL	7(1)	0	0	0	0	0

TOTAL APPS	7(1)
TOTAL GOALS	0

Albert Abraham GOODMAN, 1925-26

Born in Dalston, London on 3 September 1890, Abe Goodman, a full-back who was affectionately known as 'kosher' during his playing days, was one of only a handful of Jewish players to appear for O's throughout the years. Goodman started off playing as a schoolboy with London Fields, and then he joined Tufnell Park in 1911, before becoming an amateur with Tottenham Hotspur in 1913. He then played for Green Old Boys and Maidstone United in 1913. During 1914 he made 21 Southern League appearances with Reading, scoring 3 goals. In 1915 he played for Croydon Common, and he guested for the O's in the First World War. After the war he signed for Spurs, and made 17 senior appearances in 1919/20 (scoring once), which was enough to qualify him for a Second Division Championship medal. In February 1921 he joined Charlton Athletic, and made 126 League appearances during his four-year stay, scoring 15 goals. In June 1925, he moved to Gillingham, making just 6 appearances before becoming an 'Oriental' on 8 March 1926. He was not a regular with O's, playing just a handful of matches, although he was picked at centre forward (due to an injury to Donald Cock) for the visit to Nottingham Forest on 5 April 1926, and managed to get himself sent off! He moved to non-League Guildford City in November 1927, where he won Kent Cup honours, and he later coached Tooting City. It was reported in January 1935 that he was a get-away driver involved with a robbery of a tailor's shop at Ilford, and he received a year's sentence. Goodman proved throughout his career to be 'unorthodox', unpredictable and perplexing. He died in Ilford on 7 December 1959, following a road accident.

G

SEASON	LEAGUE		FA CUP		TOTAL	
	Apps	Gls	Apps	Gls	Apps	Gls
1925/26	10	0	0	0	10	0
1926/27	2	0	0	0	2	0
TOTAL	12	0	0	0	12	0

Frederick Leslie GORE, 1939-46

Les Gore will be best remembered for his service to the O's as coach, trainer, care-taker-manager and manager between 1951 and 1966. Yet Gore was also a successful player, and appeared for O's during the war years, featuring in both FA Cup ties against Newport Isle of Wight in 1945/46. Born in Coventry on 21 January 1914, Gore started his playing career with Birmingham's Morris Metalworks side. He joined Fulham as a professional in June 1953, but it was whilst with Stockport County that he made his League debut against Port Vale on 26 September 1936. He made 7 League appearances and scored once for County. He joined Carlisle United in September 1937, but after just 3 League matches he joined Bradford City in February 1938, where he was more successful, playing in 33 League games and netting 8 goals. He joined O's on 8 May 1939, scoring on his O's League debut at outside right in a fixture against Ipswich Town on 26 August 1939 (the result of which was later expunged, due to the start of the Second World War). He played in 25 wartime matches for O's, netting 5 times. He scored one of the goals in that FA Cup tie against Newport (IOW) on 17 November 1945, but it was not enough, and the O's were eliminated from the competition over the two-legged tie (2-3). In 1946 he moved to Yeovil Town, where he and his colleague (and former 'Oriental') Johnny Hartburn netted nearly 60 goals between them. His next move was to Gravesend & Northfleet in 1948, from whom he re-joined O's as assistant coach in 1951. Gore left Orient in November 1967 and then joined Charlton Athletic as chief scout. After his retirement in the mid-1980s, he scouted for Millwall. Les Gore died on 22 January 1991, the day after his seventy-seventh birthday. Gore should hold a permanent and prominent place in the history of Leyton Orient Football Club.

SEASON	LEAGUE		FA CUP		TOTAL	
	Apps	Gls	Apps	Gls	Apps	Gls
1939/40*	3	1	0	0	3	1
1945/46**	-	-	2	1	2	1
TOTAL	-	-	2	1	2	1

* All records for the 3 League matches (including appearances and goals) in 1939/40 were expunged from the record books due to the start of the Second World War, when all League matches were suspended.

** No League matches were played in 1945/46.

Cecil William GOUGH, 1925-26, 1928-29

Cecil Gough was born in Cirencester, Gloucestershire on 17 October 1901. He started as a young boy with Cirencester Town Juniors, and at the age of twelve he was elected captain – a position he held for three years. After playing for South Cirney FC for two seasons, Gough spent a similar period with Cirencester Town in the Stroud & District League. He then joined Cirencester Victoria FC and then assisted Tetbury Town FC. He returned to Cirencester Town, and attracted the attention of Bristol Rovers in September 1923. Although his position was inside forward, injuries compelled them to convert him to left half. His only senior appearance for Rovers was on 5 May 1924 at Ashton Gate, and was against Bristol

City in the Gloucestershire Cup Final replay, which was lost 2-0. He became an 'Oriental' during August 1925, making his League debut against Derby County on 24 September 1925, a 1-0 defeat. He joined Queens Park Rangers in June 1926, making 19 League appearances. In June 1927 he moved to Torquay United for their inaugural League season, making 28 senior appearances. Gough rejoined O's in August 1928, but his only appearance was in the 2-0 defeat at Millfields by West Bromwich Albion on 29 December 1928, and he was only playing due to injuries to both Duffy and Galbraith. In May 1929 he joined Canterbury Waverley FC, and later played for Park Royal FC (whom he joined on 30 October 1933) and he signed for Ealing Celtic FC on 9 December 1935. During March 1948, he was appointed to the Committee of Crittall Athletic FC. Cecil Gough died in Braintree, Essex on 16 May 1963, aged sixty-one.

SEASON	LEAGUE		FA CUP		TOTAL	
	Apps	Gls	Apps	Gls	Apps	Gls
1925/26	6	0	0	0	6	0
1928/29	1	0	0	0	1	0
TOTAL	7	0	0	0	7	0

Neil GOUGH, 1999-2002

YTS player Neil Gough was born in Harlow, Essex on 1 September 1981. He attended Brays Grove School, and played for the Pitney Bowes Club, as well as representing Harlow District. The right-sided midfielder also played up front for the youth side. Gough made 23 youth appearances in 1998/99, scoring 3 goals. The highlight of the following youth campaign for Gough, was when he netted 4 goals in a 6-1 win at Gillingham, and a hat-trick in a 4-1 win over QPR. In total, he scored

17 goals from 21 appearances. His League debut was as a substitute brought on in the seventy-first minute against Torquay United on 18 September 1999. He became the 872nd player to appear for the club in League and major cup competitions. Another substitute appearance came against Grimsby Town in the Worthington Cup. His full debut came on 15 April 2000 against Chester City. He was a playing substitute in the youth team that won the FA Alliance Cup final at the Millennium Stadium on 22 April 2001, beating Bradford City 1-0. Gough signed a new one-year contract in June 2001. He was loaned out to Chelmsford City the following August, but sustained a hamstring injury. He opened his League goal account with a last-minute header to secure a 3-1 win over Bristol Rovers on 8 September. O's Captain Dean Smith praised Gough saying: 'I thought he played with a lot of maturity, in fact, he was excellent.' He joined Dr Marten's Premier Division side Chelmsford City in December 2001 on a month's loan. He was released from his O's contract in March 2002 and went on to join Hampton & Richmond FC.

SEASON	LEAGUE		FA CUP		L. CUP	
	Apps	Gls	Apps	Gls	Apps	Gls
1999/2000	1(3)	0	0	0	0(1)	0
2000/01	0	0	0	0	0	0
2001/02	1(10)	1	0	0	0	0
TOTAL	2(13)	1	0	0	0(1)	0

TOTAL APPS	2(14)
TOTAL GOALS	1

Ronald Donald GOULD, 1999-present

Ronnie Gould was born in Bethnal Green, London on 27 September 1982. The midfielder signed YTS forms on

5 July 1999, and made his League debut when coming on as a substitute on the seventy-sixth minute at Hull City on 8 April 2000. A further substitute appearance came during the final League game of the 1999/2000 season at Brisbane Road against York City on 6 May 2000. He was an unused substitute at Shrewsbury Town and at Darlington in March 2001. He was a member of the team that won the FA Alliance Cup Final over Bradford City at the Millennium Stadium on 22 April 2001. A determined midfielder, with good positional sense and composure on the ball, he became a regular in the reserves and the under-19 double-winning team, with 22 appearances and 4 goals, and was rewarded with the offer of a professional contract from Tommy Taylor in October 2001. Gould, who recently starred in the ITV documentary *The Real EastEnders*, joined Ryman League Premier Division side Heybridge Swifts in September 2001 on a month's loan, in order to gain some senior match experience.

SEASON	LEAGUE		FA CUP		L. CUP	
	Apps	Gls	Apps	Gls	Apps	Gls
1999/2000	0(2)	0	0	0	0	0
2000/01	0	0	0	0	0	0
2001/02	0	0	0	0	0	0
TOTAL	0(2)	0	0	0	0	0

TOTAL APPS	0(2)
TOTAL GOALS	0

James Arthur GRAHAM, 1937-38
Born in Corby, Northamptonshire on 13 January 1911, the brother of former O's manager Dick Graham, Jimmy Graham joined O's in May 1937 from Southend United, where he had been limited to just 4 appearances (scoring once) during his two seasons at Roots Hall. The centre forward started his career with Desborough Town, before joining Nottingham Forest in 1932. During his three years at Forest, he made 32 League appearances and scored 13 goals. In 1937 he joined York City, but after 7 appearances he was off to Hartlepool United, with whom he played 20 senior matches and scored 3 goals, before moving south to join Southend United. Graham was not a regular with O's, his only League goal came in 1-0 win over Bristol Rovers in January 1938. However, he was top scorer for the reserves with 20 goals in 1937/38. He left the club in May 1938. Graham died in Bath on 28 November 1987.

SEASON	LEAGUE		FA CUP		TOTAL	
	Apps	Gls	Apps	Gls	Apps	Gls
1937/38	9	1	1	1	10	2
TOTAL	9	1	1	1	10	2

* Jimmy Graham also appeared in a Third Division Cup match in 1937/38.

Malcolm GRAHAM, 1960-63
Malcolm Graham, a short and bustling forward, possessed a terrific shot on both feet. He will always be fondly remembered for his brace against Bury on an emotional day (28 April 1962), in the match that took O's up to the top League in the country for the only time ever in its history, as runners-up to Liverpool. Born in Wakefield on 26 January 1934, he joined Barnsley as a part-time professional from Hall Green FC in April 1953, where he combined his football with working as a miner at Haigh Colliery. During his time with Barnsley, he attracted the attention of several First Division clubs, and a deal with Newcastle

Malcolm Graham

United was set up, but they refused to pay the £20,000 asking fee. He made a total of 103 senior appearances and scored 35 goals at Oakwell, including 4 goals against Charlton Athletic in September 1958. Graham was one of several players to leave the south Yorkshire club, following their relegation at the end of 1958/59 season, joining Bristol City in May 1959 (along with left-winger Johnny McCann) for a joint fee of £7,000. He scored twice on his City League debut, yet played just 14 times for the Robins, scoring 8 goals, before joining O's on 20 June 1960 for £8,000. His first goal for O's came at Leeds United, in a 3-1 win during September 1960, however, injury restricted his progress that season. Graham came into his own during the 1961/62 promotion season, striking up a wonderful partnership with big striker Dave Dunmore – between them, the pair scored 35 League goals. He started the season off with a

bang, with a great hat-trick at Walsall in a 5-1 victory. The season's climax came with the Bury match in April 1962. Graham had arrived at the ground thinking he would be watching from the stands, but when Ronnie Foster failed a very late fitness test, in came Graham, and what a fairytale ending it turned out to be. Graham's first goal on fourteen minutes was a header, while the second came with just five minutes remaining. He picked up a loose ball, beat a defender on the right, raced into the penalty area, dribbled around Bury 'keeper Chris Harker, and joyfully drove into an empty net, to the roars of the 21,617-strong crowd. The final whistle sounded, and Sunderland had only managed a 1-1 draw at Swansea, so promotion was assured for the boys in blue, and tears of joy ran down the Yorkshireman's face. During the First Division campaign, he hit a notable goal against West Ham United to ensure a 2-0 victory. He also grabbed a hat-trick in the 9-2 demolition of Chester in the League Cup. It was, however, to be his final season at Brisbane Road. During July 1963, he (along with Derek Gibbs) joined Queens Park Rangers for a joint fee of £10,000. He scored on his Rangers debut against Oldham Athletic, and made 23 senior appearances, scoring 8 goals, before returning to Barnsley in July 1964, where he played 22 senior matches and netted a further 6 goals. Graham joined Buxton FC in June 1965, and ended his playing career with Alfreton Town. He made a total of 233 League appearances that yielded 82 goals. In recent years, Mal Graham suffered from a heart attack at his home in Barnsley, but, happily, in May 2000, he was able to attend O's 'Starman' dinner awards, an event that also celebrated the seventieth birthday of Stan

Charlton – O's skipper of that promotion campaign.

SEASON	LEAGUE		FA CUP		L. CUP	
	Apps	Gls	Apps	Gls	Apps	Gls
1960/61	19	7	0	0	1	0
1961/62	29	13	2	0	2	0
1961/62	27	9	2	0	2	5
TOTAL	75	29	4	0	5	5

TOTAL APPS	84
TOTAL GOALS	34

George GRANT, 1938-39

Born in Bonnyrigg, Scotland, George Grant, who was a tall inside forward, started his career with Tranent FC, and later played for Bonnyrigg Rose Athletic and Leith Athletic. He became an 'Oriental' in July 1938, joining from the Edinburgh club St Bernard's FC. He shared the right-wing spot with Fred Tully throughout the 1938/39 season, proving to be a dangerous attacking wingman. He left O's in July 1939, joining Ballymena.

SEASON	LEAGUE		FA CUP		TOTAL	
	Apps	Gls	Apps	Gls	Apps	Gls
1938/39	19	4	1	0	20	4
TOTAL	19	4	1	0	20	4

Lionel Oliver GRAPES, 1912 (loan)

Amateur goalkeeper L.O. Grapes joined O's in September 1912, on loan from Shepherds Bush FC, when both the regular 'keepers – Hugall and Bower – were injured. He made his League debut on 28 September 1912 against Glossop North End, and also played in the following match against Blackpool – both matches at Millfields Road resulted in 1-0 victories. *Athletic News* reported that with amateur goalkeeper L.O. Grapes in

the side, the O's fans greeted his entry onto the field with a chorus of 'Hello Grapes', (L.O.) Grapes responded with two wonderful performances. He returned to the Shepherds Bush club when Billy Bower was fit to return between the sticks for the next fixture.

SEASON	LEAGUE		FA CUP		TOTAL	
	Apps	Gls	Apps	Gls	Apps	Gls
1912/13	2	0	0	0	2	0
TOTAL	2	0	0	0	2	0

Andrew GRAY, 1994-96

Andy Gray, a diminutive striker who stood just 5ft 6in tall, was born in Southampton on 25 October 1973, and started as a trainee with Reading in July 1992. Gray made 8(9) League appearances and scored 3 goals for Reading, before a free transfer took him to O's in July 1994. He scored on his full League debut on 27 August 1994 against Hull City, having previously appeared as a

Andy Gray

substitute. After a couple of seasons at the club, he could never really command a regular first-team place, due to a number of injury setbacks. It was Gray's FA Cup goal at Tiverton on 12 November 1994, which led to a wall collapsing behind the goal. In February 1996 he was set to join Woking, but the two clubs could not agree on a suitable fee, so instead he went on loan to Enfield in the ICIS League. During May 1996 he signed for Vauxhall Conference team Slough Town for a nominal fee.

SEASON	LEAGUE		FA CUP		L. CUP	
	Apps	Gls	Apps	Gls	Apps	Gls
1994/95	13(12)	3	1	1	0(2)	0
1995/96	3(4)	0	0	0	0	0
TOTAL	16(16)	3	1	1	0(2)	0

TOTAL APPS	17(18)
TOTAL GOALS	4

* Andy Gray also appeared in 0(1) Auto Windscreens Shield match.

Mark Stuart GRAY, 1979-81

Mark Gray was born in Tenby, Pembroke, Wales on 24 November 1959. This centre forward and former Welsh youth international started off with Swansea City in September 1977, making 1(1) League appearances, before moving to Fulham in January 1978. He joined O's as part of the £100,000 deal that took Peter Kitchen to Craven Cottage in February 1979. As with his time at Fulham, he didn't cut much ice at Brisbane Road, playing mostly reserve-team football. His full League debut came in the 1-0 win at Burnley on 28 April 1979. He returned to his former club, Swansea City, on trial in 1981, but soon after drifted into non-League football.

SEASON	LEAGUE		FA CUP		L. CUP	
	Apps	Gls	Apps	Gls	Apps	Gls
1978/79	1(1)	0	0	0	0	0
TOTAL	1(1)	0	0	0	0	0

TOTAL APPS	1(1)
TOTAL GOALS	0

Nigel Robert GRAY, 1974-83

Nigel Gray was never rated as one of the club's better centre halves, yet in an organised defensive set-up, he played his part very efficiently. The 6ft 3in player performed excellently in O's great FA Cup run of 1977/78, and stayed with the club for over nine seasons. Born in Fulham, London on 2 November 1956, he signed as an associate schoolboy, having been nurtured by the local Beaumont club (under the leadership of Maurice Newman). After signing apprentice forms in 1973, he became a full-time professional in April 1974, making his League debut a year later against Bolton Wanderers. Gray didn't score many goals, but he did get on the scoresheet in a 4-1 win over a Kuwait XI in a friendly during 1982/83. Gray had loan spells with both Blackburn Rovers and Charlton Athletic, before joining Swindon Town in July 1983. He made 36 senior appearances and scored once for the Robins, before going on loan to Brentford in March 1984 (16 League appearances and a single goal), then to Aldershot in September 1984 (4 League appearances). He moved into non-League football with Enfield, and then Dagenham, and later represented an England non-League representative side. He also enjoyed spells with Wycombe Wanderers in 1987 and with Tooting & Mitcham in 1988. Forty-five-year-old Gray was still playing football at

G

Nigel Gray

the end of 2001, when turning out for a side called Van Dyke FC in the Kingston-upon-Thames area.

SEASON	LEAGUE		FA CUP		L. CUP	
	Apps	Gls	Apps	Gls	Apps	Gls
1974/75	2	0	0	0	0	0
1975/76	1	0	0	0	0	0
1976/77	22	2	0(1)	0	0	0
1977/78	22	0	8	0	2	0
1978/89	42	0	3	0	1	0
1979/80	37	0	3	0	0	0
1980/81	39	0	1	0	2	0
1981/82	38	0	5	0	1	0
1982/83	30	2	0	0	2	0
TOTAL	233	4	20(1)	0	8	0

TOTAL APPS	261(1)
TOTAL GOALS	4

* Nigel Gray also appeared in 7 Anglo-Scottish Cup matches, scoring once, and 6 Football League Groups Cup matches.

Thomas GRAY, 1919-21

Born in Portsmouth during 1891, goal-keeper Tommy 'Dolly' Gray started off with Portsmouth in September 1914, making 12 Southern League appearances. He joined O's in June 1919 as understudy to Jimmy Hugall, making his League debut against Huddersfield Town in a 1-0 home defeat. He was about to leave the club, but with the sudden death of Guy Dale in 1920, he was re-signed for a brief time, but he left to join Guildford in May 1921.

SEASON	LEAGUE		FA CUP		TOTAL	
	Apps	Gls	Apps	Gls	Apps	Gls
1919/20	6	0	0	0	6	0
1920/21	6	0	1	0	7	0
TOTAL	12	0	1	0	13	0

Wayne GRAY, 2001-2002 (loan)

Twenty-one-year-old Wayne Gray joined O's on a month's loan from Wimbledon on 30 November 2001, and made his Os debut the following day against Division Three leaders Plymouth Argyle, when replacing Steve Watts on seventy-one minutes. The striker was born in Camberwell, London on 7 November 1980, and could have become a professional sprinter had he not chosen a football career instead. He started his career with the Dons, and turned professional on 1 August 1999. He made his League debut in 1999, and played a total of 1(12) matches without finding the net, however, he did score a goal against Wycombe Wanderers in an FA Cup tie. His only full appearance came against Huddersfield Town in a 1-1 draw on 11 May 2001. During March 2000, he went on loan to Swindon Town, and he netted twice from 8(4) starts. During October 2000, he went on a month's loan to Port

Vale and made 2(1) appearances. The lively young striker showed he had lots of potential. Orient offered Wimbledon £25,000 plus a fifty per cent sell-on clause, but the Dons turned this down and Gray returned to south London on 4 March 2002.

SEASON	LEAGUE		FA CUP		L. CUP	
	Apps	Gls	Apps	Gls	Apps	Gls
2001/02	13(2)	5	2	1	0	0
TOTAL	13(2)	5	2	1	0	0

TOTAL APPS	15(2)
TOTAL GOALS	6

William Patrick GRAY, 1947-49

Born in Durham on 24 May 1927, Billy Gray came to O's as a twenty-year-old from Dinnington Colliery during May 1947. Known as Patrick in his early days with O's, he came to the club having been watched on a regular basis by O's boss Charles Hewitt, who realised his great potential. On arrival, he showed great promise with his thrusting wing play, scoring on his League debut against Newport County on 6 September 1947, which proved to be his only League goal for the club. On 27 December 1948, he had the rare distinction of playing in 2 matches for the club on the same day. In the morning he turned out for the reserves in a Combination match at Chelsea, and then rushed back to Brisbane Road to play for the first team against Port Vale that afternoon. He was transferred to Chelsea in March 1949, and did very well at Stamford Bridge, making 172 senior appearances and netting 15 goals, as well as gaining England 'B' honours. He later played for Burnley and Nottingham Forest, with whom he won an FA Cup winner's medal in 1959. He later became player-manager at Millwall and also managed Brentford. He also occupied the position of groundsman at Nottingham Forest before retiring. Billy Gray had a long and distinguished career that spanned some eighteen years, and included 505 League appearances and 79 goals

SEASON	LEAGUE		FA CUP		TOTAL	
	Apps	Gls	Apps	Gls	Apps	Gls
1947/48	11	1	1	0	12	1
1948/49	8	0	0	0	8	0
TOTAL	19	1	1	0	20	1

Anthony Patrick GREALISH, 1974-79

Tony 'Paddy' Grealish was born in Paddington, London on 21 September 1956. A product of west London football, he was another of a group of players brought to O's by Maurice Newman of the Beaumont club, signing as an apprentice in June 1972 and turning professional in 1974. Grealish made

Tony Grealish

his League debut against Nottingham Forest in November 1974, and scored a great goal. He was soon to become a great crowd favourite with his all-action midfield play. In 1973 he featured in an England youth XI, however, due to his Irish parentage, Eire invited him to represent them in an UEFA youth tournament in Switzerland. He gained further Eire youth caps in the summer of 1975, and won his first full cap in 1976 against Norway, at the age of nineteen. Grealish won 7 full caps whilst at Brisbane Road, and totalled 45 caps and 8 goals during his career. He starred in O's great FA Cup run to the semi-final in 1977/78, but the advent of Freedom of Contract saw him move to Luton Town for £150,000 in July 1979, where he made 79 appearances and scored twice. He moved to Brighton & Hove Albion in July 1981 for £100,000 (making 95(5) League appearances and scoring 6 goals) and starred in some of their FA Cup exploits during the period. During March 1984 he moved to West Bromwich Albion for £75,000, making 55(10) League matches and scoring 5 goals. In October 1976 he joined Manchester City for £20,000, but stayed only a few months, making just 11 League appearances. He then joined Rotherham United in August 1987, and featured in their promotion to the Third Division two years later. During August 1990 he was appointed player-coach at Walsall, making 32(4) League appearances and scoring once. In May 1992 he moved into the Conference with newly-elected Bromsgrove Rovers. In later years, whilst working in the insurance business, he had spells with Moor Green, Halesowen Harriers, Sutton Coldfield Town, and Evesham

United (player-coach), before returning as coach with Bromsgrove for the start of 1994/95. In September 1994 he took over as their caretaker manager when Bobby Hope resigned, and he took over the position on a permanent basis two months later. He was dismissed in March 1995, and became coach at Atherstone FC. Grealish now works in the scrap metal business, and he was a special guest at the Orient 'Star Man' dinner, held in May 2000. Grealish had a wonderful career that spanned some eighteen years, making 545(25) League appearances and scoring 31 goals.

SEASON	LEAGUE		FA CUP		L. CUP	
	Apps	Gls	Apps	Gls	Apps	Gls
1974/75	24(1)	2	2	0	0	0
1975/76	38	1	1	0	1	0
1976/77	33	2	4	0	2	0
1977/78	35(1)	0	8	0	2(1)	0
1978/79	39	5	2	0	1	0
TOTAL	169(2)	10	17	0	6(1)	0

TOTAL APPS	192(3)
TOTAL GOALS	10

* Tony Grealish also played 13 Anglo-Scottish Cup matches.

James GREECHAN, 1907-08

Jimmy Greechan joined O's from Southern League side Brentford in September 1907, and was a thrusting inside forward with plenty of skill. He spent a single season at Millfields Road and performed very well. Greechan made his League debut in a 3-0 reverse at West Bromwich Albion, but netted twice in a 6-3 home FA Cup victory over Romford in October 1907, and in November, he scored another brace against Chesterfield in a 5-1 League victory. In April 1908 he was transferred to Glossop North End, making 19 League appearances and scoring 4 goals. He joined Stockport County in 1909, playing a further 15 League matches and notching 4 goals.

SEASON	LEAGUE		FA CUP		TOTAL	
	Apps	Gls	Apps	Gls	Apps	Gls
1907/08	30	8	3	3	33	11
TOTAL	30	8	3	3	33	11

Thomas GREEN, 1923-24

Tommy Green was born in Liverpool on 25 November 1893. This well-built centre forward started his career with Southport Central FC, and guested for both Liverpool and Stockport County during the First World War. After the hostilities, he kicked off his professional career on trial with West Ham United, making his League debut in a 7-0 defeat at Barnsley in September 1919. He made just 2 further appearances before moving back to Southport Central in October 1919, where he won a Lancashire Cup winner's medal. In March 1921 he joined Accrington Stanley for their inaugural League season, and top-scored with 23 goals from 30 appearances. When he signed for Stockport County for £200 in May 1922, Green again became top scorer on 15 goals from 31 starts. He became an 'Oriental' in May 1923, and for the third consecutive season, he was the top goalscorer, netting 10 League goals (including a hat-trick against Nelson on 1 September 1923). He was transferred to Heart of Midlothian on 27 February 1924, and in June 1925 he was moved to Third Lanark. Green died in Liverpool during October 1975, aged eighty-one.

SEASON	LEAGUE		FA CUP		TOTAL	
	Apps	Gls	Apps	Gls	Apps	Gls
1923/24	24	10	3	0	27	10
TOTAL	24	10	3	0	27	10

Gordon Harold GREGORY, 1961-66

Harry Gregory was born in Hackney, London on 24 October 1943. The former Hackney schoolboy player became O's first ever apprentice professional, soon after winning an England youth cap against Switzerland – a match played at Brisbane Road in 1960. Gregory was chosen to make his League debut on 9 October 1961 at Bury, but the match was postponed and his League aspirations had to wait a further year. When he finally made that League debut at inside forward, he scored a beauty past Roy Bailey in a First Division match against Ipswich Town during November 1962, shortly after his nineteenth birthday. He only became a regular first-teamer during the 1963/64 season, forming a dangerous trio with Dave Dunmore and Ted Phillips. Gregory moved to Charlton Athletic in May 1966, a deal that brought veteran Cliff Holton and John Snedden to Brisbane Road. He made 146(3) League appearances and scored 24 goals at the Valley. He joined Aston Villa in October 1970 for £7,770, and helped them to promotion in 1971/72, playing 18(6) matches and scoring twice. In August 1972 he signed for Hereford United, making 71(2) League appearances and scoring 6 goals. He moved into non-League football in 1974.

SEASON	LEAGUE		FA CUP		L. CUP	
	Apps	Gls	Apps	Gls	Apps	Gls
1961/62	0	0	0	0	0	0
1962/63	6	1	0	0	2	1
1963/64	17	3	3	0	0	0

G

1964/65	36	6	0	0	2	2
1965/66	20	2	0	0	1	0
TOTAL	79	12	3	0	5	3

TOTAL APPS	87
TOTAL GOALS	15

Jack Leslie GREGORY, 1955-59

Born in Southampton on 25 January 1925, Jack Gregory started with Woolston youth club, before joining Southampton in 1943. Although at the Dell for more than a decade, the full-back found it difficult to maintain a regular place in the side, due to the abundance of fine defenders. He managed just 68 senior appearances for the Saints. He joined O's in May 1955 and performed creditably for four seasons. He had a firm tackle, was very courageous, and had an uncanny ability to make goal-line clearances. One recalls him dislocating his kneecap against Brentford in January 1956, but he returned to the field after a short period to battle on, as there were no substitutes in those days. He moved on to Bournemouth in July 1959, where he made 17 League appearances, and then went into non-League football with Ashford Town in August 1960. Later he moved to Hastings United and was manager-coach to Sholing Sports FC. In 1965 he returned to Southampton to work as a boilermaker on the docks until his retirement.

SEASON	LEAGUE		FA CUP		TOTAL	
	Apps	Gls	Apps	Gls	Apps	Gls
1955/56	17	0	1	0	18	0
1956/57	40	0	1	0	41	0
1957/58	27	0	2	0	29	0
1958/59	7	0	0	0	7	0
TOTAL	91	0	4	0	95	0

Dean Greygoose

Dean GREYGOOSE, 1985-86

Goalkeeper Dean Greygoose was born in Torquay on 18 December 1964. The 'keeper was a former England youth international, who started out with Cambridge United where he made 26 League appearances. He joined O's in June 1985, as cover for Peter Wells, and he did well for the reserves. His only League appearance came at Aldershot in a 1-1 draw on 4 February 1986. He moved to Crystal Palace in August 1986, then joined Crewe Alexandra in August 1997, having several good seasons and making 205 League appearances. Greygoose moved into non-League football with Holywell FC, Northwich Victoria, and more recently with Altrincham, Chester City and Witton Albion. He joined Nationwide Conference team Stevenage Borough in August 2001, making his debut against Dagenham & Redbridge the following October.

SEASON	LEAGUE		FA CUP		L. CUP	
	Apps	Gls	Apps	Gls	Apps	Gls
1985/86	1	0	0	0	0	0
TOTAL	1	0	0	0	0	0

TOTAL APPS	1
TOTAL GOALS	0

* Dean Greygoose also appeared in 3 Auto Windscreens Shield matches.

Carl GRIFFITHS, 1996-99, 1999-2001

Welshman Carl Griffiths (Super Carl) became a real favourite with the O's fans after a very successful season in 1997/98, when he scored 23 senior goals. He was good with both feet and at holding up the ball. Unfortunately, he could not find the net so regularly the following season, and rumours of a transfer to a number of clubs (including Notts County, Shrewsbury and Charlton) abounded, after he was fined by the club for his over-exuberant celebrations after scoring at Southport in the FA Cup which upset manager Taylor. On 13 January 1999, he went on a month's loan to Wrexham. It seemed clear to many supporters that Griff would not stay with the club, and it was just a matter of time before he moved on. After his loan spell with Wrexham (where he netted 4 goals from 4 League matches and an Auto Windscreen Shield appearance), goals seem to come more frequently to Griff on his return to East London, but, as expected, he was eventually sold to Division One side Port Vale for a reported £115,000, just before the transfer deadline on 24 March 1999, much to the disappointment of O's fans. It was the Port Vale manager Brian Horton who had taken Griff to Manchester City from Shrewsbury. Griff played just 3 League matches for Vale, scoring once. Happily, he returned to Brisbane Road in December 1999, and has continued his wonderful strike record. Born in Oswestry, Shropshire on 16 July 1971, he was brought up in Forden, near Welshpool in mid-Wales. Griff started as a trainee with Shrewsbury Town on 26 September 1988. He made his League debut in 1988 as a seventeen-year-old, scoring against both Leeds United and Manchester City. He became a firm favourite with the Shrewsbury fans, finding the net 62 times from 130(40) senior appearances, and winning Welsh youth, 'B' and under-21 caps. On 29 October 1993, he was transferred to Premiership side Manchester City for £500,000, but with the arrival of strikers Walsh and Rossler, he soon found himself in the reserves. On 17 August 1995, he was transferred to Portsmouth for £200,000, but never quite made it, and was soon off to Peterborough United on 28 March 1996 for £225,000. Griff was vir-

Carl Griffiths

tually unused by their manager, Barry Fry, and he didn't play a complete match in over two years at Posh. He joined O's on loan on 31 October 1996, scoring 3 goals from 5 starts. O's boss Tommy Taylor was impressed, and offered £100,000 for the player. Fry declined the offer – he wanted £200,000, which was out of O's reach. In March 1997 Taylor tried again with an offer of £100,000, and his bid was this time accepted by Fry. Griffiths was in the crowd at Rotherham, cheering on the O's in their famous semi-final penalty shoot-out victory, and at the play-off final at Wembley to watch the O's do battle with Scunthorpe United. Rumours abounded that he was about to rejoin the O's, and on 12 December 1999 he did so, for a reported £80,000, and with O's at the foot of the table (the lowest position in the club's history), he scored a hat-trick at fellow strugglers Chester City in a crushing 5-1 win. Unfortunately, injury curtailed his season, but he came back with bang in 2000/2001. The following season he was on the goal charge, and O's manager Taylor denounced rumours in March 2001 that his charge was on the way to Rotherham United as 'absolute rubbish'. Griff has found the net at irregular intervals, but has climbed up the O's all-time goals charts, with over 50 League goals now recorded. However, after his sending off at Mansfield Town on 21 April 2001, he made himself ineligible for the play-offs due to suspension. He once again fell out with boss Tommy Taylor, who stated in the club programme: 'It does not help when people are not professional enough to stay on the field'. The player promptly requested to be placed on the transfer list. O's boss Taylor stated: 'We want him at the club and scoring goals – if nobody comes in for him, I'm

not worried about that. He's a great goalscorer, but wants to play at a higher level, yet deep down, I don't believe he really wants to leave us.' Should he have stayed, he would certainly have become only the fifth player to record more than 70 League goals for the club since 1905/06. However, he made a £65,000 move to fellow Division Three side Luton Town on 9 July 2001. There he netted 3 goals in pre-season friendlies and 7 League goals in his first 9 appearances, however, after receiving a shin injury during September 2001 in a match at Orient, it is unlikely that he will play again until 2002/03. He informed the press: 'I found myself unwanted at Orient, after my suspension I was told I could not travel with the squad for the play-off final in Wales. I'm happy to be at Luton, this club has more ambition than the Orient.' By the end of February 2002, Carl Griffiths had netted 124 goals from 256(69) career League games.

SEASON	LEAGUE		FA CUP		L. CUP	
	Apps	Gls	Apps	Gls	Apps	Gls
1996/97	13	6	0	0	0	0
1997/98	31(2)	18	2	1	4	3
1998/99	21(3)	8	3	1	3(1)	0
1999/2000	11	4	0	0	0	0
2000/01	35(2)	15	3	4	2(1)	0
TOTAL	111(7)	51	8	6	9(2)	3

TOTAL APPS	128(9)
TOTAL GOALS	60

* Carl Griffiths also appeared in 2 Auto Windscreens Shield matches, without scoring.

Thomas GRIFFITHS, 1912-14

Manchester-born Tom Griffiths was a fine left half. He was initially on the books of Blackburn Rovers, before going on to join

Southern League side Exeter City in 1910, where he made his debut against Leyton FC. He joined O's in May 1912, but was denied a regular first-team place, due to the excellent form of Harold Willis. He made his League debut in a 1-1 draw at Birmingham City in March 1913, and moved on to join Llanelli FC in 1914.

SEASON	LEAGUE		FA CUP		TOTAL	
	Apps	Gls	Apps	Gls	Apps	Gls
1912/13	8	0	0	0	8	0
1913/14	4	0	1	0	5	0
TOTAL	12	0	1	0	13	0

Arthur GRIMSDELL, 1929-30

Thirty-five-year-old Arthur Grimsdell was appointed as O's first ever player-secretary-manager during May 1929, after O's had been relegated for the first time in their history to the Third Division (South), after twenty seasons as members of the Second Division. His reign lasted just ten months, and he

Arthur Grimsdell

resigned in amicable fashion during March 1930. Born on 23 March 1894 in Watford, Hertfordshire, the young Grimsdell played for the local schools XI and gained an England schoolboy cap in 1908 – an 8-0 victory against Wales at Aberdare – in only the second schoolboy international ever staged. He was spotted by Watford playing for the Watford St Stephens club, and signed amateur forms for the Southern League outfit in 1909. The following season he split his time between playing for Watford and St Albans City – making 35 senior appearances for the latter. He played for Watford in 2 Southern League games in 1910/11. The following season he had netted 3 goals from 34 games, when Tottenham Hotspur made a double swoop on the Herts club, signing eighteen-year-old Grimsdell and Walter Tattersall for a combined fee of £500 on 17 April 1912. He remained at White Hart Lane for seventeen years, making a grand total of 417 senior appearances that yielded 38 goals, and he gained 6 full England international caps. On 23 April 1921, captain Grimsdell received the FA Cup from King George V at Stamford Bridge, following their 1-0 win over Wolves. He received two benefits whilst at White Hart Lane, firstly against Chelsea on 8 October 1920 (along with Jimmy Cantrell and another former 'Oriental', Bertie Bliss) and on 20 February 1926 (with Andy Thompson). Former Spurs colleague and later O's manager Jimmy Seed wrote of Grimsdell: 'His scientific approach and cleverness of tactics caused major problems for opponents'. Grimsdell was one of the best halfbacks in the history of the game, but a number of injuries sadly restricted his appearances, although he remained club captain. Grimsdell later went into schoolboy coaching, and between 1945 and 1951 he was a director of Watford FC as well as running a sports outfitters in Romford, Essex. He died in Watford on 13 March 1963.

SEASON	LEAGUE		FA CUP		TOTAL	
	Apps	Gls	Apps	Gls	Apps	Gls
1929/30	11	0	6	2	17	2
TOTAL	11	0	6	2	17	2

David Henry GROOMBRIDGE, 1951-60
Born in Norbury, Croydon on 13 April 1930, fair-haired goalkeeper Dave Groombridge first played with the Chase of Chertsey side (Arsenal's nursery club), and was spoken of as the next England amateur international goalie whilst with Athenian League side Hayes FC. However, his international chance never came, and he joined O's as a professional in 1951. He proved to be one of O's best ever 'keepers, but due to the form of Pat Welton, he spent a fair amount of time in the reserves. He appeared in O's great FA Cup run of 1953/54, and during his final season, he was playing better than ever. Alas, he was badly injured in a minor game and forced to retire at the age of thirty. Groombridge was not a spectacular 'keeper, but he did pull off some astonishing displays, and one of those was at Sheffield Wednesday when the home players applauded him for many of his saves. He later managed Edgware Town and coached Leyton FC.

SEASON	LEAGUE		FA CUP		TOTAL	
	Apps	Gls	Apps	Gls	Apps	Gls
1951/52	5	0	0	0	5	0
1952/53	23	0	2	0	25	0
1953/54	30	0	6	0	36	0
1954/55	3	0	0	0	3	0
1955/56	0	0	0	0	0	0
1956/57	24	0	0	0	24	0
1957/58	4	0	0	0	4	0
1958/59	8	0	0	0	8	0
1959/60	36	0	1	0	37	0
TOTAL	133	0	9	0	142	0

Victor George GROVES, 1954-55
Vic Groves was born in Stepney, London on 5 November 1932. He started off with Leytonstone, before joining Tottenham Hotspur as an amateur in June 1952, where he made just 4 League appearances and scored 3 goals. He moved to Walthamstow Avenue before becoming an 'Oriental' in May 1954, turning professional five months later. Very few players have made such an impact in their first season – he was a key man in O's promotion push in 1954/55, before an injury put paid to him and O's chances

Vic Groves (right) with coach Les Gore

and they finished as runners-up to Bristol City. The following season, a move to centre forward brought him further success, as his chase-everything attitude and skill made him a firm crowd favourite. The newspapers were full of stories that he was moving to a larger club. The supporters' club started a cash fund, in the hope that the club would turn down any offers. Their efforts failed, and in November 1955, he and Stan Charlton joined Arsenal for a joint fee of £30,000. Groves had a long association with the Gunners, and was converted successfully to wing-half. He made 203 senior appearances and scored 37 goals. (He also appeared in 140 other matches for the Gunners, netting a further 43 goals.) In May 1964 he joined Canterbury City, but retired from playing football in 1965 to become a publican in Edmonton, and later in Enfield, before working as an insurance salesman, ultimately becoming branch manager with Hambros Insurance Company. He was one of the guests of honour at O's Player of the Year awards in May 2001. Whilst with O's he won 4 England amateur caps, toured the West Indies with an FA party in 1955, and played for the England 'B' team against Yugoslavia. He netted an impressive three hat-tricks – away to Torquay United and Exeter City in 1954/5, and at home to Colchester United the following season. Both of his brothers (Bunny and Reg) were top-class amateur players.

SEASON	LEAGUE		FA CUP		TOTAL	
	Apps	Gls	Apps	Gls	Apps	Gls
1954/55	30	15	2	1	32	16
1955/56	12	9	0	0	12	9
TOTAL	42	24	2	1	44	25

H

Warren James HACKETT, 1990-94

Warren Hackett, an attacking defender/midfielder, was born in Plaistow, London on 16 December 1971. He was a junior team captain with Tottenham Hotspur, winning a FA Youth Cup winner's medal, before joining O's on a free transfer on 3 July 1990, and making his League debut at Swansea City on 30 April 1991. The following season, he came into the side at the last minute against Sheffield Wednesday in a Rumbelows League Cup tie, when Steve Castle failed a very late fitness test. He played in the next 22 matches, but then suffered a serious knee injury against Birmingham City on 22 February 1992, which kept him out of the game for nearly a year. He returned to the fray on 6 February 1993 at Brighton. Hackett was surprisingly released, and joined Doncaster Rovers on a free transfer on 26 July 1994, scoring twice in 55 senior appearances. He moved to Mansfield Town for £50,000 on 20 October 1995, and made 125(3) appearances (and scored 5 goals) for the Stags. He also won 6 international caps for St Lucia. Hackett moved to Barnet on a free transfer on 25 March 1999, but despite playing 37(4) matches in the 1999/2000 campaign, he didn't play a game the following season and was released on 21 May 2001. He trained with Boston United during pre-season, before joining Ryman League side Harrow Borough in August. He was sent off in a match against Aldershot Town the following month. On 6 November 2001, Hackett joined Ryman League side Grays Athletic, and in January 2002 he moved on to play for Ford United.

H

Warren Hackett

SEASON	LEAGUE		FA CUP		L. CUP	
	Apps	Gls	Apps	Gls	Apps	Gls
1990/91	4	0	0	0	0	0
1991/92	22	0	5	0	2	0
1992/93	16(1)	0	0	0	0	0
1993/94	32(1)	3	3	2	2	0
TOTAL	74(2)	3	8	2	4	0

TOTAL APPS   86(2)

TOTAL GOALS   5

* Warren Hackett also appeared in 7 Auto Windscreens Shield matches.

Phillip Jonathan HADLAND, 2001-02

Twenty-year-old Phil Hadland joined O's on a two-year contract on 3 July 2001. He signed under the Bosman ruling, after he rejected a further one-year contract with Rochdale. Born on 20 October 1980 in Warrington, the exciting and talented right-winger started off his career as a youth trainee player with Reading, whom he joined on 1 August 1998, playing in a single League Cup tie. He moved to Dale (instead of an expected move to York City) on a free transfer on 7 August 2000, making a total 12(20) League appearances with 2 goals. His first came against Cardiff City, and the second was scored against O's in January 2001. Hadland stated: 'The move to Orient was not about money, but rather a wish to play regular first-team football in a right-sided attacking midfield role. There were seven offers available, some in higher divisions, yet in the end, a move to Orient was my best option to progress as a player.' O's boss Tommy Taylor said of his new charge: 'Phil is only young, and he has got a great deal of potential. He is pacy and he can play on either side, quite a few clubs wanted to sign him. We did not score enough goals last season, but Phil is a creator of goals and hopefully he will be able to set up a lot of chances for our strikers.' Hadland went on a month's loan to Division Three's Carlisle United on 19 November 2001, and netted on his third appearance, a 2-1 win over Scunthorpe United in December. He has struggled to make his mark in London, with only 3 substitute appearances during August, although he played regularly for the reserves, and has made with 8 appearances, scoring once. He moved on to join Brighton & Hove Albion on 20 March 2002 and has signed for them until the end of the 2001/2002 season.

SEASON	LEAGUE		FA CUP		L. CUP	
	Apps	Gls	Apps	Gls	Apps	Gls
2001/02	0(5)	1	0	0	0(1)	0
TOTAL	0(5)	1	0	0	0(1)	0

TOTAL APPS   0(6)

TOTAL GOALS   1

Paul HAGUE, 1994-96

Paul Hague was born on 16 September 1972 in Consett, Durham. The strong central defender joined Gillingham in May 1991, making 8(1) appearances. He became an 'Oriental' on 12 September 1994 for a fee of £15,000, and notched his only League goal for O's on his debut on 24 September 1994 against Oxford United. Hague was troubled with injuries throughout the 1995/96 campaign, and did not figure in new boss Pat Holland's plans. So, after a loan spell with Dagenham & Redbridge, he joined Gateshead on a free transfer in March 1996, to play alongside another former 'O', Sam Kitchen. Hague made 13(6) appearances. O's boss Holland stated: 'It's a shame things didn't work out for Paul. He's a smashing lad, he was great to have around the club, always with a big smile on his face. He took the news of his release really well.'

SEASON	LEAGUE		FA CUP		L. CUP	
	Apps	Gls	Apps	Gls	Apps	Gls
1994/95	17(1)	0	0	0	0	0
1995/96	0	0	0	0	0	0
TOTAL	17(1)	0	0	0	0	0

TOTAL APPS	17(1)
TOTAL GOALS	0

* Paul Hague also appeared in 2(1) Auto Windscreens Shield matches.

Alan Roderick HAIG-BROWN, 1905-06

Alan Haig-Brown (or 'Haigers', as he was affectionately known) was born in Godalming, Surrey on 6 September 1877. He was one of those remarkable gentleman amateur players that existed in English sport around the turn of the century. Haig-Brown was educated at Charterhouse School and at Pembroke College, where he achieved an MA. He was a brilliant sportsman, playing football for Cambridge University (attaining blues in 1898 and 1899), Old Carthusians and the Corinthians. He also represented Pembroke College at athletics and cricket. A soldier and a scholar, he was appointed to the teaching staff of Lancing College in 1899. The fleet-footed right-winger assisted both Worthing FC and Shoreham FC in the West Sussex Senior League. The talented amateur made 3 Southern League appearances for Tottenham Hotspur in 1901/02, and then played for Brighton & Hove Albion's reserve side between 1903 and 1906, again making 3 first-team appearances. His debut came against West Ham United in an FA Cup tie in October 1903. 'Haigers' became an 'Oriental' in February 1906 – when O's could not afford to pay its wage bill and several players were sold – and he came to assist the club for a short period. He made his League debut in a 3-0 win over Burnley on 24 February 1906, and his only goal for the club came in the 6-1 defeat at Chelsea the following month. He returned to Lancing College, and was involved in the school's cadet corps and officer training corps between 1906 and 1915, whilst also playing football for Shoreham FC, with whom he gained a runners-up medal in the Sussex Senior Cup in 1906. Haig-Brown was a writer of some note, and he made many contributions to the *Times*, writing more than a thousand poems and articles in all. He was the author of three books: *Sporting Sonnets*, *My Game Book* and *The OTC in the Great War*. He attained the rank of Lieutenant-Colonel during

H

the First World War, commanding the 23rd Battalion of the Middlesex Regiment. and he was twice mentioned in dispatches. In addition to all this, he was awarded the Distinguished Service Order for Bravery. Sadly, he was one of thousands of men who lost their lives in the second battle of the Somme on 25 March 1918, at the age of forty-one. His obituaries in the *Times* and *Lancing College* magazine reflected the devotion for him both of the troops under his command and of his former pupils and colleagues.

Kevin Hales

SEASON	LEAGUE		FA CUP		TOTAL	
	Apps	Gls	Apps	Gls	Apps	Gls
1905/06	4	1	0	0	4	1
TOTAL	4	1	0	0	4	1

Kevin Peter HALES, 1983-93

Kevin Hales was a grand and loyal servant to Leyton Orient, playing for the club for a decade. The 5ft 7in midfielder was rewarded with a thoroughly well-deserved testimonial match against West Ham United on 6 August 1993, after the O's had released him at the end of the 1992/93 season. Hales finished in eleventh spot in O's all-time appearance list, with over 300 senior appearances. Born in Dartford, Kent on 13 January 1961, he played cricket and soccer for Kent schools, and signed professional forms with Chelsea in January 1979. He went on to make 22(2) senior appearances (scoring twice) and over 200 reserve appearances for the Blues. His League debut was against O's on 9 November 1979 as a substitute, when O's were beaten 7-3 at home. He joined O's in August 1983, being Frank Clark's first signing, and was a member of the promotion-winning side of 1988/89. His

first-team opportunities were rather limited in the latter part of his stay, and the thirty-two-year-old was given a free transfer in May 1993, just a couple of days after Frank Clark had departed to become manager at Nottingham Forest. Hales joined Welling United in 1993 and was with the Wings for seven years, first as player and then as player-manager, signing a large number of former O's players during his stay. On 2 March 1999, Hales offered to resign as manager, due to their poor run of form, but the directors requested that he stay at the club. Unfortunately, Welling were relegated in 1999/2000. During May 2000, he did resign, and was appointed as the assistant manager with Stevenage Borough. However, he was asked to leave the club after the departure of manager Paul Fairclough. His contract was terminated at the end of March 2002.

198

SEASON	LEAGUE		FA CUP		L. CUP	
	Apps	Gls	Apps	Gls	Apps	Gls
1983/84	43	2	1	0	2	0
1984/85	32(1)	0	4	0	4	0
1985/86	31	2	6	0	4	0
1986/87	28(5)	1	3	0	0	0
1987/88	42	6	4	0	2	1
1988/89*	39	9	3	0	5	1
1989/90	36(3)	2	1	0	3	0
1990/91	3(2)	0	0	0	1	0
1991/92	6(4)	0	1(1)	0	0	0
1992/93	29	1	2	0	2	0
TOTAL	289(15)	23	25(1)	0	23	2

TOTAL APPS	337(16)
TOTAL GOALS	25

* Includes 4 play-off matches during 1988/89.

** Kevin Hales also appeared in 16 Auto Windscreens Shield matches, scoring once.

William HALES Snr, 1910-11

London-born William Hales Snr joined O's on trial between March and May 1911, having started with Walthamstow Grange FC, a leading East London amateur side. An attacking type of centre half, his only League appearance came in the 1-1 draw at Fulham on 15 April 1911. He left O's in May 1911, and after a brief trial with West Ham, he returned to Walthamstow Grange FC.

SEASON	LEAGUE		FA CUP		TOTAL	
	Apps	Gls	Apps	Gls	Apps	Gls
1910/11	1	0	0	0	1	0
TOTAL	1	0	0	0	1	0

William Alfred HALES Jnr, 1931-33

William Hales Jnr was born in Poplar, London. Son of William Hales Snr, Billy, a winger, joined O's in 1931 from Thames Association FC, where he made 3 League appearances in 1930/31, having previ-

ously played for Leytonstone. Hales Jnr made his O's debut in a 2-2 draw against Brighton & Hove Albion on 21 January 1932. He collapsed and died outside Leyton Stadium, just after watching O's lose 1-0 against Mansfield Town on 15 February 1986.

SEASON	LEAGUE		FA CUP		TOTAL	
	Apps	Gls	Apps	Gls	Apps	Gls
1931/32	9	2	0	0	9	2
1932/33	4	1	0	0	4	1
TOTAL	13	3	0	0	13	3

Stanley Arthur HALL, 1938-47

Stan Hall was born in Southgate, London on 18 February 1917. He was a slim, agile goalkeeper, who joined Orient from Finchley FC in March 1938, taking over the green jersey from Jacob Iceton in February 1939. New signing Jack Ellis was preferred to him for the start of the 1939/40 season, which was swiftly curtailed after just 3 matches due to the outbreak of the Second World War. Hall played in 120 wartime regional matches for O's, and was in the side that was knocked out of the FA Cup over two legs by Newport Isle of Wight (2-3 on aggregate) during November 1945. He also appeared in a number of matches when League action recommenced in 1946/47. He was transferred to Yeovil Town in May 1947, and figured in some of the matches in their splendid FA Cup run of 1948/49.

SEASON	LEAGUE		FA CUP		TOTAL	
	Apps	Gls	Apps	Gls	Apps	Gls
1938/39	18	0	0	0	18	0
1945/46*	-	-	2	0	2	0
1946/47	8	0	0	0	8	0
TOTAL	26	0	2	0	28	0

* No League football in 1945/46.

H

David HALLIDAY, 1933-35

Born on 11 December 1897 in Dumfries, Scotland, Dave Halliday was one of the truly great forwards to appear for O's. The 5ft 11in and 12st player, with a short shuffling stride, was a legend in his day, both for his ability and his prolific goalscoring achievements. He was a delight to watch, and it was not often that O's fans were privileged to be able to witness such a top quality forward. He became an 'Oriental' on 29 December 1933, for a record £1,500 fee from Manchester City. He netted 19 League goals from just 21 starts, and would surely have shattered O's goalscoring record, had he joined from the start of that season. He started his remarkable career in December 1919 with Queen of the South, and then went on to play for St Mirren, Dundee, Sunderland, Arsenal and then Manchester City. Halliday was a goalscoring machine – he held Dundee's Scottish Leaugue goalscoring record (38 goals in a season) for over forty years, until Alan Gilzean broke it in 1963/64. He netted 92 goals in total during his four seasons at Dens Park. He joined Sunderland for £4,000 in April 1925, and is still their record goalscorer, netting 43 First Division goals from 42 starts in 1928/29. He eventually scored a grand total of 157 senior goals from 166 appearances for the club. He joined Arsenal in November 1929 for a sizeable fee of £6,500, and despite not being a regular at Highbury, he netted 53 goals from 48 League, cup and reserve starts, before joining Manchester City in November 1930 for £5,700, where he found the net 47 times from 76 appearances. Halliday signed for O's around Christmas 1933, and although many had thought that Halliday might be past his best, the O's fans were not let down by the player. His unusual style and splendid left foot caused total panic amongst all the Third Division defences. He netted a trio of hat-tricks in his first season, and finished as the top scorer. During one spell, he netted in 9 consecutive League matches, a feat only equalled by O's legendary goal poacher Tommy Johnston in 1957/58. Halliday again top-scored in 1934/35, however, at the age of thirty-seven he decided to retire from League football to take up a position as player-manager with Southern League side Yeovil & Petters United. During 1938 he accepted the manager's job at Aberdeen – a position he held for seventeen years – winning the Scottish Cup and, in his final season, the Scottish League Championship, for the first time in their history. In July 1955, he was appointed manager of Leicester City, who had been relegated the previous season. Within two years, he had them back up to into the First Division, and clinched promotion with a 5-1 win at Brisbane Road in April 1957. He left Filbert Street in November 1958, and in March 1959 he returned to Aberdeen to run a hotel, and became a shareholder of Aberdeen FC. His record shows that in fifteen years in Scottish and English League football, he scored a total of 339 goals in 448 appearances and averaged 0.751 goals per game – a higher goals per match ratio than some of the all-time greats of British football, such as Hughie Gallacher (0.712) and Jimmy Greaves (0.691). One quite remarkable fact was that Halliday could never obtain a full Scottish cap, but this could be attributed to the fact that Hughie Gallacher – of Airdrie, Newcastle United and Chelsea – had won 20 caps, and was holding down the place at the time. Halliday died on 5 January 1970.

SEASON	LEAGUE		FA CUP		TOTAL	
	Apps	Gls	Apps	Gls	Apps	Gls
1933/34	21	19	1	0	22	19
1934/35	32	14	2	3	34	17
TOTAL	53	33	3	3	56	36

* Dave Halliday also appeared in 3 Third Division Cup matches between 1933 and 1935, scoring once.

James Michael HALLYBONE Jnr, 1981-82

Born in Leytonstone, London on 15 May 1962, Jimmy Hallybone, a small-built midfield player, was an apprentice at O's before signing professional forms in May 1980, and played regularly for the youth and reserve sides. It was during the troubled season of 1981/82 that he got his chance for League action. He was given his League debut by O's boss Paul Went in a 1-0 defeat at Crystal Palace on 22 September 1981, where he did his best, but in truth looked a little out of his depth. He moved to Halifax Town on 26 July 1982, making 13(5) League appearances. After leaving the Shay, he was a much-travelled member of the non-League circuit, and enjoyed spells at Dagenham, Barking, Billericay, Dartford, Basildon, Grays and Tilbury. His father, Jimmy Hallybone Snr (who died in April 1998), played for O's juniors just after the Second World War, before playing amateur football with Leytonstone, and later held youth coaching roles with O's during the 1970s and 1980s.

SEASON	LEAGUE		FA CUP		L. CUP	
	Apps	Gls	Apps	Gls	Apps	Gls
1981/82	5(3)	0	3	0	0	0
TOTAL	5(3)	0	3	0	0	0

TOTAL APPS	8(3)
TOTAL GOALS	0

Jimmy Hallybone Jnr (left)

* Jimmy Hallybone also appeared in 0(1) Football League Group Cup match.

Victor Lewis HALOM, 1967-68

Vic Halom, the son of a Hungarian immigrant, became O's record outgoing transfer fee at £35,000, when he was transferred from Fulham in October 1968. Derby County manager Brian Clough had planned to visit Leyton to watch Halom and start talks for a £50,000 transfer, only to be told that a deal had been concluded with the Cottagers. Born in Swadlincote, Burton-upon-Trent on 3 October 1948, he was first spotted by a Charlton Athletic scout whilst playing schools football for Coton Park. He signed as an apprentice in April 1964 at the age of fifteen. In January 1966, Halom made his League debut as a defender. Later he was converted to a forward, and scored several goals for their reserves. He then suffered ankle and cartilage injuries, which set his career at the Valley back somewhat, and he made just 9(3) League appearances. He came to O's on loan from Charlton in August 1967, and displayed his versatile qualities, playing in defence, midfield and up front. He impressed with his aggression and bustle, and by not being afraid to get stuck in, causing a real buzz amongst the O's fans. He loved his stay at Brisbane Road so much, that upon his return to the Valley, he asked if he could join the O's on a permanent basis. O's put in a formal offer, and he became an 'Oriental' in October 1967 for £3,000. During the first two months of the 1968/69 season, he hit the headlines by scoring 9 senior goals from 7 starts to make him the top marksman in the League. After his transfer to Fulham, he stayed at Craven Cottage for two years, and netted 25 goals from 76(6) senior matches. He moved to Luton Town in September 1971 for £35,000, scoring 17 goals from 57(2) League appearances. He moved to Sunderland in February 1973 for £25,000, having a long and distinguished career at Roker Park, making a total of 110(3) League appearances with 35 goals as well as appearing in their FA Cup-winning team in 1973. Oldham Athletic was his next club in July 1976 – for whom he notched his 100th League goal in a match against O's at Brisbane Road on 5 March 1977 – and he netted 43 goals from 121(2) matches for the Latics. He ended his League career with Rotherham United, signing in February 1980. He later went to manage Norwegian club Fredikstad FC, and upon his return to England, he did the managerial rounds with Rochdale (for two years), North Shields, Barrow, Burton Albion. During 1992 he contested the Sunderland North seat for the Liberal Democrats in the General Election, finishing in third spot. He also worked as a PR man for the Oldham-based firm of New Earth Plumbing as well as the Amec Computer company. Vic Halom made a total of 435(17) League appearances, netting 131 goals.

SEASON	LEAGUE		FA CUP		L. CUP	
	Apps	Gls	Apps	Gls	Apps	Gls
1967/68	39	7	5	3	0	0
1968/69	14	5	0	0	4	4
TOTAL	53	12	5	3	4	4

TOTAL APPS	62
TOTAL GOALS	19

Harold James HALSE, 1905-06

Harold Halse, who stood just 5ft 6in and weighed 10st 10lb, played only a handful of League matches for O's as an amateur in their inaugural season in the League, yet the forward was to become one of the most prolific goalscorers of his era. His masterly ball control and a very hard shot, led to him winning FA Cup and League Championship winner's medals, and he was the first man to play in the FA Cup final for three different clubs. Halse also won an England international cap against Austria in September 1908 – scoring twice in an 8-1 victory in Vienna – and represented the Football League XI five times. Born in Stratford, London on 1 January 1886, he started with Wanstead FC and then moved to Barking FC, before joining O's as a nineteen-year-old in August 1905. He made his League debut for O's in a 4-0 defeat at Manchester United on 2 December 1905, and his only goal came in a 3-0 win over Lincoln City in January 1906. After just a few League outings, he moved on to Southend United in May 1906 for their inaugural season in the

Second Division of the Southern League. Halse was snapped by up by Manchester United in March 1908 for £350, and scored within a minute of his debut against Sheffield Wednesday. During a four-year stay, he notched 56 goals from 125 senior outings, winning an FA Cup winner's medal in 1909 and a League Championship medal in 1911. Possibly his sweetest moment for United came in the Charity Shield match in September 1911 at Stamford Bridge, when he scored 6 goals against Swindon Town. In July 1913, United rather surprisingly sold him to Aston Villa for £750, and he appeared in 2 further FA Cup finals and 30 League appearances, scoring 21 goals. In May 1913 he joined Chelsea, scoring 25 goals in 111 senior appearances. During the First World War he guested for O's, but in July 1921 he returned to League action with Charlton Athletic, making 21 appearances and notching 5 goals. Halse eventually retired from the game in 1923, later becoming chief scout at the Valley, a position he held for four years. He died in Colchester on 25 March 1949, aged sixty-three.

SEASON	LEAGUE		FA CUP		TOTAL	
	Apps	Gls	Apps	Gls	Apps	Gls
1905/06	3	1	0	0	3	1
TOTAL	3	1	0	0	3	1

Stephen HAMBERGER, 1978-80

Steve Hamberger was born in Hackney, London in 1959. The central defender joined O's in December 1978 from Walthamstow Avenue as cover for Nigel Gray, but only played in one League Cup tie. Hamberger was a Millwall apprentice in 1976, in the days of manager Gordon Jago, but left the club without any League action to join Barking, before moving to Walthamstow Avenue. His sole first-team appearance came against Wimbledon in the League Cup tie at Brisbane Road on 29 August 1979, before being substituted by Alan Whittle. His only other game in first-team colours was when he replaced Tommy Taylor in a pre-season friendly against Tottenham Hotspur – O's drew 1-1 at Brisbane Road against a Spurs side that included such stars as Glenn Hoddle and Osvaldo Ardiles. He went to Portsmouth on trial in 1980, but returned to the club a week later. In November 1980 he joined Maidstone United. In 1983, he moved to Leyton-Wingate FC, and made a club record 387 senior appearances, also winning a Northern Championship Second Division medal in 1985. He was there again when they won promotion as runners-up in the Vauxhall Opel League, and was voted their Player of the Year two years running in both 1984 and 1985. In 1990 he was captain of Diadora League side Bromley.

SEASON	LEAGUE		FA CUP		L. CUP	
	Apps	Gls	Apps	Gls	Apps	Gls
1979/80	0	0	0	0	1	0
TOTAL	0	0	0	0	1	0

TOTAL APPS	1
TOTAL GOALS	0

George HAMMOND, 1904-05 and 1906

Centre forward Hammond was born in Sunderland in 1880 and began his playing career with Barrow. He made his League debut for Lincoln City against Blackpool in November 1902, scoring in what was to be his only appearance. He joined O's in May 1904 for O's Southern League and London League campaigns, scoring 12 goals. He netted in O's first ever FA Cup match, a 4-1 home win over Enfield in September

1904. He left the club in June 1905, joining Gainsborough Trinity and scored on his debut against Blackpool in September 1905. During O's financial crisis in early 1906, he returned to the club after a number of more senior players were sold, and made his League debut in a 1-1 draw at Chesterfield in February 1906.

SEASON	LEAGUE		FA CUP		TOTAL	
	Apps	Gls	Apps	Gls	Apps	Gls
1904/05*	-	-	3	2	3	2
1905/06	4	0	0	0	4	0
TOTAL	4	0	3	2	7	2

* Clapton Orient first entered the League in 1905/06.

Charles HANNAFORD, 1924-27, 1929

Born on 8 January 1896 in Finsbury Park, London, Charlie Hannaford was a star schoolboy footballer, capped for England schools against Wales in 1910. He started his playing career at Tufnell Park FC and he was an amateur with Tottenham Hotspur in December 1916. He moved on to Maidstone United in 1919, scoring 39 times in 1920/21. He joined Millwall in March 1921, making 37 appearances and scoring 12 goals. Two years later, he was on the books of Charlton Athletic, where he played 20 matches and scored 2 goals. He became an 'Oriental' in March 1924, replacing Owen Williams who had been sold to Middlesbrough. He scored on his debut in a 4-0 win over Coventry City. The swift-raiding outside left, who had a powerful run and a fierce shot, performed very well for two seasons, and was rewarded when picked to go to Australia with an FA touring party in 1925. In December 1927, he joined Manchester United for £1,000, but saw little League action at Old Trafford, making just a

dozen senior appearances in a two-year stay. He returned to O's in September 1929, but seemed to have lost much of his old sparkle, and made a handful of appearances before retiring at the end of the season. Off the field, Hannaford was an accomplished pianist, whose speciality was jazz music. He died in Aylesbury in July 1970.

SEASON	LEAGUE		FA CUP		TOTAL	
	Apps	Gls	Apps	Gls	Apps	Gls
1923/24	13	1	0	0	13	1
1924/25	34	5	1	0	35	5
1925/26	16	4	0	0	16	4
1928/29	4	0	0	0	4	0
TOTAL	67	10	1	0	68	10

David Paul HANSON, 1995-98

Dave Hanson, a striker, joined O's from Hednesford Town for a surprising £50,000 fee on 2 October 1995. A mystery virus struck him down after his arrival in East London, and it proved a real struggle for him to settle down at the club. Born in Huddersfield on 19 November 1968, he started his football trade with local side Farsley Celtic in August 1992, before joining Bury on 19 July 1993, where he made just 3 senior appearances. He joined Halifax Town on 18 August 1994, but left without experiencing any first-team action, and moved on to Hednesford Town. His move to East London came on 4 October 1995, but he was never able to hold down a regular first-team spot – his best season was during 1996/97. He went out on loan to a number of clubs, including Welling United in March 1996; Chesterfield in March 1997 (3 appearances and 1 goal); and then to Dover Athletic in September 1997 (4 appearances and 1 goal). Hanson made a few sporadic League appearances for O's in 1997/98, before being given a

Dave Hanson

free transfer to non-League Halifax Town on 23 January 1998. There he made 6(5) Conference appearances and scored twice. He was in their squad that gained re-entry in the League in 1998, and came on as a substitute against O's at the Shay in March 1999. He was released in May 1999 to join Nuneaton Borough, where he played 21(4) matches and scored 3 goals. In July 2000, he joined Hyde United.

SEASON	LEAGUE		FA CUP		L. CUP	
	Apps	Gls	Apps	Gls	Apps	Gls
1995/96	7(4)	1	0	0	0	0
1996/97	15(10)	3	0	0	1(1)	0
1997/98	4(8)	1	1(1)	0	0	0
TOTAL	26(22)	5	1(1)	0	1(1)	0

TOTAL APPS	28(24)
TOTAL GOALS	5

* Dave Hanson also appeared in 2(2) Auto Windscreens Shield matches.

David HARPER, 1967-71

Dave Harper was born on 29 September 1938 in Peckham, London. The wing-half started as a junior with Millwall and represented England at youth level. He made 165 League appearances and scored 4 goals for the Lions. In March 1965 he was transferred to Ipswich Town, playing 70(2) League games and scoring twice. He moved to Swindon Town in July 1967, but was dogged by injuries and made just 4 appearances, and moved to become an 'Oriental' in October 1967. He proved to be an excellent acquisition, and helped O's to avoid relegation in 1968/69, scoring the final goal in the safety-clinching 4-0 winning game against Shrewsbury Town in 1968/69, and was also a major influence in the promotion side of 1969/70. He scored a grand twenty-yard goal against Sheffield United in the opening fixture of the new Second Division campaign, but an injury in a match at Fulham three days later (in the League Cup) eventually ended his career. A testimonial match was staged for him against West Ham United in May 1971, with the money going towards him buying a black taxicab. Dave Harper was a hard-working player with plenty of skill, who would always soldier on when others may have given up, often working like a Trojan.

SEASON	LEAGUE		FA CUP		L. CUP	
	Apps	Gls	Apps	Gls	Apps	Gls
1967/68	22	0	5	0	0	0
1968/69	40(1)	3	1	0	3	0
1969/70	19(2)	0	0	0	2	1
1970/71	1	1	0	0	1	0
TOTAL	82(3)	4	6	0	6	1

TOTAL APPS	94(3)
TOTAL GOALS	5

Dave Harper receives his testimonial cheque

Marvin Lee HARRIOTT, 1993 (loan)

A former West Ham trainee who had also played reserve team football at Oldham Athletic, it was whilst he was at Barnsley that this full-back came to O's on loan on 1 October 1993. As a youngster he played in the same England schools team as Ryan Giggs, and while the latter went straight to the top, Harriott struggled to break through. Born in Dulwich, London on 20 April 1974, he joined Bristol City from Barnsley on 9 December 1993, and played 36 League matches for the Robins. He joined his friend Tony Woodcock (the former Nottingham Forest player), who was coach at Fortuna Dusseldorf in Germany, on a free transfer during July 1995. He returned to England and played for Gloucester City. He had a trial with Cardiff City in November 1997, but played in a single AWS Cup match and

soon drifted out of Ninian Park. In August 1998 he joined Aylesbury United, and a year later was on the books at Scarborough. On 1 August 2000, he joined Kingstonian, where he made 5(1) appearances before joining Chesham United that November, followed by Enfield.

SEASON	LEAGUE		FA CUP		L. CUP	
	Apps	Gls	Apps	Gls	Apps	Gls
1993/94	8	0	1	0	0	0
TOTAL	8	0	1	0	0	0

TOTAL APPS	9
TOTAL GOALS	0

Andrew David HARRIS, 1999-present

Twenty-two-year-old Andy Harris signed for O's on a non-contract basis from Southend United on 5 June 1999, after being released by their new manager Alan Little in June 1999. Born on 26 February 1977 in Springs, near Johannesburg in South Africa, he left the country in 1979 at the age of two, when his parents moved back to the UK, but is still eligible to play for his home country. He grew up in Liverpool, and was a product of the Liverpool youth team that produced Michael Owen. He turned professional on 23 March 1984. The player was signed on a free transfer by Ronnie Whelan (the former Liverpool player) for Division Two's Southend United on 9 July 1996. In 1997/98 he took over as captain, and was the kingpin at the heart of the defence. After some outstanding performances, England under-21 manager Peter Taylor came to Roots Hall to watch him. However, a serious injury in February 1998 curtailed his progress and he never won his place back, playing just once in February 1999 against Brighton, and he left having made a total of 78(2) senior appearances for the Shrimpers. Harris has proved himself to be an accomplished defender, who appears more at home on the right side of the defence. He is quick in the tackle, but had a tendency to over-commit himself, obtaining 15 bookings and a sending-off during his stay on the coast. Harris made his League debut at Carlisle United in August 1999. He had excellent academic grades (and is a member of Mensa with an IQ of 153), but chose to play football rather than continue his studies. Harris recovered from an injury-hit first season, and was converted to a central midfield role in 2000/01 to excellent effect. He made an appearance in the play-off final – a defeat at the hands of Blackpool (4-2 at the Millennium Stadium) in May 2001. Harris signed a new two-year contract in June 2001, and will be hoping to score his very first goal in the League and get a call-up for the country of his birth – South Africa.

SEASON	LEAGUE		FA CUP		L. CUP	
	Apps	Gls	Apps	Gls	Apps	Gls
1999/2000	11(4)	0	0	0	4	0
2000/01*	45	0	4	0	7	0
2001/02	45	1	4	0	1	0
TOTAL	101(4)	1	8	0	12	0

TOTAL APPS	121(4)
TOTAL GOALS	1

* Andy Harris's League record includes 1 play-off match in 2000/01.

Jason Andre Sebastian HARRIS, 1997-98

Jason Harris, a pacy and strong central striker, was played mostly on the left side of the forward line by boss Taylor. Born in Sutton on 24 November 1976, he joined O's on 20 September 1997 for £25,000 from Crystal Palace. Palace originally wanted £120,000 for the player, however, there was a sell-on clause in the contract. Harris made only 4 senior appearances as a substitute in his two years at Selhurst Park. He impressed during a loan spell with Bristol Rovers in November 1996, scoring twice in 5(1) appearances. He also had a loan spell with Lincoln City in August 1997, where he played just once, as a substitute against Mansfield Town. O's boss Tommy Taylor stated: 'I have high hopes for Harris, I have seen him play many times and he has lots of potential.' Harris made a lively start in the 1997/98 campaign, but could not hold down a regular first-team place. In August 1998 he went on loan to Division Two side Preston North End, where he impressed the Deepdale fans with his skill and speed, as well as by scoring a few goals. The deal with Preston was eventually made permanent at a giveaway fee of £25,000. The sell-on clause was reported to give Palace 40 per cent of the total fee if Harris was sold for more than the original fee (£25,000), which explains why Preston got such a good deal. Harris openly expressed his anger at continually being put on the bench and played out of his favourite position by the O's boss. Harris made 9(27) League appearances at Deepdale, scoring 6 goals. In July 1999 he joined his sixth club, when former PNE midfielder Warren Joyce brought him to Hull City in July 1999 for £40,000, but he only made 19(19) League appearances during his two-year stay, scoring just 4 goals. After 4 substitute appearances the following season, he eventually went on loan to Shrewsbury Town on 16 March 2001, but only made 1(3) League appearances. Harris was released by Hull City in June 2001, with one year remaining on his contract. Harris has failed to deliver during his seven-year career in the League, with a total of 65(72) appearances and just 21 goals. He joined Southend United on 7 July 2001, but after just 2(3) League starts, he cancelled his contract at the end of November in order to look for a new club. He joined Unibond League side Harrogate Town in December 2001 and in February 2002 joined Nationwide Conference League Nuneaton Borough.

SEASON	LEAGUE		FA CUP		L. CUP	
	Apps	Gls	Apps	Gls	Apps	Gls
1997/98	21(14)	6	2	0	1	0
1998/99	1(1)	1	0	0	0	0
TOTAL	22(15)	7	2	0	1	0

TOTAL APPS	25(15)
TOTAL GOALS	7

* Jason Harris also appeared in 1(1) Auto Windscreens Shield matches.

Jeffrey Bruce HARRIS, 1961-62, 1964-65
Born in Stepney, London on 11 June 1942, Jeff Harris started his career as a junior with Arsenal, and then played for Hendon and Enfield. He appeared in the FA Amateur Cup final for Hendon in their 1959/60 success, and also gained a runners-up medal with them in 1963/64, when he returned to Hendon after his first spell with O's. In addition to this, he gained a number of England amateur international caps. Harris joined O's for a second spell from Enfield in May 1964. Previously, as an amateur, he was a regular member of the reserve side that won the Midweek Section of the Football Combination in 1961/62, play-ing at left-back. He rejoined as a part-time professional, and played mostly at left half, making his League debut in a 3-2 home defeat by Norwich City during February 1965. Harris left O's in May 1965 to join Southern League side Romford, where he was able to combine playing football with his business interests.

SEASON	LEAGUE		FA CUP		L. CUP	
	Apps	Gls	Apps	Gls	Apps	Gls
1961/62	0	0	0	0	0	0
1964/65	14	0	0	0	0	0
TOTAL	14	0	0	0	0	0

TOTAL APPS	14
TOTAL GOALS	0

Paul Edwin HARRIS, 1970-75
Many ex-footballers return to their former club as coach or manager, but very few return as the club consultant chiropodist, but that is exactly what Paul

Paul Harris

Harris did! Born in Hackney, London on 19 May 1953, he was a member of the very successful Waltham Forest school-boy team that jointly held English Schools Trophy with Manchester schools when he was at Leyton County High School. The fair-haired centre half joined O's as an apprentice in 1969, and signed full-time a year later. He also showed great promise as a cricketer, but he chose football as his career, making his League debut at Cardiff City in the final fixture of the 1970/71 season. Harris more or less followed in the footsteps of Tommy Taylor, performing extremely well between 1971 and 1973. Harris appeared in O's great FA Cup run in 1972, including the superb victories over both Leicester City and Chelsea. He picked up a series of injuries thereafter, however, which affected both his form and his weight. He was transferred to Swansea City in July 1975, making 47(2) League appearances and scoring twice. Perhaps Paul Harris didn't quite achieve what seemed likely in his early years, yet he certainly played very well in his first two full campaigns during the early 1970s.

Tommy Harris

SEASON	LEAGUE		FA CUP		L. CUP	
	Apps	Gls	Apps	Gls	Apps	Gls
1970/71	1	0	0	0	0	0
1971/72	42	2	4	0	2	0
1972/73	37	2	1	0	2	0
1973/74	2	0	2	0	1(2)	0
1974/75	14	0	0	0	2	0
TOTAL	96	4	7	0	7(2)	0

TOTAL APPS	110(2)
TOTAL GOALS	4

* Paul Harris also appeared in 2 Texaco Cup matches in 1974/75.

Thomas HARRIS, 1951-53

Born in Chelsea, London on 8 November 1924, Tommy Harris started with Fulham in 1947, but only played in their reserve side. He joined O's in September 1951, where he again featured in the second string during 1951/52, but he then suddenly burst onto the scene when he played at outside right in O's 7-0 thrashing of Colchester United in January 1952 and scored twice. After an injury to O's favourite Billy Rees, Harris took over the centre forward position and scored one of the goals in O's superb win at Everton in an FA Cup third round replay. He also grabbed the only goal of the match at Birmingham City in an FA Cup fourth round tie – a stunning victory in front of 49,500 St Andrews fans. Subsequently, he lost form, and drifted in and out of the team. He was transferred to Colchester United in June 1953, making 103 League appearances and scoring 6 goals. After leaving the U's in 1962, he moved on to the non-League circuit with Tunbridge Wells, Yiewsley and Deal Town. He died on 11 October 2001.

SEASON	LEAGUE		FA CUP		TOTAL	
	Apps	Gls	Apps	Gls	Apps	Gls
1951/52	20	8	3	2	23	10
1952/53	11	3	2	0	13	3
TOTAL	31	11	5	2	36	13

John HARTBURN, 1954-58

John Hartburn, a small, quick-raiding left-winger, was a firm favourite with the O's fans, and he went into the record books when he scored a hat-trick in just three-and-a-half minutes against Shrewsbury Town at Brisbane Road on 22 January 1955, the quickest ever by an O's player. He is also one of a handful of O's players to have recorded 4 goals in a League match (against Queens Park Rangers on 3 March 1956). Born in Houghton-le-Spring, Co. Durham on 20 December 1920, Hartburn started his career with Bishop Auckland, and then played for Yeovil Town, for whom he scored 24 goals in just 25 outings. He moved to QPR in March 1947 for £1,700 winning a Third Division Championship medal in 1947/48 and netting 13 goals from 64 senior appearances. He moved to Watford in September 1949 for £1,000, where he made 71 senior appearances and scored 21 goals (4 of which were penalties). In March 1951 he joined Millwall for £2,500, and made 110 senior appearances that yielded 30 goals. The small speedy winger became an 'Oriental' in June 1954 at the age of thirty-three, yet some of his most successful seasons were still ahead of him. He scored on his debut against Torquay United in August 1954, and he simply excelled in O's Third Division

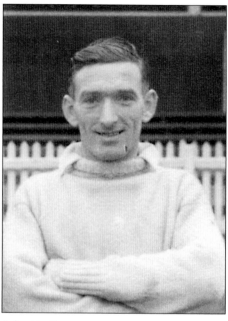

John Hartburn

Championship season (1955/56), recording 20 League goals (one of only nine players to score at least 20 League goals in a season). It was his goal direct from a corner-kick that sent O's on their way to the championship. However, age began to catch up on him, and he was not a regular during the following couple of seasons, although he still performed admirably when called upon. He left the club in July 1958 at the age of thirty-eight to join Yiewsley, but a few months later he moved on to Southern League side Guildford. He returned to O's in 1963 as the club's first pools promoter and programme editor, before leaving in 1966 and joining Fulham in a similar capacity. He was the commercial manager at Watford between July 1976 and 1981, and then Barnet's commercial manager and honorary secretary between June 1982 and 1987. His playing career spanned some twelve years, over the course of which he amassed a total of 364 senior appearances and 104 goals. Johnny Hartburn died on 21 January 2001 in Bournemouth, aged eighty-one.

SEASON	LEAGUE		FA CUP		TOTAL	
	Apps	Gls	Apps	Gls	Apps	Gls
1954/55	39	10	2	0	41	10
1955/56	40	20	4	3	44	23
1956/57	14	1	0	0	14	1
1957/58	19	5	1	0	20	5
TOTAL	112	36	7	3	119	39

Lee Derek HARVEY, 1984-93

Lee Harvey will go down in O's history as the scorer of a superb opening goal in O's 2-1 victory in the promotion play-off final, second leg match against Wrexham at Brisbane Road on 3 June 1989. The fair-haired midfield and wing player was born in Harlow, Essex on 21 December 1966. He played for Harlow and Essex schools, and scored in England youth's 5-3 win over Iceland at Maine Road in a European

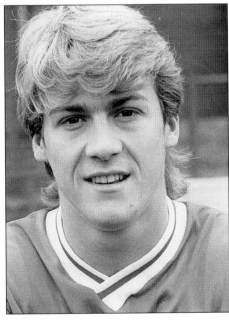

Lee Harvey

Youth Championship game. He signed as a professional on 5 December 1983 and made his League debut as a substitute in a 6-3 defeat at Sheffield United during March 1984. After the promotion play-off match, his career took a nosedive due to various injuries, and he failed to complete a full ninety minutes in 1991/92. He did, however, score a magnificent goal in an FA Cup third round replay against First Division Oldham Athletic in an extra-time 4-2 victory in January 1992. Harvey was on a weekly contract for two seasons, and then decided that after nine seasons at the club, it was time to move on and start at a new club. It was former O's boss Frank Clark who took Harvey to Nottingham Forest on trial between August and November 1993. He made just 2 appearances as a substitute, but returned to London to join Brentford on 18 November 1993. He spent four seasons at Griffin Park, making 87(18) League appearances and scoring 6 goals. He then moved to Vauxhall Conference side Stevenage Borough, playing in a more defensive midfield role. He made 64 appearances without scoring, before being released in May 2000. He joined Ryman League side St Alban's City early in the new season, but was troubled by injury after his arrival at Clarence Park. In August 2001 he moved to Ryman Premier League side Bedford, playing in the back line.

SEASON	LEAGUE		FA CUP		L. CUP	
	Apps	Gls	Apps	Gls	Apps	Gls
1983/84	0(4)	0	0	0	0	0
1984/85	2(2)	0	0(1)	0	0	0
1985/86	11(1)	2	0(1)	0	0	0
1986/87	10(5)	1	1(2)	1	2	1
1987/88	6(17)	1	1	0	0	0
1988/89*	29(4)	7	3	0	2(2)	0

1989/90	36(1)	6	0	0	4	1
1990/91	21(5)	3	3	0	5	1
1991/92	5(8)	0	2	1	0(1)	0
1992/93	19(2)	4	0	0	0	0
TOTAL	139(49)	24	10(4)	2	13(3)	3

TOTAL APPS	162(56)
TOTAL GOALS	29

* Including 4 promotion play-off matches and a goal in 1988/89.

** Lee Harvey also appeared in 15(4) Auto Windscreens Shield matches, scoring twice.

Harold HASLAM, 1948-49

Born in Manchester on 30 July 1921, Harry Haslam will be best remembered not as a player, but as a manager with Luton Town and Sheffield United, with 404 matches in charge. Haslam was a well-built fair-haired full-back who began his career playing in wartime matches as an amateur with Manchester United. He joined Rochdale in May 1945, before moving on to Oldham Athletic in May 1946, where he played in just 2 League matches. During September 1947, he moved on to Brighton & Hove Albion, where he played only reserve football. He became an 'Oriental' in July 1948, making his League debut in a 3-1 win over Torquay United on 20 November 1948. However, he was confined mostly to O's reserves, and hampered somewhat by injuries, he eventually moved to Southern League side Guildford City in October 1949. He then became manager of Hastings followed by Eastbourne United. He was manager of Barry Town between 1954 and 1959, and between 1959 and 1968, he managed Tonbridge. He moved to Fulham as chief scout in July 1968, but left five months later. He was appointed coach and promotions man-

ager at Luton Town in 1969, and then was appointed as their manager in May 1972, succeeding Alec Stock. He remained as boss until January 1978, and then moved on to Sheffield United, of whom he was boss between January 1978 and May 1981. He later had a spell as an England scout in 1981. Harry Haslam, who was known as a natural comic and motivator, died in Biggleswade on 11 September 1986, aged sixty-five.

SEASON	LEAGUE		FA CUP		TOTAL	
	Apps	Gls	Apps	Gls	Apps	Gls
1948/49	7	0	0	0	7	0
1949/50	0	0	0	0	0	0
TOTAL	7	0	0	0	7	0

Patrick Joseph HASTY, 1958-59

Northern Ireland amateur international player Paddy Hasty was born on 17 March 1932 in Belfast. He joined O's in July 1958 on amateur forms, while playing for Tooting & Mitcham. He was a real live-wire centre forward, who was only available to play for O's in midweek matches. He played in just 2 senior mid-week fixtures – both against Swansea Town during September 1958 – and he netted a brace in the 3-3 draw at Vetch Field. Patrick Hasty joined Queens Park Rangers in October 1959, where he made a single League appearance. He returned to play for Tooting & Mitcham, but then signed for Aldershot in March 1961, where he enjoyed slightly more success, notching 14 goals from 35 League appearances. In 1962 he moved on to join Guildford FC.

SEASON	LEAGUE		FA CUP		TOTAL	
	Apps	Gls	Apps	Gls	Apps	Gls
1958/59	2	2	0	0	2	2
TOTAL	2	2	0	0	2	2

Daniel HATCHER, 2000-present

Born in Newport on the Isle of Wight on 24 December 1983, seventeen-year-old first-year YTS trainee Danny Hatcher, another of O's promising youth players, was given his big chance when he was made a substitute for the big FA Cup tie against Tottenham Hotspur on 6 January 2001. Although he never came onto the field of play, it was surely a wonderful experience for the lad. He did come on as a substitute in the LDV Vans Trophy match against Wycombe Wanderers on 9 January 2001, and again four days later for his League debut, to replace Carl Griffiths in the eighty-ninth minute of a 3-2 win at Exeter City. He nearly scored when home goalkeeper Van Heusden pushed his angle shot round the post, to prevent what would have been a dramatic start to his League career. In addition to playing for O's, he is studying for a GNQV in Sport and Leisure. He was a member of the youth team that won the FA Alliance Cup final (1-0 over Bradford City) played at the Millennium Stadium, Cardiff on 22 April 2001. His father, a local publican, wanted him to join Tottenham Hotspur, where he also played for a short time, but Hatcher preferred to try his luck with O's. He played 15 under-17 games for O's in 2000/01, scoring a dozen goals, and he also made 5 starts for the under-19s, scoring twice. In addition to this, he played twice for the reserves, scoring once. Under Paul Brush, he has become a regular first-team squad player. He was involved in a car accident whilst travelling with reserve-team player Adam Levy on 13 February 2002, but fortunately neither were seriously injured and were both playing football again the following month.

SEASON	LEAGUE		FA CUP		L. CUP	
	Apps	Gls	Apps	Gls	Apps	Gls
2000/01	0(2)	0	0	0	0	0
2001/02	2	0	0(1)	0	0	0
TOTAL	2(2)	0	0(1)	0	0	0

TOTAL APPS	2(3)
TOTAL GOALS	0

* Danny Hatcher also appeared in 0(1) LDV Vans Trophy match.

Herbert Henry HAWKINS, 1951-53

Born in Lambeth, London on 15 July 1923, Bert Hawkins was a strong, forceful centre forward, who joined O's in June 1951 from Gravesend & Northfleet. His opportunities at Brisbane Road were limited, but he performed well for the reserves, yet made little impression when called up for first-team duty. He made his League debut on 29 September 1951, in a 1-0 defeat at Southend United. Unfortunately, he was not retained in May

Bert Hawkins

1953, moving back into non-League football. Bert Hawkins died in Basingstoke during March 1982.

SEASON	LEAGUE		FA CUP		TOTAL	
	Apps	Gls	Apps	Gls	Apps	Gls
1951/52	3	0	1	0	4	0
1952/53	2	0	0	0	2	0
TOTAL	5	0	1	0	6	0

John East HAWLEY, 1982 (loan)

John Hawley had a short spell with O's on loan from Arsenal in October 1982, joining at the same time as another loanee, Trevor Lee from Gillingham. Born in Partington, Yorkshire on 8 May 1954, the big striker started his career as a professional with Hull City in April 1972, scoring 22 times in 101(13) Second Division starts. He was sold to Leeds United in May 1978 for £81,000, playing 30(3) games and netting 16 goals. During October 1979 he joined Sunderland, notching a further 11 goals from

John Hawley

25 games. He moved to Arsenal for £50,000 in September 1981, playing in 21 senior matches and scoring 3 goals. After another loan spell with former club Hull City, he went to play in Hong Kong for the Happy Valley Club in 1983, but was soon back in England in 1983, playing for Bradford City and then for Scunthorpe United in 1985/86 (18(3) games and 7 goals). Hawley was always a threat in the penalty box with his strong physical presence. Nowadays, he runs an antique business in Beverley, Yorkshire.

SEASON	LEAGUE		FA CUP		L. CUP	
	Apps	Gls	Apps	Gls	Apps	Gls
1982/83	4	1	0	0	0	0
TOTAL	4	1	0	0	0	0

TOTAL APPS	4
TOTAL GOALS	1

William HAYWARD, 1926-27, 1931-32

Welshman Willie Hayward had two spells with O's. He was born in Blaina, near Brynmawr, Wales on 16 November 1907, and the right half started his career with Blaina West Side FC, after a short spell with the Abertillery club. During August 1924 he joined Newport County, making 4 League appearances. He became an 'Oriental' in September 1926, making his League debut in a 4-2 defeat at Barnsley on 19 February 1927. Two years later he joined Tottenham Hotspur, and played alongside his brother, Fred Hayward (a full-back), in their reserve side. Hayward returned to O's in 1931 – his first match back was against Mansfield Town in a 4-0 victory on 5 September 1931. He was released in May 1932. Hayward died in Newport, Gwent in 1976.

SEASON	LEAGUE		FA CUP		TOTAL	
	Apps	Gls	Apps	Gls	Apps	Gls
1926/27	1	0	0	0	1	0
1931/32	9	0	0	0	9	0
TOTAL	10	0	0	0	10	0

Paul Andrew HEALD, 1988-95

Heald, a goalkeeper, known for his extremely quick reaction saves and safe handling, spent seven seasons with O's, after transferring from Sheffield United on 2 December 1988 for £2,500. Born in Wath-on-Dearne, a small village near Rotherham, on 20 September 1968, he learnt his trade with the Blades, signing as professional on 30 June 1987. Heald was excellent in O's promotion season of 1988/89, playing in the final 32 matches (including the 4 promotion play-off matches), after making his O's debut on 17 December 1988 against Grimsby Town, replacing veteran Peter Wells in goal. In the 1990/91, season he was voted Player of the Year. A couple of seasons later, he ended a personal fifteen-month injury nightmare, when he ran onto the Brisbane Road turf against Mansfield Town on 28 November 1992 – O's celebrated with a 5-1 victory. It was Heald's first game back since he had undergone major back surgery that threatened his career. He was sent on loan to a number of different clubs in order for him to gain his confidence back. These included Coventry City (in March 1992), Crystal Palace, Leeds United, Malmo FC (in Sweden) and Swindon Town (in March 1994). He was transferred to Premiership club Wimbledon for £250,000 on 25 July 1995, as cover for Scottish international 'keeper Neil Sullivan. Heald had played just 28 senior matches in five seasons for the Dons, but with the transfer of Sullivan to Tottenham Hotspur in May 2000 (after

Paul Heald

their relegation to Division One), Heald was hoping to make the number one jersey his own. However, the Dons signed Kelvin Davis from Luton Town for £600,000, and Heald only appeared in the first team twice in 2000/01, as a substitute for the injured Davis. In January 2002, Heald went on loan with Sheffield Wednesday and went stright into their Worthington Cup semi-final second leg tie against Blackburn Rovers, but they went out 6-2 on aggregate.

SEASON	LEAGUE		FA CUP		L. CUP	
	Apps	Gls	Apps	Gls	Apps	Gls
1988/89*	32	0	0	0	0	0
1989/90	37	0	1	0	4	0
1990/91	38	0	5	0	6	0
1991/92	2	0	0	0	1	0
1992/93	26	0	1	0	0	0
1993/94	0	0	0	0	0	0
1994/95	45	0	2	0	2	0
TOTAL	180	0	9	0	13	0

TOTAL APPS 202

TOTAL GOALS 0

* Includes 4 promotion play-off matches in 1988/89.

** Paul Heald also appeared in 17 Auto Windscreens Shield matches.

Hugh HEARTY, 1936-39

Born in Lesmahagow, Lanarkshire, Scotland on 22 March 1913, Hugh Hearty started with Scottish junior side Royal Albert FC in Larkhill. He joined Heart of Midlothian for £40 in January 1933, playing in 37 senior matches, before signing for Cardiff City on a free transfer in May 1935, where he made 18 League appearances. This steady, reliable left-back became an 'Oriental' in August 1936, and he was in the side for O's first match at Brisbane Road, against Cardiff City on 28 August 1937. He was a regular for three seasons, proving to be a very useful player, and even captained the side for a

Hugh Hearty

short period. Hearty decided to retire from football to join the Rochester City police force in April 1939.

SEASON	LEAGUE		FA CUP		TOTAL	
	Apps	Gls	Apps	Gls	Apps	Gls
1936/37	35	1	2	0	37	1
1937/38	37	1	2	0	39	1
1938/39	26	0	2	0	28	0
TOTAL	98	2	6	0	104	2

* Hugh Hearty also appeared in 4 Third Division Cup matches between 1936 and 1939.

John Thomas HEBDON, 1932-33

Born on 12 November 1900 in Castleford, Yorkshire, John Hebdon started his professional career at Castleford Town before moving on to Bradford City, where he made 3 League appearances. The strong-tackling full-back moved to West Ham United in May 1921, where he played 116 senior games. He then moved to Fulham in December 1927, along with fellow full-back George Horlor for £850, and made 24 senior appearances. Hebdon joined Thames Association in August 1929, captaining them in their inaugural League season played at the old West Ham stadium in Prince Regent Lane. However, after a few years the team disbanded – in one Third Division match against Luton Town on 6 December 1930, they attracted an attendance of only 469 people. He became an 'Oriental' in June 1932, making his League debut in the opening match of the 1932/33 season in a 2-0 home win over Newport County. He lost his place after just a handful of appearances, and signed for Halifax Town in October 1932. He moved back to East London and worked for the electricity works department in East Ham.

John Hebdon

SEASON	LEAGUE		FA CUP		TOTAL	
	Apps	Gls	Apps	Gls	Apps	Gls
1932/33	4	0	0	0	4	0
TOTAL	4	0	0	0	4	0

Ronald Ernest HECKMAN, 1955-58

Ronnie Heckman is the only O's player to have scored 5 goals in a senior match – he did so against Lovells Athletic in an FA Cup first round tie at Brisbane Road on 19 November 1955, which O's won 7-1. He is also one of only nine players to have notched 20 or more League goals in a season, scoring 23 League goals in 1955/56. He also hit 6 FA Cup goals that season. Born in Peckham, London on 23 November 1929, Heckman was a late-comer to the professional game, having previously displayed his tremendous talent at amateur clubs Ilford and Southall. Having gained 7 England amateur international caps between 1953 and 1955, he joined O's from Bromley in July 1955. He

showed excellent ball-playing ability, with some utterly devastating finishing from the inside-left position. Some of his goals in the 1955/56 championship-winning side were out of the top drawer. He played most of the season with a broken wrist, but a broken jaw obtained at Brighton in April 1956 kept him out of O's vital run-in at the end of the season, although they did eventually win the Third Division (South) Championship. He was chosen to tour South Africa with an FA touring party, but due to his injury, he missed out. Heckman never quite recaptured his early form, and joined Millwall in November 1957, netting a total of 21 League goals from 90 appearances. In July 1960 he moved to Crystal Palace, and was a member of their Third Division promotion team of 1960/61, and scored 25 League goals from 84 appearances. He later became player-manager of Bedford Town. Heckman died in Bracknell on 26 November 1990.

Ronnie Heckman (left) with coach Les Gore

SEASON	LEAGUE		FA CUP		TOTAL	
	Apps	Gls	Apps	Gls	Apps	Gls
1955/56	36	23	4	6	40	29
1956/57	37	11	1	0	38	11
1957/58	14	4	0	0	14	4
TOTAL	87	38	5	6	92	44

Rudolph HEDMAN, 1989-90 (loan)

Rudi Hedman had a loan spell with O's during December 1989, staying for two months. Born in Lambeth, London on 16 November 1964, this tall, gangly, yet strong right-back made his O's debut against Northampton Town on Boxing Day. He started with Colchester United in February 1984, and proved to be a versatile player – very good in the air, and deceptively skilful on the deck. He made 166(10) League appearances during a five-year spell with the 'U's', scoring a total of 10 goals. He moved to Crystal Palace in December 1968, making 10(11) League appearances. He left Palace in May 1992, and drifted away from League

Rudi Hedman

football to join the Sing Tao club in Hong Kong.

SEASON	LEAGUE		FA CUP		L. CUP	
	Apps	Gls	Apps	Gls	Apps	Gls
1989/90	5	0	0	0	0	0
TOTAL	5	0	0	0	0	0

TOTAL APPS	5
TOTAL GOALS	0

Bjorn HEIDENSTROM, 1997 (trial)

Bjorn Heidenstrom, a midfielder born in Porsgrunn, Norway on 15 January 1968, first came to O's on trial from Norwegian First Division club Odd BK Grenland on 20 December 1996, making his League debut against Brighton & Hove Albion two days later. He returned home in February 1997 to continue his career with Norwegian Second Division club Tollnes. He later played for another Norwegian club – Drobak-Frogn FC. Heidenstrom later won 10 Norwegian caps at under-21 level, and played in the European Cup competition with Lillestrom FC.

SEASON	LEAGUE		FA CUP		L. CUP	
	Apps	Gls	Apps	Gls	Apps	Gls
1996/97	3(1)	0	0	0	0	0
TOTAL	3(1)	0	0	0	0	0

TOTAL APPS	3(1)
TOTAL GOALS	0

George Henry HEINEMANN, 1935-38

Born in Stafford on 17 December 1905, George Heinemann was an industrious and hard-tackling wing-half, who started his career with Stafford Rangers. He moved to Manchester City on 29 October 1928, making 24 senior appearances before joining Coventry City in May 1931. He stayed at Coventry for two seasons, starting 58 matches and scoring once – against Fulham, in a remarkable 5-5 draw in January 1932. During August 1935, he moved south to join Crystal Palace, making 26 senior appearances. He became an 'Oriental' in August 1935, playing regularly for three seasons, and starred in a 3-0 FA Cup victory over the all-conquering Charlton Athletic in January 1935. Heinemann left O's in January 1938, joining Wellington Town, and he gained a Welsh Cup winner's medal in June 1940. Heinemann died in Wellington, Shropshire in 1970.

SEASON	LEAGUE		FA CUP		TOTAL	
	Apps	Gls	Apps	Gls	Apps	Gls
1935/36	41	0	5	0	46	0
1936/37	30	1	2	0	32	1
1937/38	15	0	0	0	15	0
TOTAL	86	1	7	0	93	1

* George Heinemann also appeared in 4 Third Division Cup matches between 1935 and 1937.

Alastair Ian HENDERSON, 1933-35

Born in Anderston, Glasgow in 1911, Henderson started his career with Scottish junior side Yoker Athletic, before he moved to Liverpool in July 1931, where he made 5 League appearances. It was from the Merseysiders that he joined O's in June 1933, making his League debut in the opening fixture of the 1933/34 season – a 3-0 defeat at Norwich City. He could not hold down a regular first-team place, and left O's in May 1935.

SEASON	LEAGUE		FA CUP		TOTAL	
	Apps	Gls	Apps	Gls	Apps	Gls
1933/34	14	0	3	0	17	0
1934/35	4	0	0	0	4	0
TOTAL	18	0	3	0	21	0

James Thomas HENDERSON, 1909-10

Born in Morpeth, Northumberland in 1877, the inside right started his career with local sides Morpeth Harriers and Morpeth Town. He moved into the Southern League with Reading during 1903/04, and then moved on to Bradford City in May 1904, making 14 League appearances. He joined Leeds City in July 1905 for their inaugural season in the League, making 80 senior appearances during his three-year stay. Henderson joined Preston North End in July 1908, playing 7 matches for the Deepdale club. He came south to join O's in May 1910, but after just a single season at Millfields Road, he joined Rochdale of the Lancashire League in June 1910, staying with them for over twenty years. He made 192 senior appearances before retiring in December 1919, aged forty-two. He was appointed trainer until his resignation in July 1930. His younger brother, William Henderson, played for O's between 1910 and 1912.

SEASON	LEAGUE		FA CUP		TOTAL	
	Apps	Gls	Apps	Gls	Apps	Gls
1909/10	26	4	1	0	27	4
TOTAL	26	4	1	0	27	4

William HENDERSON, 1906-08

Right-back Bill Henderson was captain of the O's in 1907/08, and was thought of as one of the finest full-backs in the Second Division that season. Born in Linlithgow, near Broxburn, Scotland in 1878, the player started his football career with Scottish junior side Broxburn Athletic. He joined Everton in November 1886, but made only reserve appearances. He moved to Reading in 1897 and enjoyed 3 successful seasons with the Berkshire club, making 86 Southern League appearances. In June 1901 he moved on to Southern League side Southampton, and made 20 senior appearances in 1901/02. The following season he re-joined Everton, making his League debut at Goodison against Newcastle United on 13 September 1902. He made 15 senior appearances that season, but could only manage 2 games throughout the following season, his last match being against Liverpool in October 1903. During June 1904 he re-joined Reading, and was a regular in their Southern League campaign of 1904/05, making a total of 52 senior appearances during his two-year stay. In July 1906 he became an 'Oriental', making his League debut against Stockport County on 1 September. He stayed at Millfields Road for two seasons, before signing for Southern League side New Brompton (later Gillingham) in May 1909, making 10 appearances.

SEASON	LEAGUE		FA CUP		TOTAL	
	Apps	Gls	Apps	Gls	Apps	Gls
1906/07*	24	0	-	-	24	0
1907/08	23	0	4	0	27	0
TOTAL	47	0	4	0	51	0

* Clapton Orient did not enter the FA Cup competition in 1906/07.

William HENDERSON, 1910-12

William Henderson was introduced to the club by his older brother, James Henderson, before he moved on to Rochdale in May 1910. Morpeth-born William Henderson joined O's in May 1910 from Morpeth Town. The half-back was signed as cover for William Hind, and only came into the side when Hind was injured. He made his League debut in a 1-0 defeat at Chelsea in February 1911, and played for the remainder of that season. Henderson left O's in May 1912.

SEASON	LEAGUE		FA CUP		TOTAL	
	Apps	Gls	Apps	Gls	Apps	Gls
1910/11	15	0	0	0	15	0
1911/12	1	0	0	0	1	0
TOTAL	16	0	0	0	16	0

William HENDERSON, 1925-26

The third and final player named William Henderson to appear for the O's was born in Edinburgh in 1898. The centre forward made his name in Scottish football, with his bustle and speed. He started out at St Bernard's, but it was whilst with Airdrieonians that he came to the public attention, when he netted 36 Scottish League goals from 39 appearances. Manchester United came with an offer of £1,750 for his services in November 1921, and he scored on his United debut against Aston Villa. However, he did little else in a season that saw United relegated to the Second Division, and he languished in the reserves for a couple of seasons. When United were promoted in 1924, he was reinstated, and netted 14 goals from 36 senior appearances. Despite being transferred to Preston North End during that season, he still finished as United's top scorer. His stay at Deepdale lasted just a few months, and he made only 9 League appearances, scoring once. He came south to join O's in July 1925, and figured prominently in the great FA Cup run of 1925/26, scoring one of the goals that knocked out Middlesbrough in a fourth round tie. He left O's in 1926 in order to join Heart of Midlothian, and a year later moved on to Greenock Morton. During August 1928, Henderson was back in the League with Torquay United, and netted 10 goals from

15 starts. June 1930 saw him on the books of Exeter City, but after just 5 League appearances he was injured, and decided to retire in 1930. Henderson died in Rosyth, Scotland in 1964, aged sixty-six.

SEASON	LEAGUE		FA CUP		TOTAL	
	Apps	Gls	Apps	Gls	Apps	Gls
1925/26	29	7	4	1	33	8
TOTAL	29	7	4	1	33	8

Ian HENDON, 1991-92 (loan), 1993-97
Hendon was an excellent attacking wing-back who had two spells with O's, after having been at Tottenham Hotspur since the age of ten. This former England under-21 skipper made just 1 (4) League and cup appearances for Spurs, having signed apprentice forms with the club on 20 December 1989. He represented Havering Schools, and captained their FA Youth Cup-winning side, and also skippered the England youth side which took part in the Youth World Cup com-

Ian Hendon

petition in Portugal. Hendon also tasted European Cup action for Spurs, when he came on as a substitute against Sparkasse Stockerau in Austria, and against Hadjuk Split at White Hart Lane. Born in Ilford, Essex on 5 December 1971, he moved to Romford at a young age. He had a number of loan spells during his early days at Spurs – first with Portsmouth (4 appearances), O's, and then with Barnsley (6 appearances), before signing for the O's on 5 August 1993 for £50,000. During his loan spell at O's, Hendon played in midfield, but it was as an attacking wing-back that he made his mark, and O's manager Taylor said that he was the best wing-back in the Third Division. After four seasons in East London, Hendon's contract was coming to an end, and he was soon to became a free agent. The club were concerned that they would not receive a fee for him, so he went on loan to Birmingham City on 23 March 1995 with a view to a possible permanent move. He made 4 League appearances at St Andrews, but returned to Brisbane Road. He played under four managers during his time with O's and chalked up 150 senior appearances, and was voted Player of the Year by the fans in 1995/96. He was then transferred to Notts County on 24 February 1997 for £100,000. Hendon was appointed as County's club captain in 1997/98, and had the distinction of leading them to the Division Three Championship. He proved to be an inspirational leader, and was selected for the PFA squad for two successive years, making 95 senior appearances and scoring 6 goals. He also gained 7 England under-21 caps. He was transferred to Northampton Town on 25 March 1999 for £25,000, making 60 League appearances and scoring on 3 occasions. With

Hendon's contract running out at the end of the 2000/01 season, the Cobblers decided to cash in by selling him on 12 October 2000 for £55,000 to Division One strugglers Sheffield Wednesday, where he made over 40 senior appearances.

SEASON	LEAGUE		FA CUP		L. CUP	
	Apps	Gls	Apps	Gls	Apps	Gls
1991/92	5(1)	0	0	0	0	0
1993/94	35(1)	2	3	0	2	0
1994/95	29	0	1	0	2	0
1995/96	38	2	1	0	2	0
1996/97	28	1	2	0	2	0
TOTAL	135(2)	5	7	0	8	0

TOTAL APPS	150(2)
TOTAL GOALS	5

* Ian Hendon also appeared in 12 Auto Windscreens Shield matches, scoring once.

Ricky Heppolette

Richard Alfred HEPPOLETTE, 1972-77

Ricky Heppolette lived up to his nickname of 'Tricky Ricky', being a clever and constructive player. Even though he looked a shade slow on occasion, there was a touch of class about him and all that he did. Born in Bhusawal, Bombay, India on 8 April 1949, he came to England as a three-year-old and was brought up in Bolton. He arrived at Preston North End straight from school, and signed apprentice forms at Deepdale in September 1964. He made his League debut in April 1968, and he made 149(5) senior appearances and scored 12 goals. His headed goal against leaders Fulham on May Day 1971 gave Preston promotion to the Second Division. However, with Preston in debt, he was sold to O's for a bargain fee of £43,000 in December 1972. He played very well on the left side of midfield, and eventually linked up effectively with Laurie Cunningham. He was a member of the side that narrowly missed out on promotion to the First Division in 1974, and will be remembered for the picture of him and Barrie Fairbrother both crying in the dressing room after the match at Aston Villa on 3 May 1974. He lost his place in 1976 to fit-again Peter Bennett, and he was transferred to Crystal Palace in October 1976 for £15,000. After just a few months and only 13(2) League appearances, he moved to Chesterfield in February 1977 for another £15,000 fee. He stayed for two years making 46(1) League appearances and scoring 3 goals. In August 1979 he joined Peterborough United, but after just 5 appearances he went to Hong Kong to play for the Eastern Athletic club, before moving back to the Peterborough area to set up a business.

SEASON	LEAGUE		FA CUP		L. CUP	
	Apps	Gls	Apps	Gls	Apps	Gls
1972/73	15	0	1	0	0	0
1973/74	34	6	4	0	1	0
1974/75	22	2	0	0	0	0
1975/76	34	2	1	0	0	0
1976/77	8	0	0	0	2	0
TOTAL	113	10	6	0	3	0

TOTAL APPS	122
TOTAL GOALS	10

* Ricky Heppolette also appeared in 3 Texaco Cup matches in 1974/75 and 3 Anglo-Scottish Cup matches.

Edwin Redvers Baden HEROD, 1935-37

Baden Herod, as he always known, was born in Ilford, Essex on 16 May 1900. He started his career with Barking FC and then moved on to Ilford FC, gaining an Essex FA senior cap in 1920/21 and 6 Essex County caps. The left-back went on to have a long career, first joining Charlton Athletic in November 1921. He stayed at the Valley for seven years, amassing 213 League appearances and scoring twice. In June 1928 he moved to Brentford, playing a further 57 League matches and scoring once. During March 1929, Tottenham Hotspur paid a £4,000 fee for his services, and he made a total of 57 League appearances and scored twice. A further move took place, this time to Chester in July 1931, and he made 71 League appearances and scored once, also winning a Welsh Cup winner's medal in 1933. In July 1933 he was on the books of Swindon Town, and played another 80 League matches. On 1 July 1935 he became an 'Oriental', and he held a regular spot in his first campaign, but the following season he was injured at Newport County in December 1936, and

was replaced by Hugh Hearty. He never managed to win his place back, so he decided to retire from the game at the age of thirty-six. Baden Herod was a credit to the game, he had a long and distinguished career that spanned some fifteen years and 502 League appearances. He died in Redbridge, Essex on 9 May 1973.

SEASON	LEAGUE		FA CUP		TOTAL	
	Apps	Gls	Apps	Gls	Apps	Gls
1935/36	36	0	5	0	41	0
1936/37	17	0	2	0	19	0
TOTAL	53	0	7	0	60	0

* Baden Herod also appeared in 2 Third Division Cup matches in 1936/37.

Roberto HERRERA, 2001

Robbie Herrera, the experienced thirty-one-year-old left-back, was the last player to be signed by Tommy Taylor before his resignation on 15 October 2001. Herrera signed a one-month contract, as cover for the injured Matthew Lockwood, on 4 October, , after impressing in a reserve fixture against Millwall a few days earlier. He made his debut in a 4-2 home defeat by Shrewsbury Town. He was born in Torquay on 12 June 1970, and started his career with his hometown club as a schoolboy. He joined Queens Park Rangers as a trainee in June 1969, and signed professional forms on 1 March 1988. He made his League debut against Liverpool at Anfield in April 1990. During his five-year stay at Loftus Road, his chances were limited, with just 6(5) senior appearances. He did, however, play 139(6) reserve games – a post-war record. Herrera returned to Torquay United on loan in March 1992 and made 11 appearances, with a further 5 loan appearances coming in October 1992. He then went on loan to Fulham in October 1993, and a mystery benefactor paid his £40,000 transfer fee when he moved to Craven Cottage permanently in March 1994. He had an excellent season, as the Cottagers finished runners-up in Division Three in 1996/67. He suffered with injuries under Ray Wilkins' reign, and when Kevin Keegan took charge, he was allowed to return to Torquay, after playing 171(2) senior matches and scoring twice. He joined the Gulls for £30,000 in August 1998. After three years, he was released by boss Colin Lee in May 2001, but re-joined the Plainmoor club under new manager Roy McFarland the following August. He started the campaign, but after 3 appearances he left by mutual consent, after a total of 117(3) senior appearances and a single goal. He joined Dr Marten's Premier League side Merthyr Tydfil in December 2001.

Gary Hibbs

SEASON	LEAGUE		FA CUP		L. CUP	
	Apps	Gls	Apps	Gls	Apps	Gls
2001/02	2	0	0(1)	0	0	0
TOTAL	2	0	0(1)	0	0	0

TOTAL APPS	2(1)
TOTAL GOALS	0

Gary Thomas HIBBS, 1974-77

Born in Hammersmith, London on 26 January 1957, midfielder Gary Hibbs became an apprentice in February 1972, and was a member of a very good O's youth squad between 1972 and 1974. He turned professional in August 1974, and looked a very promising prospect. He managed just a single League appearance in the final match of the 1975/76 season at Notts County, and he also made an appearance in an Anglo-Scottish Cup tie against Fulham on 11 August 1976. Hibbs was released in February 1977, joining Aldershot and making 4(2) League appearances. He left the Shots in 1978, and later appeared for Salisbury Town.

SEASON	LEAGUE		FA CUP		L. CUP	
	Apps	Gls	Apps	Gls	Apps	Gls
1975/76	1	0	0	0	0	0
1976/77	0	0	0	0	0	0
TOTAL	1	0	0	0	0	0

TOTAL APPS	1
TOTAL GOALS	0

* Gary Hibbs also appeared in an Anglo-Scottish Cup match in 1976/77.

Stuart Jason HICKS, 1997-2000

This big, strong, vastly experienced central defender was known as 'Psycho'. He was signed from Scarborough as cover for defenders Clark and Smith, but with his uncompromising defending and his skill in the air, he soon established himself in a three-man defensive formation, nicknamed the 'Three Amigos' by the fans. Quite amazingly, Hicks played for nine different clubs during his career, yet never commanded any transfer fees. Born in Peterborough on 30 May 1967, he joined Colchester United from Wisbech Town on 24 March 1988. He played 69 senior matches and scored once. On 19 August 1990 he moved to Scunthorpe United, and played a further 83 matches and scored 2 goals. He moved on to Doncaster Rovers on 9 August 1992, and 41 matches later, he was on his travels to Huddersfield Town in August 1993, making 27 appearances and scoring once. On 24 March 1994 he was on the books of Preston North End, playing 14 times and again scoring once. His next port of call was Scarborough, and he joined on 23 February 1995 and

Stuart Hicks

played 93 matches, scoring twice. He became an 'Oriental' on 4 August 1997 and became a constant rock in the centre of the defence. However, during the 1997/98 season he received 7 yellow cards and a red one, and the following season he had received another 8 yellows by Christmas. On 13 December 1997 he took over in goal at Shrewsbury, when 'keeper Chris Mackenzie – making his League debut – was sent off for a handling offence. Hicks kept goal for thirty-five minutes, keeping the home team at bay for the O's to record a creditable 2-1 win. He scored his first and only goal for the club on tour in Antigua during the summer of 1999. The 1999/2000 League season started off in the same 'bad' fashion for Hicks, with yet another sending-off, and he was eventually released. In February 2000 he joined Chester City, making 14 League appearances, but could not help them avoid losing their League status. On 12 July 2000 he signed for Mansfield Town, on yet another free transfer, and thirty-three-year-old Hicks became a regular in the Stags side. He has made over 450 senior career appearances during his seventeen years in the professional game before retiring due to a knee injury on 26 February 2002. He later moved into the Unibond League with Hucknall Town.

SEASON	LEAGUE		FA CUP		L. CUP	
	Apps	Gls	Apps	Gls	Apps	Gls
1997/98	35	0	2	0	4	0
1998/99*	30(1)	0	3	0	3	0
1999/2000	13(1)	0	1	0	2	0
TOTAL	78(2)	0	6	0	9	0

TOTAL APPS   93(2)

TOTAL GOALS   0

H

* Stuart Hicks' League record includes 1(1) promotion play-off matches in 1998/99. He also
appeared in an Auto Windscreens Shield match in
1999/2000.

Henry HIGGINBOTHAM, 1922-24

A strong forward, Henry Higginbotham
was born in Sydney, Australia on 27 July
1894. He started his League career just
after the First World War, making a total
of 7 appearances with North Eastern club
South Shields. He moved to Luton Town
in 1920, spending three seasons at
Kenilworth Road, playing 81 times and
scoring 26 goals. He became an 'Oriental'
in February 1922, making his League
debut in a 3-1 win over Crystal Palace. He
was not always a regular choice, but he
did play a handful of matches at inside
right during his second campaign. He
joined Nelson in February 1924, where he
had just 4 outings. He moved to Reading
in May 1924, making 25 League appearances and scoring 3 goals. In 1926 he
was on the books of Pontypridd FC.
Higginbotham died in Springbok in
Glasgow on 5 June 1950, a month before
his fifty-sixth birthday.

SEASON	LEAGUE		FA CUP		TOTAL	
	Apps	Gls	Apps	Gls	Apps	Gls
1922/23	14	1	0	0	14	1
1923/24	5	0	0	0	5	0
TOTAL	19	1	0	0	19	1

Ronald Valentine HIGGINS, 1949-50

Ronnie Higgins was born in Silvertown,
London on 14 February 1923. He came to
O's as an amateur in December 1949
from local works team Green & Siley
Weir. He was given a try in the first team
at centre forward, but he did not impress
and was released in May 1950 to join non-
League Tonbridge. He moved to Brighton
& Hove Albion in January 1952, where he
made 9 League outings without finding
the net. A further move took him to
Queens Park Rangers in January 1933,
where he played a further 3 League
matches and scored once. Higgins was
not a great success during his time in the
League, and eventually moved back into
non-League football.

SEASON	LEAGUE		FA CUP		TOTAL	
	Apps	Gls	Apps	Gls	Apps	Gls
1949/50	2	0	0	0	2	0
TOTAL	2	0	0	0	2	0

Charles Emmanuel HILLAM, 1934-38

Charlie Hillam was probably one of the
best O's goalkeepers of the 1930s, he was
fearless and strong in the air. Born in
Burnley on 6 October 1908, the 6ft tall
goalie played for Burnley Schools. In
1922 he worked in the local collieries and
played football as an amateur with
Nelson, who were then in the Third
Division (North) and with Clitheroe
(Lancashire Combination League). He
joined Burnley in May 1932, and made his
League debut in a 4-4 draw against West
Ham United during October 1932. He
made 21 senior appearances at Turf Moor
before joining Manchester United, along
with Tommy Manns in May 1933, but he
went on to make just 8 appearances for
United. Both Hillam and Manns were on
their travels together again, joining O's in
May 1934 for a joint fee of £100. He eventually ousted regular 'keeper Alf
Robertson in 1935/36, and played in the
famous FA Cup third round victory over
high-flying Charlton Athletic – 3-0 at Lea
Bridge Road in January 1936. He was also
in goal when O's played their first League
match at Brisbane Road against Cardiff
City in August 1937. Hillam played a total

of 116 consecutive League matches for O's. He was transferred to Southend in June 1938, and was appointed trainer at Chingford Town during 1948/49. He died in North Walsham, Norfolk in April 1958.

SEASON	LEAGUE		FA CUP		TOTAL	
	Apps	Gls	Apps	Gls	Apps	Gls
1934/35	15	0	0	0	15	0
1935/36	42	0	5	0	47	0
1936/37	42	0	2	0	44	0
1937/38	26	0	2	0	28	0
TOTAL	125	0	9	0	134	0

* Charlie Hillam also appeared in 4 Third Division Cup matches between 1935 and 1937.

Jack HILLS, 1899-1906

Londoner Jack Hills joined O's from East London amateur football in 1899. He scored on his O's debut in a London League match against Kent side Bromley during August 1899, a match that ended 1-1 at the old Whittle's Athletic Ground. He figured prominently in O's non-League years. Hills, was noted for his powerful shooting, and he captained the team when the O's won their first two major trophies – the Middlesex Charity Cup and the West Ham Charity Cup – in 1901/02. During the following three seasons, he made 47 appearances in the London League and scored 12 goals. He also appeared in O's only campaign in the Second Division of the Southern League in 1904/05, netting 5 goals. He was one of a few players to be retained when O's were elected into the League in May 1905. He made his League debut in a 3-0 victory over Lincoln City on 20 January 1906. In May 1906 he decided to leave the club and return to non-League football. Jack Hills was one of O's better players in their pre-League days.

SEASON	LEAGUE		FA CUP		TOTAL	
	Apps	Gls	Apps	Gls	Apps	Gls
1904/05*	-	-	5	0	5	0
1905/06	2	0	2	0	4	0
TOTAL	2	0	7	0	9	0

* Clapton Orient didn't join the League until 1905/06.

William HIND, 1908-20

Billy Hind was born in Percy Main, Newcastle-upon-Tyne during April 1885. He was a gangly wing-half, who also occasionally played at full-back, serving O's splendidly over eight seasons. He started his career with Willington Athletic before joining Fulham in May 1907, making his League debut against Clapton Orient on 26 October 1907. He made 2 further League appearances at Craven Cottage before signing for O's in June 1908. He was a regular member of the team that finished in fourth spot in the Second Divison in both 1910/11 and 1911/12. He

Billy Hind

was also in the side that won the London Challenge Cup in 1911/12 with a 3-0 win over Millwall, a match played at White Hart Lane on 4 December 1912. He continued at the club after the First World War, and appeared in several matches in 1919/20 before hanging up his boots and joining Welsh side Ton Pentre as trainer in 1920. He re-joined O's as assistant trainer in 1921, a position he held until 1925.

SEASON	LEAGUE		FA CUP		TOTAL	
	Apps	Gls	Apps	Gls	Apps	Gls
1908/09	37	1	1	0	38	1
1909/10	19	0	0	0	19	0
1910/11	24	0	1	0	25	0
1911/12	38	3	1	0	39	3
1912/13	26	1	1	0	27	1
1913/14	31	2	2	0	33	2
1914/15	15	0	0	0	15	0
1919/20	8	0	0	0	8	0
TOTAL	198	7	6	0	204	7

Philip Frederick HOADLEY, 1971-78

Phil Hoadley was a strong, solid and very consistent central defender with a fierce shot, who skippered O's for several seasons. At £30,000, he was a real bargain buy by O's boss George Petchey from his old club Crystal Palace, and proved to be a fine player and skipper. Born in Battersea, London on 6 January 1952, he represented Surrey, South London and the South of England as a schoolboy. He signed as a professional with Crystal Palace in January 1969, although he made his League debut at Bolton in April 1968 when only sixteen years of age. At that time he was the youngest ever player to appear for the Eagles in the League. He made 63(11) senior appearances for them (scoring once), before being released by manager Malcolm Allison in

Phil Hoadley

September 1971. He made his O's debut at full-back in a 3-2 win over Charlton Athletic on 2 October 1971, but he was soon converted to the centre of the defence where he formed a highly effective partnership with Tom Walley. It was his unforgettable goal against Chelsea in the FA Cup in February 1972 that started the memorable comeback, which led to a famous 3-2 victory. Hoadley was the first player to a make a freedom-of-contract move to Norwich City in 1979, the £110,000 fee being fixed by a tribunal. He made 89 senior appearances for the Canaries, before going on-loan to play in Hong Kong for the Eastern Athletic club in 1982. He then sustained a serious knee ligament injury, ending his professional playing career. He moved into non-League football with Loddon United, Norwich United and Holt United as manager. He was assistant manager with Jewson Eastern League side Fakenham

Town. He started a building business and then spent three years running a public house. In August 1987 he returned to Carrow Road as Norwich's 'Football in the Community' officer, a position he still holds.

SEASON	LEAGUE		FA CUP		L. CUP	
	Apps	Gls	Apps	Gls	Apps	Gls
1971/72	32	0	4	1	0	0
1972/73	42	3	1	0	2	0
1973/74	42	1	4	0	4	0
1974/75	38	1	2	0	2	1
1975/76	40	1	1	0	1	0
1976/77	22	3	4	1	4	0
1977/78	39	0	8	0	3	0
TOTAL	255	9	24	2	16	1

TOTAL APPS	295
TOTAL GOALS	12

* Phil Hoadley also appeared in 3 Texaco Cup matches in 1974/75 and 12 Anglo-Scottish Cup matches, scoring once.

Sidney Walter HOAR, 1929-30

Sid Hoar was born on 28 November 1895 in Leagrave, near Luton. The 5ft 8in winger started off with amateur clubs Toddington, Leagrave and Luton Clarence, before signing for Luton Town in 1911. He made 160 League appearances and scored 27 goals over the six seasons he was at Kenilworth Road. Hoar was a victim of poisonous gas whilst serving in France during the First World War, and this put his future as a footballer in doubt. However, he recovered and joined Arsenal from the Hatters on 22 November 1924 for £1,250. He won a runners-up medal with the Gunners in their 1927 FA Cup final match against Cardiff City. He made 117 senior appearances and scored 18 goals, and also featured in 56 other matches (7 goals) whilst at Highbury. In addition, he featured in an England trial match in 1924/25. The thirty-three-year-old Hoar was on the verge of retirement at the end of the 1928/29 season, but was eventually persuaded by O's new boss (Arthur Grimsdell) to sign, and he joined O's on 12 September 1929 for £470. He made his debut against Torquay United, and scored the following week against Charlton Athletic. He broke his leg at Southend United on 12 April 1930, and he decided to call it a day. He went on to become a shopkeeper in Luton until his death on 4 May 1969, a few months before his seventy-fourth birthday.

SEASON	LEAGUE		FA CUP		TOTAL	
	Apps	Gls	Apps	Gls	Apps	Gls
1929/30	26	3	5	0	31	3
TOTAL	26	3	5	0	31	3

Sidney George HOBBINS, 1949-50

Born in Plumstead, London on 16 May 1916, goalkeeper Sid Hobbins started out with Bromley, before joining Charlton Athletic in 1937. He remained at the Valley until 1946, although largely as understudy to the ever-green Sam Bartram. He did, however, play many matches during wartime, and he kept goal for them in the wartime FA Cup final at Wembley, but, unfortunately, Arsenal put seven goals past him that day. Hobbins moved on to Millwall in May 1948, where he made 16 League appearances. He became an 'Oriental' in December 1949 at the age of thirty-three, when the O's were grooming young goalkeeper Pat Welton, and he assisted in Welton's development, but he made his debut in a 2-1 home win over Reading on Christmas Eve 1949. His final League appearance was in a 2-7 defeat by Aldershot at Brisbane Road in February 1950, and Pat Welton came on to replace him. He retired soon afterwards, and was appointed a club representative and then chief scout. He left the club under a cloud during the 1957/58 season when Orient were fined £2,000 for 'financial irregularities', and both Arthur Huggett (club secretary) and Hobbins were asked to leave the club. It was rather unfortunate, because only a few months later it was revealed that the problem was down to a misunderstanding. Hobbins died in Greenwich, London on 16 March 1984.

SEASON	LEAGUE		FA CUP		TOTAL	
	Apps	Gls	Apps	Gls	Apps	Gls
1949/50	11	0	0	0	11	0

Daniel HOCKTON, 1999/2000 (loan)

Danny Hockton joined O's on loan on 14 September 1999 from Division Two side Millwall, after an injury crisis at the Matchroom had left O's without a recognised striker. Hockton was born on 7 February 1979 in Barking, London, and started as a trainee with the Lions, and he progressed rapidly through the youth and reserve ranks at the Den. He was reported to be a player with a lot of pace, who could shoot with both feet, was good in the air, and held up the ball well. He made his debut for the Lions against Stockport County on 21 October 1996, and made 13(31) senior appearances and scored 7 goals for them, including a brace against Northampton Town in a Coca-Cola Cup tie. When he arrived at O's, Hockton went straight into the side to face Grimsby Town in a Rumbelows Cup match at Blundell Park. Unfortunately, he sustained a hamstring injury and had to go off, and was only able to play a hand-ful of games before returning to the Den. On 7 January 2000, he joined Stevenage Borough, where he scored 6 goals from 18(2) appearances. More recently, he has played for Dover Athletic, but after just 12(4) appearances and 9 goals, he joined Chelmsford City for £7,500 on 29 August 2001.

SEASON	LEAGUE		FA CUP		L. CUP	
	Apps	Gls	Apps	Gls	Apps	Gls
1999/2000	1(4)	0	0	0	1	0
TOTAL	1(4)	0	0	0	1	0

TOTAL APPS	2(4)
TOTAL GOALS	0

Carl HODDLE, 1989-91

Carl Hoddle is the brother of current Tottenham Hotspur boss, Glenn Hoddle. Carl Hoddle came to O's from Bishop Stortford for a reported fee of £10,000, having previously been at Barnet. However, he could never hold down a

Carl Hoddle

regular first-team place at Brisbane Road. A 6ft 4in tall midfielder, he was born in Harlow, Essex on 8 March 1967. He started his career at Tottenham Hotspur as an apprentice in July 1984, at a time when his brother was starring in the first team. His most productive season with O's was during 1989/90, after spending some time in France on loan with Caen. His best match was on October 21 1989 where he produced a sparkling performance and a goal against Reading. Hoddle asked to be placed on the transfer list in 1990. He joined Barnet in July 1991, and scored 3 goals from 80(12) senior appearances during the four seasons he was with the Bees. He later played for Woking, Aylesbury and Enfield (by whom he was fired for his 'lack of discipline') and he became a postman. More recently, he has worked as a car salesman for Gates of Harlow in Essex. It must have been extremely difficult for Carl Hoddle, constantly living in the shadow of his more famous brother.

SEASON	LEAGUE		FA CUP		L. CUP	
	Apps	Gls	Apps	Gls	Apps	Gls
1989/90	19(7)	2	0	0	1	0
1990/91	0(2)	0	0	0	0	0
TOTAL	19(9)	2	0	0	1	0

TOTAL APPS	20(9)	
TOTAL GOALS	2	

* Carl Hoddle also appeared in 3 Auto Windscreens Shield matches.

Stephen Brian HODGE, 1997 (trial)

Steve Hodge, the former England international midfielder, joined Orient on 15 August 1997 on a non-contract basis. At the age of thirty-four, he was in the twilight of his career, and joined O's after a spell in Hong Kong. He played just sixty minutes on 16 August 1997 at Scunthorpe United before being substituted, having looked useful but very unfit. Born in Nottingham on 25 October 1962, he was capped 24 times for England and played at the highest level with Nottingham Forest, Aston Villa, Tottenham Hotspur, Leeds United, Derby County (loan), Queens Park Rangers and Watford. Hodge amassed a total of 385 League appearances and 81 goals during his long career. O's boss Tommy Taylor stated: 'Steve (Hodge) has not been offered a contract, he felt the division was too physical and decided to retire from the game.' After his retirement, he became a media pundit in the Midlands, and was under-14 coach at Notts County.

SEASON	LEAGUE		FA CUP		L. CUP	
	Apps	Gls	Apps	Gls	Apps	Gls
1997/98	1	0	0	0	0	0
TOTAL	1	0	0	0	0	0

TOTAL APPS	1	
TOTAL GOALS	0	

Lee Leslie HODGES, 1997 (loan)

This small midfielder, standing just 5ft 4in tall, came to O's on loan from West Ham United on 28 February 1997. He made his League debut a few days later against Barnet, but he was sent back to the Hammers earlier than anticipated. Born in Newham, London on 2 March 1978, he looked a fast, elusive player. He turned professional in July 1996, after playing for England schoolboys, and went on to have a number of loan spells with various clubs over the years, including Exeter City, Plymouth Argyle, Ipswich Town and, more recently, Southend United (March 1999). He had an excellent match against

O's in April 1999 in the Blues' shock 3-0 win at the Matchroom Stadium. He made just 6 senior appearances (all as substitute) during his four years at Upton Park. Hodges joined newly promoted Scunthorpe United in June 1999 for an initial £50,000 down payment, set to rise after 25 appearances and eventually netting West Ham £130,000. Up to the end of 2000/01, he had made 81(7) senior appearances and scored 15 goals, but his contract expires at the end of April 2002.

SEASON	LEAGUE		FA CUP		L. CUP	
	Apps	Gls	Apps	Gls	Apps	Gls
1996/97	3	0	0	0	0	0
TOTAL	3	0	0	0	0	0

TOTAL APPS	3
TOTAL GOALS	0

Jonathan Jack HOLLAND, 1927-29

Born in Preston on 3 April 1901, inside forward John Holland started as a nineteen-year-old with Preston North End in 1920, spending two seasons at Deepdale but making just 5 League appearances. He joined Swansea Town in June 1922, and spent two seasons in Wales, making 23 senior appearances and scoring on 3 occasions. In 1925 he signed up with Wrexham, but after 9 appearances and 3 goals, he was off to Crewe Alexandra before the season was even over. He made 23 League appearances and scored 3 times for Crewe. The following season he was on his travels yet again, this time earning his trade with Newport County, where another 10 appearances brought him 2 goals. He became an 'Oriental' in October 1927, and made his debut in a 2-1 win over Leeds United in December 1927, but again he had to be content with reserve-team football. He moved on to

Carlisle United in July 1929, where he had his best ever spell, making 34 League appearances and finding the net 13 times. His League career ended with Barrow in 1931/32, where he made 8 appearances at the age of thirty-one. John Holland, who had spent much of the time playing reserve football, spent a total of twelve years on the League circuit and amassed a total of 131 League appearances and 35 goals, before joining amateur side Darvel Blackpool FC.

SEASON	LEAGUE		FA CUP		TOTAL	
	Apps	Gls	Apps	Gls	Apps	Gls
1927/28	6	2	0	0	6	2
1928/29	13	2	0	0	13	2
TOTAL	19	4	0	0	19	4

Gavin Victor HOLLIGAN, 1999 (loan)

Gavin Holligan, a nineteen-year-old striker, came to O's on loan from West Ham on 17 September 1999, during a serious injury crisis. The striker was no stranger to the O's fans, having scored for Kingstonian in their 2-1 FA Cup replay defeat at Brisbane Road on 15 December 1988, tapping in from two yards in the seventy-fourth minute, after O's goalkeeper Mackenzie had dropped the ball into his path. A few months after that defeat, Holligan joined West Ham United for a reported £100,000 on 5 March 1999. Born in Lambeth, London on 5 August 1980, the youngster started with Walton & Hersham in August 1997, joining Kingstonian in June 1998. When he moved to West Ham, he soon made his mark by scoring freely for the youth and reserve sides. He made a dramatic first-team entrance when he came on as a substitute against Liverpool at Anfield, and in the final seconds was only just foiled by home 'keeper David James in a one-on-

one situation. He was brought back to reality when playing against Millwall reserves, yet still managed to score a hat-trick. O's fans were hoping that Holligan was the player to kick start the 1999/2000 season, as did a young Kevin Campbell some ten years earlier. He made his debut in a 2-0 home defeat by Torquay United, and he also played against Grimsby Town in the Worthington Cup. However, he could not meet the high expectations and returned to Upton Park on 17 October 1999, after just those 2 appearances. In October 2000 he joined Division Three side Exeter City on loan, but after just 3 League appearances he returned to Upton Park. In March 2001 he went back on loan to Kingstonian, and scored a couple of goals from his first 6 appearances, but could not stop them from being relegated. His short West Ham career came to an end in May 2001, when he was given a free transfer to Wycombe Wanderers on 9 August 2001.

SEASON	LEAGUE		FA CUP		L. CUP	
	Apps	Gls	Apps	Gls	Apps	Gls
1999/2000	1	0	0	0	1	0
TOTAL	1	0	0	0	1	0

TOTAL APPS	2
TOTAL GOALS	0

Michael John HOLLOW, 1961-65

Mike Hollow came to O's as an eighteen-year-old from Bishop Stortford in December 1961, and scored on his reserve debut in a 7-0 thrashing of Southend reserves on 13 December. He appeared at centre forward for O's in a friendly against Scottish side Greenock Morton at Brisbane Road on 5 April 1963, scoring once in a 4-0 win. Born in Nazeing, Essex on 5 September 1943, he

moved to Bishop Stortford as a youngster and represented the Herts county youth side. He was converted to right full-back and made his O's League debut in March 1964, when he replaced the injured Eddie Lewis at Portsmouth in a 4-3 defeat. He played more regularly during the following season. When manager Benny Fenton departed and was replaced by Dave Sexton, like a number of the more established players, Hollow fell out of favour and was allowed to leave. He joined Peterborough United in July 1965, where he made 14 League appearances and scored once, before moving on to Southern League side Cambridge City in 1966. Hollow was not a hard-tackling type of defender, but was a more constructive type of player who held off from making rash tackles.

SEASON	LEAGUE		FA CUP		L. CUP	
	Apps	Gls	Apps	Gls	Apps	Gls
1963/64	12	0	0	0	0	0
1964/65	22	0	0	0	1	0
TOTAL	34	0	0	0	1	0

TOTAL APPS	35
TOTAL GOALS	0

Norman HOLMES, 1910-13

Norman Holmes was born in Darley Hillside, Matlock during 1891. He was the younger brother of O's manager William Holmes, who signed him from Leeds City reserves side in 1910 as cover for J.T. Johnston. The 5ft 10in right-back made his League debut in a 3-1 win at Glossop North End in March 1911, but could not make any impact at Millfields Road. He was transferred to Huddersfield Town on 16 June 1913, making just 3 further League appearances before going to York City of the Midlands League in July

1914. During the First World War, he returned to London to enlist in the army alongside his brother and former O's colleagues. L/Cpl Holmes was seriously wounded, and was not able to play football again after the hostilities had ceased.

SEASON	LEAGUE		FA CUP		TOTAL	
	Apps	Gls	Apps	Gls	Apps	Gls
1910/11	2	0	0	0	2	0
1911/12	2	0	0	0	2	0
TOTAL	4	0	0	0	4	0

William Marsden HOLMES, 1905-08

Billy 'Doc' Holmes, as he was known, was born in Darley Hillside, Matlock in 1875. The defender started his playing career with Darley Dale FC. He moved on to Chesterfield Town of the Sheffield League (making 38 appearances), before moving to Manchester City in July 1896. He made his League debut for City at centre half against Notts County on 31 October 1896, and stayed at Hyde Road for nine years, making 166 senior appearances and scoring 4 goals. He won a Second Divison Championship medal in 1899, and a Lancashire Combination Championship medal in 1902. He represented a League XI against Irish League in an 8-1 win during November 1897. Holmes was omitted for City's 1-0 FA Cup win over Bolton Wanderers on 23 April 1904 at the Crystal Palace, a decision that prompted him to throw his football boots through the team's dressing-room window in disgust. He was suspended and was handed a hefty suspension by the FA, along with sixteen other Manchester City players between May 1906 and January 1907 – this was eventually rescinded in 1908. He was also fined £50 fine for his part in the infamous illegal payments and irregular bonuses scandal in 1904/05, often

referred to as the Billy Meredith case. Holmes joined O's on 19 August 1905 for £10, and made his debut in O's inaugural League fixture at Leicester Fosse on 2 September 1905. He was appointed player-manager in March 1906, after boss Samuel Ormerod had resigned, and was appointed manager in March 1908. His management acumen was particularly evident between 1910 and 1912, when his team twice finished in fourth position in the Second Division. Holmes died in Hackney, London on 22 February 1922 after collapsing, aged just forty-seven, after sixteen years with the club.

SEASON	LEAGUE		FA CUP		TOTAL	
	Apps	Gls	Apps	Gls	Apps	Gls
1905/06	27	0	3	0	30	0
1906/07	17	0	0	0	17	0
1907/08	2	0	2	0	4	0
TOTAL	46	0	5	0	51	0

Clifford Charles HOLTON, 1966-67

The grand job thirty-eight-year-old Cliff Holton did for the O's in 1966/67, and the vital goals he scored deserve a prominent place in this book. 'Big Cliff' had probably the hardest shot of any post-war player. Born in Oxford on 29 April 1929, he started as a full-back with junior side Marston Minors. He joined Arsenal in November 1947 from Isthmian League side Oxford City, where his potential as a dangerous striker had come to the fore, making his Gunners debut on Boxing Day 1950. He made 198 League appearances for Arsenal, scoring 82 goals, and winning a League Championship medal and an FA Cup runners-up medal. He moved to Watford in October 1958 for £10,000, and broke their goalscoring record with 42 League goals in 1959/60. He joined Northampton Town for £7,000 in September 1961, where he also broke their club record, scoring 36 goals in 41 League appearances – both of these records are still unbroken. In December 1962 he moved to Crystal Palace for £4,000, netting a further 40 goals from 101 League appearances. He returned to Watford in May 1965 for £5,000, and then moved on to Charlton Athletic in February 1966. Holton joined O's in June 1966, along with defender John Snedden, in exchange for young O's favourite Harry Gregory. The O's were in dire financial straits, and it was the veteran Holton who inspired the players to beat off the threat of relegation with his skilful play and powerful shooting, the like of which had not seen at the club since the days of Frank Neary in the 1940s. A leg injury and vein problem ended his playing days, falling just half-a-dozen goals short of a remarkable total of 300 League goals. His 294 goals came from 570 League appearances with seven clubs. After retiring, he became the MD of Stonebridge Jigs & Tools in Hadley Wood. Cliff Holton died from a heart attack whilst on a golfing holiday in Almeria, Spain on 4 June 1996, aged sixty-seven.

SEASON	LEAGUE		FA CUP		L. CUP	
	Apps	Gls	Apps	Gls	Apps	Gls
1966/67	44	17	3	0	1	0
1967/68	3	0	0	0	1	1
TOTAL	47	17	3	0	2	1

TOTAL APPS	52
TOTAL GOALS	18

Philip HOPE, 1927-28

Born in Kimblesworth, Co. Durham on 24 April 1897, full-back Phil Hope started his career with Durham City, before moving to Norwich City in January 1920. He spent four seasons with the Norfolk club, making 109 senior appearances and scoring just once. In May 1924 he was transferred to Blackburn Rovers, but his chances were limited with just 6 outings in two seasons. In June 1926 he made the move to Southend United, but played only 9 games. He joined O's in June 1927, playing in both full-back positions, but he lost his place to Bob MacDonald in May 1928. After a short spell with Washington Colliery during October 1928, he joined Rochdale, making 13 senior appearances and scoring once. Hope died in Ouston, Co. Durham on 3 January 1969.

SEASON	LEAGUE		FA CUP		TOTAL	
	Apps	Gls	Apps	Gls	Apps	Gls
1927/28	18	0	1	0	19	0
TOTAL	18	0	1	0	19	0

Keith Morton HOUCHEN, 1982-84

Keith Houchen joined O's from Hartlepool United in March 1982 for £25,000,

Keith Houchen

with a reputation for being a good striker and an excellent header of the ball. Probably the highlight of his football career was playing for Coventry City in the 1987 FA Cup final against Tottenham Hotspur. City won 3-2, and Houchen scored in the sixty-second minute with a typical flying header. Born in Middlesbrough on 25 July 1960, Houchen started off as a junior with Chesterfield. In February 1968 he signed for Hartlepool United, and went on to notch 65 League goals from 160(10) starts. His transfer to O's came in the midst of a relegation battle, but he looked impressive and was an excellent penalty taker. Unfortunately, his form soon dipped, and his aspirations of playing a higher grade of football took a severe knock when O's were relegated to the Third Divison. He moved to York City for £15,000 in March 1984, and his debut was quite eventful. Coming on as a substitute, he scored one, missed a penalty and was booked. He made 56(11) League

Keith Houchen scores with a flying header

appearances and scored 19 goals for the Minstermen. He signed for Scunthorpe United for £40,000 in March 1986, but his stay was short-lived, making just 9 League appearances and scoring 3 goals. He joined Coventry City in June 1986 for £50,000 (50(13) senior appearances and 12 goals), and he was then sold to Scottish side Hibernians for £300,000 and did quite well during his stay at Easter Road. He moved to Port Vale in August 1991 for a £100,000 fee, and made 44(15) appearances, scoring 10 goals. He concluded his career with another spell at Hartlepool in August 1993, scoring a further 27 goals from 104(5) League appearances. He was later appointed their player-manager in 1996. After his retirement from the game, he lived in the North-East and worked as a property developer, as well as doing some football reporting for the Press Association. In a League career that spanned some eighteen years, Keith Houchen netted some 152 goals from 574(44) League appearances.

SEASON	LEAGUE		FA CUP		L. CUP	
	Apps	Gls	Apps	Gls	Apps	Gls
1981/82	14	1	0	0	0	0
1982/83	32	10	2	0	1	0
1983/84	28(2)	9	1	0	2	1
TOTAL	74(2)	20	3	0	3	1

TOTAL APPS	80(2)
TOTAL GOALS	21

* Keith Houchen also appeared in 3 Football League Groups Cup matches and 0(1) Auto Windscreens Shield match.

Scott Arron HOUGHTON, 2000-2002
Much travelled winger Scott Houghton came to O's on a free transfer from

Scott Houghton

Excellence, signing as a trainee in July 1988 and turning professional May 1990. He made 14 senior appearances with Spurs (all as substitute), including a couple of matches in Europe. He won various honours as a youngster, including 8 England schoolboy caps, 10 youth caps and 6 under-19 caps. He was also a member of Spurs FA Youth Cup-winning team in 1990.He had a number of loan periods at other clubs whilst at White Hart Lane, including Ipswich Town, Gillingham and Charlton Athletic, before a free transfer took him to Luton Town in August 1993. In September 1994 he joined Walsall for £20,000, playing 76(2) matches and scoring 14 goals. He moved to Peterborough United in July 1996 for £60,000, and netted 13 League goals from 57(13) starts. He spent a couple of loan periods with Southend United, before joining them on a permanent basis on 1 June 1999. He went on to make 69(4) League appearances and score 9 goals for the club. Houghton is a player who has certainly done the rounds, playing for nine different clubs before his move to O's, and making a career total of 213(39) League appearances with 38 goals. The thirty-year-old certainly looked a useful and experienced acquisition in O's push for promotion in 2001, however, a number of injuries curtailed his progress. He scored a cracker in the play-off final at the Millennium Stadium, Cardiff, but it wasn't enough to stop O's eventually going down 4-2 to Blackpool. He was substituted after eighty-two minutes, and upon the leaving the field, he threw down his jersey in disgust. Houghton went on to play for Halifax Town, but was released in March 2002. He had a clause in his contract that allowed him to leave the Yorkshire side

Southend United on 6 October 2000, after having been a target of O's boss Tommy Taylor for some time. His debut came at Torquay United on 7 October 2000, where he played the first half but was injured after colliding with a perimeter fence. He only returned towards the end of November 2000. The 5ft 7in and 12st 4lb Houghton scored a vital goal that brought three points against Darlington in December, and soon after scored the winner against Northwich Victoria in an FA Cup second round replay, thus securing a 3-2 win in extra time and a lucrative tie against his first club Tottenham Hotspur. His winner came in the 116th minute – when a clearance from visiting goalkeeper Lance Key was charged down by Houghton, the ball looped over Key into an unguarded net to sink the non-League team. Born in Hitchen on 22 October 1971, Houghton started with Tottenham Hotspur at their School of

if another club came in with a long-term contract, which is what Stevenage Borough did. Thirty-year-old Houghton was released from his contract in January 2002. After training with Peterborough, he signed for Halifax Town the following month. He played for the Yorkshire side at Brisbane Road in a 3-1 defeat on 2 March and was warmly applauded by O's fans before the game. After just 7 appearances at The Shay, he moved into the Football Conference with Stevenage Borough on 7 March 2002. So ended a League career for Houghton that spanned some twelve years and 247(54) League matches with 44 goals.

SEASON	LEAGUE		FA CUP		L. CUP	
	Apps	Gls	Apps	Gls	Apps	Gls
2000/01*	21(3)	2	3	1	0	0
2001/02	10(11)	5	0	0	1	1
TOTAL	31(14)	7	3	1	1	1

TOTAL APPS	35(14)
TOTAL GOALS	9

* Houghton played in an LDV Vans Trophy match in 2000/01. He also made 3 play-off appearances and scored a goal in 2000/01.

Terence HOWARD, 1987-95

Quite remarkably, O's cult hero and stalwart Terry Howard – dubbed 'Oooh' by O's fans – was sensationally sacked by John Sitton during the half-time break in the home match against Blackpool on 7 February 1995, after 8 years of loyal service with O's. He is one of only a handful of players to have made over 300 League appearances for the club. After his sacking, Howard was left bemused, sitting in the dressing-room all on his own. Not surprisingly, O's went onto lose the match 1-0, and were eventually relegated

after finishing in bottom place on just 26 points, 3 adrift of Chester City and 12 points behind Cardiff City. Born in Stepney, London on 26 February 1966, he started as an apprentice with Chelsea in February 1984, making 6 League appearances. After loan spells with Crystal Palace and Chester City, he joined O's in March 1987 for £10,000. Howard showed good touches for a big man, and was accurate with his passing. He played 50 matches in O's promotion season of 1988/89, including 4 play-off matches. His run of 114 consecutive League matches ended on the final day of the 1991/92 season, because of blisters on his feet. He scored his first ever hat-trick playing in a midfield role in a match against Mansfield Town on 28 November 1992, his third coming from the penalty spot. Howard, a player who had stayed remarkably fit and free from any serious injuries, was on course to possibly break Peter Allen's long-standing League appearance record until that

Terry Howard

remarkable sacking – a sad time in the club's history. Wycombe Wanderers manager Martin O'Neill signed Howard on 11 February 1995, and he made a total of 20 appearances for the Chairboys in the 1994/95 season. This makes him one of just a handful of players to have made more than the 46 full League appearances in a single season (excluding play-off matches), playing on 47 occasions. Howard made an emotional return to Brisbane Road with Wycombe for the final League match of the 1994/95 season. He said: 'Despite what happened, I still have a great affection for Orient. I still see a lot of people connected with the club, and I got a lot of letters from fans when I left.' His last Wycombe match was on 6 August 1996 at Hull City, when he was substituted for the first time during his 63-match run, and ended his time at the club with 3 goals. Howard joined Woking in the Football Conference, making 43(2) appearances and scoring once during the 1996/97 and 1997/98 seasons. He won a FA Trophy winner's medal for Woking at Wembley in 1997. After a short spell with Yeovil, he joined Aldershot Town, where he made his debut on 21 March 1998 and was appointed club captain. Howard made 60 appearances and scored 4 goals for the Shots, but he requested a transfer and left them at the end of the 1998/99 season. He joined Borehamwood for the start of the 1999/2000 season, and then moved on to Braintree Town FC for the 2000/01 season.

SEASON	LEAGUE		FA CUP		L. CUP	
	Apps	Gls	Apps	Gls	Apps	Gls
1986/87	12	2	0	0	0	0
1987/88	41	2	4	0	2	0
1988/89*	50	5	3	0	5	0
1989/90	45	7	1	0	4	1
1990/91	46	3	5	1	6	0
1991/92	45	4	5	1	4	0
1992/93	41	5	2	1	2	0
1993/94	20(5)	2	1(1)	0	2	0
1994/95	27	1	2	0	1	0
TOTAL	327(5)	31	23(1)	3	26	1

TOTAL APPS	376(5)
TOTAL GOALS	35

* Includes 4 promotion play-off matches in 1988/89.

** Terry Howard also appeared in 25 Auto Windscreens Shield matches (an O's record), scoring a single goal.

Albert Richard Henry HOWE, 1967-69

Defender Bert Howe was born in Greenwich, London on 16 November 1938. He started his career with Kent League side Faversham Town and then joined Crystal Palace in December 1958 and spent nine years at Selhurst Park, proving to be a steady left-back. He chalked up 192(1) League appearances for Palace, before re-joining his former Palace boss, Dick Graham, at O's in January 1967. He lent experience to a young O's defence, at a time when they were struggling, both on and off the field. He performed well, until being ousted by young Dennis Rofe. Howe joined Colchester United in July 1969, where he teamed up with Dick Graham for a third time. He spent just a single season at Layer Road, making 29 League appearances and scoring once. He proved to be a very good influence, being cool and sound under pressure in O's defence, just when the team needed those very qualities during an awkward period for the club. He joined Romford FC in June 1969, and later was employed as a salesman in the London area.

SEASON	LEAGUE		FA CUP		L. CUP	
	Apps	Gls	Apps	Gls	Apps	Gls
1966/67	23	0	0	0	0	0
1967/68	40	0	5	0	1	0
1968/69	28	0	0	0	4	0
TOTAL	91	0	5	0	5	0

TOTAL APPS	101
TOTAL GOALS	0

Shaun Colin HOWES, 1996-97

Shaun Howes, a promising young 5ft 10in and 10st 3lb left-sided defender, joined O's from Cambridge United on a free transfer on 18 November 1996. He started out in 1992 in Norwich City's under-14 squad and then moved to the Abbey Stadium, making just a single League appearance as a substitute between August 1994 and November 1996. Born in Norwich on 7 November 1977, he made his O's League debut in a 1-1 draw at Fulham in December 1996. However, he played only a handful of matches before a cruciate ligament injury kept him out the game for a long period. After a short loan spell with Billericay Town during March 1977, he eventually decided to retire from the professional game. He was out of work for two years whilst undertaking a sports science course in Norwich. He then joined Jewson Eastern Counties League side Wroxham FC in 1999 and is still with the club. Howes also works as a self-employed tennis coach.

SEASON	LEAGUE		FA CUP		L. CUP	
	Apps	Gls	Apps	Gls	Apps	Gls
1996/97	3(2)	0	0	0	0	0
TOTAL	3(2)	0	0	0	0	0

TOTAL APPS	3(2)
TOTAL GOALS	0

Samuel HOWSHALL, 1907-08

Outside right Sam Howshall joined O's from Salisbury City in May 1907, making his senior debut in a 3-0 FA Cup victory over Custom House on 21 September 1907. His entry into the League came against Grimsby Town on 9 April 1908. He was considered a very promising amateur player, but he never quite lived up to expectations, and returned to Salisbury Town in May 1908.

SEASON	LEAGUE		FA CUP		TOTAL	
	Apps	Gls	Apps	Gls	Apps	Gls
1907/08	2	0	1	0	3	0
TOTAL	2	0	1	0	3	0

James Cockburn HUGALL, 1910-21

Jimmy Hugall was unquestionably one of O's finest goalkeepers, and certainly ranks alongside Arthur Wood and John Jackson. He was born in Whitburn, Sunderland on 26 April 1889, and started his career with Sunderland Co-operative FC. He joined O's from Whitburn FC of the Wearside League in 1910, and was deputy to Billy Bower during his early days at Millfields Road. He made his League debut against Stockport County in December 1910, but shared the green jersey with Bower for a number of seasons, until finally displacing him in 1914/15. During the First World War, he joined the Durham Light Infantry, and received wounds to his leg, eye and shoulder that many thought would threaten his playing career. Yet remarkably, in the 1919/20 season, he only missed 7 matches. Hugall was awarded a benefit match against Tottenham Hotspur in 1920, which attracted over 10,000 spectators who turned out to honour the big custodian. During 1921/22, he lost his place to Arthur Wood, and in 1922 he moved on to join Scottish side Hamilton Academicals. However, in 1923 he joined Durham City, where he made 35 League appearances in the Third Division (North). Hugall died in Sunderland on 23 September 1927, aged thirty-eight.

SEASON	LEAGUE		FA CUP		TOTAL	
	Apps	Gls	Apps	Gls	Apps	Gls
1910/11	1	0	0	0	1	0
1911/12	18	0	0	0	18	0
1912/13	4	0	0	0	4	0
1913/14	14	0	0	0	14	0
1914/15	31	0	1	0	32	0
1919/20	35	0	1	0	36	0
1920/21	35	0	1	0	36	0
1921/22	2	0	0	0	2	0
TOTAL	140	0	3	0	143	0

Henry Hughton

Robert Arthur HUGHES, 1929-30

Bobby Hughes was born in Wrexham, Wales on 26 September 1901. He gained 2 Welsh amateur international caps in 1925/26. He joined O's from Blackpool in August 1929, having played twice for the Seasiders' first XI. He made his League debut on the left wing for O's on Christmas Day 1929, scoring the opener in a 2-1 win against Swindon Town at Millfields Road. He played just a handful of first-team matches (largely being confined to reserve football) and he left O's in July 1931, joining Altrincham before later moving to Mossley. Hughes died in 1973, aged seventy-two.

SEASON	LEAGUE		FA CUP		TOTAL	
	Apps	Gls	Apps	Gls	Apps	Gls
1929/30	6	1	0	0	6	1
TOTAL	6	1	0	0	6	1

Henry HUGHTON, 1976-1982, 1986-88

Henry Hughton was born in Stratford, London on 18 November 1959. He was an O's apprentice for almost a year, before signing professional forms in December 1976. He progressed in O's reserve side during 1977/78 (gaining an Eire youth cap), before making his League debut in a 2-1 win at Sheffield United on 19 August 1978. Hughton was a tenacious tackler, and his hard-working and bustling style made him a favourite with O's fans. He started at full-back, but soon settled into a midfield role, and after 2 successful seasons, he was transferred to Crystal Palace in July 1982, where he made 113(5) League appearances and scored once. After a short spell with Brentford – 5(3) League appearances – he returned to Brisbane Road during December 1986, but was a shadow of his former self and went off to play in Sweden in May 1988. He returned to England to play for non-League Enfield, and in 1996 he was on the books of Crockenhill FC. Henry Hughton always showed 100 per cent effort and never let the team down. Nowadays, he works for Parcel Force in Croydon.

SEASON	LEAGUE		FA CUP		L. CUP	
	Apps	Gls	Apps	Gls	Apps	Gls
1977/78	0	0	0	0	0	0
1978/79	33	2	2	0	1	0
1979/80	40	0	3	0	2	1
1980/81	8(3)	0	1	0	0	0
1981/82	23(4)	0	3	0	1	0
1986/87	10	0	0	0	0	0
1987/88	6(2)	0	0	0	1	0
TOTAL	120(9)	2	9	0	5	1

TOTAL APPS	134(9)
TOTAL GOALS	3

* Henry Hughton also appeared in 2 Anglo-Scottish Cup matches and an Auto Windscreens Shield match.

Alan Edward HULL, 1987-91

Alan Hull, a diminutive live-wire striker, joined O's from Vauxhall Opel League

Alan Hull

Alan Hull, on the way to scoring a hat-trick in the 8-0 thrashing of Colchester United in October 1988

side Barking in June 1987, firstly as a part-timer. After hitting an incredible 45 goals for Barking in the 1986/87 season, like so many non-League players, he found goals in the League a little harder to come by. Born in Rochford, Essex, on 4 September 1962, he became a Southend United apprentice before going to Barking. Early in his O's career, he scored a brace in the away win at Stockport County, but he could never hold down a regular first-team place. However, he did score a hat-trick in O's 8-0 thrashing of Colchester United on 15 October 1988. He became unsettled at Brisbane Road, and went on loan to Redbridge Forest in 1981. When he was not retained in May 1981, he joined Enfield, before later playing for Dagenham & Redbridge, Heybridge Swifts and Great Wakering Rovers, where he became assistant manager. In June 2001 he was appointed as manager of the Ryman League Second Division club.

SEASON	LEAGUE		FA CUP		L. CUP	
	Apps	Gls	Apps	Gls	Apps	Gls
1987/88	27(9)	6	2(1)	1	0(2)	0
1988/89	12(5)	5	1(2)	0	4	1
1989/90	15(9)	6	0	0	0(2)	0
1990/91	0(2)	0	0(1)	0	0	0
TOTAL	54(25)	17	3(4)	1	4(4)	1

TOTAL APPS   61(33)
TOTAL GOALS   19

* Alan Hull also appeared in 3(3) Auto Windscreens Shield matches, scoring 3 goals.

Archibald James HULL, 1930-31

Archie Hull was born in East Ham, London on 8 August 1902. He first played for Isthmian League side Ilford FC, and was rated as one of the best amateur centre halves in London. Having played for West Ham in 1927 (2 League appearances), he became an 'Oriental' in July 1930, making just a single League appearance in the 3-0 defeat at Thames Association during September 1930. He rejoined Ilford a few months later. Away from football, Archie Hull was a chemist, and was also renowned for his talent as a singer, performing in many concerts. He died in Windlesham, Surrey on 6 March 1978, aged seventy-six.

SEASON	LEAGUE		FA CUP		TOTAL	
	Apps	Gls	Apps	Gls	Apps	Gls
1930/31	1	0	0	0	1	0
TOTAL	1	0	0	0	1	0

Douglas Arthur HUNT, 1946-48

Centre forward Doug Hunt was born in Shipton Bellinger, Andover on 19 May 1914. His early football career was spent with Northfleet FC, before joining Spurs in March 1934 and making 17 League appearances with 6 goals. He moved to Barnsley in March 1937, and during his two-year stay netted 17 goals from 36 League appearances. He then joined Sheffield Wednesday in March 1938, and experienced a very successful spell, scoring 31 goals from just 45 League appearances (including 6 goals against Norwich City in a Second Division fixture on 19 November 1938). During the Second World War, he guested for Brentford. It was O's boss Charles Hewitt who brought thirty-two-year-old Hunt to Brisbane Road in April 1946, and he was O's joint-top League scorer (with Wally Pullen) in 1946/47. He did a good job for O's during a difficult period, and his cool play and smart headwork were assets to the team. In June 1948 he was appointed player-manager of Gloucester City, and was later coach at Yeovil. Hunt died in Yeovil during May 1989, aged seventy-five.

SEASON	LEAGUE		FA CUP		TOTAL	
	Apps	Gls	Apps	Gls	Apps	Gls
1946/47	39	13	1	1	40	14
1947/48	22	3	1	0	23	3
TOTAL	61	16	2	1	63	17

Harold HUNT, 1905-06

Amateur Harry Hunt, a reserve centre forward, played just a single League match for O's, a 1-0 defeat at Bristol City on 31 March 1906. Very little else is known about this player, who returned to the amateur ranks in May 1906.

SEASON	LEAGUE		FA CUP		TOTAL	
	Apps	Gls	Apps	Gls	Apps	Gls
1905/06	1	0	0	0	1	0
TOTAL	1	0	0	0	1	0

H

William HUNTER, 1913-14

Billy Hunter was born in Sunderland in 1888. He was a live-wire centre forward who started his career with Sunderland West End FC. He joined Liverpool in December 1908, making his League debut against Preston North End in March 1909. After a short trial with Sunderland in May 1909, he signed for Lincoln City in August 1909, making 35 senior appearances with 8 goals during a three-year stay. In 1911 he left and had trials with Wingate Albion, Airdrieonians and South Shields, before making 2 League appearances for Barnsley in 1912. Hunter then moved to Manchester United, making his debut against his old club Liverpool in March 1913. A few weeks later, he netted a brace against Newcastle , but he never fitted in at Old Trafford and came south to become an 'Oriental' in July 1913 after only 3 appearances. He spent a season mostly in the reserves, but made his League debut in a 1-0 win over Fulham on 6 September 1913, and a week later scored in a 3-0 win at Glossop North End. In May 1914 he joined Southern League Lincoln City, scoring once from 5 appearances. A player for whom there had been high hopes, Hunter unfortunately did not fulfil these expectations. In five years he played for ten different clubs, making just 55 senior career appearances and scoring 13 goals.

Billy Hurley

SEASON	LEAGUE		FA CUP		TOTAL	
	Apps	Gls	Apps	Gls	Apps	Gls
1913/14	9	1	1	0	10	1
TOTAL	9	1	1	0	10	1

William Henry HURLEY, 1976-78

Billy Hurley was born in Leytonstone, London on 11 December 1959. He was on schoolboy forms with O's when he starred at centre forward with England schoolboys. He became an apprentice professional in May 1976, and signed full-time in January 1977. He was hailed as a great prospect, and the club had high hopes of him, but unfortunately he never fulfilled them. He made his League debut in a 1-1 draw at Hull City on 19 April 1977. He does, however, jointly hold one O's record, that of fastest goal scored. His goal against Colchester United reserves on 9 September 1975 was scored after just seven seconds after the start of the match (he was only fifteen years old at the time), equalling a goal scored from Mike Burgess against Fulham Reserves on 8 January 1955. Billy Hurley's stay with O's was short, and it was reported that he gave up the game in May 1997.

SEASON	LEAGUE		FA CUP		L. CUP	
	Apps	Gls	Apps	Gls	Apps	Gls
1976/77	1(1)	0	0	0	0	0
TOTAL	1(1)	0	0	0	0	0

TOTAL APPS   1(1)
TOTAL GOALS   0

Aaron HURST, 1935-36

Aaron Hurst was born in Bolton on 1 December 1912, and he joined O's from Blackpool in June 1935, having played only reserve football for the Seasiders. His only League appearance for O's was at right-back, in a 3-1 win against Brighton & Hove Albion on 25 April 1936. He moved to Bury in May 1936, but once again he played only reserve football. Hurst died in Bolton on 3 January 1979, aged sixty-seven.

SEASON	LEAGUE		FA CUP		TOTAL	
	Apps	Gls	Apps	Gls	Apps	Gls
1935/36	1	0	0	0	1	0
TOTAL	1	0	0	0	1	0

Carl Emil HUTCHINGS, 2002-present

The dread-locked 6ft tall midfielder was born in Hammersmith, London on 24 September 1974. He started off as a Brentford trainee in July 1993 and went on to make 172(18) senior appearances and score 10 goals at Griffin Park before a £130,000 move took him to Bristol City on 6 July 1998 – despite Brentford's valuation of £500,000. Hutchings fell out of favour at City and after loan spells with Brentford in February 2000 (7(1) League appearances) and Exeter City in December 2000 (2 League appearances), he joined Southend United on a free transfer on 29 December 2000. After playing 47(1) senior matches and scoring 4 goals for the Shrimpers, the versatile midfielder or defender was snapped up by O's boss Paul Brush on 12 February 2002 on a free transfer. He signed with O's for a year after his monthly contract with Southend had expired.

SEASON	LEAGUE		FA CUP		L. CUP	
	Apps	Gls	Apps	Gls	Apps	Gls
2001/02	9(1)	1	0	0	0	0
TOTAL	9(1)	1	0	0	0	0

TOTAL APPS   9(1)
TOTAL GOALS   1

Paul David HYDE, 1996-99

Paul Hyde, the 6ft 1in goalkeeper, was an excellent shot-stopper, who made the 'keeper's jersey his own until a tragic injury at Exeter City on 31 January 1998 occurred, following a terrible tackle by Exeter's substitute John Williams. This resulted in Hyde breaking his leg in three places and sustaining considerable bruising to his chest. With Hyde crying out in pain, the ball ran loose for the home team to score. The referee did not stop play, and the O's players, led by skipper Dominic Naylor, engulfed the referee to show their anger. Paul Hyde never played League football again, and retired from

Paul Hyde

the senior game in December 1998 after a long struggle to regain his fitness. Hyde was born in Hayes on 7 April 1963, and started his football career with his home side Hayes. He was spotted by Wycombe Wanderers and signed for £15,000 on 6 July 1993. He was a member of the Wycombe team that won promotion into the League, and was also a member of their FA Trophy-winning side. He played 141 senior games for the Chairboys before joining Leicester City on a free transfer on 15 February 1996, as cover for American international Kasey Keller. Hyde joined O's on loan on 3 February 1997, as a replacement for Luke Weaver, who had sustained a nasty eye injury at Exeter City a couple of days before. He played just 4 matches before returning to Leicester. However, when Weaver went on loan to West Ham, the club decided to sign Hyde on a free transfer on 14 March 1997. Hyde proved dependable throughout his stay until the terrible injury that ended his career. The fans showed their appreciation by helping to raise over £2,000 for Hyde's autistic twin boys when walking to a match at Barnet on 11 April 1998. He said: 'It was a magnificent effort, I can't thank the O's fans enough.' O's awarded Hyde a testimonial match, which was played against West Ham United on 29 March 1999. At the end of April of that year, Hyde helped out Harrow Borough when they were short of a 'keeper, playing a match for their reserve side. Upon leaving O's he joined Football Conference side Dover Athletic as player-coach on 1 August 1999, and had made over 80 appearances up to the end of December 2000. He played a blinder to help Dover to a 1-1 draw with AFC Bournemouth in an LDV Vans Trophy match, and played his 120th senior match

for Dover during September 2001. He was rewarded when picked to represent an FA XI against the Combined Services, and played alongside his Dover colleague and former 'Oriental' Lee Shearer in a 6-1 victory. Hyde, the Dover club captain, also won the Dover supporters' Player of the Year award two years running.

SEASON	LEAGUE		FA CUP		L. CUP	
	Apps	Gls	Apps	Gls	Apps	Gls
1996/97	13	0	0	0	0	0
1997/98	28	0	2	0	4	0
1998/99	0	0	0	0	0	0
TOTAL	41	0	2	0	4	0

TOTAL APPS	47
TOTAL GOALS	0

* Paul Hyde also appeared in an Auto Windscreens Shield match.

I

Jabo Oshevire IBEHRE, 1999-present

A promising youth-team player, who was born in Islington, London on 28 January 1983, the 6ft 2in forward signed YTS forms on 1 July 1999. He started in O's School of Excellence and surprised many with a wonderful performance as a substitute in the 1-1 Worthington Cup tie against Premiership side Newcastle United at home in September 2000. Striker Ibehre was a regular in O's successful youth side in 1999, and after a training spell with Chelsea, he also had a training session with the England under-17s in October 1999. Ibehre was given his League debut as a substitute at Northampton Town on 7 March 2000, when he came on for the final five minutes, and he had 2 further substitute appearances – at Swansea City and Hull City – in the 1999/2000 season. In August 2000 he turned down a loan move to Irish side Bohemians, and a chance to appear in UEFA Cup competition along with former 'Orientals' Mark Dempsey, Dave Morrison and Simon Webb. He netted four goals against Portsmouth in a 5-1 Football Youth Alliance League under-19 match during September 2000, and was a member of the youth team that won the FA Alliance Cup final 1-0 over Bradford City at the Millennium Stadium in Cardiff on 22 April 2001. The eighteen-year-old rookie came up trumps on his full League debut in the final match of the 2000/01 season at Macclesfield Town, having signed a two-year contract prior to the game. Having only been told on the day before that he was playing, remarkably, he scoring twice (on forty-four and seventy-nine minutes) to secure O's fifth spot and a place in the play-offs. He played in the two play-off matches against Hull City, and in the final against Blackpool at the Millennium Stadium – a disappointing 4-2 defeat. He netted a total of 19 goals from 26 under-19 appearances in the 2000/01 season. During the first pre-season friendly match at Devon League champions Buckfastleigh, he netted four goals in O's 13-1 victory on 22 July 2001. He has the potential to become a star in the future, but a groin injury has hampered his progress in 2002.

SEASON	LEAGUE		FA CUP		L. CUP	
	Apps	Gls	Apps	Gls	Apps	Gls
1999/2000	0(3)	0	0	0	0	0
2000/01*	4(4)	2	0	0	0(1)	0
2001/02	21(7)	4	2(1)	1	1	0
TOTAL	25(14)	6	2(1)	1	1(1)	0

TOTAL APPS	28(16)
TOTAL GOALS	7

* Jabo Ibehre's record includes 3 play-off appearances in 2000/01.

Jacob ICETON, 1936-37

Goalkeeper Jake Iceton was born in West Auckland on 22 October 1903. He worked down the mines as a young man and played football with Shildon FC. He went to Hull City but never made the grade, and moved south to join Fulham in August 1930. He stayed at the London club for four seasons, making 99 senior appearances and winning a Third Division Championship medal. During May 1935 he joined Aldershot, making a further 10 League appearances. He joined O's in August 1936 (as understudy to Charlie Hillam), but had to wait fifteen months for his first-team debut on 18 December 1937 in a 2-1 win over Exeter City. He stayed for 2 more seasons

Jake Iceton

before joining Worcester City just prior to the outbreak of the Second World War. Iceton guested for O's in a regional wartime match in 1942/43 at the age of forty. After the war he returned to his native West Auckland, where he died in April 1981, aged seventy-seven.

SEASON	LEAGUE		FA CUP		TOTAL	
	Apps	Gls	Apps	Gls	Apps	Gls
1936/37	0	0	0	0	0	0
1937/38	16	0	1	0	17	0
1938/39	24	0	2	0	26	0
TOTAL	40	0	3	0	43	0

* Jacob Iceton also appeared in a Third Division Cup match in 1938/39.

David IMRIE, 1931-33

Centre forward Dave Imrie, a Scotsman, joined O's in August 1931, after spending sometime in the USA. He became known at O's as 'Al Capone', due to his Chicago links! He had to be content with mostly reserve football during his two seasons in London. He made his League debut on 5 September 1931 in a 4-0 win over Mansfield Town, and netted a hat-trick in a rare appearance on 21 April 1932, a 4-3 defeat at Northampton Town. He was always likely to score when given a chance, but could never replace regular forwards, Fletcher and Tricker. He topped O's reserve goalscoring charts with 19 goals in 1931/32, and scored frequently for the second-string side the following season, but he left the club in May 1932.

SEASON	LEAGUE		FA CUP		TOTAL	
	Apps	Gls	Apps	Gls	Apps	Gls
1931/32	6	3	0	0	6	3
1932/33	6	4	0	0	6	4
TOTAL	12	7	0	0	12	7

Joseph Charles ING, 1916-20

Walthamstow-born Joe Ing was on O's books in 1915/1916, and was one of over forty O's players and officials who enlisted in the forces to fight in the First World War. The wing-half joined O's from Clapton Warwick FC, and made his League debut at Nottingham Forest on 6 December 1919. He left O's in July 1920 to join Northfleet FC (the club under Spurs' wing), and later had a short spell with Southern League side Swindon Town.

SEASON	LEAGUE		FA CUP		TOTAL	
	Apps	Gls	Apps	Gls	Apps	Gls
1915/16	0	0	0	0	0	0
1919/20	17	0	1	0	18	0
TOTAL	17	0	1	0	18	0

Alexander INGLETHORPE, 1995-2000

Alex Inglethorpe came to O's from Watford with a reputation for scoring goals – he had been their top reserve-team scorer for the previous four seasons, having made just 3(13) senior appearances for the Hornets and scored 3 goals. He also went on loan to Barnet, playing 5(1) matches and finding the net 3 times. Born in Epsom on 14 November 1971, the forward had been with Watford since signing as a junior in July 1990. O's boss Pat Holland signed him on 12 May 1995 for £25,000, in an attempt to rebuild a battered squad that had been humiliated in the 1994/95 relegation season. Inglethorpe will be remembered for his last-minute winner at Northampton on 12 September 1995 that gave O's their first away win in nearly two years, and what a celebration it was on the way back to London. Unfortunately, he was plagued with injury problems that kept him out of the team for long periods. He

Alex Inglethorpe

was on the verge of joining Welling United for a nominal fee, until Barry Fry (the Peterborough boss) unexpectedly re-called on-loan Carl Griffiths, and the Inglethorpe deal was cancelled. He found his goalscoring form in 1996/97, and was top League goalscorer, scoring 8 goals from just 10(6) appearances. Although still injury-prone, Inglethorpe had proved to be a hard-working and valuable squad member who, after the transfer of Mark Warren to Oxford United in January 1999, was the longest serving player at the club. Inglethorpe came on as a substitute for the second half of the Division Three play-off final against Scunthorpe at Wembley in May 1999. In the final minutes, his shot was superbly saved by Scunthorpe's 'keeper Evans. Inglethorpe did not go on O's tour of Antigua in July 1999 – instead, he was having talks with Exeter City, and Barry Hearn stated that they would release him if he found another club. O's longest serving player seemed to be on his way, yet Inglethorpe was in the line-up for the first match of the 1999/2000 season at Carlisle United, scoring O's first goal of the new campaign. Inglethorpe stated: 'I'm planning to stay at the club and do not want to leave Orient. If I was offered a ten-year contract, I would sign it.' It was further reported that he was helping out with coaching of the youth and reserve sides of his local club, Leatherhead. He went on loan to Exeter City on 24 February 2000, a free transfer deal was made permanent in June 2000, and he netted for City in their 2-1 defeat at the Matchroom on 28 August 2000. On 4 December 2000 he went on loan to Canvey Island, making his debut six days later in the 2-1 defeat by Southend United in the FA Cup. He returned to Exeter on 4 February 2001, and made a total of 13(8) senior appearances and 2 goals up to the end of the 2000/01 season. Twenty-nine-year-old Inglethorpe was released from his contract on 9 May 2001. He was appointed joint manager of Leatherhead United on 12 July 2001 on a three-year contract, in partnership with Chick Botley.

SEASON	LEAGUE		FA CUP		L. CUP	
	Apps	Gls	Apps	Gls	Apps	Gls
1995/96	30	9	0	0	2	0
1996/97	10(6)	8	0(1)	0	0	0
1997/98	38	9	1	0	2	2
1998/99*	15(8)	4	2(2)	0	1	1
1999/2000	12(4)	2	0(2)	0	1	0
TOTAL	105(21)	32	4(3)	0	7	3

TOTAL APPS	114(23)
TOTAL GOALS	35

* Alex Inglethorpe's League total includes 0(2) promotion play-off appearances in 1998/99.

** Inglethorpe also appeared in 3(1) Auto Windscreens Shield matches, scoring once.

Charles Benjamin IVES, 1919-20

Ben Ives was born in Tottenham, London in 1889. The thrusting outside left started with Page Green Old Boys club, then played for Romford FC and Tufnell Park, and was on Spurs' books in September 1908, before moving to Exeter City. He joined O's from Queens Park Rangers in June 1919, after making 32 Southern League matches and scoring 2 goals. He started as first choice for O's, and notched a hat-trick in a 4-0 win over South Shields on 27 September 1919. However, he later lost his place to Owen Williams, who was to become O's most outstanding forward of the 1920s. Ives left the club to join Ton Pentre in August 1920, a club newly managed by former 'Oriental' Robert Dalrymple. Ives was Spurs' assistant trainer in January 1922, and later their chief scout until his retirement in 1947. He died in Margate on 14 April 1962, aged seventy-three.

SEASON	LEAGUE		FA CUP		TOTAL	
	Apps	Gls	Apps	Gls	Apps	Gls
1919/20	17	4	0	0	17	4
TOTAL	17	4	0	0	17	4

J

Robert Rollo JACK, 1929-31

Rollo Jack was born in Bolton on 2 April 1902 and was one of the Jack brothers, the most famous of whom was David, who scored the first ever FA Cup goal at Wembley Stadium for Bolton Wanderers. Rollo Jack started his career with Plymouth Argyle, managed by his father Bob Jack, and he scored 4 goals in 15 League appearances for the club. He then joined Bolton Wanderers for a small fee, but was always overshadowed by his more famous brother at Burnden Park, making just 29 League appearances and scoring 9 goals during six seasons. He became an 'Oriental' in September 1929 for a reported £1,500, but O's only ever paid a small portion of this fee due to their financial situation. Jack was a versatile player and was used mostly at outside right, where he proved to be a dangerous raider who liked to cut in and shoot for goal. He featured in O's two League matches at Wembley Stadium in 1930. He moved to Yeovil & Petters United in November 1932, and then on to Swindon Town in 1934, playing 20 League matches and scoring twice. In 1936 he was appointed assistant manager at Plymouth Argyle, before rejoining O's for a season (1946/47) as assistant secretary. Rollo

Rollo Jack

Jack died in Lambeth, London during April 1994, aged ninety-two.

SEASON	LEAGUE		FA CUP		TOTAL	
	Apps	Gls	Apps	Gls	Apps	Gls
1929/30	24	5	2	0	26	5
1930/31	25	6	2	0	27	6
1931/32	30	11	0	0	30	11
TOTAL	79	22	4	0	83	22

Frank JACKETT, 1953-54

Welshman Frank Jackett was born in Ystalyfera, Glamorgan on 5 July 1927. He represented South Wales at youth level, and whilst at Swansea Town between 1947 and 1949, he played in their youth and reserve teams. In May 1949 he joined Portardawe Athletic, before joining Watford as a professional in November 1949, where they converted him from an inside forward to a strong-tackling wing-half. He made 14 League appearances for the club. He joined O's in July 1953 on a free transfer, but was mostly a reserve player for whom he did quite well as captain with his forceful style of play. He made his League debut in a 3-1 defeat at Ipswich Town on 5 September 1953. He was transferred to Ramsgate Athletic – where former 'Oriental' Jimmy Blair was player-manager – in 1954. He later played for Margate in 1958 and then had a spell at Adeyfield Athletic as player-coach between January 1960 and 1962. Frank Jackett was the senior half of the only father and son pair ever to represent Watford. His son, Kenny, played for the Hornets between 1979-1990, making 330(7) League appearances and scoring 25 goals.

SEASON	LEAGUE		FA CUP		TOTAL	
	Apps	Gls	Apps	Gls	Apps	Gls
1953/54	4	0	0	0	4	0
TOTAL	4	0	0	0	4	0

Brian Harvill JACKSON, 1950-52

Born in Walton-on-Thames, Surrey on 1 April 1933, young Brian Jackson was just seventeen years old when he made his League debut. He was hailed by many as a great prospect, and was better than any other young O's star up to that time, even better than Tommy Mills or Billy Gray. He joined O's from the Chase of Chertsey club in October 1950, and made his League debut at Brisbane Road against Southend United in December 1950. He performed so well at outside right that he soon became a target of scouts from several First Divison clubs. He would take on and beat opposing defenders with ease, and he certainly benefited from playing alongside ex-internationals such as Billy Rees, Jimmy Blair and Tommy Brown. In November 1951 he was eventually snapped up by Liverpool (for £7,500 and winger Don Woan), and went on to score on his 'Pool debut against Bolton Wanderers. He stayed for seven seasons at Anfield, making 124 League appearances and scoring 12 goals during his time there. In July 1958 he joined Port Vale for £1,700, and won a Fourth Division Championship medal in 1959, and went on to make 178 senior appearances and score 34 goals (including 9 penalties). In July 1962 he signed for Peterborough United for £2,000, making a further 51 senior appearances from which he scored 4 goals. Jackson then had a short spell with Lincoln City between May and December 1964, but he made just 10 League appearances and scored once. He acted as assistant manager at Sincil Bank, and later held managerial positions at both Burton Albion and Boston United.

SEASON	LEAGUE		FA CUP		TOTAL	
	Apps	Gls	Apps	Gls	Apps	Gls
1950/51	21	2	0	0	21	2
1951/52	17	0	0	0	17	0
TOTAL	38	2	0	0	38	2

John Keith JACKSON, 1973-79

Goalkeeper John Jackson joined O's in October 1973, but at first his move was not greeted terribly enthusiastically by O's fans because he displaced O's popular 'keeper Ray Goddard. Yet over time, Jackson went onto to become one of O's finest 'keepers, along with the likes of legendary Arthur Wood of the 1920s. Born in Hammersmith, London on 5 September 1942, he joined Crystal Palace after leaving Westminster School and excelled at Selhurst Park, making 346 League and 47 cup appearances. This total included 222 consecutive appearances between August 1967 and October 1972, missing just 12 matches over eight seasons with the Eagles. His first season at Brisbane Road was not one of his best, as he was troubled with a leg injury, but from 1974/75 onwards, he did not miss a League match for five seasons, making 210 consecutive League appearances. He was quite superb during O's great FA Cup run in 1977/78, including making one magnificent save at home to Chelsea in the dying minutes to ensure a replay. During his stay with O's, Jackson guested for American sides St Louis Stars and California Surf, making 32 appearances. When Jimmy Bloomfield signed Mervyn Day from West Ham United for £100,000 in July 1979, thirty-six-year-old Jackson became unsettled, and he joined his former O's boss George Petchey at Millwall for £7,500 the following August. He made his 600th League appearance (against Oxford United) whilst at the Den, and

John Jackson

after 79 appearances for the Lions, he joined Ipswich Town in August 1981, making his League debut (and indeed his only appearance) in a win over Manchester United in July 1982, at the age of thirty-nine. He moved to Hereford United in August 1982, making a further 4 League appearances during his fortieth year. Altogether he totalled 656 League appearances, spanning eighteen seasons. Only the form of Gordon Banks and Ray Clemence denied him a full England cap, and he had to be content with England youth caps and a single appearance for a League XI against the Scottish League at Hampden Park. He held the position of youth development officer at Brighton & Hove Albion between June 1996 and May 1998, whilst George Petchey was the Seagulls' assistant manager. He later became the goalkeeping coach for Sussex School of Excellence, and more recently worked for the Lewes Council.

SEASON	LEAGUE		FA CUP		L. CUP	
	Apps	Gls	Apps	Gls	Apps	Gls
1973/74	16	0	1	0	2	0
1974/75	42	0	2	0	2	0
1975/76	42	0	1	0	1	0
1976/77	42	0	4	0	4	0
1977/78	42	0	8	0	1	0
1978/79	42	0	3	0	1	0
TOTAL	226	0	19	0	11	0

TOTAL APPS	256
TOTAL GOALS	0

* John Jackson also appeared in 3 Texaco Cup matches in 1974/75, as well as 9 Anglo-Scottish Cup matches.

Robin JACQUES, 1922-23

He was always referred to as Lieutenant Jacques, in deference to the rank he reached in the RAF. Born in London during 1897, he joined O's on 1 October 1923, having previously played football for the RAF and for West Norwood. He scored on his O's League debut in a 3-0 win over Leeds City on 7 October 1922, and his second goal came a few weeks later in a 2-2 draw at Millfields against Sheffield Wednesday. In July 1923 he signed for Fulham, but never got a chance to show the Craven Cottage fans what he was capable of, as he was tragically killed in an air crash over Grantham during August 1923, aged just twenty-six.

SEASON	LEAGUE		FA CUP		TOTAL	
	Apps	Gls	Apps	Gls	Apps	Gls
1922/23	4	2	0	0	4	2
TOTAL	4	2	0	0	4	2

Thomas Ernest JENKINS, 1966-67

Born on 2 December 1947 in Bethnal Green, London, Tommy Jenkins came to O's in early 1966, after being spotted playing on Hackney Marshes. He played for the youth and reserve sides, and showed great promise with his good ball skills and his turn of speed. Yet he made just a single League appearance – at Bristol City on 30 April 1966. Outside left Jenkins was allowed to leave due to the financial crisis at the club. He was snapped up for a trial by West Ham United in December 1967, but he was not kept on. He then signed for Margate in February 1968, making 69 appearances and scoring 12 goals, where his fine displays came to the attention of Reading, who signed him in July 1969. Jenkins went on to make 21 League appearances and score 5 goals. He stepped up to a higher grade when joining Southampton for £60,000 in December 1969, and at the Dell he made 84 League appearances, scoring 4 goals. His next club was Swindon Town in November 1972, where he made 89(11) League appearances and netted 4 goals. He moved to America in 1976 to join

Tommy Jenkins

Seattle Sounders, and after 5 seasons there he moved on to play in the Indoor League for 3 seasons between 1981 and 1984 with Pittsburgh and Phoenix. He then held various managerial positions and in 2002 became the coaching director of women's side Club Dosvedanya.

SEASON	LEAGUE		FA CUP		L. CUP	
	Apps	Gls	Apps	Gls	Apps	Gls
1965/66	1	0	0	0	0	0
TOTAL	1	0	0	0	0	0

TOTAL APPS	1
TOTAL GOALS	0

Percival JENNINGS, 1930-33

Percy Jennings joined O's from Blackpool in August 1930, having made 3 League appearances for the Seasiders in 1929/30. He made his O's League debut in a 2-1 win over Thames Association on 18 September 1930. Born in Consett, Gateshead on 27 March 1907, Jennings could not gain a regular place in the first team, the full-back positions being held by Broadbent and Morley. He left in July 1933 to join non-League Annfields Plain FC.

SEASON	LEAGUE		FA CUP		TOTAL	
	Apps	Gls	Apps	Gls	Apps	Gls
1930/31	11	0	0	0	11	0
1931/32	8	0	0	0	8	0
1932/33	0	0	0	0	0	0
TOTAL	19	0	0	0	19	0

William John JENNINGS, 1979-1982

Billy Jennings was born in Hackney, London on 20 February 1952. For such a small and lightweight man, – he was just 5ft 9in tall and weighed 10st 2lb – he seemed to be able to hang in the air and rise above most defenders. During his school days, he played on the famous Hackney Marshes, and attended training sessions at Tottenham Hotspur. But it was with Watford that he first made his mark, joining the Hertfordshire club as an amateur in March 1969, and turning professional in April 1970. He also gained England youth caps. He made 87(13) senior appearances for the Hornets, scoring 37 goals. His 26 League goals in 1973/74 prompted West Ham United to splash out £110,000 in September 1974, and his arrival coincided with a distinct revival of Hammers' fortunes, culminating in their 1975 FA Cup win over Fulham. An Achilles tendon injury threatened to cut short his career, but he recovered and made 124 senior appearances with 39 goals whilst at Upton Park, before taking the well-worn transfer trail to Brisbane Road for £100,000 in August 1979. He never seemed to hit it off with O's, yet he still showed his marksmanship qualities. Arguably his best goals for O's were against Charlton Athletic in September 1979 and against Altrincham in January 1980 in the FA Cup, both splendid shots after he had manoeuvred skilfully past opposing defenders. He finished as joint top scorer in 1979/80 with Joe Mayo, both with 11 goals. He was allowed to move to Luton Town in March 1982, but made just 2 appearances as substitute, scoring once. After a short rebel soccer tour to South Africa, he joined Dagenham & Redbridge in March 1993, and later had brief spells with Bishop Stortford and Heybridge Swifts in 1984/85. After his retirement from the game, he spent three years running a Fleet Street wine bar/restaurant, and was later reported to be the owner of a Brentwood brasserie and another restaurant in London.

Billy Jennings (left)

appeared in their first ever professional fixture – a Southern League match against Norwich City on 28 August 1920. He made 23 Southern League and 9 League appearances and scored twice, before joining Southend United in February 1924. Jewhurst spent three years down by the seaside, making 126 senior appearances. He joined O's in June 1927, but the thirty-year-old only made a single League appearance against Manchester City on 19 November 1927. He joined Dartford in August 1929. On leaving full-time football, he became a licensed victualler in Plumstead. Jewhurst died at the Seaman's Hospital, Greenwich, London on 17 May 1949, at the age of fifty-one.

SEASON	LEAGUE		FA CUP		TOTAL	
	Apps	Gls	Apps	Gls	Apps	Gls
1927/28	1	0	0	0	1	0
1928/29	0	0	0	0	0	0
TOTAL	1	0	0	0	1	0

James JEYES, 1914-15

Little is known about this London-born amateur player (sometimes referred to as Jayes). He played in the reserves and made just a single League appearance (at left half) in a 1-0 victory over Leeds City on 3 January 1915. Jeyes left the club in May 1915, returning to non-League football before going off to war.

SEASON	LEAGUE		FA CUP		TOTAL	
	Apps	Gls	Apps	Gls	Apps	Gls
1914/15	1	0	0	0	1	0
TOTAL	1	0	0	0	1	0

Stephen Paul JOHN, 1984-88

Steve John was born in Brentwood, Essex on 22 December 1966. He signed YTS forms for O's in 1982, and turned pro-

SEASON	LEAGUE		FA CUP		L. CUP	
	Apps	Gls	Apps	Gls	Apps	Gls
1979/80	32(2)	11	3	2	2	0
1980/81	22(1)	7	1	1	2	1
1981/82	10	3	1	0	2	1
TOTAL	64(3)	21	5	3	6	2

TOTAL APPS	75(3)
TOTAL GOALS	26

* Billy Jennings also appeared in 3 Anglo-Scottish matches, scoring once, and in 3 Football League Groups Cup matches, again scoring once.

Frederick Harold JEWHURST, 1927-28

Born on 30 September 1897 in Hoxton, London, Fred Jewhurst spent five years playing football for the Army, before being wounded out of service in 1917. After guesting for Charlton Athletic during the First World War, he joined Northfleet FC in 1919. The wing-half signed for Charlton in June 1920, and

fessional in December 1984. A calm, steady defender, he could play either at full-back or in the centre of defence. He had the ability to read dangerous situations and step in and halt opposing attacks. He made his League debut in a 1-0 win over Swindon Town on 30 November 1985. His football career was halted by a bad injury while still only twenty-two years old, however, he later made a successful new career, as a male model!

SEASON	LEAGUE		FA CUP		L. CUP	
	Apps	Gls	Apps	Gls	Apps	Gls
1985/86	8	0	1	0	0	0
1986/87	15	0	2	0	0	0
TOTAL	23	0	3	0	0	0

TOTAL APPS	26
TOTAL GOALS	0

* Stephen John also appeared in 4(1) Auto Windscreens Shield matches.

Steve John

Geoffrey Harold JOHNSON, 1908-12

Geoff Johnson (often called George in the press) formed a most notable full-back partnership with John Johnston for over three seasons. They were often referred to as 'the two 'J's' duo. Fulham-born Johnson joined O's from Southend United in 1908, was reserve for Jumbo Reason in his first season, but played steadily over the following three seasons. The 5ft 10in defender is one of a handful of O's players to score two penalties in the same match – he achieved this feat against Birmingham City on 25 March 1911 to give O's a 2-1 win. In March 1912 he was transferred to Chelsea, for a record fee of £650. He stayed at Stamford Bridge for two seasons, yet surprisingly made just 5 senior appearances. He then moved to Southern League Portsmouth in 1913, after just 3 Southern League and 10 Southern Alliance appearances for Pompey, before moving in 1914 to South Eastern League side Bournemouth & Boscombe Athletic. He later appeared for Merthyr Town.

SEASON	LEAGUE		FA CUP		TOTAL	
	Apps	Gls	Apps	Gls	Apps	Gls
1908/09	4	0	0	0	4	0
1909/10	22	0	1	0	23	0
1910/11	38	4	1	0	39	4
1911/12	18	0	0	0	18	0
TOTAL	82	4	2	0	84	4

John Joseph JOHNSON, 1912-13

John Johnson had the unenviable task of trying to dislodge the brilliant Richard McFadden from the O's team. Like so many others, he failed, yet he proved to be a worthy reserve-team player. Born in Rossendale, Lancashire in 1882, he started out with local side Rossendale United, before moving into the League with Grimsby Town in 1905, where he made 19 League appearances and scored 3 goals, before joining Carlisle United in the Lancashire Combination League in 1906. During May 1907, he came south to play in the Southern League with Millwall Athletic, and scored 6 goals in 30 senior appearances for them. In June 1908 he signed for fellow Southern Leaguers Luton Town and stayed with the club for three seasons, making 37 Southern League appearances and scoring 6 goals. In August 1912 he became an 'Oriental', making his League debut in a 2-1 win over Hull City in January 1913. He also played in the two following matches in place of the injured McFadden. He left the club in June 1913, joining Southern League outfit Brentford.

SEASON	LEAGUE		FA CUP		TOTAL	
	Apps	Gls	Apps	Gls	Apps	Gls
1912/13	3	0	0	0	3	0
TOTAL	3	0	0	0	3	0

Peter James JOHNSON, 1972-74

Born in Hackney, London on 18 February 1954, Peter Johnson was a tricky winger, who came to O's in March 1972 from Tottenham Hotspur's youth side. He played quite well for the reserves, but sometimes his tricky wing-play was a little overdone. Johnson made his League debut in a 2-2 draw at Swindon Town on 29 April 1972. He was released in May 1974, and after a short spell in Greek football he joined Crystal Palace in January 1975, making 5(2) League appearances. In June 1976 he moved on to join AFC Bournemouth, where he had 2 successful seasons, making 99(8) League appearances and scoring 11 goals. In 1978 he joined Weymouth FC.

SEASON	LEAGUE		FA CUP		L. CUP	
	Apps	Gls	Apps	Gls	Apps	Gls
1971/72	1	0	0	0	0	0
1972/73	0(2)	0	0	0	0	0
1973/74	0	0	0	0	0	0
TOTAL	1(2)	0	0	0	0	0

TOTAL APPS	1(2)
TOTAL GOALS	0

NB. Peter Johnson's appearances record for 1972/73 was incorrectly printed in the *Complete Record* of October 1990.

Victor Ralph JOHNSON, 1947-49

Ralph Johnson (or 'Vic', as he was known), was a bustling, ginger-haired centre forward, who was born in Hethersett, Norfolk on 15 April 1922. He started as an amateur with Chesterfield, before joining Norwich City in May 1946. He once scored a goal for the Canaries after only ten seconds, against the O's in a Third Division (South) game on 19 October 1946, which at that time was the quickest goal ever scored at Carrow Road. In 1946/47, he netted 10 goals from 24 senior appearances. He amassed a remarkable 123 goals from 107 wartime appearances for Norwich. Johnson signed for O's in May 1947, although he ended up mostly playing for the reserves. He top scored for the second string in 1948/49, including four goals against West Ham United reserves in a Combination match. He made his League debut in a 2-2 draw with Newport County in September 1947, but he couldn't replace Frank Neary, and moved on to Lowestoft Town in May 1949.

SEASON	LEAGUE		FA CUP		TOTAL	
	Apps	Gls	Apps	Gls	Apps	Gls
1947/48	5	1	0	0	5	1
1948/49	2	1	0	0	2	1
TOTAL	7	2	0	0	7	2

Ralph Johnson

John Thompson JOHNSTON, 1908-15

Sunderland-born John Johnston was a small but strong full-back, who was renowned for his excellent passing skills and was regarded as one of O's finest backs prior to the First World War. He started with Sunderland Royal Rovers, and joined O's from Middlesbrough groundstaff in June 1908, having played only reserve football. He made his League debut against Hull City during September 1908, and he missed just 10 League matches in four seasons. Many of the sports writers of his day suggested he should be picked for England, but he had to be content representing the League XI against the Southern League at White Hart Lane on 14 November 1910 – a 3-2 win for the Southern Leaguers. Johnston joined both Fred Parker and George Scott as the only O's players to have made over 200 League appearances before the First World War. He was

awarded a benefit in 1914 for his service to the club. His only senior goal came against Oldham Athletic in December 1909. Due to serious wounds, Johnston never played football again after the war.

SEASON	LEAGUE		FA CUP		TOTAL	
	Apps	Gls	Apps	Gls	Apps	Gls
1908/09	38	0	1	0	39	0
1909/10	36	1	1	0	37	1
1910/11	36	0	1	0	37	0
1911/12	36	0	1	0	37	0
1912/13	34	0	0	0	34	0
1913/14	11	0	1	0	12	0
1914/15	27	0	1	0	28	0
TOTAL	218	1	6	0	224	1

Thomas JOHNSTON, 1956-58, 1959-61

This brief record of O's seasonal and aggregate goalscoring record holder can hardly do justice to a player who was voted by O's supporters as the club's greatest player of all-time in a Millennium poll, gaining over 20 per cent of all votes cast. He will go down in the record books as one of the country's most remarkable players. He played in every class of professional football with three Scottish League clubs, one Welsh and seven English clubs. That means he played in the First Division, Second Division, Third Division (North), Third Division (South) and Fourth Division, as well as in the Southern League. Thomas Bourhill Johnston (Bourhill was his mother's maiden name) – 'Tommy' or 'Tom', as he was affectionately known – was born in Loanhead, a small mining village five miles from Edinburgh, Scotland on 18 August 1927. As a boy, Tommy worked down the local coal mine, along with his father and brother, but he wanted to follow in the footsteps of his two brothers, who had played for Falkirk and Hibernian. At the age of seventeen, a serious mining accident nearly cost him his life. Tommy suffered a broken leg and a badly crushed arm, which nearly ended his dream of playing professional football. It was touch-and-go as to whether his left arm would have to be amputated, but the doctors managed to save it after a series of skin grafts. The injury meant he had to stop playing football for two years, and he subsequently wore a bandage on his wrist for every match, to protect it in case he should fall on it. Tommy started on the road to fame when he joined juvenile team Gilmerton Drumbirds, and then moved on to Scottish junior side Loanhead Mayflower who played in the shadow of Scott's Monument in Princess Street, Edinburgh. He progressed to Peebles Rovers (who played in the East of Scotland League) in 1947/48, and trials with Falkirk and Third Lanark soon followed. Bolton Wanderers offered him a month's trial, but he turned down the chance of playing in the English League, as he wanted to stay in Scotland. In 1949, at the age of twenty, he joined Scottish First Division side Kilmarnock. He stayed two seasons at Rugby Park, but then asked for a transfer, feeling that the time was now right to try his hand south of the Border. He had short spells with Third Division (North) side Darlington in 1950/51, but he could not settle and so returned to Scotland. The following week he received several telegrams from Oldham Athletic, Arbroath and Dundee United. He decided on Oldham, joining in March 1952 for a £500 signing-on fee. He scored a hat-trick in the final match of the season against Carlisle United. In the crowd was Tom Bradshaw, a scout for Norwich City. City offered £2,500 for his services,

and he scored on his League debut for the Canaries on 23 August 1952. He started off very well, netting 10 goals from 10 matches, but a serious leg muscle injury then kept him out of the side for a while. The years were drifting by for Tommy, and it did not seem possible that he would ever be more than a moderately successful Third Divison player. However, one match seemed to turn it all around for him. It was the end of January 1954, and Norwich were facing an FA Cup fourth round tie against Arsenal at Highbury. Due to a number of injuries, he was drafted into the side to lead the attack. He soon shot to fame by rocketing home two wonderful headers for a 2-1 victory. He scored 33 goals in two seasons at Carrow Road, yet it wasn't until he joined Billy Lucas at Newport County for £2,100 in October 1954 that he became a nationally recognised player. The Welsh air seemed to agree with him, and he bagged 26 goals in 1954/55. A further 21 goals followed up to February 1956, including a hat-trick against the O's. At the end of January 1956, when O's were returning home from an away fixture, the players and management were discussing with chairman Harry Zussman the need for a quality striker to cement their push for the Third Division title. Zussman asked captain Stan Aldous if he had any suggestions. He said 'Yes, I reckon we ought to go for that fellow Johnston at Newport. He always plays a blinder against me, in fact, he is an absolute menace to play against, and in the air, he is unplayable.' Well no one was more surprised than Aldous when he was told by caretaker manager Les Gore that Zussman had paid money from his own pocket to get Johnston. On 24 February

1956, Zussman had heard that Newport were desperate for cash to make ends meet, and they accepted an offer of £4,500 plus O's Canadian-born forward Mike Burgess, as part of the deal, and so started the extraordinary goalscoring feats of Tommy Johnston. He scored on 25 February 1956 on his debut at Swindon Town with a wonderful trademark header, and he also scored the goal that clinched the title against Millwall the following April, thus winning a championship medal for the first time in his career. In one spell of 82 matches, he found the net 67 times. In a further spell of 10 consecutive games (from November 1957), he notched 19 goals. He took Second Division football in his stride, and finished the 1957/58 season on 27 League goals, surpassing Frank Neary's record of 25 League goals in 1948/49. During the following season, Johnston looked the complete centre forward, rattling in goal after goal, and some of the headed goals in particular were truly magnificent. There was much talk of him surpassing Dixie Dean's record of 60 goals in a season from just 39 matches, a feat achieved some thirty years earlier. He was the talk of the country, having scored a remarkable 37 goals from just 27 matches. He was itching to represent his country, and feeling that he could only achieve this by playing First Division football, he became unsettled at Brisbane Road. Three clubs – Newcastle United, Sunderland and Blackburn Rovers – were showing interest, and it was the latter who came in with a £15,000 offer. O's boss Gore and chairman Zussman, although both were very upset at losing their star man, didn't want to stand in Johnston's way. Blackburn Rovers were pushing for promotion to the First Division, and in the final match of that campaign they had to beat Charlton away to go up. If they didn't win, then it would be the Londoners who would be promoted in second spot. It was quite a match, and it was the Lancashire side who got through in an exciting tussle by 4-3 in front of 56,000 fans. So, Tommy achieved his goal of First Divison football, and having netted 8 goals from 11 starts, he ended the 1957/58 season as the League's top scorer on 43 League goals. His baptism into the First Division proved a successful one, scoring twice on the opening day of the season in a 5-1 win over Newcastle United, and netting 5 times in the opening 3 fixtures. At the age of thirty-one, he was proving to be well up to football at the highest level. However, as the season progressed, one thing was noticeable – he was slowing down a little, but he continued to play well and, of course, score goals. Rovers started to give more youngsters a run in their side, and as the team began to struggle, Tommy was not happy at losing his first-team place. At the same time, O's were in the middle of a relegation battle, and Johnston phoned O's boss Les Gore to ask about re-joining. Gore met with Harry Zussman, and then put in a bid of £7,500 – Johnston was on his way back 'home' to Brisbane Road, re-signing on 14 February 1959, with the move, his dream of a Scottish cap now a thing of the past. However, he had certainly been no failure with Rovers, scoring 23 goals from 36 senior appearances. He joined up at O's with fellow veterans Eddie Baily and Eddie Brown, who combined to steer O's out of the relegation zone. Tommy had a fine season in 1959/60, notching 25 League goals, but he was clearly slowing, and with the

Tommy Johnston

appearances, but he never played in any Southern League matches. In 1964 he retired and moved to Poulton-le-Fylde (just outside Blackpool) to open a betting shop. However, in October 1965 he was approached by Lytham St Annes FC, so at the age of thirty-eight he made a total of 10 appearances for the club. On 3 February 1972 he and his family emigrated to Australia, and he coached the Lysaghts works football team. He and his son Neil played 4 games, netting 15 goals between them. Tommy Johnston was primarily a great goalscorer, but he was also extremely useful at leading the attack with astute distribution. His ability as a schemer or forager wasn't always recognised. He was a strong and tough Scotsman, and could give and take the hard knocks. Above all, however, his heading ability was his greatest asset, in fact, he was a genius in this respect. Quite simply, he was an excellent player – he must go down as one of the greatest centre forwards of all-time. Tommy Johnston has every reason to feel proud of his achievements in football. He now lives in Sanctuary Point, NSW, Australia. In 1991 he was diagnosed with bowel cancer, and had to undergo a long operation and three weeks in intensive care. However, he pulled through, and though he cannot play golf anymore, he still enjoys a game of bowls or snooker. Tommy Johnston scored a total of 257 English and Scottish League goals from 431 appearances.

arrival of Johnny Carey as new manager in the summer of 1961, it was to be the end of Johnston's wonderful O's career. His number 9 jersey went to new signing Dave Dunmore. Carey called Johnston into his office and informed him that he might call him up into the first team from time to time, but he mainly wanted him to play in the reserves and help the younger players. Johnston agreed, as long as he received first-team wages. Carey refused, and Johnston was on his way out of Brisbane Road. At the end of September 1961, he joined Gillingham for £3,000. He scored on his League debut for the Gills, but he did not enjoy his stay at Priestfield Stadium. In July 1962 he was appointed player-coach at Folkestone Town, and within a season they had won the Southern League Championship. He spent a couple of happy seasons with them, scoring 40 goals from 68 Kent League and FA Cup

SEASON	LEAGUE		FA CUP		L. CUP	
	Apps	Gls	Apps	Gls	Apps	Gls
1955/56	15	8	0	0	-	-
1956/57	42	27	1	0	-	-
1957/58	30	35*	2	1	-	-
1958/59	14	10	0	0	-	-

1959/60	39	25	1	0	-	-
1960/61**	40	16	3	1	3	0
TOTAL	180	121	7	2	3	0

TOTAL APPS	190
TOTAL GOALS	123

* Club record.

** First season of the League Cup competition.

William JONAS, 1912-15

Twenty-two-year-old Willie Jonas joined O's in 1912, after a personal recommendation from his friend and O's brilliant forward Richard McFadden, having both grown up together in Blyth. Jonas proved to be a great capture, and played his part as the O's rose to be one the top teams in the Second Division over the following few seasons leading up to the First World War. Born in Blyth, Northumberland in 1892, he started his career with Jarrow Croft FC, scoring twice for them in the Gateshead Charity Cup final. He turned down an offer of a trial with Barnsley, and instead joined Havanna Rovers in 1910, going on to net 68 goals in two seasons. He became an 'Oriental' in June 1912, and his fearless and dashing play made him a firm favourite with O's fans. He showed great skill, and his distribution of the ball was excellent, which meant that he was often the target of crude tackles by defenders. He also donned the goalkeeper's jersey during a number of League matches when Hugall became injured. He came to the fore in 1913/14, scoring 10 League and 17 reserve goals. Jonas became a great heart-throb amongst the lady supporters, and it was reported that he received over fifty letters a week from his adoring fans. Things got so bad that he requested the club to place a special notice in the match-day programme, to the effect that he was very happily married to his sweetheart, a charming young lady called Mary Jane. Jonas was once sent off in an FA Cup tie at Millwall in January 1915 for fighting with home 'keeper Orme. The incident resulted in a riot on the terraces, and the local newspaper reported that police on horseback had to be brought in to stop the fighting and escort the O's fans out of the old Den Stadium. Jonas and friend McFadden were among forty-one O's players and officials to enlist in the Footballers' Battalion of the Middlesex Regiment. Both men were killed in action, along with a third player, George Scott. Jonas was killed in action on 27 July 1916, aged twenty-six. Although Jonas never reached the heights of his friend McFadden, he was still a very impressive player, and his contribution to O's cause will not be forgotten.

SEASON	LEAGUE		FA CUP		TOTAL	
	Apps	Gls	Apps	Gls	Apps	Gls
1912/13	13	0	0	0	13	0
1913/14	26	10	3	1	29	11
1914/15	31	11	1	1	32	12
TOTAL	70	21	4	2	74	23

Andrew Mark JONES, 1991-93

Andy Jones, the twenty-eight-year-old former Welsh international (6 caps and a goal), joined O's in October 1991. He had a reputation of being a goalpoacher of note, having netted 76 League goals from 184(33) career appearances. He had bagged 37 goals from 43 appearances whilst with Port Vale in 1986, including 5 goals in a single League match against Newport County, equalling Vale's post-war record. Born in Wrexham, Wales on 9 January 1963, he began his career with Rhyl FC, before

Andy Jones is welcomed by Ken Knighton

joining Port Vale for £3,000 in June 1985. He went on to make 115(4) senior appearances and score 64 goals for Vale. He moved to First Division side Charlton Athletic in September 1987 for £350,000, and found the net 15 times from 51(15) League matches. After a loan spell with Port Vale in February 1989 (where he made a further 8(9) League appearances and scored 3 goals), and then with Bristol City in November 1989 (2 League appearances and a goal), he signed for AFC Bournemouth for £100,000 in October 1990, netting 8 goals from his 36(4) League appearances. O's management team of Frank Clark and Peter Eustace had high hopes for their new charge. He scored a great individual goal against Chester City on 12 October 1991 with a well-struck cross-shot from the edge of the box after a powerful run. That goal won him the O's Goal of the Season competition for 1991/92. Jones

was forced to retire in 1993 due to a serious injury, and he went on to work as an accounts manager for British Telecom in Bournemouth.

SEASON	LEAGUE		FA CUP		L. CUP	
	Apps	Gls	Apps	Gls	Apps	Gls
1991/92	20(10)	5	4(1)	0	0	0
1992/93	24(5)	8	0(1)	1	2	0
TOTAL	44(15)	13	4(2)	1	2	0

TOTAL APPS	50(17)
TOTAL GOALS	14

* Andy Jones also appeared in 7(1) Auto Windscreens Shield matches, scoring 5 goals.

Christopher Harry JONES, 1984-87

Chris Jones was born in Jersey on 18 April 1956. He first made a name for himself with Tottenham Hotspur, having signed as a apprentice in May 1971. He signed a on a full-time basis two years later, and made 164 League appearances, scoring

Chris Jones

37 goals. He went on loan to Manchester City in September 1982, where he made 3 League appearances. Two months later he went to Crystal Palace, where he made a further 18 League appearances. In September 1983 he joined Charlton Athletic, and scored twice in 29 matches. He was signed by O's boss Frank Clark on a two-month trial and then on a permanent basis in September 1984. The centre forward specialised in holding the ball at feet and feeding his fellow strikers, in a similar manner to Mickey Bullock some ten years earlier. Jones became less effective in his final season at Brisbane Road, and was released in May 1987, moving into non-League football with St Albans City. During the 1990s he became player-manager at St Peter's FC in Jersey.

SEASON	LEAGUE		FA CUP		L. CUP	
	Apps	Gls	Apps	Gls	Apps	Gls
1984/85	36	4	4	1	1	0
1985/86	40(1)	9	4	1	3	1
1986/87	30	6	3	0	1	0
TOTAL	106(1)	19	11	2	5	1

TOTAL APPS 122(1)
TOTAL GOALS 22

* Chris Jones also appeared in 5(1) Auto Windscreens Shield matches, scoring twice.

David Owen JONES, 1931-33

David 'Dai' Jones was born in Cardiff, Wales on Friday 28 October 1910, and proved to be a most outstanding full-back. Having started his career with Ely United whilst working as a trawlerman, he joined O's from Ebbw Vale FC in August 1931, after trials with both Charlton Athletic (May 1930) and Millwall (July 1931). The O's were going through a period of struggles, both on and off the field, yet he impressed with his steady and stylish defensive play. At the end of the 1932/33 season, O's financial plight became dire, and Jones was sold to Leicester City for just £200. He was ever-present in City's 1937 promotion campaign, and made 238 senior appearances and scored 4 goals. He also won 7 Welsh international caps between 1933 and 1937. He played during the war years for City, Notts County and West Ham United, and notched City's first goal after the return to League football on 31 August 1946. He was almost thirty-seven years old when he moved to Mansfield Town in October 1947, yet he made a further 74 League appearances. During 1949 he was appointed player-manager at Hinckley Athletic. On retirement from the game, he became a partner in the Leicester firm Day & Jones Leather Company, and later worked as a sales executive in the shoe trade until his death in Oadby, Leicestershire on 20 May 1971.

SEASON	LEAGUE		FA CUP		TOTAL	
	Apps	Gls	Apps	Gls	Apps	Gls
1931/32	22	0	3	0	25	0
1932/33	33	0	1	0	34	0
TOTAL	55	0	4	0	59	0

Michael Keith JONES, 1966-71

Right full-back Mike Jones arrived at O's at the end of February 1966 as a replacement for David Webb, and did a first-rate job for the seven seasons he was at Brisbane Road. Born in Birkhampstead on 8 January 1945, he started his career with Slough-based junior side Pathfinders FC, also representing Berkshire, Buckinghamshire and Oxon county schoolboys. He joined Fulham as an apprentice in 1961, and

Mike Jones

SEASON	LEAGUE		FA CUP		L. CUP	
	Apps	Gls	Apps	Gls	Apps	Gls
1965/66	13	0	0	0	0	0
1966/67	43	7	3	0	1	0
1967/68	39(1)	2	5	0	0	0
1968/69	31(3)	3	2	0	4	0
1969/70	46	3	2	0	2	0
1970/71	41	1	3	0	1	0
1971/72	10(1)	0	0	0	2	0
TOTAL	223(5)	16	15	0	10	0

TOTAL APPS	248(5)
TOTAL GOALS	16

Selwyn Thomas JONES, 1952-53

Born in Rhos, North Wales on 3 April 1929, the slim, nippy right-winger started out at Everton in July 1949, but failing to make the grade there, he moved to Sheffield Wednesday in August 1951. Once again, he could not break into the first team, but during his season with the Owls, he played 22 reserve matches and scored 8 times.

turned professional in January 1963. He only played a single League Cup tie against Reading in October 1964, before joining Chelsea two months later for £3,000 where he only played reserve football. He became an 'Oriental' in February 1966 for a £3,000 fee, and soon became a crowd favourite with his never-give-up attitude and his wonderful overlapping runs down the right wing. With the club short of strikers, he was moved up front and scored a great hat-trick against Doncaster Rovers in April 1967. Jones was ever-present in the 1969/70 championship-winning season, and he netted a remarkable goal against Stockport County in March 1971 with a shot-cum-cross from the right-hand touchline. He moved to Charlton Athletic for £7,000 on 28 December 1971, making 66(2) senior appearances without scoring, before joining Burnham FC in June 1974, where later he was appointed player-manager.

Selwyn Jones

He also made a further 10 appearances for their third team in the Hatchard League, scoring 4 goals. He joined O's in July 1952, where he also played mostly reserve football, being overshadowed by George Poulton. He made his League debut in the 3-0 defeat at Coventry City on 1 September 1952, and played in only a handful of matches before being released in May 1953. Jones died in Chesterfield during September 1995.

SEASON	LEAGUE		FA CUP		TOTAL	
	Apps	Gls	Apps	Gls	Apps	Gls
1952/53	6	0	0	0	6	0
TOTAL	6	0	0	0	6	0

William Kenneth JONES, 1999-present
Highly rated left-back Billy Jones was born in Gillingham, Kent on 26 June 1983. He signed YTS forms with O's on 5 July 1999. Jones made his League debut on 17 February 2001 against Kidderminster

Billy Jones

Harriers in a 0-0 draw at Brisbane Road. Jones played well on his debut, and although a little nervous early on, he came into his own and his confidence grew. The 6ft and 11st 7lb player looks to have a good future ahead of him. Jones scored a penalty in the forty-first minute to secure O's under-19 youth side victory in the FA Alliance Youth Cup final, beating Bradford City 1-0 at the Millennium Stadium in Cardiff on 22 April 2001. The new first-year professional made 32 appearances for the under-19 side in 2000/01, more than any other player. He made his second League appearance in a 0-0 draw at Halifax Town on 22 September 2001, and he held his spot after the injury to Matt Lockwood. He is maturing into a solid all-round defender and has become a regular in the side.

SEASON	LEAGUE		FA CUP		L. CUP	
	Apps	Gls	Apps	Gls	Apps	Gls
2000/01	1	0	0	0	0	0
2001/02	16	0	3(1)	0	0	0
TOTAL	17	0	3(1)	0	0	0

TOTAL APPS	20(1)
TOTAL GOALS	0

David JONES-QUARTEY, 1988 (trial)
David Jones, as he was known during his footballing career, made little impact at most of the twelve clubs he played for (mostly on trial), and it was only in the latter part of his career with Doncaster Rovers that he finally achieved much. Born in Harrow, Middlesex on 3 July 1964, he started as a youth player with Watford. He joined O's from non-League Barnet on a non-contract basis on 1 December 1988, and played just 2 matches – both as a substitute – against Wrexham and Rochdale. The tall, gangly striker – he was

6ft 3in and weighed 13st 4lb – appeared slow and cumbersome, and was not kept on. He moved to Burnley in February 1989, making 4 League appearances. He joined Doncaster Rovers in November 1989, notched a hat-trick against Rochdale on his debut, and made a total of 38 senior appearances, from which he scored 15 goals. In September 1991 he joined Bury, making 3(8) senior appearances, before moving to Hull City in February 1993, making 11(1) League appearances. In January 1995 he had a week's trial with Bradford City, but made a single Central League appearance. During nine years of professional football, he had spells with Crystal Palace, Chelsea, Barnet (Vauxhall Conference), Bury, Welling United (Vauxhall Conference), Burnley, Ipswich Town, Doncaster Rovers, Bury, Hull City and Bradford City, as well as O's. He had a short spell with Watford, where he played just once, in a reserve match. He also had spells in both New Zealand and United States. He made a total of 49(10) League appearances and scored 15 goals. After retiring, he worked as a cameraman for Sky TV.

SEASON	LEAGUE		FA CUP		L. CUP	
	Apps	Gls	Apps	Gls	Apps	Gls
1988/89	0(2)	0	0	0	0	0
TOTAL	0(2)	0	0	0	0	0

TOTAL APPS	0(2)
TOTAL GOALS	0

* David Jones also appeared in 1(1) Auto Windscreens Shield matches, scoring 1 goal.

Matthew Nathan JOSEPH, 1998-present

Despite a lack of height, the former England youth international has proved to be an excellent right wing-back and a tenacious tackler, difficult to beat in the air and possessing good ball control. He was rewarded after many fine displays when voted 'Starman' – O's Player of the Year – in 1999/2000. He also won 2 full international cap for Barbados in 2000. Born in Bethnal Green, London on 30 September 1972, he joined O's on 20 January 1998 for £20,000 from Cambridge United – another of Tommy Taylor's signings from his former club. Matthew Joseph began as a first-year YTS trainee with Arsenal on 11 November 1990. He moved to Gillingham on a free transfer on 12 December 1992, yet seemed to be lost to League football when he joined Finnish side Ilves FC in May 1993, without having played any League matches. It was Cambridge manager Gary Johnson who gave Joseph his chance in November 1993, and he went on to make 175(3) senior appearances for the U's, scoring 6 goals before being snapped up by O's boss Taylor. He was a mainstay in the team during O's push for promotion during the 1998/99 season, and in subsequent seasons has proved to be one of the best defenders in the division. He signed a new three-year contract in February 2000, and captained the side in the absence of Dean Smith for the Worthington Cup tie against Reading in August 2000. Joseph's form for his club was rewarded by gaining his first full cap for Barbados – a highlight of his career – against Guatemala, in the semi-final of the Football Confederation qualifying round (World Cup) on 9 October 2000, which they lost 1-3. He was O's thirteenth full international player. He won a second cap on 15 November against the USA at the Waterford National Stadium in Bridgetown, losing 0-4. He was again voted O's Player of the Year for the

2000/01 season, and was presented with the bronze trophy before the match against Cheltenham on 28 April. He appeared in all 3 play-off matches, including the 4-2 defeat by Blackpool at the Millennium Stadium in Cardiff on 26 May 2001. None were happier than Joseph after O's 4-2 win over Rochdale on 27 October 2001 – he had scored only his second League goal in almost four years with the club. He netted with a diving header to record O's fourth goal.

SEASON	LEAGUE		FA CUP		L. CUP	
	Apps	Gls	Apps	Gls	Apps	Gls
1997/98	14	1	0	0	0	0
1998/99*	35	0	3(1)	0	2	0
1999/2000	38(3)	0	2	0	2(1)	0
2000/01**	47	0	4	0	3	0
2001/02	29(1)	1	3	0	1	0
TOTAL	163(4)	2	12(1)	0	8	0

TOTAL APPS	183(5)
TOTAL GOALS	2

Matthew Joseph

* Matthew Joseph's League record in 1998/99 includes a promotion play-off appearance.

** Joseph's League record in 2000/01 includes 3 promotion play-off appearances. He also played in 0(1) Auto Windscreens Shield match in 1999/2000, and an LDV Vans Trophy match in 2000/01.

Roger JOSEPH, 1996-97, 1998-2000

Roger Joseph, a hard-tackling defender, was a member of Wimbledon's Crazy Gang during their remarkable rise to the top division. Born in Paddington, London on Friday 24 December 1965, the right-back started his career with Southall in June 1983. He joined Brentford on a free transfer on 4 October 1985, playing 119(1) senior matches and scoring twice. Moving to Wimbledon for £150,000 on 25 August 1988, he played well for the Dons over a number of seasons, making 189(12) appearances. After a short loan spell at Millwall (5 League appearances), Joseph joined O's on a non-contract basis on 22 November 1996, staying just over three months. He joined West Bromwich Albion in February 1997, but only made a couple of appearances as a substitute. He returned to London, and was offered a contract by O's boss Tommy Taylor, signing on 3 August 1998. Roger Joseph proved to be a valuable squad member, making his 300th League career appearance during the 1998/99 season. He signed a new one-year contract in March 1999, but missed most of the 1999/2000 season through a serious calf injury, playing just once as a substitute at Swansea Town on 25 March 2000. The thirty-five-year-old Joseph was given a free transfer in May 2000, but due to an ongoing injury problem, he decided to retire. It was a real surprise to see Joseph back at the club in July 2001 on trial, playing in a number of pre-season friendlies. He net-

Roger Joseph

ted a goal in O's 9-1 win at Essex senior side Saffron Walden on 23 July, and he also came on as a substitute in the friendly against Chelsea two days later. He left O's during early November 2001, after playing 3 reserve matches, and signed for Dr Martens side Kings Lynn, on a game-by-game basis. He made his debut at centre half in a 2-1 defeat at Weymouth in front of just 778 spectators. He left Kings Lynn on 8 December 2001 after 6 games.

SEASON	LEAGUE		FA CUP		L. CUP	
	Apps	Gls	Apps	Gls	Apps	Gls
1996/97	15	0	0	0	0	0
1997/98	13(12)	0	0(1)	0	2(1)	0
1998/99*	16(10)	0	1(1)	0	1(1)	0
1999/2000	0(1)	0	0	0	0	0
TOTAL	44(23)	0	1(2)	0	3(2)	0

TOTAL APPS	48(27)
TOTAL GOALS	0

* Joseph's League record includes 3 promotion play-off matches in 1998/99.

** Roger Joseph also appeared in 2 Auto Windscreens Shield matches.

Leonard Bruce JULIANS, 1955-59

Len Julians was born in Tottenham, London on 19 June 1933, and followed Spurs as a youngster. He represented Rowland High School and Tottenham boys. On leaving school, he joined Harris Lebus youth club, and then played for Spurs juniors. He moved away from White Hart Lane after leaving the Army, and joined Leytonstone. Shortly thereafter he moved to Walthamstow Avenue, and was their leading scorer with over 40 goals. He joined O's in June 1955, and made an excellent start when scoring twice against Brentford in January 1956. He scored 11 League goals from just 9 starts in O's League championship success in 1955/56, and he also netted a goal in a 7-0 trouncing of East Fife in a friendly during 1957/58. However, despite scoring 45 goals for the reserves in 1956/57, he could never achieve a regular first-team place, due to the brilliant form of Tommy Johnston, yet still managed 36 senior goals for the O's. He was transferred to Arsenal for a £12,000 fee in December 1958, but made just 18 League appearances, scoring 7 goals, before signing for Nottingham Forest for £10,000 in June 1960. He stayed at the City Ground for three seasons, making 59 League appearances and scoring 24 goals. In January 1964 he moved on to Millwall, where he made 125 League appearances as well as notching 58 goals for the Lions. He left the League in May 1966 to play for Detroit Cougars in the USA. Julians was

J

Len Julians

a very deceptive player, who scored 124 League goals in a career that spanned twelve years. He died in Southend-on-Sea on 17 December 1993, at the age of sixty.

SEASON	LEAGUE		FA CUP		TOTAL	
	Apps	Gls	Apps	Gls	Apps	Gls
1955/56	9	11	0	0	9	11
1956/57	1	0	0	0	1	0
1957/58	34	16	2	1	36	17
1958/59	22	8	0	0	22	8
TOTAL	66	35	2	1	68	36

Edward JUNIPER, 1920-21

Ted Juniper was born in Shadwell on 3 December 1901. As an amateur, Juniper was a sturdy centre forward who was given a run of 8 matches, making his League debut in a 2-0 win against Leicester City on 28 August 1920. His only goal came in a 2-2 draw at Blackpool the following month. He

soon lost his place to Ernie Cockle. (Six different centre forwards were tried that season, without much success.) Juniper made a single further appearance – at wing-half – in a 3-0 defeat at Hull City in December 1922, but was released in May 1922 and returned to non-League football. He died in Havering, Essex during April 1990.

SEASON	LEAGUE		FA CUP		TOTAL	
	Apps	Gls	Apps	Gls	Apps	Gls
1920/21	9	1	0	0	9	1
TOTAL	9	1	0	0	9	1

Ian Martin JURYEFF, 1984-89

Ian Juryeff will best be remembered for a wonderful spell he had with O's between Christmas 1987 and May 1988, when he scored 16 League goals from just 21 starts. He spent five seasons at Brisbane Road without being a regular, yet still netted 55 senior goals. One of his goals, witnessed by millions around the world, was an FA Cup strike against Nottingham Forest on 30 January 1988. Born on 24 November 1962 in Gosport, Hampshire, he progressed through the ranks of Southampton's youth and reserve sides. He went on loan to Mansfield Town in March 1984 (scoring 5 goals from 12 starts) and with Reading in November 1984 (making 7 appearances and scoring 2 goals). He joined O's in February 1985 for £10,000, but despite producing some classy displays early in his stay, he never quite held on to that form, and Second Division side Ipswich Town took him on trial in February 1989. He was named substitute 7 times and came on twice, and he also scored 3 goals in 6 reserve appearances at Portman Road, but returned to Brisbane Road in April 1989. Juryeff holds one record: he is O's leading goalscorer in the Auto Windscreens Shield competition with 6 goals. He declined a move to Gillingham, but eventually signed for Halifax Town in August 1989 for £40,000, and made 15(2) League appearances, scoring 7 goals. He was transferred to Hereford for £50,000 in December 1989, and netted a further 13 goals from 72 League starts. In June 1991 he was back at Halifax Town, and netted 4 goals from 37 starts during the 1991/92 season. In August 1992 Juryeff joined Darlington on a free transfer, netting 6 goals from 26(8) senior matches. A further transfer took him to Scunthorpe United for £5,000, making 41(3) League appearances and scoring 13 goals between 1993 and 1995. In 1995/96 he played for non-League Havant Town, and in 1997 became a coach involved with Charlton Athletic's and Southampton's 'Football in the Community' schemes.

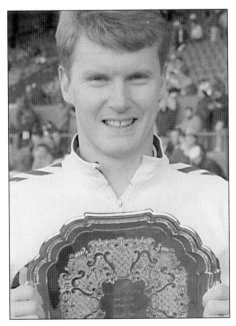

Ian Juryeff

SEASON	LEAGUE		FA CUP		L. CUP	
	Apps	Gls	Apps	Gls	Apps	Gls
1984/85	19	7	0	0	0	0
1985/86	25(2)	10	5	3	1	0
1986/87	11(2)	2	0	0	2	1
1987/88	23	16	2	2	1	0
1988/89	28(1)	10	3	2	5	2
TOTAL	106(5)	45	10	7	9	3

TOTAL APPS	125(5)
TOTAL GOALS	55

* Ian Juryeff also appeared in 9(1) Auto Windscreens Shield matches, scoring a club record 6 goals.

K

John Peter KANE, 1978-80

Born in Hackney, London on 15 December 1960, central defender John Kane progressed through O's junior ranks, signing professional forms in July 1978. He played regularly for the reserves but made a single senior appearance as a substitute in the 3-0 defeat at Blackburn Rovers on 2 September 1978. He never made the anticipated progress, and was released in May 1980 to join Rainham Town. Later he had a spell with Walthamstow Avenue, and then moved to Leytonstone & Ilford FC.

SEASON	LEAGUE		FA CUP		L. CUP	
	Apps	Gls	Apps	Gls	Apps	Gls
1978/79	0(1)	0	0	0	0	0
TOTAL	0(1)	0	0	0	0	0

TOTAL APPS	0(1)
TOTAL GOALS	0

* John Kane also appeared in an Anglo-Scottish Cup match in 1978/79.

K

Archibald KEAN, 1921-22

Born on 30 September 1894 in Barrhead, Glasgow, Archie Kean started his career with Parkhead FC, moving to Croy Celtic FC in 1920. He became an 'Oriental' in July 1921, after a trial with Southend. He was a neat and clever inside left, but after a short run in the first team, he was demoted to the reserves. Unable to regain his place, he left to join Lincoln City in August 1922, making 76 League appearances and scoring 11 goals. In April 1924 he joined Blackburn Rovers, but never made the first XI, and in September 1925, he joined Grantham Town of the Midland League.

SEASON	LEAGUE		FA CUP		TOTAL	
	Apps	Gls	Apps	Gls	Apps	Gls
1921/22	11	0	0	0	11	0
TOTAL	11	0	0	0	11	0

Walter James KEEN, 1932-35

Wally Keen was born in April 1904 in Loudwater, Buckinghamshire. Starting his career with Wycombe Wanderers, he joined Fulham from Millwall in May 1930, making a single FA Cup appearance against Yeovil & Petters United in December 1931. The solid defender joined O's in May 1932, and despite appearing initially in both the centre half and right half positions, he soon settled down at right-back under David Pratt's management. He scored just 2 goals for O's – both came in a 7-1 defeat of Swindon Town in January 1933, the first time O's had scored so many goals in a League match. One of only three players to be retained at the end of the 1932/33 season, Keen was in the side that defeated Aldershot 9-2 in February 1934. This makes him one of only two men (along with Tommy Mills) to have played in O's two highest ever scores in League football before the Second World War. He lost his place to Frank Searle in October 1934, and joined London Transport (Tramway Central) in June 1935. Keen was the uncle of 1960s QPR player, Mike Keen, and great-uncle of Kevin Keen, the former West Ham United, Wolves and Stoke City player. Walter Keen died in New Cross, London on 6 May 1968, aged sixty-four.

SEASON	LEAGUE		FA CUP		TOTAL	
	Apps	Gls	Apps	Gls	Apps	Gls
1932/33	31	2	1	0	32	2
1933/34	19	0	0	0	19	0
1934/35	3	0	0	0	3	0
TOTAL	53	2	1	0	54	2

* Wally Keen also appeared in 2 Third Division Cup matches between 1933 and 1935.

Nyree Anthony Okpara KELLY, 1995-96

Winger Tony Kelly, as he was known during his footballing days, was born in

Wally Keen

Meridan on 14 February 1966. He was a player who did the rounds with a number of clubs, having joined O's from Bury for £30,000 on 1 July 1995. He started as a junior with Bristol City, and made his League debut in September 1982, making a total of 2(4) appearances and scoring once. He then joined non-League St Albans, before moving on to Stoke City in January 1990 for £20,000, making 33(25) League appearances and scoring 5 goals. Two loan spells then followed – with Hull City and Cardiff City – before signing for Bury in September 1993 for £10,000, where he went on to score 10 goals from 53(4) League appearances. During his stay at Brisbane Road, he was fined a week's wages and given a severe warning by O's boss Pat Holland for costing O's an FA Cup tie at Torquay United in November 1995, when he was sent off for taking a kick at Chris Curran. The game turned from that point, and O's went out of the FA Cup by a goal to nil. Kelly did not feature in new O's manager Tommy Taylor's plans, and the boss stated that Kelly did not fit in and terminated his contract. He had a trial with Colchester United in October 1996, but after only 2(1) League appearances, he moved back to one of his earlier clubs St Albans. However, after only a handful of games, he joined Ryman League side Billericay, and stayed for a year. In July 1998 he joined another Ryman League side – Harlow Town – for whom he netted 35 goals and made 130 appearances. During May 2000 he joined Arlesey Town, but after receiving a suspension he left the club.

SEASON	LEAGUE		FA CUP		L. CUP	
	Apps	Gls	Apps	Gls	Apps	Gls
1995/96	32(2)	3	1	0	1	0

Tony Kelly

1996/97	6(3)	1	0	0	1	0
TOTAL	38(5)	4	1	0	2	0

TOTAL APPS	41(5)
TOTAL GOALS	4

* Tony Kelly also appeared in 2 Auto Windscreens Shield matches.

Russell KELLY, 1995-96

Irishman Russell Kelly was born in Ballymoney, Co. Antrim on 9 August 1976. He joined O's from Chelsea on a non-contract basis on 1 March 1996, having played only reserve-team football at Stamford Bridge since he joined in July 1995. The versatile Irish youth international could play either in defence or midfield, and made his League debut as a substitute for Greg Berry against Bury on 30 March 1996. The O's coach said of his charge: 'We were quite happy with the way he played, but he is only nineteen years old and inexperienced, so we released him.' Kelly joined Darlington on a free transfer on 16 August 1996, making 13(8) League appearances and scoring twice for them. He moved to St Mirren in Scotland on 8 January 1997, thereafter playing for Scottish League clubs Dundee, Ayr United and Partick Thistle between August 1997 and May 2000, making 31(16) Scottish League appearances and scoring 4 goals. After a short spell in Iceland and a brief trial with Cheltenham Town, he finally returned to Ireland and joined Linfield in July 2001.

SEASON	LEAGUE		FA CUP		L. CUP	
	Apps	Gls	Apps	Gls	Apps	Gls
1995/96	5(1)	0	0	0	0	0
TOTAL	5(1)	0	0	0	0	0

TOTAL APPS	5(1)
TOTAL GOALS	0

Robert Charles KERR, 1927-29

Born in Larkhall, Lanarkshire in 1904, Bobby Kerr started his career with Heart of Midlothian, before joining Wolverhampton Wanderers from Oadby Town in June 1925. He scored on his debut against Portsmouth on 12 September 1925, and stayed at Molineux for two years, making 18 League appearances and scoring 7 goals. He became an 'Oriental' in July 1927, and also scored on his debut in a 2-2 draw at Grimsby Town on 27 August 1927. He looked to be a stylish and clever type of centre forward during his first season, but his form waned the following season and he left O's in August 1927 for Worcester City. He later played for both Kettering and Grantham.

SEASON	LEAGUE		FA CUP		TOTAL	
	Apps	Gls	Apps	Gls	Apps	Gls
1927/28	23	8	0	0	23	8
1928/29	8	0	0	0	8	0
TOTAL	31	8	0	0	31	8

Wayne Michael KERRINS, 1989 (loan)

Left-back Wayne Kerrins had a short loan spell with O's in March 1989, joining from Fulham. Born in Brentwood, Essex on 5 August 1965, he joined Fulham as an associate schoolboy at the age of thirteen in August 1983, and stayed at Craven Cottage for five years, making 60(16) senior appearances and scoring once. After a loan spell with Port Vale, he joined Sutton United in September 1989. He played for many years on the non-League circuit in London, and after a spell at Croydon, he had a succesful time at Dulwich Hamlet, helping them gain promotion to the Premier Division of the Isthmian League and reach the final of the London Challenge Cup in 1992. He also had spells with Chesham United, Farnborough, Woking and Kingstonian. Kerrins was signed by Orient on loan for the run-in to the end of the season because the club were short on left-sided players and he could be used as cover for Kevin Dickenson. He was, in fact, required to deputise on three separate occasions – against York City, Cambridge United and Carlisle United – and he did not let the team down. He was one of those players who could do a reasonable job, but perhaps just lacked that something to make him into a regular first-team player. Manager Frank Clark did, however, give credit to him for his efforts in his three performances for Orient, saying that the team did not miss Dickenson too much because of Kerrins' displays.

SEASON	LEAGUE		FA CUP		L. CUP	
	Apps	Gls	Apps	Gls	Apps	Gls
1988/89	3	0	0	0	0	0
TOTAL	3	0	0	0	0	0

TOTAL APPS	3
TOTAL GOALS	0

Stephen Jack KETTERIDGE, 1987-89

Steve Ketteridge, an elegant midfielder, was born in Stevenage on 7 November 1959. He commenced his career as an apprentice with Derby County during the mid-1970s. He left the Baseball Ground without having experienced first-team football, in order to join Wimbledon for £2,000 in April 1978, where he went on to make 229(8) League appearances and score 32 goals between 1978 and 1985. He also had a loan spell in the Finnish Premier League during the summer of 1979. Ketteridge made the short journey from Plough Lane to Crystal Palace in August 1985, scoring 6 goals and making

Steve Ketteridge

58(1) League appearances for the Eagles. He joined O's in July 1987, and his first appearance came in the 1-1 draw at Cardiff City during August 1987, but he didn't really shine at Brisbane Road. His only senior goal came in a 4-1 defeat at Rotherham United in September 1988. After a loan spell with Cardiff City in October 1988 (where he made 6 League appearances and scored 2 goals), he moved to Aylesbury United in May 1989, and then joined Diadora League side St Albans City in 1991 as assistant player-manager. He later became manager, but parted company with the club in 1994.

SEASON	LEAGUE		FA CUP		L. CUP	
	Apps	Gls	Apps	Gls	Apps	Gls
1987/88	21(5)	0	0(1)	0	2	0
1988/89	5	1	0	0	0(3)	0
TOTAL	26(5)	1	0(1)	0	2(3)	0

TOTAL APPS	28(9)
TOTAL GOALS	1

* Steve Ketteridge also appeared in an Auto Windscreens Shield match.

John Peter KEY, 1968-69

Johnny Key was born in Chelsea, London on Friday 5 November 1937. He joined the Fulham groundstaff in May 1956, and the right-winger showed a lot of promise with his fast, direct style of play. He played regular First Division football, and was at Craven Cottage for more than nine years, making 181 senior appearances and scoring 37 goals. Key was one of a number of experienced players sold by manager Vic Buckingham, and he joined Coventry City in May 1966 on a free transfer, rejoining former Fulham colleague and City manager, Jimmy Hill. He helped the Sky Blues to win the Second Division

Championship in 1966/67, and after 7 goals and 33(1) senior appearances , he joined O's in March 1968. He was desperately unlucky at O's, becoming badly injured soon after signing, and he never got over a severe Achilles heel injury which forced him to retire in 1969.

SEASON	LEAGUE		FA CUP		L. CUP	
	Apps	Gls	Apps	Gls	Apps	Gls
1967/68	8	0	0	0	0	0
1968/69	1(1)	0	0	0	0(2)	0
TOTAL	9(1)	0	0	0	0(2)	0

TOTAL APPS	9(3)
TOTAL GOALS	0

Richard Martin KEY, 1983-84

Goalkeeper Richard Key was born in Coventry on Friday 13 April 1956. He started at Coventry City as a junior, but it was whilst with Exeter City (whom he joined in July 1975) that he made his mark, making 109 League appearances for the Devon club. His progress was halted when he broke his leg, and he later moved to Cambridge United in August 1978, where he made a further 52 League appearances. After a short loan spell with Northampton Town (2 League appearances), he joined O's in August 1983 to replace Mervyn Day, and proved a worthy successor between the sticks. After just one campaign, he moved to Brentford in August 1984, but only appeared once. After loan spells with both Sunderland and Swindon Town, he went back to Cambridge United (on loan), making a further 13 appearances in 1984/85. He was back at Brentford in 1985/86 and made 3 appearances, before finally ending his League career with further loan spells at Millwall and Cambridge United. Key played for eight League clubs, mak-

ing a career total of 222 League appearances over eleven years.

SEASON	LEAGUE		FA CUP		L. CUP	
	Apps	Gls	Apps	Gls	Apps	Gls
1983/84	42	0	1	0	2	0
TOTAL	42	0	1	0	2	0

TOTAL APPS	45
TOTAL GOALS	0

* Richard Key also appeared in an Auto Windscreens Shield match.

Edward KING, 1914-15

Eddie King was born in 1890 in Blyth, Northumberland. The half-back joined Woolwich Arsenal from Southern League outfit Leyton FC in August 1912, whose ground was at Brisbane Road over twenty years before O's moved there. He made 13 senior appearances and 53 reserve appearances, and scored 2 goals for the Gunners between 1912 and 1914. King joined O's as a right half on 30 June 1914 and made his League debut in a 0-0 draw at Wolves in September 1914. However, later in the 1914/15 season, he was moved to centre forward. He left O's in May 1915.

SEASON	LEAGUE		FA CUP		TOTAL	
	Apps	Gls	Apps	Gls	Apps	Gls
1914/15	17	0	0	0	17	0
TOTAL	17	0	0	0	17	0

Raymond KING, 1946-47

Goalkeeper Ray King was born in Warkworth, Northumberland on Friday 15 August 1924. He was a tall goalkeeper (6ft 3in) who began his career with non-League Ashington as an outfield player, before moving on to Amble. He joined Newcastle United in April 1942 for £10, and played in the unofficial regional war Leagues. He broke both wrists when saving a penalty from Everton's legendary forward Tommy Lawton, and played several matches without realising the extent of his injury. This ultimately led to his release from Gallowgate, having made 31 wartime appearances and played in 2 FA Cup matches. He joined O's on a free transfer in October 1946, and made his debut in a 4-1 defeat at Northampton Town on 2 November 1946. Unbelievably, in that match, he broke his wrist again! He thought that the weakness in his wrists would mean the end of his career, and he left Brisbane Road to play non-League football for Ashington. In May 1949 he was offered a trial with Port Vale, and he went on to have 7 wonderful seasons with them, making 275 senior appearances. During his time at Vale, he won a Third Division (North) Championship medal and reached the FA Cup semi-final, after beating O's 1-0 at Brisbane Road in the quarter-final in front of 31,000 fans. He also won an England 'B' cap against Switzerland in 1954. He was transferred to Boston United for £2,500 in July 1957, and in 1959 was appointed player-manager. He also managed Poole Town and Sittingbourne. On his retirement from the game, he returned to his native Northumberland and settled in Amble practising shiatsu, a form of physiotherapy.

SEASON	LEAGUE		FA CUP		TOTAL	
	Apps	Gls	Apps	Gls	Apps	Gls
1946/47	1	0	0	0	1	0
TOTAL	1	0	0	0	1	0

Herbert Charles KINGABY, 1904-06

Bert Kingaby is in the record books as the scorer of O's first ever goal in the League. He achieved this feat at Leicester Fosse on 2 September 1905, when heading home from a Richard Bourne cross in the sixty-second minute of the match. Born in Hackney, London during January 1880, he joined O's from the West Hampstead club in 1904, and played extremely well in O's only season in the Second Division of the Southern League. He was also on the team-sheet for O's first ever FA Cup venture – a tie against Enfield on 17 September 1904. He also netted twice in an FA Cup replay against Cheshunt in a 4-1 win the following month. He remained a part-timer earning £2 per week – the normal wage for professional players was £4 – and because he worked for a woollen merchant, he was rarely able to play any weekday matches. Kingaby was a very fast right-winger, with excellent ball control and tricky dribbling skills. His form was such that he attracted scouts from the First Division clubs, including both Arsenal and Aston Villa. With O's experiencing a serious financial crisis during 1906, Kingaby was sold to Aston Villa for £300 on 7 March 1906, receiving a £10 signing-on fee. However, he did not fare too well at Villa Park, making just 4 League appearances for the club – in fact, Villa offered him back to O's for £150, but they just could not afford it. Kingaby is best remembered for his landmark legal case against Villa, claiming that he was denied freedom to move to another League club. He went to the High Court, but the protracted legal case only reached the King's bench on 26 March 1912. Throughout this long period, Kingaby was only allowed to play for teams outside the League. He eventually lost the case against Villa, and it was the Player's Union who paid the legal costs of £725. During September 1906 he joined Southern League Fulham, and was a member of their side that won the Southern League Championship. He made 37 senior appearances for Fulham and scored 3 goals, but had to leave Craven Cottage in 1907 when they were elected to the League, as the Villa board refused Fulham's plea to allow him to play in the League. He joined Southern League side Leyton FC in 1907, staying with then for three seasons before joining Peterborough City in 1910. He then moved to Croydon Common in 1913. Unfortunately, Kingaby is remembered mainly for the legal wrangle with Aston Villa, yet during his time at Millfields Road he looked a wonderful player. Bert Kingaby died in Hackney, London during 1957, aged seventy-seven.

Sam Kitchen

SEASON	LEAGUE		FA CUP		TOTAL	
	Apps	Gls	Apps	Gls	Apps	Gls
1904/05*	-	-	5	3	5	3
1905/06	26	4	5	0	31	4
TOTAL	26	4	10	3	36	7

* Clapton Orient first entered the League in 1905/06.

David Edward Samuel KITCHEN, 1992-94

Sam Kitchen, as he was always known, was a strong, quick-tackling Yorkshireman, who came into the League at the late age of twenty-five. He joined O's on a trial at the end of the 1991/92 season from Frickley Town, signing a permanent contract on 11 August 1992 for £10,000. Born in Rintein, Germany on 11 June 1967, he had previously had trials with both Cambridge United and Rotherham United, before having short spells with Stafford Rangers and Goole Town. He joined Frickley Town of the HFS Loans League, spending two seasons there.

Kitchen stated: 'It's not easy trying to fit in a job and making a career in non-League football. Having spent four-and-a-half years working for a Doncaster-based tarmac firm, it meant I was often up at 5 a.m. to start work at 6 a.m. tarmacking motorways, then on to training in the evenings.' He made his O's debut at centre-half in the League Cup tie against Millwall in August 1992, earning plenty of praise for his performance. Manager Eustace said: 'It was a marvellous performance, considering it was his first game at this level – he made it look so easy.' Kitchen had a good season, and scored his only goal for the club against West Bromwich Albion on 7 November 1992. The following season he struggled to find his form, and was released in February 1994. He joined Doncaster Rovers, where he made 21 League appearances and scored once. In May 1995 he moved to Gateshead, making over

100 Conference appearances. In July 2001, he joined Bishop Auckland, playing 16(1) games, but returned to Gateshead the following December.

SEASON	LEAGUE		FA CUP		L. CUP	
	Apps	Gls	Apps	Gls	Apps	Gls
1992/93	28(4)	1	2	0	1	0
1993/94	7(4)	0	2	0	1	0
TOTAL	35(8)	1	4	0	2	0

TOTAL APPS	41(8)
TOTAL GOALS	1

* Sam Kitchen also appeared in 3(1) Auto Windscreens Shield matches.

Michael KITCHEN, 1977-79, 1982-84

Peter Kitchen joined O's for £40,000 from Doncaster Rovers in July 1977, with a reputation of being a hotshot goalscorer. Upon his arrival, the 5ft 8in and 11st player promised the fans goals, having previously notched 89 goals from 221(7) League appearances and 13 goals from 28 cup matches. Most certainly he lived up to his promise, and was arguably O's greatest forward of the past few decades. Many of his goals were sheer magic – older O's fans will never forget his two marvellous strikes at Stamford Bridge that knocked Chelsea out of the FA Cup. Nor will they forget his goal against Middlesbrough that helped to take O's to a semi-final match against Arsenal at Stamford Bridge in April 1978 – a goal he himself ranks as his greatest scored for O's. Born in Mexborough on 16 February 1952, Kitchen joined Doncaster Rovers as a junior. He made his debut in 1970/71, and his record at the Belle Vue speaks for itself. He was signed by George Petchey, just before he the manager was fired, and after his wonderful first spell with O's, he

moved to Fulham. The £150,000 deal, which took place in February 1979, also included Fulham youngster Mark Gray. His stay at Craven Cottage was not a happy one – he netted just 6 goals from 21(3) appearances – so he moved on to Cardiff City for £150,000 in August 1980. He topped City's goalscoring chart in his first season, and netted a total of 21 League goals from 64(3) outings. He was given a free transfer in May 1982, and went to team up with former O's colleague Joe Mayo at the Happy Valley club in Hong Kong. However, a few days after signing, he was approached by top Dutch side Sparta Rottadam for a trial, but it was too late, he was on his way to Hong Kong. During December 1982 it was manager Ken Knighton who brought 'Kitch' back to Brisbane Road. After a reserve match against Southend United, he returned to first-team action against Preston North End, scoring the winner. If not the Kitchen of old, he certainly had not lost

Peter Kitchen

L

his knack of scoring goals, as was evident in a match against Millwall in April 1984, when he bagged 4 goals in a thrilling 5-3 win. He left the club in May 1984, and went to play indoor soccer in America for a couple of months. In July 1994 he joined Dagenham & Redbridge, and in March 1995 he briefly returned to the League with Chester City, scoring a single goal from 3(2) League appearances. These days he lives in the Essex area, works as a reporter and plays his football in the Epping five-a-side League to keep fit. He also runs the White Oak Leisure Centre.

SEASON	LEAGUE		FA CUP		L. CUP	
	Apps	Gls	Apps	Gls	Apps	Gls
1977/78	42	21	8	7	3	1
1978/79	22(1)	7	3	2	1	0
1982/83	20	9	0	0	0	0
1983/84	26(3)	12	1	0	1(1)	1
TOTAL	110(4)	49	12	9	5(1)	2

TOTAL APPS	127(5)
TOTAL GOALS	60

* Peter Kitchen also appeared in 6 Anglo-Scottish Cup matches without scoring, and also appeared in an Auto Windscreens Shield match, scoring twice.

L

Barry LAKIN, 1992-96

Barry Lakin was born in Dartford, Kent on 19 September 1973. As a schoolboy he was on Gillingham's books, but when John Gorman took over as O's youth coach on leaving the Gills, he brought Lakin with him. The young energetic mid-fielder/striker represented an England XI against the Army under-18s, scoring in an 8-0 victory. Lakin made his League debut when coming on as a substitute on 18 December 1992. He had a run of 7 League games at the end of the season, and scored in 2 successive games against Stockport County and Preston North End in April 1993. He also scored the opener in a 2-2 draw in a friendly against a Caribbean All-Star XI in 1993/94. He went on loan to Vauxhall Conference side Woking in 1994. He played without disturbing the net in the League for the following three seasons, and was one of eight players released during May 1996 by O's boss Pat Holland. Holland said: 'Barry has been unlucky with injuries, and we will do all we can to find him another club.' He joined former 'Oriental' Kevin Hales – manager at Welling United – playing 38(4) matches during his time with the club. In 1997 he joined Chelmsford City and appeared 78 times for the Clarets, scoring 16 goals. In 2000 he left

Barry Lakin

and had spells with Erith & Belvadere and Enfield before going to Massachusetts, USA as the assistant coach of Cape Cod Crusaders, a semi-pro team who play in the Premier Development League. He returned to England in March 2002 and was appointed youth development officer with Chelmsford City.

SEASON	LEAGUE		FA CUP		L. CUP	
	Apps	Gls	Apps	Gls	Apps	Gls
1992/93	8(1)	2	0	0	0	0
1993/94	11(4)	0	2	1	2	0
1994/95	17(5)	0	0(2)	0	2	0
1995/96	5(3)	0	0	0	0	0
TOTAL	41(13)	2	2(2)	1	4	0

TOTAL APPS	47(15)
TOTAL GOALS	3

* Barry Lakin also appeared in 3(1) Auto Windscreens Shield matches.

George LAMBERTON, 1905-06

George Lamberton was one of two brothers – the other being older brother James – who both played for O's in the inaugural League season of 1905/06, including the first League match at Leicester Fosse on 2 September 1905. Born in Rossendale on 24 December 1880, he started off as a youngster with spells at Berry's Association FC and Tonge FC. George Lamberton, an inside forward, commenced his professional career with Bury, whom he joined in June 1899. He scored on his debut, and went on to make 23 senior appearances at Gigg Lane and score 8 goals. He moved to Luton Town in May 1904, playing 33 matches and scoring 8 goals. He joined O's in July 1905, and appeared together with his brother in 24 League and 6 FA Cup matches. He scored 4 goals in 3 FA Cup ties – netting

twice against Felstead, and scoring a goal each against Barking and Leyton. George Lamberton joined Norwich City on 1 May 1906, making 36 senior appearances and scoring 11 goals. He died in Middleton on 18 May 1954.

SEASON	LEAGUE		FA CUP		TOTAL	
	Apps	Gls	Apps	Gls	Apps	Gls
1905/06	26	3	6	4	32	7
TOTAL	26	3	6	4	32	7

James LAMBERTON, 1905-06

Born in Haslingden on 9 February 1877, the elder brother of George Lamberton joined O's for the first League campaign in 1905 from Stalybridge Celtic. The right full-back first started his career with Middleton FC and Berry's Association FC. In 1899 he joined Bury, making his debut against Wolverhampton Wanderers in September 1899. In 1902 he joined Bristol City, playing in 3 League matches. Between 1903 and 1905, he played for Wellingborough FC, Crewe Alexandra and Stalybridge before becoming an 'Oriental'. He did well during his season with O's, but decided to leave to join his brother at Southern League Norwich City in June 1906, where he appeared once in the Southern League and 5 times in the United League. He later had spells with West Bromwich Albion (October 1907) and Bury (1908). James Lamberton died in Oldham during 1929, aged fifty-two.

SEASON	LEAGUE		FA CUP		TOTAL	
	Apps	Gls	Apps	Gls	Apps	Gls
1905/06	33	0	6	0	39	0
TOTAL	33	0	6	0	39	0

Jack John LANDELLS, 1937-38

Despite being born in Gateshead on 11 November 1904, Landells played most of his football in the south, after his family moved to Essex. The scheming inside forward spent his early years with local Thames Board Mills in Tilbury, Grays Athletic and Grays Thurrock. He moved to Millwall in 1925, and had eight wonderful years at the Den. It was Landells and another former 'Oriental', Wilf Phillips, who contributed 33 and 26 goals respectively in the Lions' championship-winning side of 1928. Landells totalled 176 League appearances and scored 69 goals for Millwall, and he also toured South Africa with an FA XI in 1926. He moved across the Thames in May 1933 to join West Ham United, making 21 senior appearances and scoring 3 goals. Landells moved to Bristol City in July 1934, making a further 30 senior appearances and scoring 4 goals. He joined Carlisle United in May 1935, where he made a further 33 League appearances and scored 6 goals, but soon afterwards signed for Walsall in 1936, where he made 20 senior appearances and scored once. In June 1937 the thirty-two-year-old signed for O's and appeared to be past his best, making just 2 League appearances. His debut came in the 1-0 defeat at Notts County on 13 November 1937. He moved on to Chelmsford City in 1938. Landells went into the motor trade before hanging up his boots, and also acted as the Midlands scout for Arsenal. He died in Durham in 1960.

SEASON	LEAGUE		FA CUP		TOTAL	
	Apps	Gls	Apps	Gls	Apps	Gls
1937/38	2	0	0	0	2	0
TOTAL	2	0	0	0	2	0

William LANE, 1904-05

Hackney-born Billy Lane joined O's from non-League football for the first campaign in the Second Division of the Southern League, and played in the first ever fixture against Brighton & Hove Albion at Millfields Road on 8 October 1904, in front of 3,000 spectators. He also featured in O's first FA Cup fixture against Enfield on 17 September 1904, scoring the fourth goal in a 4-1 win, and played in all 6 FA Cup matches that season. He played regularly in both the Southern League and the London League, but decided against turning professional when O's were elected to the League in 1905, and returned to non-League football.

SEASON	LEAGUE		FA CUP		TOTAL	
	Apps	Gls	Apps	Gls	Apps	Gls
1904/05*	-	-	6	1	6	1
TOTAL	-	-	6	1	6	1

* Clapton Orient did not enter the League until 1905/06.

William Henry Charles LANE, 1937-38

Billy Lohn was born in Tottenham, London on 28 October 1903, and later changed his name to Lane. The goalscoring centre forward had a long and distinguished career, and it was whilst with Watford that he recorded a hat-trick against O's in just three minutes during 1933/34 season. He also recorded another hat-trick against O's in the following season, but not such a quick one! He began his career with London City Mission, and then went on to Gnome Athletic followed by Park Avondale. He joined Barnet in January 1924 from Summerstown FC. He turned professional when joining Tottenham Hotspur in July 1924, and made 26 League appearances and scored 7 goals. In November 1926 he signed for Leicester City for a

Billy Lane (1937-38)

moved to Guildford City in 1947, and returned to Brighton between 1950 and May 1961. During his stay with the Seagulls, they were promoted to the Second Division for the first time in their history. He then managed Gravesend & Northfleet between 1961 and 1963. After retiring, he scouted for Arsenal, QPR and Brighton. William Lane died in Chelmsford, Essex on 9 November 1985, aged eighty-two.

SEASON	LEAGUE		FA CUP		TOTAL	
	Apps	Gls	Apps	Gls	Apps	Gls
1937/38	12	1	2	1	14	2
TOTAL	12	1	2	1	14	2

Hubert Henry LAPPIN, 1906-07

Harry Lappin was born in Manchester in January 1879. The small, nippy and clever winger started with Springfield FC and then with Oldham Athletic when they were operating in the Manchester Alliance League. He was spotted by Newton Heath in 1901, and he was still with the club when they changed their name to Manchester United. He played 27 Second Division matches and scored 4 times, before joining Grimsby Town in August 1903. A year later he moved on to non-League Rossendale United, and he joined O's in August 1906. He was ever-present in 1906/07, and proved to be a goal-maker rather than a goalscorer. His only goal for O's came against Hull City in January 1907. The following season he joined Chester, and he played for them in the Welsh Cup final of 1909, losing 1-0 to Wrexham. In 1909 he was on the books of Birmingham, and thereafter he played for a number of non-League clubs, including Chirk FC (1910), Hurst FC and then Macclesfield Town. He died in Liverpool during May 1925, aged forty-six.

£2,250 fee, and stayed for two seasons, yet he only made 5 League appearances, scoring twice. He moved to Reading in May 1928 for £450, but made just half-a-dozen League appearances (scoring two goals) during his only season there. In May 1929 he was on his travels again, this time to Brentford. In three years at Griffin Park, he notched 84 goals from 114 League appearances. This record encouraged Watford to pay a four-figure fee for him in May 1932, and he went on to record a total of 68 League goals from 124 appearances for the club. In January 1936 he joined Bristol City for £200, making 31 senior appearances and notching a further 11 goals. In July 1937, the thirty-four-year-old Lane became an 'Oriental' on a free transfer, appearing in O's first League match at Brisbane Road against Cardiff City on 28 August 1937. At the end of the season he retired, and was appointed manager of Brentford. Lane

SEASON	LEAGUE		FA CUP		TOTAL	
	Apps	Gls	Apps	Gls	Apps	Gls
1906/07*	38	1	-	-	38	1
TOTAL	38	1	-	-	38	1

* Clapton Orient did not enter the FA Cup in 1906/07.

Edward LAWRENCE, 1928-31 and 1937-38

Welshman Eddie Lawrence was born in Cefn Mawr, near Wrexham on 24 August 1907. The left half started his career with Druids FC, and then joined Wrexham as an amateur in 1925, making 22 League appearances for the club before leaving in 1928. He became an 'Oriental' in August 1928, and his debut came in a splendid 3-0 win over Middlesbrough. This very shrewd player – noted for his no-nonsense manner – distributed the ball extremely accurately. His fine play was recognised by the Welsh selectors in 1930 when he gained a full cap against Northern Ireland. In May 1931, he was transferred to Notts County for £275, scoring twice and making 143 senior appearances. He also gained a further international cap against Scotland in 1932. He moved to Bournemouth & Boscome Athletic in August 1936, making 39 League appearances and scoring once. He rejoined O's in May 1937, but returned to Notts County in 1939, and later served them as a scout. Lawrence died in Nottingham on 20 July 1989.

SEASON	LEAGUE		FA CUP		TOTAL	
	Apps	Gls	Apps	Gls	Apps	Gls
1928/29	26	0	2	0	28	0
1929/30	37	2	5	0	42	2
1930/31	37	0	2	0	39	0
1937/38	21	0	3	0	24	0
TOTAL	121	2	12	0	133	2

Arthur Richard LAYTON, 1914-20

Arthur Layton was born in West Ham, London in 1890. He joined O's from Spittlefields Athletic in September 1914, showing considerable promise. He had few opportunities, but played and scored in the final League match to take place before the players went off to fight in the First World War – a 2-0 win over Leicester Fosse at Millfields on 24 April 1915. He was also the top goalscorer for the reserves in 1914/15 with 26 goals, as well as top scoring with 32 goals in O's wartime regional matches. Layton was one of the players who returned to the club after the First World War, making a number of appearances. He left in May 1920 to join Northfleet FC, and died in London in 1962.

SEASON	LEAGUE		FA CUP		TOTAL	
	Apps	Gls	Apps	Gls	Apps	Gls
1914/15	3	1	1	0	4	1
1919/20	23	3	1	0	24	3
TOTAL	26	4	2	0	28	4

Mark LAZARUS, 1957-60 and 1969-72

As a Jew, Lazarus had to endure taunts and insults from fans and players alike – one of the worst occasions being the match against Millwall at the Den on 6 March 1971 – yet he came through it with honour, and was a member of promotion sides for four consecutive seasons during his career. He collected a Third Division Championship medal with Queens Park Rangers in 1967, Second Division runners-up medals with Rangers and Crystal Palace in seasons 1968 and 1969 respectively, and then figured in O's Third Division Championship triumph in 1970. He also gained a League Cup winner's medal with QPR in 1967, when he scored a goal against West Bromwich Albion at

Mark Lazarus

Wembley. Born in Stepney, London on 5 December 1938, he was a member of a great Jewish sporting family of thirteen brothers – two being famous boxers Harry and Lew Lazar. He joined O's from Barking as an amateur, whilst serving in the armed forces, and made his debut in a London Challenge Cup match against Charlton Athletic, scoring two brilliant goals. He signed professional forms on 26 November 1957, and played his first professional match for the reserves against Southend United, scoring in the thirty-fifth minute. His first-team debut came in an FA Cup tie against Reading in January 1958, but his League debut did not transpire until the following season at Swansea City on 11 September 1958, the match ending 3-3. Two days later, during his home debut against Scunthorpe United, he set up the first goal for Len Julians, and scored the second himself, O's winning 2-1. However, he could not

establish himself in the side, and jumped at the chance of joining former O's boss Alec Stock at Queens Park Rangers for £3,000 in September 1960. The following September he moved to Wolves for £27,500, and from there Lazarus did the rounds in London, enjoying spells with QPR, Brentford, Crystal Palace, and again with O's, giving great pleasure to many. In 1971/72 he retired from League football, and played with Folkestone Town in the Southern League for a while, and then with Athenian League side Wingate. Mark Lazarus will always be remembered fondly as a colourful character – he always loved to do a lap of honour in celebration, every time he scored a goal. The winger's career tally was 134 goals from 439(3) League appearances – not bad for a player whose transfer fees totalled only £154,000 from seven moves. Nowadays, he runs his own transport business in Romford, Essex.

SEASON	LEAGUE		FA CUP		L. CUP	
	Apps	Gls	Apps	Gls	Apps	Gls
1957/58	0	0	1	0	-	-
1958/59	15	4	0	0	-	-
1959/60	0	0	0	0	-	-
1960/61*	5	0	0	0	0	0
1969/70	29	7	2	0	0	0
1970/71	32	6	3	1	1	0
1971/72	20(1)	1	0	0	2	1
TOTAL	101(1)	18	6	1	3	1

TOTAL APPS	110(1)
TOTAL GOALS	20

* The League Cup commenced in 1960/61.

Cyril LEA, 1957-64

Born in Moss, near Wrexham on 5 August 1934, left half Lea was just 5ft 9in tall, yet was strong in the tackle and was noted for his excellent ball distribution. The Welsh amateur international joined O's from Bradley Rangers as a full-back in May 1957, but Lea blossomed into a left half at Brisbane Road. He formed part of the famous Lucas, Bishop and Lea half-back line, who were considered to be as good as any middle line fielded previously. Their most successful season came in 1961/62, when all three were ever-present in the season they won promotion to the First Division. It was something of a mystery that he never gained a full Welsh cap whilst with O's, although his partner Lucas did. He was transferred to Ipswich Town on 17 November 1964 for £20,000, and did eventually gain 2 well-deserved Welsh caps. He had a long stay at Portman Road, making 103(4) League appearances, scoring 2 goals. After he retired form playing during May 1969, he joined the Ipswich coaching staff and went on to coach the Welsh national squad. Lea finally left Portman Road on

13 August 1979, to become assistant manager to Alan Durban at Stoke City. He then managed Hull City in 1983 and Colchester United between May 1983 and 1986 – they just missed promotion in each of the three seasons he was in charge, but, incredibly, he was sacked anyway, along with his assistant Stewart Houston. He went on from there to become youth development officer with Leicester City between May 1987 and May 1989, and then youth coach with West Bromwich Albion in July 1989. More recently, he has enjoyed a role of chief scout with Rushden & Diamonds FC. Cyril Lea will be remembered by older O's fans for his rugged yet skilful defensive play.

SEASON	LEAGUE		FA CUP		L. CUP	
	Apps	Gls	Apps	Gls	Apps	Gls
1957/58	13	0	0	0	-	-
1958/59	14	0	0	0	-	-
1959/60	14	0	0	0	-	-
1960/61*	33	0	3	0	-	-
1961/62	42	0	4	0	3	0
1962/63	40	0	4	0	4	0
1963/64	42	0	3	0	1	0
1964/65	7	0	0	0	1	0
TOTAL	205	0	14	0	9	0

TOTAL APPS   228
TOTAL GOALS   0

* The League Cup commenced in 1960/61.

John George LEATHER, 1926

Born in Bethnal Green, London on 9 May 1901, goalkeeper John Leather came to O's from local amateur football in December 1926, after both Arthur Wood and his understudy, Arthur Slater, were sidelined. He played in a single League match – a 6-0 defeat at Blackpool on

Cyril Lea

11 December 1926 – but left soon after, when both Wood and Slater were fit again.

SEASON	LEAGUE		FA CUP		TOTAL	
	Apps	Gls	Apps	Gls	Apps	Gls
1926/27	1	0	0	0	1	0
TOTAL	1	0	0	0	1	0

Christian LEE, 2001 (loan)

Christian Lee joined O's on a month's loan from Gillingham on 30 January 2001, after Steve Watts sustained a cartilage injury. Born in Aylesbury on 8 October 1976, the striker started his career as a junior with Doncaster Rovers in August 1994. A year later, he moved to Northampton Town, where he made a total of 26(34) League appearances and scored 8 goals. Lee was transferred to Gillingham for a tribunal fee of £35,000 in August 1999, and showed considerable promise in his early games, scoring against Brighton in the Worthington Cup and also against Stoke City. However, he sustained a knee injury that required complex surgery, and he did not start training again until early 2000, making just 3(3) senior appearances for Division One side Gills. He went on loan to Rochdale in October 2000, scoring once (against Macclesfield) in 1(2) League matches. His loan spell was cut short, after Bristol Rovers signed him on a free transfer on 20 March 2001, and he netted 2 goals from 8(1) League appearances. However, his contract was not renewed and he left on 17 May 2001. He held talks with Carlisle United at the end of August 2001, but after a single reserve match, it was decided he wasn't the player they were looking for. He then joined Nationwide Conference side Farn-borough Town on 7 September (playing 4(1) games and scoring once), before going on to join newly promoted League side Rushden & Diamonds at the end of September, and making his debut in a 2-1 win over Hartlepool United on 5 October. After just two months with the Diamonds where he made 2 appearances – including a 7-1 defeat at Cardiff City in an LDV Vans Trophy match – he moved to Unibond League side Eastwood Town on 20 November 2001. In January 2002, he joined Farnborough Town.

SEASON	LEAGUE		FA CUP		L. CUP	
	Apps	Gls	Apps	Gls	Apps	Gls
2000/01	2(1)	0	0	0	0	0
TOTAL	2(1)	0	0	0	0	0

TOTAL APPS	2(1)
TOTAL GOALS	0

James LEE, 1954-56

Tough-tackling Yorkshireman Jimmy Lee was born in Rotherham on 26 January 1926. He came to O's from Chelsea in July 1954, having spent three seasons at Stamford Bridge without featuring in their first XI. He started his career with Wath FC, before moving to Wolves in February 1945, where he did not feature. In October 1948 he went to Hull City, playing just 3 League matches scoring once. In February 1951 he joined Halifax Town, making 26 League appearances, and the following October, he moved to Chelsea. This formidable full-back formed a solid partnership with Stan Charlton in 1954/55, when O's finished runners-up to Bristol City (only one team was promoted in those days). However, he could never quite recapture that earlier form, and moved to Swindon Town in November 1956, along with Stan Earl, making 35 League appearances. In 1958, he moved to Hereford United.

SEASON	LEAGUE		FA CUP		TOTAL	
	Apps	Gls	Apps	Gls	Apps	Gls
1954/55	43	1	2	0	45	1
1955/56	24	0	2	0	26	0
1956/57	0	0	0	0	0	0
TOTAL	67	1	4	0	71	1

John Charles LEE, 1910-13

Morpeth-born John Lee joined O's from his local side, Morpeth Town, in March 1910. The young, nippy outside left got his chance against Leicester Fosse at Millfields on 25 April 1910, due to an injury to O's regular winger Austin Underwood. The following season, he was understudy to record signing Joe Dix. In July 1913, he moved to Southern League side Exeter City, making 6 appearances and scoring once.

SEASON	LEAGUE		FA CUP		TOTAL	
	Apps	Gls	Apps	Gls	Apps	Gls
1909/10	1	0	0	0	1	0
1910/11	17	1	0	0	17	1
1911/12	0	0	0	0	0	0
1912/13	2	0	0	0	2	0
TOTAL	20	1	0	0	20	1

Trevor Carl LEE, 1982 (loan)

Born in Lewisham, London on 3 July 1954, the hard-running striker joined O's on loan from Gillingham during October 1982, along with John Hawley, who came on loan from Arsenal. The duo made their O's debut in a 5-1 home defeat at the hands of Bristol Rovers. Lee started his career an apprentice with Fulham in 1970, moving to Epsom & Ewell in 1972. In October 1975 he joined Millwall, and made 114(11) League appearances, scoring 27 goals. He moved to Colchester United in November 1978 for £15,000, making 95(1) League appearances and netting 36 goals. Lee's next club was Gillingham, to whom he moved in January 1981 for £90,000, but he played in just 18 League matches and scored 6 goals. After his loan spell at O's, he signed for AFC Bournemouth in November 1982 for £5,000, making 28(6) senior appearances and scoring 9 goals. He then moved on to Cardiff City in December 1983, and made 21 appearances and scored 5 goals. In July 1984 he went to Northampton Town, where he made another 24 appearances, after which he played a single match on loan with Fulham in March 1985. Lee moved into non-League football with Bromley FC in July 1995, and later was moved back to one of his first clubs, Epsom & Ewell.

SEASON	LEAGUE		FA CUP		L. CUP	
	Apps	Gls	Apps	Gls	Apps	Gls
1982/83	5	0	0	0	0	0
TOTAL	5	0	0	0	0	0

TOTAL APPS	5
TOTAL GOALS	0

Trevor Lee

Richard Peter LE FLEM, 1966-67

Dick – or 'Flip' Le Flem, as he was known – was born in Bradford-on-Avon, Wiltshire on 12 July 1942, moving to Guernsey at a young age. The big, strong and quick outside left joined O's, having made a name for himself with Nottingham Forest between May 1960 and 1964, during which time he had gained an England under-23 cap against Holland in 1962. Le Flem made 132 League appearances at the City Ground, scoring 18 goals, before joining Wolverhampton Wanderers in an exchange deal involving Alan Hinton in January 1964. He made just 19 League appearances and scored 5 goals, before moving on to Middlesbrough for a fee of £10,000 in February 1965. His stay lasted thirteen months, and saw just 9 League appearances and a single goal. He became an 'Oriental' in March 1966 when signed by Les Gore for £2,000, and briefly showed some of his old ability with his attacking style of wing-play. He scored a cracking thirty-five-yard goal at home to Ipswich Town, yet O's still lost 1-4. When Dick Graham took over the reins from Gore, Le Flem's form dipped and he was promptly dropped. Graham wanted him to be more than simply an out-and-out winger. He sustained an injury in a reserve match, became disenchanted with football, and decided to retire at the age of twenty-four, returning to Guernsey. It was not really Dick Graham's fault that the talented Le Flem's form and interest declined after his injury. Yet, once recovered, he could have played a part in combating O's struggles of that season. However, at the time football managers were taking away the emphasis from individual abil-

Dick Le Flem

ity, and concentrating on work-rate and collective methods.

SEASON	LEAGUE		FA CUP		L. CUP	
	Apps	Gls	Apps	Gls	Apps	Gls
1965/66	9	2	0	0	0	0
1966/67	2	0	0	0	0	0
TOTAL	11	2	0	0	0	0

TOTAL APPS	11
TOTAL GOALS	2

Sydney LEGGETT, 1914-21

Born in Clapton, London in 1897, Syd Leggett was an amateur with Fulham before joining O's in February 1914. He played in the reserves, and was one of forty players and officials who went off to fight in the First World War. He rejoined the O's in 1919, and got his only opportunity in a 2-2 draw at Blackpool on 13 September 1920, this after O's had taken a six-goal drubbing at Stockport

County only two days earlier. Manager Holmes was so upset with his charges that he gave a number of reserve players (including Leggett) their League debuts, but he was never given another chance. He left O's in May 1921, joining Tunbridge Wells Rangers.

SEASON	LEAGUE		FA CUP		TOTAL	
	Apps	Gls	Apps	Gls	Apps	Gls
1914/15	0	0	0	0	0	0
1919/20	0	0	0	0	0	0
1920/21	1	0	0	0	1	0
TOTAL	1	0	0	0	1	0

Mikele LEIGERTWOOD, 2001-2002

A highly-rated, tough-tackling 6ft 1in central defender, Leigertwood joined O's from Wimbledon on 19 November 2001 on a month's loan. He is thought to have a big future at Selhurst Park, having been on the bench 8 times for the Dons. Born in Enfield on 12 January 1982, he came through the Dons' regional coaching centres, and signed on professional forms during August 2001. He impressed in their youth team as well as for the reserves. He made his League debut in O's 3-0 win over Oxford United on 20 November, and the defence did not concede a goal during his first 5 games in the defence. He returned to Wimbledon after O's boss Paul Brush decided not to extend his stay, wanting a rather more experienced defender.

SEASON	LEAGUE		FA CUP		L. CUP	
	Apps	Gls	Apps	Gls	Apps	Gls
2001/02	8	0	2	0	0	0
TOTAL	8	0	2	0	0	0

TOTAL APPS	10
TOTAL GOALS	0

Walter LEIGH, 1905-06 and 1907-08

Smethwick-born Walter Leigh was a very dashing centre forward, who had the distinction of being the leading goalscorer in O's first League campaign in 1905/06. He was also the first player to grab four goals in a League match – this happened against Bradford City during April 1906. 'Swappy', as he was known, started his career with Cadishead Athletic, and was on Aston Villa's books in 1898, making a single First Division appearance against Everton. He moved to Altrincham in May 1899, and he joined Grimsby Town in June 1900, where his stay was more productive. There he scored 12 goals in 48 senior appearances, as well as gaining a Second Division Championship medal. In May 1902 he signed for Bristol City, making 30 League appearances. He moved to Southern League side New Brompton (later to become Gillingham) in June 1903, for whom he made 38 appearances and netted 14 goals. He came to Millfields Road in May 1905, and was played in O's first League match at Leicester Fosse in September 1905. It was rather a surprise that he was allowed to move on to Hastings United in May 1906, but he returned to Millfields in June 1907, and found the net twice in the FA Cup ties against Romford and Old Newportonians. At the end of the 1907/08 season, he moved on again to assist Kettering Town.

SEASON	LEAGUE		FA CUP		TOTAL	
	Apps	Gls	Apps	Gls	Apps	Gls
1905/06	23	8	2	0	25	8
1907/08	17	3	5	4	22	7
TOTAL	40	11	7	4	47	15

Frederick John Sidney LE MAY, 1932-33

Outside right Fred Le May is recognised by football historians as the shortest ever player to appear in the League, standing exactly 5ft tall and weighing just 8st 10lb. Born in Bethnal Green, London on 2 February 1907, he started off with Bulpham FC, Laindon Hills FC and Tilbury FC. He then spent some time in Southend United's reserve side, before playing for Grays Thurrock FC, Grays Athletic FC and Woking FC. In July 1930 Le May signed amateur forms with the ill-fated Thames Association, making a total of 34 League appearances and scoring 4 goals. He joined his brother (Leslie) at Watford for a small fee in July 1931, making his League debut against Clapton Orient on 21 January 1932. After just 4 League appearances, he became an 'Oriental' in August 1932, along with his brother, but Leslie only ever played for the reserves. Le May made his League debut against old club Watford – a 2-0 victory during December 1932 – and he also starred in O's 7-1 defeat of Swindon Town on 21 January 1933, providing a number of goals in the match. After just a season, he moved on to Margate FC, and in 1936 moved to Chelmsford FC. Le May died in Debenham, Suffolk during September 1988, aged eighty-one.

SEASON	LEAGUE		FA CUP		TOTAL	
	Apps	Gls	Apps	Gls	Apps	Gls
1932/33	10	0	0	0	10	0
TOTAL	10	0	0	0	10	0

Anthony Michael LEONARD, 1906-07

Irishman Micky Leonard joined O's from Irish football, having already represented Ireland at amateur level. He only had a season at Millfields Road, but he made a good impression. He was a sharp and artistic forward, missing a single match all season, and made his League debut in a 2-0 defeat at Hull City on 8 September 1906. Leonard joined Southern League outfit Plymouth Argyle, playing in a total of 34 matches and scoring 9 goals. Argyle finished as runners-up during his stay, but he left in 1908. Despite rumours in the local press that he would return to O's, he never did, and joined Reading in 1908. Leonard was also a top-class baseball player.

SEASON	LEAGUE		FA CUP		TOTAL	
	Apps	Gls	Apps	Gls	Apps	Gls
1906/07*	37	7	-	-	37	7
TOTAL	37	7	-	-	37	7

* Clapton Orient did not enter the FA Cup in 1906/07.

Edward LEWIS, 1946-47

Born in West Bromwich on 21 June 1926, he joined Albion as an amateur player in October 1944, before signing on professional terms a month later, spending two seasons at the Hawthorns. He appeared

Micky Leonard

in 28 matches in the Northern Section in wartime games, and came south to join O's in March 1946, playing in 7 wartime matches in 1945/46. He was given the first-team jersey for the start of the 1946/47 season, the first one back after the Second World War, and showed a couple of eccentricities, such as sitting at the foot of the post whilst O's were on the attack. Lewis went back to live in the Midlands in December 1946, after retiring through injury.

SEASON	LEAGUE		FA CUP		TOTAL	
	Apps	Gls	Apps	Gls	Apps	Gls
1946/47	5	0	0	0	5	0
TOTAL	5	0	0	0	5	0

Edward LEWIS, 1958-64

Eddie Lewis was one of the 'Busby babes' of the 1950s, and he was the full-back in O's great side that won promotion to the First Division in 1962. Over the past thirty years, he has become one of the great coaches in South African football. Born in Manchester on 3 January 1935, he joined Manchester United as an amateur after playing just 4 matches for local side Goslings FC in 1950. He made his name as a centre forward, and scored on his League debut at West Bromwich Albion in November 1952 at the age of seventeen. He went onto score 9 goals from 20 appearances, netting a further 2 FA Cup goals. He was transferred to Preston North End for £9,000 in December 1955, making 12 League appearances and scoring twice. He came south to join West Ham United during November 1956 – a deal that resulted in Frank O'Farrell going to Deepdale – and helped the Hammers to promotion from the Second Division. He scored a creditable 15 goals from 36 senior appearances, and also netted

Eddie Lewis

23 goals from 29 reserve outings. He joined O's together with full-back George Wright, and was also converted to a full-back by manager Alec Stock. In 1958/59 he was given an extended run in the team at left-back, and held that position for several seasons. He was at his peak during the promotion season of 1961/62, missing just a single match through injury, and his display against Stanley Matthews at Stoke City brought rave notices. He was in the side for the start of the First Division campaign until being ousted by Billy Taylor, but soon regained the position. Lewis moved to Folkestone Town in May 1964. He later managed Ford Sports FC in the Greater London League, and in 1965 coached Clapton FC. Lewis emigrated to South Africa during April 1970 and began a long and successful coaching career. He first coached Border Schools, then in 1971 he coached Jewish Guild FC, and a year later became man-

ager of Highlands North. In 1973, he coached Lusitano FC. In 1974, he became the coach of famous Soweto side Kaiser Chiefs, and a year later he was appointed director of soccer at Wits University. It was Lewis who sent over youngsters Gary Bailey and Richard Gough to play in England, and he also coached the Continental XI in the first ever multi-racial tournament held in South Africa. In 1988 he took Giant Blackpool FC to promotion to the SA Premier League, and in 1989 he took over the reins of Moroko Swallows and acted as director of soccer at Ellis Park for former Rugby supremo Louis Luyt. During recent years, he has coached a number of clubs, including D'Alberton Callies, Moroko Swallows, Manning Rangers, Wits FC and Free State Stars. He was appointed to the South African Football Association's technical team for the 1998 World Cup finals in France, and for the African Cup of Nations finals during early 2000, held in both Ghana and Nigeria. Lewis also works as a soccer commentator for the South African Broadcasting Corporation's sports programme *Topsport*, and on 5 April 2000 he celebrated thirty years' service to South African football. After retirement in 2001, he took up coaching at a number of local schools, and also helps run a family garden service company in Johannesburg. Lewis still follows the fortunes of his two favourite teams, Manchester United and the O's.

SEASON	LEAGUE		FA CUP		L. CUP	
	Apps	Gls	Apps	Gls	Apps	Gls
1958/59	14	2	1	2	-	-
1959/60	13	0	0	0	-	-
1960/61*	17	2	3	2	0	0
1961/62	41	1	4	0	3	0
1962/63	28	0	4	0	2	0
1963/64	30	0	3	0	1	0
TOTAL	143	5	15	4	6	0

TOTAL APPS	164
TOTAL GOALS	9

* The League Cup commenced in 1960/61.

James Leonard LEWIS, 1950-51

Born in Hackney, London on 26 June 1927, centre forward Jim Lewis signed for O's on amateur forms in November 1950, while playing for Walthamtow Avenue, who had first priority on his services. Lewis was a regular England amateur international player, having been capped 49 times, and he also represented Great Britain in the Olympic Games. He cut his ties with O's in May 1951, but continued to play well for Avenue, and then signed for Chelsea on amateur forms in September 1952. He spent six years at Stamford Bridge, making 90 League appearances and scoring 38 goals. He also won a League Championship medal in 1954/55. He returned to Avenue in May 1958, seeing out his football career with them.

SEASON	LEAGUE		FA CUP		TOTAL	
	Apps	Gls	Apps	Gls	Apps	Gls
1950/51	4	0	0	0	4	0
TOTAL	4	0	0	0	4	0

John George LEWIS, 1972-74

Born in Hackney, London on 9 May 1954, John Lewis, a small midfielder, was a former England youth international. He played for O's juniors, having previously been on Tottenham Hotspur's groundstaff. He was a lively and energetic performer and, for a short period, he was on the fringe of O's first team. However, he never quite made the grade. Lewis

293

made his League debut as a playing substitute in the 3-2 win over Sheffield Wednesday on 25 November 1972, and his only other first-team appearance came as a substitute in a 1-0 win over Brighton & Hove Albion the following month. In May 1974 he joined Southern League side Romford, and later turned out for both Walthamstow Avenue and Tilbury.

SEASON	LEAGUE		FA CUP		L. CUP	
	Apps	Gls	Apps	Gls	Apps	Gls
1972/73	0(2)	0	0	0	0	0
TOTAL	0(2)	0	0	0	0	0

TOTAL APPS	0(2)
TOTAL GOALS	0

Edward LIDDELL, 1907-13

Ned Liddell was born in Sunderland on 27 May 1878. He was a strong and powerful centre half, who weighed 12st 6lb and stood 6ft tall. He graduated through the local Wearside Leagues with East End Blackwatch FC in 1901, and then with Whitburn FC and Seaham White Stars (1903), while at the same time working for Wearside Shipyards. He signed for Sunderland in 1904, but never played any first-team games at Roker Park. He was about to sign for Lincoln City when he heard that Southern Leaguers Southampton wanted to give him a trial, and he signed for them in August 1905. After playing a single Southern League match at the Dell in January 1906 – a 9-1 win over Northampton Town – he moved on to Gainsborough Trinity in August 1906. He spent a year there, making 10 League appearances, before becoming an 'Oriental' in July 1907. He played at left half at first, but he soon settled in at centre half to form the wonderful defensive trio of Hind-Liddell-Willis, who were a prominent force for several seasons. During 1909/10 he was chosen to keep goal in a League match at Glossop North End on 13 November 1909, when both the O's goalkeepers Bower and Whittaker were injured – O's lost 3-1. After half-a-dozen seasons at Millfields Road, he joined Southend United in October 1913, appearing 26 times. He was then transferred to Arsenal on 1 September 1914, where he made 2 League and 46 reserve appearances, scoring twice for the Gunners. He also featured in 68 wartime football matches. After the First World War, he was appointed manager at Southend United in July 1919, and he also made a Southern League appearance as a player. He managed QPR in 1923/24, and then became Fulham scout in 1924, before becoming manager in 1929. He was West Ham United's assistant manager and scout from 1931, before his appointment as manager of Luton Town between August 1936 and February 1938. He later scouted for Chelsea, Portsmouth, and Brentford. Ned Liddell eventually retired in January 1966, after serving Tottenham Hotspur as scout for over twenty years. He died in Redbridge, Essex on 22 November 1968, aged ninety.

SEASON	LEAGUE		FA CUP		TOTAL	
	Apps	Gls	Apps	Gls	Apps	Gls
1907/08	30	0	3	0	33	0
1908/09	35	0	1	0	36	0
1909/10	27	1	1	0	28	1
1910/11	37	2	1	0	38	2
1911/12	35	0	1	0	36	0
1912/13	29	0	1	0	30	0
1913/14	0	0	0	0	0	0
TOTAL	193	3	8	0	201	3

John Gilbert Hay LIDDELL, 1944-46

Born in Edinburgh on 17 April 1915, John Liddell moved south of the Border to join Bolton Wanderers as a wartime guest player during the 1943/44 season. He joined O's in February 1944, and scored on his debut – a 5-1 defeat at Millwall in a wartime match on 12 February. He made 61 wartime appearances and scored 3 goals for O's between 1944 and 1946. After being demobbed he returned home to Scotland, before joining Bolton Wanderers in September 1946, spending seven months in their reserve side. He joined Brighton & Hove Albion in March 1947, but after just 4 League outings and a single goal, he joined Gravesend & Northfleet in September 1947. In June 1948 he moved to newly formed Hastings United, appearing in their first ever Southern League fixture at Tonbridge. John Liddell died in 1986, aged seventy-one.

SEASON	LEAGUE		FA CUP		TOTAL	
	Apps	Gls	Apps	Gls	Apps	Gls
1945/46*	-	-	2	0	2	0
TOTAL	-	-	2	0	2	0

* The League re-commenced in 1946/47, after the Second World War.

John LILLIE, 1925-26

Full-back John Lillie was born in Newcastle-upon-Tyne, Staffordshire. He started off with Liverpool, before moving to Queens Park Rangers in July 1924, making 3 League appearances. He joined O's in July 1925, and had early opportunities in the side in both full-back positions. He made his League debut in a 3-1 defeat at Derby County in August 1926, and his final appearance came in the 4-1 defeat at Preston North End in December 1925. Lillie moved to Blyth Spartans in August 1926, and then to New Brighton in October 1926.

SEASON	LEAGUE		FA CUP		TOTAL	
	Apps	Gls	Apps	Gls	Apps	Gls
1925/26	5	0	0	0	5	0
TOTAL	5	0	0	0	5	0

Martin LING, 1996-2001

Martin Ling, a midfielder with great balance, captured the imagination of all O's fans with a display of sparkling performances in 1997/98. His excellent passing showed he had recaptured the form which had made him a top-class Premiership player a few years before. This form earned him a place in the PFA Division Three team of 1998, and also made him O's Player of the Year. Born in West Ham, London on 15 July 1966, he started as a junior with the Hammers, but gained his apprenticeship at Exeter City in January 1984, going on to make

Martin Ling

109(8) League appearances and score 14 goals. He joined Swindon Town for £25,000 in July 1986, but after just 3(1) senior appearances, he moved on to Southend United for £15,000 on 16 October 1986. He had a wonderful spell, scoring 31 goals from 126(12) games. After a loan spell with Mansfield Town in January 1991 (which lasted just 3 matches), he returned to Swindon Town for £15,000 on 28 March 1991, and had 6 wonderful seasons in Wiltshire. He made 132(18) League appearances and scored 10 goals, and also won the Man of the Match award in Swindon's Division One play-off final at Wembley Stadium in 1995. Ling joined O's on a free transfer on 22 July 1996. He did not play well in his first season, under the tactics of O's manager Pat Holland, but under new boss Tommy Taylor, he seemed to blossom, and was ever-present in 1997/98, playing in all 52 senior matches. At the age of thirty-three, Ling found his form again, and was one of the stars when O's climbed up the League table in their push for promotion in 1998/99. He also performed well in O's second-half fight-back in the play-off final against Scunthorpe at Wembley in May 1999, and will be remembered for one remarkable clearance off the line, but to no avail, as O's went down 1-0. He continued in the line-up for the 1999/2000 season, even though it was reported that he would mostly sit on the bench. Ling was sent off in a last-minute incident during O's Worthington Cup first round second leg tie against Swindon Town in August 1999, and scored the winner at Rotherham on 13 November 1999 to end O's terrible run of matches without a win. Due to a large number of youth players having

their chance in the side, he had talks to return to Swindon Town in January 2000, but refusing terms, he instead joined Brighton & Hove Albion on a short-term contract on 23 March 2000, making 3(6) senior appearances and scoring once. O's fans were happy to read that Ling rejoined O's on 6 June 2000, as youth-team coach, as well as being on non-contract terms, should the need arise for first-team duty. To stay match-fit, he went on loan with Purfleet in February 2001 – the situation of a League team coach playing elsewhere was not unique, as another former 'Oriental' Paul Raynor combined a coaching job at Sheffield United and playing for non-League Boston United. His O's under-19 youth side won the FA Alliance Cup final over Bradford City (1-0) at the Millennium Stadium, Cardiff on 22 April 2001. Ling made a total of 639(55) senior appearances with 75 goals in a playing career that spanned some sixteen years. LIng was appointed assistant manager to Paul Brush on 15 October 2001 after the resignation of Tommy Taylor.

SEASON	LEAGUE		FA CUP		L. CUP	
	Apps	Gls	Apps	Gls	Apps	Gls
1996/97	39(5)	1	2	0	2	0
1997/98	46	2	2	0	4	0
1998/99*	47	4	5	0	4	0
1999/2000	14	1	0(1)	0	3	0
2000/01	0	0	0	0	0	0
TOTAL	146(5)	8	9(1)	0	13	0

TOTAL APPS	168(6)
TOTAL GOALS	8

* Martin Ling's League record includes 3 promotion play-off matches in 1998/99.

** Ling also appeared in 2 Auto Windscreens Shield matches, scoring once.

Paul Hayden LINGER, 1997-98

Paul Linger was born in Stepney, London on 20 December 1974. The diminutive midfielder stood just 5ft 6in tall, and came to O's on a month-by-month contract from Charlton Athletic on 24 September 1997. He started off his career with the Addicks as a junior in July 1991, making 5(18) League appearances and scoring once, before breaking his leg in April 1997. Linger made a single full appearance for O's – against Notts County in November 1997 – and he was released a month later, joining Brighton & Hove Albion on 17 December 1997. After an impressive debut, he made 17(2) League appearances, before being released in May 1998. He then joined Welling United in July 1998, but was placed on the transfer list after manager Kevin Hales was unhappy with Linger's attitude to being placed on the bench. He joined Billericay Town in 1998 and moved to Ryman League side Purfleet in July 1999, where he has made over 100 appearances up to the end of February 2002. He also appears in Sky's *Dream Team* programme.

Malcolm Linton

SEASON	LEAGUE		FA CUP		L. CUP	
	Apps	Gls	Apps	Gls	Apps	Gls
1997/98	1(2)	0	0(1)	0	0	0
TOTAL	1(2)	0	0(1)	0	0	0

TOTAL APPS	1(3)
TOTAL GOALS	0

Malcolm Wilton LINTON, 1972-75

Malcolm Linton – the son of Falkirk-born Tom Linton, who played 68 League matches for Southend United between 1946 and 1948 – joined O's in August 1968 from Southend United, where he had been an amateur, but he could never follow in his father's footsteps at Roots Hall. He previously had a spell with West Ham United juniors. Born in Southend-on-Sea on 13 February 1952, the tall, well-built central defender signed after a short trial, and got his chance in December 1972 in the 3-1 defeat at Queens Park Rangers, when both Peter Bennett and Phil Hoadley were injured. He was a reasonable defender, if a bit limited to play at League level. In December 1974 he was loaned to Bath City, and then left O's to play for Tampa Bay Rowdies in America during March 1975.

SEASON	LEAGUE		FA CUP		L. CUP	
	Apps	Gls	Apps	Gls	Apps	Gls
1972/73	11	0	1	0	0	0
1973/74	2(5)	0	2	0	0(1)	0
1974/75	1	0	0	0	0	0
TOTAL	14(5)	0	3	0	0(1)	0

TOTAL APPS	17(6)
TOTAL GOALS	0

L

Walter James LITTLE, 1929-30

Born on 9 November 1897 in Southall, Middlesex, Wally Little joined Southern League side Brighton & Hove Albion for a reserve-team trial in August 1919, after his demob from the Army. He signed a permanent contract the following month and stayed for ten years, becoming a great favourite with many excellent displays that endeared him to the Hove fans. Little was small in stature at just 5ft 8in, and was bandy-legged and tenacious with his no-frills style of play. He made his senior debut in the Seagulls' first ever League fixture in the Third Division (South), playing at left-back against Southend United on 28 August 1920. He made 332 senior appearances whilst at the Goldstone Ground, scoring 36 goals. He was credited with having converted 26 penalties – a club record. He joined O's on a free transfer in May 1929, aged thirty-two, and made his debut in a 3-1 defeat at Brentford that September. He finally decided to call it a day the following May, due to injury. Little died in Exeter, Devon on 15 August 1976, aged seventy-eight.

SEASON	LEAGUE		FA CUP		TOTAL	
	Apps	Gls	Apps	Gls	Apps	Gls
1929/30	24	0	1	0	25	0
TOTAL	24	0	1	0	25	0

Simon Robert LIVETT, 1992-93

Born in Newham on 8 January 1969, Simon Livett stayed a number of seasons with West Ham United, but the creative midfielder only appeared once in the League for the Hammers (against Wolves in September 1990), and was forced out of the match due to a knee injury. His only other competitive senior appearance was as a substitute for Colin

Simon Livett

Foster against Aldershot in a FA Cup tie in January 1991. He joined O's on a free transfer just nine days before the start of the 1992/93 season, having been impresseive in pre-season friendlies. He considered an offer from Exeter City, but Livett wanted to remain in London. He made his League debut against Brighton & Hove Albion in August 1992. Unable to command a regular place, he went on loan to Cambridge United in October 1993. He joined them on a full-time contract in 1994, but spent the latter part of the season with Dagenham & Redbridge on loan. He soon drifted into non-League football, first with Grays and then Billericay. It was Alvin Martin (then manager with Southend United) who gave Livett a chance to revitalise his League career. In July 1998 he came on as a substitute in the Blues' surprise 3-0 win at the Matchroom Stadium in April 1999. He made 19(4)

League appearances and scored once, before joining Conference side Dover Athletic on 29 January 2000, where he appeared just once as a substitute, before joining Boston United in June 2000 and making 2(4) Conference appearances. He then took up an offer to play in Chicago, USA, before returning home to England in December 2001 to play for Ford United.

SEASON	LEAGUE		FA CUP		L. CUP	
	Apps	Gls	Apps	Gls	Apps	Gls
1992/93	16(7)	0	2	0	2	0
1993/94	0(1)	0	0	0	0	0
TOTAL	16(8)	0	2	0	2	0

TOTAL APPS	20(8)
TOTAL GOALS	0

* Simon Livett also appeared in 1 Auto Windscreens Shield match, scoring once.

Allan LIVINGSTONE, 1927 (trial)

Over the course of twelve years, Allan Livingstone was on the books of, or on trial with, no less than seventeen clubs. Born in Alexandria, Dumbartonshire, Scotland on 2 December 1899, the inside forward started as an amateur with Vale United, and then went on to Dumbarton Harps. In March 1922 he joined Hull City, making a single League appearance – against Clapton Orient at Millfields Road on 3 February 1923, O's won 2-0. He then did the rounds with Crewe Alexandra, Scunthorpe, Lindsay United, Hartlepool United, New Brighton, Merthyr Town, Swansea Town, Ayr United, East Fife, Walsall, Colwyn Bay United, Chester, Mansfield Town and Stockport County between 1922 and 1936. A forward in his early days, he later tried his hand at half-back and at centre half. His one and only appearance for O's was at Blackpool on 11 December 1926 – O's lost 6-0. His best spells were with Merthyr Town (where he made 25 League appearances and scored 3 goals) and with Mansfield Town (where he scored once in 43 League appearances). In total, he made 80 League appearances throughout his career and scored 5 goals. He was the younger brother of Dougald Livingstone, a Glasgow Celtic and Everton defender, who went on to become the well-known manager of Newcastle United, Fulham and Chesterfield during the 1950s.

SEASON	LEAGUE		FA CUP		TOTAL	
	Apps	Gls	Apps	Gls	Apps	Gls
1926/27	1	0	0	0	1	0
TOTAL	1	0	0	0	1	0

Matthew LOCKWOOD, 1998-present

Matt Lockwood, a talented and highly rated left-wing back and midfield player, joined O's from Bristol Rovers on a free transfer on 7 August 1998, having turned down an approach from Division One side Bury. Lockwood has proved to be a versatile and talented player as well as a creator of goals, and his accurate crosses have provided many opportunities for the strikers. More recently he has become known as a deadly penalty taker. Born in Rochford, near Southend-on-Sea on 17 October 1976, he spent six years with West Ham as a schoolboy, but served his apprenticeship with Southend United. He was offered a contract by Queens Park Rangers on 2 May 1995, although he did not figure in the first team at Loftus Road. He was one of three QPR players recruited by Bristol Rovers' new manager Ian Holloway (a former

Matt Lockwood

Rangers player himself) on 24 July 1996. Lockwood made a total of 66(6) senior appearances with Rovers, scoring once against Wycombe, and turned in some outstanding performances, both at left-back and on the left of midfield. Quite remarkably, his first season with O's saw him face his old club, Bristol Rovers, twice – in the League Cup and FA Cup. Rover's loss has undoubtedly been O's gain: he has given the O's good balance by offering astute defensive qualities and an attacking option down the left flank, and he proved to be one of the star players of the 1998/99 season. He played well in O's 1-0 defeat by Scunthorpe at Wembley in the play-off final in May 1999, and was rewarded with a new two-year contract in April 2000. The highly-rated player is now valued in the £1 million bracket, and could become O's highest incoming transfer since the £600,000 deal with Notts County for John Chiedozie

back in August 1981. It was reported (but unconfirmed) that during February 2001, the club turned down a £750,000 offer from Reading, and that Lockwood was being watched by Charlton Athletic, Ipswich Town, Tottenham Hotspur and West Ham United. However, there have many been stories about Lockwood moving on, yet, unless a very large offer comes in, it is unlikely that he will be moving on. Lockwood was rewarded for his consistent play by being named in the PFA Division Three team of the 2000/01 season. It was his stunning goal against Hull City that took O's to the play-off final against Blackpool at the Millennium Stadium in Cardiff, where they unfortunately lost 4-2. The new season was unsettling for Lockwood – he went on trial with Millwall, but O's turned down their £150,000 offer. Unfortunately, he suffered a serious injury at York City on 25 August, and a scan revealed a ruptured spleen. He was later informed that he could have died, as the doctors had failed to diagnose the rupture for two days. Lockwood made a welcome return when coming on a substitute in a 1-1 draw at Exeter City on 24 November 2001. In January 2002, Lockwood was placed on the transfer list. After trials with both Sheffield Wednesday and Peterborough United, he returned to Brisbane Road and regained his place in the first-team squad. To the delight of all, he signed a new two-year contract in March 2002.

SEASON	LEAGUE		FA CUP		L. CUP	
	Apps	Gls	Apps	Gls	Apps	Gls
1998/99*	39(1)	3	4	0	2	0
1999/2000	41	6	2	0	4	2
2000/01**	34(1)	7	4	0	4	0
2001/02	20(4)	2	1	0	1	0
TOTAL	134(6)	21	11	0	11	2

| TOTAL APPS | 156(6) |
| TOTAL GOALS | 21 |

* Matt Lockwood's League record includes 3 promotion play-off appearances in 1998/99.

** Lockwood's League record includes 3 promotion play-off appearances in 2000/01 and an LDV Vans Trophy match in 2000/01.

William LOMAS, 1913-14

Willie Lomas was born in Pendelton, Lancashire on 4 July 1885. The lively centre forward started his career with Heywood United in 1908, before moving to Burnley in 1909, where he notched 21 goals in 36 games. He joined Bury in 1910, and made 15 First Division appearances. He became an 'Oriental' in June 1913 (joining from York City) and was given a run in the first team during October 1913, but he had to be content to play reserve football a lot of the time. However, he did gain a winner's medal for his appearance in the final of the London Challenge Cup in 1913. Lomas joined Tranmere Rovers in August 1914, playing a further 25 League matches and finding the net twice. He played for Manchester City during wartime, scoring 23 goals from 45 appearances. He died in Pendelton on 17 June 1976.

SEASON	LEAGUE		FA CUP		TOTAL	
	Apps	Gls	Apps	Gls	Apps	Gls
1913/14	5	0	0	0	5	0
TOTAL	5	0	0	0	5	0

Lionel Arthur LOUCH, 1908-10

L.A. Louch was born in Brentford, Middlesex on 4 July 1888, and he was to become O's first international player – albeit at amateur level. Louch was one of the most prominent amateur players of his era to play in the League. He started

with Southall Schools, but his senior career started with Shepherds Bush FC. He then joined Southern League side Portsmouth on 23 November 1907, where he made 56 senior appearances that yielded 23 goals. He joined O's in December 1908 and stayed for two seasons. He scored on his debut in a 1-1 draw against Barnsley on Christmas Day 1908. The stylish forward gained his England amateur caps against Sweden (1909), France and Denmark (1910). He gained further caps against Wales and Belgium in 1914, scoring 7 international goals. L.A. Louch certainly had the ability to join the paid ranks, but preferred to remain as an amateur. In July 1910 he joined Southend, making 28 Southern League appearances and scoring 9 goals. He returned to play for Pompey between 1912 and 1915. He died in February 1967, aged seventy-nine.

SEASON	LEAGUE		FA CUP		TOTAL	
	Apps	Gls	Apps	Gls	Apps	Gls
1908/09	14	5	1	0	15	5
1909/10	22	5	1	0	23	5
TOTAL	36	10	2	0	38	10

Joshua David LOW, 1999

Josh Low joined O's on 27 May 1999. He was a product of Bristol Rovers' youth programme, having joined that club at the age of twelve. Born in Bristol on 15 February 1979, this tall, tricky right-winger made his League debut for Rovers as a last-minute substitute against Wycombe Wanderers on the final day of the 1995/96 season. He obtained a professional contract on 19 August 1996, after just a year as a trainee. He could play in midfield or on either flank, and was an exciting young talent. He proved to be a threat with his pace and ability to

Josh Low

take on defenders, and he could also provide quality crosses into the penalty area. He played for the Welsh youth side in Italy during March 1997. His biggest disappointment was his sending-off at Wigan Athletic in December 1997 after two bookable offences. Three more of his Rovers team-mates were also sent off, thus equalling a League record of four players from one team sent off in the same match. During January 1999 he went on a month's loan to Farnborough, making 4(1) Football Conference appearances and scoring twice. The following month he had a trial with Portsmouth, where it was reported that he impressed, but he returned to Bristol in March. Low made a total of 15(1) senior appearances for Rovers, without finding the net. It was reported that in training Low was one of the most talented players his Rovers' team-mates had ever seen, yet he never could display that talent when it mat-

tered. In League matches he seemed to have a mental block – the fans got on his back and he totally lost his confidence. He joined O's on 27 May 1999 on a free transfer (but with a 50 per cent sell-on clause in the contract) and came on as a substitute during the first match of the 1999/2000 season at Carlisle United in August 1999. He also came on as a substitute at Southend United, yet after just fifteen minutes, he was also substituted – it was a very disappointing and embarrassing start to his O's career. Manager Tommy Taylor sent Low home for a week, as he was homesick. The break seemed to do the trick, and Low looked a different player on his return, showing plenty of pace and skill, and scoring in the 2-1 home win over Hartlepool United on 25 September. Yet, the powers-that-be decided to let him go on loan to Cardiff City on 11 October 1999. He made his debut in a minor cup match at Newtown. The free transfer move became permanent on 18 November 1999. Low has proved to be a great success at Ninian Park, putting in a number of Man of the Match performances for the Welsh club. He helped City in their push for promotion from Division Three, playing in over 50 senior games for the Bluebirds and scoring 6 goals during 2000/01 season. He was rewarded for his fine play by being selected for the PFA Division Three team of the 2000/01 season as a wingback.

SEASON	LEAGUE		FA CUP		L. CUP	
	Apps	Gls	Apps	Gls	Apps	Gls
1999/2000	2(3)	1	0	0	1	0
TOTAL	2(3)	1	0	0	1	0

TOTAL APPS	3(3)
TOTAL GOALS	1

George Richard LUCAS, 1942-46

Londoner Dickie Lucas played for O's juniors in 1942, and he turned out as an amateur towards the end of the Second World War. He could operate either as a wing-half or inside forward, and made 5 wartime appearances for O's. He made his senior debut at centre forward in an FA Cup tie against Newport Isle of Wight on 24 November 1945. O's lost 2-1 and therefore went out of the competition 2-3 on aggregate over the two-legged tie. He left in 1946 and played for both Leyton Amateurs and St Albans. He later turned out for Walthamstow Avenue in 1950, and gave splendid service to the A's for several seasons. He appeared for them in the 1952 Amateur Cup final – a 2-1 win over Leyton – and also appeared in the Avenue team that drew 1-1 at Manchester United in the FA Cup fourth round in 1953.

SEASON	LEAGUE		FA CUP		TOTAL	
	Apps	Gls	Apps	Gls	Apps	Gls
1945/46*	-	-	1	0	1	0
TOTAL	-	-	1	0	1	0

* The League re-commenced after the Second World War in 1946/47.

Oliver Henry LUCAS, 1948-50

Oliver Lucas was born in Paisley, Scotland on 14 January 1923. The full-back joined O's from St Mirren in July 1948, and impressed in two public trial matches when marking Frank Neary. He made his League debut in the final match of the 1948/49 season, a 1-0 defeat against Reading in May. His only other appearance came the following season, in a 2-0 defeat at Aldershot during October 1949. Lucas could never break into the first-team squad, and returned home to Scotland in May 1950.

SEASON	LEAGUE		FA CUP		TOTAL	
	Apps	Gls	Apps	Gls	Apps	Gls
1948/49	1	0	0	0	1	0
1949/50	1	0	0	0	1	0
TOTAL	2	0	0	0	2	0

Peter Malcolm LUCAS, 1958-64

Welshman Mal Lucas, as he was known, was born in Bradley, near Wrexham on 7 October 1938. He started as a youth player with Wrexham, and after a short trial with Bolton Wanderers, he returned to Wales to play for Bradley Rangers in the Wrexham & District League, and also gained Welsh youth caps. The half-back joined Liverpool on trial, playing a few reserve games, but on the recommendation of friend Cyril Lea, he came to O's for a trial in August 1958, signing professional forms on 5 September 1958. Lucas progressed rapidly, excelling as a quick-tackling and hard-working player. He didn't score many goals, but did grab one in a friendly game against German side Wormatia Worms: a 5-1 victory in 1960/61. Lucas formed part of arguably O's best half-back line (Lucas-Bishop-Lea) that played such an important role in O's promotion to the First Division in 1962. He gained his first of 4 full Welsh caps in 1962 against Northern Ireland – the other caps came against Mexico (1962), Scotland and England (1963). He was transferred to Norwich City in September 1964 for £15,000, with full-back Colin Worrell coming to Brisbane Road. Lucas made 201(3) senior appearances at Carrow Road, scoring 10 goals. He moved to Torquay United in March 1970, and stayed for four seasons, making 118(4) League matches and scoring 3 goals. He retired in 1964, having made a career total of 454(7) League appearances from which he'd scored 17 goals. A few years ago he assisted Dale Gordon, the manager at Gorleston, but more recently he has been living in the Norwich area and working for Brent Leisure.

SEASON	LEAGUE		FA CUP		L. CUP	
	Apps	Gls	Apps	Gls	Apps	Gls
1958/59	17	0	1	0	-	-
1959/60	3	0	0	0	-	-
1960/61*	13	0	1	0	1	0
1961/62	42	3	4	0	3	0
1962/63	37	0	2	0	3	0
1963/64	40	3	3	0	1	0
1964/65	5	0	0	0	0	0
TOTAL	157	6	11	0	8	0

TOTAL APPS	176
TOTAL GOALS	6

* The League Cup commenced in 1960/61.

Thomas LUCAS, 1933-34

Born in St Helens on 20 September 1895, left-back Tommy Lucas started his football career with a number of junior clubs: Sherdley Villa, Sutton Commercial, Heywood United, Peasley Cross and Eccles Borough. He joined Manchester United on trial in March 1916, making 3 appearances in a Lancashire tournament after the First World War, before signing for Liverpool, for whom he played regularly for thirteen years. His League debut was on 13 September 1919, and his final appearance was against Arsenal on 22 October 1932. Lucas made a total of 366 senior appearances whilst at Anfield and scored 3 goals. He won 3 England caps and appeared 4 times for an England League XI. O's manager David Pratt (who had played in the same Liverpool side as Lucas) signed the thirty-seven-year-old veteran early in the 1933/34 campaign. He made his debut in

a 3-0 defeat at Norwich City in August 1933, but, unfortunately, age caught up with him and Walter Keen replaced him in the side. Lucas was appointed manager of O's nursery club Ashford Town in May 1934. On leaving fulltime football, he became a licensee in Stoke Mandeville, Buckinghamshire in 1935. He stayed in the area for eighteen years until he died on 11 December 1953, aged fifty-eight.

SEASON	LEAGUE		FA CUP		TOTAL	
	Apps	Gls	Apps	Gls	Apps	Gls
1933/34	21	0	4	0	25	0
TOTAL	21	0	4	0	25	0

Dominic James LUDDEN, 1992-94

Dom Ludden's decision to turn his back on a university place to try and make it as a professional footballer certainly paid off during his early career, but in recent seasons he has battled with a number of injuries. Whilst most footballers spend their time passing a ball around, Ludden was just as good at passing exams gaining 10 GCSEs and 4 A-levels. Born in Basildon, Essex on 30 March 1974, he first hit the headlines as a sixteen-year-old with Billericay in the Diadora League. He was invited to train at Tottenham, but turned down the chance to join their YTS Scheme, choosing instead to join O's on a two-year contract. He gained schoolboy international honours for England against Eire at Yeovil in March 1992, and made his O's debut as an eighteen-year-old, when he came on as a substitute against Blackpool. He made his full League debut against Huddersfield Town on 1 September 1992, scoring in the eleventh minute. However, it was to be the only senior goal he ever scored for the club. Ludden was strong in the

Dominic Ludden

SEASON	LEAGUE		FA CUP		L. CUP	
	Apps	Gls	Apps	Gls	Apps	Gls
1992/93	21(3)	1	0	0	0	0
1993/94	29(5)	0	0(1)	0	1	0
TOTAL	50(8)	1	0(1)	0	1	0

TOTAL APPS	51(9)
TOTAL GOALS	1

* Dominic Ludden also appeared in 6 Auto Windscreens Shield matches, scoring once.

Leslie Reginald LUSTED, 1952-54

Born in Reading on 20 September 1931, Leslie Lusted was a member of O's successful junior team of 1949/50, who were unbeaten throughout the season. He usually appeared at outside left. Lusted left O's in 1951 and joined Harwich & Parkeston, however, he returned to Brisbane Road as an amateur in August 1952. He made his League debut at inside left and scored O's fourth goal in a 4-1 win over Walsall in October 1952. He looked set for brighter things, scoring some wonderful goals, but lost form the following season and spent most of his time in the reserves. He was transferred to Aldershot in July 1954, and spent two seasons there, making just 9 League appearances and scoring once. He then moved on to the non-League circuit with Tonbridge, and ended his career playing left-back for both Canterbury FC and Sittingbourne FC.

SEASON	LEAGUE		FA CUP		TOTAL	
	Apps	Gls	Apps	Gls	Apps	Gls
1952/53	19	6	0	0	19	6
1953/54	4	0	0	0	4	0
TOTAL	23	6	0	0	23	6

Albert Thomas LYONS, 1926-30

Born in Hednesford on 5 March 1902, Bert Lyons, a full-back, was signed by O's

tackle and looked good when going forward as a left-wing back. He had a couple of good seasons at O's, and was snapped up by Watford on 7 August 1994 for £100,000. His career at Vicarage Road never quite took off, as he suffered a serious back injury, and made just 28(5) League appearances in four seasons. He moved to Preston North End on a free transfer on 1 July 1998, and made 31(8) League appearances without scoring up to the end of December 2000. He did not appear in the League during 2001, but he did play regularly in the reserves. In May 2001, twenty-seven-year-old Ludden was released from his contract, and on 6 June he signed a two-year deal with Halifax Town, where he eventually made his debut in November 2001, following an injury-prone start to his career with the Shaymen. However, after just 3 starts he injured his knee again and was out for another long period.

boss Peter Proudfoot from the Army in September 1926, and made his League debut the following month against Barnsley. Lyons converted a spot-kick in an FA Cup third round tie against Bristol Rovers at Millfields Road in January 1930. His goal secured the match for O's, after the visitors' Ronnie Dix had crashed a penalty against the bar. This was Lyons' only senior goal. He excelled in O's first season of Third Division (South) football in 1929/30, and was later transferred to Tottenham Hotspur on 30 May 1930. After a couple of seasons languishing in the reserves, he joined Colwyn Bay in August 1932. Lyons died in Great Yarmouth on 9 May 1981, aged seventy-eight.

SEASON	LEAGUE		FA CUP		TOTAL	
	Apps	Gls	Apps	Gls	Apps	Gls
1926/27	16	0	0	0	16	0
1927/28	9	0	0	0	9	0
1928/29	12	0	0	0	12	0
1929/30	39	0	6	1	45	1
TOTAL	76	0	6	1	82	1

Robert James MacDONALD, 1927-29

Bob MacDonald was born in Inverness, Scotland on 25 February 1895. The full-back started his career with local club Inverness Caledonians, before joining Tottenham Hotspur in August 1919 for £25. He made 125 senior appearances for Spurs between 1919 and 1925. MacDonald was in the Spurs side that won the 1921 FA Cup final, but during August 1927 he returned to Scotland for a month's trial with Heart of Midlothian. However, he could not make the first XI,

and returned south of the Border to become an 'Oriental' on 11 October 1927. The thirty-two-year-old defender, although looking reasonable, seemed past his prime and a bit short of pace. Upon his retirement from football, he ran a drapery shop in Glasgow until he died on 1 April 1971, aged seventy-six.

SEASON	LEAGUE		FA CUP		TOTAL	
	Apps	Gls	Apps	Gls	Apps	Gls
1927/28	28	0	1	0	29	0
1928/29	9	0	0	0	9	0
TOTAL	37	0	1	0	38	0

Christopher Neil MacKENZIE, 1997-99

'Macca', as he was known, joined O's from Hereford United on a week-by-week contract on 17 October 1997. The goalkeeper had quite an eventful start to his O's career, saving a penalty in an Auto Windscreen match against Colchester United, when he read Paul Buckle's spot-kick well and dived to his left to palm the ball away. His handling was good despite the difficult conditions that night, and his overall distribution was excellent. O's boss Taylor said of his charge: 'He did very well and proved what a good goalie he could be, and with Hyde and Weaver both injured, Chris was prepared to help us out.' During his League debut at Shrewsbury Town on 13 December 1997, he rushed out of his penalty area in the fifty-fifth minute to parry Devon White's shot, and was shown the red card for deliberate handball – but O's held out to win 2-1. He signed a permanent contract in March 1998. Born in Northampton on 14 May 1972, he started his career with Corby Town, before joining Hereford United on 20 July 1994 for £15,000. He was voted the Player of the Year at Edgar Street, and played 65(1) senior matches for

Chris Mackenzie

SEASON	LEAGUE		FA CUP		L. CUP	
	Apps	Gls	Apps	Gls	Apps	Gls
1997/98	4	0	0	0	0	0
1998/99	26	0	5	0	3	0
TOTAL	30	0	5	0	3	0

TOTAL APPS	38
TOTAL GOALS	0

* Chris Mackenzie also appeared in 2 Auto Windscreens Shield matches.

Joseph MALLETT, 1953-55

Born in Dunstan-on-Tyne, Gateshead on 8 January 1916, Joe Mallett started his career with Dunstan CWS, before joining Charlton Athletic in November 1936, where he made a handful of League matches. He went on loan to Queens Park Rangers between April 1937 and May 1938, eventually signing for £800 in February 1939. He made a total of 70 League appearances and scored 11 goals. The wing-half moved to Southampton for £5,000 in February 1947, and was very successful in the side that just missed out on promotion three times. He made 223 senior appearances for the Hampshire club, scoring 3 goals. He joined O's in July 1953 at the age of thirty-seven, yet when called upon he displayed constructive, clever and methodical ability. He made his debut at Exeter City in August 1953, and also had a superb match in O's FA Cup fifth round tie against Doncaster Rovers in February 1954. The following year he was appointed as coach, and continued to play in the reserve side. He joined Nottingham Forest as coach in September 1954 and stayed for three years, before returning to Brisbane Road as coach in June 1957. He had further successful coaching spells with Nottingham Forest (from July 1959) and with Birmingham City. He was coach

Hereford, and even scored a goal! Macca's goal came in the first game of the 1995/96 season against Barnet on 12 August 1995. In the forty-fourth minute, he hit a long clearance that bounced over the Barnet 'keeper's head and into the net. He was only the tenth goalkeeper to score from his own penalty area since the Second World War (Peter Shilton was another to achieve this feat). Mackenzie was ever-present during the 1998/99 season, until suffering a loss of form which caused him to flap at crosses and high balls into the area. This prompted O's boss Taylor to sign Scott Barrett from Cambridge United. He went on a short loan spell to Nuneaton Borough, but returned to the club during March 1999, before being released during May 1999. He had an unsuccessful trial at Plymouth Argyle in July 1999, and he eventually returned to Nuneaton Borough that August, playing 75 senior matches up to the end of 2000/01.

and manager at St Andrews between June 1964 and December 1965. He then went on to coach the Panionios club in Greece (August 1970), the Washington Diplomats (August 1975), and the San Jose Earthquakes (1982). The following year he returned to the England to become chief scout at Southampton. Mallett had since retired, and now lives in St Leonards, Sussex.

SEASON	LEAGUE		FA CUP		TOTAL	
	Apps	Gls	Apps	Gls	Apps	Gls
1953/54	23	1	3	0	26	1
1954/55	4	0	0	0	4	0
TOTAL	27	1	3	0	30	1

Michael Leonard MANCINI, 1984

Born in Hammersmith, London on 8 June 1956, Mike Mancini was the younger brother of former 'Oriental' favourite Terry Mancini. He joined O's in March 1984 on a non-contract basis from Fulham, for whom he had only made reserve outings. The midfielder was given a couple of opportunities, making his League debut in a 2-0 defeat at Port Vale on 9 April 1984. He played again the following week in a 3-1 loss at Preston North End. He was not kept on and retired from the game to go into commerce.

SEASON	LEAGUE		FA CUP		L. CUP	
	Apps	Gls	Apps	Gls	Apps	Gls
1983/84	2	0	0	0	0	0
TOTAL	2	0	0	0	0	0

TOTAL APPS	2
TOTAL GOALS	0

Terence John MANCINI, 1967-71

In October 1967, Terry Mancini walked into the office of O's boss Dick Graham with a letter from old friend Cliff Holton, asking for a trial. Three years later he captained the side that won promotion as champions to the Second Division. Later in his career, he gained 5 Eire international caps whilst at Queens Park Rangers and Arsenal. He was born in Camden Town, London on 4 October 1942. After a brief association with Fulham, he joined Watford as a junior in September 1959, turning professional in July 1961. The tall centre half made 75(1) senior appearances for the Hertfordshire club. In 1965 he was one of a number of British players who received attractive offers to play in South Africa, and he skippered Port Elizabeth FC to the championship. When he wanted to return to England, he contacted O's because three former colleagues who played with him in South Africa were on their books – namely Tom Anderson, Roger Hugo (on trial) and Eddie Werge. Mancini impressed Graham, and within two

Terry Mancini

weeks he had signed a contract, and so began his long association with O's. He was skipper for nearly four seasons up to the championship year in 1970. He broke a leg on 31 January 1970 against Tranmere Rovers, but, remarkably, he returned just two months later to lead the side on to the championship. The broken leg ended a run of 105 consecutive League outings. On 16 October 1971 he signed for Queens Park Rangers for £30,000, and went on to make 94 League appearances and score 3 goals. It was whilst at Loftus Road that he won the first of his international caps. During October 1974 came the surprise announcement that he had signed for Arsenal for £22,500, and he played 52 League matches for the Gunners, scoring once. Between April and August 1977, he played in the USA for the Los Angeles Aztecs. Mancini later held a coaching position at Fulham in September 1978, and was assistant manager at Luton Town in 1989, as well as acting as a scout for Blackburn Rovers. After retirement from football, he ran a car hire business, but for the past eight years Mancini has worked for Barwood Leisure, a sports travel company, as their sports events director.

SEASON	LEAGUE		FA CUP		L. CUP	
	Apps	Gls	Apps	Gls	Apps	Gls
1967/68	31	3	5	1	0	0
1968/69	46	7	2	0	4	0
1969/70	38	4	2	0	2	0
1970/71	42	1	3	0	1	0
1971/72	10	1	0	0	2	0
TOTAL	167	16	12	1	9	0

TOTAL APPS	188
TOTAL GOALS	17

James Anthony MANKELOW, 1982-83

Born on 4 September 1964 in Highams Park, Essex, Jamie Mankelow was a regular goalscorer for O's juniors, before signing a full contract on 1 September 1982. He made his full League debut in a 3-3 draw against Reading on 20 February 1983, although he had come on as a substitute earlier that month against Lincoln City. In truth, he wasn't quite up to League standard, and the striker was released in May 1983, joining Walthamstow Avenue. He later moved on to play for Epping.

SEASON	LEAGUE		FA CUP		L. CUP	
	Apps	Gls	Apps	Gls	Apps	Gls
1982/83	1(1)	0	0	0	0	0
TOTAL	1(1)	0	0	0	0	0

TOTAL APPS	1(1)
TOTAL GOALS	0

Thomas MANNS, 1934-35

Tommy Manns was born in Eastwood Vale, Rotherham on 2 May 1908. He started off with local side Eastwood United, and then joined big brother club Rotherham United as an amateur in December 1930, playing in their reserve side. In May 1931 the right-back joined Burnley, making 10 League appearances and also winning an East Lancashire Cup winner's medal. He joined Manchester United, along with fellow Burnley goalkeeper Charlie Hillam, in June 1933. Manns had to wait nine months for his League debut at Old Trafford, playing against his old colleagues at Burnley in February 1934. He appeared just once more for the first team, before he and Hillam joined O's in June 1934. He showed his versatility by playing at right-back, left-back and outside right in his

3 League appearances, and scored at Aldershot on 1 May 1935. He left O's in July 1935, joining Carlisle United. There he had a much more successful run of 22 matches, before moving on to Yeovil & Petters United in July 1936.

SEASON	LEAGUE		FA CUP		TOTAL	
	Apps	Gls	Apps	Gls	Apps	Gls
1934/35	3	1	2	0	5	1
TOTAL	3	1	2	0	5	1

* Tommy Manns also appeared in a Third Division Cup match, a 4-0 defeat at Northampton Town on 1 October 1934.

Chad Andrew MANSLEY, 2000/01

Young Aussie striker Chad Mansley came to O's from Watford on a non-contract basis on 7 December 2000. Born on 13 November 1980 in Newcastle, New South Wales, Australia, he played for the Australian schoolboy side whilst he was at Whitebridge High School in Newcastle, gaining 3 caps. He played for the Newcastle Breakers in the Northern Division of the NSW Youth League in 1997/98, and stayed with them for the following two seasons. His only senior appearance for the club was in 1999/2000, before leaving and trying his hand in the English League. He joined Watford and impressed them by scoring 6 goals whilst on trial during the pre-season. They invited him to stay for an extended period, and the striker scored on his debut at Cheshunt in a Herts Senior Cup match on 26 October 2000. He made 6 appearances for the reserves, scoring twice. The twenty-year-old made his O's League debut as a substitute when coming on for Billy Beall in the sixty-first minute of the 1-0 win over Darlington on 16 December 2000. He made a nervous start, which was understandable, but he looked strong and assured in his English senior debut. Four days later, he came on as a substitute in the FA Cup tie against Northwich Victoria on forty-six minutes. The club offered Mansley a contract, but he decided to return home to Australia to continue his career – a decision that coincided with a period of cold weather in England! His last match was against Wycombe Wanderers, a 0-2 defeat in the LDV Vans Trophy on 9 January 2001. He rejoined Newcastle United in NSW, and scored on his debut in mid-March, playing alongside another former 'Oriental' Chris Zoricich.

SEASON	LEAGUE		FA CUP		L. CUP	
	Apps	Gls	Apps	Gls	Apps	Gls
2000/01	0(1)	0	0(1)	0	0	0
TOTAL	0(1)	0	0(1)	0	0	0

TOTAL APPS	0(2)
TOTAL GOALS	0

* Chad Mansley also appeared in 0(1) LDV Vans Trophy match in 2000/01.

Vincent Clifford MANSLEY, 1952-53

Wing-half Cliff Mansley was born in Skipton on 5 April 1921. He started off with Preston North End in September 1940, but never made the first team. He joined Barnsley in November 1945, making 31 League appearances. He moved on to Chester during June 1948, and made a further 22 appearances, before dropping out of the League with Yeovil. He joined O's in July 1952, making his debut in a 4-1 win over Torquay in September 1952. He did quite well for a short period with his mixture of constructive and tenacious play, but soon found it difficult to dislodge first-teamers Deverall, Blizzard,

Cliff Mansley

Brown and McMahon. He moved back into non-League football in May 1953.

SEASON	LEAGUE		FA CUP		TOTAL	
	Apps	Gls	Apps	Gls	Apps	Gls
1952/53	10	0	0	0	10	0
TOTAL	10	0	0	0	10	0

John William MARGERRISON, 1979-82

Born on 20 October 1955 in Bushey, Hertfordshire, he started as an apprentice with Tottenham Hotspur, gaining a FA Youth Cup winner's medal when Spurs defeated Huddersfield Town in the 1974 final. His opportunities were limited at White Hart Lane, so he moved on to Fulham in July 1975, making his League debut in April 1976. He made 70(9) senior appearances at Craven Cottage and scored 11 goals, playing his final match against O's in April 1979. Jimmy Bloomfield persuaded him to come to Brisbane Road in July 1979, and he signed for £65,000. Despite appearing somewhat slow and cumbersome, he was a constructive midfield player with good ball distribution, getting through a good deal of work. He spent three seasons at Brisbane Road, and perhaps his best display was in November 1981 in a 3-0 victory over Sheffield Wednesday. He left O's in May 1982 to play in the USA with Kansas City Comets. Upon his return to England, he joined Borehamwood. He later played for Wealdstone, before enjoying a long career with non-League Barnet, for whom he made 194(4) appearances. He was capped at England semi-professional level against Wales in March 1987. Margerrison broke his leg in 1987 and left football to work in his father's sign-writing business. More recently, he has been playing football again with Brache Sparta FC in the South Midlands League and played cricket for Elstree in 1998. He also turned out in a few games for Harrow Borough in January 2001, aged forty-four.

John Margerrison

Margerrison (right) scores for O's

scoring 10 goals. He is reported to be the youngest ever Lion's player to score a hat-trick. Mike Marks came to O's from the Den for £25,000 in February 1988, after he had a brief loan spell with Mansfield Town, where he'd made a single substitute appearance. The striker made his debut in the 2-1 win over Wrexham on 27 February 1988, but had a continuous string of injuries and illnesses whilst at Brisbane Road. It would be fair to say that he was one of the unluckiest footballers of his time, and never fulfilled the early potential he showed whilst at the Den. He moved to Fisher Athletic in May 1989.

SEASON	LEAGUE		FA CUP		L. CUP	
	Apps	Gls	Apps	Gls	Apps	Gls
1987/88	3	0	0	0	0	0
1988/89	0	0	0	0	0	0
TOTAL	3	0	0	0	0	0

TOTAL APPS	3
TOTAL GOALS	0

His midfield partner in the side was another former 'Oriental' – forty-eight-year-old Barry Silkman.

SEASON	LEAGUE		FA CUP		L. CUP	
	Apps	Gls	Apps	Gls	Apps	Gls
1979/80	22(2)	2	1	0	2	1
1980/81	21(1)	1	0	0	1	0
1981/82	34	3	5	0	2	0
TOTAL	77(3)	6	6	0	5	1

TOTAL APPS	88(3)
TOTAL GOALS	7

* John Margerrison also appeared in 2 Anglo-Scottish Cup matches, scoring twice, and also appeared in a Football League Groups Cup match.

Michael David MARKS, 1988-89
Born in Waterloo, London on 23 March 1968, Marks became an apprentice with Millwall in 1985. He did quite well with the Lions, playing 36 League matches and

Mike Marks

* Michael Marks also appeared in 0(1) Auto Windscreens Shield match.

Alvin Edward MARTIN, 1996-97

On 1 July 1996 O's boss Pat Holland and chairman Barry Hearn unveiled two veteran signings from West Ham United to the press – Alvin Martin and Les Sealey. Thirty-six-year-old Martin – one of West Ham's all-time greats – signed a one-year contract, and was installed as club captain. In twenty wonderful years at Upton Park, he had made 463(7) League and 110 cup appearances, and scored 33 goals. He also gained 17 England international caps, making his debut against Brazil in May 1981. The central defender was born in Bootle on 29 July 1958. He arrived at Upton Park as a schoolboy in 1974, having impressed for Bootle and Lancashire schoolboys, but having been turned down by his local club, Everton. He played in the Hammers side that reached the FA Youth Cup final in 1975, and signed professional forms on 29 July 1976, making his League debut at Aston Villa during March 1978. His last few seasons at Upton Park were punctuated by injuries, but somehow he continued to defy his age. He made his O's debut against Scunthorpe United on 12 August 1996, however, with the sacking of boss Holland in October and the appointment of Tommy Taylor, the new 'gaffer' was not at all impressed with either of his two veterans. In a match at Doncaster Rovers on 5 October 1996, Martin had to come off the field after thirty minutes, grimacing in pain. It seemed to the fans that perhaps the time was right for him to retire, but he carried on a little longer. His final match for O's was at Wigan Athletic on 25 January 1997, and he had made a total of more than 600 senior appearances dur-

Alvin Martin

ing his career. Martin was appointed manager of Southend United on 15 July 1997, but they struggled under his leadership and he resigned at the end of March 1999. More recently, he was a *Talk Sport* presenter.

SEASON	LEAGUE		FA CUP		L. CUP	
	Apps	Gls	Apps	Gls	Apps	Gls
1996/97	16(1)	0	0	0	2	0
TOTAL	16(1)	0	0	0	2	0

TOTAL APPS	18(1)
TOTAL GOALS	0

David MARTIN, 1996

Thirty-three-year-old midfielder Dave Martin looked a basic player when he arrived at Brisbane Road from Gillingham on 30 July 1996, having made 31 appearances as the Kent side won promotion to Division Two during 1996/67. Martin had a long career in the lower divisions, making up for his lack of ability with his motivational and battling qualities. Born in East Ham, London on 25 April 1963, he began his career with Millwall. He turned professional in 1980, and made 131(9) League appearances, scoring 6 goals. He then did the rounds with Wimbledon (who paid £35,000 for his services), Southend United (with whom he stayed for a total of seven years), Bristol City, Northampton and Gillingham. His time at Southend was by far his best period in the League, the Essex side wining promotion three times in five seasons, and he made 212(9) League appearances and netted 19 goals. He also spent time on loan with Colchester United in 1991/92, during their run-in to the Conference title, and appeared in their FA Trophy-winning side in 1993. His stay with O's lasted just four months, and he left when informed by management that he didn't fit into O's style of attacking play. It is believed he received a cash settlement

Dave Martin

before agreeing to end his contract and move on to Northampton Town on a free transfer in October 1996. He then moved to Brighton & Hove Albion in March 1997, making a single League appearance before drifting into non-League football with Welling United. Dave Martin's League career spanned seventeen years, and totalled 462(31) appearances and 31 goals.

SEASON	LEAGUE		FA CUP		L. CUP	
	Apps	Gls	Apps	Gls	Apps	Gls
1996/97	8	0	0	0	2	0
TOTAL	8	0	0	0	2	0

TOTAL APPS	10
TOTAL GOALS	0

Jae Andrew MARTIN, 1994 (loan)

Jae Martin, a lively winger, was born in Hampstead, London on 5 February 1976. The 5ft 9in and 11st midfielder started off as a trainee with Southend United in May 1993, making 1(7) League appearances with the Shrimpers. He joined O's on a month's loan from Southend on 9 September 1994, playing in 4 League matches and making a single appearance in the Auto Windscreen Trophy at Colchester United. He moved on to Birmingham City in July 1995, playing a further 1(6) matches, and then moved on to Lincoln City for £25,000 in August 1996, where he achieved his best run with 27(12) League appearances and 5 goals. He had a disappointing season in 1997/98, after a hernia operation ruled him out, and he was released in 1998. Martin joined Peterborough United on a free transfer in July 1998, playing 7(11) League matches and scoring once. After a loan spell with Grantham between March and May 1999, he moved into the

Conference with Welling United in February 2000, making 14 appearances and scoring 4 goals. June 2000 saw him on the books of Woking, before he joined Moor Green FC on 8 January 2001.

SEASON	LEAGUE		FA CUP		L. CUP	
	Apps	Gls	Apps	Gls	Apps	Gls
1994/95	1(3)	0	0	0	0	0
TOTAL	1(3)	0	0	0	0	0

TOTAL APPS	1(3)
TOTAL GOALS	0

* Jae Martin also appeared in an Auto Windscreens Shield match.

John MARTIN, 1997-present

Left-footed midfielder John Martin was born in Bethnal Green, London on 15 July 1981. As a boy, he was selected for England trials, and reached the last thirty at under-16 level. He joined O's on YTS forms in 1995/96, turning professional in July 1998. Martin, although appearing a little lightweight at 5ft 6in tall and just 9st 12lb, made his League debut as a seventeen-year-old, when coming on as a substitute in the ninetieth minute against Scunthorpe United on 21 April 1998. Despite being one of the smallest players in the current League, he is extremely determined and has the skill to beat players on the ball. His full debut came at Chester City on 8 August 1998, where he did not look out of place, yet was subbed in the fifty-second minute. Martin said: 'I enjoyed my first professional outing, I just kept going and got behind the ball, it was great to win 2-0.' In 1998/99 he played 21 times for the youth team, scoring 5 times, and in 1999/2000 he played a further 9 times, and scored twice. He made his debut for the reserve side in

John Martin

1997/98, and played a dozen times in 1999/2000, scoring 3 goals to add to the 4 goals that he notched the previous season. He also scored from the penalty spot in O's 3-0 friendly victory over Antigua in July 2000. He started the 2000/01 season in midfield, but was then left out of the side in favour of more experienced players. However, his chance came later in the campaign to help O's maintain their top six spot, and he came on in the eighty-first minute of the play-off final against Blackpool, but could not do anything to prevent the 4-2 defeat. In 2001/02, Martin came to the fore with some wonderful displays, which have seen him become more of a regular in the first team.

SEASON	LEAGUE		FA CUP		L. CUP	
	Apps	Gls	Apps	Gls	Apps	Gls
1997/98	0(1)	0	0	0	0	0
1998/99	1	0	0	0	2	0

1999/2000	8	0	0	0	0	0
2000/01*	15(4)	0	0	0	3	0
2001/02	29(2)	2	3(1)	0	0	0
TOTAL	53(9)	2	3(1)	0	5	0

TOTAL APPS	61(10)
TOTAL GOALS	2

* John Martin's record includes 0(2) substitute appearances in the play-offs in 2000/2001.

** Martin also appeared in 2 Auto Windscreens Shield matches and 0(1) LDV Vans Trophy match in 2000/01.

William Thomas John MARTIN, 1906-08

Bill Martin, a 5ft 9in defender, arrived from Hull City on a free transfer in May 1906. He went rather unnoticed, and was soon dropped after what was described by the local press as a 'brilliant own goal' at his former club in September 1906. The golden-haired player was converted to centre forward later that season, and went on to net 17 goals. Born in Poplar, London on 27 April 1883, he started his career with junior side Millwall St Johns. He moved to big brother club, Millwall Athletic of the Southern League, in October 1901, and made 21 Southern League appearances, scoring once. He then joined Second Division Hull City in August 1904, where he made 44 League appearances and netted 5 goals. In one spell with O's, he notched 11 goals from just 5 League matches, including a hat-trick against Wolves. During January 1907 he bagged the winner against Hull City, to make up for his 'own goal' earlier that season. During the 1907/08 season he topped the scoring charts again, including scoring another hat-trick against Stockport County. He became a very dangerous striker, and the Stockport directors were so impressed with his play that they signed him for £150 in May 1908. He never quite fulfilled his potential with the Cheshire club, and in February 1909 he joined Oldham Athletic. However, he made just 7 appearances during his three-year stay, before rejoining Millwall in October 1913. Martin died in Stepney, London on 11 December 1954, aged seventy-one.

SEASON	LEAGUE		FA CUP		TOTAL	
	Apps	Gls	Apps	Gls	Apps	Gls
1906/07	30	17	0	0	30	17
1907/08	31	11	3	2	34	13
TOTAL	61	28	3	2	64	30

Craig Dell MASKELL, 1997-99

This much-travelled striker was born in Aldershot on 9 April 1968. He joined O's on 26 March 1998 from the Happy Valley Club in Hong Kong. Craig Maskell was an excellent striker in his day, scoring 132 senior goals from 317(40) appearances. His career spanned some thirteen years and included various spells with Southampton (twice), Huddersfield Town, Reading, Swindon Town, Bristol City, Brighton and Dunfermline Athletic in Scotland. Transfer fees throughout his career totalled £785,000. He proved to be a good utility player, and in a number of matches showed his experience in the way he was able to hold up the ball. He joined O's on a non-contract basis on transfer deadline day in March 1998, and finished the season in spectacular fashion with a goal against Torquay United on 2 May 1998. During March 1999 he held talks with Kingstonian, but ended up remaining at O's. He came on as a substitute in the win at Halifax Town on 26 March 1999 and was praised for his performance, holding the ball up well in

Craig Maskell (right)

Robert Henry MASON, 1963-64

Bobby Mason was born in Tipton on 22 March 1936. He came to O's in March 1963 from Wolverhampton Wanderers (he was on loan with Southern League Chelmsford City at the time) for £20,000, an O's record up to that time. Mason first signed professional forms with Wolves in May 1953, and had a very successful career at Molineux. He made 173 senior appearances and scored 54 goals, and was a member of their championship-winning teams of 1957/58 and 1958/59. However, the inside forward was past his best and very disappointing at Brisbane Road, and he only occasionally showed brief glimpses of his old self. He left O's in March 1964 to join Poole Town, retiring a year later to Bournemouth.

SEASON	LEAGUE		FA CUP		L. CUP	
	Apps	Gls	Apps	Gls	Apps	Gls
1962/63	13	0	0	0	0	0

Bobby Mason

difficult situations. He also played well when coming on as a substitute in O's play-off final match at Wembley against Scunthorpe in May 1999. He was eventually released in May 1999, joining Hampton & Richmond Borough of the Ryman League Premier Division as player-coach, and notched over 30 goals for his new club.

SEASON	LEAGUE		FA CUP		L. CUP	
	Apps	Gls	Apps	Gls	Apps	Gls
1997/98	7(1)	2	0	0	0	0
1998/99*	8(9)	0	0(2)	0	2	0
TOTAL	15(10)	2	0(2)	0	2	0

TOTAL APPS	17(12)
TOTAL GOALS	2

* Craig Maskell's League record includes 0(2) promotion play-off matches in 1998/99.
** Maskell also appeared in an Auto Windscreens Shield match.

1963/64	10	0	0	0	1	0
TOTAL	23	0	0	0	1	0

TOTAL APPS	24
TOTAL GOALS	0

Roy MASSEY, 1967-69

Roy Massey was born in Mexborough, Yorkshire on 9 September 1943. The centre forward came to O's from Rotherham United in September 1967. He represented Yorkshire schools and England grammar schools, whilst he was at St Paul's College in Cheltenham. He was an amateur with Arsenal, but turned down the chance to sign professional forms at Highbury in order to return to Yorkshire. He joined Rotherham in July 1964, after completing his studies to become a schoolteacher. He scored twice on his debut for the Merry Millers at Cardiff City in April 1965, and made 15(1) League appearances for them, scoring 6 goals. Upon joining O's, he combined his football with school teaching at Lake House Junior school in Leyton. He performed very well at Brisbane Road, setting up a lively partnership with Vic Halom, and was top goalscorer in 1967/68. He scored a memorable headed goal against Bury in January 1967 to take Orient into the FA Cup fourth round. The following season he was handicapped through injury, and he could never recapture his earlier form. He moved to Colchester United for £5,000, teaming up with former O's boss Dick Graham in July 1969. He made 30(4) League League appearances and netted 11 goals, before a serious knee injury forced him to give up League football. He later played in the Eastern Counties League with Clacton, and in later years was a youth development officer for Colchester United and a PE master at Thomas Audley's School.

SEASON	LEAGUE		FA CUP		L. CUP	
	Apps	Gls	Apps	Gls	Apps	Gls
1967/68	41(1)	12	5	1	0	0
1968/69	17(4)	1	1	0	4	1
TOTAL	58(5)	13	6	1	4	1

TOTAL APPS	68(5)
TOTAL GOALS	15

Joseph MAYO, 1977-81

Big Joe Mayo came to O's with Allan Glover on 9 March 1977 from West Bromwich Albion, as part of the deal that took Laurie Cunningham to the Hawthorns in a deal worth £135,000. The striker made a significant contribution by forming a wonderful partnership with Peter Kitchen. He proved a great 'target man' in O's FA Cup run to the semi-final during 1977/78, scoring one of the goals against Middlesbrough in the quarter-final. Born in Tipton, Staffordshire on

Roy Massey

Joe Mayo

25 May 1952, he started off with Dudley Town in the Midlands League, having represented both Dudley and Kingswinford Boys whilst at school and working as a trainee accountant. After a trial with Oxford United, he moved to Walsall on a free transfer in August 1972, making just 2(5) League appearances and scoring his only goal on debut as a substitute at Notts County in September 1972. He moved on to West Brom in February 1973 for £10,000, staying for four years and netting 17 goals from 67(5) League matches. He was a member of Jimmy Giles' promotion-winning side, and scored 8 goals which saw them return to the First Division. Both Mayo and Glover scored on their O's League debuts at Blackburn Rovers, but Mayo sustained a bad knee injury that ruled him out for the most of the remainder of the season, although he returned to play in the final two League games. The following season he came to

the fore, and was voted Player of the Year. He proved to be a very versatile clubman, and played in the centre of defence on a few occasions. His wife, Pam, was secretary to O's chairman Brian Winston. He moved on to join Cambridge United in September 1981, making 39(1) senior appearances and scoring 14 goals. After a brief loan spell with Blackpool in October 1982, where he scored once from 5 starts, he went to team up once again with Peter Kitchen at the Happy Valley club in Hong Kong during June 1983. In 2002, 'big Joe' was running a hotel in Criccieth, Wales called the Plas Isa.

SEASON	LEAGUE		FA CUP		L. CUP	
	Apps	Gls	Apps	Gls	Apps	Gls
1976/77	4	1	0	0	0	0
1977/78	35(1)	9	8	2	3	0
1978/79	40	11	3	0	1	0
1979/80	39	11	2	1	2	1
1980/81	32(3)	4	0	0	2	0
1981/82	0(1)	0	0	0	0(1)	0
TOTAL	150(5)	36	13	3	8(1)	1

TOTAL APPS	171(6)
TOTAL GOALS	40

* Joe Mayo also appeared in 9 Anglo-Scottish Cup matches, scoring once, and 2(1) Football League Groups Cup matches.

John Dunnett MAYSON, 1933-36

Born on 24 October 1908 in High Park, Southport, Johnny 'Ginger' Mayson started off with Burscough Rangers, and represented both Southport and Lancashire schools. He turned professional with Bolton Wanderers in April 1932, but played only reserve football. In July 1933 O's boss David Pratt brought him to Lea Bridge Road, and he became a regular in a very impressive O's front line in 1933/34. The right-winger showed a mixture of speed and good skill, and he was in the side that trounced Aldershot 9-2 in February 1934. He also scored a goal in the 5-1 win over Irish side Belfast Celtic FC in 1934/35, but he lost his place to another conspicuously fast little wingman, Idris Miles. In May 1936 he joined Hull City, making 12 senior appearances and scoring 9 goals. In May 1937 he moved on to Tranmere Rovers, and the following year moved to Runcorn. Mayson died in Southport on 22 June 1991, aged eighty-two.

SEASON	LEAGUE		FA CUP		TOTAL	
	Apps	Gls	Apps	Gls	Apps	Gls
1933/34	39	11	4	0	43	11
1934/35	33	10	2	1	35	11
1935/36	7	1	0	0	7	1
TOTAL	79	22	6	1	85	23

* Johnny Mayson also appeared in 5 Third Division Cup matches between 1933 and 1936, scoring once.

Joseph McALEER, 1935-36

Born in Blythswood, Glasgow on 8 March 1910, Joe McAleer started his career with Arbroath. He then moved on to Rochdale in July 1931, and his two seasons at Spotland saw him make 35 League appearances and score 8 goals. After a short spell with Irish club Glenavon, the right-winger moved to Northampton Town in July 1933, notching 6 goals from just 8 starts. In August 1933, Lincoln City was McAleer's next club, where he scored a further 5 goals from 6 appearances. He left to became an 'Oriental' in July 1935, proving to be a dangerous player with a go-ahead style, who liked to cut inside for a shot on goal, as his career record suggests. He stayed only a season before moving on to Gillingham in August 1936, making 9 League appearances and scoring 3 goals.

After a short stay with Brideville FC in July 1937, he ended his career with Wrexham with a single goal from 7 appearances for the 1937/38 season.

SEASON	LEAGUE		FA CUP		TOTAL	
	Apps	Gls	Apps	Gls	Apps	Gls
1935/36	18	4	3	1	21	5
TOTAL	18	4	3	1	21	5

Alan James McCARTHY, 1995-97

Born on 11 January 1972 in Wandsworth, London, Alan McCarthy started as a trainee with QPR in December 1989, making 8(3) League appearances. After loan spells with Watford and Plymouth Argyle during the 1993/94 season, he joined O's on 14 August 1995 for £25,000. He made the highest number of League appearances of any player for O's in 1995/96, but after a fall-out with O's boss Pat Holland, he was placed on the transfer list. However, he was still at the club the following season, under new boss Tommy Taylor, but a groin injury restricted his number of appearances. McCarthy was to go on trial with Northampton Town, but his injury put paid to that. He left O's on 31 May 1997, and drifted out of League football. He trained with Woking, but joined Boreham Wood FC in August 1997, and was still on their books in 2001.

SEASON	LEAGUE		FA CUP		L. CUP	
	Apps	Gls	Apps	Gls	Apps	Gls
1995/96	40(3)	0	0	0	1	0
1996/97	3(1)	0	0	0	1	0
TOTAL	43(4)	0	0	0	2	0

TOTAL APPS	45(4)
TOTAL GOALS	0

* Alan McCarthy also appeared in 2 Auto Windscreens Shield matches.

Sidney Benjamin McCLELLAN, 1958-59

Sid McClellan was born in Dagenham, Essex on 11 June 1925. He started as an amateur with Chelmsford City in 1946, moving to Tottenham Hotspur as a professional in August 1949, where he made 70 senior appearances and scored 32 goals, and was good enough to appear in their championship-winning campaign of 1950/51. Although he did not qualify for a championship medal, he contributed 3 goals from 7 appearances. He was never a regular at White Hart Lane, but he did hit a Spurs record of 9 goals in a game when on tour in the USA and Canada, in a match against Saskatchewan in May 1952 that Spurs won 18-1. Playing mainly reserve team football, he won 2 Football Combination medals – in 1953 and 1956. In November 1956 he moved to Portsmouth for £8,500, making 37 League appearances and netting 9 goals, before joining O's in July 1958, where he had the difficult task of trying to fill the boots of departed legend Tommy Johnston. He had a few good games, playing in four out of the five forward positions, and scoring on his debut in the 2-1 win at Derby County on 30 August 1958. McClellan's great asset was his pace, and at his best he was quite a good forward. He once scored 4 goals for O's in a 5-0 win over Brentford in a London Challenge Cup tie. He also scored a goal in O's 9-1 win over QPR in a friendly match at Brisbane Road in January 1959, a match that also marked the debut of another speedster, Eddie Brown. He moved to Southern League outfit Romford in July 1959, making 26 appearances and scoring 9 goals, and helped them win promotion in their Southern League season. In 1960 he worked for the Ford Motor Company in Dagenham, and had three separate spells as coach of Dagenham FC between 1963 and 1972. He made a total of 122 senior appearances and scored 46 goals. McClellan died at his Dagenham home on 15 December 2000, aged seventy-five.

SEASON	LEAGUE		FA CUP		TOTAL	
	Apps	Gls	Apps	Gls	Apps	Gls
1958/59	12	4	1	0	13	4
TOTAL	12	4	1	0	13	4

James McCOMBE, 1936-38

Jimmy McCombe was born Bothwell, Lanarkshire, Scotland on 4 June 1915. O's boss Peter Proudfoot signed him in July 1936 from Clyde, and he made a fine start to his career at Lea Bridge Road by scoring a goal in each of his first 3 League matches. Yet during his second season, he failed to find the net at all, but he made quite a few goals for others. The winger showed some swift movement that made him a dangerous player, and he joined Dartford in August 1939. McCombe in later life continued to live in London, and attended a number of former player reunions at Brisbane Road in the 1980s.

SEASON	LEAGUE		FA CUP		TOTAL	
	Apps	Gls	Apps	Gls	Apps	Gls
1936/37	27	8	2	0	29	8
1937/38	18	0	0	0	18	0
TOTAL	45	8	2	0	47	8

* Jimmy McCombe also appeared in 3 Third Division Cup matches between 1936 and 1938.

Stephen McCORMICK, 1998 (loan)

Tall, lanky striker Steve McCormick came to O's on a three-month loan from

Scottish side Dundee on 9 September 1998. However, he lasted just a month and returned on 8 October 1998. Born in Dumbarton, Scotland on 14 August 1969, 'McLadder' (as the 6ft 4in player became known by O's fans) started his career with Queens Park. He then moved on to Stirling Albion, where he was voted the Scottish Second Division Player of the Year in 1995/96, scoring 8 goals from 29(2) starts. After a loan spell with Arbroath in December 1996 – where he scored in his only Scottish League appearance – he joined Dundee for £25,000 on 29 December 1997. He went on to win a First Division Championship medal with the Dens Park club, scoring 5 goals from 6(9) matches. The following season he didn't figure in Dundee's Premier League aspirations, and was loaned out to both O's and Greenock Morton (making 3(2) Scottish League appearances, scoring once), before joining Airdrieonians on a free transfer on 12 November 1998, where he made 21(11) senior appearances and scored 6 goals. He was later on the books of East Fife between February and August 2000, with 3 goals from 11 Scottish League starts. The highlight of his stay with O's came against Mansfield Town on 8 September 1998, his good run on the left beating three players, only to be denied a goal by the legs of Mansfield's 'keeper, Bowling. In September 2000 a move to Clyde was on the cards, but the Scotsman decided to move south of the Border to live in Shrewsbury, and he joined League of Wales side Newtown AFC on 1 October, scoring on his debut against Llanelli. During the summer of 2001, he attracted the attention of Colchester United, but nothing materialised.

SEASON	LEAGUE		FA CUP		L. CUP	
	Apps	Gls	Apps	Gls	Apps	Gls
1998/99	1(3)	0	0	0	2	0
TOTAL	1(3)	0	0	0	2	0

TOTAL APPS	3(3)
TOTAL GOALS	0

Terence James McDONALD, 1959-65

Outside left Terry McDonald, who stood 5ft 7in tall and weighed just 10st, turned professional with West Ham United in April 1956. He was a member of the team that reached the 1957 Youth Cup final against Manchester United, and was also an England youth international. He played just once for their first XI, in a friendly against Sparta Prague of Czechoslovakia. Born on 12 November 1938 in Stepney, London, McDonald joined O's in July 1959, just before completing his national service. He capped a promising League debut by scoring direct from a corner-kick against Hull

Terry McDonald

City in October 1959, but it was his sparkling performance in the 5-0 defeat of Middlesbrough a few weeks later that saw him emerge as a top-class wingman. He played a major part in O's promotion season of 1961/62, and the highlight of his career was his scorching last-minute winner against Manchester United in September 1962. He was not quite as effective in his last two seasons with O's, and in May 1965 he moved to Reading, making 13 League appearances and scoring twice during his only season at Elm Park. He moved to non-League Wimbledon, and later joined Southern League Folkestone Town as well as running a betting in Hornchurch. After retiring, he spent several summers running soccer clinics in Philadelphia, USA and also worked part-time coaching twelve-year-olds at Chelsea's football centre in Dagenham. In 2002, he runs a betting shop in Great Portland Street, London. Now sixty-three, he is often seen at O's matches and player reunion functions. To this day, people keep reminding him about his winning goal against Manchester United!

SEASON	LEAGUE		FA CUP		L. CUP	
	Apps	Gls	Apps	Gls	Apps	Gls
1959/60	28	9	1	0	-	-
1960/61*	26	3	1	1	3	1
1961/62	36	6	4	0	3	2
1962/63	20	2	0	0	4	0
1963/64	16	0	0	0	0	0
1964/65	26	3	1	0	2	0
TOTAL	152	23	7	1	12	3

TOTAL APPS	171
TOTAL GOALS	27

* The League Cup competition commenced in 1960/61.

David Eugene McDOUGALD, 1998-99
Junior McDougald, as he was known, was a very fast striker, who had played for five clubs before joining O's on a non-contract basis on 8 October 1998, but his stay at Brisbane Road was dogged by injury. Born in Big Springs, Texas, USA on 12 January 1975, his parents moved to Huntingdon, Cambridgeshire when he was just eighteen months old. He started with Spurs as a trainee in July 1993 and was at White Hart Lane for nine years. He also won an England youth cap. However, he first caught the eye whilst at Brighton & Hove Albion, whom he joined in May 1994, scoring 14 goals from 78 appearances. After a loan spell with Chesterfield in March 1996 (9 appearances and 3 goals), he was transferred to Rotherham United for £50,000 on 30 July 1996. However, in a season hampered by a niggling back injury, he played just 14(4) matches and scored 2 goals in 1996/97. McDougald went to play for Toulon in France in 1997, and scored a number of goals in pre-season friendlies. He went on to make 5(10) French League appearances without scoring. He also played against Lille in a French cup match, scoring once. After a spell with Colorado Rapids in America, he returned to Rotherham in March 1998, but declined a contract with the Millers and joined Millwall in May 1998, playing just sixteen minutes as a substitute in a Division Two match against Wigan, before joining O's. He made just 3 substitute appearances before sustaining a serious ankle ligament injury that kept him out of action for over two months. He returned in a FA Cup tie at Southport on 2 January 1999, and had a good game. He joined St Albans on loan in February 1999 to regain his match fitness, but was

back with O's the following month. He was given a rare start in the final match of the season against Barnet, but limped off after eight minutes to end a disappointing season. McDougald was released in May 1999. He went on trial with Billericay and played against O's in a pre-season friendly during July 1999, alongside a number of former 'Orientals' – Joe Baker, Lee Williams, Andy Sussex and Chris Whyte. However, McDougald started the new season with Football Conference side Dagenham & Redbridge, teaming up with former O's players Paul Cobb, Paul Newell and Dominic Naylor. McDougald found his form with the Daggers, and headed a goal against Charlton Athletic at the Valley in a surprise 1-1 draw in the FA Cup third round during January 2001 – it was his fifth goal in 4 matches. He won his first England semi-professional cap in March 2001, scoring in the game against Holland.

Junior McDougald

SEASON	LEAGUE		FA CUP		L. CUP	
	Apps	Gls	Apps	Gls	Apps	Gls
1998/99	3(5)	0	1(1)	0	0	0
TOTAL	3(5)	0	1(1)	0	0	0

TOTAL APPS	4(6)
TOTAL GOALS	0

Brendan McELHOLM, 1999-2002

Born in Omagh, Northern Ireland on 7 July 1982, the left-footed central defender has represented his country of birth as captain at under-17 and under-18 level, and was the only non-Premiership club player in their youth squad. He looked very comfortable on the ball and strong in the tackle. He came to O's on trial in July 1998, after playing for his local side Dunbreen Colts in Ireland, and signed YTS forms the following October. He made 24 youth-team appearances in 1998/99, scoring 3 goals, and played 22 youth games the following season. He also made 8(2) reserve appearances. McElholm made his League debut at Macclesfield Town on 18 December 1999. He looks set to have a very bright future at both club and international level. He was a member of the under-19 youth team that won the FA Alliance Cup final against Bradford City at the Millennium Stadium, Cardiff on 22 April 2001. He scored his only senior goal for the club in a friendly against the Indian national side in a 1-1 draw. He was unavailable for the start of 2001/02, having been called up to the Northern Ireland under-21 squad for their European Championship qualifying matches against both Denmark and Iceland. On his return he went on a month's loan on 3 September to Dr Martens Premier League side Chelmsford City. However, McElholm was released from his contract on 18 January 2002 and

Brendan McElholm

with the Petershill club in Glasgow. He moved to QPR on 4 March 1939, and served the West London club for eleven years, making 76 regional wartime matches at centre forward, and scoring 34 goals. He later made 96 League appearances at outside right, netting 17 goals. Although his stay with O's was for only a year, he came at a time when the team were struggling and his experience was invaluable. He was in the side that drew with Southend United on the last day of the 1949/50 season (and scored a goal) that saw O's escape the need to apply for re-election. He moved to Southern League side Gravesend & Northfleet in July 1951. Billy McEwan died in Gravesend during December 1991, aged seventy-seven.

SEASON	LEAGUE		FA CUP		TOTAL	
	Apps	Gls	Apps	Gls	Apps	Gls
1949/50	13	3	0	0	13	3
1950/51	8	0	0	0	8	0
TOTAL	21	3	0	0	21	3

Richard McFADDEN, 1911-15

Skilful striker Dickie McFadden stood only 5ft 8 in tall, yet he was a brilliant player, and one of only a handful of truly prolific goalscorers to have played for O's since entry into the League in 1905. Born in Cambuslang, Lanarkshire, Scotland in 1889, he moved to Blyth as a boy and became best friends with William Jonas, and they later teamed up together at Millfields Road. McFadden started with Blyth in the Northern League, and then moved to Wallsend Park Villa, before joining O's during May 1911. He made his League debut and scored against Derby County on 2 September. McFadden broke Bill Martin's O's goalscoring record of 17 goals, when bagging 19 goals in

returned to Northern Ireland to join his local side, Omagh Town, on 24 February.

SEASON	LEAGUE		FA CUP		L. CUP	
	Apps	Gls	Apps	Gls	Apps	Gls
1999/2000	3	0	0	0	0	0
2000/01	3(9)	0	0	0	1(2)	0
2001/02	0(2)	0	0	0	0	0
TOTAL	6(11)	0	0	0	1(2)	0

TOTAL APPS	7(13)
TOTAL GOALS	0

* McElholm played in 2 LDV Vans Trophy matches, one in 2000/01 and one in 2001/02.

William McEWAN, 1950-51

Billy McEwan was born in Glasgow on 29 August 1914. He was a thirty-six-year-old veteran by the time he became an 'Oriental', joining from Queens Park Rangers along with his colleague and friend John Pattison. He started his career

1911/12 – a record he himself surpassed in 1914/15 with 21 goals. He represented a Southern XI against England at Craven Cottage in November 1914, obtaining rave notices from the national press and scoring the only goal of the game. It was during the same week that Middles-brough offered over £2,000 for his services, however, after consulting the player, the club declined the offer, to the delight of all O's fans. McFadden told O's chairman, Captain Henry Wells-Holland, that he did not want to leave Orient. McFadden was very popular with the fans, and even more so when it was reported that he had saved the life of a small boy. He saw the lad floundering in the River Lea and jumped in the water to pull him out, for which he received a medal of bravery from the mayor of Hackney. He and William Jonas – friend and O's colleague – were two of the first to enlist in the Footballers' Battalion to fight in the First World War. CSM Richard McFadden died in hospital on 23 October 1916 at the age of twenty-seven, from wounds received during hostilities in the First World War. He was one of three O's players to be killed in action in the battle of the Somme, the others being William Jonas and George Scott. He is buried at the Couin British Cemetery, Pas De Calais, fifteen kilometres east of Doullens, France. McFadden was top scorer for the four seasons he played with O's, yet his only hat-trick came during O's first overseas tour to Denmark, when they beat a Copenhagen XI by 4-0 in May 1912. Had he survived the First World War, he surely would have topped 100 League goals for the club. He was a player of rare quality, who will long be remembered for his efforts, both on and off the field of play, whilst with O's.

SEASON	LEAGUE		FA CUP		TOTAL	
	Apps	Gls	Apps	Gls	Apps	Gls
1911/12	37	19	1	0	38	19
1912/13	30	10	1	0	31	10
1913/14	33	16	3	2	36	18
1914/15	37	21	0	0	37	21
TOTAL	137	66	5	2	142	68

Joseph McGEACHY, 1948-52

Joe McGeachy was born in Glasgow, Scotland on 21 April 1920. He started in junior football with Denniston Waverly FC, before joining the Navy in 1941. He played for Partick Thistle during the Second World War, and later played for Dunfermline Athletic. He then had a spell with Third Lanark, where he was spotted by O's boss Neil McBain, who signed him in May 1948. McGeachy had a good first season down the left wing, proving to be a handful for opposing defenders. The bald-headed player will be remembered by older supporters for his long baggy shorts – as he was a little on the short side, they gave him a rather comical appearance. However, this should not detract from the fact that he was a good player who always gave 100 per cent effort. He was described in a club programme of the time as one of the best 'middlers' in the division. He was transferred to Workington in September 1952, making just a couple of appearances and scoring once, and he later played for Hereford United. Joe McGeachy died during 1985.

SEASON	LEAGUE		FA CUP		TOTAL	
	Apps	Gls	Apps	Gls	Apps	Gls
1948/49	38	2	2	1	40	3
1949/50	20	1	1	0	21	1
1950/51	16	1	0	0	16	1
1951/52	0	0	0	0	0	0
TOTAL	74	4	3	1	77	5

James Lumley McGEORGE, 1965-66

Jimmy McGeorge, a slightly built inside forward, was born in Sunderland on 8 June 1945. He joined O's from Spennymoor United in March 1965, and did well for the reserves. He was given his League debut in March 1965 at Huddersfield Town. However, McGeorge was inclined to be a little dainty in his play and couldn't command a regular place in the League XI. He was transferred to Mansfield Town in July 1966, where he made just 5(4) League appearances, before joining Southern League outfit Cambridge City in May 1967.

SEASON	LEAGUE		FA CUP		L. CUP	
	Apps	Gls	Apps	Gls	Apps	Gls
1964/65	10	0	0	0	0	0
1965/66	6	0	0	0	1	0
TOTAL	16	0	0	0	1	0

TOTAL APPS	17
TOTAL GOALS	0

Jimmy McGeorge

Robert McGEORGE, 1896-98 and 1902-06

East Londoner Bob McGeorge first played for O's in the Second Division of the London League in 1897/98, making 11 appearances before leaving in 1898. He re-joined O's in May 1902 from Finchley FC (before O's had became a professional club) and played alongside his brother Kenneth McGeorge in the London League. He played in both 1902/03 and 1903/04, and also appeared in the Southern League in 1904/05. McGeorge was a very versatile player, and appeared on the wing, and at inside forward, but it was at centre half that he played in all 6 FA Cup ties in 1904/05. He had a hand in O's first ever FA Cup goal when he touched the ball on for Reynolds to score. McGeorge himself netted O's fourth goal in a 4-1 victory over Enfield on 17 September 1904. He was one a few to make the transition into the League in 1905, making his debut in a 0-0 draw against Barnsley on 7 October 1905. He returned to Finchley FC in 1906.

SEASON	LEAGUE		FA CUP		TOTAL	
	Apps	Gls	Apps	Gls	Apps	Gls
1904/05*	-	-	6	2	6	2
1905/06	14	0	1	0	15	0
TOTAL	14	0	7	2	21	2

* Clapton Orient first entered the League in 1905/06.

David McGHEE, 1999-present

Dave McGhee – or 'Mad Dog', as he is known by the fans – a 5ft 11in tall defender/midfielder, came to O's on a month's trial on 12 October 1999, and signed a full-time contract a month later. He had previously turned down a similar offer from Crewe Alexandra, wanting to stay in London. This happened after a career-threatening injury sustained whilst with Brentford and missed a whole season of football. Born in Worthing, Sussex on 19 June 1976, he grew up as a boy in Cornwall. He started as a trainee with Brentford and turned professional on 15 July 1994. He made 109(24) senior appearances for the Bees, scoring 10 goals, but was released on 22 January 1999 after his injury. After recovering, he played some non-League football in Cornwall, with a number of local sides around the Penzance area. He then moved to Stevenage Borough in July 1999, making just 2 substitute appearances, but failing to agree terms with them. He made his O's debut at Rotherham United on 12 November. McGhee has proved to be an uncompromising tackler, good in the air, and is equally as effective as a ball-winning midfielder/defender as he is a striker. His battling displays (not to mention his eight tattoos) have won over the O's faithful, and his career has most certainly been revitalised by Tommy Taylor at the Matchroom Stadium. He was a tower of strength as O's held a top five spot for most of the 2000/01 season, and appeared in all 3 play-off matches against Hull City and Blackpool in May 2001. He won the manager's Player of the Year award in May 2001. The twenty-five-year-old signed a two-year extension to his contract in June 2001.

SEASON	LEAGUE		FA CUP		L. CUP	
	Apps	Gls	Apps	Gls	Apps	Gls
1999/2000	17(6)	1	0	0	0	0
2000/01*	42	3	4	0	4	0
2001/02	39(1)	2	4	0	0	0
TOTAL	98(7)	6	8	0	4	0

TOTAL APPS	110(7)
TOTAL GOALS	6

* McGhee's League record includes 3 play-off appearances in 2000/01. He also played in an Auto Windscreens Shield match in 1999/2000, and in an LDV Vans Trophy match in 2000/01.

Scott McGLEISH, 1995 (loan) and 1996-98

McGleish is a very popular and brave striker, who showed plenty of effort and a high work-rate, and for such a small striker – he stood 5ft 9 in – he had a prodigious leap. He will be remembered for his goal celebrations, always doing double backwards somersaults! Born in Barnet, Hertfordshire on 9 February 1974, the forward started his career with Edgware Town in August 1993, but moved to Charlton Athletic on a free on 24 May 1994. However, after just 6 substitute appearances, he came to O's on loan on 9 March 1995. He found it difficult during his loan period, playing in a struggling side under constant pressure of relegation. He left Charlton for Peterborough United on a free transfer in July 1995, and teamed up with Carl Griffiths. He never made it at Boro, making just 3(10) appearances. He went on loan spells with Colchester United (scoring 6 goals from 10(5) starts) and Cambridge United (7 goals from 10 appearances), before catching the eye of O's new boss Tommy Taylor. McGleish signed for O's for £50,000 (with a sell-on clause) on 18 November 1996 – the biggest signing to date during chairman Barry Hearn's reign. Although he only scored 9 senior goals after his return to Brisbane Road, it was a great surprise to both McGleish and O's fans when news broke of his possible move. Apparently, he was phoned by O's boss Taylor very early in the morning, to be told that he might be on his way, after two clubs (Barnet and Cambridge) had shown interest in him. McGleish eventu-

Scott McGleish

ally signed for Barnet for £70,000 on 30 September 1997. He didn't disappoint in his first season at Underhill, scoring 13 goals from 37 appearances, yet in May 1999 he was suspended by Barnet boss John Still. It was a sad day when McGleish left the club, as he had endeared himself to the fans during his short stay. Up to the end of the 1999/2000 season, McGleish had made 100(23) senior appearances and scored 39 goals at Underhill. He started the new season with a bang, scoring 4 goals in as many games, but then seemed to lose form and struggled scoring just once in 15 starts. He joined Essex side Colchester United on 12 January 2001, making over 20 senior appearances and scoring twice during the season.

SEASON	LEAGUE		FA CUP		L. CUP	
	Apps	Gls	Apps	Gls	Apps	Gls
1994/95	4(2)	1	0	0	0	0
1996/97	28	7	1	0	0	0
1997/98	8	0	0	0	3	1
TOTAL	40(2)	8	1	0	3	1

TOTAL APPS   44(2)
TOTAL GOALS   9

* Scott McGleish also appeared in 2 Auto Windscreens Shield matches, scoring once.

Joseph Russell McGREA, 1930-31

Full-back Joe McGrea struggled to maintain a first-team place during his single season at the club, and was kept out of the side by Welsh international Tom Evans, managing just 4 appearances – all defeats. Born in Kirkdale, Liverpool on 24 October 1903, the 5ft 10in full-back started with local club Royal Albion. After the First World War, he joined Everton as an amateur in June 1919, making a number of reserve appearances during his six-year stay. A move to Tranmere Rovers in May 1925 saw him make 8 League appearances. However, his chance came when he joined Norwich City in August 1926. He stayed with the Carrow Road club for three years and made 124 senior appearances, scoring 3 goals. He went back north with Bradford City in May 1929, but his move turned sour, and after just a single senior appearance, the Valley Parade club were fined five guineas for giving McGrea his League debut before his registration. Thereafter, he was left in the reserves and became an 'Oriental' on 27 July 1930. After his only season –the first for the club at their new Lea Bridge Road ground – he moved to Halifax Town on 22 July 1931, and made 37 senior appearances. However, he had his contract cancelled in April 1932, and so moved to non-League Macclesfield Town. A year later he moved to Littlewoods FC, and in 1935 he became a Hyde United player. On leaving fulltime football, he became a checker at a food warehouse in Bootle, Liverpool until he died on 19 November 1975.

SEASON	LEAGUE		FA CUP		TOTAL	
	Apps	Gls	Apps	Gls	Apps	Gls
1930/31	4	0	0	0	4	0
TOTAL	4	0	0	0	4	0

James Alexander McKAY, 1924-26

Born in Custom House, London in April 1901, Jim McKay, a centre forward, started off with Custom House FC and Dartford, before joining Fulham in November 1922. He made 17 League appearances and scored 5 goals at Craven Cottage, before moving to Orient in November 1924, making his debut at Bradford City that month. He bagged a brace on his home debut against Port Vale on 15 November, but he could never replace Albert Pape, or the following season's big signing, Donald Cock. In 1926 he moved to Aldershot.

SEASON	LEAGUE		FA CUP		TOTAL	
	Apps	Gls	Apps	Gls	Apps	Gls
1924/25	5	2	0	0	5	2
1925/26	3	1	0	0	3	1
TOTAL	8	3	0	0	8	3

John James McKECHNIE, 1923-26

Inverness-born Jimmy McKechnie played for a number of clubs, before arriving at Millfields Road in May 1923. The 5ft 11in and 12st 7lb right-back had been at Newcastle United, but never tasted first-team action. He moved to Northampton Town in June 1920, and made his debut in their inaugural League fixture against Grimsby Town in August 1920, going on to play 11 senior matches. In May 1921 he moved to Exeter City, for whom he made

Jim McKay

18 appearances. The following season he joined Stockport County, making his debut against Leeds United in September 1922. He made a further 7 appearances for the club. He made his O's debut in a 1-0 defeat at Leeds United on 13 October 1923, and was an able replacement when Sam Tonner was injured. In 1925/26 he started in the side, after Tonner had left the club. McKechnie moved on to Crewe Alexandra in June 1926, playing a total of 15 League matches.

SEASON	LEAGUE		FA CUP		TOTAL	
	Apps	Gls	Apps	Gls	Apps	Gls
1923/24	12	0	3	0	15	0
1924/25	17	0	0	0	17	0
1925/26	18	0	0	0	18	0
TOTAL	47	0	3	0	50	0

Alexander McKEEMAN, 1946-47

Alex McKeeman (not McKeenan, as some reports state) was born at Carnegie Park

Gardens in Port Glasgow, Renfrewshire, Scotland on 26 February 1924. He joined O's from Port Glasgow FC in June 1946, and his only appearance was against Crystal Palace on 25 September 1946 – O's first match under their new title of Leyton Orient FC. McKeeman could never replace Doug Hunt, and after playing the whole season in the reserves, he returned home to Port Glasgow in May 1947.

SEASON	LEAGUE		FA CUP		TOTAL	
	Apps	Gls	Apps	Gls	Apps	Gls
1946/47	1	0	0	0	1	0
TOTAL	1	0	0	0	1	0

Philip McKNIGHT, 1954-61

Phil McKnight was one of the most underrated members of O's 1955/56 promotion-winning team. He seldom hit the headlines, yet his steady and consistent play, along with that of with fellow half-backs Blizzard and Aldous, was a major factor in many great League performances. The trio must rank just behind the Lucas-Bishop-Lea half-back combination of the early 1960s as the finest in the club's history. Born in Camlachie, Glasgow on 15 June 1924, he played for Alloa Athletic, before moving south of the Border to join Chelsea in January 1947. A hard-working defender, noted for his long throw-in, he stayed at Stamford Bridge for eight seasons, but managed just 33 League appearances. However, he did win 5 Combination medals. He joined O's in July 1954, proving to be a wonderful defensive player, and did well in the Second Division. Whilst at Brisbane Road, he represented London against Lausanne in the Inter Cities Fairs Cup. In 1960 he was appointed coach to the O's 'A' side, and

later managed Hendon FC. In 1965/66 he became manager of Hayes FC.

SEASON	LEAGUE		FA CUP		TOTAL	
	Apps	Gls	Apps	Gls	Apps	Gls
1954/55	42	0	2	0	44	0
1955/56	39	0	3	0	42	0
1956/57	33	1	1	0	34	1
1957/58	29	0	2	0	31	0
1958/59	18	1	0	0	18	1
TOTAL	161	2	8	0	169	2

Robert McLAUGHLAN, 1925-26

Born in Kilwinning, Ayrshire, Scotland in 1902, outside left Bob McLaughlan joined O's from Kilwinning Rangers in May 1925, after he had experienced a brief but unsuccessful spell with Cardiff City. He joined as understudy to O's wingers Peter Gavigan and Charlie Hannaford. After McLaughlan made his League debut against South Shields in October 1925, he never looked back. He had a wonderful season, and starred in O's great run to the

Phil McKnight

sixth round of the FA Cup. He performed what is surely quite a unique feat when, in two consecutive League matches, he scored direct from corner-kicks – against Barnsley at Millfields and at at Stockport County in January 1926. He left the club in May 1926.

SEASON	LEAGUE		FA CUP		TOTAL	
	Apps	Gls	Apps	Gls	Apps	Gls
1925/26	19	3	4	0	23	3
TOTAL	19	3	4	0	23	3

Aaron McLEAN, 1999-present

Born in Hammersmith, London on 25 May 1983, forward Aaron McLean signed YTS forms with O's on 1 July 1999, after playing junior football with Jays Boys club. He first appeared as a substitute in an Auto Windscreen Cup match at Reading on 8 December 1999, and he made his League debut (also as a substitute) when replacing Carl Griffiths in the seventy-sixth minute at Lincoln City on 22 April 2000. He made his full debut at Cardiff City on 6 March 2001, being replaced in the sixty-fifth minute by loan striker Christian Lee. He scored his first ever senior goal after coming on as a substitute, when he headed home a Sasha Opinel centre on seventy-four minutes to earn O's a point in a 1-1 draw at Shrewsbury Town on 17 March 2001. Unfortunately, he broke his ankle in a 3-0 win over Mansfield Town in the quarter-final of the FA Youth Alliance League on 26 March 2001, and missed out on the remainder of the season. However, he was back in the first-team squad the following season.

SEASON	LEAGUE		FA CUP		L. CUP	
	Apps	Gls	Apps	Gls	Apps	Gls
1999/2000*	0(3)	0	0	0	0	0
2000/01	1(4)	1	0	0	0	0
2001/02	4(23)	1	0(3)	0	0	0
TOTAL	5(27)	2	0(3)	0	0	0

TOTAL APPS	5(30)
TOTAL GOALS	2

* Aaron McLean played in 0(1) Auto Windscreen match in 1999/2000.

Robert McLEAN, 1908-10

Born in Glasgow, Bob McLean joined O's in October 1908 from Scottish side Bo'ness, and stayed for two seasons. The scheming inside forward, who had good dribbling skills, had a fine match in a 5-0 defeat of Stockport County in February 1909, but he was somewhat inconsistent. He ended up being transferred to Southern League side Leyton FC in 1910.

SEASON	LEAGUE		FA CUP		TOTAL	
	Apps	Gls	Apps	Gls	Apps	Gls
1908/09	25	2	0	0	25	2
1909/10	14	0	0	0	14	0
TOTAL	39	2	0	0	39	2

Edward McMAHON, 1913-14

Addleworth-born Ted McMahon joined O's from Midlands League side York City in June 1913, as cover for Richard McFadden, having previously been at Southern League side Portsmouth. The 5ft 7in tall and 10st 12lb inside forward played well in the reserves, making his League debut on 27 December 1913 in the 2-0 defeat at Fulham, but he left the club in May 1914.

SEASON	LEAGUE		FA CUP		TOTAL	
	Apps	Gls	Apps	Gls	Apps	Gls
1913/14	3	0	0	0	3	0
TOTAL	3	0	0	0	3	0

Peter John McMAHON, 1951-58

Peter McMahon was born in Marylebone, London on 30 April 1934. The wing-half came to O's from Chase of Chertsey (then Arsenal's nursery club) in May 1951, and he continued to play for them when O's took over the running of that club. He showed great promise, and made his League debut at Crystal Palace in January 1952, a few months before his eighteenth birthday. He found himself mostly in the reserves during his seven years at Brisbane Road, but took part in some vital games in the 1955/56 championship-winning season. His only senior goal for O's was in the 1-0 win against Lincoln City on 29 March 1958. He was transferred to Aldershot in October 1958, where he played a total of 39 matches. He proved to be a more than useful player, and an excellent squad member over the years, and he was rather unlucky not to have seen more regular first-team action.

Peter McMahon

SEASON	LEAGUE		FA CUP		TOTAL	
	Apps	Gls	Apps	Gls	Apps	Gls
1951/52	1	0	0	0	1	0
1952/53	13	0	0	0	13	0
1953/54	25	0	4	0	29	0
1954/55	5	0	0	0	5	0
1955/56	12	0	1	0	13	0
1956/57	2	0	0	0	2	0
1957/58	8	1	0	0	8	1
1958/59	0	0	0	0	0	0
TOTAL	66	1	5	0	71	1

TOTAL APPS 71
TOTAL GOALS 1

Stuart Thomas McMILLAN, 1928-30

Stuart McMillan was born in Leicester on 17 September 1896, and the right-winger had a long career before joining O's. He started out at Derby County, and had played once in the League for the Rams against Glossop in January 1915, as a nineteen-year-old. He served in the Derbyshire Yeomanry during the First World War, as well as guesting for Chelsea and playing in their reserve side between 1919 and 1921. He joined Gillingham in March 1921, and scored twice in 30 League appearances. He moved on to Wolverhampton Wanderers in August 1922, where he made 39 senior appearances and scored 5 goals, gaining a Third Division (North) Championship winner's medal in 1924. It was during this period that he played cricket for Derbyshire CCC, and scored 30 runs in 6 innings. McMillan moved to Bradford City for £250 on 9 May 1924 and stayed for three years, playing 73 senior matches and scoring 9 goals. In June 1927, he moved to Nottingham Forest, where he made just 10 senior appearances, before joining O's in August 1928. He scored his only goal for O's in a thrilling 3-2 loss against

Tottenham Hotspur on 16 March 1929 at Millfields Road, in front of 37,615 spectators. After sustaining a serious injury at Northampton Town on 23 November 1929, he was forced to retire from the game. He became licensee of the Nag's Head at Mickleover in Derbyshire. In March 1936 he was appointed assistant manager of Derby County, and progressed to manager in January 1946. He led County to a 4-1 win (after extra time) over Charlton Athletic in the 1946 FA Cup final at Wembley. McMillan resigned on 23 November 1953, and became the licensee of the Station Hotel in Ashbourne, Derbyshire until he died on 27 September 1963, aged sixty-seven.

SEASON	LEAGUE		FA CUP		TOTAL	
	Apps	Gls	Apps	Gls	Apps	Gls
1928/29	16	1	1	00	17	1
1929/30	7	0	0	0	7	0
TOTAL	23	1	1	0	24	1

Mark John McNEIL, 1981-84

Speedy striker Mark McNeil joined O's as an apprentice in December 1979, and got his first-team chance on 18 October 1981 against Queens Park Rangers – new boss Ken Knighton's first match in charge. Born in Bethnal Green, London on 3 December 1962, he was at his best when playing at centre forward. He looked dangerous going forward, and was the possessor of a powerful shot. He netted a couple of particularly memorable goals – against Exeter City and Preston North End in 1982/83. In the Exeter match, he was originally credited with a hat-trick, but one of the goals was later recorded as an own goal by Viney. He moved to Aldershot in November 1984, scoring twice in 20(5) appearances, and in 1986 he went to play in Sweden.

Mark McNeil

SEASON	LEAGUE		FA CUP		L. CUP	
	Apps	Gls	Apps	Gls	Apps	Gls
1981/82	20(4)	3	1(1)	0	0	0
1982/83	15(3)	5	0	0	0	0
1983/84	37(2)	4	0	0	2	0
1984/85	4(4)	0	1	1	0(2)	0
TOTAL	76(13)	12	2(1)	1	2(2)	0

TOTAL APPS	80(16)
TOTAL GOALS	13

* Mark McNeil also appeared in 0(1) Football League Groups Cup match and an Auto Windscreens Shield match.

Bertram MENLOVE, 1929-30

Bertie Menlove was born in St Albans on 8 December 1892, and played at centre forward for O's in an FA Cup tie against Folkestone Town on 30 November 1929, aged thirty-seven. He started his career with the Southern Railway club, and then moved to Barnet before moving on to

Aston Villa, where he played for their reserve side. He joined Crystal Palace in 1920, where he chalked up 48 League appearances and scored 12 goals. Sheffield United signed him in 1922, and by the time he left the Yorkshire club, had made 74 League appearances and scored 42 goals. He then had spells with Boston Town, Aldershot, Worksop Town and Bangor City, before becoming an 'Oriental' in May 1929. At O's he didn't get into the League side, but in the days when there were no substitutes, he was often twelfth man, in case someone pulled out at the last minute, and he always travelled with the squad for away matches. He moved to Coleraine in May 1930, and later played for Connah's Quay and Shotton FC. Bertie Menlove died in Bridge, Kent on 3 July 1970, aged seventy-seven.

SEASON	LEAGUE		FA CUP		TOTAL	
	Apps	Gls	Apps	Gls	Apps	Gls
1929/30	0	0	1	0	1	0
TOTAL	0	0	1	0	1	0

Harold George MERRITT, 1945-47

Harold Merritt was born in Ormskirk on 22 September 1920. He started as a junior with Everton in December 1937, and guested for them during the Second World War. He joined O's in 1945 and made 6 wartime appearances, scoring once. He appeared in the two-legged FA Cup tie against Newport Isle of Wight during November 1945, and was unfortunate to score an own goal in the away tie, which ended O's dreams of an FA Cup run, as they went out 3-2 on aggregate. The inside left was retained for the return of League football in 1946/47, but made just a single League appearance against Crystal Palace on 28 September 1946. He left in 1947.

SEASON	LEAGUE		FA CUP		TOTAL	
	Apps	Gls	Apps	Gls	Apps	Gls
1945/46*	-	-	2	0	2	0
1946/47	1	0	0	0	1	0
TOTAL	1	0	2	0	3	0

* The League re-commenced in 1946/47, after the Second World War.

David John METCHICK, 1964-67

Dave Metchick was born in Bakewell, Derbyshire on 14 August 1943. The scheming inside forward started off as a junior with Fulham, signing professional forms in August 1960. An England youth international with 7 caps to his name, he made 56 senior appearances and scored 13 goals whilst at Craven Cottage. He joined O's just before Christmas 1964, and scored with a splendid twenty-five-yarder on his debut against Charlton Athletic that Boxing Day. He was joint top scorer (with Colin Flatt) with 8 goals in the relegation season of 1965/66. He performed well the following season in the Third Division, but with O's in a financial crisis he was transferred to Peterborough United in March 1967, where he scored 6 goal in 38 League appearances. He joined Queens Park Rangers in August 1968, but made only three appearances as a substitute, scoring once. After a spell in Arsenal's reserves, he went to play in America with Atlanta Chiefs, Miami Toros and Atlanta Apollos. He returned to England with Brentford in September 1973, and in his two seasons at Griffin Park, he made 57(4) League appearances and scored 4 goals. He moved into non-League football with Hendon FC, and later joined Hillingdon Borough and Woking. Metchick, like so many former O's players of the era, worked as a black-cab driver on his retirement from football.

Dave Metchick signs for O's

SEASON	LEAGUE		FA CUP		L. CUP	
	Apps	Gls	Apps	Gls	Apps	Gls
1964/65	15	2	1	0	0	0
1965/66	37	8	1	0	1	0
1966/67	23	5	3	2	1	0
TOTAL	75	15	5	2	2	0

TOTAL APPS	82
TOTAL GOALS	17

Thomas MEYNELL, 1909-10

Born in Southwick-on-Wear, Tommy Meynell joined O's from Goole Town in June 1909. The promising young centre half performed well for O's reserves, and he was given his League chance in a 2-2 draw at Blackpool in October 1909. Meynell was often seen going forward to assist the attack, as centre halves were rather more attack-minded in that era. It was surprising that he was transferred to Lancashire League side Rochdale in June 1910, where he gained a Manchester Senior Cup winner's medal in 1912. He returned to his first club, Goole Town, in May 1912.

SEASON	LEAGUE		FA CUP		TOTAL	
	Apps	Gls	Apps	Gls	Apps	Gls
1909/10	16	2	0	0	16	2
TOTAL	16	2	0	0	16	2

Idris MILES, 1934-37

Welshman Idris Miles was nicknamed the 'flying flea' by O's fans, because he stood just 5ft 3in tall and weighed 9st 6lb, and considerably speedy. There was just one player who was smaller than him – Fred Le May, who stood just 5ft tall. Born in Neath, Glamorgan on 2 August 1908, he started off with local side Radnor Road FC, before moving to Cardiff City in May 1932, making just 3 League appearances. After a short spell with Yeovil & Petters United between May and October 1932, he moved to Leicester City and scored on his debut at Everton in October 1932. After just 7 League appearances, he suffered appalling fortune when twice breaking his collarbone. He failed to gain another first-team place, and moved to O's in May 1934, as part of the deal that took O's Welsh international Tommy Mills to Filbert Street. Miles came into his own during the 1935/36 season, with his dangerous runs down the right wing setting up a quite a number of Ted Crawford's 25 senior goals that season. He was transferred (along with Vince Farrell) to Exeter City in May 1937, where he made 10 League appearances. He then joined Worcester City, as they switched from the Birmingham League to the Southern League in 1938. Idris Miles died in Dudley during October 1983, at the age of seventy-five.

SEASON	LEAGUE		FA CUP		TOTAL	
	Apps	Gls	Apps	Gls	Apps	Gls
1934/35	10	0	0	0	10	0
1935/36	37	3	4	0	41	3
1936/37	26	3	2	0	28	3
TOTAL	73	6	6	0	79	6

* Idris Miles also appeared in 2 Third Division Cup matches between 1935 and 1937.

John MILLINGTON, 1934-35

Born in Bolton in 1916, John Millington started with Bolton Wanderers, but was unable to make the first team. He joined O's in June 1934, as understudy to regular left-winger Arthur Rigby. He made his League debut in the 4-0 defeat at Coventry City on 3 September 1934, and his only other appearance came twelve days later, in a 5-0 defeat at Watford. He did well for the reserves and played in several first-team friendly matches, scoring in one against Irish side Belfast Celtic FC in 1934/35, a 5-1 victory. He joined

Idris Miles

Notts County in May 1935, and was a little luckier there, playing 15 League matches and scoring twice. He moved to Birmingham City in June 1936, but didn't make it at St Andrews and soon moved on to Swansea Town in May 1937. It was with the Welshmen that he made the biggest impact – in the two seasons before the Second World War, he made 44 League appearances and scored 6 goals. He later joined Scunthorpe United, retiring soon after.

SEASON	LEAGUE		FA CUP		TOTAL	
	Apps	Gls	Apps	Gls	Apps	Gls
1934/35	2	0	0	0	2	0
TOTAL	2	0	0	0	2	0

* John Millington also appeared in a Third Division Cup match at Northampton Town on 1 October 1934, a 4-0 defeat.

Thomas James MILLS, 1929-34

Tommy Mills was born in Ton Pentre, Wales on 28 December 1911. Having worked as a miner in Wales, he moved to London and worked in the Trocadero Hotel. He was first spotted by an O's scout playing for Welsh schoolboys against both England and Scotland, and when the same scout saw him playing a match for the hotel staff team, new O's boss Arthur Grimsdell signed him up straight away. He made his League debut on 25 September 1929 (just before his eighteenth birthday,at Brighton & Hove Albion) and he blossomed to become a brilliant creative inside forward with splendid ball control. He played a major part in O's 9-2 trouncing of Aldershot in February 1934. He gained his first full Welsh cap – and scored the winning goal – against England at Newcastle in November 1933, and he won a further

Tommy Mills

cap against Northern Ireland. He won another two caps whilst with Leicester City. Mills was transferred to Leicester in May 1934 for over £1,500, but struggled to gain a regular first-team spot in their relegation-bound team. He could not find the form he enjoyed at Millfields, playing just 18 senior matches and scoring 5 goals, and moved to Bristol Rovers for £575. This move saw a revival of his career, and whilst at Eastville he netted 17 goals in 99 League appearances before his retirement from the game in 1939. Sadly, Tommy Mills' death came about in Bristol on 15 May 1979, as a result of being knocked down by a lorry.

SEASON	LEAGUE		FA CUP		TOTAL	
	Apps	Gls	Apps	Gls	Apps	Gls
1929/30	19	2	6	3	25	5
1930/31	7	0	0	0	7	0
1931/32	37	6	3	0	40	6
1932/33	27	7	1	0	28	7
1933/34	29	5	3	0	32	5
TOTAL	119	20	13	3	132	23

Jeffrey Simon MINTON, 2001-present

Jeff Minton was born in Hackney, London on 28 December 1973, and started his career as a trainee with Tottenham Hotspur in 1991. During his three-year stay at White Hart Lane, he made just 2(1) senior appearances. The 5ft 6in and 11st 10lb central midfielder moved to Brighton & Hove Albion on a free transfer in July 1994. He soon became a big crowd favourite, combining vision, excellent passing ability and strong tackling. During his final season with the Seagulls, he was named in the PFA Division Three team for 1998/99. Minton made 186(7) senior appearances, scoring 32 goals. He joined Port Vale under the Bosman ruling in June 1999, but sinus trouble hampered his stay at Vale Park, and he made just 42(2) senior appearances and scored 6 goals. He moved to Rotherham United on a free on 15 March 2001, scoring twice on his debut and playing his part in their surge to Division One. Minton was keen on a move back to London, and O's boss Taylor moved quickly get his man. Rotherham offered him a new contract, and offers were on the table from both Luton Town and Oxford United, but he chose to get back to his native London. Taylor stated: 'I have been trying to sign him for three years, and he has become a better player in that time, so to get him now is really good.' Minton has proved to be a great capture, and has been the star performer up to the end of 2001. After an altercation with O's boss Paul Brush during a match at Shrewsbury Town, as well as stalling on signing a new contract, Minton was placed on the transfer list in

February 2002, although he remained in the squad.

SEASON	LEAGUE		FA CUP		L. CUP	
	Apps	Gls	Apps	Gls	Apps	Gls
2001/02	32(1)	5	4	0	1	1
TOTAL	32(1)	5	4	0	1	1

TOTAL APPS	36(1)
TOTAL GOALS	6

Dean Francis MOONEY, 1973-76

Dean Mooney was O's second highest ever youth goalscorer (after Barrie Fairbrother) with over 100 goals, but unlike Fairbrother he could not hit the same heights when appearing in the first team. Born in Paddington, London on 24 July 1956, he signed apprentice forms with O's in July 1972, after a short time on QPR's books, and turned professional in November 1973 when only seventeen. He had previously represented West London, Middlesex and London schools. He burst onto the scene, netting 35 goals from 41 games for the youth side in1972/73, and he smashed 3 or more goals on 4 occasions. He also excelled the following season, when he bagged a further 37 youth goals and 10 goals for the reserve side in the Midweek League. He made his League debut as a substitute, replacing Fairbrother in the 1-0 win against Bristol Rovers in February 1974. His full debut came in the 1-0 home defeat by Notts County on 8 March. He had a longer run during the following season, scoring his first League goal in the 2-1 win at Carlisle on 22 November 1975. However, he could never quite recapture the same scoring ratios, and he was released in 1976 to join Dulwich Hamlet. He moved to Sweden to play for Gais FC. In December 1980 he joined AFC Bournemouth, and netted 10 goals from 27 League appearances. In August 1974 he signed for Torquay United – after a brief spell with non-League side RS Southampton – and made 15 League appearances and scoring twice in Devon.

SEASON	LEAGUE		FA CUP		L. CUP	
	Apps	Gls	Apps	Gls	Apps	Gls
1974/75	1(2)	0	0	0	0	0
1975/76	15(4)	3	0	0	0	0
TOTAL	16(6)	3	0	0	0	0

TOTAL APPS	16(6)
TOTAL GOALS	3

John MOONEY, 1926-27

Born in Glasgow on 1 January 1898, John Mooney first came south of the Border from Glasgow-based Perthshire FC to join Bristol City in June 1921. His two-year stay at Ashton Gate yielded just 2 League appearances. In July 1923 he returned to Scotland to play for Cowdenbeath, and

Dean Mooney

after a short spell with Queen of the South Wanderers, he moved to Barrow for the 1925/26 season, where he made 14 League outings and scored 2 goals. The inside forward joined O's in 1926, but managed a single senior appearance – an FA Cup tie against Port Vale at Millfields on 8 January 1927. He returned home to Scotland in May 1927.

SEASON	LEAGUE		FA CUP		TOTAL	
	Apps	Gls	Apps	Gls	Apps	Gls
1926/27	0	0	1	0	1	0
TOTAL	0	0	1	0	1	0

Ian Richard MOORES, 1978-82

Ian Moores joined Orient for £55,000 (along with free transfer Ralph Coates) from Tottenham Hotspur at the end of September 1978, and scored twice on his debut, a day after celebrating his twenty-fourth birthday at Charlton Athletic on 6 October 1978. Tragically, Moores succumbed to cancer, aged just forty-three, and passed away during the night of 12 January 1998 at a Stoke hospital, after being admitted the previous September. Born on 5 October 1954 in Newcastle-under-Lyme, he attended the Edward Orme Secondary School and was first spotted by Stoke City whilst playing for Staffordshire Schools. The forward joined the Potters as an apprentice, and signed professional forms in June 1972 with the club he had supported from the terraces, making his League debut in a 1-1 draw at Leicester City on 16 April 1974. He totalled 14 goals from 50 League games. He netted twice for the England under-23 side against Wales during January 1975 at Wrexham. He then joined Tottenham Hotspur on 28 August 1976 for £75,000, making 32 senior appearances and scoring 8 goals. One of the highlights of his

Ian Moores

spell in North London was his hat-trick in Spurs' 9-0 win over Bristol Rovers. During the summer of 1977, he went on loan to the Western Suburbs club in Sydney, Australia. He finished his first season at Orient as leading goalscorer on 13 goals. He spent much of his second season either in midfield or playing as an emergency centre half. With O's relegated to the Third Division during 1982, he was one of several players to be released, and he moved to Bolton Wanderers where he scored 5 goals from 30 starts. He also had a three-month loan stint with Barnsley. After Bolton were relegated to the Third Division, he started a five-year stint with APOEL in Nicosia, Cyprus during 1983, gaining a Cypriot Cup winner's medal, and helping them to a League title in 1986. On returning to the UK in 1988, he had loan spells with Port Vale and with non-League Newcastle Town, before signing for Southern League Tanworth, for whom he played in the 1989 FA Vase final at Wembley. He opened the scoring in their 3-0 victory over Sudbury Town in the replay at Peterborough four days later. Ian Moores made 254 senior career appearances with his five clubs, scoring 59 goals.

SEASON	LEAGUE		FA CUP		L. CUP	
	Apps	Gls	Apps	Gls	Apps	Gls
1978/79	30	13	3	0	0	0
1979/80	21(5)	0	3	0	0	0
1980/81	36(1)	9	1	0	0(1)	0
1981/82	23(1)	4	5	3	2	2
TOTAL	110(7)	26	12	3	2(1)	2

TOTAL APPS	124(8)
TOTAL GOALS	31

* Ian Moores also appeared in 1(1) Anglo-Scottish Cup matches and 3 Football League Groups Cup matches, scoring once.

Alfred Stanley MORGAN, 1953-56

Stan Morgan was born in Abergwynfi, Wales on 9 October 1920. He was signed by Arsenal as an outstanding prospect from Welsh junior side Gwynfi Welfare in 1938, turning professional during December 1941. While serving as a Commando, he made guest appearances for both Brighton and Swindon during the Second World War. He appeared in the Gunners' League side at outside left twice in 1946/47, before moving to Walsall in June 1948, where he made 10 League appearances and scored once. He joined Millwall in December 1948, and it was whilst at Cold Blow Lane that he came to the public attention, having 5 wonderful seasons in which he played 156 senior matches and notched 40 goals. O's boss Alec Stock brought him to Brisbane Road in May 1953, and his subtle, clever play impressed the O's fans. He figured in O's great run in the 1953/54 FA Cup, and his coolly taken goal in the fifth round against Doncaster Rovers was typical of the man. He missed only 5 matches when O's finished as runners-up in 1954/55, and he netted 4 goals against Exeter City in March 1955. Although thirty-five years old, he made 12 appearances in O's championship-winning side of 1955/56. He moved to Falmouth Town to take up the position of player-manager in May 1956, but because the club could not find him suitable accommodation in the area, he resigned after just two weeks and was appointed coach at Tunbridge Wells. He later worked as a representative for the Kenwood company.

SEASON	LEAGUE		FA CUP		TOTAL	
	Apps	Gls	Apps	Gls	Apps	Gls
1953/54	43	9	7	2	50	11
1954/55	41	12	2	0	43	12
1955/56	12	3	0	0	12	3
TOTAL	96	24	9	2	105	26

Stan Morgan

M

Ernest James MORLEY, 1928-31

Ernie Morley was born in Sketty, Swansea on 11 September 1901. The quality full-back started with local side Sketty FC, and made his League debut for Swansea Town against Watford on 3 September 1921. He won his first full Welsh cap at right-back against England on 28 February 1925, and also won a Third Division (South) Championship medal in 1924/25. After playing 123 League appearances for the Swans, he joined O's for £500 in June 1928, and was capped a further 3 times whilst at Millfields Road – against England, Scotland and Ireland in 1929. He also appeared in O's 2 League matches played at Wembley Stadium – on 2 November 1930, against Brentford, and against Southend United on 6 December 1930. Morley always marked his opposition very tightly, and was rarely beaten for pace. He was a good tackler and used the ball well, being quick and accurate in distribution. He broke his leg in a Third Division (South) match at Watford on 7 February 1931, and decided to retire from the game due to the after-effects of the injury. He returned to live in his native Swansea, and the Swans management offered him a chance of a return to League action in June 1931, but he decided against it. Ernie Morley died in Swansea on 26 January 1975, aged seventy-three.

SEASON	LEAGUE		FA CUP		TOTAL	
	Apps	Gls	Apps	Gls	Apps	Gls
1928/29	27	0	4	0	31	0
1929/30	25	0	4	0	29	0
1930/31	19	0	2	0	21	0
TOTAL	71	0	10	0	81	0

Frank George MORRAD, 1946-47

Born on 28 February 1920 in Brentford, Middlesex, Frank Morrad started out as a sixteen-year-old amateur with Brentford in 1936. He was released and then played for Southall FC in the Athenian League until the outbreak of the Second World War. During the war he guested for O's, playing 19 matches and scoring twice between 1944 and 1946. He then went to Nottingham to guest for County in a single match. He returned to Brisbane Road in November 1946, and the centre forward looked a strong resourceful and courageous player, who did well in the first League season back after the war. The centre half was then transferred to Fulham, where he had no first-team opportunities, so moved to Brighton & Hove Albion in February 1948. There he played as a part-timer whilst working as a bookmaker, making 43 senior appearances and scoring 3 goals. He joined Brentford in August 1951, netting twice from 6 matches. Morrad drifted out of the League in August 1953 with a move to Bedford Town.

SEASON	LEAGUE		FA CUP		TOTAL	
	Apps	Gls	Apps	Gls	Apps	Gls
1946/47	25	11	0	0	25	11
TOTAL	25	11	0	0	25	11

David Hyman MORRIS, 1933-4

Born on 25 November 1897 in the East End of London, cockney 'Abe' or 'Harry' Morris, as he was known, was one of only a handful of truly great Jewish players to play for O's over the years, along with the likes of Mark Lazarus and Barry Silkman. Morris had a wonderful career, having once informed a local journalist that it was his job to score goals, and that is something he most certainly did. He played with Fulham, Brentford, Millwall Swansea Town and Swindon Town, before ending his League career with O's, scoring a remarkable 290 goals from 420 League career appearances. Morris started his long playing career with the Vicar of Wakefield club as an eighteen-year-old, before joining Fulham for £250 in May 1919, where he played just 7 senior matches, scoring twice. He moved on to Brentford in June 1921, and in just one-and-a-half seasons with the Bees, he turned out 59 times and netted 29 goals. He joined Millwall in March 1923, and found the net 30 times from 74 League appearances. He moved on to Swansea Town in 1926, where he played just 8 matches and scored 5 goals. He caused quite a stir with the young Welsh ladies, earning himself the nickname of the 'Swansea Casanova' with the local South Wales press. However, he soon fell out with the club's management and joined Swindon Town for £110, becoming their all-time record goalscorer with 227 senior goals from 279 matches – 216 in the League – between 1926 and 1933. He netted 47 of Swindon's total of 100 Third Division (South) League goals in 1926/27. The following season he netted 38 goals, and bagged 20 or more League goals for 5 successive seasons for the Robins. Thirty-six-year-old Morris returned to his roots to become an 'Oriental' on a free transfer in July 1933. He held a first-team spot up until after Christmas 1933, scoring in most of his appearances, but when David Halliday joined he went into the reserves, and scored 23 goals in five months. He moved to Cheltenham Town in September 1934, playing 2 Birmingham Combination League matches, before going to coach Swedish side Gothenburg. He returned to England at the start of the Second World War, and then went to work for the British Information Bureau in New York.

Morris died in San Mateo, California on 20 December 1985, aged eighty-eight.

SEASON	LEAGUE		FA CUP		TOTAL	
	Apps	Gls	Apps	Gls	Apps	Gls
1933/34	13	8	2	3	15	11
TOTAL	13	8	2	3	15	11

James MORRIS, 1914-15

Amateur goalkeeper Jimmy Morris started his career with Bury in 1910, joining O's in May 1914 as cover for Jimmy Hugall. He came south to London to join the Metropolitan Police force. He made his O's debut against Grimsby Town at Millfields Road on 13 March 1915, having been on duty in the law courts that morning – O's won the match 2-1. Morris played in 4 first-team matches – 3 wins and a draw – before returning to Bury to enlist with a local regiment during June 1915, before the commencement of hostilities against Germany.

SEASON	LEAGUE		FA CUP		TOTAL	
	Apps	Gls	Apps	Gls	Apps	Gls
1914/15	4	0	0	0	4	0
TOTAL	4	0	0	0	4	0

David Ellison MORRISON, 1997-2000

Dave Morrison, a left-sided attacking midfielder/wing-back, showed immense pace and skill on joining O's from Peterborough United for £20,000 (plus a further £5,000 after 30 first team appearances) on 21 March 1997. Born in Walthamstow, London on 30 November 1974, he played for Fulham, Wimbledon and Brighton as a schoolboy, before joining Chelmsford City. He then moved on to Peterborough for £30,000 on 12 May 1994, making 59(18) appearances and scoring 12 goals before his transfer to Brisbane Road. Unfortunately, he suffered a serious cruciate ligament knee injury just four minutes into the start of the 1997/98 season in a match against Cardiff City, and only came back as a substitute in the ninetieth minute of the final match of that season against Torquay United. He featured in the early part of the 1998/99 season, scoring his first League goal for the club against Swansea City on 22 August 1998. As a number of injuries curtailed his progress, he went on loan to St Albans in December 1998 to gain match fitness. On his return he played as a substitute at Exeter City in April 1999. He scored one of the vital penalties in the shoot-out at Rotherham United that took O's to the play-off final against Scunthorpe at Wembley, but was not selected for the final, although his pace could possibly have been a great asset on the wide Wembley pitch. Morrison signed a new twelve-month contract with O's at the end of May 1999. He was involved in the first team up to November 1999, but then lost his place. After a couple of loan spells

Dave Morrison

with Stevenage Borough and Dover Athletic, he was given a free transfer in May 2000. He moved on to join Bohemians in Ireland in June 2000, but badly injured a fibula against Shamrock Rovers on 3 November 2000, and was forced to sit out most of the season at Dalymount.

SEASON	LEAGUE		FA CUP		L. CUP	
	Apps	Gls	Apps	Gls	Apps	Gls
1996/97	8	0	0	0	0	0
1997/98	1(1)	0	0	0	0	0
1998/99*	7(17)	3	1	0	1(3)	0
1999/2000	5(8)	0	0	0	2(1)	0
TOTAL	21(26)	3	1	0	2(5)	0

TOTAL APPS	24(31)
TOTAL GOALS	3

* Dave Morrison's League record includes 0(1) promotion play-off match in 1998/99. He also appeared in an Auto Windscreens Shield match.

Murdoch MORRISON, 1947-48

Goalkeeper Murdo Morrison was born in Glasgow on 9 October 1924, and he joined O's from Luton Town in August 1947. He started his career with Scottish club Bell Haven Stars, and came south of the Border to join the Hatters in September 1947, where he made a single League appearance. He joined O's as understudy to Stan Tolliday and fared quite well, making his League debut at Southend United in September 1947. He left the club in May 1948 and returned home to Glasgow. Morrison died in Scotland during 1975.

SEASON	LEAGUE		FA CUP		TOTAL	
	Apps	Gls	Apps	Gls	Apps	Gls
1947/48	10	0	0	0	10	0
TOTAL	10	0	0	0	10	0

Bobby Moss

Robert MOSS, 1968-72

Born in Chigwell, Essex on 13 February 1952, Bobby Moss, a quick and lively striker, did well in O's youth side and signed professional forms in 1970. He scored within five minutes of his League debut at home to Watford on 21 November 1970. However, Moss didn't progress as expected, and he found it difficult in the higher grade. He was allowed to move to Colchester United in May 1972. He had 16(1) League outings for the U's, scoring 3 goals, before dropping out of the League with Wealdstone.

SEASON	LEAGUE		FA CUP		L. CUP	
	Apps	Gls	Apps	Gls	Apps	Gls
1970/71	2(3)	1	0	0	0	0
1971/72	0	0	0	0	0	0
TOTAL	2(3)	1	0	0	0	0

TOTAL APPS	2(3)
TOTAL GOALS	1

Peter MOUNTFORD, 1985-87

Born in Stoke on 13 April 1960, the long-haired Peter Mountford started off as an apprentice with Norwich City in September 1978, playing 1(3) League matches. He moved to Charlton Athletic on a free transfer in September 1983, and made 10(1) League appearances from which he scored once. He joined O's in January 1985, making his League debut as a substitute against Wigan Athletic in a 1-1 draw on 2 March 1985. He was a good squad member and always tried very hard, but he just couldn't gain a regular first-team place. He moved to Fisher Athletic in May 1987.

SEASON	LEAGUE		FA CUP		L. CUP	
	Apps	Gls	Apps	Gls	Apps	Gls
1984/85	14(2)	1	0	0	0	0
1985/86	11(4)	1	2(2)	0	1(1)	0
1986/87	2	0	1(1)	0	0	0
TOTAL	27(6)	2	3(3)	0	1(1)	0

Peter Mountford

M

TOTAL APPS 31(10)

TOTAL GOALS 2

* Peter Mountford also appeared in 6(1) Auto Windscreens Shield matches, scoring once.

Jade Alan MURRAY, 1998-2002

Jay (as he is affectionately known by O's fans) was born on 23 September 1981 in Isling-ton, London. He joined Orient on YTS forms on 1 July 1998, after play-ing his schoolboy football with the Norsemen club. Murray looked to be a powerful striker, and good when run-ning at defenders, and he made a total of 19 youth appearances and scored 3 goals in 1998/99. He notched 15 goals from 25 games the following season, including a hat-trick, and also made 4(7) appearances for the reserve team. He made his League debut as a substi-tute against Rotherham United on 21 March 2000, playing for five minutes. His big moment was when he came on as a substitute towards the end of the home Worthington Cup tie against Newcastle United in September 2000. He went on loan to Chelmsford City on 17 January 2001, returning to the club a month later. He was a member of the under-19 youth side that won the FA Alliance Cup final against Bradford City at the Millennium Stadium on 22 April 2001. Murray signed on a month's loan with Ryman Premier Division side Sutton United during the early part of the 2001/02 season, play-ing 3 matches before being re-called by new O's boss Paul Brush in November. However, he was released from his con-tract in January 2002 and after a short trial with Billericay Town, he joined Barking & East Ham United the follow-ing month.

SEASON	LEAGUE		FA CUP		L. CUP	
	Apps	Gls	Apps	Gls	Apps	Gls
1999/2000	0(2)	0	0	0	0	0
2000/01	0	0	0	0	0(1)	0
2001/02	0	0	0	0	0	0
TOTAL	0(2)	0	0	0	0(1)	0

TOTAL APPS 0(3)

TOTAL GOALS 0

Malcolm MUSGROVE, 1962-66

Malcolm Musgrove was born on 8 July 1933 in Lynemouth, Newcastle-upon-Tyne. The left-winger started out with local side Lynemouth Colliery, before joining West Ham United in December 1952 after his demob. He went on to score the second highest number of goals ever by a West Ham winger – 89 goals from 301 senior appearances during his ten-year stay at Upton Park – only the legendary Jimmy Ruffell (164 goals) ever scored more. Musgrove also won a Second Division Championship medal. He joined O's on 20 December 1962 for £11,000, and scored with his first kick against Birmingham City in a First Division game two days later. He didn't enjoy the O's crowd, coming in for some unnecessary barracking, and he appeared to perform better away from home. He had a wonderful match at Leicester City in O's shock 3-2 victory at Filbert Street in the FA Cup, netting two goals, and another golden moment was when he scored against Cardiff City at Brisbane Road – probably his best per-formance at the ground – in April 1964. The following season he was appointed player-coach, and during his four-year stay, he served under five managers at Brisbane Road. Whilst with O's he suc-ceeded Tommy Cummings as chairman of the Professional Footballers Association.

He left Leyton Orient in May 1966 and retired from playing football, but he has remained in the game holding various managerial, coaching and physio positions with Charlton Athletic, Aston Villa, Leicester City, Manchester United, Torquay United, Exeter City and also Plymouth Argyle. He went to America and worked with the Connecticut Bi-Continentals and the Chicago Stings in the NASL. After a two-year stay in the States, he returned to the UK, spending three years as physio with Exeter City. After a spell as coach to the Qatar national side in 1994, he was appointed reserve coach with Plymouth Argyle. More recently, he was the physio at Shrewsbury Town, and today he is living in retirement.

SEASON	LEAGUE		FA CUP		L. CUP	
	Apps	Gls	Apps	Gls	Apps	Gls
1962/63	18	3	3	2	0	0
1963/64	42	11	3	2	1	0

Malcolm Musgrove

1964/65	16	0	1	0	0	0
1965/66	7	0	0	0	0	0
TOTAL	83	14	7	4	1	0

TOTAL APPS	91
TOTAL GOALS	18

N

Dominic John NAYLOR, 1996-98

This fine 5ft 9in and 13st 9lb defender joined O's from Gillingham on 15 August 1996 and had 2 good seasons. He was a player who got through a tremendous amount of work during a game. Born in Watford, Hertfordshire on 12 August 1970, he started with Watford as a trainee in July 1987, signing professional forms in September 1988. He captained the Watford youth side that won the FA Youth Cup in 1988/89. He actually made his League debut with Halifax Town whilst on a loan spell with them in December 1998 – he went on to make a total of 5(1) appearances for them, scoring once. Watford released him and he went to play in Hong Kong in October 1990. He returned to England in August 1991 and joined Barnet, making 84(1) appearances for the Bees before joining Plymouth Argyle on 17 July 1993, where he played 94(1) senior games. During August 1995 he moved on to Gillingham, and after 30 appearances he moved to O's for £25,000 on 15 August 1996. He scored twice in Peter Shilton's 1,000th League match against Brighton & Hove Albion in December 1996. Probably his happiest moment at O's was on 12 September 1995, when he captained the side that won away at Northampton Town 2-1 – their first win after 42 League

Dom Naylor

away matches. When Naylor's contract ran out, he left on a free transfer under the Bosman ruling. Naylor left the club to join Stevenage Borough in the Vauxhall Conference during June 1998. He moved on to Dagenham & Redbridge in October 1999 on loan, signing a permanent deal the following month. He played over 100 senior games and won a championship medal with them. He moved to Basingstoke Town on 19 November 2000.

SEASON	LEAGUE		FA CUP		L. CUP	
	Apps	Gls	Apps	Gls	Apps	Gls
1996/97	44	3	2	0	2	0
1997/98	43	1	2	0	4	0
TOTAL	87	4	4	0	6	0

TOTAL APPS	97
TOTAL GOALS	4

* Dominic Naylor also appeared in 3 Auto Windscreens Shield matches.

William Henry NAYLOR, 1947-50

Billy Naylor's surname was originally Barke, until he changed it by deed poll sometime before joining O's in June 1947. Born in Sheffield on 23 November 1919, he started off playing football with Hampton Sports FC before joining Crystal Palace in January 1939, where he made 18 League appearances and scored 8 goals. One of those goals – as Barke – was scored against O's in the club's first match under the name of Leyton Orient FC at Brisbane Road on 28 September 1946. Naylor joined Brentford for £6,000 in February 1947, making just 11 League appearances and scoring 2 goals for the Bees, before his move to Brisbane Road. He was undoubtedly a clever and neat forager with a good measure of skill, and his play was a major influence in an 11-match unbeaten run which meant the club avoided having to apply for re-election. He also helped create some splendid openings for Frank Neary to break the club goalscoring record with 25 League goals in 1948/49. The eighth match of the 1949/50 season, at Ipswich Town in September, saw him sustain a serious cartilage injury, which sadly ending his playing career. Naylor died in 1989.

SEASON	LEAGUE		FA CUP		TOTAL	
	Apps	Gls	Apps	Gls	Apps	Gls
1947/48	27	6	0	0	27	6
1948/49	29	8	2	0	31	8
1949/50	8	0	0	0	8	0
TOTAL	64	14	2	0	66	14

Harold Frank NEARY, 1947-49

Big centre forward Frank Neary – nick-named the 'Brown Bomber' – proved to be one of the most popular players to wear O's colours in the 1940s. This was due mainly to his very powerful shooting from all angles and distances, and his excellent goalscoring ability – something not common down Brisbane Road way – and his never-say-die attitude. He was reputed to have one of the hardest shots in football during his era. He came at a time when the O's were in the doldrums, and he not only helped O's to rise up the table, but also brought back the crowds to Brisbane Road. Attendances averaged 13,500 during his stay. Born on 6 March 1921 in Aldershot, Hampshire, he commenced his career with Finchley FC. He then moved to Queens Park Rangers in July 1945 on a free transfer and netted 4 goals from 9 League appearances. (He also scored 23 goals from 30 regional wartime matches.) He moved to West Ham United for £4,000 in January 1947, and his 15 League goals from just 14 games helped the Hammers ease away from the likelihood of relegation. He became an 'Oriental' in November 1947 for £2,000, and soon showed his ability by becoming the club's leading goalscorer for two seasons. He broke Ted Crawford's record of 23 League goals (set back in 1935/36) by scoring 25 goals in 1948/49. Neary's shooting was so powerful that he once knocked Torquay United's goalkeeper Archie McFeat unconscious with a trademark drive, and Bristol Rovers 'keeper Jack Weare, in trying to stop a Neary penalty-kick, not only found the ball in the back of the net, but himself as well! It was a sad day when he was allowed to move to QPR for £7,000 in October 1949, yet he only made 19 senior appearances and scored 5 goals for Rangers before moving on to Millwall for £6,000 in August

1950. Signed by the former O's boss Charles Hewitt, Neary netted 50 goals from 123 League appearances for the side. He ended his career in non-League football with Gravesend in May 1954. Frank Neary scored a total of 118 career goals from 245 League appearances.

SEASON	LEAGUE		FA CUP		TOTAL	
	Apps	Gls	Apps	Gls	Apps	Gls
1947/48	26	15	1	0	27	15
1948/49	39	25	2	0	41	25
1949/50	13	4	0	0	13	4
TOTAL	78	44	3	0	81	44

Andrew Nesbitt NELSON, 1964-66

Andy Nelson was born in Custom House, London on 5 July 1935. He joined the West Ham groundstaff in December 1953 as a junior, and scored once in 15 League appearances, until an approach by the Ipswich Town manager Alf Ramsey took him to Portman Road for £8,000 in June 1959. The 6ft tall centre half gained both Second and First Division Championship medals in 1961 and 1962, and made 193 League appearances for the Suffolk club during his five-year stay. He moved to Brisbane Road in September 1964, signed by O's boss Benny Fenton, and skippered the O's for a short time. He will be recalled for his brave display at Southampton in an FA Cup tie during January 1965, when he refused to leave the field despite suffering from an injury and concussion. However, his heroic efforts were to no avail, as O's lost 3-1. During October 1965 he was transferred to Plymouth Argyle for £4,000, where he totalled 94 League appearances, scoring once. In 1969, after his playing days were over, he managed both Charlton Athletic and Gillingham. More recently he was living in retirement in

Alicante, Spain and he won the Spanish Bowls Championship in 1996.

SEASON	LEAGUE		FA CUP		L. CUP	
	Apps	Gls	Apps	Gls	Apps	Gls
1964/65	36	0	1	0	2	0
1965/66	7	0	0	0	0	0
TOTAL	43	0	1	0	2	0

TOTAL APPS	46
TOTAL GOALS	0

Paul Clayton NEWELL, 1990-94

The frustrating life of being a goalkeeper is that there is room for only one in a team, so any understudy can spend more time watching from the bench or in the stand than playing. This is exactly what happened to Paul Newell, as second choice behind Paul Heald, and later Chris Turner. Born in Greenwich, London on 23 February 1969, his family later moved to South Woodham Ferrers in Essex to run a public house. He started with Southend United, joining them as a youth trainee in June 1987 and playing 18 senior matches. Newell joined O's from the Blues for £5,000 in July 1990, making his League debut against Bury on 19 February 1991, after Heald had injured his back in training. He also played the 2 League Cup ties against Sheffield Wednesday in 1991/92. He in turn broke his ankle in training before the visit of Stoke City in October 1991. After a loan spell with Colchester United in August 1992 (where he made 14 League appearances) he joined Barnet on a free transfer in July 1994, making 16 League appearances. He signed for Darlington in January 1996, appearing at Wembley in a Division Three play-off defeat against Plymouth in front of 43,000 fans. The twenty-nine-year-old made 45 appearances for them, before he

Paul Newell

moved into non-League football in January 1997 with Sittingbourne. He also had non-contract spells in 1997/98 with Colchester United and Northampton Town; in 1999 with St Albans City and Dagenham & Redbridge; and in 2000 with Grays Athletic. In October 2001, he joined Canvey Island FC as player-coach. In total, he made 161 League career appearances.

SEASON	LEAGUE		FA CUP		L. CUP	
	Apps	Gls	Apps	Gls	Apps	Gls
1990/91	8	0	0	0	0	0
1991/92	10	0	0	0	3	0
1992/93	3	0	0	0	0	0
1993/94	40	0	3	0	0	0
TOTAL	61	0	3	0	3	0

TOTAL APPS	67
TOTAL GOALS	0

* Paul Newell also appeared in 4 Auto Windscreens Shield matches.

Ronald Vernon NEWMAN, 1961-62

Born on 19 January 1934 in Portsmouth, Hampshire, he started off his career with Fareham Town in the early 1950s. He then played for Newport Isle of Wight and Woking, before signing on a free transfer with Portsmouth in January 1955. Ron Newman was with Pompey for six years, and chalked up 108 League appearances and 21 goals, showing up well with his thrusting style of play down the left wing. He joined O's on 4 January 1961 for £5,000 and did well for a while, until being replaced in favour of the youthful Terry McDonald. This largely confined him to the reserves, but he did score O's third in a 5-1 win in a friendly against German side Wormatia Worms FC in 1961. During O's promotion campaign of 1961/62, he made just 2 appearances. He didn't make any appearances for the club in the First Division, and was transferred to Crystal Palace for £4,200 in October 1962, where he made a total of 14 League matches and scored once. His stay at Selhurst Park was brief, and he moved on to Gillingham for £2,000 in September 1963, and helped them to a Fourth Division Championship in 1963/64. By the time he left the Gills in 1966, he had made 90(3) League appearances and scored 21 goals for them. Newman moved to the USA in 1968 and played for Atlanta Chiefs. Today he is alive and well in America, as a coach for Dallas Tornado and Fort Lauderdale, and as general manager of the San Diego Sockers. He still keeps in touch with the Ex-Pompey Reunion Club.

SEASON	LEAGUE		FA CUP		L. CUP	
	Apps	Gls	Apps	Gls	Apps	Gls
1960/61	12	1	2	0	0	0
1961/62	2	0	0	0	1	0
1962/63	0	0	0	0	0	0
TOTAL	14	1	2	0	1	0

TOTAL APPS	17
TOTAL GOALS	1

Adam NEWTON, 2002 (loan)

Newton, a very pacy twenty-one-year-old right-sided full-back or midfielder, joined O's on loan on 9 March 2002 from West Ham United. Born in Ascot, Berkshire on 4 December 1980, the England Under-21 international started out on YTS forms with West Ham in 1998 and has made 2 starts for the senior team. He also starred in their youth team's 9-0 aggregate victory over Coventry City in the FA Youth Cup final in 1999. In July 1999 he went on loan to Portsmouth, for whom he made 1(2) League appearances, and in November 2001 he went on loan to Notts County and made 15(7) senior starts and scored a goal. O's boss Paul Brush stated: 'If things work out, Newton's stay could

Ron Newman

be longer.' However, the player himself has hinted that he does not want to play Division Three football.

SEASON	LEAGUE		FA CUP		l. CUP	
	Apps	Gls	Apps	Gls	Apps	Gls
2001/02	10	1	0	0	0	0
TOTAL	10	1	0	0	0	0

TOTAL APPS	10
TOTAL GOALS	1

Reginald William NEWTON, 1948-49

Amateur goalkeeper Reg Newton was born in Limehouse, London on 30 June 1926. He came to O's from a Dagenham works team in April 1948, turning professional for the start of the 1948/49 season. He got his first-team chance a little earlier than expected, due to injury and illness to first choice Stan Tolliday and Polish amateur international Stan Gerula. Although not the tallest of 'keepers (5ft 10in), he was daring and proved to be an excellent shot-stopper. He made his League debut in a 2-2 draw at Southend United in September 1948. Newton was transferred to Brentford in July 1949 where he stayed for seven years. Although not always a first-teamer, he made a total of 87 League appearances, before leaving in 1958 and moving into the non-League circuit and enjoying spells with Tunbridge Wells, Yiewsley and Chelmsford City.

SEASON	LEAGUE		FA CUP		TOTAL	
	Apps	Gls	Apps	Gls	Apps	Gls
1948/49	23	0	2	0	25	0
TOTAL	23	0	2	0	25	0

Anthony Wallace NICHOLAS, 1965-66

Born in West Ham, London on 16 April 1938, big things were expected of Tony Nicholas when he signed as a professional with Chelsea in May 1955, having gained a number of England youth caps. Yet despite his early promise, he did not quite fulfil his early potential. Nicholas was a tall, long-striding inside forward, and although he might have not have reached the heights at Stamford Bridge, he did make 63 senior appearances for the Blues with 21 goals. Several clubs were interested in him, and he finally joined Brighton & Hove Albion in November 1960, signed by their manager and former 'Oriental' Billy Lane, for a record fee of £15,000. He made 70 senior appearances at the Goldstone club and scored 23 goals. He then moved out of the League in 1962, after a contractual dispute with Brighton, and joined Southern League side Chelmsford City. It was Dave Sexton who brought him to Brisbane Road in June 1965, and he became O's first ever substitute to come on to the field of play and score a goal in his final O's appearance, a 2-1 defeat against Charlton Athletic on 26 February 1966. Although he scored constantly for the reserves, he only managed a couple of first-team goals, before moving on to play for Dartford in May 1966. Two years later he joined Cambridge United, and then did the rounds of non-League football with Dartford (again), Gravesend & Northfleet, and finally with Folkestone Town, before calling it a day in 1973, at the age of thirty-five.

SEASON	LEAGUE		FA CUP		L. CUP	
	Apps	Gls	Apps	Gls	Apps	Gls
1965/66	8(1)	2	1	0	0	0
TOTAL	8(1)	2	1	0	0	0

TOTAL APPS	9(1)
TOTAL GOALS	2

Joseph Edward NICHOLLS, 1919-25

Born in Bilston, near Wolverhampton, Joe Nicholls started off with Bilston United and then, after a trial, became a reserve player for Wolverhampton Wanderers. He joined O's in June 1919, and made his League debut at Huddersfield Town on 30 August 1919 – the first League match to be played on resumption of League football after the wartime hostilities. He performed creditably for four seasons, usually playing at left-back until being replaced by Bert Rosier, and was remembered for his consistency and aggressive play, rather than any flamboyant displays. He was a reserve for his final couple of seasons at Millfields Road, and moved back to his local side, Bilston United, in August 1925.

Joe Nicholls

SEASON	LEAGUE		FA CUP		TOTAL	
	Apps	Gls	Apps	Gls	Apps	Gls
1919/20	42	1	1	0	43	1
1920/21	24	1	1	0	25	1
1921/22	17	0	0	0	17	0
1922/23	31	0	1	0	32	0
1923/24	1	0	0	0	1	0
1924/25	2	0	0	0	2	0
TOTAL	117	2	3	0	120	2

Derek NICHOLSON, 1953-58

Born in Harrow, Middlesex on 8 April 1936, Derek Nicholson was a very strong-moving outside right, who joined in November 1953 after coming up through the junior ranks via the Chase of Chertsey club. He turned professional, aged seventeen, in November 1953. He spent his days playing for the reserves either at right-back or at centre forward. He represented the Surrey County side against Middlesex, and was a regular scorer for an Army representative side. He did quite well in his League debut against Stoke City on 31 August 1957, and during the following 3 matches he set up goals for Tommy Johnston, but once Phil White had recovered from injury, Nicholson went back to the reserves. He returned to the first XI later that season, but didn't show much. He left to join Queens Park Rangers in May 1958, but made no headway at Loftus Road, and soon drifted into non-League football. Nicholson was also a top-class cricketer and badminton player.

SEASON	LEAGUE		FA CUP		TOTAL	
	Apps	Gls	Apps	Gls	Apps	Gls
1956/57	0	0	0	0	0	0
1957/58	6	0	0	0	6	0
TOTAL	6	0	0	0	6	0

George Harold NICHOLSON, 1959-60

Born in Wetherall, near Carlisle on 25 January 1932, Harry Nicholson was probably O's biggest goalkeeper since

Derek Nicholson

the days of Arthur Wood, weighing 14st. He started off as an amateur player with Carlisle United, before moving on to Grimsby Town in August 1952, chalking up 17 appearances. During July 1957 he moved to Nottingham Forest, where he had his most successful period and played in 72 League matches, including 34 in their promotion run to the First Division in 1956/57. He moved on to Accrington Stanley, but due to a number of injuries, he only managed a single appearance before joining O's for £500 in March 1959. He spent most of his time in the reserves as understudy to Dave Groombridge, however, he did feature in the final 4 League matches of 1959/60. He joined Bristol City in July 1960, playing just a single match, before going to Poole Town in June 1961. Harry Nicholson was, at his best, a good goalkeeper, and gained a reputation as a good sportsman.

SEASON	LEAGUE		FA CUP		TOTAL	
	Apps	Gls	Apps	Gls	Apps	Gls
1959/60	4	0	0	0	4	0
TOTAL	4	0	0	0	4	0

Joseph Robinson NICHOLSON, 1919-24

Joe Nicholson was born in Ryhope, near Sunderland on 4 June 1898 and started off with hometown club Ryhope. He joined O's as a wing-half in July 1919, and was a player who loved to venture forward and have a shot at goal. He proved over his four years at Millfields Road to be a great trier, but moved on to Cardiff City in May 1924, where he made 48 League appearances and also appeared for the Welshmen in the 1925 FA Cup final, losing 1-0 to Sheffield United. He later moved to Aston Villa in an exchange deal with George Blackburn, yet only played once in the League for Villa before moving to Spennymoor United. Joe Nicholson died in Durham during 1974.

SEASON	LEAGUE		FA CUP		TOTAL	
	Apps	Gls	Apps	Gls	Apps	Gls
1919/20	30	1	0	0	30	1
1920/21	39	1	0	0	39	1
1921/22	32	0	1	0	33	0
1922/23	35	2	1	0	36	2
1923/24	9	0	0	0	9	0
TOTAL	145	4	2	0	147	4

William NICOL, 1904-05

There is very little documented information about Middlesbrough-born inside forward Billy Nicol. He came to O's from non-League football during May 1904, and was present for the club's first season in the Second Division of the Southern League, and for its first entry into the FA Cup. Nicol scored a total of 13 goals in all competitions (London

Joe Nicholson

League, Southern League and FA Cup). He left the club in May 1905.

SEASON	LEAGUE		FA CUP		TOTAL	
	Apps	Gls	Apps	Gls	Apps	Gls
1904/05*	-	-	6	3	6	3
TOTAL	-	-	6	3	6	3

* Clapton Orient first entered the League in 1905/06.

Kevin Patrick NUGENT, 1987-92, 2002

Kevin Nugent, a big 6ft 1in striker, was a product of O's YTS scheme, who signed professional forms in July 1987, and scored on his League debut against Scarborough. During the early days of his professional career, he was a victim of barracking by a section of the Brisbane Road crowd, but he showed strength of character and eventually won over the O's fans. Born in Edmonton, London on 9 April 1969, he played 4 times for Eire at youth level, as both his parents were Irish. One of his most memorable matches was his double strike in the epic FA Cup victory over First Division side Oldham Athletic on 15 January 1992. Nugent was an unselfish player, whose goalscoring record did not reflect his other qualities as a player. His best season at the club was during 1991/92, when he found the net with 11 League goals and 5 goals in major cup competitions. (Some football books credit Nugent with 12 League goals – he was wrongly credited with the opening goal of the season at Brentford, this goal was scored by Wayne Burnett.) He scored the only goal of a friendly game against Spanish side Royal Vallidolid in 1991/92. After five seasons with O's, the twenty-two-year-old was transferred to Plymouth Argyle for £275,000 on 23 March 1992. He was no failure at Home Park, netting 32 League goals from 124(7) starts. In September 1995 he signed for Bristol City for £75,000, but only managed 14 goals from 48(22) appearances, which was not a good enough return for the Red Robins. He moved on to Cardiff City on 27 June 1997 for £65,000, however, he was ruled out for much of that season with injury. During 1998/99 his 18 senior goals from 48 appearances helped Cardiff gain promotion to Division Two. He scored for the Bluebirds in their 3-1 FA Cup replay victory over the O's at Ninian Park in November 1999, and he netted 29 goals from 94(5) League appearances until sustaining a serious injury in November 2000, which ruled him out from playing. He, along with Matthew Brazier, joined O's on free transfers from Cardiff City on 31 January 2002, after they had both turned down a joint £70,000 move to Colchester United. For Nugent, it was a

Kevin Nugent

1920. The biggest problem he had was trying to dislodge the outstanding Owen Williams. Twenty-one-year-old Nunn got his opportunity when Williams was injured at Port Vale in April 1921, and played the following week in a very special match – the 3-0 win over Notts County at Millfields Road on 30 April, which was attended by the Prince of Wales. This was indeed an honour for the young player. Nunn played whenever Williams was injured over the next three seasons, leaving in July 1924 to join Folkestone. He returned to League football with Luton Town (playing 14 matches in 1927/28), but was a reserve for the next two League campaigns. Nunn died on 20 February 1946 in Uxbridge, aged forty-seven.

SEASON	LEAGUE		FA CUP		TOTAL	
	Apps	Gls	Apps	Gls	Apps	Gls
1920/21	2	0	0	0	2	0
1921/22	5	0	0	0	5	0
1922/23	7	0	0	0	7	0
1923/24	5	0	0	0	5	0
TOTAL	19	0	0	0	19	0

return to the club some fourteen-and-a-half years after his debut for O's.

SEASON	LEAGUE		FA CUP		L. CUP	
	Apps	Gls	Apps	Gls	Apps	Gls
1987/88	10(1)	3	0	0	1	0
1988/89	2(1)	0	0	0	0(1)	0
1989/90	5(6)	0	0	0	0	0
1990/91	33	5	5	1	4(2)	3
1991/92	36	11	4	2	4	3
2001/02	7(2)	1	0	0	0	0
TOTAL	93(10)	20	9	3	9(3)	6

TOTAL APPS	111(13)
TOTAL GOALS	29

* Kevin Nugent also appeared in 9(1) Auto Windscreens Shield matches, scoring once.

Alfred Sydney NUNN, 1920-24
Born on 15 November 1899 in Holborn, London, outside left Alf Nunn joined O's from non-League football in December

Scott John OAKES, July-November 2001
Versatile Scott Oakes joined O's on a free transfer on 3 July 2001, signing a two-year contract. This former England under-21 player (he gained a cap against Brazil during 1993) was born in Leicester on 5 August 1972, the son of Trevor of the 1960s pop group Showadawaddy, and the brother of Leicester City's Stefan. The 5ft 11in and 11st 4lb winger or midfielder started his career as a youth trainee with

his hometown club Leicester City, and was rated as an excellent prospect, making 1(2) League appearances. Oakes joined Luton Town on 22 October 1991, and made his name with some fine match-winning performances. After playing 136(37) League matches and scoring 28 goals, he joined Premiership side Sheffield Wednesday on 7 August 1996 for £425,000, but during his four-year stay at Hillsborough he struggled with injuries, making just 7(17) League appearances and scoring once. He joined Burnley in August 2000, in the hope of reviving his career, but his move to Turf Moor didn't work out and he joined Cambridge United the following October on a free transfer. However, after just 7(11) League appearances, he was given a free transfer in May 2001 and he hopes to revive his career. He received a bad knee injury in the match at Mansfield Town on 6 October, and there were even fears he could be at the end of his playing career. Oakes was released from his contract on 26 November 2001. The parties involved reached a financial agreement, but O's boss Paul Brush told the player that he is welcome back for pre-season training. Oakes said: 'I understand what the club have done – it's a reality and I don't blame them. I'm definitely not giving up.'

SEASON	LEAGUE		FA CUP		L. CUP	
	Apps	Gls	Apps	Gls	Apps	Gls
2001/02	11	0	0	0	1	0
TOTAL	11	0	0	0	1	0

TOTAL APPS	12
TOTAL GOALS	0

George O'BRIEN, 1966

George O'Brien was born in Dunfermline, Scotland on 22 November 1935. He stood just 5ft 6in tall, but he was a prolific goalscorer with Southampton, who joined O's in March 1966, at the age of thirty-one. This was part of the deal that took young starlet David Webb to the Dell. O'Brien started his career with Blairhall Colliery, before moving to Dunfermline Athletic in 1952, playing in their first team at the age of just sixteen. He moved to Leeds United in March 1957, making 44 League appearances and scoring 6 goals. His move to Southampton took place in July 1959 for a mere £10,000, and he went on to have his best years in football there, scoring a remarkable 174 senior goals (154 in the League) from 178 appearances. He broke the Saints' aggregate goalscoring record playing against O's. In the event of his signing, the O's were relegated to the Third Division. O'Brien was troubled by injury and illness at Brisbane Road, and just couldn't seem to settle in London. He eventually moved to Aldershot in December 1966, where he made 38(3) League appearances and scored 8 goals during his two-year stay. He decided to retire from the game in May 1968, and became the landlord at the Waterloo Arms in Shirley. In 1990 he moved back to Scotland to become sub-postmaster, but within a year he had returned to Southampton in order to become the landlord at the Star & Garter Public House in Freemantle.

SEASON	LEAGUE		FA CUP		L. CUP	
	Apps	Gls	Apps	Gls	Apps	Gls
1965/66	7	0	0	0	0	0
1966/67	10	3	0	0	1	0
TOTAL	17	3	0	0	1	0

TOTAL APPS	18
TOTAL GOALS	3

O

James O'GARA, 1908-09

Jimmy O'Gara was born in Maryhill, Glasgow during 1888. The inside forward started his career with Airdrie, but moved to Middlesbrough in August 1907. He joined O's in July 1908, but was unable to gain a first-team place. O'Gara made his only League appearance in the 2-0 defeat at Chesterfield on 26 September 1908, but spent the remainder of the season as a reserve. He went on trial with Preston North End in July 1909, but never made it. He returned to Scotland to join Dundee Hibernians FC, where he spent two seasons making 23 Scottish League appearances and scoring 5 goals. In June 1911 he returned south of the Border, joining Southern League Portsmouth, but made just a single senior appearance.

Steve Okai

SEASON	LEAGUE		FA CUP		TOTAL	
	Apps	Gls	Apps	Gls	Apps	Gls
1908/09	1	0	0	0	1	0
TOTAL	1	0	0	0	1	0

Stephen Patrick OKAI, 1991-94

Wing-back Steve Okai made a dream start to his League career when scoring against Reading on his debut in the penultimate game of the 1991/92 season. His second goal came the following season, with a last-gasp winner against Bolton Wanderers on 3 October 1992, when he shot into the right corner of the net from just inside the box. Born on 3 December 1973 in Ghana, his family came to England in 1984, and he was spotted playing for Villa Court FC under-14s in Lewisham by an O's scout. Whilst at school he was selected for England schoolboy trials. He turned down a YTS place with O's to continue his A-Level studies, and only trained twice a week whilst attending St Francis Xavier College in Clapham. Okai signed

professional forms in 1991, and made just a handful of appearances between 1992 and 1994. He later played for non-League sides Barnet and Dagenham & Redbridge.

SEASON	LEAGUE		FA CUP		L. CUP	
	Apps	Gls	Apps	Gls	Apps	Gls
1991/92	1	1	0	0	0	0
1992/93	5(8)	1	0	0	1	0
1994/94	5(6)	2	1(1)	0	0(1)	0
TOTAL	11(14)	4	1(1)	0	1(1)	0

TOTAL APPS	13(16)
TOTAL GOALS	4

Frank OLIVER, 1906-09, 1912-13

Southampton-born inside forward Frank Oliver started off in the professional ranks with Southern League Brentford during the 1904/05 season, making a total of 10 appearances and scoring 3 goals. He moved to First Division Everton in June

1905, scoring a hat-trick on his League debut on 14 October 1905 against Notts County, but he went on to make just 4 more senior appearances. Oliver joined O's in August 1906 and was the second-top goalscorer on 8 goals, behind Bill Martin. His goal return was not so good over the following two seasons, so he played mainly in the reserves. He moved to Southport Central FC in May 1909, but during 1912/13, Oliver returned to O's and made a single further League appearance in a 2-0 defeat at Blackpool in February 1913.

SEASON	LEAGUE		FA CUP		TOTAL	
	Apps	Gls	Apps	Gls	Apps	Gls
1906/07*	22	9	-	-	22	9
1907/08	6	0	0	0	6	0
1908/09	10	1	1	0	11	1
1912/13	1	0	0	0	1	0
TOTAL	39	10	1	0	40	10

* Clapton Orient did not enter the FA Cup in 1906/07.

Emmanuel OMOYINMI, 1999 (loan)

Manny Omoyinmi, a strong, speedy wing-back, came to O's on loan from West Ham United on 19 March 1999, but sustained an injury in training. After just a handful of League matches during the following month, he returned to Upton Park. Born in Nigeria on 28 December 1977, he was a product of the Hammers' successful youth scheme. He became a trainee on 11 June 1984, and was a member of the side that won the South East Counties League title in 1995/96. He turned professional on 15 May 1996. He spent much of his time on loan with other clubs: in September 1996 he went on loan to AFC Bournemouth, playing 5(2) matches. During February 1998 he was at Dundee

United, where he made just 1(3) Scottish League appearances. Upon his return to Upton Park, he eventually got a first-team chance coming on as a substitute at Crystal Palace and scoring two well-taken goals. His first full start came in January 1999 in their FA Cup defeat at Swansea City, and he made a total of 2(11) senior appearances. He made his O's League debut at Scunthorpe United in March 1999, and scored in his next match at Halifax Town after just three minutes. After his return to Upton Park, he went on loan to Gillingham on 3 September 1999, playing 7(2) matches and scoring 3 goals during December 1999. He also played in 2 significant matches as a substitute in the Worthington League Cup. He returned to Upton Park and came on as a substitute in the quarter-final of the Worthington Cup against Aston Villa. In the last six minutes of extra time, the Hammers won the match, yet due to the fact that Omoyinmi was already cup-tied with Gillingham and therefore was an 'illegal' player, it was Villa who progressed to the semi-final after winning a re-match. The blunder by the Hammers secretary cost him his job, and it was former O's and Spurs secretary Peter Barnes who was appointed to replace him. During December 1999, Omoyinmi went on loan to Scunthorpe United, where he made 6 League appearances and scored once. February 2000 saw another loan spell, this time at Barnet, where he played 1(5) matches. With his career at Upton Park going nowhere, he was given a free transfer and moved to Oxford United on 23 June 2000. It was not the best of moves, as they were struggling to avoid relegation, and he played 16(8) League matches up to the end of the 2000/01 season, grabbing 3 goals.

O

SEASON	LEAGUE		FA CUP		L. CUP	
	Apps	Gls	Apps	Gls	Apps	Gls
1998/99	3(1)	1	0	0	0	0
TOTAL	3(1)	1	0	0	0	0

TOTAL APPS	3(1)
TOTAL GOALS	1

Kelechi-Krisantos OPARA, 2000/01

K.K. Opara came to O's for a reported fee of £2,500, after having his contract cancelled by Colchester United for what was reported as 'persistent misconduct'. He was in the same U's youth side as Lumana Tresor Lua Lua, who joined Newcastle United in 2001 for a big fee. Born in Oweri, Nigeria (the same town as John Chiedozie) on 21 December 1981, the striker started with Colchester's youth team, signing professional forms in August 1998 at the age of seventeen. His first-team debut came at the end of the 1998/99 season. He built on that start with a series of substitute appearances, and made 2 starts in 1999/2000. Opara made a further 3 senior starts in September 2000, and made 2(18) senior appearances in total, without finding the net. His O's debut came against Darlington on 16 December 2000, and he received a warm ovation on what was an impressive performance. He showed a lot of maturity, despite having only just turned nineteen the previous Thursday. He got a surprise call-up for the FA Cup third round tie against Tottenham Hotspur on 6 January 2001, after top scorer Carl Griffiths was injured during training the previous day. He impressed the television commentators with his deft touches in a match televised worldwide via Sky. After the arrival of Italian-born Pinamonte on loan from Brentford in February 2001, Opara went on loan himself to Dagenham & Redbridge on 9 February 2001, along with Finnish trialist Juno Rantala. Opara played for the Daggers at Nuneaton Borough, facing former 'Oriental' goalie Chris Mackenzie. He scored in their 5-1 win over Kettering eight days later, and appeared in 4 straight wins for the Daggers. He returned to O's in March and played in the 1-1 draw at Shrewsbury Town on 17 March. He was a member of O's under-19 youth team that won the FA Alliance Cup final against Bradford City at the Millennium Stadium on 22 April 2001. He went on loan to Ryman League side Billericay Town for three months in August 2001, playing alongside another former 'Oriental' Amara Simba. He started off very well, netting 5 goals in 4 games before being sent off against Hampton & Richmond on 1 September. It was then incorrectly reported that Opara had gone to earn his living in Hong Kong, but the truth of the matter was that he had gone to Essex side Purfleet on a month's loan. Opara was sold to Billericay Town in November for £3,000 with a 40 per cent sell-on clause in the contract. Billericay released him in in March 2002.

SEASON	LEAGUE		FA CUP		L. CUP	
	Apps	Gls	Apps	Gls	Apps	Gls
2000/01	3(3)	0	1	0	0	0
2001/02	0	0	0	0	0	0
TOTAL	3(3)	0	1	0	0	0

TOTAL APPS	4(3)
TOTAL GOALS	0

* K.K. Opara also played in an LDV Vans Trophy match in 2000/01.

Sasha Fernand Henry OPINEL, 2001

Frenchman Sasha Opinel was a surprise inclusion on the bench, and came on at half-time for a Division Three match against Kidderminster on 16 February 2001. He had actually played against O's reserves the previous Wednesday for AFC Bournemouth, with whom he was on trial. Born in Bourge-Saint-Maurice, close to the French Alps, on 9 April 1977, the defender started his career with Cannes, Ile Rousse FC, Lille and Corsican side AC Ajaccio. After a trial with Stockport County, he moved as a free agent to Scottish First Division side Raith Rovers on 27 December 1999. He made an immediate impact at Stark's Park in his first reserve match, by crocking an East Fife player within the first two minutes, and he followed that up with another crunching tackle twenty minutes later, receiving the first of many yellow cards. He made his Scottish League debut at Morton on 27 December, and soon established himself as the regular left-back. He was dropped for the final match of the 1999/2000 season because of an alleged drinking incident the previous night. He signed a two-year contract during the summer break, but red cards in his first 2 starts led to him being dropped. He got injured in a reserve match, and in November 2000 went on trial with Notts County, but he returned to Kirkaldy. He was released from contract on 8 December 2000 after making 24(1) senior appearances, picking up 16 yellow cards and 4 red cards. A spokesman for Raith stated that both club and player thought it was best he left, and they wished him all the best for the future. He went on trial with Plymouth Argyle on 21 December 2000, and made a single appearance in an LDV Vans Trophy match at Bristol Rovers on 9 January 2001. He then moved to AFC Bournemouth on trial. Opinel joined O's on 15 February

2001, and showed up well against Kidderminster as an attacking full-back, causing the 'Kiddie' defence a few headaches. He played in a reserve fixture a few days later, picking up a yellow card. He was an unused substitute in the 1-1 draw at Scunthorpe United on 20 February. He made his League debut in the 3-2 win at Lincoln City on 26 February, and according to assistant manager Paul Clark 'Sasha did a fine job at right-back'. He scored a brilliant goal at Cardiff City on 6 March 2001 when he cut inside the home defence and put a curling twenty-yarder into the top left-hand corner of the net. He also made O's equaliser at Shrewsbury Town for McLean to head home, but unfortunately picked up another yellow card. Sasha Opinel played his last game (and picked up yet another booking) against Cheltenham Town on 28 April, and was not seen again. He turned down the chance of a two-year contract with O's in May 2001, in order to try his luck with French Second Division side Nancy FC. However, things didn't worked out in France, and he returned to England looking for a club. To keep fit he played for Chelten United in the Barking & District Sunday League, helping out a couple of mates. He joined Billericay Town and made his Ryman Premier League debut alongside another French former O's star, Amara Simba, against Purfleet on 9 November 2001, a match that featured seven former O's players.

SEASON	LEAGUE		FA CUP		L. CUP	
	Apps	Gls	Apps	Gls	Apps	Gls
2000/01	9(2)	1	0	0	0	0
TOTAL	9(2)	1	0	0	0	0

TOTAL APPS		9(2)
TOTAL GOALS		1

O

Richard William ORTON, 1905-06

London-born amateur reserve centre forward Dick Orton made his League debut in the 6-1 defeat at Chelsea in March 1905. The following week, he scored the only goal of the game against Gainsborough Trinity. During April, he assisted Walter Leigh, bagging 4 goals against Bradford. There is little else that is known about Orton – he was not retained and left in May 1906, supposedly returning to non-League ranks.

SEASON	LEAGUE		FA CUP		TOTAL	
	Apps	Gls	Apps	Gls	Apps	Gls
1905/06	8	1	0	0	8	1
TOTAL	8	1	0	0	8	1

Keith OSGOOD, 1981-84

Keith Osgood could be described as a rather unlucky player, his career being interrupted by constant injury. The 5ft 11in centre half, was a cool and steady defender, who impressed with his speed and agility, but perhaps was not so impressive in the air. Born in Ealing, London on 8 May 1955, he gained both England schoolboy and youth caps, assisting them to win the 'Little' World Cup in 1973. He started with Tottenham Hotspur as an apprentice in 1971, and scored 13 goals from 112(13) League appearances for Spurs between 1973 and 1977. He moved to Coventry City in January 1978 for £130,000, but after just 24(1) League appearances and a single goal, he joined Derby County in October 1979 for £150,000, recapturing his old form and making 66(8) senior appearances as well as scoring 10 goals. O's boss Ken Knighton brought him to Brisbane Road for £20,000 in December 1981, in the hope that his experience would help O's in their fight against relegation. Sadly, Osgood suffered a serious injury, and only appeared in a handful of games that term – O's were relegated to the Third Division. His following two seasons at the club were troubled by injuries, and he moved on to Cambridge United in November 1984, making 34(1) League appearances and scoring once during his two-year stay.

SEASON	LEAGUE		FA CUP		L. CUP	
	Apps	Gls	Apps	Gls	Apps	Gls
1981/82	6	0	3	0	0	0
1982/83	18	0	2	0	1	1
1983/84	12	0	0	0	0	0
TOTAL	36	0	5	0	1	1

TOTAL APPS	42
TOTAL GOALS	1

* Keith Osgood appeared in a Football League Group Cup match and an Auto Windscreens Shield match.

Keith Osgood

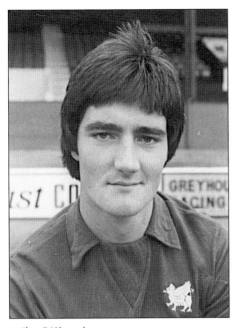

Mike O'Shaughnessy

Michael John O'SHAUGHNESSY, 1973-75

Born in Bow, London on 15 April 1955, 'keeper Mike O'Shaughnessy was in the East London Schools side that won the English Schools Shield. He came through O's youth ranks and signed as an apprentice in 1970, turning professional in August 1973. The goalie, who performed well for the reserves as understudy to both John Jackson and Ray Goddard, made a single League appearance at Hull City in October 1973. He performed very well and was only beaten by a penalty-kick. Perhaps his best display came in the London Challenge Cup final against Dagenham, when he made several fine saves to help the team to victory. He moved to Harlow Town in May 1975.

SEASON	LEAGUE		FA CUP		L. CUP	
	Apps	Gls	Apps	Gls	Apps	Gls
1973/74	1	0	0	0	0	0
TOTAL	1	0	0	0	0	0

TOTAL APPS	1
TOTAL GOALS	0

Timothy James O'SHEA, 1988-89

Tim O'Shea was born in Westminster, London on 12 November 1966. He started his football career as a schoolboy with Arsenal, moving across north London to Tottenham Hotspur as an apprentice player in September 1983. However, he made just 1(2) League appearances for Spurs. He went on loan to Newport County in October 1986, making 10 League appearances before transferring to O's in July 1988. Although he did look slightly better going forward than he did defending, he was released to join Gillingham in February 1989, where he performed a lot better. He made 102(10) League appearances, scoring twice for the Gills before going to play in Hong Kong in March 1992 with Easterns FC. He later represented Hong Kong against South

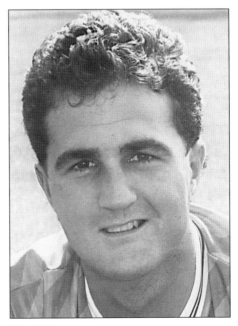

Tim O'Shea

O

Korea in March 1998. O'Shea returned to the United Kingdom in July 1999, signing for non-League side Farnborough Town.

SEASON	LEAGUE		FA CUP		L. CUP	
	Apps	Gls	Apps	Gls	Apps	Gls
1988/89	7(2)	1	2	0	0	0
TOTAL	7(2)	1	2	0	0	0

TOTAL APPS	9(2)
TOTAL GOALS	1

* Tim O'Shea also appeared in 2 Auto Windscreens Shield matches, scoring once.

Joseph Edward OSMOND, 1919-23

Joe Osmond was born in 1897 in Seaham Harbour, Sunderland, and started out with local side Sunderland West End. The O's, who had strong scouting connections in the North-East, brought him to Millfields Road in June 1919. He was equally at home in either full-back position, and made his League debut (which turned out to be his only appearance that season) in a 4-2 defeat at Port Vale during November 1919. He proved to be a strong-kicking, reliable defender over the following couple of seasons, but he was transferred to Hartlepool United in July 1924. He played just once for them in November. Joe Osmond died in Ryhope, County Durham on 1 June 1955, aged fifty-eight.

SEASON	LEAGUE		FA CUP		TOTAL	
	Apps	Gls	Apps	Gls	Apps	Gls
1919/20	1	0	0	0	1	0
1920/21	19	0	1	0	20	0
1921/22	28	0	1	0	29	0
1922/23	2	0	0	0	2	0
TOTAL	50	0	2	0	52	0

Ricky OTTO, 1990-93

Ricky Otto was born in Hackney, London on 9 November 1967. During his early days in Hackney, he played for local sides Clapton Rangers FC and Puma FC. After trials with both Spurs and West Ham, he served three years in prison for robbery. He played football for the prison team and also became a gym orderly, which meant he could work out every day. After leaving prison he played for Haringey Borough and Dartford, and was watched by a number of O's personnel. Eventually, the wing-man signed for the club on 6 November 1990. Otto stated: 'I'll never forget my first taste of Football League action, when I came on as a substitute at Fulham, running all around the ground and hearing the vibe of the crowd before entering the fray. I got a great buzz when I made my full League debut at Brentford in the first match of the 1991/92 season, but turning professional with Orient is something that really made me happy. I owe a great deal to both Frank Clark and Peter Eustace, they were tremendous to me.' 'Tricky Ricky', with his unusual hairstyle, his great pace, his ability to get behind defences, and the mystique of his past soon made him a cult figure at the club. Otto surprisingly turned down a move to Coventry City in the summer of 1992. His most memorable match was at Brighton & Hove Albion on 6 February 1993, where he scored a brilliant hat-trick. He also scored the goal against AFC Bournemouth on 17 October 1992 that took O's to the top of Division Two, the first time that O's had reached such heights in over twenty-one years, and something still not achieved since. It was no real surprise that he would move on, but the surprise was that it was to

Southend United for £100,000 on 9 July 1993. He continued his brilliant form at Roots Hall, scoring 17 goals from 63(1) appearances. In December 1994 he moved on to Birmingham City for £800,000. Otto struggled to find a regular first-team spot at St Andrews, playing just 25(21) League matches and scoring 6 goals. During 1996 and 1997 he was loaned out – to Charlton Athletic in June 1996 (making 5(2) League appearances) and to Peterborough United in February 1997 (making 16 appearances and scoring 4 goals). On 3 September 1997 he went to Notts County on trial with a view to a permanent move, but he suffered a serious knee ligament injury after just 6 matches that put him out of action for the remainder of 1997/98 season. He returned to Birmingham City, but was released from his contract by mutual consent in December 1997. This devastating wing-man was a terrific crowd-pleaser everywhere he played, and many

soccer fans around the country were saddened and shocked by his enforced long-term absence from the game for personal reasons. It was reported that thirty-two-year-old Otto was training with Peterborough United in July 1999, with a view to getting fit and returning to League football; however, he soon left and his whereabouts remained a mystery. More recently it was reported that Otto was running a dry-cleaning business with former Birmingham City player Peter Shearer in the Birmingham area. The image of Ricky Otto tearing opposition defences apart from his left-wing position was one of the major highlights in O's history during the early 1990s. In January 2001, Otto moved to Tamworth, and in March he moved on again to Halesowen Town, making 2(8) appearances and scoring twice. He joined Midlands Combination side Romulas before signing for Dr Marten's League outfit Bloxham United. After Bloxham withdrew from their division, thirty-six-year-old Otto moved on to play for League of Wales side Rhyl, but he left the club after just 2 appearances, claiming the long rail trips from his home in the West Midlands were just too troublesome, after having been stranded for up to eight hours on his way home on two occasions. Otto decided to call it a day and hang up his boots.

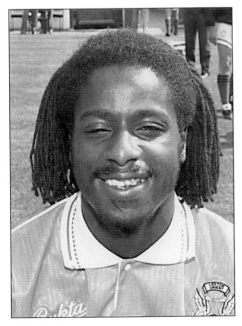

Ricky Otto

SEASON	LEAGUE		FA CUP		L. CUP	
	Apps	Gls	Apps	Gls	Apps	Gls
1990/91	0(1)	0	0	0	0	0
1991/92	23(9)	4	2	0	3	0
1992/93	18(5)	8	0(1)	0	0	0
TOTAL	41(15)	12	2(1)	0	3	0

TOTAL APPS	46(16)
TOTAL GOALS	12

*Ricky Otto also featured in 5(1) Auto Windscreen Shield matches, scoring 2 goals.

Jonathan OWEN, 1945-46

Johnny Owen came to O's in June 1945 from local football, and participated in 9 regional wartime matches in 1945/46. He performed well enough on the right wing to be given a chance in the FA Cup first round first leg tie against Newport Isle of Wight – O's won the leg 2-1, but lost 0-2 on the Isle of Wight to be eliminated from the competition. That was his only senior appearance, and he left O's in May 1946.

SEASON	LEAGUE		FA CUP		TOTAL	
	Apps	Gls	Apps	Gls	Apps	Gls
1945/46*	-	-	1	0	1	0
TOTAL	-	-	1	0	1	0

* The League re-commenced in the 1946/47 season, after the Second World War.

Trefor OWEN, 1958-61

Trefor Owen was born in Flint, Wales on 20 February 1933. He was a towering centre half, who played amateur football for Llanfair Caereinion FC (in the Mid-Wales League), Loughborough College, Barry Town, Bedworth Town and Tooting & Mitcham. The Welsh amateur international joined O's and turned professional in January 1958, after a spell on amateur forms. He was considered a very good prospect, and several League clubs were interested in signing him. He was given his League debut at the start of the 1958/59 season in preference to Sid Bishop, such were the high hopes O's had of him. Owen kept his place until that October, but Bishop was brought back in and never lost his place, except for injury, so Owen had to be content with reserve football. He was allowed to leave in May 1961, and joined Southern League Bath City. Trefor Owen never quite made it and didn't fulfil his early expectations. He was a little slow on the turn and perhaps a little cumbersome when confronted with onrushing forwards, and these things probably prevented him from reaching the top. He nevertheless achieved a lot at an amateur level.

SEASON	LEAGUE		FA CUP		L. CUP	
	Apps	Gls	Apps	Gls	Apps	Gls
1958/59	13	0	1	0	-	-
1959/60	0	0	0	0	-	-
1960/61*	2	0	0	0	1	0
TOTAL	15	0	1	0	1	0

TOTAL APPS	17
TOTAL GOALS	0

* The League Cup competition commenced in 1960/61.

Dennis Frank PACEY, 1951-54

The signing of twenty-two-year-old Dennis Pacey from Walton & Hersham in November 1951 almost went unnoticed. Three weeks after he had joined, he burst onto the scene with a hat-trick on his senior debut in an FA Cup second round replay against Gorleston at Highbury in December 1951, O's scraping home 5-4. Born in Feltham on 22 September 1928, Pacey was yet another product from the Chase of Chertsey club. Once he had finished his two-year national service stint, he played as an amateur with Woking. After unsuccessful trials with both Spurs and Arsenal, he was invited to Brisbane Road by O's boss Alec Stock. Although not doing particularly well, Stock saw something in the lad and he was offered a contract. The striker was no flash-in-the-pan, and although he looked ungainly, he was very fast for a big man and had a powerful shot. As the seasons went by, he scored some tremendous goals, including four in a match against Colchester United in a 5-3 win on 30 April 1953. He played a major part in O's great FA Cup runs of 1951/52 and 1953/54, and still holds O's all-time FA Cup goalscoring record with 12 goals. He moved to Millwall in October 1954, scoring on his debut, and he went onto grab 13 goals from 13 matches. He netted 36 goals from 132 League appearances for the Lions, before a transfer to Aldershot in September 1958, where he scored a further 13 goals from 32 appearances. He later played for Dartford and Yeovil. More recently Pacey was living in Chertsey and worked in the baggage-handling department at Heathrow Airport.

SEASON	LEAGUE		FA CUP		TOTAL	
	Apps	Gls	Apps	Gls	Apps	Gls
1951/52	25	11	7	6	32	17
1952/53	37	19	1	1	38	20
1953/54	45	16	7	5	52	21
1954/55	13	0	0	0	13	0
TOTAL	120	46	15	12	135	58

Albert Arthur PAPE, 1924-25

Albert Pape joined O's from Notts County in June 1924, and for a player who made just 24 League appearances for the club, Pape still had time to rewrite the O's record books. Firstly he netted 4 goals on his home debut against Oldham Athletic, and then came the well-documented (if somewhat bizarre) transfer to Manchester United for over £2,000, just one-and-a-half hours before O's match at Old Trafford on 7 February 1925. After saying his farewells to his O's colleagues, he rushed across to the home dressing-room, put pen to paper and changed shirts to score United's second in a 4-2 victory. He netted a total of 5 goals from 18 League appearances for the Red Devils. Born in Elsecar, near Wath-on-Dearne, Yorkshire on 13 June 1897, he started his career with local club Wath Athletic. Soon after the First World War, he moved to Bolton upon Dearne FC and, in December 1919, he joined Rotherham County. In May 1923, he moved again, this time to Notts County. During October 1925, he moved to Fulham, but still continued to live in Bolton, training at Old Trafford. He made 48 senior appearances and scored 16 goals for the Londoners. Between August 1927 and November 1933, he played for Flint Town, Rhyl Athletic, Hurst FC, Darwen (as player-coach), Manchester Central, Hartle-pool United, Halifax Town, Burscough Rangers, Horwich RMI, and finally Nelson. Pape was a man of many clubs, making 266 League appearances during his career and scoring 103 goals. He died in Doncaster on 18 November 1955.

SEASON	LEAGUE		FA CUP		TOTAL	
	Apps	Gls	Apps	Gls	Apps	Gls
1924/25	24	11	1	0	25	11
TOTAL	24	11	1	0	25	11

Frederick George PARKER, 1907-22

Fred 'Spider' Parker was one of the most popular pre-First World War players, a real character, whose antics and clowning around often had the O's fans in fits of laughter. Yet for all that, he was a wonderful inside forward. During his stay at

Millfields Road, Parker reached a number of milestones. He was the first O's player to reach 100 League appearances on 30 April 1910 at Fulham. His 200th appearance was on 11 October 1913 at Leicester Fosse, and his 300th League appearance came on 2 October 1920 at Millfields against Nottingham Forest. Parker was aged thirty-five at the time and, fittingly, O's won 2-1. Parker was born in Weymouth on 18 June 1886. He started with local side Portland Grove FC, before moving to Weymouth where he remained for two years before joining Salisbury. He joined O's on trial on his twenty-second birthday in June 1907, but manager Holmes was so impressed that he was in the side to play Hull City in September 1907, setting up the wining goal for Bill Martin. He picked up the nickname 'Spider' when, after the match, Holmes told the press that his new charge was just magnificent, and that the visitors were knocking him down so much, that whilst on the floor, he crawled around just like a spider. The account was published in the club programme and local newspapers, and the nickname was taken up by all. There was only one player to enjoy greater popularity than Parker up until the Second World War, and that man was Arthur Wood. Parker was at the club for eleven seasons and he was awarded a well-deserved benefit in 1921. It was a sad day when he decided to retire at the age of thirty-six, when age was certainly catching up on him. Although he was a member of the coaching staff for most of the 1921/22 season, his final appearance came against Leicester Fosse on 21 January 1922 – his 350th senior appearance. He won a number of honours whilst with O's, including winners' medals in the London Challenge Cup,

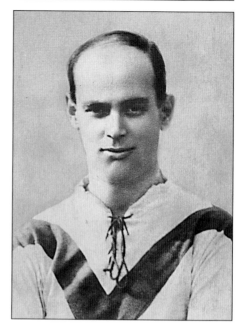

Fred Parker

London Professional Cup and West Ham Charity Cup. He also captained the side to victory over Millwall in May 1911 to lift the Dubonnet Cup in Paris, and captained a London XI against Birmingham. It was rumoured that he would stay with the club as a coach, but in the end he was appointed manager of Folkestone Town in June 1922. During later years, it was reported that he worked as a porter at King's Cross Station. Fred Parker died in the New Forest area during 1949, aged sixty-four.

SEASON	LEAGUE		FA CUP		TOTAL	
	Apps	Gls	Apps	Gls	Apps	Gls
1907/08	31	6	3	0	34	6
1908/09	36	6	1	0	37	6
1909/10	33	5	1	0	34	5
1910/11	22	1	0	0	22	1
1911/12	34	4	1	0	35	4
1912/13	38	4	1	0	39	4
1913/14	37	3	3	0	40	3

1914/15	37	2	1	0	38	2
1919/20	28	2	1	0	29	2
1920/21	33	1	2	0	35	1
1921/22	7	0	0	0	7	0
TOTAL	336	34	14	0	350	34

Alan PARKINSON, 1967

Alan Parkinson, a tall, well-built goal-keeper was born in Dagenham, Essex on 12 April 1945. He joined O's as an amateur in March 1967 from Aveley FC, having once been a youth player with Southampton. He came to O's when the club needed a goalkeeper as cover for Ron Willis, after veteran Vic Rouse decided to earn his trade with Atlanta Chiefs in America. O's boss Dick Graham, a former goalkeeper himself with Crystal Palace, offered him a professional contract, but he declined. He wanted to continue being a schoolteacher, and joined Barking of the Isthmian League. Parkinson's only League appearance came in a 1-1 draw at Mansfield Town on 22 April 1967.

SEASON	LEAGUE		FA CUP		L. CUP	
	Apps	Gls	Apps	Gls	Apps	Gls
1966/67	1	0	0	0	0	0
TOTAL	1	0	0	0	0	0

TOTAL APPS	1
TOTAL GOALS	0

Terence Leslie PARMENTER, 1969-71

Terry Parmenter was born in Romford, Essex on 21 October 1947. He joined Fulham as an apprentice in 1963 before signing professional terms the following November, making his League debut at Liverpool in March 1965. The quick-raiding outside left made 20(1) senior appearances and scored 2 goals at the Cottage, before joining O's for £7,000 in February 1969. Yet with Peter Brabrook holding down the wing berth, he often found himself in the reserves. He played in a dozen matches during O's Third Division Championship-winning campaign of 1969/70. Parmenter's most memorable feat was a goal against Sunderland on 12 September 1970, when his cross from the left touchline drifted over Montgomery and into the visitors' net for the only goal of the match. During the later stages of his O's career, he was moved to the left-back position. He joined Gillingham in August 1971, making 53(1) senior appearances (mostly at left-back), before joining Southern League outfit Romford in January 1973.

SEASON	LEAGUE		FA CUP		L. CUP	
	Apps	Gls	Apps	Gls	Apps	Gls
1968/69	18	1	0	0	0	0
1969/70	12(2)	1	0	0	0	0
1970/71	4(1)	1	0	0	0	0
TOTAL	34(3)	3	0	0	0	0

Terry Parmenter

P

TOTAL APPS   34(3)

TOTAL GOALS   3

Henry Harold PARR, 1945-46

Clever inside forward Harry Parr was born in Newark on 23 October 1915. He started off with Ransome & Miles, and then joined Newark FC in the Midlands League. He also turned out for Lincoln City reserves in 1939/40. He joined O's as an amateur in July 1945, having been spotted playing for the RAF. He played in 21 regional wartime matches, scoring 8 goals. He also appeared in both legs of the FA Cup tie against Newport Isle of Wight, scoring a goal in the 2-1 home leg victory. Parr moved to Lincoln City in August 1946, making 112 League appearances and scoring 13 goals between 1946 and 1949. He gained an England amateur international cap in February 1947 against Ireland, and then retired in 1949 to take up a civil service post in Lincoln.

SEASON	LEAGUE		FA CUP		TOTAL	
	Apps	Gls	Apps	Gls	Apps	Gls
1945/46*	-	-	2	1	2	1
TOTAL	-	-	2	1	2	1

* League matches re-commenced in 1946/47, after the Second World War.

David PARSONS, 1998-2002

Dave Parsons was born in Greenwich, London on 25 February 1982. The strong, attacking midfield player signed YTS forms on 11 July 1998, and the former Arsenal apprentice signed as a professional on 1 July 2000. He made 33 appearances and scored 5 times for the Youth side in 1998/99. He scored a further 5 goals in 28 games in 1999/2000 and also netted twice for the reserves from 10 appearances. He was an unused substitute at Swansea City during March 2000, and was given his League debut in the final match of the season against York City, showing good ball-winning and passing qualities. Parsons was an unused substitute for the Worthington Cup match on 22 August 2000 against Reading, but he did not figure for the remainder of the 2000/01 season. He went on a month's loan to Purfleet in January 2001. He returned to Brisbane Road and was a member of O's under-19 youth side that won the FA Alliance Cup final (1-0 against Bradford City) at the Millennium Stadium in Cardiff on 2 April 2001, and made 24 under-19 appearances. Parsons signed a new one-year contract in June 2001, and played regularly in pre-season matches. He was hoping for a regular place on the bench, but instead he found himself sent out on a month's loan with Nationwide Conference side Dover Athletic in mid-August 2001, but also struggled to make it into their team. He returned to Brisbane Road on 4 September after appearing just once for Dover, in a 3-0 defeat at Nuneaton on 25 August. He was released by O's in January 2002 and went on to join Purfleet. The following month, he moved on to Witham Town and then soon moved on to Dartford.

SEASON	LEAGUE		FA CUP		L. CUP	
	Apps	Gls	Apps	Gls	Apps	Gls
1999/2000	1	0	0	0	0	0
2000/01	0	0	0	0	0	0
2001/02	0	0	0	0	0	0
TOTAL	1	0	0	0	0	0

TOTAL APPS   1

TOTAL GOALS   0

Stephen Paul James PARSONS, 1980-81
Steve Parsons, who was born in Hammersmith, London on 7 October 1957, was one of a number of players to have his League career cut short by injury, after breaking a leg at Grimsby Town on 14 February 1981. The left-sided midfielder started his career with Walton & Hersham, before joining Wimbledon on a free transfer in December 1977. He contributed to some of the Dons' early League successes. He was a very talented but rather unpredictable player, who scored twice against O's in the course of 2 League Cup ties in early 1979. Altogether, he made 91(3) League appearances for the Dons, scoring 19 goals. He became an 'Oriental' in March 1980 for £42,000, his main assets being a strong tackle and an energetic style of play. In a desperate effort to return after breaking his leg, he tried his luck in the reserves, but he could never recover his old sparkle or confidence. He drifted into non-League football, having short spells with Hayes, Wembley and Dulwich Hamlet before finally calling it a day. Parsons was one of the guests of honour at O's Player of the Year awards in 2001.

SEASON	LEAGUE		FA CUP		L. CUP	
	Apps	Gls	Apps	Gls	Apps	Gls
1979/80	6	0	0	0	0	0
1980/81	30	6	1	0	2	0
TOTAL	36	6	1	0	2	0

TOTAL APPS	39
TOTAL GOALS	6

* Steve Parsons also appeared in 3 Anglo-Scottish Cup matches.

David PARTRIDGE, 2002 (loan)
Twenty-three-year-old Dave Partridge, the former Welsh Youth player, joined O's on loan on January 2002 until the end of the season, with a view to a permanent move from Scottish Premier League side Dundee United. The left-sided 6ft 1in defender was born in Westminster, London on 26 November 1978. He began his career as a trainee with West Ham United in July 1998, turning professional two years later. He made no impression on the first team at Upton Park, however, and was eventually sold to Dundee United for £40,000 on 11 March 1999. He made his senior debut against Celtic and went on to win the Young Player of the Year award during 2000/01. Partridge missed most of the season through injury and illness and was in and out of the Dundee United team during 2001/02, making a total of 72(4) senior appearances at Tannadice.

SEASON	LEAGUE		FA CUP		L. CUP	
	Apps	Gls	Apps	Gls	Apps	Gls
2001/02	6(1)	0	1	0	0	0
TOTAL	6(1)	0	1	0	0	0

TOTAL APPS	7(1)
TOTAL GOALS	0

George Edward PATEMAN, 1935
George Pateman can be described as a journeyman, having made just 86 League appearances for nine different clubs in a career that spanned some ten years. Born in Chatham, Kent on 18 May 1910, he was an accomplished schoolboy athlete, cricketer and footballer. He started his amateur days off with Aveling and Porters FC, whilst employed as a shipyard worker, and later had a spell with Canterbury Waverley FC. In June 1920 he turned professional with Gillingham, and scored on his senior debut in the League against Northampton Town in October

1929. He went on to make 17 League appearances and score 5 goals. In August 1931 he joined Portsmouth, making just 2 appearances during the season before going to Oldham Athletic in May 1932, where he made 7 appearances and scored 3 goals. June 1934 saw him move to Bradford City, where he made a single appearance. He joined O's on 31 July 1935, making his debut in a 3-0 home win over Luton Town on 31 August 1935. His only goal for the club came in a 4-0 win over Northampton Town the following October. However, the inside forward stayed for less than half the season, and was transferred to Reading for £350 on 17 October 1935, where he made a solitary senior appearance in the FA Cup, scoring in a 1-3 defeat against Liverpool during January 1936. Pateman was off on his travels again, moving to Accrington Stanley in August 1936 for £100, where he had his most successful run, scoring 8 goals from 24 senior appearances. In February 1937 he moved to Southport in a part-exchange deal. He scored twice on his debut, making 13 League appearances and scoring 3 goals in total. He went to Barrow in June 1937, and scored once in 17 appearances. In May 1939 he joined Shorts FC, combining football with their works team with the job of acting as the aircraft company's personnel manager. He was their player-manager in 1946/47. In later years he served on the committee of Kent CCC. Pateman died after a three-year battle with cancer at St Bart's Hospital in Rochester, Kent on 21 March 1973, aged sixty-two.

SEASON	LEAGUE		FA CUP		TOTAL	
	Apps	Gls	Apps	Gls	Apps	Gls
1935/36	9	1	0	0	9	1
TOTAL	9	1	0	0	9	1

* George Pateman also appeared in a Third Division Cup match in 1935/36, a 6-2 defeat at Bournemouth.

James PATERSON, 1938-39

Jimmy Paterson, yet another Scotsman to appear for the club during the 1930s, was born in St Ninians, near Stirling in 1907, and was another player who travelled around a bit. He was a very experienced and constructive centre forward, sometimes inside forward, who had started with Causewayhead FC and Camelon Juniors before joining Everton in January 1927, as an amateur playing for their reserve side. The following season he moved to St Johnstone. In 1930 he moved to Cowdenbeath, and had a very successful spell, making 74 Scottish League appearances and scoring 53 goals. He won 3 full Scottish caps (against Austria, Italy and Switzerland) whilst on a European tour in May 1931. In May 1932 he joined Leicester City, where he stayed for three years, making 48 League appearances and netting 17 goals. He was then a player with Reading, appearing in 82 senior matches and scoring 26 goals between 1935 and 1938. He joined O's in July 1938, and performed very well in pre-season trial matches, however, he played in just a handful of matches during the season, before deciding to retire in May 1939.

SEASON	LEAGUE		FA CUP		TOTAL	
	Apps	Gls	Apps	Gls	Apps	Gls
1938/39	5	0	0	0	5	0
TOTAL	5	0	0	0	5	0

Frank PATTISON, 1913-14

Frank Pattison, like a number of pre-First World War players, came down to join O's from the Sunderland & District League in

June 1913, after a short spell on amateur terms with Sunderland. Born in South Bank, Middlesbrough on 7 March 1889, the winger had to be content to play second fiddle to O's big signing, Joe Dix. He could not gain a regular place, so he moved on to Lincoln City in June 1914, and made 11 League appearances (scoring twice) in 1914/15. He continued with the Imps during wartime football, making 37 appearances and scoring 4 goals. He also played for a local works team (Rustons Airrcraftmen) that consisted almost entirely of ex-Lincoln professionals. After the First World War he played for Mid-Rhondda, and then between July 1921 and 1923, he turned out for Boston FC before retiring. He later went into the licensed trade and ran a number of public houses in Lincolnshire and the East Midlands. His last job was as licensee of the Midland Hotel in Mansfield, before he retired due to ill health in June 1949. Pattison died in Mansfield on 8 March 1950, aged sixty-one.

SEASON	LEAGUE		FA CUP		TOTAL	
	Apps	Gls	Apps	Gls	Apps	Gls
1913/14	7	0	0	0	7	0
TOTAL	7	0	0	0	7	0

John Morris PATTISON, 1949-51

Johnny Pattison was born in Eastwood, Glasgow on 19 December 1918. The outside left joined Queens Park Rangers from Motherwell in May 1937. After playing 95 League matches and scoring 26 goals for Rangers, as well as appearing in 35 regional wartime matches with 19 goals, he joined O's in February 1950, along with Billy McEwan. His great experience helped O's to stave off the threat of having to apply for re-election, and he scored a cracking thirty-yarder at South-

end United in September 1950 to secure the points. He also scored a goal in a 3-1 win over Dutch side Racing Club of Haarlem in a Festival of Britain match during 1951. At the end of the following season, age seemed to catch up with him, and he moved to Dover in May 1951. He later coached the Queensland club in Australia in 1955/56.

SEASON	LEAGUE		FA CUP		TOTAL	
	Apps	Gls	Apps	Gls	Apps	Gls
1949/50	15	4	0	0	15	4
1950/51	28	6	1	0	29	6
TOTAL	43	10	1	0	44	10

David Ronald PAYNE, 1973-78

David Payne was born in Croydon on 25 April 1947. He started his career with Crystal Palace in January 1968, and was at Selhurst Park for five years. He made 281(3) League Appearances and scored 9 goals, also gaining an England under-23 cap. Payne became another of George

John Pattison

Petchey's signings from his former club for £20,000 in August 1973. He played in either full-back or in midfield during his first season at Brisbane Road, which saw O's fail to gain promotion to the First Division by a single point. During the penultimate match at Cardiff, he had the misfortune to break his leg, so missing the vital match against Villa. The injury kept him out for a long spell, and he was never the same player again, making just 2 appearances. He played in 3 FA Cup ties on the way to the semi-finals in 1978, and it was Payne who had a hand in Joe Mayo's goal in the sixth-round victory over Middlesbrough. He re-joined his old boss Petchey at Millwall in June 1978, but did not make any first-team appearances. He retired from the game and joined the Police.

SEASON	LEAGUE		FA CUP		L. CUP	
	Apps	Gls	Apps	Gls	Apps	Gls
1973/74	34(1)	0	4	0	4	0
1974/75	2(1)	0	0	0	0	0
1975/76	19	0	0	0	0	0
1976/77	22	0	2	0	2	0
1977/78	11(3)	0	2(1)	0	2	0
TOTAL	88(5)	0	8(1)	0	8	0

TOTAL APPS	104(6)
TOTAL GOALS	0

* David Payne also appeared in 7 Anglo-Scottish Cup matches.

David Payne

David Sidney PEACH, 1982-83

Left-back David Peach was probably past his best when joining O's in March 1982 on a free transfer from Swindon Town, nevertheless, the experienced defender was a more than useful acquisition. With over 450 League appearances and a remarkable 66 goals behind him, he will be recalled as an expert free-kick and penalty-kick taker. He also played in 67(1) cup matches, scoring 9 goals during his long career. Peach was born in Bedford on 21 January 1951. He started as an apprentice with Gillingham in January 1969, and made 186(1) League appearances and scored 30 goals during his five-year stay with the Kent club. He was transferred to Southampton for £50,000 in January 1974, chalking up 221(3) matches and a further 34 goals. Whilst at the Dell he won 3 England under-21 caps and 8 England under-23 caps. Swindon Town snapped him up for £150,000 in March 1980, and he played 52(1) League matches and scored twice for them. He joined O's but couldn't help them avoid relegation into the Third Division in 1982. He still looked the part the following season at the age of thirty-two, but left the club in May 1983, joining non-League side RS Southampton FC, later moving to Andover. After retiring he worked in the

David Peach

building trade at Milford-on-Sea, Hampshire.

SEASON	LEAGUE		FA CUP		L. CUP	
	Apps	Gls	Apps	Gls	Apps	Gls
1981/82	13	0	0	0	0	0
1982/83	34	6	2	0	1	0
TOTAL	47	6	2	0	1	0

TOTAL APPS	50
TOTAL GOALS	6

* David Peach also appeared in 3 Football League Groups Cup matches.

Joseph John PEACOCK, 1931-33

Joe Peacock – sometimes referred to as Jack – was born in Wigan on 15 March 1897. He joined Everton from Atherton FC in 1919, having a couple of outings at right half before being given a go at centre forward and eventually settling at wing-half. He stayed at Goodison Park for eight years, making 151 League appearances and scoring 12 goals. He joined Middlesbrough in May 1927, making a further 85 senior appearances and scoring 4 goals. He also won 3 full England caps with the team of 1929 that toured France, Belgium and Spain, and was in the Boro side that won the Second Division Championship in 1928/29. He moved to Sheffield Wednesday for £300 in May 1930, spending just a season at Hillsborough, and making a single appearance against Chelsea in September 1930. He joined O's in May 1931 and proved to be a great asset to the Londoners at a time of great turmoil, both on and off the field. In March 1933 he joined Sliepner FC in Sweden as coach, and in July 1939 he was appointed trainer at Wrexham. Peacock died in Ince, Lancashire on 4 March 1979, just a few days before his eighty-second birthday.

SEASON	LEAGUE		FA CUP		TOTAL	
	Apps	Gls	Apps	Gls	Apps	Gls
1931/32	37	0	0	0	37	0
1932/33	17	0	1	0	18	0
TOTAL	54	0	1	0	55	0

Frank PEMBERTON, 1906-08

Londoner Frank Pemberton, a left half, joined O's from local non-League football in May 1906, and showed considerable promise in the reserve side. He made his League debut in a 3-0 win over Glossop on 15 September 1906, and his next match was a 0-5 defeat at West Bromwich Albion. He then became injured and suffered a long spell out of the game as a result. The following season he starred in a 5-1 win over Chesterfield in November 1907, but Pemberton could not gain a regular first-team place, due to the form of Liddell, and was released in May 1908.

SEASON	LEAGUE		FA CUP		TOTAL	
	Apps	Gls	Apps	Gls	Apps	Gls
1906/07	2	0	0	0	2	0
1907/08	2	0	0	0	2	0
TOTAL	4	0	0	0	4	0

Mark PENFOLD, 1979-81

Mark Penfold was born in Woolwich, London on 9 December 1956. This stocky little right-back started as an apprentice with Charlton Athletic in April 1974, and made 65(5) League appearances, but was hampered by a broken leg in 1977 and thereafter lost his way. He joined O's in July 1979, when the club were regulars in the Second Division, making his League debut in a 2-1 defeat at Wrexham during September 1979. He scored in a 2-2 draw at Preston North End in November, yet he couldn't find a regular first-team place, and was eventually transferred to Maidstone United in July 1981. Two years later he signed for Gravesend & Northfleet.

SEASON	LEAGUE		FA CUP		L. CUP	
	Apps	Gls	Apps	Gls	Apps	Gls
1979/80	3	1	0	0	0	0
1980/81	0	0	0	0	0	0
TOTAL	3	1	0	0	0	0

TOTAL APPS	3
TOTAL GOALS	1

Andrew Alfred PERCY, 1938-39

Alf Percy, a nippy, tricky right-winger, was born in Ilford, Essex in 1912. He came to O's from Ilford FC in May 1938, but had to be content with mostly reserve team football, due to the form of Les Dodds. He did get a brief run between March and April 1939 when Dodds was injured, showing pace and skill, but he left O's in May 1939. He joined Plymouth Argyle for

the 1939/40 season, which was interrupted by the Second World War.

SEASON	LEAGUE		FA CUP		TOTAL	
	Apps	Gls	Apps	Gls	Apps	Gls
1938/39	4	0	0	0	4	0
TOTAL	4	0	0	0	4	0

Christopher PERIFIMOU, 1994-95

Chris Perifimou was born in Enfield on 27 November 1975. A right-back and midfielder, this YTS player made his League debut at Cardiff City on 4 April 1995, and all 4 of his appearances occurred during an end-of-season run of 9 consecutive League defeats in 1995. O's manager Pat Holland released him in May 1995, and he went off to join Barnet, later playing for Stevenage Borough and Baldock Town. Perifimou joined amateur side Cheshunt FC in January 1998, whilst also working as a designer in an advertising agency, and made over 100 appearances. In August 2001 he joined up with former O's management personnel Tom Loizou and John Sitton – the management team at Enfield.

SEASON	LEAGUE		FA CUP		L. CUP	
	Apps	Gls	Apps	Gls	Apps	Gls
1994/95	3(1)	0	0	0	0	0
TOTAL	3(1)	0	0	0	0	0

TOTAL APPS	3(1)
TOTAL GOALS	0

Edward John PHILLIPS, 1964-65

Tall, craggy inside left Ted Phillips was noted for his powerful shooting, and joined Ipswich Town from Leiston FC on 11 December 1953 to become one of the most prolific goalscorers of the post-war years. Phillips hit the headlines with Ipswich during their 1956/57 promotion season, when he netted 41 League goals from as many matches. Born in Leiston, near Snape, Suffolk on 21 August 1933, he excelled for several seasons at Portman Road, winning Second and First Division Championship medals between 1960 and 1962, with 58 goals from 82 League appearances. Phillips totalled 160 League goals from 269 appearances (181 senior goals from 295 appearances) before being signed by O's boss Benny Fenton as a thirty-year-old on 16 March 1964, a replacement for young Gordon Bolland who had been sold to Norwich City for £30,000. Phillips commenced the 1964/65 season in fine style, scoring 3 goals in the opening match (all headers) against Portsmouth, O's winning 5-2. For a short period he struck up a fine partnership with Dave Dunmore, but later seemed to lose his form. He did, however, end the season as O's top goalscorer. He did not figure in new O's boss Dave Sexton's plans, and he was allowed to join Luton Town in February 1965, where he scored 8 goals from a dozen appearances. In September 1965 he had a spell with Colchester United, scoring a further 13 goals from 32 League appearances, before moving into the Southern League with Chelmsford City during May 1966. Phillips will be remembered for some wonderful goals for the O's, in particular against Rotherham in September 1964, and against Sunderland in April 1964, both at Brisbane Road. He fell just short of reaching a unique 200 League career goals between 1954 and 1966 by 2 goals. He also represented Suffolk at cricket and was more recently living in the Colchester area.

SEASON	LEAGUE		FA CUP		L. CUP	
	Apps	Gls	Apps	Gls	Apps	Gls
1963/64	10	4	0	0	0	0
1964/65	26	13	0	0	2	2
TOTAL	36	17	0	0	2	2

TOTAL APPS	38
TOTAL GOALS	19

George Raymond PHILLIPS, 1932-33

Inside forward George Phillips was born in Tottenham, London on 11 October 1912. He joined O's as an amateur from Northfleet United FC – a club under Tottenham's wings – in August 1932, having been on Spurs books as a junior and playing for their reserve side in 1931/32. Although he turned professional two months later, he could not make progress, and reserve football was his lot. He made his O's debut on 12 November 1932 against Queens Park Rangers, and he scored at Southend United the following week in a 3-3 draw. He moved to Millwall in September 1933, making 18 League appearances and scoring 5 goals between 1933 and 1935. George Phillips died in Southbourne, Hampshire on 13 March 1993, aged eighty.

SEASON	LEAGUE		FA CUP		TOTAL	
	Apps	Gls	Apps	Gls	Apps	Gls
1932/33	3	1	0	0	3	1
TOTAL	3	1	0	0	3	1

Wilfred John PHILLIPS, 1932-33

Born in Brierley Hill, West Midlands on 9 August 1895, Wilf Phillips is a famous name in the history of Millwall FC. Inside forward 'Peanut Winkie' Phillips, as he was tagged by the Docker's fans – one dare not ask why! – was a great practical joker. He appeared in the Lions' 1928 Third Division (South) Championship-winning side that notched a record total of 127 League goals, Phillips bagging 26 of them. Altogether, he netted a total

Wilfred Phillips

match at Reading in May 1933, but along with almost the entire playing staff, he was not retained at the close of the season by manager Jimmy Seed, and went on to join Stourbridge in August 1933. Wilf Phillips died on 25 February 1973 in Penzance, aged seventy-seven.

SEASON	LEAGUE		FA CUP		TOTAL	
	Apps	Gls	Apps	Gls	Apps	Gls
1923/33	24	4	0	0	24	4
TOTAL	24	4	0	0	24	4

William Hunter PICKERING, 1932-33

Billy Pickering was born in Murton Colliery on 13 November 1906. He was one of five brothers, of whom only one lived to the age of fifty. Upon leaving school at the age of fourteen, he worked down the local pit and played for the Murton Colliery football team at centre half. The bustling 5ft 11in and 11st 10lb Pickering joined Southport in May 1929, and made 11 League appearances, but after breaking his leg in November 1930, he could not regain his place. He joined O's in August 1932 and looked a good left half, earning a name for himself as a good 'spoiler'. (The left-half position seemed to be a bit of a problem area, with six different players filling that spot during the troubled season.) He left O's to rejoin Southport on 15 June 1933, making a further 5 League outings. After his demob from the RAF, he bought a seaside rock shop, and ran it until he was forced to retire from illness. He died from cancer in the Southport Promenade Hospital on 8 February 1952, aged forty-five.

of 58 League goals from 108 appearances for the Lions. He started his career with Bilston United, before moving onto Stoke City in 1919, making 14 League appearances and scoring 3 goals. After spells with Ebbw Vale FC and Darlaston FC, he came to the fore with Bristol Rovers between 1923 and 1926, scoring 35 goals from 90 appearances. After his feats with Millwall, who paid £600 for his services, he played for Thames Association FC in 1930, scoring 7 goals from 37 appearances. He then moved to West Ham United, who paid £500 for him, making 21 appearances and netting 3 goals in 1931/32. He joined O's in June 1932 – a month before his thirty-eighth birthday – and played over half of the matches during that season. He featured in O's 7-1 win over Swindon Town on 21 January 1933 – the first time so many goals had been scored by O's in a League match. He scored in his final League

SEASON	LEAGUE		FA CUP		TOTAL	
	Apps	Gls	Apps	Gls	Apps	Gls
1932/33	12	0	0	0	12	0
TOTAL	12	0	0	0	12	0

Geoffrey Alan PIKE, 1989-91

Geoff Pike was a highly talented and very determined midfielder, who played 30 League matches for O's in 1990/91 before a pelvic injury finally ended the thirty-five-year-old's playing career after sixteen years in the game. One of the highlights was when he scored in O's 2-2 draw at Everton in a League Cup match on 3 October 1989. He was a real workaholic, who covered every blade of grass at least twice during every game. Pike was appointed O's youth and reserve coach in June 1991, succeeding John Gorman who joined Glenn Hoddle at Swindon Town. Born in Clapton, London on 28 September 1956, he joined O's from Notts County in September 1989, after playing 80(2) League matches and scoring 17 goals. However, it was with West Ham United that he made his name, and he played 367 senior games and scored 41 goals for them after joining in 1975. He also won an FA Cup winners'

Geoff Pike

medal in 1980 and a Second Division Championship medal a year later. He made his League debut for the Hammers at Walsall on 9 September 1989, and moved to County in July 1987 for £35,000. Pike lost his coaching job in July 1993 after his two-year contract was not renewed. He said: 'I thought I was doing a good job in bringing in youngsters like Lakin, Okai and Warren through. I did learn a lot with Orient, which should hold me in good stead for my next job.' Pike went on to join Hendon, making a further 30 appearances whilst also acting as their coach. Pikey worked part-time for the FA during the early 1990s as a monitor of League clubs and their School of Excellence programmes. In 2001 he worked full-time as the PFA's south-eastern representative, helping players to gain coaching qualifications.

SEASON	LEAGUE		FA CUP		L. CUP	
	Apps	Gls	Apps	Gls	Apps	Gls
1989/90	6(8)	0	0	0	1	1
1990/91	30	1	5	2	5	0
TOTAL	36(8)	1	5	2	6	1

TOTAL APPS	47(8)
TOTAL GOALS	4

* Geoff Pike also appeared in 2 Auto Windscreens Shield matches.

Lorenzo PINAMONTE, 2001 (loan)

The signing of the twenty-three-year-old 6ft 3in Italian-born striker was completed on the afternoon of 2 February 2001. Having joined on loan from Brentford until the end of the 2000/01 season, a permanent deal seemed unlikely. Born in Foggia, Italy on 9 May 1978, he started as a boy with Verona. He moved to England as a twenty-year-old, joining Bristol City's

Youth Academy from Italian Serie B side Foggia in September 1998, where he made 7 League appearances and scored once. He spent six days training with Carlisle United during March 1999, before going on loan to Brighton & Hove Albion in December 1999 and scoring twice from 9 outings. On 2 February 2000, Brentford signed him for £75,000, and before his loan spell at the Matchroom, he had totalled 8(15) League appearances and scored twice. He was on target during his O's debut against Halifax Town on 3 February 2001, scoring after South African Andy Harris hit a low cross from the right on eighteen minutes. The Italian added the faintest of touches to help the ball onto the far post, and it drifted slowly into the net. Pinamonte made an impressive debut with his deft first touch and his aerial ability. He left the field on seventy-nine minutes, drawing a standing ovation from the crowd. However, he was yet another of the many loan players who ended up not performing as well as hoped, and he returned to Brentford. He was released in May 2001, returning home to Italy.

SEASON	LEAGUE		FA CUP		L. CUP	
	Apps	Gls	Apps	Gls	Apps	Gls
2000/01	5(6)	2	0	0	0	0
TOTAL	5(6)	2	0	0	0	0

TOTAL APPS   5(6)
TOTAL GOALS   2

Michael John PINNER, 1962-65

Mike Pinner, a solicitor by profession, was one of the most outstanding amateur goalkeepers of his era, having gained 52 England amateur international caps. Pinner was born in Boston, Lincolnshire on 16 February 1934, and started playing football with Wyberton Rangers. He played for Notts County reserves before his sixteenth birthday, and besides playing for amateur sides Pegasus, Corinthian Casuals and Hendon, he also helped out a number of League clubs between March 1954 and 1965. These included Aston Villa, Sheffield Wednesday, Queens Park Rangers, Manchester United, Chelsea and Swansea City, and he made a total of 36 League appearances with those clubs. He joined O's on amateur forms in October 1962, making his debut in the 5-1 home defeat by Tottenham Hotspur in front of 30,987 fans. Whilst with the club, he represented Great Britain against Iceland in an Olympic Games qualifying match. He signed as a part-time professional in October 1963, but when Dave Sexton became O's boss, he was not keen to have part-timers on the books. In July 1965 Pinner left, joining Distillery of the Irish League. Had he stayed, he surely would have given O's many more years of good service.

SEASON	LEAGUE		FA CUP		L. CUP	
	Apps	Gls	Apps	Gls	Apps	Gls
1962/63	19	0	0	0	1	0
1963/64	31	0	3	0	0	0
1964/65	27	0	1	0	1	0
TOTAL	77	0	4	0	2	0

TOTAL APPS   83
TOTAL GOALS   0

Darren Edward PITCHER, 1998 (loan)

Darren Pitcher, the England youth international midfielder, came to O's on loan from Crystal Palace in January 1998. He played just a single League match at Cardiff City on 19 January 1998, and was substituted five minutes into the second half, when he sustained a serious knee injury. He also played in an Auto Windshield Trophy second round match at AFC Bournemouth on 6 January – a 2-0 defeat. Born in Stepney, London on 12 October 1969, Pitcher started his career as a trainee with Charlton Athletic in January 1988. He enjoyed a long career at the Valley, playing 170(3) League appearances and scoring 8 goals. After a loan spell with Galway United in Ireland, he joined Crystal Palace for £700,000 on 5 July 1994, but after 60(4) Premier and League appearances, he suffered a cruciate knee ligament injury that kept him out of action for over a year. This hard-tackling midfield dynamo was loaned to O's in an effort to gain match fitness, but sadly the injury at Cardiff City led to his retirement from the game.

SEASON	LEAGUE		FA CUP		L. CUP	
	Apps	Gls	Apps	Gls	Apps	Gls
1997/98	1	0	0	0	0	0
TOTAL	1	0	0	0	0	0

TOTAL APPS	1
TOTAL GOALS	0

* Darren Pitcher also appeared in an Auto Windscreens Shield match.

Richard William PLUME, 1969-71

Dickie Plume was born in Tottenham, London on 9 June 1949. He started as an apprentice with Millwall in 1964 and rose through their youth ranks, going on to make 12(3) League appearances for the South London club between 1966 and 1968. He joined O's in May 1969, and was noticeably strong on his left foot. He could play at either at left half or on the left side of midfield. He was a constructive type who always tried to play methodically, however, as with his time at the Den, he was on the fringe of the first team but could never gain a regular place. However, he proved to be a useful squad member of the team that won the Third Division Championship in 1969/70. Plume was released in May 1971 and moved to Southern League side Barnet.

SEASON	LEAGUE		FA CUP		L. CUP	
	Apps	Gls	Apps	Gls	Apps	Gls
1969/70	10(5)	1	0	0	0	0
1970/71	2(1)	0	0	0	0	0
TOTAL	12(6)	1	0	0	0	0

TOTAL APPS	12(6)
TOTAL GOALS	1

Harold Edward William POLE, 1951-53

Versatile utility player Ted Pole was born in Kessingland on 25 March 1922. He joined Ipswich Town from the Forces in October 1946, making 43 senior appearances and scoring 13 goals. He joined O's on 18 July 1951. Pole could always be

Ted Pole

counted upon to give 100 per cent effort, and could play at left-back, right half, centre half, outside left, or even at centre forward, and it was in the latter position that he got his chance with O's. His best first-team game for O's was against Walsall, when he twice hit the woodwork. He moved to Southern League Chelmsford City in July 1953.

SEASON	LEAGUE		FA CUP		TOTAL	
	Apps	Gls	Apps	Gls	Apps	Gls
1951/52	10	0	0	0	10	0
1952/53	2	0	0	0	2	0
TOTAL	12	0	0	0	12	0

Derek James POSSEE, 1974-77

The nippy little 5ft 5in wing-man, Derek Possee, was born in Southwark, London on 14 February 1946. He excelled as a youth player with Tottenham Hotspur during the mid-1960s, making his League debut in 1964. However, the fierce competition for places meant that he managed just 19 League appearances, finding the net 4 times, before a £25,000 transfer took him to Millwall in August 1967. He proved to be an excellent capture, netting a total of 79 League goals from 222(1) Second Division appearances during a six-year spell. Crystal Palace stepped in with a £115,000 offer, and he scored a further 13 goals from 51(2) matches. He joined O's in July 1974 for £60,000, but seemed to be dogged by injures during his stay at Brisbane Road, and the O's fans never really got to see the best of him. Whilst with the O's he notched the 100th League goal of his career – ironically, it was against his old club, Millwall. Possee was on target for the O's in the first leg of the Anglo-Scottish Cup final against Nottingham Forest in 1977. He was released in May 1977 and went to play in Canada for Vancouver Whitecaps, but later returned to play for Dartford. Nowadays he lives in Vancouver, Canada and is Head of Soccer in British Columbia and head coach of the Canadian under-15 side.

Derek Possee

SEASON	LEAGUE		FA CUP		L. CUP	
	Apps	Gls	Apps	Gls	Apps	Gls
1974/75	34(1)	7	2	1	2	0
1975/76	21(1)	3	0	0	0	0
1976/77	22(1)	1	4	1	3	0
TOTAL	77(3)	11	6	2	5	0

TOTAL APPS	88(3)
TOTAL GOALS	13

* Derek Possee also appeared in 2 Texaco Cup matches in 1974/75, and 5 Anglo-Scottish Cup matches, scoring 3 goals.

George Henry POULTON, 1952-56

The O's may have had more skilful players than George Poulton, but very few who have battled so hard – sometimes against all the odds – and his willingness to always be in the thick of the action, made him quite a favourite with O's fans. Born in Holborn, London on 23 April 1929, the left-winger started off with Gillingham in August 1949, making 5 League appearances and scoring once, before joining O's in July 1952 on a month's trial. O's boss Alec Stock had no hesitation in signing him. Poulton netted twice on his debut against Torquay United at Brisbane Road in September 1952. He had a really memorable afternoon against Norwich City in November 1953, when he hammered home two wonderful goals – one after dribbling through the whole of City's defence, which made the 15,694-strong crowd erupt in a frenzy of excitement. His great qualities were very evident during O's great FA Cup run to the sixth round in 1953/54. Another great asset was his delivery of the hook shot on the turn, and he scored a number of goals that way. Poulton lost his place in 1954/55 after the arrival of Johnny Hartburn, and he spent his last couple of seasons in the reserves. In 1956 he left, joining Gravesend & Northfleet, and he later played for both Dover and Bexley United. He ended his playing career as a permit player with Mann Crossman FC in the Walthamstow & District League. Although lacking any kind of finesse, he was a player any manager would love to have in their side with his never-say-die attitude.

George Poulton

Thomas POULTON, 1904-06

Hackney-born Tom Poulton came to O's in 1904 from Clapton Imperial FC, about a year-and-a-half before the club's entry into the League. He was not a regular during the 1904/05 season, but played at right half or centre half when included in Southern League and London League matches. However, he never featured in any of the 6 FA Cup ties played that season. Poulton was one who was surprisingly retained for the move into the League in 1905/06, but made a single senior appearance in an FA Cup tie at Felstead on 7 October 1905. He moved back to Clapton Imperial in 1906.

SEASON	LEAGUE		FA CUP		TOTAL	
	Apps	Gls	Apps	Gls	Apps	Gls
1952/53	20	11	2	0	22	11
1953/54	34	12	7	3	41	15
1954/55	7	1	0	0	7	1
1955/56	0	0	0	0	0	0
TOTAL	61	24	9	3	70	27

SEASON	LEAGUE		FA CUP		TOTAL	
	Apps	Gls	Apps	Gls	Apps	Gls
1904/05*	-	-	0	0	0	0
1905/06	0	0	1	0	1	0
TOTAL	0	0	1	0	1	0

* Clapton Orient entered the League in 1905/06.

David James PRICE, 1983

Midfielder David Price had a long association with Arsenal, making a total of
116(10) League appearances for the
Gunners between 1973 and 1981 and
scoring 16 goals. Price also played in
50 cup matches (scoring 3 goals) and
made 210 Combination appearances
(scoring 29 goals). In January 1975 he
had a loan spell with Peterborough, making 6 appearances and scoring once. He
was in the Gunners side that defeated
the O's 3-0 in the FA Cup semi-final during April 1978, and represented them in
European competition as well as playing
in 4 FA Cup finals. Born in Caterham,
Surrey on 23 June 1955, the former
England schoolboy captain moved from
Highbury to Crystal Palace for £80,000
in March 1981, and totted up 25(2)
matches and 2 goals. He joined O's on a
non-contract basis in March 1983, and
although a bit bulkier than he was in his
Arsenal days, he still looked an efficient

David Price

player with plenty of courage. He moved
to Wealdstone in May 1983 and, upon his
retirement from football, he became a
taxi-driver in Surrey.

SEASON	LEAGUE		FA CUP		L. CUP	
	Apps	Gls	Apps	Gls	Apps	Gls
1982/83	10	0	0	0	0	0
TOTAL	10	0	0	0	0	0

TOTAL APPS	10
TOTAL GOALS	0

Terence Edmund PRICE, 1964-67

Diminutive Terry Price was born in
Colchester on 11 October 1945. He progressed through O's youth ranks and
made his League debut a few months
before his nineteenth birthday. The
game was at home to Portsmouth in
August 1964 on the opening day of the
season, and he capped a fine performance by scoring in a 5-2 victory. His
early displays at outside right suggested
he could go on to better things, but after
a couple of seasons he, like the team,
somewhat faded. At his best, he was a
tricky little winger, proving a handful for
opposing defenders. He was with the
club when they were relegated to the
Third Division in 1966/67, but due to the
club's financial crisis, he acted as a
trainer when the O's could not afford to
employ an extra person to do the job. He
was transferred to Colchester United for
£2,000 in September 1967, where he
made 55(2) League appearances and
scored 5 goals. He joined Southern
League side Chelmsford during May
1969, and ended his career playing in
the Eastern Counties League in 1985.
He retired from the game aged forty,
and opened a fish and chip shop in
Colchester.

Terry Price

SEASON	LEAGUE		FA CUP		L. CUP	
	Apps	Gls	Apps	Gls	Apps	Gls
1964/65	26	8	1	0	2	0
1965/66	26	3	1	1	0	0
1966/67	31	7	3	0	1	0
1967/68	3(1)	0	0	0	1	0
TOTAL	86(1)	18	5	1	4	0

TOTAL APPS	95(1)
TOTAL GOALS	19

Philip PRIOR, 1909-12

Phil Prior was born in Hackney, London in 1890. He was spotted playing on Hackney Marshes and was signed in June 1909. He was considered to be a very promising young winger, but the stumbling block to his progress was the form of Fred Parker. He did get the occasional game (when Parker was injured) during his three seasons at Millfields Road, and always gave a good account of himself, making his League debut in the 3-1 defeat at Glossop in November 1909. Prior was transferred to Bury in June 1912, and during his two seasons there, he made 35 senior appearances without finding the net. In 1914 he joined North Eastern League side Darlington.

SEASON	LEAGUE		FA CUP		TOTAL	
	Apps	Gls	Apps	Gls	Apps	Gls
1909/10	1	0	0	0	1	0
1910/11	15	3	1	0	16	3
1911/12	3	0	0	0	3	0
TOTAL	19	3	1	0	20	3

Andrew Smart PRITCHARD, 1938-39

Andrew Pritchard was born in Airdrie, Scotland on 23 June 1912. He started his career with Ashfield, and then played for Partick Thistle between 1933 and 1936. In May 1936 he moved to Irish League side Ards. The right half-back moved to Halifax Town on trial in August 1937, playing 18 senior games and scoring 3 goals, and came south to join O's in August 1938. He made some good performances in the reserves, but could not dislodge either Bill Dodgin or Harold Taylor from the first XI. His only senior appearance came in a 1-1 draw at Queens Park Rangers on 24 April 1939. He left the club in May 1939, but made a single League South wartime guest appearance for O's in 1944/45.

SEASON	LEAGUE		FA CUP		TOTAL	
	Apps	Gls	Apps	Gls	Apps	Gls
1938/39	1	0	0	0	1	0
TOTAL	1	0	0	0	1	0

Peter PROUDFOOT, 1905-06

Peter Proudfoot was yet another player who later became manager at the club, and went on to have three spells as O's boss – April 1922 to April 1929, April 1930 to April 1931, and January 1935 to January 1939. Born in Wishaw, Scotland on 25 November 1880, this tough-tackling wing-half started his career with local sides Wishaw FC and Wishaw United. In December 1900, he came south of the Border to join Lincoln City, and during his three-year stay, he made 79 League appearances and scored 20 goals. In 1903, Proudfoot moved back to Scotland with St Mirren, making 2 Scottish League appearances. October 1904 saw him in London with Southern Leaguers Millwall Athletic, for whom he chalked up 16 senior appearances. He joined O's in May 1905 for O's first League campaign, and made his League debut in a 2-1 home defeat by Grimsby Town on 14 October 1905. Due to O's financial crisis, he was sold to Chelsea for £120 in April 1906, after just 12 League appearances he moved to Manchester United in 1908. He then quickly moved on to Stockport County and made 34 League appearances, scoring once. Proudfoot went back to Scotland to play for Greenock Morton for a short time in 1909, but re-joined Stockport County in 1910, making a further 11 League appearances between then and 1913. He held a commission in the Army until being appointed O's manager in April 1922 after the sudden death of William Holmes, and was involved with the club until his retirement due to ill health in January 1939. He was in charge for 483 League matches – more than any other O's manager. Proudfoot died in his native Wishaw on 4 March 1941, aged sixty.

SEASON	LEAGUE		FA CUP		TOTAL	
	Apps	Gls	Apps	Gls	Apps	Gls
1905/06	26	0	6	1	32	1
TOTAL	26	0	6	1	32	1

Walter Ernest PULLEN, 1946-50

Wally Pullen was born in Ripley, Surrey on 2 August 1919. The inside forward joined O's in January 1946 from the Army, having previously been registered with Fulham as an amateur. He played for O's in the 1945/46 regional wartime League, scoring 4 goals from 20 appearances. He established himself as a first-teamer in the first peacetime season of 1946/47, and netted a hat-trick against Bristol City on 7 December 1946, scoring his final 2 goals despite limping with a badly injured leg. He always had an eye for goal, and supported big Frank Neary admirably during O's 11-match unbeaten run that saved O's from relegation in 1947/48. He will be remembered most by older fans for the goal he scored with the last kick of the match at Southend United, which saved the embarrassment of having to apply for re-election in 1949/50. The club awarded him a benefit match against West Ham United in 1950. He joined his

Wally Pullen

former colleague Doug Hunt, boss at Southern League Gloucester City. Wally Pullen died in Luton during 1977, aged fifty-eight.

SEASON	LEAGUE		FA CUP		TOTAL	
	Apps	Gls	Apps	Gls	Apps	Gls
1946/47	30	13	1	0	31	13
1947/48	37	10	1	0	38	10
1948/49	17	5	0	0	17	5
1949/50	31	9	1	0	32	9
1950/51	2	0	0	0	2	0
TOTAL	117	37	3	0	120	37

Darren John PURSE, 1993-96

Born in Stepney, London on 14 February 1977, Darren Purse was a talented centre half, who made his League debut against Wrexham in March 1994, just days after his seventeenth birthday. His first League goal was against Birmingham City – a club he now plays for – during the first match of the 1994/95 season. During a match at Torquay United on 20 January 1996, he took over in goal after O's 'keeper Fearon was sent off. Purse remarkably saved a penalty on seventy-five minutes, but, unfortunately, the home side put one past him in injury time to win the match. Purse joined Oxford United for £100,000 on 23 July 1996, the deal including a 20 per cent sell-on-clause. He played 52(7) League matches and scored 5 goals. O's gained a big cash windfall when Purse was transferred to Birmingham City for £775,000 on 16 February 1998, with tall centre forward Kevin Francis going to Oxford as part of the deal. Twenty-one-year-old Purse was bought as a player for the future, and was voted by City supporters as the club's star of the future. He was their Young Player of the Year in 2000. With the departure of Steve Bruce, he became a regular first-teamer, winning

2 England under-21 caps, and has represented a Nationwide League side against their Italian counterparts. Purse had made over 100 senior appearances up to the end of 2000/01. He appeared in Birmingham City's team for the League Cup final on 25 February 2001 against Liverpool at the Millennium Stadium in Wales, and scored the last-minute penalty that took the match into extra time. However, they eventually lost in a dramatic penalty shoot-out. His season ended in the same fashion when Birmingham failed in their quest to reach the Division One play-off final, losing to Preston North End in a penalty shoot-out on 17 May 2001.

SEASON	LEAGUE		FA CUP		L. CUP	
	Apps	Gls	Apps	Gls	Apps	Gls
1993/94	2(3)	0	0	0	0	0
1994/95	37(1)	3	1	0	2	0
1995/96	9(3)	0	0	0	0	0
TOTAL	48(7)	3	1	0	2	0

Darren Purse

TOTAL APPS   51(7)
TOTAL GOALS   3

* Darren Purse also appeared in 7(1) Auto Windscreens Shield matches, scoring 2 goals.

Trevor Anthony PUTNEY, 1993-94

Trevor Putney, the veteran midfielder, joined O's at the age of thirty-two for £40,000 from Watford in July 1993, bought with some of the money from the sale of Adrian Whitbread to Swindon Town. Born in Harold Hill, Essex on 11 February 1961, he started his career with Havering Boys FC, before having two trials with Spurs, arranged by Peter Taylor. He moved to Brentwood & Warley before joining Ipswich on 15 September 1980, where he played 94(9) League matches and scored 8 goals. He moved on to Norwich City in June 1986 (in exchange for John Deeham) and scored a further 9 goals from 76(6) appearances. Middles-brough signed him for £300,000 during July 1989, and he stayed there for two years, making 46(3) League appearances and scoring once. A £100,000 transfer took him to Watford in July 1991, where he made 20(2) appearances and netted 2 goals before his move to Brisbane Road. O's boss Eustace stated 'Trevor has all-round ability, valuable passing skills and long experience, with a wide understanding of the game'. Putney spent just a season with O's before having his contract cancelled, and he joined Colchester United on trial in August 1994. He signed permanently the following December, and made 28 League appearances and scored 2 goals. Putney retired in 1995 owing to injury, and worked for a time on the Futures Market, subsequently doing some work for the Press Association.

SEASON	LEAGUE		FA CUP		L. CUP	
	Apps	Gls	Apps	Gls	Apps	Gls
1993/94	20(2)	2	0	0	2	0
TOTAL	20(2)	2	0	0	2	0

TOTAL APPS   22(2)
TOTAL GOALS   2

* Trevor Putney also appeared in 1(1) Auto Windscreens shield matches.

Trevor Putney

Gerald QUEEN, 1972-77

Striker Gerry Queen was born in Paisley, West Glasgow on 15 January 1945. He was spotted by St Mirren whilst playing youth club football, and made his Scottish League debut in 1962/63. After 63 games (in which he scored 10 goals) he moved the short distance to Kilmarnock in 1966, where he

Gerry Queen

made 94 appearances and scored 29 goals. His performances were rewarded with Scottish under-23 honours. He moved south of the Border in July 1969, joining Crystal Palace for £80,000 and scoring on his First Division debut against Manchester United in front of nearly 50,000 fans. Queen was at Selhurst Park for three years and made 149(7) senior appearances, scoring 34 goals. Queen joined O's for a then club record fee of £70,000 in September 1972, making his debut against Queens Park Rangers. He was hailed as quite a capture, and although he was sometimes an enigma, there were times that he lived up to the high expectations. His best period was during the early stages of the 1973/74 season, and he played well in the front line with Bullock and Fairbrother. However, a back injury at Notts County checked his progress, and he was never the same player after his return. During the 1976/77 season, he scored some vital goals in O's

run to the final of the Anglo-Scottish Cup. He hit the winner against Aberdeen in the second leg of the quarter-final to secure a place in the next round, and two goals (including one penalty) against Partick Thistle for a place in the two-legged final against Nottingham Forest. Queen played in 8 Anglo-Scottish matches that season (scoring those 3 goals) and enjoyed the experience of once again playing against top Scottish sides. Queen went to South Africa to play for Arcadia Shepherds in Pretoria in 1977, but he returned to the UK a year later. Nowadays, he lives and coaches soccer in Florida, USA at the Coca Expo Sports Center.

SEASON	LEAGUE		FA CUP		L. CUP	
	Apps	Gls	Apps	Gls	Apps	Gls
1972/73	33	10	1	0	0	0
1973/74	34(2)	12	3	0	3	1
1974/75	32(2)	4	2	1	0	0
1975/76	32	6	1	0	0	0
1976/77	18(3)	2	2(1)	0	4	0
TOTAL	149(7)	34	9(1)	1	7	1

TOTAL APPS	165(8)
TOTAL GOALS	36

* Gerry Queen also appeared in 3 Texaco Cup matches in 1974/75 and 8 Anglo-Scottish Cup matches, scoring 3 goals.

Sean RAFTER, 1979-81
Born in Rochford, Essex on 20 May 1957, Sean Rafter was a safe and steady goalkeeper who started his career with Southend United in June 1975 as an apprentice. During his three-year stay, he

Sean Rafter

George McIntosh RAMAGE, 1964-65

Goalkeeper George Ramage was born in Newbattle, Midlothian, Scotland on 29 January 1937. He started out with Third Lanark, before moving south of the Border to join Colchester United in August 1961, where he made 38 League appearances during a three-year stay at Layer Road. He was signed from the U's by O's boss Benny Fenton in July 1964. He made his senior debut in the 2-1 defeat at Charlton Athletic in the League Cup on 14 October 1964. When Dave Sexton joined as O's manager, he gave Ramage his chance in the first team, but after a handful of matches he was replaced by Reg Davies. Ramage did play in the famous 2-1 win over Second Division leaders Newcastle United when O's were rooted firmly to the bottom of the table, and two goals from Joe Elwood secured the unexpected two points. Ramage was not retained for the following season, and he joined Luton Town

made 23 League appearances. Rafter joined Leicester City in January 1978, but had a frustrating spell as cover for first-team goalie Mark Wallington, and went on to join O's in July 1979, as cover for Mervyn Day. He made his senior debut when Day failed a fitness test in a FA Cup tie against West Ham United, a 2-3 defeat on 26 January 1980. His League chances came in the final couple of matches of the 1980/81 season – a 2-2 home draw against Bolton Wanderers and a 3-1 defeat at Birmingham City. Rafter left in June 1981, going into non-League football.

SEASON	LEAGUE		FA CUP		L. CUP	
	Apps	Gls	Apps	Gls	Apps	Gls
1979/80	0	0	1	0	0	0
1980/81	2	0	0	0	0	0
TOTAL	2	0	1	0	0	0

TOTAL APPS	3
TOTAL GOALS	0

George Ramage

in November 1965, making a further 7 League appearances.

SEASON	LEAGUE		FA CUP		L. CUP	
	Apps	Gls	Apps	Gls	Apps	Gls
1964/65	4	0	0	0	1	0
TOTAL	4	0	0	0	1	0

TOTAL APPS	5
TOTAL GOALS	0

John RANCE, 1904-05

London-born John Rance came to O's as a reserve player from Southern League side Queens Park Rangers in June 1904. The right-back looked a good prospect, and played regularly in O's Southern League campaign. He appeared twice with his brother – Albert, a winger – in London League matches. Rance played in all 6 FA Cup ties – O's first introduction to the famous Cup competition – albeit in the qualifying rounds. Despite his consistent displays, he was not retained for the first campaign in the League in 1905/06.

SEASON	LEAGUE		FA CUP		TOTAL	
	Apps	Gls	Apps	Gls	Apps	Gls
1904/05*	-	-	6	0	6	0
TOTAL	-	-	6	0	6	0

* Clapton Orient first entered the League in 1905/06.

Paul James RAYNOR, 1998

Paul Raynor, an attacking right midfielder, joined O's from the Guang Deong Club in China on 26 February 1998. He had previously been at Cambridge United and had left on a free in June 1997. Born in Nottingham on 29 April 1966, he became an apprentice with Nottingham Forest in April 1984, and made 4 senior appearances. His career then saw him on the books of Bristol Rovers (making 7(1) League appearances during his loan period), followed by a transfer to Huddersfield Town in August 1985, where he scored 27 goals from 28(12) appearances. He joined Swansea City on a free transfer in March 1987, and starred as the Swans clinched promotion via the Fourth Division play-offs in 1987/88. He helped them win the Welsh Cup in both 1989 and 1991, and scored 27 times from 170(21) League appearances. After a loan spell with Wrexham in October 1988, he joined Cambridge United in March 1982, making 46(3) League appearances and scoring twice. Raynor then joined Preston North End for £36,000 on 23 July 1993, playing 72(8) matches and scoring 9 goals, but returned to Cambridge in September 1995. In a career that lasted fourteen seasons, he made 420(46) League appearances and scored 54 goals before his move to Brisbane Road. O's boss Tommy Taylor signed the thirty-one-year-old on a non-contract basis on 26 February 1998, but his stay was shortlived, and after a very brief spell with Stevenage Borough in September 1998, he signed with Kettering Town on a non-contract basis, before moving to Ilkeston Town. More recently, he combined a coaching job at Sheffield United with playing for Boston United, whom he joined in February 2000, making 45(2) appearances and scoring 3 goals. He later played for Kings Lynn. During early 2001 he was player-manager at Dr Martens Premier League side Hednesford Town, however, he was sacked and on 9 October 2001, he was

Paul Raynor

appointed as Gainsborough Trinity's youth officer. However, due to cost cutting measures, he was later released from this post and joined Unibond League side Ossett Albion in January 2002.

SEASON	LEAGUE		FA CUP		L. CUP	
	Apps	Gls	Apps	Gls	Apps	Gls
1997/98	5(5)	0	0	0	0	0
1998/99	1(4)	0	0	0	1(1)	0
TOTAL	6(9)	0	0	0	1(1)	0

TOTAL APPS	7(10)
TOTAL GOALS	0

Paul Colin READ, 1995 (loan)
Ginger-haired striker Paul Read was born in Harlow, Essex on 25 September 1973. The England schoolboy international spent eight years with Arsenal and, during his last couple of seasons at Highbury, he scored an impressive 41 goals from

49 reserve appearances. He came to O's on loan in March 1995, but failed to impress, and he was unable to find the net from 11 League starts. He then went on loan to Southend United and scored once from 3(1) appearances. Read signed for Wycombe Wanderers for £35,000 (to rise to £135,000, should he achieve 75 first-team appearances) in January 1997. He scored 3 goals from his first 4 League matches, but only managed 32(25) first-team appearances and a total of 9 goals during his stay with the club. Read was given a free transfer, and went off to try his luck in Sweden with Osterunds FK in June 1999. He returned to the UK in December 1999, and had an unsuccessful spell on a non-contract basis with Luton Town (making a single League appearance) before joining Exeter City on 24 November 2000. He scored his only League goal within three minutes against the O's in January 2001, but O's came back to win 3-2 at Exeter. He has made 12(9) senior appearances and scored a goal up to the start of February 2002.

SEASON	LEAGUE		FA CUP		L. CUP	
	Apps	Gls	Apps	Gls	Apps	Gls
1994/95	11	0	0	0	0	0
TOTAL	11	0	0	0	0	0

TOTAL APPS	11
TOTAL GOALS	0

* Paul Read also appeared in an Auto Windscreens Shield match.

Herbert REASON, 1905-1910
Full-back Bert Reason was born in Wanstead, London and throughout his career he had the nickname of 'Jumbo' because of his short, stocky build. Known

for his powerful shots from free-kicks, he joined O's in May 1904 from Woodford FC, and played a number of matches in both the Southern and London Leagues. Reason was a strong and very powerful defender. During the 1908/09 season, he took over penalty duty and converted 4, but when he missed a couple the following season, someone else took over. He served the club well for six seasons, before leaving in May 1910. He enlisted for the First World War in April 1915, and was one of ten O's players and officials who were wounded in action.

SEASON	LEAGUE		FA CUP		TOTAL	
	Apps	Gls	Apps	Gls	Apps	Gls
1905/06	11	0	3	0	14	0
1906/07	5	0	0	0	5	0
1907/08	25	0	0	0	25	0
1908/09	34	4	1	0	35	4
1909/10	16	0	0	0	16	0
TOTAL	91	4	4	0	95	4

Joseph REDDING, 1904-06

Jim Redding, as he was known, joined O's from Amersham FC in May 1904. Although a little on the small side for a goalkeeper, he proved to be very daring and took over the jersey from Hugh Liles after the first match of the 1904/05 season, making it his own throughout the season. He appeared in goal for the first ever fixture in the Southern League, a 0-0 draw at Brighton & Hove Albion in October 1904, and also in O's first ever FA Cup tie, against Enfield in September 1904, a 4-1 victory. Redding lost his place to Joseph Butler for the start of the League campaign, but Butler had to be sold due to a financial crisis at the club, so Redding got his chance. However, he let in 17 goals in 4 matches, and was soon replaced by youngster Billy Bower. He

was so upset at his performance and letting the side down, that he left the club and moved back into non-League football with Amersham, whom he later coached.

SEASON	LEAGUE		FA CUP		TOTAL	
	Apps	Gls	Apps	Gls	Apps	Gls
1904/05*	-	-	6	0	6	0
1905/06	7	0	3	0	10	0
TOTAL	7	0	9	0	16	0

* Clapton Orient were elected into the League in 1905/06.

Charles REED, 1909-10

Durham-born Charles Reed joined O's from North Eastern League outfit Darlington in June 1909. This solidly-built left-back was a regular in O's reserve side, making his League debut in a 4-0 win over Barnsley on 7 April 1910. Reed was released in May 1910 and returned to the North-East.

SEASON	LEAGUE		FA CUP		TOTAL	
	Apps	Gls	Apps	Gls	Apps	Gls
1909/10	2	0	0	0	2	0
TOTAL	2	0	0	0	2	0

George REED, 1935-36

Born in Altofts, Yorkshire on 7 February 1904, George Reed started his career with Leeds United in October 1924 and stayed for six years, making 141 League appearances and scoring 2 goals. The wing-half moved to Plymouth Argyle in May 1931, where he made a further 41 League appearances and netted once. He came to London to join Crystal Palace in June 1934, but made just 2 appearances before joining O's in June 1935 as coach. The thirty-one-year-old played mainly in the reserves, but did make a League appearance in a 3-1 win over

R

Brighton & Hove Albion at Lea Bridge Road on 25 April 1936. He re-joined Plymouth Argyle in June 1936 as reserve coach.

SEASON	LEAGUE		FA CUP		TOTAL	
	Apps	Gls	Apps	Gls	Apps	Gls
1935/36	1	0	0	0	1	0
TOTAL	1	0	0	0	1	0

Melvyn John REES, 1990 (loan)

Goalkeeper Mel Rees was with O's for a two-month loan spell between January and March 1990. The Welshman died in Derby on 30 May 1993, after a long battle against cancer at the age of twenty-six. Rees was born in Cardiff on 25 January 1967, and the former Welsh youth international started off with Cardiff City in 1981 as a trainee. After a short spell with Plymouth Argyle, he returned to Cardiff in August 1983 and made 31 League appearances. He was transferred to Watford for £63,000 in July 1987, but found himself as understudy to Tony Coton, before being superceded by a young David James. After a loan spell with Crewe Alexandra in August 1989, where he made 6 appearances, he came to Brisbane Road in January 1990, whilst Paul Heald was recovering from a broken nose. He made his debut at Chester City, a 1-0 defeat. After his return to Vicarage Road, he was transferred to West Bromwich Albion for £45,000 in September 1990, and during a two-year stay, he made 18 appearances. He then moved to Sheffield United for £25,000 in March 1992, making 8 appearances. During the summer he underwent an operation which revealed the cancer. He was undergoing chemotherapy, but, sadly, he succumbed after a recurrence of the cancer and died.

SEASON	LEAGUE		FA CUP		L. CUP	
	Apps	Gls	Apps	Gls	Apps	Gls
1989/90	9	0	0	0	0	0
TOTAL	9	0	0	0	0	0

TOTAL APPS	9
TOTAL GOALS	0

* Mel Rees also appeared in an Auto Windscreens Shield match.

William Derek REES, 1950-55

Inside forward Billy Rees, a Welsh international, caused a sensation when joining O's from Tottenham Hotspur for a then club record fee of £14,500 in July 1950. O's, having outbid both Fulham and West Ham United, paid off the fee in instalments, yet attendances certainly increased, with over 21,000 witnessing his debut at Brisbane Road. Born in Blaengarw, near Bridgend, Wales on 9 March 1924, he spent seven years on the coal face whilst turning out for Carn

Billy Rees

Rovers FC and Blaengarw FC, before joining Cardiff City in February 1944. There he made 101 League appearances and scored 33 goals during his five-year stay, and he was a member of their Third Division (South) Championship side of 1947. He also won a wartime Welsh international cap within six months of turning professional. He won 3 full Welsh caps in 1949 – against Northern Ireland, Belgium and Switzerland. Rees moved to Tottenham Hotspur for £14,000 in June 1949, but made just 11 appearances and scored 3 goals during his year at White Hart Lane. However, he did win a further Welsh cap, this time against Northern Ireland in 1950. Rees made a big impact at Brisbane Road, proving his quality with some fine forceful play and scoring many wonderful goals, including 3 hat-tricks. He suffered from many injuries, but always gave 100 per cent. He left in December 1955, joining Headington United, and in 1959, he moved to Kettering. Billy Rees died in Bridgend on 25 July 1996, aged seventy-two.

SEASON	LEAGUE		FA CUP		TOTAL	
	Apps	Gls	Apps	Gls	Apps	Gls
1950/51	39	10	1	1	40	11
1951/52	39	13	6	3	45	16
1952/53	30	3	0	0	30	3
1953/54	36	15	5	4	41	19
1945/55	35	17	2	0	37	17
1955/56	5	0	0	0	5	0
TOTAL	184	58	14	8	198	66

David REGIS, 1997

This much-travelled thirty-three-year-old veteran striker came to O's on a weekly contract on 30 October 1997, but parted company with the club after making just 4 League appearances. He fell out with boss Tommy Taylor after refusing to play in a FA Cup tie at Hendon in November 1997. Born in Paddington, London on 3 March 1964, he started his long career as an apprentice with Barnet, but came into the League when joining Notts County for £25,000 in November 1990. He later played for Plymouth Argyle, AFC Bournemouth (loan), Stoke City, Birmingham City, Southend United, Barnsley (loan), Peterborough United (loan), and Notts County (loan). After leaving O's, he played for both Lincoln City and Scunthorpe United, for whom he signed in February 1998 scoring twice from 4 games before rupturing his knee ligaments. In 2000/01 the thirty-seven-year-old was on the books of Hucknell Town. During his eighteen-year career, he made 180(57) League appearances and netted 53 goals, and accumulated transfer fees totalling around £600,000.

SEASON	LEAGUE		FA CUP		L. CUP	
	Apps	Gls	Apps	Gls	Apps	Gls
1997/98	4	0	0	0	0	0
TOTAL	4	0	0	0	0	0

TOTAL APPS	4
TOTAL GOALS	0

Thomas REID, 1926-27

Tommy Reid was born in Calderbank, Airdrie, Scotland in 1901. He was a strong and fearless centre forward, who began his career with New Stevenston United. He later had trials with Clyde, Albion Rovers Dundee, and Ayr United, before moving south of the Border with Port Vale in August 1922. He stayed at the old Recreation Ground for four years, making 29 League appearances and scoring 3 goals. He joined O's for £230 in January 1927, and scored on his debut on 23 January 1927 against South Shields. However, he was mostly confined to the reserves after that. He moved to Northwich Victoria in July 1927, and later returned to the League with New Brighton, making 7 appearances and scoring once between 1928 and 1930.

SEASON	LEAGUE		FA CUP		TOTAL	
	Apps	Gls	Apps	Gls	Apps	Gls
1926/27	7	2	0	0	7	2
TOTAL	7	2	0	0	7	2

Robert Squire REINELT, 1998

Robbie Reinelt, a midfielder, joined the O's on a non-contract basis in June 1998, after being released by Brighton & Hove Albion. It was Reinelt who scored the goal for the Seagulls at Hereford United on 3 May 1997 that condemned the home side to relegation to the Football Conference, saving Brighton. Born in Loughton, Essex on 11 March 1974, he started as a trainee with Aldershot in March 1993, where he made 3(2) League appearances. He moved to Wivenhoe Town before going to Gillingham the following year, where he played 34(18) games, scoring 5 goals. He went to Colchester United in March 1995, and netted 10 times from 22(26) League appearances, before moving to the Seagulls for £15,000 in February 1997, where he hit 7 goals in 32(12) matches. He joined O's on 1 August 1998, making his debut as a substitute in the 2-0 victory at Chester City on 8 August 1998. He scored his only goal for the club in the 1-5 home League Cup defeat by Nottingham Forest in September 1998. During mid-September he was called into Taylor's office – the other players had thought that he would be offered a

contract, but instead he was informed that he was surplus to the club's requirements and that his services would no longer be required from October 1998. Reinelt trained with Gillingham, but he eventually went on to sign for Stevenage Borough and made his debut for them on 26 September 1998 at Kidderminster. He was released in January 1999, and joined St Albans, and in 2000/01 he was on the books of Braintree Town FC, for whom he has scored over 30 goals, playing alongside former O's favourite Terry Howard. Reinelt played 93(63) matches throughout his League career, scoring 22 goals.

SEASON	LEAGUE		FA CUP		L. CUP	
	Apps	Gls	Apps	Gls	Apps	Gls
1998/99	2(5)	0	0	0	0(4)	1
TOTAL	2(5)	0	0	0	0(4)	1

TOTAL APPS	2(9)
TOTAL GOALS	1

Robbie Reinelt

John Forgan RENNIE, 1938-39

Born in Kirkcaldy, Fife on 24 May 1911, John Rennie joined O's from Scottish side Hibernian in 1932. He looked to be a steady full-back, not lacking in ability, but was a reserve player during his stay at Brisbane Road. Rennie made his League debut in a 1-0 win over Port Vale on 8 September 1938. He was released in May 1939 and joined Selby Town a few months later.

SEASON	LEAGUE		FA CUP		TOTAL	
	Apps	Gls	Apps	Gls	Apps	Gls
1938/39	6	0	0	0	6	0
TOTAL	6	0	0	0	6	0

Clatworthy RENNOX, 1921-25

Blessed with such an unusual forename, it will come as no surprise to anyone that Clatworthy Rennox was always known as 'Charlie' during his career. Born in Shotts, Lanarkshire, Scotland on 25 February 1897, Rennox started off with Dykehead FC and Wishaw FC, before joining O's in July 1921. He topped the O's goal charts in his first season on 11 goals. He was a forceful type of forward, who had broad shoulders and was difficult to knock off the ball, and he was also a brilliant header of the ball. Both he and Albert Pape came under the watchful eye of Manchester United during 1925, and both moved to Old Trafford within a month of each other, helping United clinch promotion as runners-up in the Second Division. He moved to Manchester for £1,250 and had a wonderful first full season in the First Division during 1926/27, netting 17 goals from 34 League appearances and helping the Reds to finish ninth in the table. He scored 25 goals for them from 68 senior appearances, before moving to Grimsby Town for £400 in July 1927. However,

rather surprisingly, he did not feature in the Mariners first team, and was injured during pre-season. In October 1928, he moved to Bangor City, and the following month he turned out for Accrington Stanley.

SEASON	LEAGUE		FA CUP		TOTAL	
	Apps	Gls	Apps	Gls	Apps	Gl
1921/22	34	11	1	0	35	11
1922/23	13	2	0	0	13	2
1923/24	24	6	3	1	27	7
1924/25	30	5	0	0	30	5
TOTAL	101	24	4	1	105	25

Jack William REYNOLDS, 1904-05

Centre forward Billy Reynolds goes down in the O's record books as the club's first goalscorer in an FA Cup match – he netted the first goal against Enfield on 17 September 1904 in a first qualifying round tie. Midway through the first half, a scrimmage occurred after a Bert Kingaby corner-kick was not cleared, and Reynolds sent the ball on its way into the net. McGeorge had followed up, but the ball from Reynolds' kick had already crossed the line. He netted 17 senior goals that term, finishing 9 behind leading scorer Cavendish. Reynolds was born in Manchester in 1878, and he started playing junior football in Manchester, before joining Manchester City in 1901, where he played alongside his younger brother, John, in City's reserve side. Although he scored a number of goals, he could not make it into their first team, and moved to Burton United in June 1903. Reynolds and his brother made their League debuts for Burton against Lincoln City on 3 October 1903, and Jack's first goal came in a game against Gainsborough Trinity two months later. He made 7 League appearances without scoring again, before joining O's for their first venture in the Second Division of the Southern League in June 1904. His brother joined Grimsby Town, and thereafter played for The Wednesday (Sheffield Wednesday) and Watford. He played in all 6 of O's FA Cup ties, scoring 3 goals. Surprisingly, after a successful season, he was not retained for O's first season in the League, and joined his brother at Grimsby Town in June 1905, making 6 Second Division appearances without finding the net. The following season he moved to Southern League First Division side Swindon Town.

SEASON	LEAGUE		FA CUP		TOTAL	
	Apps	Gls	Apps	Gls	Apps	Gls
1904/05*	-	-	6	3	6	3
TOTAL	-	-	6	3	6	3

* Clapton Orient were elected into the League in 1905/06.

Walter REYNOLDS, 1931-32

Like a number of O's players through the years, Wally Reynolds left O's after playing just a couple of League matches, yet he went on to have a distinguished career with other clubs. All in all, he made over 220 League appearances with five different clubs. Reynolds was born in Ecclesall, Sheffield on 24 November 1906, and was a lightening fast outside right. He was an accomplished quarter and half-mile runner, and, in fact, was the Yorkshire amateur quarter-mile champion. He started off his football career with local amateur club Hathersage FC. Thereafter he tried his luck with both Sheffield Wednesday and Leeds United, but it was with Leyton Orient, whom he joined on 18 August 1931, that he first got his taste of League action. He made his debut at

Watford on 29 August 1931, and despite playing in the next fixture against Crystal Palace, he was not chosen again. He joined Burnley on 24 June 1932, and scored 3 goals in 20 senior appearances. Two year later he moved to Newport County, and during his two-year stay notched 4 goals from 59 League appearances. He was on his travels again in June 1935 and he signed for Accrington Stanley, for whom he recorded 139 senior appearances and netted 30 goals. This included a run of 102 consecutive senior appearances between August 1935 and October 1937. During the 1938/39 season he had spells with both York City (making 3 appearances) and Rochdale (4 goals from 23 senior appearances). During the early wartime years, he played for Sheffield Wednesday, and in 1942/43 he made 38 League North senior appearances. Walter Reynolds died on 4 August 1944, aged thirty-seven.

SEASON	LEAGUE		FA CUP		TOTAL	
	Apps	Gls	Apps	Gls	Apps	Gls
1931/23	2	0	0	0	2	0
TOTAL	2	0	0	0	2	0

Anthony RICHARDS, 1997-2000

Tony Richards, a striker, was signed from Cambridge United for an initial £10,000 fee (with a further £5,000 to follow after 30 senior appearances) on 21 July 1997, soon after the arrival of Tommy Taylor from the U's. Born in Newham, London on 17 September 1973, his apprenticeship started with West Ham United. After a spell in Hong Kong with HK Rovers in May 1993, he joined Sudbury Town during August 1994, and signed for Cambridge on 9 August 1995, after a short spell with Irish side Sligo Rovers. He made 29(13) League appearances and scored 5 goals for the U's. His first season at O's was interrupted by injuries, but he did score twice in O's 8-0 thrashing of Doncaster Rovers on 28 December 1997. He once took over in goal at Exeter City on 31 January 1998, after 'keeper Paul Hyde was stretched off with a broken leg. During the early part of the 1998/99, he found his true form and showed excellent touch, speed and vision. He scored a brilliant hat-trick against the 'old enemy' Brighton & Hove Albion in a 4-2 FA Cup victory during November 1998. He also scored the O's 'goal of the season' against Plymouth Argyle. Richards was in the side that played at Wembley in the play-off final against Scunthorpe in May 1999, but he did not perform to his true capabilities and was replaced at half-time. He played more as a winger during the latter stages of the 1998/99 season, but his best position was definitely as a central striker. Richards missed most of the 1999/2000 season with a knee injury, and was released to join fellow Division Three side Barnet on 11 August 2000. Up to the end of December 2000 he had notched 9 goals from 17 senior appearances, yet he only found the net once in 17 League appearances during 2001. He appeared in the 2-3 home defeat against Torquay United on 5 May 2001 that resulted in the Bees being relegated to the Football Conference, after having made a total of 29(6) appearances and scored 8 goals for the club. He joined Southend United in July 2001 for £36,000.

Tony Richards

TOTAL APPS	55(19)
TOTAL GOALS	15

* Richards' League record includes 3 promotion play-off matches in 1998/99.

** Richards also appeared in 2 Auto Windscreens Shield matches.

SEASON	LEAGUE		FA CUP		L. CUP	
	Apps	Gls	Apps	Gls	Apps	Gls
1997/98	10(7)	2	0	0	1(2)	0
1998/99*	31(1)	7	2	3	1	1
1999/2000	9(8)	2	0	0	1(1)	0
TOTAL	50(16)	11	2	3	3(3)	1

Craig Thomas RICHARDSON, 1997

Craig Richardson was born in Newham, London on 8 October 1979. He started his youth career with Charlton Athletic, but joined O's YTS Scheme in June 1997. He made his League debut against Rochdale on 23 August 1997, looking quite comfortable on the ball and attacking the opposition's defence well. He also came on as a sub in the League Cup match against Brighton & Hove Albion three days later. Richardson was released soon after by the club, due to what was reported as continued misconduct. It is believed that he gave up playing football.

SEASON	LEAGUE		FA CUP		L. CUP	
	Apps	Gls	Apps	Gls	Apps	Gls
1997/98	1	0	0	0	0(1)	0
TOTAL	1	0	0	0	0(1)	0

TOTAL APPS	1(1)
TOTAL GOALS	0

James Robert RICHARDSON, 1948

Jimmy Richardson joined O's from Millwall in January 1948 as player/assistant trainer, and was called upon a month before his thirty-seventh birthday to make his debut at inside right. His debut occurred in unusual circumstances, when big Frank Neary missed the train for the visit to Port Vale on 10 January 1948. O's went on to lose 3-0, but Richardson played so well that he kept his place and captained the side for a few matches, inspiring the team to an 11-match unbeaten run that lifted them from the foot of the table. Born in Ashington on 8 February 1911, the England schoolboy international started

Jimmy Richardson

off with Blyth Spartans in 1925, before joining Newcastle United during for £200 April 1928. He soon showed his tremendous ball control and dribbling skills. He made 136 League appearances and scored 42 goals, also winning 2 full England caps in 1933 (against Italy and Switzerland), scoring a goal in each game. He is best remembered by football historians for his infamous cross in the 1932 FA Cup final at Wembley that led to a goal for Newcastle against Arsenal, the ball appearing to cross the dead-ball line before he had centred. The goal was allowed to stand and the Geordies won the FA Cup 2-1. He also scored a hat-trick in a 3-1 victory against O's in an FA Cup fourth round tie on 25 January 1930 in front of 48,141 fans at St James Park. In October 1934, he signed for Huddersfield Town for £4,000, and during his three-year spell he played in 125 matches, netting 32 goals for the Tykes. He returned to Gallowgate for a second spell for £4,500 in October 1937, but made just 14 League appearances and scored 4 goals before moving to London. He joined Millwall for £4,000 in March 1938, making 52 League appearances and scoring 6 goals up to the start of wartime football. During the Second World War, he guested for both Charlton Athletic (in 1942/43) and O's (in 1944/45). At O's he was appointed head trainer between June 1951 and 1956. During November 1956 he returned to Millwall as assistant trainer, until ill-health forced him to retire from the game in 1957. Richardson died on 28 August 1964 in Bexley, Kent, aged fifty-three.

SEASON	LEAGUE		FA CUP		TOTAL	
	Apps	Gls	Apps	Gls	Apps	Gls
1947/48	15	0	0	0	15	0
TOTAL	15	0	0	0	15	0

Steve Riches

SEASON	LEAGUE		FA CUP		L. CUP	
	Apps	Gls	Apps	Gls	Apps	Gls
1996/97	2(3)	0	0	0	0	0
TOTAL	2(3)	0	0	0	0	0

TOTAL APPS	2(3)
TOTAL GOALS	0

Steven Alexander RICHES, 1996-97

The Australian left-winger was signed by O's boss Pat Holland via a recommendation from agent and former 'Oriental' Barry Silkman, after Riches was turned down by West Ham United. He was born in Sydney, Australia on 6 August 1976. An Australian schoolboy international in 1994, the twenty-year-old was spotted playing for New South Wales State side Warringh Dolphins, and signed for O's on 26 September 1996. After a glittering home debut against Swansea City (watched by his parents), coming on as a second-half substitute, Holland said he had unearthed a diamond. However, Riches never quite lived up to Holland's expectations, and after brief loan spells with Bradford City and Billericay Town, he returned home to Australia after being released by new O's manager Tommy Taylor. Taylor informed the press: 'He will definitely not be missed at Orient.'

William Crichton RICHMOND, 1938-39

Billy Richmond was born in Kirkcaldy, Fife on 1 March 1900. Having worked as an engineer in a Scottish shipyard, the left half started his football career with Raith Rovers and Montrose. He came south of the Border to join Carlisle United in August 1929, making 41 League appearances and scoring once. After leaving Carlisle in 1932, he went for trials with both Ayr United and Southport but he ended up moving to the south of England and signing for the Bournemouth & Boscombe Athletic side in October 1932 for whom he made 27 appearances. In June 1935 he went to Walsall, and during his three-year stay in the Midlands, he made 98 senior appearances, scoring once. The wing-half became an 'Oriental' in May 1938, but made a single League appearance against Reading on 4 March 1938, before signing for Guildford City in 1939. He later returned to Scotland to play with St Barnard's FC and Valentine Thistle, before retiring from football in 1942. He died in his native Kirkcaldy in 1973, aged seventy-three.

SEASON	LEAGUE		FA CUP		TOTAL	
	Apps	Gls	Apps	Gls	Apps	Gls
1938/39	1	0	0	0	1	0
TOTAL	1	0	0	0	1	0

Norman RIDDELL, 1911-12

Blyth-born Norman Riddell came to O's from Rochdale in May 1911, where he had made 24 League appearances in 1910/11. The left-back, who started his career with Blyth Spartans, made his O's debut on 2 September 1911 in a 3-0 win over Derby County, the same match which saw the debut of forward Richard McFadden. The left-back berth was eventually taken by Geoff Johnson, and Riddell moved on to Rossendale United in June 1912.

SEASON	LEAGUE		FA CUP		TOTAL	
	Apps	Gls	Apps	Gls	Apps	Gls
1911/12	11	0	1	0	12	0
TOTAL	11	0	1	0	12	0

Gordon George RIDDICK, 1970-73

Gordon Riddick has gone down in O's folklore as the player to record Orient's 3,000th League goal, in a 1-0 win at Middlesbrough on 20 March 1971 – the historic event was watched by a crowd of 17,017. Apart from that, Riddick made little impression at the club, and was yet

Gordon Riddick

another player who performed creditably elsewhere in his career, but with O's did little to enthuse the imagination. Born in Langlebury, near Watford, Hertfordshire on 6 November 1943, the 6ft tall striker was an amateur with his home club Watford, but he was apprenticed with Luton Town in 1961, and signed as a professional at the age of seventeen. During seven seasons at Kenilworth Road, he amassed 101(1) League appearances and scored 16 goals, but when they dropped down to the Fourth Division, he joined Gillingham for £10,000, signing just ten minutes before the transfer deadline in March 1966. He impressed during his three years with the Kent club, notching 24 goals from his 114 League appearances, and Charlton Athletic came in with a £5,000 offer for him. He helped them in their fight to avoid relegation from the Second Division, even appearing at centre half a number of times due to injuries. He made 26(3) appearances during his time at the Valley, scoring 5 goals. Riddick joined O's for £7,700 as a utility player in October 1970, but he was never a favourite with certain sections of the O's crowd. He was out for lengthy periods due to injury, and was a player who seemed to perform better away from home – he would make some intelligent moves off the ball, and score some vital goals. Riddick left O's in December 1972 to join Northampton Town for £4,000, playing 28 League matches and scoring 3 goals. In October 1973 he moved to Brentford, and did quite well over three years at Griffin Park, making a total of 104(4) appearances and scoring 5 goals. After retiring, he became a good club cricketer whilst running his own building firm, and he later worked in security for Sky TV events.

SEASON	LEAGUE		FA CUP		L. CUP	
	Apps	Gls	Apps	Gls	Apps	Gls
1970/71	13(6)	3	0	0	0	0
1971/72	0(1)	0	0	0	0	0
1972/73	0(1)	0	0	0	0	0
TOTAL	13(8)	3	0	0	0	0

TOTAL APPS	13(8)
TOTAL GOALS	3

Robert RIDLEY, 1915

North-Easterner Bobby Ridley joined O's in January 1915 from Sunderland Royal Rover FC, having previously played for South Shields. Signed as a replacement for the seriously injured Joe Dix, the outside left performed very well throughout the second half of the season, setting up a number of goals for McFadden, another whose career was cut short by the First World War.

SEASON	LEAGUE		FA CUP		TOTAL	
	Apps	Gls	Apps	Gls	Apps	Gls
1914/15	17	1	0	0	17	1
TOTAL	17	1	0	0	17	1

Arthur RIGBY, 1933-35

Having been a very successful player in his day, Arthur Rigby joined O's in 1933 at the veteran age of thirty-three, yet was an important member of an excellent forward line comprised of Mayson, Crawford, Halliday, Mills and Rigby. Born in Chorlton, Manchester on 7 June 1900, the player was an electrician by trade. He was a reserve goalkeeper with Stockport County, before being converted to a forward at Crewe Alexandra after the First World War. He went on to join Bradford City in February 1921, making 121 League appearances on the left wing and scored 21 goals, before joining Blackburn Rovers for £2,500 in April 1925. He was at Ewood Park for three years and gained 5 full England international caps during this time – against Scotland, Wales, Belgium, Luxembourg and France – between April and November 1927, and an FA Cup winner's medal in 1928. He played in 156 League matches and scored 41 goals. Rigby was sold to Everton for £2,000 in November 1929, making 42 appearances and scoring a further 11 goals. He moved on to Middlesbrough in May 1932, playing just 10 matches and scoring 3 goals before becoming an 'Oriental' in August 1933. He settled quickly at Lea Bridge Road, displaying skill and cunning in helping O's play some attractive football in 1933/34. He scored a goal and made a number of others in O's memorable 9-2 League victory over Aldershot on 9 February 1934, and he also scored the winner in a 2-1 victory over Scottish side Motherwell in a friendly during 1934/35. In August 1935 he returned to Crewe Alexandra, where he went on to make a further 69 League appearances from which he scored 13 goals. He also won a Welsh Cup winner's medal before retiring in 1937 at the age of thirty-seven. Arthur Rigby died in Crewe on 25 March 1960, shortly before his sixtieth birthday.

SEASON	LEAGUE		FA CUP		TOTAL	
	Apps	Gls	Apps	Gls	Apps	Gls
1933/34	36	11	4	1	40	12
1934/35	34	7	0	0	34	7
TOTAL	70	18	4	1	74	19

* Arthur Rigby also appeared in 2 Third Division Cup matches between 1933 and 1935.

Ledger RITSON, 1946-48

Left-back Ledger Ritson was born in Gateshead on 28 April 1921. O's boss Captain Charles Hewitt signed him in

R

March 1946, after he was spotted playing Army football. He proved to be a great defender, and the club rather surprisingly turned down numerous offers for him, including a £8,000 offer from Birmingham City. Ritson formed a wonderful full-back partnership with Arthur Banner, but tragedy struck on 11 September 1948 when he broke his leg against Northampton Town. After breaking the same leg again in training, Ritson never played again, and eventually had to have his leg amputated. The club did all they could for him, including staging a benefit in April 1951. Ledger Ritson was a fair tackler and a superb defender, and one wonders what he might have achieved but for that cruel end to his career. He died in 1977, aged fifty-six.

SEASON	LEAGUE		FA CUP		TOTAL	
	Apps	Gls	Apps	Gls	Apps	Gls
1946/47	35	0	0	0	35	0
1947/48	42	0	1	0	43	0
1948/49	7	0	0	0	7	0
TOTAL	84	0	1	0	85	0

John ROACH, 1905-08

John Roach was born in Dalston, London and joined for O's first season in the League from local amateur side Clapton Wanderers in May 1905. He starred in O's reserve side, and made his senior debut at left half in an FA Cup qualifying tie at Felstead on 7 October 1905. The first team were playing a League fixture against Barnsley on the same day, so O's fielded a reserve team for the cup match. Roach was not seen again until a League match at West Bromwich Albion on 21 September 1907, playing at inside right. The club were ordered to field their first team in an FA Cup tie against Custom House, so

the reserve side played in the League match, which was lost 3-0. He was not retained and went back into non-League football in June 1908.

SEASON	LEAGUE		FA CUP		TOTAL	
	Apps	Gls	Apps	Gls	Apps	Gls
1905/06	0	0	1	0	1	0
1906/07	0	0	0	0	0	0
1907/08	1	0	0	0	1	0
TOTAL	1	0	1	0	2	0

William Lawson ROBB, 1950-51

Willie Robb, a stylish wing-half, was born in Cambuslang, Rutherglen, Scotland on 23 December 1927. He started with local side Cambuslang Rangers, before joining Aberdeen in December 1949, where he made 4 Scottish League appearances. He came south of the Border to join O's in May 1950, but was restricted due to the number of good wing-halves on the club's books. He made his League debut on 18 September 1950 in a 3-1 defeat at Millwall, but left O's in October 1951, returning to Scotland to join Albion Rovers. He signed for Bradford City for £1,000 on 4 October 1954, and scored 6 goals from 136 senior appearances during his five-year stay. He sustained a very bad knee injury against Accrington Stanley in November 1957, and eventually had to retire from playing football in March 1959 on medical advice, when his knee failed to respond to treatment. Robb was then appointed as coach at Rutherglen Glencairn FC in June 1959. He resigned from that post in October 1960, and was next appointed as the Scottish-based scout for Bradford City, a position he held until 1965. He combined his football duties with the job of working as a salesman for the Glasgow gas board.

SEASON	LEAGUE		FA CUP		TOTAL	
	Apps	Gls	Apps	Gls	Apps	Gls
1950/51	5	0	0	0	5	0
TOTAL	5	0	0	0	5	0

Frederick ROBERTS, 1946-47

Outside right Fred Roberts was born in Rhyl, North Wales on 7 May 1916. He started out with Rhyl FC, before joining Bury in April 1938. He made 12 League appearances and scored 5 goals in 1938/39, and also played for them in a number of wartime matches. He joined O's in June 1946 and looked to be a useful attacking player, making his debut in a 2-1 defeat at Brighton & Hove Albion in November 1946. He left O's in May 1947. Roberts died in Colwyn Bay during June 1985, aged sixty-nine.

SEASON	LEAGUE		FA CUP		TOTAL	
	Apps	Gls	Apps	Gls	Apps	Gls
1946/47	18	2	1	0	19	2
TOTAL	18	2	1	0	19	2

Joseph ROBERTS, 1931-32

Joe Roberts was born in Tranmere, near Birkenhead on 2 September 1900, and this widely travelled player played for ten professional clubs between 1926 and 1935. He first worked as a boilermaker on Merseyside Docks, whilst playing football for Oswestry Town. This fast, clever left-winger – who stood just 5ft 6in and weighed 10st 4lb – made his entry into the professional ranks with Watford during September 1926, making 20 League appearances. The following season he joined Queens Park Rangers on a free transfer, making just 4 appearances, before moving to Midlands League side York City in August 1928, where he made 40 Midlands League and 7 FA Cup appearances and scored 7 goals. The following

year he moved on to Halifax Town and scored just once from 22 League appearances during the season. In March 1930 he moved on to Southport and made 50 senior appearances, and whilst at Haigh Park he proved quite the billiard player. He was a member of their FA Cup side of 1930/31, and on the eve of a sixth round match at Everton, he had a disturbing experience when his landlady died – he slept elsewhere that night. On 15 May 1931 he became an 'Oriental', and made his debut against Gillingham in a 3-1 home win on 21 November 1931. Roberts was soon on his travels again, and on 14 August he joined Luton Town, making his debut against the O's on 29 August 1932. After 14 League matches and 2 goals, he signed for Millwall in March 1933, but he didn't get a look in at the Den. He joined Barrow on 14 July 1933, becoming a frequent scorer for them and netting 14 goals from 36 games. He returned to Luton Town in May 1934,

Joe Roberts

but was only a reserve player. In August 1935, he went to Wales to team up with Cardiff City and, once again, his debut was against the O's on 16 September 1935, starring in their 4-1 win. He made 23 senior appearances and netted 5 goals. In March 1936 Roberts moved out of the League to join Dartford FC, after a quite remarkable career which had taken him all around the UK. The following August he moved to Worcester City. On leaving full-time football, he took over his father-in-law's newsagent's business near the Watford football ground in Vicarage Road, which he ran until his death on 9 March 1984, aged eighty-three.

SEASON	LEAGUE		FA CUP		TOTAL	
	Apps	Gls	Apps	Gls	Apps	Gls
1931/32	2	0	3	0	5	0
TOTAL	2	0	3	0	5	0

Alfred Joseph ROBERTSON, 1933-35

Goalkeeper Alf Robertson was born in Sunderland on 2 July 1908. He started as an amateur with Notts County, before moving on to Grantham FC. The 6ft tall 'keeper joined Bradford Park Avenue in May 1930 and made 43 League appearances. He came south to join O's in June 1933, spending the first half of the season as understudy to Joshua Gill. Robertson received some rave notices playing in the reserves, and he got his first-team chance in a 3-1 defeat at Coventry City on 23 December 1933, keeping the green jersey for the remainder of that season. He was in goal for O's historic 9-2 victory over Aldershot during February 1934. He lost his place to Charlie Hillam in February 1935, and soon moved on to Bristol Rovers, making 8 League appearances in 1935/36. The following season he joined Accrington Stanley, and played

81 League matches over the course of three seasons, before moving into non-League football. Alf Robertson died in Clayton-Le-Moors, Lancashire in May 1984, aged seventy-seven.

SEASON	LEAGUE		FA CUP		TOTAL	
	Apps	Gls	Apps	Gls	Apps	Gls
1933/34	23	0	1	0	24	0
1934/35	27	0	2	0	29	0
TOTAL	50	0	3	0	53	0

* Alf Robertson also appeared in 3 Third Division Cup matches between 1933 and 1935.

Robert ROBERTSON, 1901-05

Londoner Bob Robertson joined O's in 1904 and played in the four seasons prior to O's entry into the League. He was a utility player and appeared mostly at right half and centre half, but in emergencies he turned out on the wing. He scored the only goal of the match to win the West Ham Charity Cup final against Clapton FC in 1901/02. Robertson also appeared in Orient's first match in Second Division of the Southern League, against Brighton & Hove Albion during August 1904. He also played in an FA Cup tie for O's against Leytonstone FC – a replay which took place during October 1904.

SEASON	LEAGUE		FA CUP		TOTAL	
	Apps	Gls	Apps	Gls	Apps	Gls
1904/05*	-	-	1	0	1	0
TOTAL	-	-	1	0	1	0

* Clapton Orient were elected to the League in 1905/06.

William Gibb ROBERTSON, 1960-63

Well-built goalkeeper Bill Robertson was born in Glasgow on 13 November 1928, and he joined Chelsea from the Scottish

Bill Robertson

junior club Arthurlie during July 1946. Robertson was very patient in serving a five-year apprenticeship in the reserves as understudy to Harry Medhurst. He went on to make a total of 215 senior appearances (including an appearance in both the Charity Shield and the Fairs Cup), and also won a League Championship medal in 1955. He also won a Charity Shield winner's medal for the Blues the following September, in a 3-0 win over Newcastle United. He joined O's for £1,000 in September 1960, after Dave Groombridge was seriously injured. He made his debut in a 3-1 defeat at Brisbane Road against Liverpool on 24 September, but played in some of O's most vital matches during his stay, including the victory over Bury in April 1962 which took O's up to the First Division. The following season he lost his first-team place to Mike Pinner, and at the age of thirty-four he left to join Dover Athletic in May 1963.

Robertson died in June 1973 in Tadworth, aged forty-four.

SEASON	LEAGUE		FA CUP		L. CUP	
	Apps	Gls	Apps	Gls	Apps	Gls
1960/61	15	0	0	0	0	0
1961/62	16	0	0	0	0	0
1962/63	16	0	2	0	2	0
TOTAL	47	0	2	0	2	0

TOTAL APPS	51
TOTAL GOALS	0

Samuel Henry ROBINSON, 1933-34

Steady right-back Sam Robinson was born in Hucknall on 15 December 1910. He started as an amateur with Luton Town, before moving to Bournemouth & Boscombe in 1929 where he made 11 League appearances and scored once. In 1931, after failing a trial with Derby County, he moved to Mansfield Town and made 61 League appearances, scoring once. He joined O's in June 1933 and was a reserve to veteran Tommy Lucas. He made his debut in a 2-3 home defeat by Watford on 21 April 1934, and he also played the following week – a 4-0 defeat at Reading. Robinson left the club in August 1934, joining Guildford City.

SEASON	LEAGUE		FA CUP		TOTAL	
	Apps	Gls	Apps	Gls	Apps	Gls
1933/34	2	0	0	0	2	0
TOTAL	2	0	0	0	2	0

Glenn Victor ROEDER, 1974-78 and 1992

It was quite remarkable that Glenn Roeder, the former O's favourite, should return to the club in January 1992 for five months – some thirteen years and eight months after his last League match for the O's at Cardiff City on 8 May 1978. It was even more remarkable that he was appointed as the manager of West Ham United nine years later! The 6ft 2in and 12st 8lb defender had a long and distinguished career, and no older O's fans will ever forget the elegant upright player. He showed style and class, especially when going forward, which was tinged with a touch of arrogance – he also performed a crowd-pleasing double shuffle, which often confounded opponents. Born in Woodford, Essex on 13 December 1955, Roeder joined Arsenal as schoolboy in December 1969. He came to O's, along with Laurie Cunningham, after both were released by Arsenal as schoolboys in August 1972. Roeder first played football for Gidea Park Rangers, and represented both Essex and London schools. He started his O's career in midfield, but was later switched to central defender, and was sometimes deployed as sweeper. He was a vital member of the club's exciting Second Division squad, and helped steer Orient to their only FA Cup semi-final appearance, against Arsenal at Stamford Bridge in 1978. He was transferred to QPR for £250,000 in August 1978, after he toured New Zealand with an England party. He captained QPR to promotion and to a FA Cup final, and made 181 senior appearances for Rangers, and was also on the verge of a full England cap. After a loan spell with Notts County in November 1983 (4 appearances), he joined Newcastle United for a bargain £125,000 fee in December 1983, and captained them for nearly for six years, mak-ing 219 senior appearances and scoring 10 goals. He won 6 England 'B' caps between 1978 and 1982, a Second Division Championship medal in 1983, and won promotion from the Second Division in 1984. He moved to Watford on a free transfer in July 1989 and was at

Glenn Roeder

Vicarage Road for two years, playing 74(4) matches and scoring twice. He later acted as reserve-team coach until August 1991. When he retired he went to Italy to act as Paul Gascoigne's 'minder', but soon changed his mind and returned home. After a couple of reserve outings for Millwall, he joined O's. After a handful of appearances during his second spell at Orient, the thirty-two-year-old Roeder joined Purfleet FC in October 1992, and moved to Gillingham in November 1992 as player-manager, where he made 6 appearances including a match against the O's. In July 1993 he was appointed as manager of Watford, and stayed for three years before being sacked in February 1996 and joined the England scouting team. Roeder joined Burnley as assistant manager to Chris Waddle in July 1997. In 1998, he became part of England's coaching staff under boss Glenn Hoddle. In February 1999 he joined the coaching staff of West Ham United, a week before Hoddle's departure as the England boss. After the shock departure of Harry Redknapp as the Hammers boss, it was Glenn Roeder who took charge as caretaker-manager of the team for the final match of the season at Middlesbrough in May 2001 – a 2-1 defeat. The forty-five-year-old was appointed on a two-year contract as the Hammers' ninth manager on 14 June 2001, but the first four months were a struggle for Roeder to prove himself. As a player, Glenn Roeder made 547(14) League appearances and scored 31 goals in a career that spanned some twenty years.

SEASON	LEAGUE		FA CUP		L. CUP	
	Apps	Gls	Apps	Gls	Apps	Gls
1974/75	3(3)	0	0	0	0	0
1975/76	20(5)	2	1	0	1	0
1976/77	42	2	4	0	4	0
1977/78	42	0	8	0	3	0
1991/92	6(2)	0	1	0	0	0
TOTAL	113(10)	4	14	0	8	0

TOTAL APPS	135(10)
TOTAL GOALS	4

* Glenn Roeder also appeared in 12 Anglo-Scottish Cup matches and an Auto Windscreens Shield match.

Dennis ROFE, 1967-72

Dennis Rofe was a fast, tough-tackling left-back and he was one of the most admired Second Division defenders of his era. Rofe was born in Epping, Essex on 1 June 1950, and was a class-mate of another O's youth player, Terry Brisley, and appeared in the same East London schools side as another former 'Oriental', Paul Went. Rofe started as an inside forward in the O's youth side, but he was converted to a full-back by manager Dick Graham. He was given his League debut by boss Jimmy Bloomfield on a cold winter's night in April 1968 at Bristol Rovers – a club he was later to manage – when he came on as a substitute for winger John Key. He scored by playing a quick one-two with Dave Harper, picking up the return to slide the ball past the advancing 'keeper. Rofe was a key member of O's championship-winning side of 1969/70. He left O's to follow Jimmy Bloomfield to Leicester City on 23 August 1972 for a record fee for a full-back of £112,000. After eight years with Leicester (323 senior appearances and 6 goals), he joined Chelsea for £80,000 in February 1980, and was appointed club captain. He made 58(1) League appearances, before joining Southampton on a free transfer in July 1982, where he made 18(2) League appearances. Rofe won a single England under-23 international cap during his career. After retiring from

Dennis Rofe

playing, he was appointed to the coaching staff at the Dell. In January 1992 he was appointed as manager at Bristol Rovers, but ten months later Malcolm Allison was drafted in as a coaching consultant. Soon after, Rofe was asked to relinquish control of the first team – he refused and then resigned. He was then appointed reserve coach at Stoke City. At the end of the 2000/01 season, it was reported that he was back at the Dell in a coaching capacity, after the departure of both Glenn Hoddle and John Gorman to Spurs, and after turning down a coaching position with Wolves, he was still around when the Saints moved to their new ground, St Mary's.

SEASON	LEAGUE		FA CUP		L. CUP	
	Apps	Gls	Apps	Gls	Apps	Gls
1967/68	3(1)	1	0	0	0	0
1968/69	38	2	2	0	1	0
1969/70	45	3	2	0	2	0
1970/71	42	0	3	0	1	0
1971/72	40	0	4	0	2	0
1972/73	2	0	0	0	1	0
TOTAL	170(1)	6	11	0	7	0

TOTAL APPS 188(1)

TOTAL GOALS 6

William Robert ROFFEY, 1973-84
This attacking full-back with a very powerful kick joined O's from Crystal Palace in October 1973 and stayed for eleven seasons. During his first few seasons he was often overlooked by boss George Petchey, and that caused him to miss out on becoming one of a only few players to have reached the 400 senior appearances mark for the club. Only Peter Allen and Stan Charlton have achieved this wonderful feat. However, Roffey does feature in the record books as the scorer of O's 3,500th League goal – his second against Brentford in a 3-3 draw in a game on 18 September 1982. Born in Stepney, London on 6 February 1954, Bill Roffey signed as an apprentice with Crystal Palace in May 1971, making 24 League appearances before joining O's for a modest £5,000. He performed very well, and was in the side that reached the semi-final of the FA Cup against Arsenal in April 1978. In March 1984 he went on loan to Brentford, making 13 League appearances and scoring once. He went to Millwall on a free transfer in August 1984 and stayed at the Den for two years, making 36(1) appearances and scoring once. In June 1986 he went to play in the USA, and upon his return, he became manager of Tonbridge.

SEASON	LEAGUE		FA CUP		L. CUP	
	Apps	Gls	Apps	Gls	Apps	Gls
1973/74	20(1)	1	0	0	1	0
1974/75	6	0	0	0	0	0

Bill Roffey

Season	Apps	Gls	Apps	Gls	Apps	Gls
1975/76	13(1)	0	0	0	1	0
1976/77	34(1)	2	0(1)	1	3	0
1977/78	42	1	8	0	1(1)	0
1978/79	39	0	3	0	1	0
1979/80	40	1	3	0	2	0
1980/81	42	0	1	0	2	0
1981/82	18	0	0	0	2	0
1982/83	42	3	2	0	2	0
1983/84	28(1)	0	1	0	1	0
TOTAL	324(4)	8	18(1)	11	16(1)	0

TOTAL APPS 358(6)

TOTAL GOALS 9

* Bill Roffey also appeared in 3 Texaco Cup matches in 1974/75, 13(1) Anglo-Scottish Cup matches, 3 Football League Groups Cup matches and an Auto Windscreens Shield match.

William ROGERS, 1933-34

Right half Billy Rogers was born in Summerhill, near Wrexham in 1905. He started off with Flint Town, before moving to Wrexham in 1926, where he made 171 League appearances and scored 23 goals, twice being capped for Wales (against England and Scotland) in 1931. In August 1932 he joined Newport County, and hit 3 goals from 21 League appearances. In August 1933 the twenty-eight-year-old Rogers moved to Bristol Rovers, but he could not get into their first team and so joined Orient in November 1933. He could not gain a place in O's first team either at first, due to the form of Billy Fogg, but finally he got his chance and made his debut at Queens Park Rangers on Christmas Day 1933, and played in the following 2 matches. He joined Bangor City in September 1934. Rogers died from tuberculosis on 14 January 1936, at the age of just thirty-one, in Penyffordd, near Wrexham.

SEASON	LEAGUE		FA CUP		TOTAL	
	Apps	Gls	Apps	Gls	Apps	Gls
1933/34	3	0	0	0	3	0
TOTAL	3	0	0	0	3	0

Robert ROONEY, 1948-51

Big, strong and powerful centre half Bob Rooney, a former Scottish schoolboy international, joined O's from Clyde, signed by O's Scottish-born manager Neil McBain in May 1948. Born on 26 October 1920 in Glasgow, Rooney, who had started off with Falkirk before joining Clyde, proved to be the mainstay of O's defence with Arthur Banner. He scored a memorable last-minute equaliser in a 4-4 draw at Ipswich Town in September 1948, and was ever-present in 1949/50. Rooney stood no nonsense from any bustling forwards, but a cartilage injury halted his run of 59 consecutive appearances and thereafter he struggled to replace Stan Aldous in the centre of defence. He was transferred to Workington Town in June 1951, where he made 27 League appearances, however, serious injury curtailed his career and he was appointed their assistant trainer. Rooney died in 1992.

SEASON	LEAGUE		FA CUP		TOTAL	
	Apps	Gls	Apps	Gls	Apps	Gls
1948/49	15	0	0	0	15	0
1949/50	42	2	1	0	43	2
1950/51	9	0	0	0	9	0
TOTAL	66	2	1	0	67	2

Stephen Benjamin ROSE, 1922-23

Stephen Rose, another Jewish player to appear for the club, was born in the East End of London on 10 January 1895. He was a bombardier in the Army during the First World War, and played in two friendlies for Arsenal at the end of 1919/20. He did not make it into a strong Arsenal side, but played in 60 London Combination matches, netting 3 goals. He also appeared in 24 other cup matches for the Gunners, scoring once. He moved to O's in June 1922, but found it impossible to replace such established players as Dixon and Galbraith. He made his League debut in a 2-0 win over Leicester City on 9 September 1922, but was not retained and left in May 1923.

SEASON	LEAGUE		FA CUP		TOTAL	
	Apps	Gls	Apps	Gls	Apps	Gls
1922/23	3	0	0	0	3	0
TOTAL	3	0	0	0	3	0

Edward ROSEBOOM, 1924

Scottish-born centre forward Teddy Roseboom was another of the few great Jewish players to play in the League for O's. He was born in Govan, Glasgow on 24 November 1896. He was rather short for a forward at 5ft 8in, and he weighed 11st 8lb. He started off with Strathclyde FC, whilst serving during the First World War in the Highland Light Infantry. After the war, he came south to London and joined Fulham on trial, but soon left to try his hand in Wales with Ton Pentre, Pontypridd and, in April 1921, Cardiff City. It was with Blackpool that he came to the fore, and he made his League debut in December 1921, scoring 2 goals and making 21 senior appearances. In August 1923 he joined Nelson, and made his debut at inside right in a 5-1 drubbing at Clapton Orient on 1 September 1923. He made 12 League appearances and scored once before joining O's in February 1924, making his debut in a 0-0 draw against Southampton on 5 April 1924. He played in the following couple of matches and was then replaced by George Waite. He was not retained and joined Rochdale in

July 1924, making 32 senior appearances and scoring 4 goals. The following May he signed for Chesterfield, where he had his most successful period in professional football. His four-year stay resulted in 45 goals from 133 senior appearances. He then moved out of the League with Midlands League side Mansfield Town, for whom he made 32 appearances and scored a further 5 goals. In August 1930, he moved to another Midlands League side, Newark Town, finally ending his career with Mexborough FC in October 1931. Ted Roseboom died during 1980 in Kensington, London, aged eighty-three.

SEASON	LEAGUE		FA CUP		TOTAL	
	Apps	Gls	Apps	Gls	Apps	Gls
1923/24	3	0	0	0	3	0
TOTAL	3	0	0	0	3	0

Bertram Leonard ROSIER, 1923-27

Bertie Rosier was born in Hanwell on 21 March 1893. He was a small, but tenacious left-back, who attended St Anne's School in Hanwell and played for Hanwell North End, Uxbridge Town and Southall, before signing for Brentford as a professional in July 1914. Rosier spent a total of seventeen months in a POW camp during the First World War before being released. He later helped the Bees take the London Combination title in 1918/19. He made 127 appearances for Brentford, before O's boss Peter Proudfoot signed him in March 1923, giving him his debut on 17 March 1923 in a 3-1 defeat at Notts County. He was noted for his no-nonsense approach, and was one of the better full-backs during the 1920s. He was transferred to Southend United in June 1927, making 42 appearances, and then moved to Fulham in July 1928, where he made 57 senior appearances. He moved

Bertie Rosier

into non-League football with Folkestone Town in September 1930. His only ever League goal – out of a total of 367 senior appearances – came for Orient from the penalty spot and it secured a 2-1 win against Wolverhampton Wanderers in April 1925. Bert Rosier died in Ealing, London on 18 February 1939, aged forty-five.

SEASON	LEAGUE		FA CUP		TOTAL	
	Apps	Gls	Apps	Gls	Apps	Gls
1922/23	10	0	0	0	10	0
1923/24	34	0	0	0	34	0
1924/25	33	1	1	0	34	1
1925/26	26	0	2	0	28	0
1926/27	33	0	2	0	35	0
TOTAL	136	1	5	0	141	1

Ambrose ROSSITER, 1936-37

'Bud' Rossiter, as he was always known, was born on 24 November 1907 in West Ashford, Kent. The full-back started his career with Margate FC in 1930, and then moved on to Folkestone Town in 1932. In 1933 he joined Crystal Palace, making 27 senior appearances before joining Gillingham in July 1935, where he made a further 11 League appearances. Rossiter became an 'Oriental' in July 1936, and made his debut in the 2-0 win over Brighton & Hove Albion on 17 September 1936. He was later tried out in the reserves as a centre forward. Due to injuries to Ted Crawford and a number of other forwards, he was played at centre forward in the first team between April and May 1937. His big day came when he netted twice in a 3-0 win over Southend United on 29 April 1937, but, unfortunately, he broke his leg in the final match of the season at Brighton, and the injury forced him to retire from the professional ranks. He died in Wellingborough in September 1993, aged eighty-five.

SEASON	LEAGUE		FA CUP		TOTAL	
	Apps	Gls	Apps	Gls	Apps	Gls
1936/37	7	2	0	0	7	2
TOTAL	7	2	0	0	7	2

Donald Paul ROSSITER, 1956

Don Rossiter, a methodical inside forward, was born in Strood, Kent on 8 June 1935. He played his early football for Temple County Secondary School, and at the age of eleven he was playing for Chatham and Rochester boys, before progressing to local side Temple Parish FC. At thirteen years of age, he represented both Kent and Middlesex schoolboys at football and cricket, won an *Evening Standard* award for the best young cricketer, and became an England youth international in 1951/52. Rossiter joined Arsenal's groundstaff in August 1950 at the age of fifteen. He went on

Don Rossiter

loan to Walthamstow Avenue for the 1951/52 season when still an amateur, and the right-winger assisted them in winning the FA Amateur Cup final – a 2-1 win over Leyton FC at Wembley Stadium – at the age of just sixteen. He turned professional on 9 June 1952. During his national service in the Army, he was loaned to Hartlepool United during March 1954, returning to Highbury the following year. He never got a chance of first-team football with the Gunners, but appeared in 131 reserve matches and scored 39 goals. He was transferred to O's in March 1956 and played some fine games for the reserves, but could not break into the First XI. He appeared in the League just once, in a 7-1 thrashing at Stoke City on 22 September 1956. In November 1956 he moved to Dartford, and in July 1957 he moved from there to Gillingham, making only a single League appearance. Later he played for Dover,

Chatham, and Ashford. Don Rossiter was a player who never quite fulfilled his early potential.

SEASON	LEAGUE		FA CUP		TOTAL	
	Apps	Gls	Apps	Gls	Apps	Gls
1955/56	0	0	0	0	0	0
1956/57	1	0	0	0	1	0
TOTAL	1	0	0	0	1	0

Joseph ROULSON, 1924-25

Born in Sheffield on 7 October 1891, Joe Roulson started out with Cammell Laird FC. He moved to Birmingham City in 1912 and stayed for ten years, making 115 League appearances and scoring a total of 4 goals. This top quality left half moved on to Swansea Town in May 1922, and during his two-year spell, he made a further 48 League appearances and scored 2 goals. He joined O's at the veteran stage, a few months before his thirty-third birthday, making his debut in a 0-0 draw with Chelsea on 20 September 1924. After playing a number of games, he decided to retire at the end of the season. Joe Roulson died in Sheffield on 7 December 1952, aged sixty-one.

SEASON	LEAGUE		FA CUP		TOTAL	
	Apps	Gls	Apps	Gls	Apps	Gls
1924/25	16	0	0	0	16	0
TOTAL	16	0	0	0	16	0

Raymond Victor ROUSE, 1965-66

Goalkeeper Vic Rouse will be remembered as the first player to gain a full international cap whilst playing for a Fourth Division side. He played for Wales whilst at Crystal Palace – against Northern Ireland in 1959 – but this was his only cap, and throughout his career, he was known as the Welshman with the English accent. His only Welsh under-23 cap came against

Scotland in Edinburgh, and he had to fly straight back to London afterwards, in order to play for Palace in an FA Cup third-round replay against Shrewsbury twenty-four hours later. Born on 16 March in Swanse 1936, six-footer Rouse started as a junior with Millwall in May 1953, but after a number of reserve matches, he moved to Crystal Palace in August 1956. He was at Selhurst Park for seven years, making 238 League appearances, and was ever-present when Palace gained promotion to the Third Division in 1960/61, enjoying a wonderful season. He moved to Northampton Town in April 1963, but only spent five months with the Cobblers in their reserve side, before moving on to Oxford United the following August in their first season in the League. His two-year-long stay with the League's 'babes' included six months out of action with a broken leg, but he still made 22 League appearances. He was released in May 1965 and became an 'Oriental' just two

months later. He performed quite well for O's during their relegation battle of 1965/66. However, at the start of the following season, an injury and the form of young Ron Willis kept him out of the side, and in December 1966, he went out to the USA to play for Atlanta Chiefs. He stayed there for five years and made a total of 70 appearances. More recently, he became coach of the Metropolitan Police football team.

SEASON	LEAGUE		FA CUP		L. CUP	
	Apps	Gls	Apps	Gls	Apps	Gls
1965/66	37	0	1	0	1	0
1966/67	3	0	0	0	0	0
TOTAL	40	0	1	0	1	0

TOTAL APPS	42
TOTAL GOALS	0

Darren ROWBOTHAM, 1999 (loan)

The much-travelled veteran Welsh striker, Darren Rowbotham, joined O's on a two-month loan from Exeter City in November 1999, after training at Brisbane Road during the late summer months. He proved, like so many on-loan strikers, not to be the answer to O's goalscoring woes, and eventually returned to Devon. Rowbotham was born on 22 October 1966 in Cardiff, and the Welsh youth international started off with Plymouth Argyle as a junior in November 1984, for whom he made 22(24) League appearances and scored 2 goals. He then joined Exeter City in October 1987 and during a four-year stay he notched 47 League goals from 110(8) appearances. From September 1991, his career took off with spells at Torquay United, Birmingham City, Mansfield Town, Hereford United, Crewe Alexandra and Shrewsbury. However, in October 1996 he returned to Exeter City,

Vic Rouse

and scored 37 goals from a further 108(10) matches. He came to O's after a 'personality clash' with Exeter boss Peter Fox. He made his debut in the 1-0 win at Rotherham United on 12 November 1999, and his final match for O's was as a substitute in the 5-1 win at Chester City on 28 December. Thirty-five-year-old Rowbotham – who was idolised by the Grecians' fans, having scored 127 League career goals from 387(58) appearances – joined Weymouth in the Dr Martens League in August 2000.

SEASON	LEAGUE		FA CUP		L. CUP	
	Apps	Gls	Apps	Gls	Apps	Gls
1999/2000	4(2)	0	0	0	0	0
TOTAL	4(2)	0	0	0	0	0

TOTAL APPS	4(2)
TOTAL GOALS	0

* Darren Rowbotham also appeared in 0(1) Auto Windscreens Shield match in 1999/2000.

Marvin Marcel RUFUS, 1995

Marvin Rufus, the younger brother of Charlton player Richard Rufus, was born in Lewisham, London on 11 September 1976. The midfielder joined O's from Charlton Athletic in March 1995, where he started as a trainee. Rufus appeared in 7 matches during O's poor end-of-season run of 9 consecutive League defeats in 1994/95. He had his contract cancelled at the end of that season and later played for Romford. In August 2001 he joined Enfield Town with two former 'Orientals' – Chris Perifimou and Glen Wilkie.

SEASON	LEAGUE		FA CUP		L. CUP	
	Apps	Gls	Apps	Gls	Apps	Gls
1994/95	5(2)	0	0	0	0	0
TOTAL	5(2)	0	0	0	0	0

TOTAL APPS	5(2)
TOTAL GOALS	0

George Arthur RUMBOLD, 1937-46

George Rumbold was born in Alton, Hampshire on 9 July 1911. The left full-back started his career with Farringdon FC, before moving to Crystal Palace on 20 October 1934. He made his League debut the following year, in a 6-1 win over Northampton Town, and made 5 appearances before joining O's in June 1937, for whom Rumbold made his debut at Cardiff City on New Years Day 1938. He was in the side for the three matches of 1939/40 that were later expunged from the record books due to the outbreak of the Second World War. He made 89 regional wartime appearances, and was a member of the O's team who were eliminated by Newport Isle of Wight from the FA Cup in 1945/46. He moved to Ipswich Town on 15 May 1946, and made his debut on 31 August against O's in a match that was drawn 2-2. He was an ever-present between 1946 and 1948, making 127 consecutive senior appearances, and his final appearance – his 130th – eventually came on his thirty-ninth birthday against West Ham United in January 1950. He became a penalty and free-kick specialist, scoring 11 goals for the Blues. Rumbold joined Kings Lynn in July 1949, and later played for Whitton United. He died in Ipswich on 12 December 1995, aged eighty-four.

SEASON	LEAGUE		FA CUP		TOTAL	
	Apps	Gls	Apps	Gls	Apps	Gls
1937/38	17	0	0	0	17	0
1938/39	35	0	2	0	37	0
1945/46*	-	-	2	0	2	0
TOTAL	52	0	4	0	56	0

* No League matches were played that season.

** George Rumbold also appeared in a Third Division Cup match in 1938/39.

John RUTHERFORD, 1926-27

'Jackie' or 'Jock' Rutherford, as he was often called, was one of the most outstanding forwards in football history, enjoying wonderful spells with both Newcastle United and Woolwich Arsenal between 1902 and 1926. He played for O's at the end of his career, and, in fact, played his final League match for O's on 2 April 1927 against Portsmouth, a 4-5 defeat. At the time he was 43 years and 172 days old – still the oldest ever O's outfield player. Born in Percy Main, near Newcastle-upon-Tyne on 12 October 1884, he started his career as a thirteen-year-old with Percy Main FC in 1897. He moved on to Willington United in 1900, before moving to Newcastle United for a fee of £75 in January 1902. He soon became a big favourite with the Geordie fans, scoring on his debut as a seventeen-year-old. Rutherford started as a centre forward, but soon switched to the right wing, and before he was twenty, he won his first full England international cap against Scotland in 1904. He won numerous medals during Newcastle's great Edwardian period, and for over twelve seasons he showed great skill, speed and consistency down the right wing, as well as possessing a great ability to cut inside the box to score. In October 1913, the prematurely balding thirty-year-old fell into dispute with United, and surprisingly he moved to Woolwich Arsenal for £800, after making 336 senior appearances and scoring 94 goals for the Tynesiders. He won 11 full England caps, 3 First Division Championship medals, an FA Cup winner's medal and 4 FA Cup runners-up medals. Many felt his career was over when he joined the Gunners, yet he appeared in a further 366 matches in all competitions, scoring 81 goals. During the First World War he guested for Chelsea, and scored a brace in the war-time Victory Cup final during 1919. His final competitive appearance for the Gunners was in a Combination match against Clapton Orient on 27 March 1926. Rutherford briefly became player-manager at Stoke City between March and April 1923, but returned to Arsenal in September 1923. Rutherford joined O's on 17 August 1926, and his debut came at Preston North End eleven days later. He retired from playing in May 1927. Rutherford became an off-licensee in Neasden, but then in September 1928 he joined Tunbridge Wells Rangers as trainer, and in 1929 he was appointed trainer of Tufnell Park FC. In a friendly against Dutch side Ajax, when they heard who the trainer was they pleaded with him to play so their players could learn football skills from the old master. It was reported that although some of the speed was missing, the skill was still there, and he received a standing ovation from all players and spectators. John Rutherford died in Neasden, London on 21 April 1963, aged seventy-eight.

SEASON	LEAGUE		FA CUP		TOTAL	
	Apps	Gls	Apps	Gls	Apps	Gls
1926/27	9	0	0	0	9	0
TOTAL	9	0	0	0	9	0

Vaughan William RYAN, 1992-95

This tough-tackling midfielder joined O's in August 1992, just forty-eight hours prior to the start of the 1992/93 season, as part of the deal that took Greg Berry to Wimbledon for £250,000. He made his

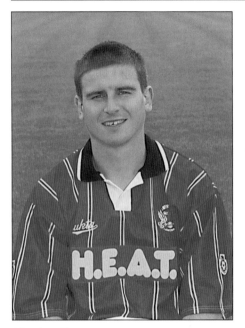

Vaughan Ryan

ances. During his time at O's, John Sitton suspended Ryan for being overweight, and then new boss Pat Holland released him from his contract in May 1995. In June 1995 he joined Dundee on trial, and more recently has been working as a black-cab driver in London.

SEASON	LEAGUE		FA CUP		L. CUP	
	Apps	Gls	Apps	Gls	Apps	Gls
1992/93	18(2)	0	1	0	1(1)	0
1993/94	16(1)	0	2	0	1	0
1994/95	6(1)	0	0	0	0	0
TOTAL	40(4)	0	3	0	2(1)	0

TOTAL APPS	45(5)
TOTAL GOALS	0

* Vaughan Ryan also appeared in an Auto Windscreens Shield match.

S

debut as a substitute in the 3-2 win over Brighton & Hove Albion on 15 August 1992, and his full debut came the following week at Reading. Ryan missed the end of the 1992/93 season after injuring his stomach in a freak accident at home, and he later received an injury to his ankle that kept him out for a further two months. Born in Westminster, London on 2 September 1968, the player joined Wimbledon as an associate schoolboy in 1984. He represented the England under-17 side, and went on to make 67(15) League appearances for the Dons, scoring 3 goals. He played in every round up to the semi-final of the Dons' famous FA Cup run in 1988, before injury ruled him out of their famous final win over Liverpool. Some consolation for Ryan was that he played in the Charity Shield match at Wembley as a nineteen-year-old. In January 1991 he went on loan to Sheffield United, and made 2(1) League appear-

William SAGE, 1927-28
William Sage was born in Edmonton, London on 11 November 1893. He started out with junior side Tottenham Thursday FC, and then joined Corinthians FC after leaving the Army. In October 1919, he joined Tottenham Hotspur and made 12 League appearances. He also represented an FA XI on tours to South Africa in 1920 and to Australia in 1925. He joined O's in July 1927 and made his debut at centre half in a 3-0 win over Reading in September 1927 – he later appeared at wing-half and was a steady performer. He moved on to Dartford in July 1928, and was appointed coach-manager of the London Omnibus Co. FC in December 1929. Sage died in Enfield on 21 June 1968.

SEASON	LEAGUE		FA CUP		L. CUP	
	Apps	Gls	Apps	Gls	Apps	Gls
1927/28	12	0	0	0	12	0
TOTAL	12	0	0	0	12	0

Ronald Duncan SALES, 1947-50

Born in South Shields on 19 September 1920, Ronnie Sales, the tough-tackling centre half, started his career with Westoe Central School. He then played for South Shields Town alongside Stan Mortensen, who later went on to glory with both Blackpool and England. Sales started work at the Reyrolles factory and played in their football team before being spotted by Newcastle United in 1942. He made 42 appearances in the wartime League, but lost his place after an appendix operation. After failing to regain his place, he came south to join O's in May 1947, taking over from Fred Bartlett. He scored from the penalty spot on his debut against Crystal Palace in August 1947, and performed creditably that season. He will be remembered for a grand display against the legendary Tommy Lawton in O's surprise 4-1 win at Notts County on 7 February 1948. An injury restricted his progress during the following season, and he went out on loan to Chelmsford City in 1949/50. He was eventually transferred to Hartlepool United in June 1950, playing just 3 League matches before joining his hometown club South Shields FC at the end of August 1951. He had to take early retirement due to his knee problems, and he went back to work at Reyrolles as a fitter, but Newcastle United and Reyrolles paid for him to go to London for a private operation on his knees. Sales was very proud that United had not forgotten him, and that Reyrolles treated him so well. Like so many footballers of his period, Sales did not make a lot of money playing football, but he deemed it a privilege to be paid anything for playing the game he loved – he was one of many true working-class footballing heroes. Ronnie Sales spent the last year of his life on earth in hospital in South Shields, suffering from Alzheimer's disease, yet he could still recall his days with Newcastle United, O's and Hartlepool with much fondness. His daughter stated that during this time he received a smashing letter from Kevin Keegan, then the Magpies boss, wishing him well, which cheered him up no end. Sales died in August 1995, aged seventy-five.

SEASON	LEAGUE		FA CUP		TOTAL	
	Apps	Gls	Apps	Gls	Apps	Gls
1947/48	26	3	0	0	26	3
1948/49	20	0	2	0	22	0
1949/50	0	0	0	0	0	0
TOTAL	46	3	2	0	48	3

Arthur William SANDERS, 1929-33

Arthur Sanders was born in Edmonton, London on 8 May 1901. He played football for both Raynham Road School and Latymer School. During the First World War, he guested for the Rosario club in Argentina whilst serving with the Merchant Navy. After the war he went to London University, before playing for Fletton United. In December 1923, centre forward Sanders joined Tottenham Hotspur as an amateur. He then joined their nursery club Northfleet United, before returning to Spurs in 1927, making 13 League appearances and scoring 7 goals. He joined O's in July 1929, but spent most of his time in the reserves. He made his debut in a 1-1 draw at Queens Park Rangers during September 1929, and he netted twice in a 3-1 victory over Coventry City in February 1930. The following season he made just a handful of appearances, but he came to the fore in 1932/33, playing at right half in an unsuccessful team. His final match for Orient was at Reading on 6 May 1933, when he decided to retire from the game to concentrate on his profession as a school teacher. Sanders died on 26 September 1983 in Winchmore Hill, London.

Andy Sayer

SEASON	LEAGUE		FA CUP		TOTAL	
	Apps	Gls	Apps	Gls	Apps	Gls
1929/30	5	3	0	0	5	3
1930/31	9	2	0	0	9	2
1931/32	7	0	3	1	10	1
1932/33	32	0	0	0	32	0
TOTAL	53	5	3	1	56	6

Andrew Clive SAYER, 1990-92

Andy Sayer, a striker, joined O's from Fulham for £70,000 in February 1990, having played 44(10) senior matches and scored 16 goals at Craven Cottage. Born in Park Royal, Brent on 6 June 1966, he started his career as an apprentice with Wimbledon in 1982 and signed as a professional in June 1984. He had a good spell with the Dons under manager Dave Bassett, with 15 goals from 51(13) senior appearances. However, towards the end he was not a regular at Plough Lane, and he went on loan to Cambridge United (making 5 League appearances) before joining Fulham for £70,000 in August 1988. He scored with a brilliant volley on his O's debut against Huddersfield Town on 6 March 1990, but he never settled at the club due to loss of form and injuries that resulted in him putting on weight. In 1991 he went on loan to First Division Sheffield United, teaming up with his former Dons boss Dave Bassett. Everyone

had thought that Sayer would sign, but after just 3 appearances he returned to Brisbane Road with the deal having fallen through. Sayer was given a free transfer at the end of the 1991/92 season, joining Slough Town and playing against O's in a friendly. He netted 19 goals that season from 42 appearances. He subsequently moved to Enfield, who paid £11,000 for his services. During April 1996 he signed for Walton & Hersham, and more recently it was reported he was playing for Hampton & Richmond, whilst working as a customs officer at Heathrow Airport. Later he managed a restaurant in Surbiton, Surrey.

SEASON	LEAGUE		FA CUP		L. CUP	
	Apps	Gls	Apps	Gls	Apps	Gls
1989/90	9(1)	1	0	0	0	0
1990/91	6(5)	2	0	0	2	0
1991/92	8(1)	3	0	0	2	1
TOTAL	23(7)	6	0	0	4	1

TOTAL APPS	27(7)					
TOTAL GOALS	7					

* Andy Sayer also appeared in an Auto Windscreens Shield match.

1910/11	32	9	1	0	33	9
1911/12	21	5	0	0	21	5
1912/13	37	4	1	0	38	4
1913/14	27	1	3	1	30	2
1914/15	37	2	1	0	38	2
TOTAL	205	33	8	1	213	34

George SCOTT, 1908-1915

Born in West Stanley near Sunderland, George Scott started his career with local sides Braeside FC and Sunderland West End FC, both of the Sunderland District amateur Leagues. Scott joined O's in July 1908 to become the greatest of pre-First World War players. Tragically, he was one of three O's players (along with Jonas and McFadden) killed in action during the war. The highly versatile player made his League debut at centre half in a 2-0 win over Oldham Athletic on 12 December 1908, yet he also appeared in various forward positions later that season. He was a model of consistency, and his fine play was rewarded when being picked to represent a London FA XI against a Paris XI in France during in 1911. Scott was a splendid servant over the years and scored many wonderful goals, but none was better than the winning goal he scored against Tottenham Hotspur at White Hart Lane on Boxing Day 1909. He also hit a hat-trick against Leicester Fosse on 30 September 1911. He was a vital member of a great O's squad that finished in the top ten for four seasons before the First World War. Private George Scott was killed in action on 16 August 1916, and is buried in St Souplet British Cemetery, about six kilometres south of Le Cateau in France.

SEASON	LEAGUE		FA CUP		TOTAL	
	Apps	Gls	Apps	Gls	Apps	Gls
1908/09	21	6	1	0	22	6
1909/10	30	6	1	0	31	6

James Dennis SCOTT, 1962-66

Jimmy Scott was born in Dagenham, Essex on 5 September 1945. He started off as a youth player with Chelsea and showed great promise, playing in a number of reserve matches. He joined O's in November 1962 and made his League debut in a 4-1 reverse at Sunderland on 16 November 1963. He was probably best at wing-half, though he could operate at inside forward. When tactical changes took place in the game in the mid-1960s, he could probably best be described as an attacking and constructive midfield player. When Dave Sexton took over as O's manager in January 1965, he appointed Scott as captain. At nineteen years old, he was the youngest skipper throughout the League, but despite O's poor showing in 1965/66, he played quite well. He was the first ever player to sit on the bench as a non-playing substitute on 21 August 1965 against Huddersfield Town. Scott left O's March 1966 and moved out to South Africa to play for Durban FC. He was their leading marksman in South Africa for a total of five seasons, before moving into the hotel business.

SEASON	LEAGUE		FA CUP		L. CUP	
	Apps	Gls	Apps	Gls	Apps	Gls
1962/63	0	0	0	0	0	0
1963/64	1	0	0	0	0	0
1964/65	12	2	0	0	0	0
1965/66	9(1)	4	0	0	0	0
TOTAL	22(1)	6	0	0	0	0

TOTAL APPS 22(1)

TOTAL GOALS 6

Alan William SEALEY, 1959-61

Alan Sealey, a cousin of Les Sealey, caused quite a sensation when, after making just 4(1) League appearances for O's, he moved to West Ham United in an exchange deal for big David Dunmore in March 1961. He went on to became a hero for the Hammers by scoring the two goals that won the 1965 European Cupwinners' Cup against TSV Munich 1860 at Wembley Stadium. Born in Canning Town, London on 22 April 1942, he was spotted by talent scout Eddie Heath playing for local side Memorial Sports. He was signed by O's boss Les Gore in August 1959, netted 5 goals in a trial match, and thereafter played regularly for the youth and reserve sides, learning his skills from O's coach Eddie Baily. He made his League debut at Swansea Town on 4 March 1961, and a week later he scored a dramatic winner against Luton Town by back-heeling the ball into the net. His move to Upton Park was completed in unusual circumstances. Ted Fenton has just left the Hammers as boss and Ron Greenwood was yet to be confirmed in charge. Sealey was actually signed by the chairman Reg Pratt, and he made 128 senior appearances and scored 26 goals between 1961 and 1967. He would have played even more matches had it not been for a serious injury sustained by falling over a wooden bench during a practice cricket match at Chadwell Heath. He was transferred to Plymouth Argyle in November 1967, but made just 4 appearances before joining Bedford Town. He then played for Southern League side Romford in 1969, before taking over the family business of distributing bookmaker's lists. However, he retained his connection with the Hammers as a scout. Sadly, Alan Sealey died from a liver complaint on 4 February 1996, a few months before his fifty-fourth birthday.

SEASON	LEAGUE		FA CUP		L. CUP	
	Apps	Gls	Apps	Gls	Apps	Gls
1960/61	4	1	0	0	0	0
TOTAL	4	1	0	0	0	0

TOTAL APPS 4

TOTAL GOALS 1

Leslie Jesse SEALEY, 1996

Veteran Les Sealey was signed for O's (along with Alvin Martin) from West Ham United on 17 July 1996 by boss Pat Holland. Sealey was a real character and an excellent shot-stopper who had had a long and distinguished career between the sticks and made over 457(2) League appearances. He was a cousin of former

Les Sealey

'Oriental' and West Ham star Alan Sealey. The 6ft 1in tall and 13st 6lb goalkeeper was born in Bethnal Green, London on 29 September 1957. He began his career as an apprentice with Coventry City in 1976. His various clubs included Luton, Plymouth Argyle (on loan), Manchester United (twice), Aston Villa, Coventry City (loan), Birmingham City (loan), Blackpool, West Ham (twice), and finally Bury (loan) between 1976 and March 1998. He made his O's debut on 17 August 1996 at home to Scunthorpe United, but with the arrival of new boss Tommy Taylor, things turned sour for him. A swap deal was arranged with West Ham boss Harry Redknapp on 29 November 1996, sending Sealey to West Ham and bringing legendary 'keeper Peter Shilton to O's. One of Sealey's career highlights was when he kept the mighty Barcelona at bay in the 1991 European Cup-winners' Cup final for Manchester United, which helped bring home the trophy to Old Trafford. His final League appearance was for the Hammers – fittingly, it took place against Man United –when he came on as a substitute for the injured Miklosko on 11 May 1997. He left Upton Park in May 2001. The football world was shocked at the news of the passing of Les Sealey in Southend on 19 August 2001. O's chairman Barry Hearn stated: 'It is always sad when someone dies before his time, and Les was a great character. We all enjoyed having him around in the short time he was here, and it a great loss to football.' West Ham boss and former O's star Glenn Roeder said: 'When told, I was unable to take it in. It is difficult to know what words one can say to express our sadness, and my sympathies are with his wife Elaine and two boys Joe and George, both of whom are trainee goalkeepers with the club.' A minute's silence was held for Sealey at Brisbane Road before the Worthington Cup tie against Crystal Palace.

SEASON	LEAGUE		FA CUP		L. CUP	
	Apps	Gls	Apps	Gls	Apps	Gls
1996/97	12	0	0	0	2	0
TOTAL	12	0	0	0	2	0

TOTAL APPS	14
TOTAL GOALS	0

Frank Burnett SEARLE, 1934-38

Frank Searle was born in Hednesford, Staffordshire on 30 January 1906. The defender started off as an amateur with Stoke City in 1924, before joining Willenhall FC in 1925. It was with Bristol City that he made his League debut in a 5-0 defeat at Fulham in March 1926, and that was to be his only senior appearance before joining Charlton Athletic for £200 in May 1928, making 70 senior appearances and scoring twice. After a 4-match loan spell with Chester in February 1933, he moved to Watford on a free transfer in July 1933. After making a single appearance at left half, he was pushed up to centre forward for 3 matches later in the season, in an effort to ginger up their attack, but he was soon relieved of his duties. He joined O's in September 1934 and was in the side that defeated his former club Charlton Athletic 3-0 in an epic FA Cup third round tie during January 1936, when they were beating all before them in their rise to the First Division. He also captained the side that drew 1-1 with Cardiff City in the first ever League fixture at Brisbane Road on 28 August 1937. Searle retired in 1938 and died in Wanstead, London on 16 June 1977, aged seventy-one.

Frank Searle

SEASON	LEAGUE		FA CUP		TOTAL	
	Apps	Gls	Apps	Gls	Apps	Gls
1934/35	33	0	0	0	33	0
1935/36	38	1	5	0	43	1
1936/37	26	0	0	0	26	0
1937/38	25	0	3	0	28	0
TOTAL	122	1	8	0	130	1

* Frank Searle also appeared in 3 Third Division Cup matches between 1935 and 1937.

Arnold William SEIGEL, 1946-47

Jewish-born player Arnold Seigel is one of just four known players to have worn spectacles whilst playing in the League. Seigel was born in Islington, London on 21 March 1919, and joined O's from Hendon FC in June 1946. He proved to be very versatile, playing at centre forward, inside left and at left half. In his limited senior appearances for O's, he looked quite sharp when leading the attack, and had what looked like a good

goal disallowed on 21 September 1946 at Reading. He was also very close to scoring a couple of times in the 3-1 win over Mansfield Town during the following month. Later that season he was mostly confined to the reserves, and returned to non-League ranks with Hendon in May 1947.

SEASON	LEAGUE		FA CUP		TOTAL	
	Apps	Gls	Apps	Gls	Apps	Gls
1946/47	9	0	0	0	9	0
TOTAL	9	0	0	0	9	0

John David SEWELL, 1971-72

John Sewell came to O's as a thirty-five-year-old veteran, who had a long and distinguished career with both Charlton Athletic (185 League appearances and 5 goals between 1957 and 1963) and Crystal Palace (228(3) League appearances and 6 goals between 1963 and 1970). Born on 7 July 1936 in Deptford, London, the full-back was signed by O's boss George Petchey in August 1971. He had a few outings early in the season, before going to America to play for the St Louis All Stars in March 1972. After retiring from football, he ran a teashop and later became an antiques dealer in America.

SEASON	LEAGUE		FA CUP		L. CUP	
	Apps	Gls	Apps	Gls	Apps	Gls
1971/72	5(2)	0	0	0	0(1)	0
TOTAL	5(2)	0	0	0	0(1)	0

TOTAL APPS	5(3)
TOTAL GOALS	0

David James SEXTON, 1956-57

Born in Islington, London on 6 April 1930, David was the son of Archie Sexton, the celebrated middleweight boxer who fought Jock McAvoy for the British title in 1933. Dave Sexton won the middleweight boxing championship whilst doing his national service. The 5ft 9in and 11st 7lb Sexton enjoyed a rather chequered career, but was a forward of some repute. He started his career with Newmarket Town in 1949, and then moved to Southern League Chelmsford City in 1950 after his demob from the Army. He then signed for Luton Town and stayed for two seasons, making 9 League appearances and scoring once. In April 1952 he joined West Ham United, and in just over three seasons at Upton Park he made 77 senior appearances, scoring 29 goals. During his stay, he represented the FA against the RAF in 1953. In June 1956 he became an 'Oriental' for £2,000, and scored on his debut with a header against Nottingham Forest in O's return to the Second Division. He had a reasonable season but struggled to gain a first-team place the following term, and was signed by former O's player Billy Lane for Brighton & Hove Albion for £3,000 in October 1957, and he played a big part in their promotion campaign. He was picked for the Third Division (South) representative side that faced their northern counterparts in March 1958. He made 53 senior appearances at the Goldstone Ground and netted 28 goals. He then moved to Crystal Palace in May 1959, but after 27 League appearances and 11 goals, he was forced to retire from playing at the age of thirty-one, after a serious knee injury in January 1962. Sexton made 181 League appearances and scored 67 goals between 1951 and 1961. He also managed O's from 1964 until 1965 and afterwards went on to have a long and distinguished managerial career with Chelsea, QPR, Manchester United and Coventry City. He has held various positions within the England national set-up, and in 2002 he acted as chief scout for Sven-Goran Eriksson.

SEASON	LEAGUE		FA CUP		TOTAL	
	Apps	Gls	Apps	Gls	Apps	Gls
1956/57	20	4	1	0	21	4
1957/58	4	0	0	0	4	0
TOTAL	24	4	1	0	25	4

Robert SHANKLY, 1937-43

'Bob' or 'Rob' Shankly, as he was known – no relation to Bill Shankly of Liverpool fame – was born in Douglas, Lanarkshire, Scotland on 11 February 1909. He was rather small for a centre forward, standing just 5ft 6in tall. He started off with Hull City in May 1931, but never made it into their first team and moved to Glasgow, joining Carluke Rovers in 1932. He then moved on to join Scottish League side Rutherglen Glencairn FC a year later, making 47 senior appearances

Bob Shankly

in his single season and scoring 29 goals. He moved back south of the Border with Newcastle United in June 1934, making just 6 League appearances, but he was a force in their reserve side. He moved to Aldershot in July 1935, making 28 League appearances and netting 6 goals. The following season he was moved to Barrow, scoring 5 goals in 30 matches. He became an 'Oriental' in July 1937, but could never replace the in-form Ted Crawford, yet he did notch 17 reserve goals. The following season it was Rod Williams who kept Shankly out of the First XI but, once again, he hit 17 goals for the reserves. Shankly came into his own during the wartime regional games, and he notched 24 goals from 24 appearances in 1939/40. In total, he scored an impressive 29 goals from 32 appearances between 1939 and 1943. It is reported that he died in Maryland, USA.

SEASON	LEAGUE		FA CUP		TOTAL	
	Apps	Gls	Apps	Gls	Apps	Gls
1937/38	10	0	0	0	10	0
1938/39	3	0	0	0	3	0
TOTAL	13	0	0	0	13	0

* Bob Shankly also appeared in a Third Division Cup match in 1937/38.

Colin Michael SHAW, 1965-66

Born in St Albans on 19 June 1943, the former England youth international joined Chelsea as a junior in May 1960 and made a single League appearance. The small, but lively inside forward moved on to Norwich City for £3,500 in August 1963, and made 4 senior appearances the following season. Shaw joined O's in March 1965, and made his League debut in the same match as fifteen-year-old Paul Went, in a 2-2 draw against Preston North End on 4 September 1965. However, he was confined mostly to the reserves. He moved to South Africa in 1966 to join Natal FC, for whom he scored many goals – he was top League scorer for a number of seasons. He always tried hard, but just couldn't quite fulfil the early promise he showed whilst at Stamford Bridge. In 2002 he was MD of Hi-Tech Sports distributors in Johannesburg, South Africa.

SEASON	LEAGUE		FA CUP		L. CUP	
	Apps	Gls	Apps	Gls	Apps	Gls
1965/66	7	0	0	0	0	0
TOTAL	7	0	0	0	0	0

TOTAL APPS	7
TOTAL GOALS	0

Jonathan Frederick SHAW, 1908-09

North-Easterner Jon Shaw came to O's in July 1908 from Wallsend Park Villa FC. He made his O's debut in a 2-0 defeat at Glossop North End in October 1908 and scored the following week against Stockport County. The centre forward showed some good touches and played in half of the matches for the only season he spent with the club. The local press reported that he moved into the Southern League in May 1909, but little else was reported about him.

SEASON	LEAGUE		FA CUP		TOTAL	
	Apps	Gls	Apps	Gls	Apps	Gls
1908/09	19	2	0	0	19	2
TOTAL	19	2	0	0	19	2

Daniel Harold SHEA, 1925-26

Danny Shea was one of the most outstanding inside forwards of his era, and was particularly noted for his dribbling skill and close ball control. He scored

235 career goals from 526 senior appearances in the Southern League, League and FA Cup between 1907 and 1926. Born on 6 November 1887 in Wapping, London, he started off with local side Manor Park Albion, before joining West Ham United in the Southern League in 1907. During his six-year stay at Upton Park, he made 166 appearances and scored 113 goals. He was transferred to Blackburn Rovers for £2,000 in 1913 – the world's highest transfer fee at the time – and helped Rovers to win the League Championship in 1913/14 by scoring 28 goals. He was also capped for England twice (against Wales and Ireland in 1914) and he represented both the Southern and Football League representative sides. During the war, he guested for Fulham, but Shea returned to the Hammers in 1919. However, he struggled to find a regular place, making just 16 League appearances and scoring only once. He

moved to Fulham in November 1920, and made his debut against Clapton Orient the following month. He was a regular at Craven Cottage for three seasons, making a total of 107 senior appearances and scoring 24 goals. In November 1923, he joined Coventry City, playing 64 senior matches and scoring 12 goals, before joining O's on a free transfer in February 1925. Although thirty-eight years old (and a little portly), he still showed touches of real class. He stayed for two seasons before joining Sheppey United in May 1926, and he later coached in Switzer-land, before becoming Woking's coach. Shea spent his later years back working in the docks in the East End of London, and he died in Wapping in 1960, aged seventy-three.

SEASON	LEAGUE		FA CUP		TOTAL	
	Apps	Gls	Apps	Gls	Apps	Gls
1924/25	10	3	0	0	10	3
1925/26	23	5	0	0	23	5
TOTAL	33	8	0	0	33	8

James SHEARER, 1920-21

Stylish outside right Jimmy Shearer was born in Inverkeithling, Fife, Scotland, and he came south of the Border to join O's in January 1921. Signing from Dundee Hibs FC, he made his League debut in the 1-0 win over South Shields on 5 February 1921. He made a further 3 appearances and was never on the losing side, but he had to be satisfied with reserve football, due to the consistent play of Harry Smith. Shearer was not retained and he returned to Scotland in May 1921.

Danny Shea

SEASON	LEAGUE		FA CUP		TOTAL	
	Apps	Gls	Apps	Gls	Apps	Gls
1920/21	4	0	0	0	4	0
TOTAL	4	0	0	0	4	0

Lee Sean SHEARER, 1994-97

This big defender – 6ft 3in and 12st – signed professional forms on the pitch at Brisbane Road just before O's League game against Wrexham on 18 February 1995. He made his League debut against Brentford on 17 April 1995, just before his eighteenth birthday. Born in Southend on 23 October 1977, this former England under-16 international played just a handful of matches during his three seasons at the club, but he did score the opener in a 2-1 friendly victory over the Welsh national team in May 1996. He went on loan to Hastings United for a couple of months in January 1997, before being sent away to Finland for undisclosed 'personal reasons'. In November 1997 he joined Conference side Dover Athletic on loan for a season, the deal being made permanent the following July. He established himself as a firm favourite with the Crabble fans (especially with the young ladies) and

Lee Shearer

had played 83 senior games by the end of May 2001, scoring a total of 22 goals. He is likely to pass the 200-appearance mark at the end of 2001/02. He captained an FA XI against a Combined Services side in 2000/01, scoring in a 6-1 win.

SEASON	LEAGUE		FA CUP		L. CUP	
	Apps	Gls	Apps	Gls	Apps	Gls
1994/95	2	0	0	0	0	0
1995/96	5(3)	1	0	0	1(1)	0
1996/97	7(1)	0	1	0	0	0
TOTAL	14(4)	1	1	0	1(1)	0

TOTAL APPS	16(5)
TOTAL GOALS	1

Geoffrey SHELLEY, 1907-09 and 1910-12

Kent-born centre half Geoff Shelley had two spells with O's. He originally joined the club in May 1907 from Tunbridge Wells Rangers as understudy to Mark Bell, and made his League debut in a 1-0 win over Hull City on 2 September 1907. In May 1909 he returned to the Kent club, but was back on O's books as a reserve between 1910 and 1912. In September 1911, the club arranged for him to play for Halifax Town in their first ever professional match. He was sent a telegram, but in the end (according to the official club records) he did not bother to reply, not wanting to leave the south of England. He left O's in May 1912.

SEASON	LEAGUE		FA CUP		TOTAL	
	Apps	Gls	Apps	Gls	Apps	Gls
1907/08	7	0	0	0	7	0
1908/09	2	0	0	0	2	0
1910/11	0	0	0	0	0	0
1911/12	0	0	0	0	0	0
TOTAL	9	0	0	0	9	0

Geoff Shelley

James Aaron SHERRATT, 1949-52

Jimmy Sherratt was born in Warrington on 24 December 1921. This rugged, but big-hearted, full-back started out with Arsenal, and played in the reserves between 1946 and 1948. He came to the notice of O's management when he netted a hat-trick against O's reserves in 1947/48. He signed for Hartlepool United in December 1948, and made 20 League appearances in the forward line, scoring 4 goals. He was signed by O's boss Alec Stock in August 1948, and was first tried at centre forward. The following season he was switched between defence and attack. He had a couple of quite memorable matches for O's – in March 1951, he scored the winning goal at top-of-the table Nottingham Forest. On Boxing Day 1951, he battled on despite a bad head injury which had to be bandaged heavily, and he received a warm standing ovation from the Brisbane Road crowd. He was

transferred to Workington Town in August 1952, and scored 3 goals from 48 League appearances,.

SEASON	LEAGUE		FA CUP		TOTAL	
	Apps	Gls	Apps	Gls	Apps	Gls
1949/50	13	3	1	0	14	3
1950/51	22	4	1	0	23	4
1951/52	4	1	0	0	4	1
TOTAL	39	8	2	0	41	8

Peter Leslie SHILTON, 1996-97

A footballing legend, Peter Shilton made his O's League debut at home to Cardiff City on 30 November 1996. At the age of 47 years and 72 days, he became the oldest player to play in the League for the club. He chalked up a remarkable 1,000th League appearance when playing for Leyton Orient in the 2-0 victory over Brighton & Hove Albion on 22 December 1996. He kept the 333rd clean-sheet of his career at the age of 47 years and 94 days. Like Bradman's test average of 99.94, and the 25 successful heavyweight defences of boxer Joe Louis, Shilton's record is also likely to stand for many decades to come. He also holds the record for the most international caps for a British player, winning 125 caps for England between 1970 and 1990 and keeping a record 67 clean sheets. This brief profile cannot do justice to the thirty-one-year career of Peter Shilton. 'Shilts' was born on 18 September 1949 in Leicester, and his first appearance came for City as a sixteen-year-old in May 1966. Thirty years later, he fulfilled his dream of 1,000 League appearances, but not until a long and frustrating spell on the bench at West Ham, match number 996 having been played some nineteen months previously. Shilton said: 'I think I could have reached the milestone in the

Premiership, but having been on the bench for so long, it was the right time to leave Upton Park and see what I could do at Orient.' Shilton swapped clubs with another veteran goalie – Les Sealey – on 28 November 1996. His 999th game was at Barnet on 3 December 1996, and in the sixtieth minute of the match, Shilton flew to the right to punch away a shot from Hodges, which he soon followed up by making a two-handed save from Gale. Alan Mullery – Barnet's director of football and an England team-mate in Shilton's first international – said it was Shilton's blinding saves that kept Orient in the match. Shilton's big day – his 1,000th League match – began with the Coldstream Guards accompanying his arrival onto the pitch with a fanfare. This was followed by the presentation, by former World Cup referee Jack Taylor, of a silver trophy and a certificate from the *Guinness Book of Records* for the first English player to achieve such a feat. The

script went to plan, with Shilton having little to do in a 2-0 victory. Shilton's last League match with O's was against Wigan Athletic on 21 January 1997, at the age of 47 years and 124 days. He left the League and, after a spell in Hong Kong, he more recently became goalkeeping coach at Middlesbrough, until leaving the Riverside at the start of the 2000/01 season to become a soccer consultant.

SEASON	LEAGUE		FA CUP		L. CUP	
	Apps	Gls	Apps	Gls	Apps	Gls
1996/97	9	0	1	0	0	0
TOTAL	9	0	1	0	0	0

TOTAL APPS	10
TOTAL GOALS	0

Paul SHINNERS, 1985-89

Born on 8 January 1959 in Westminster, London, Paul Shinners began his career with Fisher Athletic. The 6ft 2in tall and 13st bustling striker, although often looking ponderous, topped the Southern League goalscoring charts in 1983/84 with 31 strikes. He joined Gillingham in October 1984, but made just 1(3) League appearances without finding the net. After a brief loan spell with Colchester United during March 1985 (6 League appearances and a goal), he was transferred to O's in July 1985. Shinners soon became popular with the O's faithful, being nicknamed 'Rambo'. He looked to be a useful Fourth Division player and topped the O's goal-scoring charts in 1985/86. The remainder of his stay was dogged by injuries, and eventually he left to join GM Vauxhall Conference side Barnet in January 1989. However, ongoing injuries meant that he retired at the end of the 1988/89 season. His bustling play and scoring ability helped O's to

Peter Shilton

Paul Shinners

become one of the top-scoring clubs in the League between 1986 and 1988.

SEASON	LEAGUE		FA CUP		L. CUP	
	Apps	Gls	Apps	Gls	Apps	Gls
1985/86	32(2)	16	5	2	2(1)	1
1986/87	13	5	1(1)	0	0	0
1987/88	24	11	4	2	0	0
1988/89	4(2)	0	0	0	1(1)	0
TOTAL	73(4)	32	10(1)	4	3(2)	1

TOTAL APPS	86(7)
TOTAL GOALS	37

* Paul Shinners also appeared in 5 Auto Windscreens Shield matches, scoring 2 goals.

Kevin Paul SHOEMAKE, 1983-84

Born in Wickford, Essex on 28 January 1965, Kevin Shoemake, a goalkeeper, was an O's apprentice in 1981/82 and turned professional in January 1983. He looked like a promising prospect, but he only managed a handful of first-team appearances. 'Shoey' made his League debut in a 3-2 defeat at AFC Bournemouth on 24 April 1984. He was one of O's many players who were 'nearly good enough', and in later years he actually reached quite a good standard of playing. He moved to Welling United in May 1984, but in September 1986 he returned to the League with Peterborough United, and during a two-year spell made 40 League appearances. In later seasons, he had spells with Harlow Town, Dartford and Chelmsford City. He played for Kettering Town between 1996 and 1998, and for Nuneaton Borough in 1999/2000, before being replaced by former 'Oriental' Chris Mackenzie.

SEASON	LEAGUE		FA CUP		L. CUP	
	Apps	Gls	Apps	Gls	Apps	Gls
1983/84	4	0	0	0	0	0
TOTAL	4	0	0	0	0	0

TOTAL APPS	4
TOTAL GOALS	0

Nicholas Robert SHOREY, 1998-2001

Nicky Shorey, the son of former O's scout Steve Shorey, was another one of O's excellent young prospects who was sold in his prime. He signed a three-and-a-half year contract with Reading on 9 February 2001 for an initial £25,000 (with further increments to be paid after an agreed number of senior appearances have been made). He made his senior debut for the Royals in a 4-0 win over Luton Town in the Worthington Cup on 21 August 2001. He played his first League match for them in a 3-1 home reverse against Swindon Town the following October. Born in Romford, Essex on 19 February 1981, the left sided-defender/midfielder had been on O's books since he was ten years old, and signed as a professional on 5 July 1999. He made 30 appearances and scored 3 goals for O's successful youth side in 1998/99, and was voted the Young Player of the Year. He scored twice from 18 appearances for the reserves in 1998/99. He showed that he could be a free-kick specialist, scoring a nice set-piece goal against Antigua in a pre-season friendly at the Matchroom in July 2000. Shorey made his League debut when coming on as a substitute (replacing Steve Watts) in the eighty-second minute at Shrewsbury Town on 12 February 2000. His full debut came at Northampton Town on 7 March 2000.

SEASON	LEAGUE		FA CUP		L. CUP	
	Apps	Gls	Apps	Gls	Apps	Gls
1999/2000	4(3)	0	0	0	0	0
2000/01	8	0	1	0	0	0
TOTAL	12(3)	0	1	0	0	0

TOTAL APPS	13(3)
TOTAL GOALS	0

Barry SILKMAN, 1981-85

Barry Silkman, one of a handful of successful Jewish players to play for O's through the years, was born in Stepney, London on 29 June 1952. He was a man of many clubs, whose four-year stint at Brisbane Road was one of the longest in his League career. Altogether, he made 340 League appearances and scored some 32 goals over a period of some twelve years, having commenced his career as an amateur with Barnet during the early 1970s. He was signed from Queens Park Rangers by O's boss Paul Went in September 1981. Barry Silkman also played for Hereford United, Crystal Palace, Plymouth Argyle, Luton Town, Manchester City, Maccabi Tel Aviv (Israel) and Brentford. Flamboyant Silkman was a skilful, stylish midfield player, who was unfortunate to have been with O's during some of their most unsuccessful seasons, going from the Second Division down to the Fourth Division. During the latter part of his stay, he undertook coaching duties, but moved to Southend United in July 1985, where he made 38(2) League appearances. He then joined Crewe Alexandra in September 1986, but after just 1(1) appearances he moved into the non-League circuit, playing half-a-dozen times for Isthmian League club Wycombe Wanderers (in 1987) and then with Jewish club Wingate & Finchley FC. Silkman then turned his hand to greyhound racing with a great deal of success, and in recent years trained at the Canterbury Stadium in Kent. He also acts as a player's agent, and it was Silkman who tried to get pop singer Rod Stewart to buy O's in January 1995. He was also instrumental in bringing

Barry Silkman

Aussie winger Steve Riches to Brisbane Road in September 1996. The spring 2001 report from the Association of Football Statisticians (AFS) reports that Silkman became the oldest player to appear in the FA Cup competition since Sir Stanley Matthews in the 1960s. He came on as a substitute for Harrow Borough against Wycombe Wanderers on 18 November 2000, aged 48 years and 142 days.

SEASON	LEAGUE		FA CUP		L. CUP	
	Apps	Gls	Apps	Gls	Apps	Gls
1981/82	33(2)	5	4(1)	0	0	0
1982/83	17(5)	2	0	0	1	0
1983/84	41	4	1	0	2	0
1984/85	42	3	4	1	4	1
TOTAL	133(7)	14	9(1)	1	7	1

TOTAL APPS	149(8)
TOTAL GOALS	16

* Barry Silkman also appeared in 2 Football League Groups Cup matches and 6 Auto Windscreens Shield matches.

Bertram Edward SILVESTER, 1911-12

Stortford-born Bertie Silvester, a 5ft 8in and 11st right half, was a reserve player who was called upon to play just once for the senior XI in a 4-0 defeat at Birmingham City on 23 March 1912. He was not retained and went back into non-League football during June 1912.

SEASON	LEAGUE		FA CUP		TOTAL	
	Apps	Gls	Apps	Gls	Apps	Gls
1911/12	1	0	0	0	1	0
TOTAL	1	0	0	0	1	0

Amara Sylla SIMBA, 1998-2000

The French influence had already left its mark on Premiership football with the likes of Anelka, Ginola, Henry, Petit and Vieira, and during October 1998, Amara Simba (the thirty-seven-year-old former French international player) joined O's on a free transfer from Mexican Club FC Leon. He signed on a one-year contract on 8 October 1998, having joined the Mexican club the previous year. It was an opportunity he wasn't prepared to miss out on, as it meant he would be closer to his wife and two children who living in Paris. Simba scored on his O's League debut with a bullet-like header against Exeter City on 9 October 1998. Born on 23 December 1961 at Dakar in Senegal, he didn't kick a football until he moved to Paris in 1981, aged nineteen. A natural athlete, he played for Versailles as an amateur before obtaining a professional contract with Paris St Germain in 1986/87, where he became an instant hero. The high point in his career came when he won 3 French international caps, scoring twice. He played against Poland, Iceland and England at Wembley, when he almost scored – his shot hitting a post – in their 2-0 defeat on 19 February 1992. This was their first defeat in three years. Simba was in the same PSG side as Eric Cantona, and at Monaco, his manager was the current Arsenal manager, Arsene Wenger. Simba scored 49 League and cup goals in France from 205 appearances – with Paris St Germain, Cannes, AS Monaco, Caen and Lille. He invented the back-flip goal celebration, later copied by Faustino Asprilla. Simba won the French Goal of the Season competition for three years running, scoring some stunning goals. When he came to England, he found himself living in a hotel in Woodford and playing in Division Three with O's. A spokesman for the club stated that Simba was possibly one of the most talented players ever to wear the O's colours. Simba said: 'The

Amara Simba

Orient fans motivated me, I'm aware people are watching me. If the team do well, I would like to stay longer, if I'm still fit. The club has a real family atmosphere, but it is very professional, even though it is a lower division club.' After Christmas 1998, he returned after injury to score some vital League and FA Cup goals, showing sublime touch. He proved to be a most talented player, even at the age of thirty-seven, although he did show lack of pace over short distances. Simba featured in O's play-off matches in May 1999, and signed a new one-year contract with the club. He was the club's top League goalscorer in 1998/99 with 10 goals. He has proved to be a very popular at the club, none more so when playing against Halifax Town in August 1999 after learning that his father had just died. He scored his first goal of the new season that day and clenched both his fists to the sky, in tribute to his father. Simba was released to join Kingstonian on 23 March 2000, and he scored their winning goal against Kettering in the FA Trophy final at Wembley Stadium in May 2000, at last winning at the famous stadium in his third attempt. He made 15(2) Football Conference appearances, scoring 9 goals. He joined St Albans on 8 October 2000, staying for just one month before signing for Kettering on 24 November 2000, and the forty-year-old was in their side that lost 2-0 to Yeovil in a Conference Trophy match in January 2001. It proved to be his last ever senior match for the club. A surprise announcement came when Simba signed for Barnet on transfer deadline day (25 March 2001) on a non-contract basis, acquired by John Still as cover. He remained at Kettering Town, but could be called upon as and when required by the Bees, but alas he was never chosen, and the Bees were relegated to the Football Conference, his contract with them expiring on 5 May 2001. With just a few months to go until his fortieth birthday, he took just three minutes to open his account for Billericay Town with a neat lob, after an 'assist' from another former 'Oriental' Joe Baker. This took place in a pre-season friendly against Chelmsford City on 7 August 2001, and earned Simba a loud cheer from the 273-strong crowd. The local newspaper stated: 'Even at the autumn stage of his career, there's no substitute for the pure class of one A. Simba.' Forty-year-old Simba finally retired from the game in January 2002.

SEASON	LEAGUE		FA CUP		L. CUP	
	Apps	Gls	Apps	Gls	Apps	Gls
1998/99*	22(5)	10	3(2)	1	0	0
1999/2000	8(5)	3	2	0	0(2)	0
TOTAL	30(10)	13	5(2)	1	0(2)	0

TOTAL APPS 37(12)
TOTAL GOALS 14

* Simba's League record includes 3 promotion play-off matches in 1998/99.

Christopher SIMMONDS, 1950-51

Chris Simmonds was born in Plymouth on 5 August 1920. He started his career with Southern League side Barry Town, before joining Millwall in May 1947. A tall, hefty centre forward, he was a clever player despite his heavy build, who gained quite a high reputation with his tricky play. He made 67 League appearances and scored 14 goals for the Lions, before joining O's in June 1950. He scored with a brilliant diving header on his home debut for O's – against Reading on 26 August 1950, in front of 21,298 fans – his only senior goal for O's. However, he soon found himself in the reserves, as cover for Billy Rees and George Sutherland. He was transferred to Workington Town in June 1951, and did very well during his three-year stay, scoring 34 goals in 119 League appearances. Simmonds died in 1982.

SEASON	LEAGUE		FA CUP		TOTAL	
	Apps	Gls	Apps	Gls	Apps	Gls
1950/51	15	1	1	0	16	1
TOTAL	15	1	1	0	16	1

Henry Thomas SIMONS, 1906

Inside forward Henry Simons was another of football's great travellers, playing for eleven different clubs during his career. Although he made few appearances, he had a knack of being able to score goals, yet he never stayed at any one club long enough to show his true worth. Born in Hackney, London on 26 November 1887, he started off with Peel Institute, before joining O's in March 1906. This was at a time when O's were trying out young amateurs, after selling off their star players in order to pay off their debts. He made his League debut on 24 March 1906 in a 1-0 win over Gainsborough Trinity, and his only senior goal came on 21 April to secure two points against Stockport County. He was kept on for the following season and played in the opening fixture against Stockport on 1 September 1906, but shortly thereafter he moved to Southern League outfit Leyton FC and made 7 appearances for them, scoring once. Simons then made a name for himself with the Tufnell Park club between 1908 and 1910, before signing for Sheffield United, where he made 68 League appearances and a total of scored 22 goals between 1910 and 1912. After brief spells with Halifax Town, Merthyr Town and Brentford, he moved to Fulham during April 1914, and made 9 League appearances, scoring 4 goals for the club. He was transferred to Queens Park Rangers in November 1914, and scored 8 goals in 19 matches. During the First World War, he was a guest player for Tottenham Hotspur, making 3 appearances. After the war, he was on the books of Norwich City, for whom he made 3 appearances. He then had short spells with Merthyr Town and Margate. Simons died in Stoke Newington, London on 26 August 1956, just before his sixty-ninth birthday.

SEASON	LEAGUE		FA CUP		TOTAL	
	Apps	Gls	Apps	Gls	Apps	Gls
1905/06	6	1	0	0	6	1
1906/07	1	0	0	0	1	0
TOTAL	7	1	0	0	7	1

S

Colin Robertson SIMPSON, 1997-99

This gangly twenty-one-year-old striker signed for Orient on a trial basis in December 1997. He was brought in from Hendon, after having scored twice against the O's in the FA Cup at Clarement Road. His first goal came when O's goalkeeper Hyde's attempted clearance thudded into the back of Simpson and bounced back into an empty net. His second came in the fifty-fifth minute with a header. However, one always felt when watching him play that he was never up to League grade, and so it proved. Born in Oxford on 30 April 1976, he started as a trainee with Watford in July 1994, but played just once as a substitute. He joined Enfield in 1997, and then played in Japan for a while, before returning to the UK to play for Welling United. He joined Orient on 8 December 1997. Simpson made his O's debut as a substitute, coming on after thirty minutes in an Auto Windscreen Cup match against Colchester United on 9 December 1997. O's boss Taylor said: 'He looked very bright, we simply got him to have a look at him, I am not putting any pressure on, but tonight I was impressed.' He bagged 3 League goals in his first season, including a goal on his debut against Shrewsbury Town on 13 December 1997. After twenty-one minutes, he was one of a group of players that had latched onto an in-swinging corner from Naylor. Town defender Brian Gayle admitted that he thought he had touched the ball last, but the League awarded the goal to Simpson. However Simpson only played in a handful of matches in 1998, and never featured in a first-team match during 1998/99. He spent most of the time on loan to a number of non-League teams, which included Hendon and Boreham Wood. He then

Colin Simpson

moved to Sutton United, before moving to Farnborough during February 1999. Simpson returned to the club in March 1999, but was given a free transfer a couple of months later to join Sutton United. More recently, he has played for Billericay, Braintree Town and Purfleet.

SEASON	LEAGUE		FA CUP		L. CUP	
	Apps	Gls	Apps	Gls	Apps	Gls
1997/98	9(5)	3	0	0	0	0
1998/99	0	0	0	0	0	0
TOTAL	9(5)	3	0	0	0	0

TOTAL APPS	9(5)
TOTAL GOALS	3

* Colin Simpson also appeared in 1(1) Auto Windscreens Shield matches.

Owen SIMPSON, 1967-68

Left-back Owen Simpson came to O's in September 1967, along with striker Roy

Massey from Rotherham United. O's boss Dick Graham played him down the left wing, and his powerful left-footed shooting was always a danger to opposing defences. However, he moved back to his usual role later that season. Born in Prudhoe near Stockfield on 18 September 1943, he started out as a junior with Rotherham United in October 1962, and made 6 League appearances for them between 1964 and 1966. After Graham was replaced with Jimmy Bloomfield, Simpson did not fit into his plans, and he was released to join Colchester United in August 1968, where he made 41(2) League appearances and scored 4 goals. During the following few seasons, he moved around the League with Southend United (64 senior matches and a goal), Darlington (11 matches), and Grimsby Town (6(1) appearances). He was with Boston United between 1972 and 1975, making 100 appearances and scoring 3 goals. After his retirement from the game, he became a rep for an upholstery firm in Grimsby.

SEASON	LEAGUE		FA CUP		L. CUP	
	Apps	Gls	Apps	Gls	Apps	Gls
1967/68	36	4	5	1	0	0
TOTAL	36	4	5	1	0	0

TOTAL APPS	41
TOTAL GOALS	5

John Edmund SITTON, 1985-89

Born in Hackney, London on 21 October 1959, the 5ft 11in and 12st 4lb defender started his career as an apprentice with Chelsea in October 1977, making 11(2) League appearances. In February 1980 he joined Millwall for £10,000, making 43(2) League appearances and scoring once. During September 1981 he moved to Gillingham for another £10,000 fee, and during his four-year stay made 102(5) League appearances and scored 5 goals. He joined O's on a free transfer from Gillingham in July 1985, and was a member of O's promotion-winning team of 1988/89, playing in all 4 promotion play-off matches. Sitton was released on a free transfer in May 1991. Having a full FA coaching badge, he applied for a number of coaching jobs, including player-coach at Exeter City and the manager's job at Maidstone United, but neither came to fruition. He worked in a part-time capacity with O's School of Excellence Academy whilst playing for Slough Town, making 4 appearances in 1991/92. Sitton was joint Leyton Orient manager (with Chris Turner) in 1994/95.

SEASON	LEAGUE		FA CUP		L. CUP	
	Apps	Gls	Apps	Gls	Apps	Gls
1985/86	39	0	2	0	4	0
1986/87	13	0	2	0	2	0

John Sitton

1987/88	19(1)	1	0(1)	0	1(1)	0
1988/89*	41	4	3	0	2	0
1989/90	36(1)	2	1	0	4	0
1990/91	22(2)	0	5	0	6	0
TOTAL	170(4)	7	13(1)	0	19(1)	0

TOTAL APPS	202(6)
TOTAL GOALS	7

* John Sitton's record includes 4 matches in the promotion play-offs in 1988/89. Sitton also appeared in 10 Auto Windscreen matches, scoring once.

George Alfred SKELTON, 1947-48

Well-built inside forward George Skelton was born in Thurcroft, near Rotherham on 27 November 1919. He started off with local side Thurcroft Welfare FC, before joining Huddersfield Town on amateur forms on 18 February 1945. After demobilsation from the Army, he became a professional footballer on 20 December 1945. During the war he appeared as a guest for Leytonstone FC, and he also represented the Royal Engineers, for whom he scored against the Western Command on 20 February 1946 in a 4-2 defeat at Maine Road, Manchester. After the Second World War, he returned to Leeds Road and made one League appearance for Town on 4 September 1946 at Sunderland. He joined O's on 29 July 1947, for what was reported in the club programme as a 'substantial fee'. It was further reported that the player was good with both feet, had above average ability and a quick swerve on the run that would leave many defenders going the wrong way. Skelton made his League debut in the 1-1 draw with Crystal Palace on 25 August 1947. However, during a 6-0 defeat at Bristol City on 17 September 1947, he sustained a serious rib injury. He could not play professional football again, was released in May 1948, and drifted into non-League football. A lifelong bachelor, who was known by his family as Alec, he died at his home in Thurcroft during September 1994, just before his seventy-fifth birthday.

SEASON	LEAGUE		FA CUP		TOTAL	
	Apps	Gls	Apps	Gls	Apps	Gls
1947/48	3	0	0	0	3	0
TOTAL	3	0	0	0	3	0

Michael Noel SKIVINGTON, 1949-50

Mick Skivington was born in Glasgow on 24 December 1921. The centre half started his career in June 1947 as a reserve player with Bury, but moved to Rochdale in January 1948, making a single League appearance. He joined Irish club Dundalk in 1948, and represented the League of Ireland against the Football League in May 1949. He became an 'Oriental' in October 1949, and made his

George Skelton

League debut in a 1-1 draw at Exeter City on 14 January 1950. He couldn't command a regular first-team spot, which was held by Rooney, so he moved to Gillingham on trial in July 1950. He played 8 League matches, but was not retained. In May 1951 he moved to Brentford, but never featured in their First XI.

SEASON	LEAGUE		FA CUP		TOTAL	
	Apps	Gls	Apps	Gls	Apps	Gls
1949/50	5	0	0	0	5	0
TOTAL	5	0	0	0	5	0

Malcolm Bruce SLATER, 1966-70

The tricky, slightly-built right-winger Malcolm Slater was born in Buckie, Scotland on 22 October 1939. He began his career as a fifteen-year-old with local Highland League Club Buckie Thistle, before joining Glasgow Celtic three years later. He won 3 Scottish amateur international caps, and was on the verge of signing professional forms with Celtic when two of his brothers were killed in a drowning accident. He decided to leave football and become a civil servant, playing only minor football. He was tempted back to the professional ranks to join Montrose in 1961, and was transferred to Southend United for £2,000 in November 1963. He made 82 League appearances and scored 6 goals before falling out with boss Ted Fenton, so he joined O's for a small fee in January 1967, only a month before they had turned down a £15,000 offer from Middlesbrough for him. Slater proved to be a difficult customer for defenders during his four seasons at Brisbane Road. With the arrival of Mark Lazarus in 1969, he lost his place and went on loan to Colchester United, making 4 League appearances. United could not match O's asking price of £5,000, so

Malcolm Slater

he returned to Leyton, but was released in May 1967. He returned to Scotland and played for Inverness Caledonian and then for Ross County, both in the Highland League.

SEASON	LEAGUE		FA CUP		L. CUP	
	Apps	Gls	Apps	Gls	Apps	Gls
1966/67	22	1	0	0	0	0
1967/68	35	2	5	0	1	0
1968/69	45	1	2	1	4	0
1969/70	9	0	0	0	2	0
TOTAL	111	4	7	1	7	0

TOTAL APPS	125
TOTAL GOALS	5

Thomas Arthur SLATER, 1926-1932

Arthur Slater – or Jim as he was also known – had to be content to be understudy to the legendary goalkeeper Arthur Wood during his four seasons at Millfields Road. Born on 25 February 1908 in

Chester-le-Street, Slater started his career with Horden Colliery FC, before playing for Easington Colliery and Murton Colliery Welfare, from whom he joined O's in August 1926. The 'keeper made his League debut in a 3-0 defeat at Port Vale on 27 December 1926. In 1930 he even lost his role as understudy to Wood, when O's signed amateur international goalkeeper Monty Garland-Wells. Slater was transferred to Port Vale in June 1930, but after 20 League appearances he lost his place. He moved to Watford on a free transfer in August 1932, where he spent a couple of seasons making a further 29 League appearances. Slater moved to the Vauxhall Motors works team in Luton during August 1934. He died in 1976 in Luton.

Mark Smalley

SEASON	LEAGUE		FA CUP		L. CUP	
	Apps	Gls	Apps	Gls	Apps	Gls
1926/27	1	0	2	0	3	0
1927/28	4	0	0	0	4	0
1928/29	6	0	0	0	6	0
1929/30	9	0	0	0	9	0
TOTAL	20	0	2	0	22	0

Mark Anthony SMALLEY, 1987-89

Tall central defender Mark Smalley was born in Newark-on-Trent, Nottinghamshire on 2 January 1965. He started out as an apprentice with Nottingham Forest in January 1983, and made 1(2) League appearances for Forest. After loan spells at both Birmingham City in March 1986 (7 League matches) and Bristol Rovers in August 1986 (10 League appearances), he moved to O's in March 1967. He formed part of the deal that took O's young defender Colin Foster to the City Ground for £50,000. Smalley proved to be a cool and calm defender, but injuries during his last two years at the club caused him to miss many matches, and he could never regain his place from either Tommy Cunningham or Keith Day. He moved on loan to Mansfield Town in November 1969, before a permanent move took place in January 1990. He made a total of 49 League appearances and scored twice before joining Maidstone United in May 1991, where he played a further 33(1) League matches and appeared in their last ever League fixture in May 1992. He moved into non-League football in August 1992 as player/coach with Kettering Town, Erith & Belvedere, Sutton Town, Shepshed Dynamos. Finally, in February 1995, he moved to Hucknall Town.

SEASON	LEAGUE		FA CUP		L. CUP	
	Apps	Gls	Apps	Gls	Apps	Gls
1986/87	22	1	0	0	0	0
1987/88	33(2)	3	4	0	2	0
1988/89	3(1)	0	0	0	0	0

1989/90	1(2)	0	0	0	0	0
TOTAL	59(5)	4	4	0	2	0

TOTAL APPS	65(5)
TOTAL GOALS	4

* Mark Smalley also appeared in 4 Auto Windscreens Shield matches.

John SMEULDERS, 1974-1979

Born in Hackney, London on 28 March 1957, John Smeulders, a 5ft 8in and 13st goalkeeper, signed with O's as an apprentice in July 1972 and turned professional during July 1974. He was just a shade short for a goalkeeper, often looking vulnerable under high crosses, but he was a good shot-stopper and represented England at youth level. He had the daunting task of being the understudy to firstly Ray Goddard and later John Jackson, and so had to be satisfied with reserve football during the five seasons he was at Brisbane Road. He got his chance of first-team football during August 1977, whilst Jackson was away fulfilling commitments playing and coaching in USA. Smeulders played in the 2 League Cup ties against Fulham, which O's won 3-2 on aggregate. With the arrival of Mervyn Day from West Ham United, Smeulders moved to AFC Bournemouth on a free transfer in July 1979, making 14 League appearances for the Cherries over the following two seasons, before moving to Trowbridge Town on a free. He then moved on to Weymouth, before he was re-signed by AFC Bournemouth for £4,000 in January 1984. He became a regular feature between the sticks over the next two-and-a-half seasons, and set a club record 'shut-out' period. He made a further 75 senior appearances at Dean Court, before joining Torquay United on a free transfer in July 1986. There he made another 18 League appearances in 1986/87, although he was loaned out to Peterborough United, for whom he made a solitary appearance in December 1987. Smeulders then reverted to non-League football with Poole Town, before remarkably re-signing for Bournemouth for a third spell in August 1987, as understudy to Gerry Peyton. He made 8 League appearances over the next two seasons, plus a further 8 appearances whilst on loan to Brentford in October 1988. He finally took his leave of the League scene, after making a total of 125 League appearances during fourteen years in the game.

SEASON	LEAGUE		FA CUP		L. CUP	
	Apps	Gls	Apps	Gls	Apps	Gls
1974/75	0	0	0	0	0	0
1975/76	0	0	0	0	0	0
1976/77	0	0	0	0	0	0
1977/78	0	0	0	0	2	0
1978/79	0	0	0	0	0	0
TOTAL	0	0	0	0	2	0

TOTAL APPS	2
TOTAL GOALS	0

* John Smeulders also appeared in 6 Anglo-Scottish Cup matches – 3 in 1977/78 and 3 in 1978/79.

Alan SMITH, 1949-50

Outside left Alan Smith was born in Newcastle on 15 October 1921. He began his professional career with Arsenal in May 1946, and made a total of 3 League appearances for the Gunners. He joined Brentford in December 1946, and had 13 games for the Bees during a three-year stay, scoring 4 goals. Smith moved to O's in July 1949, and scored on his debut in a 4-1 win over Exeter City on 9 September

1949. He could not gain a regular spot in the First XI, due to the form of left-wingers John Pattison and Joe McGeachy, so in May 1950 he joined non-League Tonbridge.

SEASON	LEAGUE		FA CUP		TOTAL	
	Apps	Gls	Apps	Gls	Apps	Gls
1949/50	6	1	0	0	6	1
TOTAL	6	1	0	0	6	1

Dean SMITH, 1997-present

'Deano' joined the club on 2 June 1997, proving to be a strong defender who looked equally good in the air. He shouldered the responsibility of taking the penalties, and employed his style of 'busting the net'. However, he missed a vital spot-kick against Southend in April 1999, and was thereafter reluctant to take them, eventually giving the responsibility to Matthew Lockwood. A confident leader and good professional, he was appointed club captain in 1998/99. He

Dean Smith

was born West Bromwich on 19 March 1971, and started as a trainee with Walsall in July 1989. He signed a professional contract as an eighteen-year-old and played regularly for the Saddlers for over 5 years, making 137(5) League appearances and scoring 2 goals. He also played in 24 cup matches. The defender became Hereford United's record signing when he joined for £75,000 on 17 June 1994. He found the net 19 times from 116(1) League appearances, and 7 times from 28(1) Cup matches. When the Worcestershire side dropped out of the League on the last day of the 1996/97 season, O's manager Taylor quickly moved in for his signature – Hereford wanted £200,000 for Smith, so the matter went to a tribunal. Hereford's manager Graham Taylor was angry at the tribunal's decision to take the Bosman ruling into account for the first time ever, when cutting the price from the required £200,000 to only £42,500 on 16 June 1997. Graham Taylor said 'I'm staggered and gob-smacked at the low valuation of our record signing, this is going to send shock waves throughout football.' Smith has proved to be an excellent capture and fine skipper, and he converted one of the penalties in the shoot-out at Rotherham to take O's into the play-off final. He had the honour of leading the team out at Wembley in the Division Three play-off final against Scunthorpe United in May 1999, but the tears flowed visibly when O's went down 1-0. Smith is now one of the longest-serving players at the club, and has an enviable record of scoring a goal in nearly every 6 games, not bad for a central defender. Thirty-year-old Smith has now scored more than 50 senior career goals from over 450 appearances. His fiftieth League goal came at Rochdale on 28 January 2001, and his 200th senior appearance for O's was in the 2-0 victory over Hull City which was to take O's to the play-off finals. Sadly, Smith captained O's to his second play-off final defeat in three years, this time losing 4-2 to Blackpool at the Millennium Stadium in Cardiff during May 2001. After describing Smith as the best centre half in Divison Three, O's boss Taylor turned down an offer of a large-fee-plus-player deal for his captain from Rushden & Diamonds in September 2001, saying he was not willing to do business.

SEASON	LEAGUE		FA CUP		L. CUP	
	Apps	Gls	Apps	Gls	Apps	Gls
1997/98	43	9	2	1	4	0
1998/99*	40	9	5	1	4	0
1999/2000	44	4	2	1	4	0
2000/01**	46	5	4	0	3	0
2001/02	45	2	4	1	1	0
TOTAL	218	29	17	4	16	0

TOTAL APPS	251
TOTAL GOALS	33

* Dean Smith's League record includes 3 play-off matches in 1988/99.

** Smith's League record includes 3 play-off matches in 2000/01.

*** Smith also appeared in 2 Auto Windscreens Shield matches and an LDV Vans Trophy match in 2000/01.

George SMITH, 1914-15

Londoner George Smith was an amateur goalkeeper with Tottenham Hotspur, but his only senior appearance for Spurs was against Clapton Orient in a London League fixture in September 1914. He joined O's on loan when the club's three regular goalkeepers – Bower, Hugall and Morris – were all injured. His 2 League appearances came in a 1-3 defeat at Glossop on 2 April 1915, and a 0-3 defeat at Bury the following day. Smith was on standby two days later, but it was Jim Morris who was between the sticks for a 5-2 defeat of Glossop at Millfields Road. Smith returned to White Hart Lane, but never made the grade and went back into non-League football.

SEASON	LEAGUE		FA CUP		TOTAL	
	Apps	Gls	Apps	Gls	Apps	Gls
1914/15	2	0	0	0	2	0
TOTAL	2	0	0	0	2	0

George SMITH, 1932-33

Born in Sunderland, Co. Durham on 20 November 1908, centre half George Smith started off playing football with Easington Colliery. He came to O's on trial in November 1929, but was not kept and joined Watford in November 1932. He only appeared once in the senior team at Vicarage Road, in a 1-0 win at Norwich City on the final day of the 1930/31 season. The Hornets had four players by the name of Smith in the side that day, and George and Joe Smith were making their one and only League appearances for the club. He returned to O's on a free transfer in August 1932, and made his League debut in a 2-0 win over Coventry City on 8 October 1932, but was unable to gain preference over either Keen or Vango. Smith moved to Darlington in July 1933, making a total of 13 League appearances, and the following season moved to Southern League outfit Yeovil & Petters United.

SEASON	LEAGUE		FA CUP		TOTAL	
	Apps	Gls	Apps	Gls	Apps	Gls
1932/33	2	0	0	0	2	0
TOTAL	2	0	0	0	2	0

Harold McPherson SMITH, 1934-39

Harry Smith was born in Dundee on 5 May 1911. He started off with Dundee in 1928 and, after a spell with Dunfermline, he signed for near neighbours Dundee United in December 1933. He played 12 senior matches for the Terrors, scoring twice. After a short spell with Raith Rovers, the lively inside forward came south of the Border to join O's in August 1934, signed by boss David Pratt, a Scotsman himself. Smith made a slow start, but he did score in a friendly game against Austrian side Sportclub Rapid – a 2-3 defeat in 1934/35. He was in the side that defeated the high-flying Charlton Athletic in an FA Cup third round tie in January 1936, in front of a record attendance at Lea Bridge Road of 18,658. He also appeared in the first fixture at Brisbane Road against Cardiff City on 28 August 1937. Smith was also in the side at Watford on 2 September 1939 – the last match before the outbreak of the Second World War – a game that ended 1-1. This result, like the previous 2 matches, was expunged from the record books. Smith played in 12 regional wartime matches, scoring 6 goals before deciding to retire after the war.

SEASON	LEAGUE		FA CUP		TOTAL	
	Apps	Gls	Apps	Gls	Apps	Gls
1934/35	11	1	2	0	13	1
1935/36	28	5	5	0	33	5
1936/37	38	10	2	1	40	11
1937/38	40	11	3	1	43	12
1938/39	31	7	2	1	33	8
TOTAL	148	34	14	3	162	37

* Harry Smith also appeared in 6 Third Division Cup matches between 1934 and 1939, scoring once.

Henry Harold SMITH, 1919-1925

Harry Smith was born in Walthamstow, London on 14 October 1901. He appeared as a guest for O's on 21 April 1919, in the final London Combination wartime match of that season. The inside forward scored in the 4-2 win over Brentford, only the third win from 36 wartime matches played. Seventeen-year-old Smith signed professional forms for O's in June 1919 for the start of the first League campaign after the hostilities. Manager Holmes converted Smith to a right-winger, and he became a regular for six seasons. Smith was a good player, if a little underrated – he was fast and strong, he cut out the frills and made direct runs down the wing, making quite a number goals for others. However, he had a cartilage operation during the summer of 1925, which proved very slow to heal, and this eventually put paid to his professional career at Millfields Road. In 1932/33 he turned out for amateur side Royal London United Sports FC.

Harry Smith

S

SEASON	LEAGUE		FA CUP		TOTAL	
	Apps	Gls	Apps	Gls	Apps	Gls
1919/20	18	1	0	0	18	1
1920/21	31	4	2	1	33	5
1921/22	32	3	1	0	33	3
1922/23	22	0	0	0	22	0
1923/24	40	1	1	0	41	1
1924/25	24	0	1	0	25	0
TOTAL	167	9	5	1	172	10

James SMITH, 1946-48

Right-winger Jim Smith joined O's in April 1946, after spending three years in Burnley's youth and reserve sides. He made his League debut in a 2-2 draw against Ipswich Town on 31 August 1946. Smith looked to be quite a good winger during 1947/48, but his progress was restricted due to a number of injuries. He moved first to Croydon Rovers, before leaving to play for Gloucester City.

Jimmy Smith

SEASON	LEAGUE		FA CUP		TOTAL	
	Apps	Gls	Apps	Gls	Apps	Gls
1946/47	17	2	0	0	17	2
1947/48	5	1	0	0	5	1
TOTAL	22	3	0	0	22	3

James Harold SMITH, 1955-58

Jimmy Smith was born in Sheffield on 6 December 1930 and worked as a bricklayer whilst playing for Shildon FC. He joined Chelsea in April 1951, but was not a first-team choice at Stamford Bridge. His career was halted for eighteen months (and almost ended) due to serious illness, but he bounced back, making a total of 19 League appearances and scoring 3 goals. He joined O's in July 1955, but found it difficult to gain a place in the First XI. He came to the fore in 1956/57, proving to be a great trier who could play equally well on either wing, and he was also one of those players capa-

ble of running all day. However, he sustained a very bad leg injury at Fulham in October 1957, and, sadly, that was to be the end his playing career at the age of just twenty-seven. The club staged a benefit match for him in September 1958.

SEASON	LEAGUE		FA CUP		TOTAL	
	Apps	Gls	Apps	Gls	Apps	Gls
1955/56	7	0	1	0	8	0
1956/57	20	3	1	0	21	3
1957/58	10	0	0	0	10	0
TOTAL	37	3	2	0	39	3

John SMITH, 1965-66

Sturdily-built wing-half John Smith was born in Shoreditch, London on 4 January 1939. He joined the groundstaff at West Ham United in 1954, signing as a full professional two years later, having won honours with East London, Middlesex and London schoolboys. In addition, he won both youth and under-23 caps for

445

John Smith

England whilst at Upton Park, and he was instrumental in the Hammers' 1957/58 Second Division promotion-winning side. Smith was one of Hammers' finest ever discoveries, and in 1959/60 he was on the verge of winning full international honours, twice being selected as an England reserve. However, his career took a downward spiral, and after making 132 senior appearances and scoring 22 goals, he joined Tottenham Hotspur during March 1960, in exchange for another former 'Oriental' David Dunmore. He stayed at White Hart Lane for four years, making just 21 League appearances and scoring once. He moved to Coventry City for £9,000 in March 1964, assisting them to promotion in 1963/64 and making 38(1) senior appearances and scoring once. He was signed for O's by Dave Sexton in October 1965, and scored a wonderful twenty-five-yard winning goal against Bolton

Wanderers. He later captained O's during the unfortunate relegation season. When Dick Graham took over at O's, things did not go so smoothly for Smith. He moved to Torquay United in October 1966, staying for two seasons and scoring 8 goals from 68 League appearances. He moved on to Swindon Town in June 1968, and his three-year stay brought 79(5) League appearances and 9 goals, as well as a League Cup winner's medal in 1969. Smith ended his League career with Walsall in 1971/72, making 15(1) appearances and scoring once. He was then appointed manager, but he resigned in March 1973. He next managed Irish League side Dundalk. John Smith died in 1988 at the age of forty-nine, whilst managing a social club in Harlesden.

SEASON	LEAGUE		FA CUP		TOTAL	
	Apps	Gls	Apps	Gls	Apps	Gls
1965/66	30	2	1	0	0	0
1966/67	8(1)	1	0	0	0	0
TOTAL	38(1)	3	1	0	0	0

TOTAL APPS	39(1)
TOTAL GOALS	3

John 'Jack' William SMITH, 1936-37

Jack Smith was born in Whitburn, Co. Durham on 20 October 1898. The inside right started his professional career with South Shields, and between 1919 and 1927 he made 260 League appearances, scoring 82 goals. He moved to Portsmouth in May 1927 and continued his impressive form, making a further 262 League matches and scoring 60 goals. Whilst at Pompey he gained 3 full England caps – against Ireland, Wales and Spain in 1932 – and was chosen for an FA XI that toured Canada. Smith joined Bournemouth in May 1935, making 41 League appearances and scoring 2 goals, but he had also turned main provider for centre forward Riley, who netted 25 goals. Smith became an 'Oriental' in the twilight of his career in October 1936, and made his debut in a 2-1 win over Bristol Rovers on 31 October 1936. Yet even at thirty-eight years old, he still showed touches in the few matches he played to remind one of his great past. He was appointed O's reserve coach during December 1936 and held that post until retiring in May 1937. Smith made a total of 568 League appearances during his eighteen-year career, scoring 144 goals.

SEASON	LEAGUE		FA CUP		TOTAL	
	Apps	Gls	Apps	Gls	Apps	Gls
1936/37	5	0	2	0	7	0
TOTAL	5	0	2	0	7	0

Keith Wilson SMITH, 1967

Born in Woodville on 15 September 1940, Keith Smith came to O's on a non-contract basis in May 1967. It was a surprise that he was not signed on a permanent basis, having notched 73 League career goals. This tally includes one of the fastest goals in League history, which he scored for Crystal Palace against Derby County in a Second Division fixture on 12 December 1964 after just six seconds. The quick, lively striker started off as a junior with West Bromwich Albion in January 1958, and scored 30 goals from 63 League appearances between 1959 and 1962. He moved to Peterborough United in June 1963, netting 28 goals from 55 matches. He moved to London to join Crystal Palace under boss Dick Graham in November 1964, and chalked up a further 47(3) matches and 13 goals. He moved on to Darlington in November 1966, and after 2 goals from 17 League

matches, he joined O's. After his short stint at Brisbane Road he signed for Notts County, and during his two years at Meadow Lane he notched 7 goals from 85(4) League appearances. In 1970 he joined non-League Kidderminster, before moving to Tamworth in 1971. He was appointed player-manager of Bromsgrove in 1972.

SEASON	LEAGUE		FA CUP		L. CUP	
	Apps	Gls	Apps	Gls	Apps	Gls
1966/67	3	0	0	0	0	0
TOTAL	3	0	0	0	0	0

TOTAL APPS	3
TOTAL GOALS	0

Mark Stuart SMITH, 1979-81

Mark Smith a tall, well-built full-back, was born in Carlisle on 4 April 1962. He came through O's youth ranks – and was capped for the England youth team – and looked to be a very good prospect, but as with so many players, somehow it didn't quite work out for him. The probable reasons in Smith's case were that he was a bit slow on the turn and also rather cumbersome. He made his League debut on 26 August 1978 in a 0-1 home loss to Wrexham. His last appearance was in a 0-4 defeat by West Ham at Brisbane Road on 1 January 1980, in front of 23,885. He moved to Tilbury in May 1981.

SEASON	LEAGUE		FA CUP		L. CUP	
	Apps	Gls	Apps	Gls	Apps	Gls
1978/79	1	0	0	0	0	0
1979/80	2	0	0	0	0	0
1980/81	0	0	0	0	0	0
TOTAL	3	0	0	0	0	0

TOTAL APPS	3
TOTAL GOALS	0

Matthew SMITH, 1937-39

Grimsby-born centre half Matt Smith was a reserve player for Notts County and Watford before joining O's in June 1937. He struggled to make it into the First XI and could not dislodge the splendid David Affleck from the pivotal position. When Affleck was sold to Southampton in 1937, his replacement, Fred Bartlett, was almost as formidable a stumbling block, and Smith played out his two seasons at the club in the reserves. He made his League debut in a 2-0 defeat at Walsall on 15 January 1938, and left O's in June 1939, joining Tunbridge Wells Rangers.

SEASON	LEAGUE		FA CUP		TOTAL	
	Apps	Gls	Apps	Gls	Apps	Gls
1937/38	3	0	0	0	3	0
1938/39	2	0	0	0	2	0
TOTAL	5	0	0	0	5	0

Peter Alec SMITH, 1982-83

Tall, rangy centre half and midfielder Peter Smith was born in Islington, London on 20 November 1964. He graduated through the youth ranks before signing professional forms in August 1982. He got into the first team when the club were struggling to find players of quality. He made his League debut in a 2-0 defeat at Plymouth Argyle on 11 September 1982. He appeared at centre half at a time when Orient suffered some heavy defeats – 6-0 at Huddersfield, 3-0 at Reading, 1-5 at home to Newport County and 4-0 at Gillingham – and it seemed very unfair to expect such a young player to have the required experience in such situations. However, he did experience some success when coming on as a substitute in a 5-0 win over AFC Bournemouth on 28 December 1982. However, Smith was not quite the answer to O's defensive problems at that time, and was not on the retained list released in May 1983. He signed for Barking and later played for Dagenham.

SEASON	LEAGUE		FA CUP		L. CUP	
	Apps	Gls	Apps	Gls	Apps	Gls
1982/83	8(6)	0	0	0	0	0
TOTAL	8(6)	0	0	0	0	0

TOTAL APPS	8(6)
TOTAL GOALS	0

Stephen Charles SMITH, 1927-28

Born in Hednesford on 27 March 1896, Stephen Smith started his career before the First World War with Portsmouth, but he left without any first-team experience. He joined West Ham in 1919 and had a good run in their inaugural League season during 1919/20 with 23 Second Division appearances, yet could only manage 4 outings during the next couple of seasons. He was a lively raider and able to centre accurately on the run. The left-winger was transferred to Charlton in June 1922 and did well at the Valley, making 90 League appearances and scoring 8 goals. He was a part of their giant-killing FA Cup side of 1922/23, before moving on to Southend United in August 1925. There he made 86 senior appearances and scored 11 goals during his two-year stay. He became an 'Oriental' in May 1927, but could not dislodge Billy Corkindale or Jesse Williams from the left-wing spot. However, he did score on his debut in a 2-2 draw at Hull City on 12 November 1927. Smith moved to Queens Park Rangers in May 1928, staying for one season and scoring once in 25 senior appearances, before moving to Mansfield Town on trial in June 1929. He died on 16 December 1980 in Southbourne, Sussex.

SEASON	LEAGUE		FA CUP		TOTAL	
	Apps	Gls	Apps	Gls	Apps	Gls
1927/28	6	1	1	0	7	1
TOTAL	6	1	1	0	7	1

John Duncan SNEDDEN, 1966-67

John Snedden was born in Bonnybridge, Scotland on 3 February 1942. The Scottish schoolboy international had progressed through Arsenal's youth and reserve ranks, signing professional terms on his seventeenth birthday in 1952. The burly centre half did well at Highbury, making 83 League appearances before moving to Charlton Athletic in March 1965. Injury curtailed his career at the Valley, and he only made 18(2) League appearances before becoming an 'Oriental' in July 1966. He came to the club along with veteran forward Cliff Holton, as part of the deal that took Harry Gregory to the Valley. Unfortunately, Snedden's time at Brisbane Road was blighted by injury troubles, yet he did

John Snedden

have his moments for the O's. When playing as an auxiliary striker at promotion-chasing Watford in March 1967, he dented their hopes with two goals in a rare 3-1 away win. In November 1967 he had a loan spell at Halifax Town, where he made 5 appearances. He left O's in May 1968 and went to play in South Africa. Snedden proved with Arsenal that he was a good player, but he was injured far too often whilst with O's to be able to show his true worth. He married a German girl and moved to her homeland.

SEASON	LEAGUE		FA CUP		L. CUP	
	Apps	Gls	Apps	Gls	Apps	Gls
1966/67	15	2	0	0	1	0
1967/68	11(1)	1	0	0	1	0
TOTAL	26(1)	3	0	0	2	0

TOTAL APPS	28(1)
TOTAL GOALS	3

Dennis SORRELL, 1957-62, 1964-67

Dennis Sorrell is one of just a few of players to have had two spells with the O's. Born in Lambeth, London on 7 October 1940, he was a small wing-half who started as a junior with O's, before moving on to Woodford Town. It was an O's supporter who tipped off the club about him, and he returned to sign professional forms with O's on 28 October 1957, making his League debut at the age of nineteen in a 3-1 win at Barnsley on 29 April 1959. He was very quick, with good movement off the ball, and a tenacious tackler. Sorrell created lots of attention with some gritty displays, none more so than his performance that completely subdued Huddersfield Town's rising star Denis Law at Brisbane Road in January 1960. Newcastle United then put in an offer for O's young trio of Sorrell,

Dennis Sorrell

1964/65	35	1	1	0	1	0
1965/66	31	1	1	0	1	0
1966/67	8	1	0	0	0	0
TOTAL	111	4	3	0	5	0

| TOTAL APPS | 119 |
| TOTAL GOALS | 4 |

* The League Cup competition commenced in 1960.

James Frederick SPENCE, 1926-30

Jim Spence was born in Uphall, Hertfordshire on 19 January 1904. He started off as a reserve with Watford before joining Pumpherston Rangers. He joined O's in August 1926, as cover for John Townrow and Tommy Dixon. He made his League debut at wing-half in a 6-0 defeat at Blackpool on 11 December 1926, and was not seen again that season. He was being groomed to take over Townrow's centre-half berth, yet when Townrow moved to Chelsea in February 1927, it was John Gailbraith who took over his position. Spence was given a run between 1927 and 1929, and he gave O's good service but lost his place to Gailbraith again in 1929/30. He eventually joined Thames Association in June 1930, and during his two years with the League's new boys, he made 47 League appearances. He moved to Aldershot in May 1932, and in his only season there made 17 League outings. Spence died in Tonbridge, Kent in 1968.

Foster and McDonald, which was turned down by chairman Harry Zussman. Sorrell could not break into the side during O's rise to the top of the Second Division in 1961/62, and he moved to Chelsea for £10,000 in February 1962. He spent most of his two years there in the reserves, making just 4 senior appearances and scoring once (in an FA Cup tie). He returned to Brisbane Road for £3,000 in September 1964, and helped the team to avoid relegation in 1964/65. The following season, O's were relegated and he was one of a number of experienced players to be released by boss Dave Sexton. He joined Romford in December 1966.

SEASON	LEAGUE		FA CUP		L. CUP	
	Apps	Gls	Apps	Gls	Apps	Gls
1958/59	1	0	0	0	-	-
1959/60*	26	1	1	0	-	-
1960/61	10	0	0	0	3	0
1961/62	0	0	0	0	0	0

SEASON	LEAGUE		FA CUP		TOTAL	
	Apps	Gls	Apps	Gls	Apps	Gls
1926/27	1	0	0	0	1	0
1927/28	13	0	1	0	14	0
1928/29	14	3	0	0	14	3
1929/30	2	0	0	0	2	0
TOTAL	30	3	1	0	31	3

Alfred SPENCER, 1913-15

Alfred Spencer joined O's in May 1913, after playing his early football in India, where he was serving with the British Army. Whilst there, he represented an Indian international team. He returned to England and made his League debut as a replacement for the injured Robert Dalrymple in a 1-0 defeat at Leicester Fosse on 14 February 1914. Spencer remained in the reserves in the following season. He was one of a number of O's players who were wounded in the First World War; in fact, Spencer suffered two serious wounds which resulted in him having to retire from football.

SEASON	LEAGUE		FA CUP		TOTAL	
	Apps	Gls	Apps	Gls	Apps	Gls
1913/14	1	0	0	0	1	0
1914/15	0	0	0	0	0	0
TOTAL	1	0	0	0	1	0

Robert SPOTTISWOOD, 1919-20

Crewe-born Bob Spottiswood started off as a junior with Crewe Alexandra. He came to O's from Southern League outfit Crystal Palace in October 1919, having been playing for Palace in the wartime Leagues. His season at Millfields Road was not as successful, and he appeared just once in the League – at right half in a 0-4 home defeat at the hands of Tottenham Hotspur on 18 October 1919. He joined Welsh side Caerphilly Town in July 1920.

SEASON	LEAGUE		FA CUP		TOTAL	
	Apps	Gls	Apps	Gls	Apps	Gls
1919/20	1	0	0	0	1	0
TOTAL	1	0	0	0	1	0

Roger Edmund STANISLAUS, 1995-96

Roger Stanislaus became the first British footballer to be banned for taking drugs. He was given a twelve-month ban on 1 February 1996, having tested positive for taking cocaine, a performance-enhancing drug. The club booted out the twenty-seven-year-old left-back. O's chairman Barry Hearn stated: 'Roger was resigned to it and took our decision with grace. He is a nice lad, but my overall interest is in the club's name.' Stanislaus was caught when tested after an Endsleigh League Division Three match at Barnet on 25 November 1995, and it was the first time in two years that an O's player had been picked out – O's lost the match 3-0. Born in Hammersmith, London on 2 November 1968, the player started as a trainee with Arsenal in July 1986. He moved to Brentford on 18 September 1987, making 109(2) League appearances and scoring 4 goals. He then joined Bury for £90,000 on 30 July 1990, making 167(9) League appearances and scoring 5 goals. He joined O's from Bury for £40,000 on 11 July 1995, and played his last match for the club on 6 January 1996 at Cardiff City. Hearn stated: 'The fact that Roger's version of events that led to him testing positive was heavily contradictory left us no alternative. Drugs have no place in football and particularly not at Leyton Orient.' After his ban ended, the defender was briefly on the books of Peterborough United on a non-contract basis in March 1997, but he never featured in their first team.

SEASON	LEAGUE		FA CUP		L. CUP	
	Apps	Gls	Apps	Gls	Apps	Gls
1995/96	20(1)	0	1	0	1	0
TOTAL	20(1)	0	1	0	1	0

TOTAL APPS	22(1)
TOTAL GOALS	0

* Roger Stanislaus also appeared in an Auto Windscreens Shield match.

Daniel STEEL, 1914-15

Danny Steel was born in Newmilns, Scotland on 2 May 1884. He started his career with local side Newmilns FC, and then played as an amateur for both Airdrie and Glasgow Rangers, before moving south of the Border to join Tottenham Hotspur in May 1906. He made 31 Southern League appearances and, between 1909 and 1912, he amassed 129 League appearances and scored a total of 4 goals. He also represented a London representative side om two occasions. Steel returned to Scotland in December 1912 to join Third Lanark. In July 1914 the thirty-year-old became an 'Oriental', and at Millfields he showed his vast experience with some competent displays at centre half. When the First World War was declared, he returned home to Scotland. He died in Marylebone, London on 29 April 1931.

SEASON	LEAGUE		FA CUP		TOTAL	
	Apps	Gls	Apps	Gls	Apps	Gls
1914/15	23	0	1	0	24	0
TOTAL	23	0	1	0	24	0

George James STEVENS, 1914-15

Hackney-born George Stevens joined O's from local amateur football in May 1914. The inside forward made little impact, playing just once in the League on 6 February 1915 in a 5-1 defeat at Blackpool. He left the club before the end of the 1914/15 season, and was not on the list of O's players who enlisted for the war in May 1915.

SEASON	LEAGUE		FA CUP		TOTAL	
	Apps	Gls	Apps	Gls	Apps	Gls
1914/15	1	0	0	0	1	0
TOTAL	1	0	0	0	1	0

Thomas Worley STEWART, 1906-08

Left-back Tom Stewart was one of a number of pre-First World War O's players to have played for top North-East side Sunderland Royal Rovers FC, who were champions of the Wearside League between 1900 and 1904. Stewart, who was born in Sunderland in 1881, attracted the attention of the local senior club and joined the Sunderland staff as an amateur, making his League debut during December 1904 in a 1-0 over Nottingham Forest. Three weeks later he was offered a professional contact, and played in a further 4 first-team matches. In May 1905 he joined Southern League side Portsmouth, but played just a couple of minor matches for the Fratton Park club before returning to Sunderland Royal Rovers. He joined O's in June 1906 and played consistently well for two seasons. He was persuaded to join Southern League side Brighton & Hove Albion in June 1908, and he captained Albion as they struggled to avoid relegation. He had a storming game against Manchester United in the FA Cup, when his timely tackles frustrated the legendary Billy Meredith, and the 'Welsh Wizard' was sent off for lashing out at the Albion player. He moved to Southern Leaguers Brentford in May 1909, but retired from the first-class game in disgust after failing to make the Bee's First XI.

SEASON	LEAGUE		FA CUP		TOTAL	
	Apps	Gls	Apps	Gls	Apps	Gls
1906/07	31	0	0	0	31	0
1907/08	19	0	4	0	23	0
TOTAL	50	0	4	0	54	0

John Leonard STILL, 1967-68

John Still was born in West Ham, London on 24 April 1950. The very tall central defender played for O's youth side and turned professional in May 1967. He made his only League appearance just a few months after his seventeenth birthday – against Torquay on 26 August 1967 – O's lost 0-2. Still was often troubled by injuries at Brisbane Road, and joined Charlton Athletic on trial in 1967. He later played for Dagenham, Bishop Stortford, Ilford and Leytonstone. However, it is as a manager that Still will be remembered. He started with Leytonstone & Ilford FC, winning both the Isthmian League First Division and Premier titles, and then moved on to Dartford. In November 1987 he took over at Maidstone United and they won the GM Vauxhall Conference Championship. However, he refused a new contract to lead them into the League, so it was Keith Peacock and his assistant Tommy Taylor who were in charge for their new venture during 1989/90. Still moved on to manage Redbridge Forest and was in charge of their climb up GM Vauxhall Conference in 1991/92. He was also manager when the club became Dagenham & Redbridge FC, and nearly knocked O's out of the FA Cup in the first round on 14 November 1992, eventually going down 4-5 in a classic home match. On 1 August 1994 he was appointed manager of Peterborough United, and stayed until 24 October 1995. Still was appointed boss at Barnet on 30 June 1997, and was in charge for over 150 League matches until Tony Cottee was appointed as their player-manager on 1 November 2000. Still was then made director of football with a seat on the London club's board. After Cottee's short reign ended on 16 March 2001, Still was reinstated as boss until the end of the 2000/01 season. Unfortunately, the Bees were relegated from the League to the Football Conference after losing their final match of the season – a 2-3 home reverse to Torquay United.

SEASON	LEAGUE		FA CUP		L. CUP	
	Apps	Gls	Apps	Gls	Apps	Gls
1967/68	1	0	0	0	0	0
TOTAL	1	0	0	0	0	0

TOTAL APPS	1
TOTAL GOALS	0

Mark Nicholas STIMSON, 1988, 1999
Mark Stimson began his career at Tottenham Hotspur in July 1985, making his League debut at Everton on 11 May 1987. After 1(1) League appearances, he joined O's on loan on 15 March 1988, where he played 10 League matches. He also went on loan to Gillingham in January 1989, making another 18 League appearances. Stimson rejoined O's some nine years later as a utility defender, after his contract with Southend United was cancelled by mutual consent early in March 1999. Stimson was a player who never shirked a tackle, which is possibly why he spent so much time on the physio's couch during his career. Born in Plaistow, London on 27 December 1967, he was transferred to Newcastle United for £200,000 on 16 June 1989. There he had a long run in the side, playing 82(4) League games and scoring twice. After a loan period with Portsmouth, he was eventually signed for £100,000 on 23 July 1993, and he scored 2 goals for them and played 57(1) League matches. He went on loan to Barnet in September 1995 and played 6 matches. He joined Southend United for £25,000 on 15 March 1996, appearing 57(5) times. During an FA Cup tie defeat by Doncaster Rovers in 1998, he was substituted by manager Alvin

Martin at half-time and he did not bother to stay around after the match to receive Martin's dressing-down. He was fined a week's wages for this misdemeanour, but on appeal (supported by the PFA), he had his money reinstated. However, he fell from grace and was asked to leave the Shrimpers after having made 34(5) appearances. He was on the bench for O's during the Wembley play-off final against Scunthorpe in May 1999, but never came on. Tommy Taylor released Stimson at the end of that month. He joined Ryman Premier League side Canvey Island in August 1999, and 'Stimmo' was still on their books in 2001, appearing for them at Villa Park in the FA Trophy final against Forest Green Rovers in May 2001, aged thirty-four. He is also the under-10s coach at Tottenham Hotspur.

SEASON	LEAGUE		FA CUP		L. CUP	
	Apps	Gls	Apps	Gls	Apps	Gls
1987/88	10	0	0	0	0	0
1989/99*	3(1)	0	0	0	0	0
TOTAL	13(1)	0	0	0	0	0

TOTAL APPS	13(1)
TOTAL GOALS	0

* Stimson's League record includes 1(1) promotion play-off matches in 1998/99.

George STONEHOUSE, 1911-12

Wallsend-born George Stonehouse joined O's from his local club Wallsend Park Villa in May 1911. The centre half played mostly in the reserves during his two-year stay at Millfields Road. He made his League debut in a 4-0 win over Bristol City on 16 March 1912. He was not retained in May 1913 and returned to the North-East.

SEASON	LEAGUE		FA CUP		TOTAL	
	Apps	Gls	Apps	Gls	Apps	Gls
1911/12	3	0	0	0	3	0
1912/13	0	0	0	0	0	0
TOTAL	3	0	0	0	3	0

Terence Edward STREET, 1966-67

Midfielder Terry Street was born in Poplar, London on 9 December 1948. He produced some extremely polished displays for O's youth and reserve sides, and looked to be a very dainty player with a great measure of skill. He made his only League appearance in a 2-0 defeat against Bristol Rovers on 27 December 1966. He was released by O's in May 1967 and went on to join Ashford Town.

SEASON	LEAGUE		FA CUP		L. CUP	
	Apps	Gls	Apps	Gls	Apps	Gls
1966/67	1	0	0	0	0	0
TOTAL	1	0	0	0	0	0

TOTAL APPS	1
TOTAL GOALS	0

Stanley Edward STREETS, 1926-28

Stanley Streets was born in Grantham on 25 June 1901. The stocky inside forward started off at Grantham FC, before joining Blackpool in May 1924, and during his two-year stay at the seaside, he made 20 League appearances and scored 4 goals. He joined O's in March 1926, making his debut in a 1-1 draw at Oldham Athletic on 20 March 1926. He netted in his final senior appearance – on 18 February 1928 in a 5-1 defeat at Bristol City. He moved on to Exeter City in June 1928, making 9 League appearances and scoring 2 goals. Stanley Streets died in Newark on 29 January 1961.

SEASON	LEAGUE		FA CUP		TOTAL	
	Apps	Gls	Apps	Gls	Apps	Gls
1925/26	3	0	0	0	3	0
1926/27	7	0	1	0	8	0
1927/28	2	1	0	0	2	1
TOTAL	12	1	1	0	13	1

David Roy STRIDE, 1984-85

David Stride was born in Lymington on 14 March 1958, and the defender started his career as an apprentice with Chelsea in January 1976, making 37 senior appearances between 1978 and 1980. He was transferred to the Memphis club in America for £90,000, but came back to London to join Millwall for £25,000 in January 1983, where he made 55 League appearances and scored 3 goals. He joined O's in July 1984 and had a run in an O's side that played reasonably well, and he looked good at going forward but was a little weak defensively. Stride went back to America in May 1985 to play indoor soccer.

David Stride

SEASON	LEAGUE		FA CUP		L. CUP	
	Apps	Gls	Apps	Gls	Apps	Gls
1984/85	29	0	1	0	4	0
TOTAL	29	0	1	0	4	0

TOTAL APPS	34
TOTAL GOALS	0

* David Stride also appeared in an Auto Windscreens Shield match.

William James Alfred STROUD, 1947-50

Billy Stroud was born in Hammersmith, London on 7 July 1919. He began his career as an amateur with Southampton in May 1938, and captained their reserve side, scoring 36 goals from the inside forward position. Over the next six years (during the Second World War) he was converted to half-back, and made 175 wartime appearances for the Saints. The 5ft 10in and 11st Stroud turned professional in June 1945, and made 34 senior appearances during 1946/47, scoring 4 goals. He joined O's in June 1946 – in exchange for Os defender Edgar Ballard and £3,000 – and was appointed O's captain. He worked tirelessly and was ever-present in his first season. When Jackie Deverall came into the side, Stroud's appearances were restricted. In June 1950, he was transferred to Newport County, making 63 League appearances and scoring once. He moved to Hastings United in August 1963. He returned to Newport in November 1963 as their reserve-team coach, but he developed tuberculosis, which forced him to retire from the game. He went into business as an electrician. In 1963 Southampton boss Ted Bates offered him a coaching position at the Dell, and many Saints youngsters reaped the benefits of his

Billy Stroud

November 1926 and made 6 senior appearances for the club before coming to Millfields in July 1927, but he was confined to the reserves at O's, his only League appearance taking place on 21 January 1928 in a 5-2 defeat at Blackpool. Surtees moved to Wellington Town in August 1928 and died in Millom on 30 July 1963.

SEASON	LEAGUE		FA CUP		L. CUP	
	Apps	Gls	Apps	Gls	Apps	Gls
1927/28	1	0	1	0	2	0
TOTAL	1	0	1	0	2	0

Andrew Robert SUSSEX, 1981-88

Andy Sussex was born in Islington, London on 23 November 1964. He hit the headlines by making his Orient League debut at the age of 16 years and 10 months, when starring in O's 3-0 win over Sheffield Wednesday on 7 November 1981 and scoring one of the goals with a superb chip from sixteen yards. He signed professional forms a year later. The tall, lanky, constructive left-sided midfielder often had a casual look about him, but he played for seven seasons. Yet he was never a regular – in fact, he was in and out of the team for long periods, his place often being given to a more all-action type of player. During his stay, he was often played out of position. His best season at Brisbane Road was in the Fourth Division during 1985/86. He was transferred to Crewe Alexandra for £16,000 in June 1988 (managed by former O's youth-team manager Dario Gradi) and Sussex helped them to gain promotion in 1988/89. He stayed at Gresty Road for three seasons, making 125 appearances and scoring 36 goals. He was transferred to Southend United

enthusiasm for the game before he called it a day in January 1989. Nowadays, Stroud lives in retirement in Southampton.

SEASON	LEAGUE		FA CUP		TOTAL	
	Apps	Gls	Apps	Gls	Apps	Gls
1947/48	42	0	1	0	43	0
1948/49	13	0	0	0	13	0
1949/50	10	1	0	0	10	1
TOTAL	65	1	1	0	66	1

Albert Edward SURTEES, 1927-28

Inside forward Albert Surtees was born in Wellington Quay in 1902. He started his career with Durham City, but moved to Aston Villa in 1922 and made 30 League appearances. He then joined West Ham United in 1924, but the move proved unproductive for him, as he was unable to gain a place in the Hammers first team between 1924 and 1926. He then joined Southend in

for £100,000 in July 1991, and made a total of 63(13) appearances and scored 14 goals. In December 1995 he had a loan spell at Brentford, where he made just 3 League appearances. After having enjoyed a six-year-spell with the Shrimpers, he signed for Canvey Island on 8 January 1997 and stayed until May 2000, before joining Barking. Thirty-seven-year-old Sussex joined Ryman League Grays Athletic in August 2001 whilst also working as a tiler. He has won both Ryman League First and Second Division Championship medals in a career spanning some twenty-one years.

SEASON	LEAGUE		FA CUP		L. CUP	
	Apps	Gls	Apps	Gls	Apps	Gls
1981/82	8	1	0	0	0	0
1982/83	24	2	2	1	0	0
1983/84	24(5)	6	0	0	0(1)	0
1984/85	15(4)	2	1	0	3	1
1985/86	35(1)	4	5	0	4	1
1986/87	15(5)	1	0	0	0	0
1987/88	5(3)	1	0	0	0	0
TOTAL	126(18)	17	8	1	7(1)	2

TOTAL APPS	141(19)
TOTAL GOALS	20

* Andy Sussex also appeared in 3 Football League Groups Cup matches and 5(3) Auto Windscreens Shield matches.

Andy Sussex

George Burns SUTHERLAND, 1949-51

Centre forward George Sutherland is the only O's player to have recorded a hat-trick against the same club – Ipswich Town – twice during the same season. In 1949/50 he netted three in a 4-4 draw at Portman Road (September 1949) and three more in the 4-0 win at Brisbane Road (January 1950). Born in Bathgate, Glasgow on 11 September 1923, he joined O's from Partick Thistle in August 1949, having scored 33 times for Thistle. Sutherland lacked any finesse, but his dashing never-give-up attitude was very admirable. Typical of the man was his goal against top-of-the-table Notts County in February 1950 – hobbling with a painful injury (there were no substitutes in those days), he was still determined to get on the end of a through ball, and he rifled the ball into the net. He was a grand trier who would chase everything. He topped O's goalscoring charts in 1949/50, but a loss of form meant his place went to Chris Simmonds the following season, and he was then transferred to Southern League side Hereford United.

SEASON	LEAGUE		FA CUP		TOTAL	
	Apps	Gls	Apps	Gls	Apps	Gls
1949/50	29	16	0	0	29	16
1950/51	13	6	0	0	13	6
TOTAL	42	22	0	0	42	22

Chris Tate

T

Christopher TATE, 2000-present

Striker Chris Tate came to O's on a month's loan from Football Conference side Scarborough on 3 November 2000. He made his debut when coming on as a substitute the following day in a 2-1 win over Mansfield Town, replacing Nicky Shorey after eighty-one minutes. Tate's move from the McCain Stadium was made permanent for a reported £25,000 on 14 November, after news that forward Richard Garcia's injury would keep him out for the season. Born in York on 27 December 1977, Tate started off as a trainee with local club York City in August 1995. The following August he moved to Sunderland, where his time was spent in the youth and reserve sides, and during August 1977, he signed for Scarborough on a free transfer. He was top scorer for their reserves, and he also finished his first campaign with 12 goals from 19 League starts. The following season he finished joint top scorer for the relegated club with 13 goals from 22(28) League starts. In May 1999 he returned to the Nationwide League when joining Halifax Town for £150,000. However, he did not settle at the Shay, and after just 19 League appearances and 4 goals, he returned to Scarborough for a fee of £80,000 on 17 December 1999. In March 2000, Scarborough FC turned down a reported £250,000 bid from Rushden & Diamonds, but with the club in financial difficulty, Tate was one of the players to be off-loaded and he moved to O's. He has not yet shown his true potential at the Matchroom. His first goal for the club came in the 3-3 FA Cup draw at Northwich Victoria – it was only his second goal from 17 starts for both Scarborough and O's during the campaign. However, he did net a couple of vital goals, the second of which was a wonderful overhead kick at Barnet in April 2001 to secure three points and keep O's on the road for a play-off position. He also netted the opener in the play-off final against Blackpool within the first minute at the Millennium Stadium, Cardiff in May 2001, but it wasn't enough as O's went down 4-2. He started the pre-season with a bang, netting a hat-trick in a 13-1 victory over Devon League champions Buckfastleigh FC on 22 July 2001. However, the striker was unable to find a regular first-team place and went out on a month's loan to Nationwide Conference side Stevenage Borough, who were interested in the possibility of a permanent deal. He had an eventful start, both scoring and being sent off on his Borough debut. He performed quite well with Borough with 2 goals from 6 appearances, but did not sign for them because his wage demands were too high. He returned to Brisbane Road during October. He was placed on the transfer list during February 2002 and he went on a month's loan to Nationwide side Chester City on 3 March with a possible transfer to follow.

SEASON	LEAGUE		FA CUP		L. CUP	
	Apps	Gls	Apps	Gls	Apps	Gls
2000/01*	10(15)	4	1(2)	1	0	0
2001/02	1(6)	0	0	0	0	0
TOTAL	11(21)	4	1(2)	1	0	0

TOTAL APPS	12(23)
TOTAL GOALS	5

* Chris Tate's League record includes 1(2) appearances and a goal in the play-offs in 2000/01.

Archibald TAYLOR, 1948-51

Archie Taylor was born in Glasgow on 4 October 1918. After playing starting out playing junior football in Scotland, he began his professional career with Burnley before moving to Reading during June 1939 and played for them throughout the Second World War. After the hostilities had ended, he played for the Berkshire club for two seasons, and the inside forward made 15 League appearances and scored 2 goals. He was signed by O's boss Neil McBain in August 1948, and proved to be a good ball-playing wing-half. Taylor came into his own during 1949/50, but the following season he lost his place to his former Reading colleague Jackie Deverall. The Scotsman moved on to Bath City during early 1951, and died in Scotland during 1976.

SEASON	LEAGUE		FA CUP		TOTAL	
	Apps	Gls	Apps	Gls	Apps	Gls
1948/49	9	1	0	0	9	1
1949/50	34	0	1	0	35	0
1950/51	3	0	0	0	3	0
TOTAL	46	1	1	0	47	1

Harold William TAYLOR, 1933-39

Harold Taylor was affectionately referred to as 'Lal' during his playing career, and was one of the most impressive wing-halves on the club's books during the 1930s. His consistency was a feature of O's play during those years, and he proved to be a wonderful servant for seven seasons. Born on 20 December 1910 in Boston, Lincolnshire, he moved from Lincolnshire to Southport with his family in 1921, and started his amateur career with local Southport sides Vulcans FC and High Park FC. He joined Southport in November 1929 and made his senior debut (scoring 2 goals) against New Brighton in the Lancashire Senior Cup on 13 October 1931. His League debut – and only first-team appearance – came four days later against Gateshead. He also notched two hat-tricks for the reserves during his stay at Haig Avenue. He joined O's on the 16 July 1933, in a double transfer along with Jackie Mayson. His first opportunities came in attack, but he soon established himself in the half-back line during 1936/37. He played in O's first League match at Brisbane Road against Cardiff City in August 1937, and two years later he was in the side that faced Ipswich Town and Southend United in a season that lasted just 3 matches due to the Second World War. These two appearances were later expunged from the record books. He appeared in 29 wartime matches in 1939/40, before returning to play for

Southport as a guest player. He retired from the game after the war and died in Southport Infirmary on 15 November 1970, aged fifty-nine.

SEASON	LEAGUE		FA CUP		TOTAL	
	Apps	Gls	Apps	Gls	Apps	Gls
1933/34	15	4	4	2	19	6
1934/35	19	3	1	0	20	3
1935/36	27	3	4	1	31	4
1936/37	40	2	2	0	42	2
1937/38	40	1	3	0	43	1
1938/39	33	0	2	0	35	0
TOTAL	174	13	16	3	190	16

* Harold Taylor also appeared in 4 Third Division Cup matches between 1934 and 1939.

John Swinley TAYLOR, 1935-37

Left-back Jock Taylor was born in Cowdenbeath, Scotland on 17 August 1909. He started out with Raith Rovers before joining Bristol City in July 1927, where he made 159 senior appearances without scoring. He left to join Halifax Town on 14 May 1934 and played in 34 senior matches. He became an 'Oriental' in August 1935 and did well in his first season, playing for a time at left-back, but when Dave Affleck was injured, Taylor got the centre-half berth. The following season he started the first 6 matches, but was then dropped and never won back his place. He returned to Bristol City in October 1936, but never appeared in the League again. Taylor made a career total of 228 senior appearances without ever scoring a goal. He died in Bristol on 7 March 1964.

SEASON	LEAGUE		FA CUP		TOTAL	
	Apps	Gls	Apps	Gls	Apps	Gls
1935/36	25	0	2	0	27	0
1936/37	5	0	0	0	5	0
TOTAL	30	0	2	0	32	0

* Jock Taylor also appeared in 2 Third Division Cup matches in 1935/36.

Peter John TAYLOR, 1980-82

Peter Taylor has enjoyed a quite remarkable playing and managerial career. As a player, he won 4 England under-23 caps and 4 full international caps before joining O's in November 1980 from Tottenham Hotspur, for a then record fee of £150,000 – a record only broken by the signing of Paul Beesley in 1989 for £175,000. As a manager, he has taken Gillingham to promotion via the play-offs; led Leicester City in the Premiership; and had the honour of leading England as caretaker-manager in Italy during November 2000. Born in Southend-on-Sea on 3 January 1953, the winger began his career as a junior at Southend United in July 1970, and scored 12 goals from

Peter Taylor

57(18) League appearances. He moved to Crystal Palace for £120,000 in October 1993, where he made 142 senior appearances and scored 38 goals. He was snapped up by Tottenham Hotpur for £400,000 in September 1976, and scored 33 goals from 128(9) senior matches. The clever winger started off well with O's, scoring on his debut against Bristol Rovers on 15 November 1980, and he went on to net 5 goals from his first 6 appearances. After a number of injuries and a loan spell with Oldham Athletic in January 1983 (4 League matches), he eventually joined Maidstone United as player-coach in March 1983. He moved to Exeter City in September 1983, but left after a row with one of the directors, having made just 8 League appearances. He returned to Maidstone United as first-team coach, and in 1984 he went on to become Chelmsford City's coach. He later had a spell with Heybridge Swifts, and became manager of Dartford in 1989. He returned to the League as assistant manager of Watford in 1992/93, and then became boss at Dover Athletic. He managed Southend United between 1993 and 1995, before becoming England under-21 chief in 1996. He enjoyed a very successful stint as boss, before being replaced by Howard Wilkinson in 1999, after Glenn Hoddle's reign as England manager ended. He took over as boss of Gillingham on a non-contract basis on 7 July 1999, replacing Tony Pullis and taking the Gills to promotion via the play-offs. Taylor was appointed manager of Premiership side Leicester City on 12 June 2000, taking them to the top of the League during October 2000 and a top five spot in March 2001, but loss of form saw them drift down the League. In June 2001 the FA lined him up to take over from Howard Wilkinson as manager of the England under-21 side; however he remained with Leicester City for a short while, before being sacked on 30 September 2001. He was next appointed manager of high-flying Brighton & Hove Albion on 18 October 2001, and with Bobby Zamora knocking in the goals, they successfully won promotion to Division One bet. Peter Taylor is the only man to play for England at under-23, semi-professional and full international level, and to manage the under-21 side as well as becoming caretaker manager of the full England team.

SEASON	LEAGUE		FA CUP		L. CUP	
	Apps	Gls	Apps	Gls	Apps	Gls
1980/81	24	8	1	0	0	0
1981/82	10(3)	2	0	0	2	0
1982/83	15(4)	1	1	0	2	0
TOTAL	49(7)	11	2	0	4	0

TOTAL APPS	55(7)
TOTAL GOALS	11

* Peter Taylor also appeared in 6 Football League Groups Cup matches, scoring once.

Robert TAYLOR, 1991 (loan), 1991-94

Robert Taylor came to O's on loan from Norwich City on 28 March 1991. He played 3 games as a substitute, before having to be rushed back to Norwich for an emergency appendix operation – he was at the club for just ten days. After a two-month lay-off and an unsuccessful trial with Birmingham City, he found himself without a club. It was a chance call to O's boss Peter Eustace that brought him back to Brisbane Road – he had left in such a hurry that he had left a pair of his boots at the club. He was invited back for a trial by Eustace, and impressed so much

T

Robert Taylor

that he was offered an eighteen-month contract. Born in Norwich on 30 April 1971, Taylor was a trainee at Carrow Road and scored 28 goals from left midfield for their reserve side. He had been spotted playing for his local side Witton United in the Jewson Eastern League. He was a college student at the time, studying for a recreation and leisure qualification. Witton played against Norwich City reserves, and after the match he was invited for a trial and immediately offered a contract. In 1990 he went on loan to Norwegian side Mjolner. During his short loan spell with O's in March 1991, he hit a spectacular goal at Crewe in a 3-3 draw, but after his operation, he was released by the Canaries in May 1991. His most productive spell with O's was in 1992/93, when he scored 18 League goals, and in March 1994, Taylor joined Brentford for £100,000 in a transfer-deadline move. This was a surprise for a player who had

suffered a loss of form after yet another operation, this time for a double hernia. However, Taylor was no failure with the Bees, bagging 74 senior goals from 212(1) appearances, and he was their top scorer in 1997/98. When when the Bees were relegated, he joined Gillingham for £500,000 in August 1998, scoring 21 goals from 51 senior appearances. This tally includes 5 goals at Burnley in February 1999 and a purple patch of 10 goals from 5 matches. He was a major influence in the Gills getting to the Second Division play-off final against Manchester City in May 1999. Taylor scored the Gills' second goal in the eighty-sixth minute for a 2-0 lead and it looked like they were heading for Division One, but with just seconds remaining, City sensationally scored twice to force extra-time and eventually won the match 3-1 on penalties. Twenty-eight-year-old Taylor joined Manchester City on 29 November 1999 for £1.5 million, scoring on his third appearance. He also scored the goal – against Birmingham City on 28 April 2000 – that took City up to the Premiership, thus earning himself instant cult status. Unfortunately, he never got the chance to taste Premiership football, when after just 11(1) League appearances and 5 goals, he was offered the chance of a £1.55 million move to either Wolves or Portsmouth. Taylor chose the former, joining the Division One side on 15 August. He had scored just once from 9(4) senior starts – at Oxford in the League Cup – up to the end of the year, when injury curtailed his progress and meant he required an operation on both calf muscles. He joined QPR on a month's loan on 29 August 2001, but did not find the net from his 3 starts. He then went back to Gillingham on a three-month loan on 3 October, and hoped that this might signal the end of his injury problems. He made his debut as a playing substitute against first club Norwich City on 13 October and played 3(8) games In January 2002 he went on loan to Grimsby Town, where he made a appearances and netted his first League goal in over 18 months, but returned to Molineux the following month. Robert Taylor is a striker who can produce deft flicks from both head and feet, possessed good passing ability, and has an eye for goal – he has scored over 130 senior career goals. If it weren't for that chance phone call to Peter Eustace those eight or so years ago, this talent would have been lost to senior football.

SEASON	LEAGUE		FA CUP		L. CUP	
	Apps	Gls	Apps	Gls	Apps	Gls
1990/91	0(3)	1	0	0	0	0
1991/92	6(5)	1	0(1)	0	0	0
1992/93	36(3)	18	2	0	0(1)	0
1993/94	12(11)	1	0	0	1	0
TOTAL	54(22)	21	2(1)	0	1(1)	0

TOTAL APPS	57(24)
TOTAL GOALS	21

* Robert Taylor also appeared in 2(1) Auto Windscreens Shield matches.

Thomas TAYLOR, 1967-70, 1979-82

Taylor is the second youngest player ever to appear in the League for O's at the age of 15 years and 334 days. The only man to beat that record is Paul Went, who made his League debut at 15 years and 327 days. Taylor made his League bow alongside another debutant, John Still, against Torquay United on 26 August 1967. He went on to have a wonderful career in East London with both O's and West Ham United, and was

appointed O's manager on 7 November 1996, a position he still holds. Born in Hornchurch, Essex on 26 September 1951, Taylor joined O's as a ten-year-old, having played for Hornchurch District schools and captained England schools on 6 occasions. Taylor showed a maturity way beyond his years, and teamed up well with Terry Mancini in the centre of defence, especially during O's championship-winning side of 1969/70. He was transferred to West Ham United (for £78,000 plus Peter Bennett) in October 1970. He had a brilliant career at Upton Park, winning an FA Cup winner's medal in 1975, and totalling 340 League and 58 FA Cup appearances. During his stay at Upton Park, he also won 16 England under-23 caps (some of those appearances were made as part of the over-age rule) and was on the verge of a full cap. Taylor rejoined O's in May 1979 after losing his place at Upton Park to Alvin Martin. He

Tommy Taylor

was appointed team captain and stayed for three years. It was after an infamous row with boss Ken Knighton at half-time in an FA Cup tie against Crystal Palace on 16 February 1982 that he lost his place for a while. In May 1982 he joined Charlton Athletic on a free transfer, and in August 1982, he played in Belgium for Antwerp and then Beerschot. After taking up various coaching and managerial positions, Taylor then became manager of O's on 7 November 1996. After five years in charage and two defeats in play-off finals, he resigned on 15 October 2001. He was in charge for 271 matches, winning 98, drawing 78, and losing 95 of them. He was then appointed manager of Darlington on 29 October 2001.

SEASON	LEAGUE		FA CUP		L. CUP	
	Apps	Gls	Apps	Gls	Apps	Gls
1967/68	16(1)	0	0	0	0	0
1968/69	39(1)	2	2	0	4	0
1969/70	46	2	2	0	2	0
1970/71	11	0	0	0	1	0
1979/80	42	5	3	1	2	0
1980/81	41	0	1	0	2	0
1981/82	33	0	5	0	2	0
TOTAL	228(2)	9	13	1	13	0

TOTAL APPS	254(2)
TOTAL GOALS	10

* Tommy Taylor also appeared in 2 Anglo-Scottish Cup matches and 3 Football League Groups Cup matches.

William TAYLOR, 1959-63

Billy Taylor was born in Edinburgh on 31 July 1939. He started with local junior club Bonnyrigg Rose, before becoming an 'Oriental' at the age of nineteen during August 1959, on the recommendation of O's legendary centre forward Tommy Johnston. He showed great promise playing at inside forward for the reserves at Brisbane Road, and made his League debut at Lincoln City on 29 April 1961. He made 6 appearances in O's memorable season of 1961/62, when promotion to the First Division was achieved. It was during the First Division season of 1962/63 that he was successfully converted to the left-back position by boss Johnny Carey, and replaced Eddie Lewis for a few games. When manager Carey moved on to take over Nottingham Forest, he returned to sign Taylor in August 1963. He was mostly a reserve player, making just 10(9) League appearances for Forest between 1963 and 1968. He moved to Lincoln City in May 1969 and in two seasons at Sincil Bank, he made 74(5) League appearances and scored 6 goals as an inside forward. He retired in May 1971 and went on to become the Fulham reserve coach, work-

Billy Taylor

ing his way up to first-team coach and taking the club to the 1975 FA Cup final. During October 1974, Taylor was on the coaching staff of the England national squad, and in May 1976 he was appointed as Manchester City's assistant manager. He then became coach at Oldham Athletic in July 1979. A couple of years later, Taylor suffered a viral infection which attacked his nervous system, and although he recovered, he fell ill again on 18 November. He went into a coma before passing away twelve days later in Oldham. At the time of his death, he was still the coach with both Oldham and England.

SEASON	LEAGUE		FA CUP		L. CUP	
	Apps	Gls	Apps	Gls	Apps	Gls
1959/60	0	0	0	0	0	0
1960/61	1	0	0	0	0	0
1961/62	6	0	0	0	0	0
1962/63	16	0	0	0	4	0
TOTAL	23	0	0	0	4	0

TOTAL APPS	27
TOTAL GOALS	0

Francis William THACKER, 1906-07

Frank Thacker was a real character: he was one of the toughest players of his era, as hard as nails and with a biting tackle. He was not scared to 'mix it' with anyone, and was often in trouble with referees. The wing half, who stood just 5ft 8in and weighed 11st 4lb, was involved in some notoriously dirty games for Chesterfield Town, none more so than an FA Cup first round replay against Clapton Orient on 17 January 1906. A local newspaper reported that the match, which O's lost 3-0, resembled an ice hockey match not so much for the playing conditions, but for Thacker's (and many other players') fighting behaviour! Having been at Chesterfield Town for seven years, he was asked which club he would like to play against for his benefit match and he chose Clapton Orient, of all clubs. Some said it was an apology, but others say it was just to sound out a possible move to London. Born in Sheepbridge in 1876, he worked at a forge before beginning his football career with local side Sheepbridge Red Rose FC. He later played for the Sheepbridge works team in July 1897, before moving to Sheffield United in February 1898, making 2 League appearances. However, it was with Chesterfield Town (whom he joined for £10 in July 1899) that he made his mark, playing in their very first League match at the Wednesday in September 1899. He went on to chalk up 250 senior appearances and 26 goals for the club. He supposedly fell into dispute with the Chesterfield management over new terms, and so the thirty-year-old signed for O's in September 1906, making his debut at left half in a 3-1 win at Blackpool on 22 September 1906. This was only O's second ever League away victory, achieved after twenty attempts. He brought some steel to an O's team that struggled to adapt to League football, but after a year he had enough of the capital and went on to join Rotherham County as coach. Thacker rejoined Chesterfield Town as player-trainer in 1909, when they were in the Midlands League, and made a further 120 appearances and netted 7 goals. In 1912 he was appointed player-trainer of Sheepsbridge, but returned to Chesterfield a year later as trainer. He remained in that position until Town were liquidated in 1915. He played wartime football with the former Town players and made a few appearances in his fortieth year.

After the First World War had ended, he was appointed trainer of newly formed Chesterfield FC, and continued to serve them until May 1925. After his retirement, he worked for the Chesterfield Corporation Cleansing Depart-ment, and then as a canteen attendant at the Sheepbridge works until his retirement. He died in Chester-field on 8 September 1949, aged seventy-three.

SEASON	LEAGUE		FA CUP		TOTAL	
	Apps	Gls	Apps	Gls	Apps	Gls
1906/07*	25	1	-	-	25	1
1907/08	9	0	3	0	12	0
TOTAL	34	1	3	0	37	1

* Clapton Orient did not enter the FA Cup in 1906/07.

Edward THOMAS, 1967-68

Inside forward Eddie Thomas had a very good League career with a number of clubs, scoring 113 career goals from 293(3) appearances before joining O's in September 1967 for £5,000 from Derby County. He was a deceptive player with a powerful kick, though he was not very big physically. Born in Newton-le-Willows on 23 October 1933, he started off as a junior with Everton in October 1951, but his League debut did not come until some five years later. He netted 39 goals from 86 League appearances whilst at Goodison. He moved on to Blackburn Rovers in February 1960, staying for two years, and after 37 matches and 9 goals, he moved on to Swansea City in July 1962, where 21 goals from 68 matches fol-lowed. His best career spell came with Derby County, whom he joined in August 1964, where he notched 44 goals from 102(3) League matches. His stay at Brisbane Road was beset by injuries and illness, and he only managed to score twice, but one was a real cracker – a thirty-yarder against Southport at Leyton on 14 October 1967. Thomas moved to Nuneaton Borough in March 1968, and later played for Heanor FC.

SEASON	LEAGUE		FA CUP		L. CUP	
	Apps	Gls	Apps	Gls	Apps	Gls
1967/68	11	2	0	0	0	0
TOTAL	11	2	0	0	0	0

TOTAL APPS	11
TOTAL GOALS	2

Louis Lionel THOMAS, 1906-07

London-born inside left Louis Thomas was an amateur with Fulham in May 1905, and played in a single Southern League match for them during November 1905 at Reading. He joined O's on 24 November 1906, scoring against Stockport County on his League debut in the opening fix-ture of the 1906/07 season. He found it difficult to hold down a regular place, due to the form of Richard Bourne, and he moved on to Tunbridge Wells Rangers on 13 September 1907.

SEASON	LEAGUE		FA CUP		TOTAL	
	Apps	Gls	Apps	Gls	Apps	Gls
1906/07	6	1	0	0	6	1
1907/08	0	0	0	0	0	0
TOTAL	6	1	0	0	6	1

Martin Russell THOMAS, 1993-94

Martin Thomas was born in Lymington on 12 September 1973. He started off with Southampton as a junior, turning professional in June 1992, but did not fea-ture in their first team. The lightweight but competitive ball-winning midfielder joined O's from Southampton on a non-contract basis on 24 March 1994, on the recommendation of former 'Saint' Glenn Cockerill. He scored on his debut against Fulham two days later, but after playing just a handful of League matches and scoring twice, Thomas was dropped when the Sitton/Turner duo took over the reins at the club. He never featured again, but found himself back at the Dell in July 1994. He was released at the end of the season and joined Fulham on a free transfer in July 1994, spending four seasons at Craven Cottage and scoring 9 goals from 69(32) senior matches. In June 1998 he joined Swansea City on a free transfer, and netted 3 goals from 20 matches as they qualified for the Division Three play-offs in 1998/99. He has since made 72(21) appearances for the Swans and scored 8 goals. Thomas joined Brighton & Hove Albion on a free transfer on 22 March 2001, making 1(7) League appearances without scoring. He was released in May, and the twenty-seven-year-old held talks with Oxford

Martin Thomas

United and signed on 3 July 2001, but missed the early part of the season with a broken toe.

SEASON	LEAGUE		FA CUP		L. CUP	
	Apps	Gls	Apps	Gls	Apps	Gls
1993/94	5	2	0	0	0	0
TOTAL	5	2	0	0	0	0

TOTAL APPS	5
TOTAL GOALS	2

Andrew THOMPSON, 1932-33

Andy Thompson was born in Newcastle-under-Lyme on 21 January 1899. He started out with local junior sides Newburn FC and Whickham Park Villa. The inside forward moved to Tottenham Hotspur in November 1920 and stayed for eleven years, making 166 senior appearances and scoring 21 goals. He moved to Norwich City in November 1931, but after just 14 senior matches and 3 goals. he was off to Chester City during July 1932. However, he stayed only three months, making 7 League appearances and scoring 2 goals, before becoming an 'Oriental' in October 1932 at the age of thirty-three. He played in three different forward positions, and proved a useful capture during a difficult season for O's. Thompson made his debut in a 0-0 draw at Brighton on 22 October 1932, and had a useful little run in January 1933 when netting 4 goals in 3 League matches, including a goal in a 7-1 thrashing of Swindon Town on 21 January. During the 1933/34 season, he helped out as a coach whilst playing for the reserves. In March 1934, he was appointed player-coach of Ashford Town, and the following August joined Northfleet United in the same capacity. He was appointed assistant coach at Tottenham Hotspur in the

1938/39 season, and stayed as a member of the backroom staff and as a scout until the late 1960s. Thompson died in Leyton, London on 1 January 1970.

SEASON	LEAGUE		FA CUP		TOTAL	
	Apps	Gls	Apps	Gls	Apps	Gls
1932/33	18	5	1	0	19	5
1933/34	0	0	0	0	0	0
TOTAL	18	5	1	0	19	5

Benjamin Swinhoe THOMPSON, 1908-09

Ben Thompson was born in Southwick, Sunderland in July 1882. The outside left started his career with local side Southwick FC, before going to play for Sunderland in 1903, but after not making the first team, he returned to Southwick on 30 July 1904. He came south to join Southern League outfit Fulham in May 1906, and scored on his debut at Crystal Palace in September 1906. He made 8 Southern League appearances and scored 2 goals before joining O's on

Ben Thompson

22 May 1908. The small and lightweight winger made his debut at Hull City – a 3-2 defeat on 5 September 1908 – and played in 5 matches at the start of the season. He was dropped and only played once more – in a 0-0 draw against Leeds United in April 1909. He moved to West Hartlepool United in May 1909 and scored 3 goals for the North Eastern League side from 20 or so appearances.

SEASON	LEAGUE		FA CUP		TOTAL	
	Apps	Gls	Apps	Gls	Apps	Gls
1908/09	6	0	0	0	6	0
TOTAL	6	0	0	0	6	0

James William THOMPSON, 1924-25

Although he only played a single senior game for O's, Thompson had a wonderful career after leaving Millfields Road, netting a total of 94 League goals from 140 matches. However, he will probably be remembered best as the man who first spotted the legendary Jimmy Greaves and brought him to Chelsea as a boy. Born in Plaistow, London on 19 April 1898, the big left-winger started his amateur career with Custom House FC in February 1921. He turned professional with Charlton Athletic the following year, making 2 League appearances. After a short loan spell at Wimbledon FC, he moved on to Millwall in March 1922, playing in 7 League matches and scoring 3 goals. He joined Coventry City in June 1923, but after just 2 appearances he became an 'Oriental' in August 1924, only appearing in the first match of the season at Blackpool on 30 August 1924. He moved to Luton Town for the 1925/26 season, and a change of position (to centre forward) brought a change of fortune, as he netted 42 League goals from a total of 71 games. He went to Chelsea in May

1927, and he really hit the headlines there by notching 33 League goals from just 37 appearances. He was snapped up by Norwich for a large fee, and 17 League goals were netted from only 28 appearances. As he was now approaching the veteran stage, he moved to Sunderland in 1930, but quickly moved on to Fulham, who paid £300 for his services. However, after just 5 senior appearances he went to Hull City in October 1931, but made only a single appearance for them before leaving the League to join Tunbridge Wells Rangers in December 1931. He was later appointed as a scout for Chelsea. Thompson died at Epsom racecourse on 27 August 1984.

SEASON	LEAGUE		FA CUP		TOTAL	
	Apps	Gls	Apps	Gls	Apps	Gls
1924/25	1	0	0	0	1	0
TOTAL	1	0	0	0	1	0

Thomas THOMPSON, 1906-07
Goalkeeper Tommy Thompson was an amateur with Norwich City who came to O's in July 1906 as an understudy to Billy Bower. He got his chance when Bower was injured for the home match against Lincoln City on 27 October 1906, which ended 1-1. He did not feature again and left in May 1907.

SEASON	LEAGUE		FA CUP		TOTAL	
	Apps	Gls	Apps	Gls	Apps	Gls
1906/07	1	0	0	0	1	0
TOTAL	1	0	0	0	1	0

Norman Shaw THOMSON, 1926-27
Born in Glasgow on 20 February 1901, Norman Thomson started his nomadic professional career with Dumbarton in July 1921, after playing for the renowned Glasgow junior club St Anthony's as a youngster. Three years later he joined Hibernian, before migrating south of the Border to sign for Luton Town in August 1925. There he made 42 League appearances and scored 8 goals to earn himself a move to O's in January 1927. He was given a run in both inside positions, making his debut in a 1-1 home draw with Preston North End on 15 January 1927. His stay at Millfields Road was brief, and Brighton & Hove Albion were the next to obtain his services, but his sojourn at the Goldstone was mixed, and he languished in the reserves after making only 11 League appearances and scoring 5 goals. He joined Southern League Norwich City for a fee of £125, but after 16 appearances he moved on to Swindon Town in August 1932. After just another 3 matches, he sustained a knee injury and left the League to join Southern League Folkestone Town for a short while, but he eventually had to pack in the game. On his retirement from football, he started a motorcar repair business close to West Ham's Upton Park ground which still exists to this day and is run by his son. He moved to Sussex and lived there for many years until his death on 6 June 1984 in Ferning, at the age of eighty-three. His sister was married to former 'Oriental' Alf Edmonds, while one of his sons, Ian, made his name as a pace bowler with Sussex CCC and England.

SEASON	LEAGUE		FA CUP		TOTAL	
	Apps	Gls	Apps	Gls	Apps	Gls
1926/27	10	2	0	0	10	2
TOTAL	10	2	0	0	10	2

Adrian Ernest THORNE, 1965-66
Born in Hove, Sussex on 2 August 1937, Adrian Thorne attended Brighton Grammar School and played for Brighton Boys,

before graduating through the ranks of the Sussex County League with Old Grammarians whilst still at school. It was whilst playing for a Sussex representative youth side that he was spotted by Brighton & Hove Albion, and he signed for the south coast club on his seventeenth birthday in August 1954. In only his seventh League match for Albion, the strong-running attacker bagged 5 goals. This included a hat-trick within the first ten minutes of the 6-0 win over Watford at the Goldstone, which took place during April 1958 – Thorne was only playing due to an injury to Dave Sexton! He could never keep a regular place in their side, but he still managed to maintain a scoring record of a goal every other game, ending with 44 goals from 84 senior appearances. After being demoted for the umpteenth time, he handed in a transfer request and eventually joined Plymouth Argyle for £8,000 in June 1961. He stayed at Home Park for two years, but only managed 2 goals from 11 League appearances before moving on to Exeter City, where he scored on his debut in a 2-1 win at Brighton. He made a total of 41 League appearances, scoring 9 goals, and helped them clinch promotion to the Third Division. Thorne was signed by new O's boss (and former Brighton colleague) Dave Sexton in July 1965. He started in the opening fixture of the season against Huddersfield Town on 21 August 1965, but was then dropped for the reserves, where he played regularly on the left wing and scored a number of goals. He moved on to join Southern League side Cheltenham Town in July 1966, and became their leading marksman in 1966/67, scoring a total of 31 goals from 115 Southern League appearances prior to joining Barnet in July 1969. After leaving football he become a PE teacher in Ealing, West London.

SEASON	LEAGUE		FA CUP		L. CUP	
	Apps	Gls	Apps	Gls	Apps	Gls
1965/66	2	0	0	0	0	0
TOTAL	2	0	0	0	0	0

TOTAL APPS	2
TOTAL GOALS	0

Oliver Eustace TIDMAN, 1937-38

Oliver Tidman was born in Margate, Kent on 16 March 1911. The outside left started with Middlesex Wanderers FC before joining Tufnell Park FC in 1928, where he played well for a number of seasons. Eventually, the twenty-one-year-old was snapped up by Aston Villa in May 1932, but although he stayed at Villa Park for three years, he managed a single solitary League appearance. He moved to Stockport County in May 1935, making 24 League appearances and scoring a total of 4 goals. He joined Bristol Rovers on 7 May 1936, and appeared in the first 9 games of the season for the Eastville club, but then lost his place. He went on to help the reserves win the Western League Championship, and after a single goal from 16 League appearances, he moved to O's in July 1937. Tidman did not get a League game until almost the end of the season, appearing at wing-half in a 2-0 defeat at Watford in April 1938. Tidman moved on to Southern League side Chelmsford City, and played in their first ever professional match in August 1938, against Bristol Rovers reserves. He went on to appear in 16 Southern League matches. During the Second World War he guested for Watford and obtained a military MBE. After the war he returned to play for Chelmsford, and appeared in

2 Southern League matches over Christmas 1947. However, Tidman was released in May 1948 and retired from the game.

SEASON	LEAGUE		FA CUP		TOTAL	
	Apps	Gls	Apps	Gls	Apps	Gls
1937/38	1	0	0	0	1	0
TOTAL	1	0	0	0	1	0

Arthur William TILLEY, 1912-14

Born in West Calder, Wellingborough, Arthur Tilley, an outside right, joined O's from Fletton United in July 1912. He did well and looked promising in the reserve team, and he eventually got his first-team chance when playing in a 3-1 defeat by Grimsby Town on 29 March 1913. Unfortunately, he didn't quite fulfil his early potential and wasn't helped when picking up a nasty injury during the following reserve campaign. He was released in May 1914 and went on trial with Lincoln City in July 1914, but wasn't signed.

SEASON	LEAGUE		FA CUP		TOTAL	
	Apps	Gls	Apps	Gls	Apps	Gls
1912/13	1	0	0	0	1	0
1913/14	0	0	0	0	0	0
TOTAL	1	0	0	0	1	0

Christopher Bryan TIMONS, 1997

The defender Chris Timons came to O's on a non-contract basis on 21 March 1997, after being released by Chesterfield. Born in Old Langworth, Shirebrook on 8 December 1974, he started out with Clipstone Miners' Welfare Colliery FC, before joining Mansfield Town in August 1986 as a twelve-year-old. He spent eight years as a junior and reserve player before making his League debut in February 1994, and he went on to make a total of 35(4) League appearances and score 2 goals. Timons spent the follow-ing year with Gainsborough Trinity on loan and in the reserve side of Chesterfield, before coming to Brisbane Road. He scored on his debut in a 2-3 home defeat by Lincoln City on 22 March 1997, and followed up the next week with the opener in a 2-1 win at Scunthorpe United – out of his 6 League appearances, 4 were victories. During the 1997/98 season, he returned to Gainsborough Trinity, and in May 1998 he joined Altrincham for £20,000, making 35(2) Football Conference and FA Cup appearances up to the 1999/2000 season. More recently, he joined Ilkeston Town in June 2001.

SEASON	LEAGUE		FA CUP		L. CUP	
	Apps	Gls	Apps	Gls	Apps	Gls
1996/97	6	2	0	0	0	0
TOTAL	6	2	0	0	0	0

TOTAL APPS	6
TOTAL GOALS	2

Stanley Albert TOLLIDAY, 1946-49

Goalkeeper Stan Tolliday was a player dogged by injury and misfortune – with a better run of luck, he could have achieved much more whilst at Brisbane Road. Born in Hackney, London on 6 August 1922, he joined O's from local football in July 1946. Tolliday was one of four goalkeepers tried during the 1946/47 season, Hall, King and Lewis being the others. When the latter was injured, O's manager Captain Charles Hewitt decided to give the inexperienced, but highly promising Tolliday his League debut in a 2-1 defeat at Brighton in November 1946. Although he looked a bit nervous, he played quite well and held the position for the remainder of the season. The following season he started by saving a penalty in the first home match against Crystal Palace, and continued to do well, playing a major part in Orient's 11-match unbeaten run that saw them clear from the threat of having to apply for re-election. In one match at high-flying Notts County, his goalkeeping was described by the press as 'amazing'. During the 1948/49 season, injury and then illness curtailed his progress, and his position was taken over by Polish amateur international goalie Stan Gerula. After a lengthy lay-off, Tolliday was released and joined Walsall in June 1950. He was not able to play and was sadly killed in a motorcar accident early in 1951, aged twenty-nine.

Mickey Tomlinson

SEASON	LEAGUE		FA CUP		TOTAL	
	Apps	Gls	Apps	Gls	Apps	Gls
1946/47	28	0	1	0	29	0
1947/48	32	0	1	0	33	0
1948/49	4	0	0	0	4	0
TOTAL	64	0	2	0	66	0

Michael Lloyd TOMLINSON, 1990-94

Mickey Tomlinson was born in Lambeth, London on 15 September 1972. He made the most of a dramatic entry into the League by scoring within minutes of coming on as a substitute against Wigan on 23 April 1991, after latching on to a Kenny Achampong cross. On his arrival at the ground, he had expected only to be watching from the stands, but he went into the dressing-room to show his face and wish the team well and was handed the number 14 shirt, and was apparently more shocked than nervous. Tomlinson only made his full League debut in the 3-2 home win over Brighton & Hove Albion on 15 August 1992. The winger signed with O's as a professional in April 1990, after joining a year earlier on YTS forms. He had come to the attention of

the club through the father of another O's youngster Bradley Gamble. He was at O's for four seasons, but only managed a handful of League appearances before moving to Barnet on a free on 21 March 1994. After making 67(26) League appearances and scoring 4 goals during his four-year stay, he moved on to Harrow Borough in March 1998.

SEASON	LEAGUE		FA CUP		L. CUP	
	Apps	Gls	Apps	Gls	Apps	Gls
1990/91	0(1)	1	0	0	0	0
1991/92	0(1)	0	0	0	0	0
1992/93	3(5)	0	0	0	2	1
1993/94	4	0	1	0	2	0
TOTAL	7(7)	1	1	0	4	1

TOTAL APPS	12(7)
TOTAL GOALS	2

* Mickey Tomlinson also appeared in 0(1) Auto Windscreens Shield match.

James Edward TONNER, 1919-20

The least known of the three Tonner brothers, James, was born on 31 March 1896 in Bridgetown, Glasgow. Unlike the other two, he was not a regular in O's first team due to the form of veteran Fred Parker. Jimmy Tonner started his career playing in Fife junior football with Linlithgow Port FC, and then with Dunfermline Athletic in 1912. He joined O's in 1919 and made his League debut alongside his two brothers in a 1-0 win over Nottingham Forest on 13 December 1919. He left O's in July 1920 to join Lochgelly United during their first season in the 'rebel' Central League, but they ended the season at the foot of the table. The following season, when all Central League sides were admitted to the Scottish League, he joined one of those sides, Bo'ness FC. In 1923/24 he appeared for them against former club Lochgelly in a home Scottish League fixture on 8 March 1924, in a match that later was discovered by the police to have been fixed. Two Lochgelly players – Browning and Kyle – had approached and offered the Bo'ness skipper Peter Brown £30 to 'throw' the match. Although he was not a party to the offer, Lochgelly managed to win 2-0 and when they came to give Brown the money, they were arrested and received sixty days' hard labour. Many Bo'ness players were unhappy at the situation, and Tonner was transferred to English First Division side Burnley in October 1924. He was more or less a regular in 1924/25, playing in 27 League matches and scoring twice. However, he played in just 10 League matches the following season without scoring. He did not feature at all the following season, and he was eventually transferred to Hamilton Academical in October 1926. He made his debut against Dundee United at Douglas Park on 9 October, when it was reported that he shaped up well and could not be criticised following his first appearance for the men in hoops. He made 44 Scottish League appearances and scored 6 goals, and also scored a goal from 2 Scottish Cup matches, as well as making an appearance in the Lanarkshire Cup. Tonner was another of the Scots during that period to seek fame and fortune in America, but he returned in 1932 and went on to turn out for Portsmouth reserves. When Dunfermline played Aberdeen on 7 August 1985 to celebrate their centenary, Jimmy Tonner, aged eighty-nine, was guest of honour. He was believed to be the club's oldest living player at the time, having first played in 1912. He died shortly thereafter.

SEASON	LEAGUE		FA CUP		TOTAL	
	Apps	Gls	Apps	Gls	Apps	Gls
1919/20	12	0	1	0	13	0
TOTAL	12	0	1	0	13	0

John TONNER, 1919-26

Born on 20 February 1898 in Holytown, Lanarkshire, Jack (as he was also known), the youngest of the three brothers, also progressed through local junior football in Fife before signing for Dunfermline, and he joined O's in September 1919. He proved to be a full-blooded footballer who seldom shirked a hard tackle and loved to hassle the opposition. The inside left scored on his League debut at Hull City on 13 October 1919, and he topped the goalscoring charts during his first season. The following season, despite playing in not much more than half of the first-team matches, he still managed to notch 23 goals for the reserves. In December 1922 he bagged a League hat-trick against Rotherham County in a 5-1 win, but suffered from injuries between 1923 and 1925 which affected his progress somewhat. After seven seasons at Millfields Road, he joined Fulham in June 1926. He again scored on his debut (against Manchester City at Craven Cottage on 28 August 1926), and he went on to make 30 senior appearances and score 15 goals. In May 1927 he moved on to Crystal Palace, and netted 8 goals from 24 appearances. The thirty-year-old Tonner left the League to join Southern League side Thames Association in June 1928. Tonner was later O's groundsman at Brisbane Road between 1951 and 1966. During a career that lasted some nine seasons, Jack Tonner recorded a career total of 208 League appearances and 62 goals. He died in Southend-on-Sea, Essex in 1978, aged eighty.

Jack Tonner

SEASON	LEAGUE		FA CUP		TOTAL	
	Apps	Gls	Apps	Gls	Apps	Gls
1919/20	30	12	1	1	31	13
1920/21	24	5	2	0	26	5
1921/22	13	2	0	0	13	2
1922/23	22	7	1	0	23	7
1923/24	7	2	3	0	10	2
1924/25	16	3	0	0	16	3
1925/26	31	4	4	3	35	7
TOTAL	143	35	11	4	154	39

Samuel TONNER, 1919-25

Sam Tonner was born in Dunfermline on 9 August 1894, and was the eldest of the three brothers. He started with junior side Inverkeithing FC, before joining Dunfermline Athletic as a junior. He turned professional in 1914, and then moved to East Fife in 1918, finally joining O's in May 1919. Tonner made his League debut for O's at Huddersfield Town on 30 August, and he soon became known for his powerful long-range shooting. He scored a great goal from fully thirty-five yards at Wolves on 20 September to help O's secure their first win of the 1919/20 campaign. He was a full-back who could play on either flank, possessing remarkable speed and, during the First World War, he was the quarter-mile champion for the British Army for four years. Tonner's rather robust defensive play subjected him to barracking at most away grounds, and this spilled over even to the away fans at Millfields Road in a number of matches. This upset him so much that he asked for a transfer, but instead the O's directors awarded him a benefit match during August 1924 against Spurs reserves, which attracted many thousands of fans. In July 1925, after six seasons at Millfields, he was transferred to Bristol City and made his

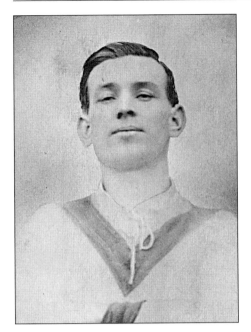

Sam Tonner

debut the following month against Norwich City. His only goal for City came from a penalty in October against Brentford. He made just 6 League appearances before joining Crystal Palace in August 1926. His debut for the Eagles came in a 5-3 win over Southend United on 13 November 1926, but he could only manage 2 further senior appearances before joining non-League side Armadale FC in 1927. Tonner was still playing football in the mid-1950s at the age of fifty-five in the Manchester Hotels League, whilst running a family-owned wholesale ice-cream business with a cousin. Sam Tonner died in Fleetwood during 1976, aged eighty-two.

SEASON	LEAGUE		FA CUP		TOTAL	
	Apps	Gls	Apps	Gls	Apps	Gls
1919/20	36	6	1	0	37	6
1920/21	31	5	2	0	33	5
1921/22	17	1	0	0	17	1
1922/23	40	1	1	0	41	1
1923/24	37	0	3	0	40	0
1924/25	25	0	1	0	26	0
TOTAL	186	13	8	0	194	13

James Chadwick TOWNLEY, 1929-31

Jimmy Townley was born in Blackburn, Lancashire on 2 May 1902, but spent most of his youth in Germany where his father – William Townley, a former Blackburn Rovers and England footballer – held a coaching post. He played as a youth for Hamburg Victoria FC, and then played in Switzerland for St Gallen. He returned to England in 1924 and joined Chelsea on trial, but made his League debut with Tottenham Hotspur in February 1925. He went on to make 3 appearances and score twice during a three-year stay at White Hart Lane. In July 1928, the outside left moved to Brighton & Hove Albion for £600, but failed to make any great impression with only 9 League appearances. He became an 'Oriental' on 1 February 1930, but was not a great deal luckier, spending most of his two years in the reserves. He made his League debut in a 4-0 defeat at Exeter City on 5 February 1930. The following season, he played at inside and centre forward, but without much success. He was released in May 1931 and moved to Switzerland three months later to continue his football career. Townley died in Thur, Switzerland on 3 February 1983, a few months before his eighty-first birthday.

SEASON	LEAGUE		FA CUP		TOTAL	
	Apps	Gls	Apps	Gls	Apps	Gls
1929/30	12	1	0	0	12	1
1930/31	7	1	0	0	7	1
TOTAL	19	2	0	0	19	2

T

John Ernest TOWNROW, 1919- 27

John Townrow was undoubtedly one of the finest defenders in the history of the club, and it was a surprise that he didn't win more than 2 full England international caps during his career. Born in Stratford, London on 28 March 1901, he started as a schoolboy with Pelly Memorial School. He was first spotted by O's boss William Holmes as a fifteen-year-old, playing for England schoolboys against both Scotland and Wales in 1915. He was one of the first players to be signed by O's as a youth player, whilst still playing for Fairburn House as an amateur. He turned professional after the First World War in July 1919. The centre half made his League debut at just eighteen years of age in a 2-1 defeat at Fulham on 15 September 1919. Taking over from another youngster, Alf Worboys, Townrow made the position his own over the next seven seasons. His class was obvious, and he was a player of resource and power, noted for his coolness, great heading and brilliant passing ability. He was often referred to by the local press as a great all-round player. He became the second O's player to gain full England international honours (after Owen Williams), gaining a cap against Scotland, when he subdued the legendary Hughie Gallacher at Hampden Park on 4 April 1925. His second cap came against Wales on 1 March 1926 at the Crystal Palace, and he also represented the League. Townrow was a tower of strength in O's famous 2-0 FA Cup fifth round victory over Newcastle United on 20 February 1926, once again outplaying Gallacher. In February 1927, Chelsea came in with a record £4,000 offer for him, which the O's Directors just could not refuse. He went on to make 140 senior appearances whilst at Stamford Bridge, scoring 3 goals before moving to Bristol Rovers in May 1932, where he played just 10 senior games. In later years he became coach and groundsman at Fairbairn House School, and was also employed at Becton gas works, and was also a publican in Harrogate for a time. He died in Knaresborough on 11 April 1969, aged sixty-eight.

John Townrow

SEASON	LEAGUE		FA CUP		TOTAL	
	Apps	Gls	Apps	Gls	Apps	Gls
1919/20	29	1	0	0	29	1
1920/21	37	1	2	0	39	1
1921/22	20	0	0	0	20	0
1922/23	23	1	0	0	23	1
1923/24	39	1	3	0	42	1
1924/25	39	0	1	0	40	0
1925/26	40	1	4	0	44	1
1926/27	26	0	2	0	28	0
TOTAL	253	5	12	0	265	5

Cyril Henry TRAILOR, 1949-51

Cyril Trailor was born in Merthyr Tydfil, Wales on 15 May 1919. The wing-half was a Welsh schoolboy international during 1932/33, scoring 3 goals from 2 appearances. He was an amateur player with Tottenham Hotspur in 1933/34, and he learnt his trade with Spurs' nursery club Northfleet United in 1937/38. He turned professional with Spurs in October 1938, and went on to to make 11 League appearances. He also appeared in their FA Cup sixth round victory at Southampton in February 1948. He joined O's for £600 on 29 July 1949, and his experience shone through in an O's team that was struggling. He made his debut for the club in a 0-0 draw against Watford on 20 August 1949. However, the following season, the thirty-one-year-old struggled to come by a first-team place, with wing-halves like Brown and Deverall holding down the position. Trailor was not retained, and in June 1951 he joined Bedford Town. After recovering from a broken ankle, he joined Merthyr on trial, but his ankle could not stand up to training and he retired from the game. He then worked for the Hoover company before developing Parkinson's disease and spending the final three years of his life bedridden. He died in Merthyr Tydfil on 28 August 1986.

SEASON	LEAGUE		FA CUP		TOTAL	
	Apps	Gls	Apps	Gls	Apps	Gls
1949/50	33	0	1	0	34	0
1950/51	6	0	0	0	6	0
TOTAL	39	0	1	0	40	0

Reginald William TRICKER, 1929-33

Reg Tricker was born in Karachi, India on 5 October 1904 (Karachi later became part of the newly-formed Pakistan in

Reg Tricker

1947). His parents returned to England in 1908, when he was a four-year-old, and settled in Suffolk. He was a fine athlete and held the Norfolk and Suffolk 120-yard Hurdles Championship for two years. He started his football career with Beccles Town in the Suffolk Amateur League. Tricker moved south to study at the Borough Road Training College in Islewoth, Middlesex and was appointed as a schoolteacher at Crouch Hill School. He played for Alexandra Park before joining Luton Town on amateur forms in 1924, making his League debut at centre forward against Watford on 25 December 1924. He made a total of 4 senior appearances for the club. He moved to Charlton Athletic in June 1925, still combining his football with his teaching career. He scored his first League goal after fifty minutes against Exeter City on 12 September 1925, and netted a total of 18 goals from 41 senior appearances. He turned professional just before signing for Arsenal for £2,250 on 12 March 1927, and made his debut against Everton. However, he could never gain a regular first-team spot during his three-year stay at Highbury, making just 12 League appearances and scoring 5 goals, although he did make 40 appearances for the Gunners in the London Combination, netting 10 goals and winning a London Combination Championship medal in 1927/28. He joined O's for £1,000 on 8 February 1929 – a substantial fee for the O's, which was payable in instalments and linked to the number of his senior appearances. It took Tricker a while to settle down in the Third Division, but the forward really came to the fore in 1930/31, showing some skilful touches and an eye for goal. He top scored with 18 goals from just 29 appearances, and remained the club's top marksman for the following two seasons. He netted in both O's League matches played at Wembley Stadium in 1930. He moved to Margate FC in October 1933, and later played for Ramsgate. In September 1954 he was appointed coach of Old Owens FC. Reg Tricker died in Hendon on 9 June 1990, aged eighty-five.

SEASON	LEAGUE		FA CUP		TOTAL	
	Apps	Gls	Apps	Gls	Apps	Gls
1928/29	11	0	0	0	11	0
1929/30	23	9	1	0	24	9
1930/31	29	18	2	2	31	20
1931/32	39	19	3	1	42	20
1932/33	29	14	0	0	29	14
TOTAL	131	60	6	3	137	63

Frederick Charles Arnold TULLY, 1937-39

Right-winger Fred Tully goes into the record books as the scorer of the very first O's League goal at Brisbane Road, against Cardiff City on 28 August 1937. Despite his un-athletic stocky build, he was always busy down the right wing, and at his best was quite a dangerous attacker. Born in St Pancras, London on 4 July 1907, Tully played for Priory and Tynemouth Schools. He then played for amateur sides Rosehill Villa, Preston Colliery and Chaddleton, before joining the paid ranks with Aston Villa. Between 1927 and 1932, he made just 8 League appearances. He joined Southampton during August 1937, and soon after made his debut against Bradford. He gave four years of grand service to the Saints, making 103 senior appearances and scoring 9 goals. He returned to his native London to join O's in June 1933. He showed plenty of thrust and enterprise, and was the top scorer in 1937/38. He performed very well the following season, and was still with O's during wartime football, making 73 appearances and scoring a total of 7 goals between 1939 and 1943. On retirement from football, he joined his father's carpentry business and later worked as an attendant at Cheddeston Mental Hospital in North Staffordshire.

SEASON	LEAGUE		FA CUP		TOTAL	
	Apps	Gls	Apps	Gls	Apps	Gls
1937/38	30	13	3	1	33	14
1938/39	27	5	1	0	28	5
TOTAL	57	18	4	1	61	19

* Fred Tully also appeared in a Third Division Cup match in 1938/39.

James Andrew TULLY, 1909-11

Born in Newcastle-on-Tyne in 1885, Jimmy Tully joined O's from the West Stanley Club in 1909. He stayed for two seasons, but played only a handful of first-team matches. The inside left made his debut in the 3-1 defeat at Wolverhampton

Wanderers on 13 September 1909. He scored his only senior goal for O's the following season to secure two points in a 1-0 win over Leeds City on 17 April 1911. Tully was not retained in May 1911 and rejoined West Stanley FC. He had a long spell with Rochdale, playing in the Lancashire Combination between 1912 and 1919, and in 1920 he had a season with Pontypridd FC. He rejoined Rochdale for their entry into the Third Division (North), and made 44 senior appearances between 1921 and 1923.

SEASON	LEAGUE		FA CUP		TOTAL	
	Apps	Gls	Apps	Gls	Apps	Gls
1909/10	2	0	0	0	2	0
1910/11	3	1	0	0	3	1
TOTAL	5	1	0	0	5	1

William Lee TURLEY, 1998 (loan)

Goalkeeper Billy Turley joined O's on loan on 5 February 1998 from Northampton Town, after a serious injury to regular goalkeeper Paul Hyde. Born in Wolverhampton on 15 July 1973, he signed for the Cobblers on a free transfer from Evesham United during July 1995. He made 28 League appearances before moving on to Kettering Town in March 1997. He made his O's League debut in a 1-0 win over Peterborough United, a match covered by Sky TV in February 1998. Turley rejoined Northampton in April 1998, and was their first-choice 'keeper for the 1998/99 season. However, he was sold to Football Conference neighbours Rushden & Diamonds for a reported £120,000 on 14 June 1999. Up to the end of May 2001, he had made over 100 senior appearances for the team that gained promotion to Division Three in May 2001. He made an unhappy return to Brisbane Road on 15 September 2001,

being sent off for in the first ever meeting between the clubs, which the O's won 2-1.

SEASON	LEAGUE		FA CUP		L. CUP	
	Apps	Gls	Apps	Gls	Apps	Gls
1997/98	14	0	0	0	0	0
TOTAL	14	0	0	0	0	0

TOTAL APPS	14
TOTAL GOALS	0

Robert Hamilton TURNBULL, 1928-29

Born in Dumbarton, Scotland on 22 June 1894, Bob Turbull was originally a full-back during his time at Arsenal, but was converted to the centre forward position with great effect. He scored 28 goals from 66 senior outings for the Gunners between 1922 and 1925. After a short spell with Charlton Athletic in 1924/25 (6 League appearances and 2 goals), he moved on to Chelsea in February 1925 and notched 51 goals from 87 senior appearances. He became an 'Oriental' in February 1928 and soon found his shooting boots, scoring on his debut in a 3-2 win over Stoke City on 25 February 1928. He also scored a brace on 31 March in a thrilling 5-3 defeat at Manchester City. The following season he was top scorer, and bagged a hat-trick against Middlesbrough on 24 November 1928. He joined Southend United in November 1929, but made just 2 League appearances and later played for Chatham FC. In 1932/33 he moved to Crystal Palace, where a further 2 League matches followed. Turnbull died in Burton-on-Trent in December 1944.

SEASON	LEAGUE		FA CUP		TOTAL	
	Apps	Gls	Apps	Gls	Apps	Gls
1927/28	9	5	0	0	9	5

1928/29	28	13	4	0	32	13
1929/30	2	0	0	0	2	0
TOTAL	39	18	4	0	43	18

Christopher Robert TURNER, 1991-95

Chris Turner joined O's on loan from Sheffield Wednesday on 25 October 1991, and the move was made permanent for £75,000 on 21 November 1991, as part of the deal that took Chris Bart-Williams to Hillsborough. This highly rated goal-keeper was born on 15 September 1958 in Sheffield. He was an apprentice at Sheffield Wednesday at the age of sixteen, making his League debut just a year later in 1976/77. He went on to make a total of 91 League appearances during his time with the Hillsborough club. After a loan spell with Lincoln City during October 1978 (5 League appearances), he was transferred to Sunderland for £80,000 in July 1979 and stayed for six years, making 195 League appearances. He joined Manchester United in August 1985 for £275,000, and played 75 League matches during three years at Old Trafford. He then re-joined Sheffield Wednesday for £175,000, making 75 appearances. The vastly experienced Turner was an immediate success at O's, making his League debut at Stoke City on 26 October 1991. The quality of his performances that season earned him a place in the PFA Third Division team of the year, for which he was presented with a special medal. Turner played his final League match for O's at the age of thirty-six – against Hull City in a 2-0 defeat on 11 March 1995, due to an injury to Paul Heald. He made 490 League appearances in a playing career that spanned fifteen years. In 1992 he was appointed assistant manager to Peter Eustace, and in April 1994, after the sacking of Eustace, he was appointed

Chris Turner

joint manager at the club, along with John Sitton. Both men were sacked on 17 April 1995. Turner was then appointed as youth coach with Leicester City and later enjoyed three successful years in the same role for Wolverhampton Wanderers. On 24 February 1999, he became the manager of Third Division side Hartlepool United.

SEASON	LEAGUE		FA CUP		L. CUP	
	Apps	Gls	Apps	Gls	Apps	Gls
1991/92	34	0	5	0	0	0
1992/93	17	0	1	0	2	0
1993/94	6	0	0	0	2	0
1994/95	1	0	0	0	0	0
TOTAL	58	0	6	0	4	0

TOTAL APPS	68
TOTAL GOALS	0

* Chris Turner also appeared in 4 Auto Windscreens Shield matches.

U

Austin Toby UNDERWOOD, 1909-10

'Tosher' Underwood, as he was affectionately nicknamed, was born in Street, Somerset in 1880. He started his professional career with Southern League Second Division outfit Fulham, but made just 3 appearances for them between 1900 and 1902. Underwood joined Brentford of the Southern League First Division in May 1902, and made a total of 175 Southern League appearances during a six-year stay, scoring 26 goals. In 1908 he joined Second Division side Glossop, making his debut at outside left against Fulham in September 1908, going on to make 18 League appearances. Underwood became an 'Oriental' in May 1909, and was a regular on the left wing with his fast raids. During his single season at Milfields Road, he looked a player capable of creating goals. On leaving football he returned to Middlesex, where he set up business as a boot and shoe manufacturer in Windmill Road, Brentford.

SEASON	LEAGUE		FA CUP		TOTAL	
	Apps	Gls	Apps	Gls	Apps	Gls
1909/10	37	1	1	0	38	1
TOTAL	37	1	1	0	38	1

V

Ike VAN DEN EYNDEN, 1913-14

Ike Van Den Eynden won 17 amateur international caps for Belgium, and was the first foreign-born player to appear for O's when he joined in February 1914, taking over from the injured George Scott. He made his League debut on 28 February, and 'Vandy', as he became known, had a great match – every time he touched the ball, a great cheer came from the home fans amongst the 17,000 crowd. However, trouble occurred in the crowd when the visiting Hull fans started to boo the home players. Police on horseback had to act quickly and moved into the crowd to break up the disturbance. O's won the match 3-0, and Van Den Eyden was cheered off the park with shouts of 'play up, Vandy'. He starred in a match at the new Highbury Stadium when O's visited Arsenal on 18 April 1914 – a match the Gunners had to win to ensure promotion – and a crowd of 35,500 thought it was all over as they led 2-0 with just five minutes remaining. The O's, however, made a spirited fightback, sending both Forrest and Van Den Eynden upfield to join McFadden and Jonas down the middle. The move by manager Holmes paid off with two late goals from Parker and McFadden, who hit the equaliser with just seconds remaining. Van Den Eynden looked a very solid, although sometimes slightly unorthodox centre half. During his run of 12 matches O's lost just 3 times, which ensured an excellent sixth spot in the Second Division. He returned to Belgium in May 1914.

SEASON	LEAGUE		FA CUP		TOTAL	
	Apps	Gls	Apps	Gls	Apps	Gls
1913/14	12	0	0	0	12	0
TOTAL	12	0	0	0	12	0

Alfred James VANGO, 1932-33

Alf Vango was born on 23 December 1900 in Bethnal Green, London. He started off with local side Gnome Athletic, a team that featured a number of experienced players. In 1924 he went on to play for Gillingham, making 5 League appearances. He then joined up-and-coming amateur side Walthamstow Avenue in 1925 and stayed for six years, remaining on their books as an amateur during his exploits in the League. He joined Queens Park Rangers from the Third Division on 14 January 1931, making 12 League appearances between 1931 and 1932. He then joined O's in June 1932, and performed creditably at centre half in a very difficult season. He left O's in August 1933 and played for the London paperworks side. Vango died in Erith, Kent on 24 November 1977, a month before his seventy-seventh birthday.

SEASON	LEAGUE		FA CUP		TOTAL	
	Apps	Gls	Apps	Gls	Apps	Gls
1932/33	23	0	0	0	23	0
TOTAL	23	0	0	0	23	0

Alf Vango

Richard Thomas VANNER, 1929-31

Richard Vanner was born in Farnham, Surrey on 14 November 1903. He started his career with the works team of the Aldershot Traction Company before joining Tottenham Hotspur as a professional in March 1925. However, he was only a reserve during his four years at White Hart Lane. Vanner joined O's in September 1929, playing the majority of matches in the second half of the 1929/30 season at outside right. He scored the last League goal at Millfields Road against Brighton & Hove Albion on 3 May 1930. During the latter part of the following season, he was replaced on the wing by Rollo Jack. He was not retained in May 1931, moving on to join Aldershot. He could be described as a useful, rather than a particularly inspirational player. He died in Farnham on 15 July 1978, aged seventy-four.

SEASON	LEAGUE		FA CUP		TOTAL	
	Apps	Gls	Apps	Gls	Apps	Gls
1929/30	19	1	2	1	21	2
1930/31	16	3	0	0	16	3
TOTAL	35	4	2	1	37	5

Emmanuel VASSEUR, February-May 2001

Emmanuel Vasseur was born in Calais, France on 3 September 1976. The midfielder started his career with Calais FC, and after a period with the Gravelines club, he returned to Calais in 1998. Amateur left-sided midfield playmaker Vasseur, who worked in the Channel Tunnel as a painter, guided Fourth Division side Calais to the Coupe de France (the French Cup final) last season, putting out a lot of big name clubs before eventually losing in the final to Nantes, 2-1 after extra time. Early in

January 2001, he informed Calais director Claude Thirot that he had signed a two-year contract with Leyton Orient. There had been a lot of interest in Vasseur from many foreign clubs, but he chose to come to the East End of London, waiting for a over a month for his international clearance from Calais to come through. He made his League debut when coming on as a substitute in the eighty-third minute of a game against Halifax on 3 February 2001, setting up O's third goal within a minute of arriving on the pitch. His incisive pass set up Carl Griffiths, whose shot was saved before Watts headed home. Vasseur, with only minutes remaining, hit a shot just over the bar that would have made it a fairy-tale day for the Frenchman. His next appearance was as a non-playing sub at Cardiff City on 6 March. It was a surprise that more was not seen of him, but the part-timer first suffered a hamstring injury, before being involved in a car-crash in Paris, and then suffering a death in his family. He was released in June 2001. The player was unsettled throughout his short stay at Brisbane Road, and was set to rejoin his old club Calais after his remaining one-year contract was cancelled. O's boss Tommy Taylor stated: 'He couldn't come to terms with living away from Calais. He's lived there all his life and he just couldn't settle in London.'

SEASON	LEAGUE		FA CUP		L. CUP	
	Apps	Gls	Apps	Gls	Apps	Gls
2000/01	0(2)	0	0	0	0	0
TOTAL	0(2)	0	0	0	0	0

TOTAL APPS   0(2)

TOTAL GOALS   0

Robert George VINCENT, 1982-83

Robbie Vincent was born in Newcastle-upon-Tyne on 23 November 1962. He gained an England schoolboy cap against Ireland in 1978/79, whilst on the books of Sunderland. He made 1(1) League appearances for the North-East club, before joining O's in March 1982. He joined a squad that really struggled for survival in the Second Division, and during some reserve matches he hardly looked like he was the player to lift the team – unfortunately, not many others looked the part either. He made his League debut in a 3-0 win over Leicester City on 18 May 1982, O's last match in the Second Division. The following season he made just a handful of Third Division appearances, before leaving on New Year's Eve 1982 to play in Australia for the Brisbane Lions side. Vincent returned to England a few years later (in 1985) and played for Whitley Bay FC.

Robbie Vincent

SEASON	LEAGUE		FA CUP		L. CUP	
	Apps	Gls	Apps	Gls	Apps	Gls
1981/82	1	0	0	0	0	0
1982/83	7(1)	0	0	0	2	0
TOTAL	8(1)	0	0	0	2	0

TOTAL APPS	10(1)
TOTAL GOALS	0

* Robbie Vincent also appeared in 2 Football League Groups Cup matches.

W

George Henry WAITE, 1923-26

Centre forward George Waite was noted as being one of the tallest and fastest players of his day in the League. Born in Bradford on 1 March 1894, he joined Bradford Park Avenue in June 1919, after serving in the Royal Artillery during the First World War, and made 6 First Division outings for the Yorkshire club. On 29 April 1920 he moved to Scotland to play for Raith Rovers, scoring 11 goals in 23 Scottish League appearances and , and helping them finish third in the table behind the 'Old Firm' of Celtic and Rangers. From 29 January 1921, he spent a couple of months on loan at Clydebank before joining Welsh side Pontypridd in March 1921. In May 1922 he moved back into the League with Leicester City, making 30 senior appearances and netting 12 goals. He became an 'Oriental' in March 1923, shifting to play on the right wing, and helping O's to escape the threat of relegation. He scored on his home debut against Notts County, and had a very good campaign the following season, but over the next few seasons, he

George Waite

drifted in and out of the first team. He was transferred to Hartlepool United in July 1926, and scored 7 goals from 26 League appearances before moving to Midlands League side York City in 1927. Waite died in his native Bradford during April 1972, aged seventy-eight.

SEASON	LEAGUE		FA CUP		TOTAL	
	Apps	Gls	Apps	Gls	Apps	Gls
1922/23	10	2	0	0	10	2
1923/24	30	4	2	0	32	4
1924/25	16	3	1	0	17	3
1925/26	6	0	0	0	6	0
TOTAL	62	9	3	0	65	9

George Edward WAITES, 1958-61, 1962

Born in Stepney, London on 12 March 1938, the right-winger started his career playing junior football in Norfolk. Whilst serving in the Army, he turned out for the Harwich & Parkeston club in the Eastern Counties League.

The Cockney winger signed for O's as an amateur in September 1958, and turned professional three months later. Waites made his senior debut in a 3-1 home defeat by Derby County on 3 January 1959, playing in place of the injured Phil White. He found it a daunting task replacing White, even though he appeared a stronger and more direct player. Waites did very well at times, but was never a regular in the side, and in January 1961 he moved to Norwich City in a deal that brought Canadian-born Errol Crossan to Brisbane Road. The Canaries were trying to strengthen their squad after winning promotion to the Second Division. He proved to be quite a success at Carrow Road, scoring 11 goals from 40 senior appearances. Surprisingly, he was allowed to return to Brisbane Road in July 1962 for O's first ever venture in the First Division, but he played just 2 League matches (against Blackpool and Aston Villa). He did, however, notch a hat-trick that season in O's 9-2 League Cup victory over Chester on 17 October 1962. In December 1962 he moved to Brighton & Hove Albion for £8,000 – the money from his sale was used to bring Malcolm Musgrove to O's from West Ham United – during a season which eventually saw Albion relegated to the Fourth Division. He could not settle at the Goldstone, and was one of five players given a free transfer at the end of the 1963/64 season, after making just 24 senior appearances and scoring once. He had a spell with Millwall in April 1965, but did not feature at the Den, joining Southern League Gravesend & Northfleet in 1967. George Waites showed his best form whilst with O's and Norwich City, and on his day, he baffled most opposing full-backs with his trickery and direct play. During a professional career that spanned some nine years, he played just 121 senior games that yielded 24 goals. Sadly, George Waites died on 24 August 2000, after a short illness. His wife requested that flowers for his funeral be in red and white to reflect the O's club colours, as she stated his heart was always firmly with the O's.

George Waites

SEASON	LEAGUE		FA CUP		L. CUP	
	Apps	Gls	Apps	Gls	Apps	Gls
1958/59	4	0	0	0	-	-
1959/60	26	7	0	0	-	-
1960/61*	13	2	0	0	0	0
1962/63	2	0	0	0	2	3
TOTAL	45	9	0	0	2	3

TOTAL APPS	47
TOTAL GOALS	12

* The League Cup commenced in 1960/61.

W

Thomas Peter WALL, 1972-73 (loan)

Born in Brockton, Salop on 13 September 1944, Peter Wall was a good quality utility defender, who started his career as an apprentice with Shrewsbury Town during September 1964. However, after playing 18 League games, he joined Wrexham for £3,000 in November 1965, and he went on to make 22 League appearances and score once for the Welshmen. Full-back Wall was snapped up by Liverpool in October 1966, staying at Anfield for two seasons and making 31 League appearances. In June 1970 he came to London to join Crystal Palace for £35,000, and during a wonderful seven-year stint at Selhurst Park, he made 167(10) League appearances and scored 3 goals. It was during his time at Palace that Wall came to O's on loan in December 1972. He stayed for two months, making his debut in a 1-0 defeat on 16 December at Aston Villa, as well as featuring in an exciting 4-0 home win over Villa in February 1973.

SEASON	LEAGUE		FA CUP		L. CUP	
	Apps	Gls	Apps	Gls	Apps	Gls
1972/73	10	0	0	0	0	0
TOTAL	10	0	0	0	0	0

TOTAL APPS	10
TOTAL GOALS	0

Henry Harold WALLER, 1947-48

Born in Ashington, Northumberland on 20 August 1917, Harry Waller, a strong two-footed centre half, started out with his local side Ashington FC, before joining Arsenal in October 1937. He went to learn his trade with the Gunners' nursery team – Margate FC – until May 1938. He made his first-team debut for

Harry Waller

Arsenal in an FA Cup tie against West Ham United in January 1946, and then made a further 8 League appearances. He also played 66 reserve matches, winning a Football Combination winner's medal in 1946/47, in addition to playing in 11 wartime matches, during which time he served with the Army in Sicily. Waller was signed by O's boss Captain Charles Hewitt on 16 July 1947, for what was reported in the club magazine *Spotlight* in August 1947 as a 'large fee'. He possessed a throw-in that was as good as a corner. He made his debut in a 1-1 draw with Crystal Palace on 23 August 1947, but in 1948 he lost his place to Cyril Bacon and played mostly for the reserves. He stayed just one season at Brisbane Road before moving back to the North-East to his first club, Ashington, in May 1947. He later played for Consett FC. Waller died in 1984, aged sixty-seven.

SEASON	LEAGUE		FA CUP		TOTAL	
	Apps	Gls	Apps	Gls	Apps	Gls
1947/48	17	0	1	0	18	0
TOTAL	17	0	1	0	18	0

John Thomas WALLEY, 1971-76

Tom Walley was born in Caernarvon, Wales on 27 February 1945. As a boy, he was encouraged to play football by his older brother, Ernie, then a professional with Tottenham Hotspur and later a coach at Crystal Palace. Tom Walley was an amateur player with Caernarvon Town, before joining Wrexham in November 1963. He was not keen to move out of Wales, but was lured by an offer to join Arsenal and signed for the Gunners for £3,000 in December 1964. He made 10(4) First Division appearances and scored once, and also gained Welsh under-23 honours. After eighteen months at Highbury, where he was never really given the opportunity to establish himself, he moved to Watford in March 1967. He soon made a big impact there, playing a major role in their team which won the Third Division championship in 1969. The following year, he was also part of the Watford team to reach the semi-final of the FA Cup before going out to Chelsea, and the season after that, he gained rave reviews for marking George Best out of the game, in an FA Cup tie against Manchester United. He gained his only full international cap during October 1971 against Czechoslovakia, a 1-0 defeat in Prague. Walley stepped out at Watford to play against O's on 4 December 1971, not dreaming that forty-eight hours later he would be an 'Oriental'. The two clubs had agreed a £25,000 fee for him, but the player wasn't told until after the match. He knew that a club was watching him, but had no idea that it was the O's.

He happily signed for the club on 6 December. Walley was a determined, hard-working model professional, and after a spell in midfield where he scored a cracking twenty-five-yard goal against Sunderland, he then formed a very effective partnership in defence with Phil Hoadley. He missed just a single match during his last three seasons at the club, and was always on the verge of another full Welsh cap. He was appointed captain of the side in 1975/76, and it was a surprise when, at the age of thirty-one, he joined Watford for £3,000 in May 1976 – the first signing under their new chairman, singer Elton John. After playing 12(1) League matches, a serious injury ended Walley's career and he was appointed youth-team coach in August 1977. The following year he was made first-team coach, a position he held until March 1990. During this period, his older brother was reserve coach. In August 1990 he was appointed youth coach at

Tom Walley

Millwall, a position he held before leaving in February 1996 to take up positions as Welsh under-21 manager and as Arsenal youth manager. He left Highbury in May 1997 and returned to Watford as reserve-team manager in July 1997, and in July 2001 he was appointed first-team coach. To characterise his wonderful work, he took both his Watford and Millwall charges to the final of the FA Youth Cup.

SEASON	LEAGUE		FA CUP		L. CUP	
	Apps	Gls	Apps	Gls	Apps	Gls
1971/72	22	2	4	0	0	0
1972/73	8(2)	0	0	0	0	0
1973/74	42	1	4	0	4	0
1974/75	41	2	2	0	2	0
1975/76	42	1	1	0	1	0
TOTAL	155(2)	6	11	0	7	0

TOTAL APPS	173(2)
TOTAL GOALS	6

* Tom Walley also appeared in 3 Texaco Cup matches in 1974/75.

Wim WALSCHAERTS, 1998 -2001

This tough-tackling midfielder, who can also play at right wing-back, was signed by O's boss Tommy Taylor from Belgian Second Division side KFC Tielen of Antwerp, who had withdrawn from the professional League during 1998 due to financial problems. He joined O's on a free transfer under the Bosman ruling on 1 July 1998, having declined a move to another Belgium Premier side, Oostende. He made an immediate impression with his tremendous stamina, energy and hard work. He also weighed in with some important goals during his three years at Brisbane Road. Born in Antwerp on 5 November 1972, Walschaerts started his career with FC Beerschot in 1994, appear-ing on the right wing in their youth side. He made his first-team debut in 1995/96, and was voted their most valuable player in that season, before moving on to join KFC Tielen in June 1996. He proved to be a more than useful player for O's, turning in many excellent performances on a regular basis. He opened his goal account against 'old foes' Brighton & Hove Albion in a FA Cup tie, and also scored a vital goal against Kingstonian in an FA Cup replay to secure a 2-1 win. Walschaerts stated: 'I was brought here to play in midfield, that is my true position, but I do not mind playing wing-back. Wherever I am asked to play, I will give 100 per cent for the team.' He originally signed a two-year contract with the club in February 1999 that was later extended. A player with an obvious rapport with the fans, he sadly missed all 3 promotion play-off matches due to suspension, after receiving a rather harsh red card at Peterborough United. He missed the early part of the

Wim Walschaerts scores against Brighton.

1999/2000 season after breaking his arm in a training mishap with Simon Clark during September 1999, and was one of twelve first-team players out for the start of the 1999/2000 season. Although linked with Luton Town, he has remained committed to the O's. He has continued to be a regular during the 2000/01 season, and featured in the side that lost 4-2 in the play-off final against Blackpool at the Millennium Stadium in May 2001. He was released under the Bosman ruling in June 2001, and it was reported that he was informed of his release by letter. O's boss Tommy Taylor reported: 'His agent said he is talking to a Second Division side KFC Strombeek in Belgium, which is fair enough.' He signed for them in June 2001, but missed the early part of the season through injury.

Tom Walters

SEASON	LEAGUE		FA CUP		L. CUP	
	Apps	Gls	Apps	Gls	Apps	Gls
1998/99	44	3	5	2	4	0
1999/2000	32(4)	3	1	0	2(1)	0
2000/01*	47(1)	3	4	0	3	0
TOTAL	123(5)	9	10	2	9(1)	0

TOTAL APPS	142(6)
TOTAL GOALS	11

* Wim Walschaert's League record includes 3 play-off appearances in 2000/01. Walschaerts also played in an Auto Windscreens Shield match in 1999/2000, and in an LDV Vans Trophy match in 2000/01.

Thomas Charles WALTERS, 1938-39

Tom Walters was born in Trealaw, near Pontypridd, Wales on 15 June 1909. He was a coalminer in the valleys, before embarking on his football career. Walters was a strong centre forward, who notched 64 career League goals between 1931 and 1939. He started off as an ama-teur with Merthyr Town in 1930, before joining Bolton Wanderers in May 1931, and during his one season he made 5 League appearances and scored once. He moved to London in June 1932 to play for Crystal Palace, and scored 4 goals from his 14 League appearances. Walters then moved to Devon with Exeter City in August 1933, making 6 League appearances and scoring 4 goals. He then moved to Torquay United in November 1933, showing his best return thus far – 12 goals from 25 League matches. He had an even better spell with Watford, whom he joined in May 1935, scoring in each of his first 3 matches, and in his first season, he hit two hat-tricks in the space of 5 games. He stayed at Vicarage Road for three seasons, netting 25 goals from 59 senior appearances. He became an 'Oriental' on a free transfer in June 1938, and looked a good signing. Later in the season, he formed a grand partnership with Rod Williams and made 23 League appearances, scoring 9 goals. He was released in May 1939, after O's had signed famous Scottish forward William McFadyen for the 1939/40 season, which was eventually cancelled after just 3 matches owing to the outbreak of the Second World War. Walters signed for Dartford in August 1939, but was a guest player for Watford during the Second World War, playing 34 matches and scoring 16 goals between April 1940 and 1942. After the war he ran public houses in Watford, Abbotts Langley and Croxley Green. He died on 27 January 1968, a few weeks after retiring to Torquay, aged fifty-eight.

SEASON	LEAGUE		FA CUP		TOTAL	
	Apps	Gls	Apps	Gls	Apps	Gls
1938/39	23	9	0	0	23	9
TOTAL	23	9	0	0	23	9

Dick Walton

Richard WALTON, 1948-51

Hefty fair-haired full-back Dick Walton was born in Hull on 12 September 1924. He first joined Leicester City as an amateur in June 1942, and then stepped up to the senior ranks in January 1943. He played 25 consecutive matches during the Second World War regional League in 1942/43. The following season he also guested for Chester, Middlesbrough and Third Lanark. He was discharged from the Army in early 1944, but immediately signed up with the Palestine Police force for the duration of hostilities. He joined O's in July 1948, after Leicester City released his registration. He made his League debut in a 1-1 draw against Bristol Rovers on 12 March 1949, but played mostly in the reserves. His best spell at Brisbane Road came during the following season – in 1950/51 he was tried at centre forward, and scored a very

memorable goal with a forty-five-yard dipping free-kick into the top corner of the net against Crystal Palace on 9 February 1951. Bumpstead (the Palace 'keeper) had just been carried off, and their winger, Stevens, took over between the sticks, but had no chance with Walton's long kick. In 1951, Richard could not find a regular place in the team and he was transferred to Exeter in December 1951. Just a month later, he netted two goals against the O's in City's 6-1 victory. However, he only scored 6 goals from 135 League appearances during his stay at St James Park. He joined Tonbridge in May 1956, making 31 appearances, later playing for Sittingbourne.

SEASON	LEAGUE		FA CUP		TOTAL	
	Apps	Gls	Apps	Gls	Apps	Gls
1948/49	10	0	0	0	10	0
1949/50	31	0	0	0	31	0
1950/51	20	4	0	0	20	4

1951/52	2	0	0	0	2	0
TOTAL	63	4	0	0	63	4

Felix WARD, 1908-09

Born in Seaham Harbour in 1886, Felix Ward was a small, lightweight outside right. He started off with local side Seaham White Star, before joining Fulham in May 1907 and making his League debut at Clapton Orient on 26 November 1907 – a 1-0 win to the Cottagers. Ward made just three further appearances before becoming an 'Oriental' on 17 August 1908. He had just a single season at Millfields Road, playing mainly down the left wing and missing just 5 matches all season. His only goal for O's came on his debut at Hull City on 5 September 1908. He was then transferred to Southern League Southend United, for whom he played 9 times during 1909/10.

SEASON	LEAGUE		FA CUP		TOTAL	
	Apps	Gls	Apps	Gls	Apps	Gls
1908/09	33	1	0	0	33	1
TOTAL	33	1	0	0	33	1

Gerald WARD, 1963-65

Born in Stepney, London on 5 October 1936, Gerry Ward represented Leytonstone, London and Essex schoolboys. He was also an England schoolboy and youth international, and he later appeared for the England amateur team. He joined Arsenal as an amateur on 17 June 1952, and signed as a professional on his birthday in 1953. He made his League debut on 22 August 1953, and at the time was the youngest ever player to appear for the Gunners first team at 16 years and 321 days. Ward made 84 senior appearances and scored 10 goals, as well as playing in 307 reserve fixtures and scoring 78 goals between 1952 and 1963. He won numerous reserve-team Combination winner's medals. He joined O's for £8,000 on 12 July 1963, and played at inside forward during his first campaign, but moved to right half the following season. He did not fit in with the helter-skelter work-rate required by new O's boss Dave Sexton, and moved to Southern League side Cambridge City in May 1965. He then became a part-time player (and later manager) with Barnet until 1972, before moving to Sheffield and working for Midland Bank. He died in Sheffield in January 1994.

SEASON	LEAGUE		FA CUP		L. CUP	
	Apps	Gls	Apps	Gls	Apps	Gls
1963/64	22	2	0	0	1	0
1964/65	22	0	1	0	2	0
TOTAL	44	2	1	0	3	0

TOTAL APPS	48
TOTAL GOALS	2

Paul Terence WARD, 1988-89

Paul Ward – or 'Biffa', as he was nicknamed – was born on 15 September 1963 in Fishburn, Sedgefield, Durham. He came to O's in July 1988 as an experienced player with over 200 League appearances under his belt, and was a part of the team that secured promotion via the play-offs in June 1990, playing as a substitute in the two-legged final against Wrexham. Midfielder Ward started his career as an apprentice with Chelsea in August 1981, but made his mark at Middlesbrough after joining them in September 1982. During his three-year stay, he made 69(7) League appearances and scored once before signing for Darlington in September 1985. There he stayed for a further three

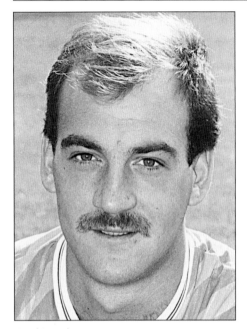

Paul Ward

SEASON	LEAGUE		FA CUP		L. CUP	
	Apps	Gls	Apps	Gls	Apps	Gls
1989/90*	28(3)	1	3	1	5	0
1990/91	2(1)	0	0	0	0	0
TOTAL	30(4)	1	3	1	5	0

TOTAL APPS	38(4)
TOTAL GOALS	2

* Paul Ward's record includes 3 playing appearances as a substitute in the play-offs during 1989/90. Ward also appeared in 3 Auto Windscreens Shield matches, scoring once.

years, making 124 League appearances and netting 9 goals. He became an 'Oriental' for £10,000 in July 1988, and he did well during the first part of the season at Brisbane Road. He looked to be a reasonably constructive and competitive player, and was appointed team captain. He appeared to suffer a loss of form and lost his first-team place for a while, but came good in the final matches when coming on as a substitute in those three play-off matches. After just a few starts the following season, he was sold to Scunthorpe United for an inflated fee of £45,000 in October 1989, staying for two seasons and scoring 7 goals from 64 (2) senior appearances. He moved to Lincoln City for £30,000 in March 1991, playing 38 League matches. Ward moved into management with Harrogate Town in February 1999, but left the following September.

Edward Alfred George WARE, 1933-36
Eddie Ware was born in Chatham, Kent on 17 September 1906. The left half started off with Chatham FC, before joining Brentford in 1928 and going on to make 96 League appearances during his six-year stay. He joined O's in August 1933 and proved to be another of O's boss Dave Pratt's shrewd captures – he was ever-present in his first season and spent two further wonderful seasons at Lea Bridge Road. Ware scored two goals when O's swamped Aldershot 9-2 in February 1934, and he also scored a goal in the 4-6 defeat by Scottish side Motherwell in a friendly in 1933/34. He was in the side that recorded a memorable 3-0 win over high-flying Charlton Athletic in the third round of the FA Cup in January 1936. With players Fogg, Heinemann and Taylor all pressing for his position, he was transferred to Swindon Town in July 1936 and played 5 League matches. In May 1937 he moved to Crewe Alexandra, and was ever-present in the 1937/38 season, making a total of 68 senior appearances. Ware was a hard-working industrious player, who would have succeeded in the modern game where a 'dynamo' was required.

He died in his native Chatham on 9 September 1976, one week before his seventieth birthday.

SEASON	LEAGUE		FA CUP		TOTAL	
	Apps	Gls	Apps	Gls	Apps	Gls
1933/34	42	2	3	0	45	2
1934/35	41	1	2	1	43	2
1935/36	23	0	3	0	26	0
TOTAL	106	3	8	1	114	4

* Eddie Ware also appeared in 2 Third Division Cup matches between 1933 and 1935.

Mark Wayne WARREN, 1991-99

It's quite ironic that Mark Warren should now be playing for Notts County because some six years earlier, a proposed £170,000 transfer to Nottingham Forest (to be Frank Clark's first signing as boss) was scuppered after a scan revealed an injury on the left side of his back. At the time this was a bitter blow for the youngster. Warren was, until his transfer, the

Mark Warren

longest serving player on O's books, having signed with the club on 8 July 1991. He made his O's League debut at Chester City on 2 May 1992, aged just seventeen. He made just over 150 League appearances during his eight seasons with the club, and was a player with good pace who always gave 100 per cent, despite sometimes getting into trouble with referees for his robust play. Born in Hackney, London on 12 November 1974, the defender was first spotted by O's scout Jimmy Hallybone whilst playing for the Cornet FC under-12 team. He then trained with O's before signing on as a YTS player. He played district football for Barking & Dagenham, and represented Essex schools at both under-15 and under-16 levels. Warren had an impressive run in 1992/93 before injuring his back at Bolton in March 1993. In February 1995 he scored a hat-trick, playing up front in O's 4-1 win over Peterborough United. He was voted Player of the Year in 1996/97, and the following season carried on from where he had left off, having his most productive season at the club and playing 41 matches. In September 1997 he scored O's fourth goal in a thrilling 4-4 draw against Bolton Wanderers at their new Reebok Stadium, and in August 1998 he hit O's extra-time winner in a 2-1 League Cup win at Bristol Rovers. During 1998/99 he refused to sign a new contract, and had loan spells with West Ham and Northampton Town. After another loan spell, this time with Oxford United in December 1998 (for whom he made 4 League appearances), the twenty-four-year-old Warren was snapped up by Notts County manager Sam Allardyce on 28 January 1999. Allardyce stated that he had long admired the player, and that he had bought him for a 'steal'. Warren has been a regular and has made over 90 senior appearances for County up to February 2002, scoring once.

SEASON	LEAGUE		FA CUP		L. CUP	
	Apps	Gls	Apps	Gls	Apps	Gls
1991/92	0(1)	0	0	0	0	0
1992/93	14	0	1	0	0	0
1993/94	5(1)	0	0	0	0	0
1994/95	24(7)	3	0	0	1	0
1995/96	15(7)	1	0	0	2	0
1996/97	25(2)	1	2	0	0	0
1997/98	41	0	2	0	4	1
1998/99	10	0	0(1)	0	1(1)	1
TOTAL	134(18)	5	5(1)	0	8(1)	2

TOTAL APPS	147(20)
TOTAL GOALS	7

* Mark Warren also appeared in 10(4) Auto Windscreens Shield matches, scoring once.

Albert WATERALL, 1926-27

Albert Waterall joined O's from Queens Park Rangers in October 1926 at the veteran age of almost thirty-nine. He scored on his debut against Nottingham Forest in a 2-2 draw on 23 October. After playing at centre half in the following match – a 6-1 defeat at Manchester City – he was not seen ever again. Born in Radford, Nottingham on 1 March 1887, Waterall started as an inside forward with local side Notts County in 1910, and during three seasons he made 26 League appearances and scored once. He moved to Stockport in 1913, and had a wonderful nine years with Cheshire club, making a grand total of 289 League appearances and scoring 36 goals. He joined Queens Park Rangers in 1926, where he made just two League appearances. Waterall died on 8 March 1963 (just a week after

his seventy-sixth birthday) in Basford, Nottingham.

SEASON	LEAGUE		FA CUP		TOTAL	
	Apps	Gls	Apps	Gls	Apps	Gls
1926/27	2	1	0	0	2	1
TOTAL	2	1	0	0	2	1

George Sutton WATSON, 1931

Born in Milton Regis on 9 April 1907, Watson started his career with Casuals FC before joining Charlton Athletic in 1929, making 14 League appearances and scoring twice. After a short spell with Maidstone United in March 1930, he signed for Crystal Palace the following August, but made just 2 League appearances. The winger joined O's in August 1931, getting his chance due to injuries to both Hales and Rollo Jack. He played 2 matches over the Christmas holiday period – both of which were against Bournemouth & Boscombe – losing at home on Christmas Day (1-2) and then winning away on Boxing Day (1-0). He joined Nuneaton Borough in January 1932. Watson died in Guildford on 1 April 1974, nine days before his sixty-seventh birthday.

SEASON	LEAGUE		FA CUP		TOTAL	
	Apps	Gls	Apps	Gls	Apps	Gls
1931/32	2	0	0	0	2	0
TOTAL	2	0	0	0	2	0

Mark Leon WATSON, 1995 (loan)

Born in Birmingham on 28 December 1973, Watson hit the headlines when he scored over 60 goals for Sutton United between 1994 and 1995. He signed for the Hammers in a £50,000 deal during May 1995, after performing well on their pre-season tour of Australia, but made just a single League appearance as a substitute. The striker came to O's on loan from West Ham United on 4 September 1995, appearing just once as a substitute and scoring with a corker of an overhead kick at Plymouth Argyle on 9 September in a 1-1 draw. To celebrate Watson's goal, one visiting O's fan will be remembered for doing an impressive break-dance routine in front of the bemused home fans. After his very brief spell at Brisbane Road, he then went on loan to Cambridge United in October 1995 and scored once from 1(3) League appearances. During February 1996 he was on loan at Shrewsbury Town, but made just a single League appearance. Watson was transferred to Shrewsbury permanently for £100,000 on February 1996, making just 6(9) League matches and netting once. He then drifted into non-League football in August 1997, moving to Welling United on a free transfer and making 4 senior appearances. He moved back to Sutton United in March 1998, and found his scoring boots again, with 11 goals from 24(11) matches. He scored a total of 78 goals from 163 games during his two spells with Sutton. He signed for Football Conference side Woking for £8,000 in May 2000. Having made 8(5) Football Conference appearances, he scored once up to October 2000. He then joined Chesham United and then Aldershot Town in March 2001.

SEASON	LEAGUE		FA CUP		L. CUP	
	Apps	Gls	Apps	Gls	Apps	Gls
1995/96	0(1)	1	0	0	0	0
TOTAL	0(1)	1	0	0	0	0

TOTAL APPS	0(1)	
TOTAL GOALS	1	

Ernest Albert WATTS, 1906-07

Ernie Watts played at right half in Reading's very first senior fixture at Elm Park against a Mr A. Roston Bourke's London XI on 5 September 1896. He later played at right half for both Reading (in the Southern League between 1896 and 1898) and First Division side Notts County (in 1898), yet with O's he made his only 2 League appearances in 1906/07 as an emergency goalkeeper. Born in Woolhampton, near Newbury, Berkshire in 1874 (some records show 1872), he started his career with Reading and made his senior debut in an FA Cup tie against Bedminster FC in September 1896. He made 2 further FA Cup appearances that season. He then joined Notts County in 1898 and made his League debut at right half in a First Division fixture against Liverpool on 27 December 1898, which ended 1-1. He made 17 senior appearances for County in 1898/99, and wore the number four shirt in 11 games and the number six shirt on 7 occasions. In August 1899 he returned to Reading, who were then playing in the First Division of the Southern League, and appeared in their 8-0 victory over Wycombe Wanderers in an FA Cup third qualifying round tie during October 1899. During his six-year stay, he made over 100 Southern League appearances and appeared in 17 FA Cup ties. He was also an excellent cricketer and represented Berkshire. He joined O's in May 1906, and was in the squad of players that went away over the Christmas and New Year period, when O's had three consecutive away League fixtures. In the first match at Wolverhampton Wanderers on 27 December, goalkeeper Billy Bower received an injury early on in the match and had to leave the field – the match was lost 6-1. Bower was not fit enough to play in the second match two days later at Stockport County, so Ernie Watts stepped in between the sticks and he played quite well in a 1-1 draw. He kept his place at Barnsley on News Year's Day, but O's went down 3-2, so the stand-in goalkeeper had done quite well. A local paper reported that he enjoyed the experience so much that in a reserve fixture against Eastbourne FC he again played in goal. He strode out of his goal and ran up the field to slam home a great goal from fully fifty yards. Watts left O's in May 1907 and returned to play for Reading.

SEASON	LEAGUE		FA CUP		TOTAL	
	Apps	Gls	Apps	Gls	Apps	Gls
1906/07	2	0	0	0	2	0
TOTAL	2	0	0	0	2	0

Steven WATTS, 1998-present

Steve Watts' story is quite the fairy-tale: the twenty-three-year-old was chosen

Steve Watts

from 850 hopefuls who entered the *Sun* newspaper/Bravo TV 'Search for a Striker' competition, the prize from which was a professional contract with the O's. It was Watts who won the competition, and he signed a two-year contract on 14 October 1998, with a fee of £6,000 going to Fisher Athletic. Born in Peckham, London on 11 July 1976, Watts had spells as a schoolboy with both Millwall and Tottenham Hotspur, but both rejected him for being too small. He played non-League football for Dulwich Hamlet and was then was spotted by a scout from Charlton Athletic. He went for a trial but received an injury to his knee ligaments and was out of action of eight months. By the time he had recovered, his chance at the Valley had gone. Watts was signed by Fisher Athletic – a Dr Martens Southern Division side – on 1 August 1997 and he scored 29 goals for them. He had already struck 9 goals from 11 matches in 1998/99 when he joined O's. O's chief scout Len Cheesewright said: 'Steve has two good feet, is very good in the air and is very competitive. Most importantly, he can make and score goals. I've watched him five times and he has scored every time.' Watts himself admitted: 'I saw details about the competition, but I was so nervous before the trial, I almost threw up. I've never been so close before, I just wanted to prove I was good enough.' Watts was a printer by trade, but he gave that up to become a professional footballer. He soon showed the O's fans of his potential, scoring twice from 4 substitute starts, including the winning goal against Brentford and a wonderful twenty-yard strike at Plymouth Argyle. There were rumours of interest in Watts from a number of clubs, including Birmingham City, Queens Park

Rangers and Torquay United. In the end he went on a month's loan to Welling United in November 1999, and scored 3 goals from 4 starts at Park View Road. He also had a loan spell with Aldershot Town in July 2000. During the 2000/01 season, he become known as the 'super sub', coming off the bench to score a number of important goals, but with the abundance of 'loan' strikers at the club, he found it difficult to break into the team. However, it was Watts who scored the goal against Newcastle United to earn a 1-1 draw in the Worthington Cup in September 2000, and he also showed some neat touches in an FA Cup third round match against Tottenham Hotspur on 6 January 2001 – a game that O's lost 1-0 in the ninety-second minute. He sustained a bad cartilage injury against Brighton & Hove Albion on 3 March 2001, which kept him out of the side for over a month. Watts has not really lived up to expectations, but then again, some may say he hasn't really been given a regular opportunity to show his worth. However, he scored the opener against Hull City just before half-time in the second leg of the play-off, heading home a Houghton cross to help O's on their way to the final against Blackpool. Sadly, Watts received a second yellow card late in the game and was sent off, so like his strike partner Carl Griffiths (also under suspension), he missed the play-off final at the Millennium Stadium. Watts was offered a one-year extension to his contract during June 2001, but rumour had it that he might possibly be off to Millwall. He committed himself to O's by signing a three-year contract in July 2001, but he struggled during the early part of the new season with a prolonged back injury.

SEASON	LEAGUE		FA CUP		L. CUP	
	Apps	Gls	Apps	Gls	Apps	Gls
1998/99*	13(18)	6	0	0	0	0
1999/2000	21(11)	6	1(1)	0	2(1)	1
2000/01**	16(22)	9	3(1)	1	2(1)	1
2001/02	22(8)	9	4	3	1	0
TOTAL	72(59)	30	8(2)	4	5(2)	2

TOTAL APPS	85(63)	
TOTAL GOALS	36	

* Steve Watts' League record includes 3 play-off appearances in 1998/99.

** Watts' League record includes 2 play-off appearances and a goal in 2000/01. Watts also appeared in an Auto Windscreens Shield match.

Luke Dennis Spencer WEAVER, 1996-97
Weaver was born in Woolwich, London on 26 June 1979. He was capped by England at youth level and signed for O's on 26 June 1996. Weaver made his League debut as a seventeen-year-old against Scarborough on 29 October 1996. He soon impressed and he was watched by scouts from West Ham United, Manchester United, Sunderland, Sheffield Wednesday, Coventry City and Aston Villa. Weaver went on loan to the Hammers on 19 March 1997 for a couple of months, and he also spent some time with Peter Schmeichel at Old Trafford to learn his trade. O's chairman Barry Hearn informed the press: 'I've ruled out any possibility of selling Weaver. He's not going anywhere, but if he did, it would be for a lot of money.' However, on 9 January 1998, Sunderland boss Peter Reid came in with a firm offer of £250,000 for the 'keeper, after he had trained in the North-East for a few days. Weaver said: 'I was a bit surprised with how it all happened within a week, it hasn't really sunk in yet, they offered me quite a good deal, I don't

mind moving away especially as Sunderland are a very big club.' Unfortunately, Weaver suffered a broken jaw in his first reserve match for Sunderland, which ruled him out for the rest of the season. On 10 December 1998, he went on loan to Scarborough in order to gain a taste of first-team action – there he made 6 League appearances. Peter Reid said: 'We rate Luke very highly, but we have got Thomas Sorenson and Andy Marriott ahead of him at senior level.' His loan spell with Scarborough was not too happy, Weaver conceding 11 goals in 4 defeats. He returned to Sunderland in January 1999 after sustaining a knee injury, and was still yet to make that first-team debut. In fact, he made just a single reserve appearance for Sunderland in 1998/99. The twenty-year-old 'keeper joined Carlisle United on a month's loan for the start of the 1999/2000 season, making his debut in their 2-1 win over O's on 7 August 1999. He signed a four-year contract with Carlisle on 26 August 1999, joining on a free transfer plus 50 per cent of any future fee. Remarkably, Luke Weaver left Sunderland without ever having made a first-team appearance. After 39 senior appearances for Carlisle, his last match being on 21 October 2000 – a 4-2 defeat at Torquay United. Weaver did not feature again due to an ongoing injury – he was placed on the transfer list in February 2001 and was not on the retained list the following May. Weaver was still in the Carlisle squad for the 2001/02 season, and starred when helping Carlisle to a share of the points in a 0-0 draw at Brisbane Road in August 2001. However, his season turned sour with a run of poor displays, leaking 14 goals in 7 matches. He lost confidence and was ordered by the Carlisle manager, Roddy

Collins, to take a three-week break and stay well away from football in order to get his head right. After leaving Carlisle, Luke Weaver went to Northampton Town on trial. He made his debut for the Cobblers in their 3-1 defeat at Leyton Orient.

SEASON	LEAGUE		FA CUP		L. CUP	
	Apps	Gls	Apps	Gls	Apps	Gls
1996/97	9	0	1	0	0	0
TOTAL	9	0	1	0	0	0

TOTAL APPS	10
TOTAL GOALS	0

* Luke Weaver also appeared in an Auto Windscreens Shield match.

David James WEBB, 1964-66

Young David Webb joined O's from West Ham juniors in May 1963 and became one of the great talents of the post-war era. The player with the famous crew-cut hairstyle was an all-action player, a hard runner and a strong tackler, and he was to become the darling of the O's fans. He was a player with a great sense of humour who would do anything for a laugh. Born in Stratford, London on 9 April 1946, he made his League debut in a 5-2 victory over Portsmouth on 22 August 1964. Also making his League debut that day was another youngster, Terry Price. Webb played at centre half that day, but soon settled down in the full-back position. He played his part in O's battle to avoid relegation in 1965/66, and it was no surprise that with O's so close to the drop into the Third Division, he was transferred to Southampton in March 1966. The fee was £23,000, with George O'Brien making the trip to London as part of the deal. He stayed at the Dell for two seasons, mak-

David Webb

ing 75 League appearances and scoring 2 goals. He then joined Chelsea for £40,000, with defender Joe Kirkup going to the Saints. Webb scored the Blues' winner when he rose to head home in the 104th minute of extra time in an FA Cup final replay against Leeds United at Old Trafford in May 1970 – the first ever 'replayed' final. He was in the winning side that beat Real Madrid in the 1971 European Cup-winner's Cup final after a replay, and he was also in their side that was dumped out of the FA Cup by the O's at Brisbane Road. It was Barrie Fairbrother who slipped the ball past a diving Webb to secure a famous 3-2 victory in the final minute in February 1972. As a midfielder, he played in their League Cup final defeat by Stoke City in 1972. He remained at Stamford Bridge for six seasons, making 299 senior appearances and scoring 33 goals. In July 1974 he moved on to Queens Park Rangers for £100,000,

making a further 116 League appearances and scoring 7 goals. He moved to Leicester City in September 1977 for £50,000, making 32(1) League appearances. Webb later played for Derby County, AFC Bournemouth and Torquay United. Webb made a career total of 550(2) League appearances and scored 34 goals. He began his managerial career with AFC Bournemouth from December 1980 and stayed for fourteen months. His next post was at Torquay United, where he remained for eighteen months. A year after leaving Torquay, he began a long association with Southend United, and during the 1986/87 season, he took them to 20 wins from 37 games with 10 losses. After a short time away, he rejoined the 'Shrimpers' in November 1988, and stayed until May 1992, taking charge for a total of 181 games. In 1993 he had a brief spell as caretaker boss of Chelsea, spending three months in charge before the appointment of Glenn Hoddle. After his short time at Stamford Bridge, he went to Brentford and stayed there for over four years until August 1997. There he got a further 216 games under his belt, winning 85 and losing 66. He was given a place on the club's board, but left Griffin Park under a cloud when Ron Noades took over. After a successful six months with Football Conference side Yeovil, he went back to the 'Shrimpers' in October 2000, saying he wanted to bring back the fun, laughter and joy of his previous time on the coast. Webb also runs a wholesale/retail business and a successful property company in Dorset. He missed the start of the 2001/02 season, after being told by doctors to take a rest, and his future at Roots Hall was in doubt. Fifty-five-year-old Webb decided to quit, but had not ruled out going back into soccer management at a later time. For now he just watches his son, Daniel, play.

SEASON	LEAGUE		FA CUP		L. CUP	
	Apps	Gls	Apps	Gls	Apps	Gls
1964/65	33	0	0	0	2	0
1965/66	29	3	1	0	1	0
TOTAL	63	3	1	0	3	0

TOTAL APPS	66
TOTAL GOALS	3

Simon WEBB, 1999/2000

Born in Castle Bar, Dublin on 19 January 1978, the left-back/midfielder started as a trainee with Tottenham Hotspur in July 1994, signing professional forms in January 1995. He won 13 Eire schoolboy caps, as well as caps at under-18 level. After playing 7(3) reserve matches during 1998/99 and playing just twice during 1999/2000 due to an injury, he joined O's on 8 October 1999 and made his debut at York City the following day. However, he could not find a regular place in the first team and went on trial with Chester City in February 2000 and on loan the following month with Purfleet. In July 2000 he moved back to Ireland to join Bohemians, teaming up with former 'Orientals' Mark Dempsey and Dave Morrison and appearing in the 'Bohs' UEFA campaign.

SEASON	LEAGUE		FA CUP		L. CUP	
	Apps	Gls	Apps	Gls	Apps	Gls
1999/2000	3(1)	0	0	0	0	0
TOTAL	3(1)	0	0	0	0	0

TOTAL APPS	3(1)
TOTAL GOALS	0

Roger WEDGE, 1961-63

Roger Wedge, the 5ft 11in winger, was a player who showed a lot of promise. He was adept at running with the ball and had a good eye for goal, but was never given a chance in the first team. Born on 6 March 1944 in Preston Park, Brighton, his family had moved from the Leyton area to Brighton during the Second World War. Upon leaving school he joined the groundstaff at Brighton & Hove Albion in 1958 and played at centre forward for the club. His family later moved back to the East End of London, and he was signed up by the West Ham United scout, Wally St Pier. He made his youth debut on 4 March 1961 and netted 7 goals from just 4 matches. When he was seventeen he went to see Hammers boss Ron Greenwood about a professional contract, but was told to wait for another six months. Wedge disagreed and stormed out of the boss's office. A couple of weeks later, Wedge received a call from O's coach Eddie Baily, who asked him to come to Brisbane Road for a trial. He played alongside Harry Gregory up front against Crittals Athletic in an FA Cup youth match – O's won 14-2, Wedge hit 4 goals and Gregory a hat-trick. He was then given a run-out in a reserve fixture against Birmingham City, scoring twice in a 4-0 victory. Wedge signed professional forms on 30 October 1961. He thought his big chance had come in the FA Cup replay against high-flying Burnley in February 1962 when Phil White reported in with 'flu, but in the end, O's manager Johnny Carey decided to play a 60 per cent fit White, and Wedge watched the match from the dugout. He could never break into the first team, with McDonald, White, Elwood and new signing Musgrove fighting for the wing berths, boss Carey preferring to stick to experience. He did get one run-out and played in the record 9-2 win over Chester City in the

League Cup on 17 October 1962. He played reasonably well and deserved another chance, but it never came. In May 1963 he was given a free transfer and joined Tunbridge Wells. Wedge then spent three years at Margate (25 appearances and 7 goals) and later joined Peter Sillett at Ashford Town. Between 1978 and 1980 he was at Hastings United and then Canterbury City. In 1982 he was appointed as the manager of Eastbourne United, and more recently he has been involved with Horsham FC and Shoreham FC. He gave up his involvement in football about four years ago to run the Preston Park Sports Tavern and has just signed a new fifteen-year lease. Wedge is a great follower of Brighton & Hove Albion, and often travelled to the Matchroom to watch the Seagulls in action to relive what might have been.

SEASON	LEAGUE		FA CUP		L. CUP	
	Apps	Gls	Apps	Gls	Apps	Gls
1962/63	0	0	0	0	1	0
TOTAL	0	0	0	0	1	0

TOTAL APPS	1
TOTAL GOALS	0

Peter Alan WELLS, 1985-89

Born in Nottingham on 13 August 1956, goalkeeper Peter Wells started off as an apprentice with Nottingham Forest in October 1974, making his debut in May 1975 and chalking up a total of 27 League appearances. He joined Southampton for £8,000 in December 1976 and stayed for seven years, making 141 League appearances before losing his place to Peter Shilton. He joined Millwall in February 1983. After playing 33 League matches for the Lions, he joined O's in July 1985 and proved to be a very reliable goalie for three seasons, until he broke a bone in his ankle during training and was replaced by David Cass. His days were numbered with the arrival of young Paul Heald from Sheffield United in December 1988, and he was released in May 1989 to join Fisher Athletic.

SEASON	LEAGUE		FA CUP		L. CUP	
	Apps	Gls	Apps	Gls	Apps	Gls
1985/86	45	0	6	0	4	0
1986/87	39	0	4	0	2	0
1987/88	46	0	4	0	2	0
1988/89	18	0	3	0	5	0
TOTAL	148	0	17	0	13	0

TOTAL APPS	178
TOTAL GOALS	0

* Peter Wells also appeared in 8 Auto Windscreens Shield matches.

Thomas Charles WELLS, 1936-37

Tommy Wells was born in Nunhead near Peckham, London on 21 September 1905. He started off as an amateur with Arsenal in 1925, but it was with Northampton Town that the winger made his mark. He joined them in May 1926 and scored 74 goals from his 279 League appearances for the Cobblers. He was a first-team regular throughout his nine years with the club. Wells moved to Swindon Town in May 1935 and during his only season at the County Ground, he made 34 League appearances and scored 7 goals. He also won a Third Division (South) runners-up medal. The thirty-two-year-old became an 'Oriental' in May 1936, and was one of seven players tried at outside left during the season. He retired from the game in May 1937. Wells died in Eastbourne on 13 August 1971, a month before his sixty-sixth birthday.

SEASON	LEAGUE		FA CUP		TOTAL	
	Apps	Gls	Apps	Gls	Apps	Gls
1936/37	4	1	0	0	4	1
TOTAL	4	1	0	0	4	1

* Tommy Wells also appeared in a Third Division Cup match in 1936/37, scoring once.

Roy Patrick WELTON, 1949-58

Pat Welton was one of O's finest goal-keepers of the post-war era. Born in Eltham on 3 May 1928, he started off with Chiselhurst FC before joining O's in May 1949 as an amateur. He was a PE teacher at a public school before turning professional later in that season. The solidly built goalkeeper had a traumatic baptism into the League when Notts County (with the legendary Tommy Lawton) hit 7 goals past him on 1 October 1949. The following week, O's lost 2-0 at Aldershot. He was replaced by Polish goalkeeper Stan Gerula for a while, but O's boss Alec Stock restored Welton to the team in

Pat Welton

December. However, after two further defeats he was again replaced, this time replaced by Sid Hobbins. Welton came back in March 1950 and was the regular 'keeper for the following six seasons. However, he had to share the green jersey with Dave Groombridge and Frank George between 1956 and 1958. He was a member of the team that won the Third Division (South) Championship in May 1956. Thirty-year-old Welton was transferred to Queens Park Rangers in March 1958, playing just 3 League matches and letting in 7 goals. He was appointed manager of St Albans FC, and later managed Walthamstow Avenue. He held a coaching position with the England youth side and was a youth-team coach at Tottenham Hotspur from 1969 to July 1976. He was then appointed Spurs' assistant manager, before moving overseas.

SEASON	LEAGUE		FA CUP		TOTAL	
	Apps	Gls	Apps	Gls	Apps	Gls
1949/50	16	0	0	0	16	0
1950/51	46	0	1	0	47	0
1951/52	41	0	9	0	50	0
1952/53	23	0	0	0	23	0
1953/54	16	0	1	0	17	0
1954/55	43	0	2	0	45	0
1955/56	46	0	4	0	50	0
1956/57	17	0	1	0	18	0
1957/58	15	0	0	0	15	0
TOTAL	263	0	18	0	281	0

Paul Frank WENT, 1965-67

Paul Went holds some unique records in the folklore of the club. He is the youngest player ever to appear for the O's in the League, at the age of 15 years and 327 days. He also holds the record for the shortest time spent as manager of the O's manager – he spent just twenty-one days in charge between September

Paul Went

then record fee of £24,250 to help O's out of one of its worst financial crises, and it was this money which saved the club from closure. He was the kingpin at the Valley for five seasons, making 160(3) League appearances and scoring a total of 15 goals. He was signed by Fulham for £80,000 on 7 July 1982 (on the same day as Alan Mullery) by boss Alec Stock, in an attempt to strengthen an ailing side. However, eighteen months later, after appearing in 58 League matches and scoring 3 goals, he moved to Portsmouth for £155,000 in December 1973, a then club record fee. Both he and Steve Earle were sacrificed in an effort to repay some of monies due on their new Riverside Stand and keep Fulham afloat. He stayed at Pompey for nearly three years, making 92 League appearances and scoring 5 goals, before yet again Went was sold for a give-away fee of £30,000 to Cardiff City on 8 October 1976, in order to help the club stave off the threat of bankruptcy. He was with the Bluebirds for two years, making 71(1) League appearances and scoring 11 goals, before returning 'home' to become an 'Oriental' for the second time on 7 September 1978. This time the fee was £20,000 and the transfer took place a month before his twenty-ninth birthday. During his second spell with O's, Went was troubled with leg and shoulder injuries, and his last League appearance was in the 7-3 home defeat by Chelsea in November 1979. He retired from playing and was appointed reserve coach and club scout. He took charge of the side during the latter part of the 1980/81 season as caretaker manager, when boss Jimmy Bloomfield was hospitalised. Went made a career total of 474(6) League appearances and scored 42 goals between 1965 and 1979.

and October 1981, one of the shortest reigns in League history. Went also spent his whole career playing for a series of hard-up teams, and often found himself being sold to keep clubs like O's, Fulham and Portsmouth afloat. Born in Bromley-By-Bow, London on 12 October 1949, the son of an Italian mother, he attended a number of local schools in the area, including Whitechapel, St Agnes School, St Bernard's Secondary School and Morpeth School in Bethnal Green. He also represented East London schools and won 6 caps for England schoolboys and 10 youth caps. He started with O's as an apprentice in August 1965, and he made his League debut on 4 September 1965 against Preston North End in a 2-2 draw – O's first point of that season. Went signed professional forms in October 1966 and he shone regularly during the following season. He was sold to Charlton Athletic on 8 June 1967 for a

SEASON	LEAGUE		FA CUP		L. CUP	
	Apps	Gls	Apps	Gls	Apps	Gls
1965/66	9(2)	0	0	0	1	0
1966/67	39	5	3	0	1	0
1967/68	37	2	3	0	0	0
1968/69	8	1	0	0	0	0
TOTAL	93(2)	8	6	0	2	0

TOTAL APPS	101(2)
TOTAL GOALS	8

Edwin WERGE, 1966-68

Eddie Werge was born in Sidcup, Kent on 9 September 1936. He started his career as a junior with Bexleyheath FC, before joining Charlton Athletic in May 1955. He spent several seasons at the Valley, making 44 League appearances and scoring 19 goals. The winger moved to Crystal Palace in May 1961 for £3,160 and stayed with the Eagles for four years, making 82 League matches and netting 6 goals. He moved to South Africa and played for Pretoria-based side Arcadia Shepherds during the 1965/66 season. He returned to England in November 1966 and joined up with his former Palace team boss Dick Graham at cash-strapped O's. He proved to be a useful capture due to his versatility, and played in midfield, on the wing and at full-back, assisting O's through a tough period when the boss often struggled to put out a fit team. In January 1968 he left to join Bexley United.

SEASON	LEAGUE		FA CUP		L. CUP	
	Apps	Gls	Apps	Gls	Apps	Gls
1966/67	22	0	1	0	0	0
1967/68	8(3)	0	0(1)	0	1	0
TOTAL	30(3)	0	1(1)	0	1	0

TOTAL APPS	32(4)
TOTAL GOALS	0

Colin WEST, 1993-98

A proven striker over the years, West has not always been a crowd-pleaser, but he has let his goalscoring ability do his talking for him. The thirty-year-old came to O's with a wealth of valuable experience, and there linked up with Peter Eustace and Chris Turner, following his time with them at both Sunderland and Sheffield Wednesday. West joined Orient from Swansea City on 9 July 1993, after a long and distinguished career of 86 League goals for seven clubs. His goalscoring didn't stop there, and he went on to become a member of the 100 League goals club. He has proved to be one of the most prolific goalscorers at the club, along with Mark Cooper, over the past decade. Born on 13 November 1962 in Wallsend, West started his career with Sunderland as an apprentice. Perhaps the highlight of his career came during the mid-1980s when winning a Scottish League title and a Scottish Cup winner's

Colin West

medal with Glasgow Rangers. It was reported that 'Westie' came to O's from Swansea on a free transfer, but in fact, the friendly Geordie had another year to run on his contract at Vetch Field, and according to O's boss Eustace, the club had to pay a 'reasonable fee' for him. Eustace said: 'I wanted to bring Colin to this club when he was at West Brom last year, but we didn't have the financial resources at the time. He is vastly experienced, has power and a brilliant goal-scoring record – his ability just what this club needs.' West scored on his O's debut against Burnley and he certainly didn't let O's down, scoring 46 senior goals whilst at the club. He seemed to come in for some rough treatment from the 'boo boys' though, and was barracked on numerous occasions. In one match against Hartlepool United, he gave the proverbial two fingers to the 'boo boys', scoring twice and setting up two more goals in a 4-1 win on 16 September 1995. Westie's goals rank him in the top twenty in O's all-time goalscoring list since 1905. After a loan spell with Rushden & Diamonds in the Football Conference during January 1998, the move was made permanent a month later, for the same fee that was paid for him by O's back in 1993. At the age of thirty-six he was still amongst the goals, hitting a brace in Rushden's 4-2 FA Cup victory that gave them a place in the third round against Leeds United in January 1999. He netted 5 League and cup goals from 19 starts in 1998/99. He was then appointed Rushden's reserve-team manager, and his charges were reserve League champions and also won the Capital League Cup. He moved to Northwich Victoria before being appointed as the assistant manager and coach for former 'Oriental' Chris Turner

at Hartlepool United on 2 November 1999. They retained his player registration, and he made two substitute appearances in 1999/2000. Turner stated: 'I am delighted to have Colin on the staff. He will be a major help to myself, but most importantly to the players. His experience within the game is there for all to see, and the list of clubs and managers he has played with speaks for itself – he has scored over 150 senior goals.' Turner and West took Hartlepool to a top four spot within two years, but were knocked out by Blackpool in the play-off semi-final, 5-1 on aggregate.

SEASON	LEAGUE		FA CUP		L. CUP	
	Apps	Gls	Apps	Gls	Apps	Gls
1993/94	42(1)	15	2	0	0	0
1994/95	27(3)	9	2	1	2	0
1995/96	39	16	1	0	1	1
1996/97	22(1)	3	2	1	2	1
1997/98	2(5)	0	0	0	1	0
TOTAL	132(10)	43	7	2	6	2

TOTAL APPS	145(10)
TOTAL GOALS	46

* Colin West also appeared in 9 Auto Windscreens Shield matches, scoring 4 goals.

** West also scored 29 Cup goals from 72(12) appearances.

Jonathan WESTCOTT, 1905-06

Shoreditch-born John Westcott joined O's from local amateur football and played out the season in the reserves. He got his chance in an FA Cup first round qualifying match playing at centre forward at Felstead on 7 October 1905 – three other players were making their only first-team appearance that day as well. The chance came only because the first team were ordered by the Football

Association to play a League fixture at Millfields Road against Barnsley on the same day as the Felstead Cup tie. Westcott left the club in May 1905.

SEASON	LEAGUE		FA CUP		TOTAL	
	Apps	Gls	Apps	Gls	Apps	Gls
1905/06	0	0	1	0	1	0
TOTAL	0	0	1	0	1	0

Percival WHIPP, 1921-22, 1927-29

Percy Whipp was born in the Gorbals, Glasgow on 28 June 1897. He moved to London as a boy and started his career with junior side West London Old Boys FC. He first attracted attention when showing excellent skill for a Hammersmith League XI against Fulham reserves. His first professional outfit in May 1920 was Welsh side Ton Pentre FC, and he then became an 'Oriental' in May 1921. The inside forward was given an opportunity by O's boss 'Doc' Holmes at Notts County on 22 October 1921, and he looked a lively player with an eye for goal, notching 8 goals for the season and finishing just three behind top scorer Clatworthy Rennox. Sunderland signed Whipp for £500 on 1 June 1922, as understudy to the famous Charles Buchan. He made his only League appearance at Bolton Wanderers in September 1922. After just five months at Roker Park, he joined Leeds United for £750 on 3 November 1922 and scored three goals (including a penalty) on his senior debut against West Ham United in November 1922. He ended the season as their top goal scorer on 16 senior goals. A player of rare cunning, Whipp (who was nicknamed 'The Arch General' by Leeds fans) was at Elland Road for five seasons, winning a Second Division Championship medal in 1924 and scoring 47 goals from

154 senior appearances. He rejoined O's in June 1927 and topped the goal charts, playing in the epic FA Cup fourth round tie at Aston Villa. O's held the mighty Villa to a 0-0 draw in the Midlands on 26 January 1929, in front of a 53,086-strong crowd – the largest ever to witness a match featuring O's. In May 1929 he joined Brentford, making just 7 League appearances and scoring 2 goals. The following season, the thirty-three-year-old Whipp signed for Swindon Town and netted 5 goals from 9 League appearances. In August 1931, he moved to Bath City.

SEASON	LEAGUE		FA CUP		TOTAL	
	Apps	Gls	Apps	Gls	Apps	Gls
1921/22	20	8	1	0	21	8
1927/28	39	12	1	1	40	13
1928/29	29	5	4	0	33	5
TOTAL	88	25	6	1	94	26

Adrian Richard WHITBREAD, 1989-93

Twenty-year-old Adrian Whitbread was handed the team captaincy in 1992 to become the youngest skipper in the League at that time. The role was to be awarded to Terry Howard, but at the time, he was out of contract. Whitbread was a dominant centre-back, who was always cool under pressure. He was born in Epping, Essex on 22 October 1971, and joined the club's School of Excellence Academy at the age of twelve. He came up through the ranks and served his apprenticeship, finally signing as a professional on 13 November 1989. He made his League debut at Brentford on 3 December 1989, and after four seasons at the club, he was transferred to newly promoted Premiership side Swindon Town for £500,000 on 30 July 1993. O's boss Peter Eustace stated: 'Adrian has done every-

Adrian Whitbread

Town in November 2000 and made a total of 13 senior appearances. Twenty-nine-year-old Whitbread went on loan to Division Two side Reading, making his debut in their 2-1 win at Brentford on 9 February 2001, and made over 20 League appearances up to the end of the season. He finally signed a two-year contract with the Royals on 5 July 2001.

SEASON	LEAGUE		FA CUP		L. CUP	
	Apps	Gls	Apps	Gls	Apps	Gls
1989/90	8	0	0	0	0	0
1990/91	38	0	5	0	5(1)	0
1991/92	43	1	5	0	3	0
1992/93	36	1	1	1	2	0
TOTAL	125	2	11	1	10(1)	0

TOTAL APPS	146(1)
TOTAL GOALS	3

* Adrian Whitbread also appeared in 8 Auto Windscreens matches.

thing I've asked of him since I joined the club, now he's going to a Premier League side. He deserves his chance.' He made 35(1) League appearances and scored once for the Wiltshire side, before being snapped up by West Ham United for £650,000 on 17 August 1994. A foot injury sidelined him for six months at Upton Park, and he failed in to break into the first team, playing just 5(7) senior matches. He went on a three-month loan spell at Portsmouth from November 1995, and made 13 League appearances before the move was made permanent in October 1996 for £250,000. He became Pompey's team captain and made 133(1) League appearances (scoring 2 goals). A knee injury ruled him out of the start of the 2000/01 season, and he then fell out of favour with player-manager Steve Claridge and was told he could leave. He went on a two-month loan period to Division Two side Luton

Philip George John WHITE, 1953-64

Phil White was an exceptionally gifted right-winger who would have received international honours, had he played for a more glamorous club. When his chance did come for a £15,000 move to Liverpool, White himself turned down the chance, deciding to remain with O's throughout his professional career. He was a frail-looking player who relied on both skill and speed. White was born on 29 December 1930 near Craven Cottage in Fulham. He was signed by Alec Stock from Wealdstone FC and was brought along slowly in the reserves. When Vic Groves moved to Arsenal, he became an automatic choice. He came to the fore during the championship-winning season of 1955/56, turning in some scintillating displays. He played a

Phil White

SEASON	LEAGUE		FA CUP		L. CUP	
	Apps	Gls	Apps	Gls	Apps	Gls
1953/54	5	2	0	0	-	-
1954/55	3	0	0	0	-	-
1955/56	28	3	2	0	-	-
1956/57	36	6	1	0	-	-
1957/58	29	5	1	0	-	-
1958/59	35	5	0	0	-	-
1959/60	23	0	1	0	-	-
1960/61	23	1	1	0	3	0
1961/62	30	6	4	0	3	0
1962/63	0	0	0	0	0	0
1963/64	5	0	0	0	0	0
TOTAL	217	28	10	0	6	0

TOTAL APPS   233

TOTAL GOALS   28

* The League Cup competition commenced in 1960/61.

big part in the O's side that gained promotion to the First Division in 1961/62, but he then sustained a very bad leg injury. This denied him a run in the First Division, and after a handful of matches between October and November 1963, he eventually retired in 1964, and the club staged a well-earned benefit for him. Phil White is perhaps one of football's most underrated players ever. Away from Brisbane Road, he was hardly known, which is a travesty of justice for such a great player. The last word on Phil White goes to the legendary Tommy Johnston: 'Whitey was a superb player, absolutely brilliant at crossing the ball, and I headed many goals from his passes. We had an understanding that's hard to explain, the ball seemed to come at just the right angle and speed'. Phil White sadly died in June 2000, just a few months before his seventieth birthday.

Thomas WHITE, 1904-05

East Londoner Tom White was born in 1883. White, who was mainly a reserve, played just a single senior match for O's. He scored once in an FA Cup third qualifying round replay at Leytonstone on 20 October 1904. He came on to replace the injured Herbert Kingaby in a 5-2 victory for O's.

SEASON	LEAGUE		FA CUP		TOTAL	
	Apps	Gls	Apps	Gls	Apps	Gls
1904/05*	-	-	1	1	1	1
TOTAL	-	-	1	1	1	1

* O's first entered the League in 1905/06.

Brian WHITEHOUSE, 1966-68

Brian Whitehouse was born in West Bromwich on 8 September 1935 and started off as a junior with West Bromwich Albion in October 1952. He began as a centre forward, making his League debut in

1955/56 and scoring a total of 13 goals from 37 League appearances. In March 1960, he moved to Norwich City for £70,000. He stayed at Carrow Road for two years, playing in 49 senior matches and netting 18 goals. He then moved on to Wrexham for £6,000 in March 1962, netting 19 goals from 45 League matches. In November 1963 he moved to London, signed for £4,000 by Dick Graham of Crystal Palace, and over three years he made a further 82 League appearances and scored 17 goals. He teamed up again with Graham at Charlton Athletic for £8,000 in March 1966, where he made 13 League appearances and scored once. He teamed up with Graham for a third time when joining O's for £10,000 in July 1966, and he proved to be a versatile player who could play either in defence or attack. He was appointed captain and scored on his home debut against Scunthorpe United in a 3-1 win in August 1966, but was unfortunate to be at Orient during their financial crisis, so he also helped out with first-team coaching duties to save costs. A serious Achilles tendon injury, sustained against Oldham Athletic on 28 October 1967, eventually ended his playing career. He moved to Luton Town as coach in 1968 and later held similar positions with Arsenal, West Bromwich Albion, Manchester United, and was also the chief scout at Aston Villa for a while.

SEASON	LEAGUE		FA CUP		L. CUP	
	Apps	Gls	Apps	Gls	Apps	Gls
1966/67	41	3	3	1	1	0
1967/68	11	3	0	0	0	0
TOTAL	52	6	3	1	1	0

TOTAL APPS	56
TOTAL GOALS	7

Albert WHITELEY, 1952-54

Outside left Albert Whiteley was born in Sheffield on 13 July 1932. He started off as an amateur with Sheffield Wednesday, after being spotted playing in the Sheffield & District League. He joined O's in November 1952 and played regularly for the second-string, where he pleased the fans with his crowd-pleasing speedy dashes. He did get a run in the first team and made his League debut in January 1953 at Watford. It looked as though he might make the grade, but unfortunately he didn't live up to expectations and was replaced by George Poulton in 1953/54. Whiteley was transferred to Ramsgate Athletic – a club managed by former 'Oriental' Jimmy Blair – and later moved to Folkestone Town.

Brian Whitehouse

SEASON	LEAGUE		FA CUP		TOTAL	
	Apps	Gls	Apps	Gls	Apps	Gls
1952/53	18	3	0	0	18	3

1953/54	5	0	0	0	5	0
TOTAL	23	3	0	0	23	3

James Henry WHITTAKER, 1907-08

Bolton-born James Whittaker started his career with Barnsley, before joining Manchester City on 2 February 1904 as an amateur. During his three-year spell there, he played only reserve football, scoring 16 goals from 84 reserve appearances during his stay at Maine Road. The thrusting outside left got his chance with City when seventeen first-team squad members were suspended after a bribery scandal which was dubbed the Billy Meredith affair. One of the players affected was William Holmes, who was later to become O's manager. Whittaker made 6 League appearances for City, making his senior debut in October 1905 at Preston North End and scoring once. He turned professional on 16 January 1907, but never featured in the first team again. Holmes signed his former colleague on 15 August 1908, and he made his debut on the opening day of the 1907/08 season – a 1-0 win over Hull City on 2 September 1907. Whittaker left O's in May 1908.

SEASON	LEAGUE		FA CUP		TOTAL	
	Apps	Gls	Apps	Gls	Apps	Gls
1907/08	17	1	5	2	22	3
TOTAL	17	1	5	2	22	3

Walter WHITTAKER, 1907-10

Walt Whittaker was a fine custodian, who stood 6ft 1in and weighed nearly 14st. He played for eleven senior clubs during a career that spanned some nineteen years and more than 500 senior matches. He was one of the finest goalkeepers of his era, and was not far short of international class. His longest spell at a club was the three-year period he spent with O's. He was born in Manchester on 20 September 1878, and started playing in the Manchester League in 1894 with Molyneaux FC. After a three-month trial with Buxton FC, he returned to Molyneaux in December 1894. His big chance came when he joined Second Division side Newton Heath (later Manchester United) in February 1895, making his League debut against Grimsby Town on 14 March 1896 in a 2-4 defeat. He made a further two appearances before moving back into the Manchester League with Fairfield FC during May 1896. The following year he joined Grimsby Town for a fee of £60, making a total of 28 League appearances. Whittaker came south to join Reading in May 1898, and made 38 Southern League appearances and 8 FA Cup appearances during his two-year stay. He moved up to League football when joining First Division side Blackburn Rovers in February 1900, where he made 53 senior appearances and also won a Lancashire Cup winner's medal. He returned to Grimsby Town for £150 in December 1901, and after a further two years he chalked up another 49 senior appearances. In April 1903, he was off on his travels again, this time to Derby County. During his only season at the Baseball Ground, he made 12 League appearances. He joined Brentford in May 1906, and during his two year spell played 63 Southern League matches before joining Reading again in May 1906. This time, he made 37 senior appearances for the club. Towards the end of his spell the Reading, it is said that after some poor displays between the posts, he was instructed by management to visit the club doctor for an eyesight test, but he never did. He joined O's in July 1907 – in exchange for David Dougal – and he excelled during his stay, showing great handling and wonderful anticipation. He was even made team captain for a short time in 1909/10. However, it was not long before his wanderlust got the better of him and he was transferred to Southern League side Exeter City in May 1910. He was ever-present for the Devon club, making 38 Southern League appearances. In total, he played in 66 senior matches before being appointed player-manager of newly elected Southern League side Swansea Town, and he appeared in their first ever senior fixture – a 1-1 draw against Cardiff City in September 1912. In June 1914, he was appointed manager of Llanelli FC, but had to resign due to ill health just six months later. He then ran a public house in Swansea until he died from pneumonia on 2 June 1917, aged thirty-eight.

Alan Whittle

SEASON	LEAGUE		FA CUP		TOTAL	
	Apps	Gls	Apps	Gls	Apps	Gls
1907/08	32	0	4	0	36	0
1908/09	29	0	1	0	30	0
1909/10	29	0	1	0	30	0
TOTAL	90	0	6	0	96	0

Alan WHITTLE, 1976-77 and 1979-81

Born in Liverpool on 9 March 1950, little Alan Whittle – he stood 5ft 7in and weighed just 10st 4lb – started as an apprentice with Everton in July 1965. He made his League debut as an eighteen-year-old, helping them to demolish West Bromwich Albion 6-2 in March 1968. Everton went on to to win the League Championship in 1970, and Whittle won England schoolboy, youth and under-23 caps. Everton boss Harry Catterick once described Whittle as the 'new Dennis Law' and 'the greatest Everton discovery

of all-time'. However, the gritty forward with a flair for goalscoring could not live up to those expectations over his seven years at Goodison Park, making just 72(2) League appearances and scoring 21 goals. He was transferred to Crystal Palace for £100,000 and he did well there, scoring 19 goals from 103(5) appearances. He looked set to join Wrexham in 1975, but that fell through, so he found his way to Sheffield United on trial in July 1976, but that didn't work out either. He joined O's in September 1976 and scored a wonderful debut goal when he ran through the Cardiff City defence to score in a 3-0 win on 18 September 1976. He played regularly throughout that season and also scored two goals, one a wonderful overhead kick in an FA Cup second round replay at White Hart Lane to knock out Darlington in January 1977. He performed well during his time at Brisbane Road, and was a great trier with good skill. There was none better at running at and taking on defenders during his stay at the club. In May 1977 he had a attractive offer to go and play in Iran for the Persepolis club. He returned to O's in February 1979, but did not perform quite as well and he moved on to AFC Bournemouth in October 1980. He made 8(1) League appearances for the club, before trying his luck in Australia. He then returned to play for Corinthian Casuals. Whittle returned to Everton to work on the commercial side in 1989/90.

SEASON	LEAGUE		FA CUP		L. CUP	
	Apps	Gls	Apps	Gls	Apps	Gls
1976/77	31(2)	5	3	2	2(1)	0
1978/79	10	1	0	0	0	0
1979/80	6(1)	0	0	0	0(2)	0
TOTAL	47(3)	6	3	2	2(3)	0

TOTAL APPS	52(6)
TOTAL GOALS	8

* Alan Whittle also appeared in 4(2) Anglo-Scottish Cup matches, scoring once.

Christopher Anderson WHYTE, 1997

Veteran defender Chris Whyte came to O's on a non-contract basis on 2 January 1997, after a spell with Detroit Neon in America. His only appearance for O's was against Exeter City on 1 February 1997, after a long career with over 400 senior games that spanned eighteen years. Born in Islington, London on 2 September 1961, Whyte signed for Arsenal as an apprentice in December 1979. During his five-year stay at Highbury, he made 86(4) League appearances and scored 8 goals. He also spent a few months (from August 1984 onwards) on loan at Crystal Palace, making 17 senior appearances. In May 1986 he was given a free transfer, and

Chris Whyte (left)

Whyte went to play in America with the LA Lazers. He returned to England two years later, joining West Bromwich Albion on a free transfer. He played very well during his stay at the Hawthorns, making 93(1) senior appearances and scoring 7 goals, and was then transferred to Leeds United for £400,000 in June 1990. His stay at Elland Road proved profitable, making a total of 113 League appearances and scoring 5 goals. Whyte moved to Birmingham City (at the age of thirty-two) for £250,000 in August 1993, and during a three-year spell he made 68 League appearances and scored once. In March 1996 he joined Charlton Athletic on a free transfer, making 10(1) League appearances before trying his luck in America once again. After his brief stay at Brisbane Road, he moved to Oxford United on 27 February 1997 and stayed until the end of that season, playing in 11 League matches. Whyte finally moved out of the

League when he signed for Football Conference side Rushden & Diamonds on 1 August 1997 and stayed for two years before moving on to join Harlow Town in November 1999. The thirty-nine-year-old was released from his contract in 2000 and retired from the professional game.

SEASON	LEAGUE		FA CUP		L. CUP	
	Apps	Gls	Apps	Gls	Apps	Gls
1996/97	1	0	0	0	0	0
TOTAL	1	0	0	0	0	0

TOTAL APPS	1
TOTAL GOALS	0

Crawford WHYTE, 1938-39

Born in Ryhope, Wallsend-on-Tyne on 4 December 1907, the left-back Crawford Whyte represented Wallsend Schools, before playing for Walker Park FC and then for Crawcrook Albion. He signed for Blackburn Rovers in April 1930, making 87 League appearances during a five-year stay. In July 1935 he joined Bradford Park Avenue, where he made just 8 League appearances, and on 24 August 1936 he moved to Tranmere Rovers for £200. He played 11 League matches, but at the end of October he fell out with the Tranmere management and was suspended for insubordination. He never played again for the club, and was placed on the trans-fer list at £200. He went on loan to Ashington FC, but eventually Tranmere accepted £100 for him from Hartlepool United in August 1937. He stayed at Victoria Park for a season, making half-a-dozen senior appearances before joining O's in August 1938, but he was mostly understudy to Hugh Hearty and later George Rumbold. Whyte had a few games after Rumbold decided to retire, and

made his debut at Exeter City on 9 April 1939. He was released in May 1939 and went to play in Malta for Floriana FC. He died in Exmouth on 11 August 1984.

SEASON	LEAGUE		FA CUP		TOTAL	
	Apps	Gls	Apps	Gls	Apps	Gls
1938/39	6	0	0	0	6	0
TOTAL	6	0	0	0	6	0

Thomas WIGHTMAN, 1905-06

Full-back Tom Wightman joined O's on amateur terms in July 1905 and played for the reserves. He made his only senior appearance on 7 October 1905 in an FA Cup match against Felstead. He only played because the first team was on duty in a League fixture on the same day. He was not up to League standard and moved back into non-League football in 1906.

SEASON	LEAGUE		FA CUP		TOTAL	
	Apps	Gls	Apps	Gls	Apps	Gls
1905/06	0	0	1	0	1	0
TOTAL	0	0	1	0	1	0

Christopher John WILDER, 1992 (loan)

On 27 February 1992, right-back Chris Wilder joined O's on loan from Sheffield United, after a previous loan spell with Charlton Athletic. He stayed at Brisbane Road until the end of that season, prov-ing to be a very capable defender. He scored in a 4-0 win over Bury in March, and he brought some composure to the team. Remarkably, up to that point, he had scored only once in the League – for Sheffield United, also against Bury. O's manager Peter Eustace wanted to sign Wilder and stated: 'The club could not afford a signing-on fee, and Wilder refused to sign as he found London too expensive to live in.' Born in Stocksbridge on 23 September 1967, he became an apprentice at Southampton as a teenager in September 1984. He then moved to Sheffield United in August 1986, playing 89(40) matches and scoring once. In 1989 he had a loan spell at Walsall, and moved to Rotherham United for £50,000 in July 1992, making 129(3) League appearances and scoring a total of 11 goals. In January 1996, he went to Notts County for £150,000 and made 46 League appearances during a ten-month stay. Another £150,000 move, this time to Bradford City, took place in January 1996, but he stayed for just a season and played 35(7) games. He joined Sheffield United for yet another £150,000 fee in March 1998, but he never fitted in at Bramall Lane. After loan spells with both Northampton Town and Lincoln City, he signed on a non-contract basis with Brighton & Hove Albion in July 1999, making 11 League appearances. Wilder elected to return north in October 1999, joining Halifax Town, and proved in a key figure in the Shaymen's defence, making 56 senior appearances and scoring just once up to the end of December 2000. However, he didn't play at all in 2001. Wilder had a remarkable professional career that has spanned sixteen years, and he has made over 450 senior appearances and scored 32 goals. He was forced to retire from the game after sustaining a serious back injury against Blackpool on 26 December 2000. In September 2001, he joined Northern Counties League club Alfreton Town and a month later was appointed their manager.

SEASON	LEAGUE		FA CUP		L. CUP	
	Apps	Gls	Apps	Gls	Apps	Gls
1991/92	16	1	0	0	0	0
TOTAL	16	1	0	0	0	0

TOTAL APPS	16
TOTAL GOALS	1

* Chris Wilder also appeared in an Auto Windscreens Shield match.

Glen Alan WILKIE, 1994-96

Glen Wilkie, a full-back/midfielder, was born on 22 January 1977 in Bethnal Green, London. He started as a junior with Tottenham Hotspur, before signing professional forms with Leyton Orient on 18 February 1995. He was pressed into first-team duty early on in his career because of O's financial difficulties – the club were not allowed by the FA to sign any new players, as wages were being paid by the PFA. Wilkie made his League debut as a substitute in a 3-0 defeat at Crewe Alexandra on 31 December 1994. His full appearance came in March 1985 in a 0-0 draw at Cambridge United. He missed just a single match of the final 11 League matches of the 1994/95 season,

Glen Wilkie

the last 9 all being defeats. He suffered with injuries throughout the 1995/96 campaign and was released on 31 May 1996. Wilkie was allowed to continue training at Brisbane Road to regain fitness before going on loan to Kettering in September 1996. He later played for IFK Mariehamn in Finland, before returning to England to play for Cheshunt FC. He made his debut for Cheshunt against Canvey Island on 10 January 1998, and was on their books at the start of 2000/01. He joined Enfield Town in August 2001.

SEASON	LEAGUE		FA CUP		L. CUP	
	Apps	Gls	Apps	Gls	Apps	Gls
1994/95	10(1)	0	0	0	0	0
1995/96	0	0	0	0	0	0
TOTAL	10(1)	0	0	0	0	0

TOTAL APPS	10(1)
TOTAL GOALS	0

Dean Mark WILKINS, 1984 (loan)

Born in Hillingdon, Middlesex on 12 July 1962, Dean Wilkins came on loan to O's in March 1984 from Brighton & Hove Albion. A member of the Wilkins football dynasty, he is the younger brother of Ray (also to appear for O's in later seasons), Graham and Steve, as well as the son of George Wilkins. As a schoolboy, Wilkins represented Middlesex and trained with Chelsea and Manchester United, but it was with Queens Park Rangers that he was apprenticed before turning professional in May 1980. He started off as a defender, but it was as a midfielder that he made 1(5) League appearances. However, after three years he joined Brighton on a free transfer in August 1993, but was released after just 3 senior appearances. Wilkins spent three seasons in the Netherlands with PEC Zwolle. In

July 1987, Brighton manager Barry Lloyd brought the twenty-five-year-old back to the Goldstone for a £10,000 fee, and he played an important part in their promotion back to the Second Division in 1987/88, making a total of 123 consecutive appearances and also captaining the side. After playing 358(17) senior matches and netting 31 goals for Brighton, he was beset by injuries and was rewarded with a testimonial in 1995/96, when brother Ray brought his Queens Park Rangers side along to provide the opposition. He was released at the end of that season, and after subsequent trials with Worthing and Torquay United, he moved to Crawley Town in 1996. He then played for Bognor Regis Town, before being appointed youth-team coach at Brighton June 1998.

SEASON	LEAGUE		FA CUP		L. CUP	
	Apps	Gls	Apps	Gls	Apps	Gls
1983/84	10	0	0	0	0	0
TOTAL	10	0	0	0	0	0

TOTAL APPS	10
TOTAL GOALS	0

Raymond Colin WILKINS, 1997

Born in Hillingdon, Middlesex, Ray 'Butch' Wilkins began his career as an apprentice with Chelsea, turning professional in 1973. He made 177(3) appearances and scored 30 goals for the Blues, before an £825,000 transfer to Manchester United in 1979, where he made 190(3) appearances and scored 10 goals. He then moved to AC Milan for £1.5 million, before signing for Paris St Germain in 1987. He then joined Glasgow Rangers for £250,000 two years later. In his later years, he turned out for Hibernian, Wycombe Wanderers and Millwall. The

W

Ray Wilkins

midfielder joined O's on a match-by-match contract on 27 February 1997 – his fourth club of the 1996/97 season – and he became the second member of the Wilkins family to play for O's, Dean having been on loan with the club thirteen years earlier. His debut was at Brisbane Road against Barnet on 1 March 1997 – Wilkins rolled back the years and the forty-year-old maestro had the fans drooling over his trademark ball-spraying ability. Barry Hearn said: 'He is still head and shoulders above a lot of players in this League.' His next match was a remarkable affair at Brighton: the match ended 4-4 and turned out to be more of a boxing match. O's boss Tommy Taylor announced that after just 3 matches, Wilkins had decided to leave the club, although he would continue to train with the team. Taylor said: 'He was outstanding in the second-half at Brighton, but there is no point in playing him in a team

and paying his high wages when our players choose to bypass him.' Wilkins was appointed assistant manager to Kevin Keegan at Fulham on 25 September 1997, but was sacked by Keegan in May 1998. This was his second spell at management, having been player-manager at Queens Park Rangers between 1994 and 1996. More recently, he was on the coaching staff at Chelsea, but with the arrival of Italian Claudio Ranieri, both he and Graham Rix were sacked on 28 November 2000. Throughout his long and distinguished playing career, Wilkins made scored 48 goals from 691 League appearances with twelve clubs, and he won 84 England international caps. He was a guest speaker on Sky TV for O's play-off final match against Blackpool at the Millennium Stadium in May 2001. The 2001/02 season saw him as head coach at Watford.

SEASON	LEAGUE		FA CUP		L. CUP	
	Apps	Gls	Apps	Gls	Apps	Gls
1996/97	3	0	0	0	0	0
TOTAL	3	0	0	0	0	0

TOTAL APPS	3
TOTAL GOALS	0

Stanley Bernard WILLEMSE, 1956-58

Stan Willemse was born in Hove, Sussex on 23 August 1924. He was famed for the ferocity of his tackling, and was one of the most successful footballers to come out of Sussex. He earned a reputation during his time at Brighton as the 'dirtiest player in football'. He arrived at Brighton & Hove Albion in August 1940 at the age of fifteen, after playing for Hove Penguins FC and Southwick. Just eight days after his sixteenth birthday, he appeared for Brighton against Southampton in a wartime regional match. During the Second World War, he joined the Royal Marine Commando and trained as a PE instructor. After the war, he made 99 senior appearances and scored 4 goals for Brighton, before joining Chelsea for £6,500. He enjoyed seven wonderful seasons at Stamford Bridge, making a total of 221 appearances, and his rugged style won him the adulation of the fans and the dread of many First Division wingers. He won a League Championship medal in 1954/55, and he also represented the League. He won England 'B' caps, and was only denied full honours by the brilliance of Manchester United's Roger Byrne. Willemse travelled all over Europe with the London XI, and took part in the first floodlit game staged at Wembley Stadium when London took on Frankfurt in the Inter Cities Fairs Cup (predecessor of the UEFA Cup) tie in 1955. He moved to O's in June 1956, and he certainly lived up to his reputation of ruggedness. He

Stan Willemse

scored with a memorable twenty-yard headed goal against Bury in a 4-3 win during September 1956. He lost his form the following season, but when Tommy Johnston was transferred to Blackburn Rovers, he was tried at centre forward for a few games, and netted a goal in a 3-1 win against Huddersfield Town in April 1958. At the age of thirty-four, he decided to hang up his boots. He then became the landlord of the Eagle public house in Gloucester Road, Brighton, and later ran a betting-shop in Southwick. He then moved on to work as security officer at London University, before retiring to Hove.

SEASON	LEAGUE		FA CUP		TOTAL	
	Apps	Gls	Apps	Gls	Apps	Gls
1956/57	40	1	1	0	41	1
1957/58	19	1	0	0	19	1
TOTAL	59	2	1	0	60	2

Emlyn WILLIAMS, 1928-29

Centre forward Emlyn Williams was born in Aberaman, South Wales in 1903. He began his career as an amateur with Aberdare Town in 1926/27, making a dozen League appearances and bagging 8 goals. He joined O's in May 1928 and scored on his debut in a 5-2 defeat at Preston North End on 17 November 1928. He moved to Hull City in June 1929 to become one of only three O's to have moved to the Tigers – Edmund Edwards and Johnny Mayson being the others. His only senior appearance for Hull came five days before their FA Cup semi-final, in a team made up of mostly reserves that lost 4-0 at Charlton Athletic on 17 March 1930. He moved to Merthyr Town (who had just lost their League status) in July 1930, and then joined Bournemouth & Boscombe Athletic in December 1931, where he netted twice from 6 League appearances. In 1932 he played for Ramsgate Athletic.

SEASON	LEAGUE		FA CUP		TOTAL	
	Apps	Gls	Apps	Gls	Apps	Gls
1928/29	3	1	0	0	3	1
TOTAL	3	1	0	0	3	1

Ernest Harold WILLIAMS, 1907-08

Welshman Ernie Williams joined O's as an amateur from Rhyl FC in May 1907. The reserve right-back made his League debut in a 0-0 draw at Gainsborough Trinity on 21 December 1907, and played in the following 4 matches, replacing the injured William Henderson. He spent the remainder of the season in the reserves, and returned to Wales after his release in May 1908.

SEASON	LEAGUE		FA CUP		TOTAL	
	Apps	Gls	Apps	Gls	Apps	Gls
1907/08	5	0	0	0	5	0
TOTAL	5	0	0	0	5	0

Jack Walter WILLIAMS, 1909-10

Jack Williams joined O's from Bury in June 1909, where he had been a reserve player. He made his League debut on 4 September 1909 in a good 2-0 win over Gainsborough Trinity . This was the first match in which O's wore their brand new colours of white shirts with a red chevron. His one and only claim to fame occurred on 8 January 1910, when he set an O's reserve record by scoring 8 goals in a South Eastern Counties League match against Leyton FC in an 8-2 victory. He was recalled to the first team soon after, and scored against both Bradford and Blackpool to secure full points. Williams was not retained and joined Brisbane Road-based Southern League side Leyton FC in June 1910.

SEASON	LEAGUE		FA CUP		TOTAL	
	Apps	Gls	Apps	Gls	Apps	Gls
1909/10	12	3	0	0	12	3
TOTAL	12	3	0	0	12	3

Jesse Thomas WILLIAMS, 1928-29

Born in Cefn-y-Bedd, near Wrexham on 24 June 1903, Jesse Williams started off with Wrexham in 1922, making 34 League appearances and scoring 3 goals. He moved to Middlesbrough in May 1924 and played regularly in his first season, scoring 4 goals from 28 senior appearances, as well as gaining a full Welsh international cap against Northern Ireland in 1925. However, the left-winger was overshadowed eventually by former 'Oriental' Owen Williams (no relation), who had joined Boro' from O's in March 1924. He spent most of the following season in the reserves, and in 1926/27 he topped the reserve goalscoring chart with 20 goals, but managed just 4 first-team appearances as promotion was

Jesse Williams

achieved. He also spent the 1927/28 season in the reserves, so after just 38 senior appearances and 8 goals during his four seasons, he joined O's on a free transfer in January 1928. Williams performed well at Millfields Road, making his debut against Blackpool on 21 January 1928. The following season he played on the right wing, but after sustaining an injury at Barnsley on 26 December 1928, he never played in the first team again, and was eventually transferred to Rhyl Athletic in July 1929. After a spell in Wales as a referee, he emmigrated to Toronto, Canada, although he did once return to Ayresome Park for a nostalgic visit in 1965. Williams died on 20 October 1972 in Toronto, aged sixty-nine.

Lee Williams

SEASON	LEAGUE		FA CUP		TOTAL	
	Apps	Gls	Apps	Gls	Apps	Gls
1927/28	15	1	0	0	15	1
1928/29	17	2	1	0	18	2
TOTAL	32	3	1	0	33	3

Lee WILLIAMS, 1995-96

Williams was born in Harol Hill, Essex, on 13 March 1977. The midfielder-cum-striker joined Purfleet at the start of the 1994/95 season, playing for their successful youth team before joining O's in 1995. A YTS player, who made just a handful of League appearances for the club, his full debut came against Exeter City in December 1995. He was a non-playing substitute on 11 occasions. After a spell in Finland with BK-IFK, he rejoined non-League Purfleet in December 1996. Soon afterwards, he joined Grays Athletic, and in December 1997 he moved to Enfield, scoring 3 goals in 20 appearances. However, a broken foot curtailed his progress, so he moved to Billericay Town in June 1999. He was still performing in the front line in 2002, after making over 100 appearances.

SEASON	LEAGUE		FA CUP		L. CUP	
	Apps	Gls	Apps	Gls	Apps	Gls
1995/96	1(2)	0	1	0	0	0
TOTAL	1(2)	0	1	0	0	0

TOTAL APPS	2(2)
TOTAL GOALS	0

* Lee Williams also appeared in 1 Auto Windscreens Shield match.

Michael John WILLIAMS, 1997-98

Born in Stepney, London on 9 October 1978, this trainee made his only senior appearance when coming on as a substitute in the eighty-second minute against Rotherham United on 11 October 1997. A first-year professional who signed in July 1997, he performed equally well up front or in central defence, but he was released in May 1998, joining Sligo Rovers in Ireland.

SEASON	LEAGUE		FA CUP		L. CUP	
	Apps	Gls	Apps	Gls	Apps	Gls
1997/98	0(1)	0	0	0	0	0
TOTAL	0(1)	0	0	0	0	0

TOTAL APPS	0(1)
TOTAL GOALS	0

Owen WILLIAMS, 1919-24

Owen Williams, a small and stocky player, was arguably the finest outside left in the club's history. He was fast, tricky and direct, and caused havoc for opposing defenders. Like another wonderful winger – Alan Comfort – he later joined Middlesbrough. Williams had the honour of becoming O's first full international player when he was picked to represent England against Ireland at West Bromwich on 22 October 1923. He set up both goals in a 2-0 victory – no mean feat for a player with unfashionable Second Division Clapton Orient. Born on 23 September 1895 in Ryhope, Co. Durham, he was an England schoolboy international before joining his local side, Ryhope Colliery. After unsuccessful trials with both Sunderland and Manchester United, he joined Easington Colliery. He was spotted by an O's scout and came to Millfields Road for a trial in July 1919, signing professional forms in August. He made his debut on the right wing against Wolverhampton Wanderers on 17 September 1919, but soon found himself as reserve for Ben Ives. However, once Ives became injured at the end of November, Williams came in and played for the remainder of the season. He proved to be one of the speediest

Owen Williams

wingers of his day, with excellent ball-control, and he often went on long dribbling runs, drifting past full-backs with ease. His perfect crosses proved crucial for the likes of Rennox, Whipp and Green over the years. There was reluctance from the England selectors to pick a player from a lower division, but in the end they couldn't leave him out, and really he should won more than 2 caps. He moved to Middlesbrough for a record fee of £2,525 in March 1924, but experienced relegation in his first season. However, he and Boro bounced back, and Williams won two Second Division Championship medals – in 1927 and 1929. He experienced the humiliation of defeat with Boro against O's in an FA Cup fourth round tie at Millfields Road – 4-2 on 30 January 1926 – but he still received a rousing reception from the 24,247 O's fans present, which he acknowledged with a wave to each corner of the ground. He stayed at Ayresome Park for seven seasons, making 194 senior appearances and scoring 43 goals. He was approaching thirty-five years of age when placed on the transfer list at £400, joining Southend United for a cut-price £200 in July 1930, for whom he made 16 League appearances and scored 4 goals before retiring in May 1931. He lived in Easington, Co. Durham until he died on 9 December 1960, aged sixty-five. His brother, Tom, played with him at O's between 1921 and 1923, and died just days after his brother.

SEASON	LEAGUE		FA CUP		TOTAL	
	Apps	Gls	Apps	Gls	Apps	Gls
1919/20	28	6	1	0	29	6
1920/21	40	9	2	0	42	9
1921/22	33	6	1	0	34	6
1922/23	37	7	1	0	38	7
1923/24	24	5	3	2	27	7
TOTAL	162	33	8	2	170	35

Roderick WILLIAMS, 1938-42

Rod Williams was born in Newport, Monmouthshire, Wales on 2 December 1909, but moved with his family to London as a youngster. The robust centre forward started as an amateur his career with spells at Sutton United, Epsom Town, Uxbridge Town and Crystal Palace, before joining Norwich City on trial in May 1933 and signing professional forms a month later. He scored a goal on his League debut at Crystal Palace in December 1933, and during his three years at Carrow Road, he made 20 senior appearances and scored 12 goals. He was credited with having scored a phenomenal 106 goals for the club's reserve side – particularly notable was his impressive tally of 45 goals in 1933/34, which included 4 goals against both Bedford Town and Great Yarmouth, as well as hat-tricks against Clapton Orient reserves, Bournemouth & Boscome Athletic reserves, Dartford, Millwall reserves and Stamford Town. He moved to Exeter City in May 1936 and scored twice on his debut against Torquay United in September 1936. He was their leading scorer in 1936/37, with 37 senior goals from 48 appearances. He joined Reading in June 1937, and once again netted on debut against Millwall in August 1937. There he scored a total of 12 goals from 15 senior matches. On 13 November 1937, he joined West Ham United for £4,000 as cover for Samuel Small. He cracked 5 goals in 9 Second Division appearances, before moving to O's on 24 September 1938, making his debut and scoring in a 4-2 defeat at Crystal Palace on 1 October 1938. Two weeks later, he bagged a hat-trick in a 5-0 win over Southend United, and scored regularly throughout the season to end as top scorer with 18 senior goals. Forming a formidable partnership with Tom Walters, Williams was a difficult man to stop when going forward. He commenced the 1939/40 season in fine style, linking well with veteran Scottish hotshot William McFadyen and scoring goals against Ipswich Town and Watford. However, the season was brought to an abrupt end due to the outbreak of the Second World War, and his goals were expunged from the record books. Many felt he could have scored more than 20 goals for the season. He made just 5 wartime appearances without scoring for O's between 1939 and 1942, before retiring from the professional game at the age of thirty-three. In October 1994, he was reported as living in the Norfolk area.

SEASON	LEAGUE		FA CUP		TOTAL	
	Apps	Gls	Apps	Gls	Apps	Gls
1938/39*	35	16	2	2	37	18
1939/40**	3	2	0	0	0	0
TOTAL	35	16	2	2	37	18

* Rod Williams also appeared in a Third Division Cup match in 1938/39.

** The 1939/40 season was abandoned after three games due to war – all records were expunged.

Thomas Hutchinson WILLIAMS, 1921-23

Tommy Williams – the younger brother of O's England international wing-man, Owen Williams – was born in Easington, Co. Durham on 23 May 1899. The centre forward started, like his brother, with Ryhope Colliery, having previously failed a trial with Huddersfield Town in February 1921. He joined O's in August 1921 on the recommendation of his brother, and made a very bright start. He scored a brace in only his second match – a 3-2 win over Derby County on 4 February 1922 – the second after a wonderful run and cross from his brother Owen, to the delight of the 15,000 crowd. He looked lively and skilful, and notched the winner at West Ham United in April 1922 to secure a 2-1 win. He played 25 League matches, together with his brother, during his two-year stay at Millfields, of which 12 were victories. Williams moved to Charlton Athletic in August 1923, but he only made 5 appearances in the League, being kept out of the side for most of the time by another former 'Oriental', Albert 'Abe' Goodman. Williams later moved to Gillingham in February 1924 and made 16 League appearances, scoring 9 times. He then moved to Third Division (North) side Ashington in August 1924, scoring 5 goals from 12 League appearances. In 1925 he played for Mid-Rhondda United,

and then he moved on to Bristol Rovers in January 1926. During his two years with Rovers, he netted 27 League goals from 75 matches. In June 1928, he moved across town to join Bristol City, but his stay was not long, making just 8 League appearances and scoring a total of 4 goals. In February 1929, he returned to Wales to join Merthyr Town, notching 19 goals from 49 League matches. In 1930, another move took him to Norwich City, where he bagged a further 13 goals from 27 League appearances. Finally, he left the League game in August 1934, and moved on to Frost's Athletic at the age of thirty-five. Williams' career spanned thirteen years, and he totalled 81 goals from 218 League appearances. Williams died 14 December 1960, aged sixty-one, just five days after his younger brother, Owen, had died.

SEASON	LEAGUE		FA CUP		TOTAL	
	Apps	Gls	Apps	Gls	Apps	Gls
1921/22	16	3	0	0	16	3
1922/23	10	3	0	0	10	3
TOTAL	26	6	0	0	26	6

Alfred WILLINGHAM, 1910-11

East-London born Alf Willingham came to O's in July 1910, after being spotted playing his football on Hackney Marshes. The centre forward showed plenty of dash, but he perhaps was not quite up to standard. He made his League debut in the 1-0 win over Stockport County on 31 December 1910. Willingham left O's in May 1911 and went for an unsuccessful trial with Millwall that summer. He then returned to the non-League ranks.

SEASON	LEAGUE		FA CUP		TOTAL	
	Apps	Gls	Apps	Gls	Apps	Gls
1910/11	1	0	0	0	1	0
TOTAL	1	0	0	0	1	0

Harold Herbert WILLIS, 1908-14

Clapton-born Harry Willis was a talented wing-half, who joined O's in May 1908 from local club Clapton Warwick FC. He made his League debut in a 1-1 draw at Stockport County on 9 October 1908, but he did not get many first-team outings during his first two seasons at the club. However, he came to the fore during 1910/11, forming part of the grand middle line of Hind, Liddell and Willis. The three players only missed a few matches together during the following few seasons, and helped the club to maintain their fourth position in the Second Division. Willis scored just once in the League throughout his career – against Leicester Fosse on 30 September 1911 in a 4-1 win. He was one of O's unsung heroes during the pre-First World War period, whose hard work did not always get the praise it really deserved. His form suffered a bit in 1914, when injuries prevented him from playing during the latter half of the 1913/14 season. He joined Maidstone United on a free transfer in June 1914.

SEASON	LEAGUE		FA CUP		TOTAL	
	Apps	Gls	Apps	Gls	Apps	Gls
1908/09	3	0	0	0	3	0
1909/10	13	0	0	0	13	0
1910/11	37	0	1	0	38	0
1911/12	37	1	1	0	38	1
1912/13	27	0	1	0	28	0
1913/14	19	0	2	0	21	0
TOTAL	136	1	5	0	141	1

Ronald Ian WILLIS, 1966-67

Goalkeeper Ron Willis was born in Romford, Essex on 27 December 1947. After trials with Coventry City and Tottenham Hotspur, he joined O's in January 1966. Willis, who was rather on the small side for a 'keeper, played regularly for O's colts and reserves, and got his first-team chance when Vic Rouse was injured during summer training. He played in the opening fixture of the 1966/67 season – a 3-1 defeat at Oldham Athletic on 20 August. He rose to the occasion and performed creditably throughout the season. Included amongst his credits was a great penalty save against Lowestoft in an FA Cup first round tie to secure a 2-1 victory in November 1966. The following season, injury and the emergence of Ray Goddard both kept him out of the side, and he was transferred to Charlton Athletic for £3,000 in October 1967. However, during his one-year stay at the Valley, he managed just a single League appearance. He went on loan to Brentford in September 1968, appearing once before joining Colchester United for £2,000 in October 1968. He played half-a-dozen League matches whilst at Layer Road. He later went to play in South Africa, and nowadays lives in KwaZulu, Natal.

SEASON	LEAGUE		FA CUP		L. CUP	
	Apps	Gls	Apps	Gls	Apps	Gls
1966/67	41	0	3	0	1	0
1967/68	4	0	0	0	1	0
TOTAL	45	0	3	0	2	0
TOTAL APPS		50				
TOTAL GOALS		0				

George James WILLSHAW, 1939-47

George Willshaw was born in Hackney, London on 18 October 1912. The outside left started his career as an amateur with Walthamstow Avenue and Southall FC, before joining Southend United in February 1936. He scored on his debut the next month in a 3-1 win at Swindon

Town. He was with the Blues for two years, making 34 senior appearances and scoring 7 goals. He was transferred to Bristol City in June 1938 and again scored on his debut, this time against Watford on 27 August 1938. He made 37 senior matches and netted 10 goals for City. He became an 'Oriental' in July 1939, and played in all 3 matches in the 1939/40 season – against Ipswich Town, Southend United and Watford – but the records were expunged due to the Second World War. He played in 72 wartime regional matches, and scored 28 goals between 1939 and 1943. He missed the two-legged FA Cup tie against Newport Isle of Wight during November 1945, due to serving abroad in the forces, but he returned to the club for the resumption of the League in 1946/47. He made his League debut and scored in the opening fixture against Ipswich Town on 31 August 1946, in front of 12,530 fans at Brisbane Road. He played a total of 6 matches at outside-left, 5 matches at centre forward and a match at inside left. At the age of thirty-five, he decided to retire at the end of that season. Willshaw died in Portsmouth during September 1993, just a month before his eighty-first birthday.

SEASON	LEAGUE		FA CUP		TOTAL	
	Apps	Gls	Apps	Gls	Apps	Gls
1939/40*	3	0	0	0	3	0
1946/47	12	2	0	0	12	2
TOTAL	12	2	0	0	12	2

* The 1939/40 season was abandoned after 3 League matches due to the Second World War and all records were expunged.

Rhys James WILMOT, 1984-85

Goalkeeper Rhys Wilmot was born in Rogiet, Newport, Wales on 21 February 1962. He started off with local junior side Rogiet FC, before joining Arsenal as a schoolboy in 1977, later turning professional in January 1980. He won Welsh caps at schoolboy, youth and under-21 level. The 6ft 1in and 12st 'keeper made 426 junior and reserve appearances for the Gunners, and was a member of their Football Combination Championship-winning side in 1993/94. He went on loan to Hereford United in May 1983, where he made 9 League appearances. He joined O's on a season's loan in May 1984 and looked very shaky early on. Although he later improved, it was not enough to prevent O's from being relegated to the Fourth Division. Wilmot returned to Highbury in May 1985, and made his senior debut in a League Cup tie against Aston Villa in January 1986. However, he only made 8 League appearances in total at Highbury. In August 1988 he went on loan to Swansea City, making 16 League appearances. During March

Rhys Wilmot

1989, he went on loan to Plymouth Argyle, impressing during a 17-match run. Wilmot was eventually transferred to Argyle for £100,000 in July 1989, and made a further 116 League appearances during his three-year stay. He was transferred to Grimsby Town for £87,500 in July 1992, and made 33 appearances before returning to London in August 1994. He joined Crystal Palace for £80,000, but only made 5(1) League appearances. In August 1996 he moved to Devon to join Torquay United on a free transfer, and made 34 League matches during the 1996/97 season at the age of thirty-five. In August 1997, he ended his long career with Ryman Premier League side Aylesbury United.

SEASON	LEAGUE		FA CUP		L. CUP	
	Apps	Gls	Apps	Gls	Apps	Gls
1984/85	46	0	4	0	4	0
TOTAL	46	0	4	0	4	0

TOTAL APPS	54
TOTAL GOALS	0

* Rhys Wilmot also appeared in 3 Auto Windscreens Shield matches.

Harold Charles WINGHAM, 1924-25

Born in Selsey, Sussex on 25 June 1895, full-back Harry Wingham started off with the Southampton-based submarine works team called Thorneycrofts. He was snapped up by Bournemouth & Boscome Athletic during June 1923, and made 18 League appearances for the Cherries, appearing in their first League fixture at Swindon, a 3-1 defeat. He joined O's in May 1924, making his debut in a 1-1 draw against Stockport County on 16 February 1925. However, he found it difficult to displace the consistent Bert Rosier, and moved to Norwich City in July 1925, where he made a further 44 senior appearances and scored once before he left in May 1926. Wingham died in Cowes on the Isle of Wight on 24 April 1969, a couple of months before his seventy-fourth birthday.

SEASON	LEAGUE		FA CUP		TOTAL	
	Apps	Gls	Apps	Gls	Apps	Gls
1924/25	5	0	0	0	5	0
TOTAL	5	0	0	0	5	0

Samuel Anthony WINSTON, 1996-97

Sammy Winston was born in Islington, London on 6 August 1978. His father was the former Arsenal professional Tony Winston. The forward started as a trainee with Tottenham Hotspur, and was part of their team that reached the final of the Southern Floodlit Cup. He joined Norwich City in 1994 and turned professional on 1 August 1995. The eighteen-year-old made 36 appearances for their youth side and scored 9 goals, as well as making 3 substitute appearances for the reserves. He joined O's on a free transfer on 1 July 1996. He will not forget his senior debut in a hurry: he came on as a substitute in the seventy-third minute of a FA Cup tie against Merthyr Tydfil on 16 November 1996, and hooked home an Ian Hendon corner to give Tommy Taylor his first win as manager. Winston never quite fitted in at Brisbane Road, and he was sent to Australia on loan in 1996, but he decided to return home early. This upset Orient's management, and he left the club in December 1997 after a row. He joined Yeovil Town in the Football Conference on 6 March 1998, making 5(9) appearances and scoring 6 goals. He later played for Chesham United, before joining Sutton United on 1 August 1999, where he made 34(4) appearances and scored once. He joined Kingstonian for a fee of £13,000 on 9 July 2000. Winston netted twice in their surprise 3-1 FA Cup victory at Brentford in November 2000, and also starred in a 1-0 victory at Southend United in the next round. Up to the end of the season, he had played 40 senior matches and scored 6 goals. He moved to Kingstonian on 7 October 2000, but when the club found themselves in a serious financial position, Winston, along with a number of first-team players, was placed on the transfer list because the club could not pay their wages. Winston was eventually released by Kingstonian in October 2001 and moved on to play for Slough Town on 11 November.

SEASON	LEAGUE		FA CUP		L. CUP	
	Apps	Gls	Apps	Gls	Apps	Gls
1996/97	3(8)	1	0(2)	1	0	0
TOTAL	3(8)	1	0(2)	1	0	0

Sammy Winston

TOTAL APPS	3(10)
TOTAL GOALS	2

Thomas Henry WITHERIDGE, 1931-32

Born in Amersham on 25 May 1911, inside forward Tommy Witheridge joined O's in July 1931 from local non-League football, making his only League appearance in a 4-3 defeat at Northampton Town on 21 April 1932. He was not retained, and left O's on 9 May 1932. He died in Newham, London on 7 March 1985, a few months before his seventy-fourth birthday.

SEASON	LEAGUE		FA CUP		TOTAL	
	Apps	Gls	Apps	Gls	Apps	Gls
1931/32	1	0	0	0	1	0
TOTAL	1	0	0	0	1	0

Donald WOAN, 1951-52

Sturdy, strong-running right-winger Don Woan was born in Bootle, Liverpool on 7 November 1927. The elder brother of Alan Woan and uncle of Ian Woan (the former Nottingham Forest and Shrewsbury Town star), Don started his career with Lancashire League side Bootle FC, before joining Liverpool for £1,000 in October 1950. He made his League debut at Derby County in January 1951, but made just a single further appearance before joining O's as makeweight in the transfer of young Brian Jackson to Liverpool for £6,500 on 5 November 1951. Woan scored a brace of goals on his home debut against Port Vale, and played very well in O's great cup run of 1951/52, but he moved to Bradford City on 3 October 1952 for £1,500. At 5ft 7in and 11st 7lb, he was the tallest in a Bradford forward line that remarkably averaged just 5ft 3in. He made 24 senior appearances and scored 4 goals, before moving to Tran-

Don Woan

mere Rovers in another player-exchange deal, this time involving Tommy Mycock in February 1924. His stay at Prenton Park lasted just a year, and after he'd made 27 League appearances and scored twice, he joined Southern League Yeovil Town in July 1955.

SEASON	LEAGUE		FA CUP		TOTAL	
	Apps	Gls	Apps	Gls	Apps	Gls
1951/52	18	4	9	0	27	4
1952/53	7	1	0	0	7	1
TOTAL	25	5	9	0	34	5

Arthur WOOD, 1921-31

Legendary goalkeeper Arthur Wood was born in Walsall on 14 January 1894. He was the son of the great Southampton stalwart Harry Wood – a great forward, who played for Wolverhampton Wanderers and won 2 caps for England, as well as scoring 65 goals from 180 Southern League and FA Cup appearances for the Saints. Arthur Wood first watched his father at Southampton as a boy, and he represented Porstmouth schoolboys before joining Portsmouth as a sixteen-year-old amateur in 1910, where his father was trainer. He first played as a full-back, but due to his heavy weight, he was converted to a goalkeeper. When his father retired from football to run The Milton Arms public house near Fratton Park, Wood went to the Dell for a trial in April 1913. He was duly taken on, and made his senior debut in a 3-2 defeat at Luton Town in a Southern League fixture on 9 September 1914, with his proud father in attendance. Wood had his career interrupted, like so many young players, by the First World War, and he served in the Royal Engineers, but still played for the Saints in wartime matches. He served in France, Palestine and Salonika, and received two medals for bravery. He rejoined the Southampton groundstaff after his demobilisation, and made his League debut in a 1-1 draw at Brentford on 30 October 1920. He seemed to have a long career ahead of him at the Dell, but with the arrival of experienced goalie Tommy Allen, he lost his place. Not being content with reserve football, the opportunity arose to come to London and he signed for O's in May 1921, after making 41 Southern League, 2 League and 4 FA Cup appearances for the Saints. His first outing was in a public trial match at Millfields Road in July 1921, and the 5ft 10in and 14st Wood, to the amazement of the 12,000-strong crowd, wore a large poacher's pocket sewn onto his tent-like shorts. The newspaper reports claimed that Wood kept fruit in the pocket, and it was nothing to see him whip out an apple when the home players were upfield. During the match, he was challenged by centre forward Clatworthy Rennox, and Wood lost his temper but was restrained from hitting him – quite a debut, the papers reported! Wood made his League debut in a 0-0 draw at Bury on 3 September 1921, after first-choice goalie Hugall was injured. Wood kept the jersey for the following nine seasons, although his ballooned to over 18st. He was a massive obstacle to opposing forwards, and back in the days when it was still permitted to barge a goalkeeper, not many tried it with Wood – he was truly a magnificent custodian. The Southern Press campaigned for his England call-up, but he could never replace Taylor of Huddersfield Town, Sewell of Blackburn Rovers and later Ted Hufton of West Ham United, so Wood was often to referred to in match reports as the best uncapped goalkeeper in England. After many splendid performances around the country, he was often applauded off the pitch by home fans. Wood still holds the O's record of consecutive League appearances for the club of 225 matches. The run started in that first match at Bury, and lasted until a game against Grimsby Town which took place on 4 December 1926. During this five-year spell, he also played in 10 FA Cup ties. He was eventually sidelined by a thigh strain for the match at Blackpool, so in came amateur goalie John Leather for his one and only senior appearance – a 6-0 defeat. Wood had an excellent match as captain against Newcastle United in the FA Cup fifth round at Millfields Road – a brilliant 2-0 victory – and he was chaired off the pitch by ecstatic fans. He also played in the 2 League matches staged at Wembley Stadium in 1930. His final League match was at Newport County – a 1-1 draw on 2 May 1931 – and he set O's League record of

373 appearances, which stood for forty-five years until being surpassed by Peter Allen in March 1976. He left O's at the age of thirty-seven, and joined Ryde Sports on the Isle of Wight in June 1931. He was in goal when they had one of their best FA Cup runs in 1932/33, before later moving to Newport Isle of Wight. He returned to London to watch O's play Crystal Palace on 26 February 1936, and the club programme of 7 March stated that it was splendid to see Arthur Wood at the ground again. He was now over 20st in weight – a possible reason why he died at the relatively young age of forty-seven in Portsmouth on 8 April 1941. His father, Harry, had died some ten years later, on 5 July 1951, aged eighty-three.

SEASON	LEAGUE		FA CUP		TOTAL	
	Apps	Gls	Apps	Gls	Apps	Gls
1921/22	40	0	1	0	41	0
1922/23	42	0	1	0	43	0
1923/24	42	0	3	0	45	0
1924/25	42	0	1	0	43	0
1925/26	42	0	4	0	46	0
1926/27	40	0	0	0	40	0
1927/28	37	0	1	0	38	0
1928/29	36	0	4	0	40	0
1929/30	22	0	6	0	28	0
1930/31	30	0	1	0	31	0
TOTAL	373	0	22	0	395	0

Brian Thomas WOOD, 1966-68
Born on 8 December 1940 in Hamworthy, Poole, Brian Wood, a tall centre half, started his career with Dorset League side Hamworthy Athletic, before joining West Bromwich Albion as a junior in January 1958. After three years in the reserves, he moved to Crystal Palace in May 1961, where his League debut ended in a 5-0 defeat against Swindon Town. He stayed at Selhurst Park for five years,

and missed a single game in their pro-motion-winning side of 1963/64, but he lost his place towards the end of his stay, after breaking his leg twice. After 142(1) League appearances and a goal, he joined O's in December 1966. He proved to be a dour, solid defender, who made few mistakes. He formed a good partnership with young Paul Went in the centre of the defence. He was appointed team captain in 1967/68, and he and his colleagues decided to refuse their Christmas bonus due to the club's financial plight. He moved to Colchester United in August 1968, and during his two-year stay at Layer Road, he made 71 League appear-ances before moving on to Workington Town in July 1970. He played 202(2) League games and scored 9 goals for the Reds before being appointed player-coach, but they failed to gain re-election to the League.

SEASON	LEAGUE		FA CUP		L. CUP	
	Apps	Gls	Apps	Gls	Apps	Gls
1966/67	23	1	0	0	0	0
1967/68	35	2	5	0	1	0
TOTAL	58	3	5	0	1	0

TOTAL APPS	64
TOTAL GOALS	3

Edward John WOOD, 1949-50

Born on 23 October 1919 in West Ham, London, Jackie Wood started out with Leytonstone. He won an England ama-teur cap, before signing professional forms with West Ham United in 1932, where he made 10 League appearances. Like so many youngsters of his day, his career suffered because of the Second World War. He enlisted with the Essex Territorial Regiment in 1939. He was an outstanding outside left with a good eye

for goal, and he returned to Boleyn in 1945 to play in a number of wartime regional matches. He stayed a further four years, and scored 15 goals from 61 senior appearances. Twenty-nine-year-old Wood joined O's in October 1949, and made his debut in a 2-0 defeat at Aldershot on 8 October 1949. He could not win a regular place in the side, and was released in May 1950. He then chose to move to Margate FC. Wood died in Exeter in October 1993, aged seventy-four.

SEASON	LEAGUE		FA CUP		TOTAL	
	Apps	Gls	Apps	Gls	Apps	Gls
1949/50	9	1	1	0	10	1
TOTAL	9	1	1	0	10	1

Joseph Henry WOODWARD, 1927-28

Goalkeeper Joe Woodward was born in Catford, London during February 1904. He started off with local side Catford FC, before joining Watford as an amateur in August 1926. He signed professional forms with the club the following month. He made his League debut against Newport County on 25 September 1926 in a 0-0 draw. After making just a single appearance, he moved on to Southend United in August 1927. He stayed with Southend for two months, making just 2 League appearances, before joining O's in October 1927 as understudy to Arthur Wood. He got his only chance in the first team when Wood was injured. He played in a 2-2 draw at Hull City on 12 November 1927, and according to reports, Wood-ward performed quite well. In January 1928 he moved to Queens Park Rangers, and made his debut in a 2-0 win over Crystal Palace on 3 March. He went on to make a total of 11 senior appearances. He moved to Third Division (South) side

Merthyr Town in July 1929, making 20 League appearances before moving into non-League football with Bexleyheath & Welling FC in January 1931.The following year, he joined Canterbury Waverley FC. Woodward died in Catford during 1974, aged seventy.

SEASON	LEAGUE		FA CUP		TOTAL	
	Apps	Gls	Apps	Gls	Apps	Gls
1927/28	1	0	0	0	1	0
TOTAL	1	0	0	0	1	0

Kenneth Robert WOODWARD, 1966-67

Winger Ken Woodward was born in Battersea, London on 16 November 1947. He started as an apprentice with Crystal Palace in December 1966, but he never made it into their first team, and joined O's in August 1966, when the club was struggling financially. He made his solitary senior appearance at Bournemouth in a 1-0 defeat on 24 September 1966, but was not really the answer to O's problems, and remained in the reserves until being released in May 1967, when he moved into non-League football.

SEASON	LEAGUE		FA CUP		L. CUP	
	Apps	Gls	Apps	Gls	Apps	Gls
1966/67	1	0	0	0	0	0
TOTAL	1	0	0	0	0	0

TOTAL APPS	1
TOTAL GOALS	0

Philip Abraham WOOSNAM, 1954-58

Phil Woosnam – the Welsh wizard – was a brilliant footballing genius. The inside forward had great vision, and was noted for his skill and accuracy of passing. He is one of a small band to have been capped for Wales at schoolboy, youth, amateur and professional level. Born in the small mid-Wales village of Caersws, Montgomeryshire on 22 December 1932, the farmer's son showed considerable academic ability, winning a scholarship to Newton Grammar School. He attended Bangor University in 1950 to read Physics and Mathematics, and during this time played in the university team and for a number of Welsh representative sides. A youth cap and his first of 8 amateur caps soon followed – against England at Bangor in 1951. He also captained the varsity side to the Welsh Universities' Championship. He played his early football with Wrexham, Peritas FC and Middlesex Wanderers, before joining Manchester City on amateur forms in 1952. Whilst with City, he made a lone League appearance against Cardiff City in February 1953 in a 6-0 defeat. He represented an Army XI, with such famous names as with Maurice Setters (WBA), Eddie Colman, and Duncan Edwards of Manchester United. Woosnam joined O's as an amateur from Sutton United in July 1954, and took up a science-teaching post at Leyton County High School. Despite not being the quickest of footballers, he never failed to create space for himself. He radiated class whenever on the ball, and was one of the best midfielders in the country. He made his O's debut in a 2-0 defeat at Brentford on 8 April 1954, but came to the fore the following season, when O's won the Third Division (South) Championship. He only turned professional in January 1957, and was a member of an O's side that demolished Scottish side East Fife by a scoreline of 7-0 in 1957/58, Woosnam bagging a pair. He was rewarded when he won a full Welsh cap against Scotland in October 1958. Twenty-six-year-old Woosnam moved to West Ham United for a then record fee of

£30,000 in November 1958, and made his debut against Arsenal. He was capped a further 15 times during his two-year stay at the Boleyn, and was picked in 1960 for a Multinational League XI against an Italian XI – an honour he considers to be his greatest as a player. The arrival of Johnny Bryne hastened his departure to Aston Villa for £27,000 in November 1962, after making 153 senior appearances and scoring 29 goals. He gained another 2 Welsh caps whilst in the Midlands, as well as scoring 24 goals from 111 League appearances. At the age of thirty, he emigrated to America in January 1966, in order to take up the post of player-coach for the Atlanta Chiefs. However, he nearly didn't make it when, a week after accepting the post, Tommy Docherty at Chelsea offered him a chance to remain in the First Division. As Woosnam explained: 'I hadn't signed for Atlanta, but I had given them my word and I stuck to it.' In 1968, Atlanta won the League, and he was voted Coach of the Year. He was then appointed commissioner to the American League, and probably did more to further the game of soccer in America than anyone else. Along with Henry Kissinger, he led the campaign that eventually saw the 1994 World Cup finals hosted successfully in America. Philip worked as a marketing consultant in Atlanta, and held a management position with the Atlanta committee for the Olympic Games. During 1999, aged sixty-seven and now retired, he oversaw the Women's World Cup finals held in America.

SEASON	LEAGUE		FA CUP		TOTAL	
	Apps	Gls	Apps	Gls	Apps	Gls
1954/55	5	0	0	0	5	0
1955/56	29	9	2	0	31	9

1956/57	23	4	0	0	23	4
1957/58	37	3	2	0	39	3
1958/59	14	3	0	0	14	3
TOTAL	108	19	4	0	112	19

James Thomas WOOTTEN, 1905-06

Midlands-born James Wootten was an amateur with Aston Villa before joining Leyton FC in 1904. He joined O's for the start of their League campaign in 1905, and played at inside forward for the first League match at Leicester Fosse on 2 September 1905. Wootten was not a regular in the first team, but got a little run during December and he scored in a 3-3 draw at Stockport County. He also played in an FA Cup fourth qualifying tie against Clapton, a 2-0 win. He left the club in March 1906, and rejoined his old club Leyton FC, playing in a single Southern League match at their Brisbane Road ground.

SEASON	LEAGUE		FA CUP		TOTAL	
	Apps	Gls	Apps	Gls	Apps	Gls
1905/06	10	2	1	0	11	2
TOTAL	10	2	1	0	11	2

Allen Albert Alfred WORBOYS, 1919-22

Alf Worboys was born in Barnet, North London on 7 November 1899. He joined O's in July 1919, straight after serving in the army, where he won various medals for service and bravery. Centre half Worboys spent four seasons at Millfields, the latter years as understudy to the England international John Townrow. He made his League debut in the very first match after the First World War – at Huddersfield Town on 30 August 1919 – and performed reasonably well during his stay. He played his final match at full-back in a 0-0 draw at Fulham on 9 March 1923, and soon after moved to Crawford

United. He died in Horsham on 11 May 1980, aged seventy-nine. His brother, Arthur Worboys, was an O's reserve during 1920/21.

SEASON	LEAGUE		FA CUP		TOTAL	
	Apps	Gls	Apps	Gls	Apps	Gls
1919/20	16	0	1	0	17	0
1920/21	14	1	2	0	16	1
1921/22	7	0	0	0	7	0
1922/23	6	0	0	0	6	0
TOTAL	43	1	3	0	46	1

Colin Harvey WORRELL, 1964-66

Full-back Colin Worrell was born in Great Yarmouth on 29 August 1943. He began his career as a junior with Norwich City in November 1961, signing as a professional in 1963 and making 9 League appearances. He joined O's in September 1964, as part of the deal that took Malcolm Lucas to Carrow Road. He was a quick-moving player, and only emerged as a first-team player once Dave Sexton took over as manager. He played adequately for two seasons – one of which was the 1965/66 season, when O's were relegated to the Third Division. He played in a remarkable match at Derby County on 2 April 1966, when both he and Dennis Sorrell were sent off, yet O's still held out to win 3-1 – only their second away victory of the season. Worrell was transferred to Charlton Athletic in June 1966, but was forced to retire from the game owing to a serious kidney complaint, and he never played at the Valley.

SEASON	LEAGUE		FA CUP		L. CUP	
	Apps	Gls	Apps	Gls	Apps	Gls
1964/65	17	0	1	0	0	0
1965/66	34	0	0	0	1	0
TOTAL	51	0	1	0	1	0

TOTAL APPS	53
TOTAL GOALS	0

George William WRIGHT, 1958-62

George Wright was a thickset full-back and a very good defender, who was born in Ramsgate, Kent on 19 March 1930. He began with Ramsgate Athletic, Thanet United and Margate, before joining West Ham United in September 1951. In 1957/58, the Hammers won the Second Division Championship, and although his 8 League appearances were insufficient to earn a medal, he did play in their two biggest victories of the season – 6-1 against Bristol Rovers and 8-0 against Rotherham. Neither did he make the top flight, as he became an 'Oriental' in June 1958, signing from the Hammers along with Eddie Lewis for a joint fee of £10,000. He made 170 senior appearances for West Ham in total, and whilst with the Hammers he played once for England 'B' and twice for the FA XI against Cambridge

George Wright

University. He also appeared for London in their away fixture against Barcelona in the second leg of the first ever Inter-Cities Fairs Cup final in 1958, alongside such illustrious names as Danny Blanchflower, Jack Kelsey, Noel Cantwell, Dave Bowen, Bobby Brown and Terry Medwin. However, after having drawn the first leg (2-2), the Londoners went down 0-6 in Spain. Wright made a rather unfortunate O's debut when scoring an own goal against Bristol Rovers in August 1958. When O's were promoted to the First Division in 1961/62, he played just once, in a 1-0 win at Stoke City. He moved to Gillingham in July 1962, making just 4 League appearances before moving back to Ramsgate Athletic. He made a total of 262 League career appearances and scored just once – a penalty for O's at Middlesbrough in a 4-2 defeat on 4 April 1959. Wright more recently ran his own cabinet-making business in Kent, before passing away in September 2000.

SEASON	LEAGUE		FA CUP		L. CUP	
	Apps	Gls	Apps	Gls	Apps	Gls
1958/59	40	1	1	0	-	-
1959/60	25	0	0	0	-	-
1960/61*	21	0	0	0	0	0
1961/62	1	0	0	0	0	0
TOTAL	87	1	1	0	0	0

TOTAL APPS	88
TOTAL GOALS	1

* The League Cup competition commenced in 1960/61.

William Peter WRIGHT, 1930-32

Bill Wright (not to be confused with William 'Bert' Bulloch Wright, O's manager between 1939 and 1945) was born in Sheffield in 1903. Bill, a tall centre half, was on O's book as an amateur during the mid-1920s and turned professional in August 1930. He never really made the grade at senior level, appearing just once in the League – on 9 October 1931 against Torquay United in a 3-1 defeat. He remained on the playing staff until 1935 and was then appointed asssant trainer. He took over as secretary-manager in January 1939 and remained in charge during the war years. He became coach in 1945 and left O's in May 1948 to become the manager of Chingford Town. Wright was still playing football, aged sixty-five, in the Birmingham Sunday League. He died in Birmingham during October 1983, aged eighty.

SEASON	LEAGUE		FA CUP		TOTAL	
	Apps	Gls	Apps	Gls	Apps	Gls
1930/31	0	0	0	0	0	0
1931/32	1	0	0	0	1	0
TOTAL	1	0	0	0	1	0

James YARDLEY, 1925-27

Jim Yardley was born in Wishaw, Scotland on 16 April 1903. He started his career with Wishaw FC, Overton Rangers and Bellhaven Oak FC, before coming south of the Border to join O's in January 1925. The inside forward looked quite a useful player, and made his League debut in a 2-0 win at Fulham on 18 April 1925. He stayed for two further seasons, before joining Luton Town in January 1927. During 1927/28 , he netted 23 goals and finally made a total of 173 appearances for the Hatters, scoring 78 goals. He moved to Millwall in 1934, and scored 24 goals from 78 appearances. During 1937 he moved back to Scotland, joining Third Lanark, and later played for both Ayr United and Morton. Yardley died in Carluke, Lanarkshire on 24 September 1959, aged fifty-six.

SEASON	LEAGUE		FA CUP		TOTAL	
	Apps	Gls	Apps	Gls	Apps	Gls
1924/25	3	0	0	0	3	0
1925/26	10	2	0	0	10	2
1926/27	16	1	0	0	16	1
TOTAL	29	3	0	0	29	3

Thomas Pearce YEWS, 1933-34

Born on 28 February 1902 in Wingate, Co. Durham, outside right Tom Yews began his career with the North Eastern Railways works team in Durham, before joining Hartlepool United in July 1920, for whom he made 47 senior appearances and scored 3 goals. Yews moved to West Ham for £150 in August 1923, and had a long and distinguished career

Tom Yews

at the Boleyn, making 361 senior appearances during his ten-year stay. The thirty-one-year-old became an 'Oriental' in August 1933, but had lost much of his speed. However, he still looked useful in the few matches he played. He spent much of his time in the reserves, due to the form of 'Ginger' Mayson. Yews retired in May 1934, and became an engineer at Briggs Motor Bodies company. He spent much of his spare time as ragtime pianist. Later he was a charge-hand at Ford, until passing away in Ilford, Essex on 19 August 1966.

SEASON	LEAGUE		FA CUP		TOTAL	
	Apps	Gls	Apps	Gls	Apps	Gls
1933/34	3	0	0	0	3	0
TOTAL	3	0	0	0	3	0

Z

Christopher Vincent ZORICICH, 1990-93

The New Zealand player Chris Zoricich – nicknamed 'Zoro' – jumped at the chance to come to England to play in the League. The defender originally came to England on a scholarship, having been halfway through his degree course. He later graduated with a BA in Economics and Accounting from Auckland University. He signed a contract with O's having played for the University FC and Papatoetoe FC in New Zealand, before moving on to the Sabah club in Malaysia. Born in Henderson, Auckland, New Zealand on 3 May 1969, he made his League debut at Cambridge United in October 1990 and proved to be an excellent squad member over three seasons. His only goal for

Chris Zoricich

good reader of the game, who looked a class act. During his stay at the club, he gained 3 full New Zealand caps in World Cup qualifying matches – against Fiji (a 3-0 win) and twice against Vanuatu (4-1 away and 8-0 at home). He also played 10 further times for his country, mostly against international League sides – these were not full internationals. He captained the New Zealand side in July 1999 in the Confederation Cup in Mexico, scoring their only goal of the tournament against the USA – this was the highlight of his career, after defeats by Germany and Brazil. He was their captain for the 2000/01 season, having won 62 full and 'A' caps for the New Zealand All–Whites, and continued as team captain for their World Cup campaign over the summer of 2001.

Orient in a 3-2 win over Brighton came on the opening day of the 1992/93 season,. During 1993 he was refused a new work permit – even after a petition from over 1,000 O's fans – and had to return home, where he played a few games for Central United. He then moved to Australia to play for the Brisbane Strikers in 1994/95, before giving it another try in the UK. He had trials with several clubs, before playing 7 reserve matches for Chelsea, but when Ruud Gullit left Stamford Bridge, so did Zoricich. He returned to Australia to re-join Brisbane Strikers, playing 118 matches and scoring 8 goals between 1994 and 1999. He moved to Sydney Olympic FC in May 1999, making a further 25 National Soccer League appearances, before joining Aussie side Newcastle United in May 2000. He made 20 appearances for the club up to the end of the 2000/01 season. Zoricich was a very mobile player and a

SEASON	LEAGUE		FA CUP		L. CUP	
	Apps	Gls	Apps	Gls	Apps	Gls
1990/91	24(4)	0	2(2)	0	2	0
1991/92	19(3)	0	0	0	2(1)	0
1992/93	10(2)	1	0	0	0	0
TOTAL	53(9)	1	2(2)	0	4(1)	0

TOTAL APPS	59(12)
TOTAL GOALS	1

* Chris Zoricich also appeared in 2(2) Auto Windscreens Shield matches.

PLAYER STATISTICS

THE 300 APPEARANCES CLUB

PLAYER	LEAGUE APPS	FA CUP APPS	L. CUP APPS	TOTAL
Peter Allen	424(8)	27	24	473(8)
Stan Charlton	367	28	13	408
Arthur Wood	373	22	-	395
Terry Howard*	327(5)	23(1)	26	376(6)
Bill Roffey	324(4)	18(1)	16(1)	358(6)
Bobby Fisher	308(6)	26	19(1)	353(7)
Fred Parker	336	14	-	350
Kevin Hales*	289(15)	25(1)	23	337(16)
Stan Aldous	302	25	-	327
Ken Facey	301	19	3	323
Sid Bishop	296	18	9	323
Ray Goddard	278	29	13	311

* Both Howard's and Hales' totals include 4 play-off matches.

40 GOALS OR MORE: 1905/06 TO 2000/01

PLAYER	LEAGUE GOALS	FA CUP GOALS	L. CUP GOALS	TOTAL
Tommy Johnston	121	2	0	123
Ken Facey	74	5	0	79
Ted Crawford	67	6	0	73
Kevin Godfrey	63	5	4	72
Mickey Bullock	65	1	3	69
Richard McFadden	66	2	-	68
Steve Castle	56	6	5	67
Billy Rees	58	8	-	66
Reg Tricker	60	3	-	63
Carl Griffiths	51	6	3	60
Peter Kitchen	49	9	2	60
David Dunmore	54	2	2	58
Dennis Pacey	46	12	-	58
Ian Juryeff	45	7	3	55
Mark Cooper*	48	4	2	54
Barrie Fairbrother	41	7	2	50
Alan Comfort	46	1	1	48
Colin West	43	2	2	47
Ronnie Heckman	38	6	- .	44
Frank Neary	44	0	-	44
Joe Mayo	36	3	1	40

* Cooper's record includes 3 goals in promotion play-off matches in 1988/89.

20 OR MORE LEAGUE GOALS IN A SEASON

SEASON	PLAYER	GOALS
1957/58	Tommy Johnston	35
1956/57	Tommy Johnston	27
1959/60	Tommy Johnston	25
1948/49	Frank Neary	25
1935/36	Ted Crawford	23
1955/56	Ronnie Heckman	23
1961/62	David Dunmore	22
1977/78	Peter Kitchen	21
1913/14	Richard McFadden	21
1931/32	Charlie Fletcher	20
1955/56	Johnny Hartburn	20

LEAGUE GOAL MILESTONES

1,000th goal	Arthur Cropper	*v.* Torquay United	14 March 1931
2,000th goal	Ken Facey (pen)	*v.* Southend United	27 November 1954
3,000th goal	Gordon Riddick	*v.* Middlesbrough	20 March 1971
4,000th goal	Mark Cooper	*v.* Wigan Athletic	4 April 1990

HIGHEST NUMBER OF GOALS SCORED IN A MATCH

Five Goals

Ronnie Heckman (FA Cup)	H	Lovells Athletic	19 November 1955

Four Goals (All League)

Walter Leigh	H	Bradford City	13 April 1906
Albert Pape	H	Oldham Athletic	1 September 1924
Dennis Pacey	H	Colchester United	30 April 1953
Stan Morgan	H	Exeter City	26 March 1955
Johnny Hartburn	H	QPR	3 March 1956
Len Julians	H	Middlesbrough	28 September 1957
Tommy Johnston	H	Rotherham United	25 December 1957
Joe Elwood	H	Bristol City	29 November 1958
Eddie Brown	H	Sunderland	30 March 1959
Peter Kitchen	H	Millwall	21 April 1984
Steve Castle	A	Rochdale	5 May 1986

PENALTY KINGS

PLAYER	CONVERTED	MISSED
Ken Facey	23	4
Kevin Hales	13	2

HAT-TRICK KINGS

David Halliday   4

Tommy Johnston   4

QUICKEST HAT-TRICKS

Johnny Hartburn scored the quickest hat-trick for O's in three-and-a-half minutes against Shrewsbury Town at Brisbane Road on 22 January 1955, O's won 5-0.

QUICKEST GOALS

14 seconds	John Cornwell	v. Torquay United	18 March 1986
20 seconds	Owen Williams	v. Notts County	29 October 1921
30 seconds	Phil Woosnam	v. Rotherham United	25 December 1957
30 seconds	Jimmy Andrews	v. Sheffield United	18 October 1958
30 seconds	Ian Bowyer	v. Fulham	3 April 1972
32 seconds	Peter Allen	v. Millwall	6 March 1971

Note

The quickest goal scored by an O's player at any level is attributed to Michael Burgess, who scored in just 7 seconds v. Fulham in a Football Combination fixture at Brisbane Road on 8 January 1955. Also, fifteen-year-old Billy Hurley scored in 7 seconds on his reserve debut at Colchester United in a Midweek League fixture on 9 September 1975.

PLAYER OF THE YEAR AWARD WINNERS: 1974-2001

1973/74	Barrie Fairbrother
1974/75	John Jackson
1975/76	Tom Walley
1976/77	Glenn Roeder
1977/78	Peter Kitchen
1978/79	Joe Mayo
1979/80	Bobby Fisher
1980/81	Nigel Gray
1981/82	Mervyn Day
1982/83	Bill Roffey
1983/84	Shaun Brooks
1984/85	Kevin Hales
1985/86	Kevin Dickenson
1986/87	Alan Comfort
1987/88	Steve Castle
1988/89	Terry Howard
1989/90	Paul Heald
1990/91	Paul Heald
1991/92	Keith Day
1992/93	Danny Carter
1993/94	Ian Bogie
1994/95	Glenn Cockerill
1995/96	Ian Hendon
1996/97	Mark Warren
1997/98	Martin Ling
1998/99	Simon Clark
1999/2000	Matthew Joseph
2000/01	Matthew Joseph

INTERNATIONAL PLAYERS

The following is a list of players who have made international appearances whilst with O's, some of whom made further appearances whilst with other clubs.

England

John E. Townrow (2 caps with O's)

v. Scotland	1925
v. Wales	1926

Owen Williams (2 caps with O's)

v. N. Ireland	1923
v. Wales	1923

Republic of Ireland (Eire)

Anthony P. Grealish (7 caps with O's)

v. Norway	1976
v. Poland	1976
v. Norway	1978
v. Denmark	1978
v. N. Ireland	1979
v. England	1979
v. W. Germany	1979

Grealish made a total of 45 full international appearances for his country, scoring 8 goals.

Wales

Tom Evans (3 caps with O's)

v. Scotland	1927
v. England	1928
v. Scotland	1928

Evans made a total of 4 full international appearances for his country.

Eddie Lawrence (1 cap with O's)

v. N. Ireland   1930

Lawrence made a total of 2 full international appearances for his country.

Malcolm Lucas (4 caps with O's)

v. N. Ireland   1962
v. Mexico   1962
v. Scotland   1963
v. England   1963

Thomas Mills (2 caps with O's)

v. England   1934
v. N. Ireland   1934

Mills made a total of 4 full international appearances for his country.

Ernie Morley (3 caps with O's)

v. England   1929
v. Scotland   1929
v. N. Ireland   1929

Morley made a total of 4 full international appearances for his country.

Phil Woosnam (1 cap with O's)

v. Scotland   1958

Woosnam made a total of 17 full international appearances for his country.

Barbados

Matthew Joseph (2 caps with O's)

v. Guatemala   2000
v. USA   2000

New Zealand

Chris Zoricich (3 caps with O's)

v. Fiji	1992
v. Vanuatu	1992
v. Vanuatu	1992

Zoricich played more than 60 times for his country up to December 2001.

Nigeria

Tunji Banjo (7 caps with O's)

v. Tunisia	1981
v. Tanzania	1981
v. Tanzania	1981
v. Guinea	1981
v. Guinea	1981
v. Algeria	1982
v. Algeria	1982

John Okay Chiedozie (7 caps with O's)

v. Tunisia	1981
v. Tanzania	1981
v. Tanzania	1981
v. Guinea	1981
v. Guinea	1981
v. Algeria	1982
v. Algeria	1982

Chiedozie made a total of 9 international appearances for his country. His other 2 caps came during his time at Spurs, both against Tunisia in 1995.

LEADING INTERNATIONALLY CAPPED PLAYERS

Tunji Banjo	7 caps for Nigeria
John Chiedozie	7 caps for Nigeria
Tony Grealish	7 caps for Eire